THE
unofficial GUIDE®
^{TO}New York City

5TH EDITION

THE *unofficial* GUIDE®
TO New York City

5TH EDITION

EVE ZIBART *with* RACHEL F. FREEMAN *and* LEA LANE

Please note that prices fluctuate in the course of time, and travel information changes under the impact of many factors that influence the travel industry. We therefore suggest that you write or call ahead for confirmation when making your travel plans. Every effort has been made to ensure the accuracy of information throughout this book, and the contents of this publication are believed correct at the time of printing. Nevertheless, the publishers cannot accept responsibility for errors or omissions or for changes in details given in this guide or for the consequences of any reliance on the information provided by the same. Assessments of attractions and so forth are based upon the author's own experience, and therefore, descriptions given in this guide necessarily contain an element of subjective opinion, which may not reflect the publisher's opinion or dictate a reader's own experience on another occasion. Readers are invited to write the publisher with ideas, comments, and suggestions for future editions.

Published by:
John Wiley & Sons, Inc.
111 River Street
Hoboken, NJ 07030

Produced by Menasha Ridge Press

Cover design by Michael J. Freeland

Interior design by Vertigo Design

For information on our other products and services or to obtain technical support please contact our Customer Care Department within the U.S. at 800-762-2974, outside the U.S. at 317-572-3993 or fax 317-572-4002.

John Wiley & Sons, Inc. also publishes its books in a variety of electronic formats. Some content that appears in print may not be available in electronic formats.

ISBN 0-471-76396-9

Manufactured in the United States of America

5 4 3 2 1

CONTENTS

LIST *of* MAPS

ACKNOWLEDGMENTS

MANY THANKS TO LEA LANE AND RACHEL FREEMAN for their time and taste.

As always, thanks to the folks at Menasha Ridge, particularly Molly, Holly, and Myra. Special thanks to Chris Mohney for his patience and painstaking transcription.

Many thanks to Carla Stec, the person who read about our vacations but never had the chance to take one, and to Liliane Opsomer, who came to our aid at the last minute to help with restaurant research and writing.

Special thanks to Ruben and a farewell tip of the hat to Johnny, who made the Oak Bar my favorite Manhattan sanctuary.

Finally, this book is for my brother Michael, the best companion.

—*Eve Zibart*

ABOUT *the* AUTHOR *and* CONTRIBUTORS

EVE ZIBART HAS WRITTEN MORE ABOUT dining and entertainment than most people experience in a lifetime. In her early years as the pop music and culture reporter for, first, the *Nashville Tennessean* and then for the *Washington Post*, Eve quickly exhibited a flair for scene and sensory detail coupled with an aptitude for grammar and an extensive vocabulary. She rapidly moved through the ranks of the *Post* as a Style feature writer, a Maryland columnist, the TV editor, and a Weekend assistant editor. Long known to friends and fans as "Dr. Nightlife," Eve has enough experience and knowledge to advise the Joint Chiefs of Staff on national trends. Currently, Eve is the restaurant critic for the *Washington Post's* Weekend section.

In addition to her responsibilities at the *Post*, Eve is a columnist for *Book Page* and has been a regular contributor to *USAir Inflight, New England Financial Journal, Impress,* and *Four Seasons* magazines. She has also written for *Cosmopolitan, Town and Country,* and *Playboy*. Given an amazing ability to turn 24 hours into 30, Eve has found time to author several books, including *The Ethnic Food Lover's Companion; The Eclectic Gourmet Guide to Washington, D.C.; The Unofficial Guide to New Orleans; The Unofficial Guide to Walt Disney World for Grown-Ups;* and *Inside Disney: The Incredible Story of Walt Disney World and the Man Behind the Mouse.*

NATIVE NEW YORKER RACHEL F. FREEMAN (Dining and Nightlife contributor) believes it is her duty to act as both foodie and night owl. Having lived abroad for 11 years, she returned to New York with a renewed hunger for what the city has to offer, resisting the temptation to join the ranks of the jaded. She has written for guidebooks in Warsaw, Poland, and has a passion for Edinburgh and the Highlands and Islands of Scotland. She has written for *Poland Business Guide, Wider Insider, Warsaw Insider,* and *Voyage* magazine.

LEA LANE HAS TRAVELED TO OVER 110 COUNTRIES AND has been a columnist for Gannett newspapers, a TV travel and lifestyle reporter, and managing editor of the newsletter *Travel Smart*. She writes for magazines and newspapers, including *The New York Times,* and is a major contributor to guidebooks, including those on Belgium, Greece, Italy, and New York. She has written *Steps to Better Writing, The World's Most Exciting Cruises, The Unofficial Guide to South Florida,* and *The Unofficial Guide to Bed and Breakfasts and Country Inns in New England.* Her newest book, *Solo Traveler: Tales and Tips for Great Trips*, was chosen as runner-up for "Best Travel Book of the Year" by the North American Travel Journalists Association. Lea's popular lifestyle Web site is **www.sololady.com.**

THE
unofficial GUIDE®
TO New York City

5TH EDITION

INTRODUCTION

"NEW YORK, NEW YORK, IT'S *a* HELLUVA TOWN..."

IF YOU'RE EVER A PASSENGER IN A TAXICAB IN NEW YORK, look at the city map affixed to the back of the driver's seat. Chances are, it will show only the tourist territories, cutting Manhattan off partway up Central Park, only hinting at Brooklyn, and likely dispensing with the Bronx, Long Island, and Staten Island altogether. So do most guidebooks about New York. They get you from the Staten Island Ferry (the departure point, at least) on the Battery to the Metropolitan Museum of Art at 82nd Street. Some less hidebound books mention Harlem and a few riverside attractions. But for the most part, it's "East Side, West Side" rather than "all around the town."

Worse, tour guides rarely draw connections, convey waves of progress, or point up ironies of development. In a city literally embraced by the spirits of multiculturalism—with the Statue of Liberty, that monumental icon of hope for immigrants, at one end, and the shrine of Mother Cabrini, their patron saint, at the other—most visitors peer through the most homogeneous of filters, the endless barrage of Big Apple boosterism and crime or inflation news trotted out every day. Watch enough TV and you'd think the whole city was painted with red ink, white ticker tape, and blue uniforms.

What a waste. New York City is one of the most original, elaborate, eccentric, and irresistible creatures—it clearly has a life of its own—you will ever encounter. And we want you to encounter it all, in not just three but four dimensions: underground, above the cloud line, and most definitely at street level, as well as seeing its past, present, and future. And for that, we need your cooperation. We need you to be open to the city's charm. And we need you to turn off that damn television.

We often speak of visiting a new place as "seeing" it. "See Rock City," read those famous barns. "Join the Navy and see the world." But the strange thing about sightseeing is that people get too absorbed in the "sights" and forget about the "seeing." It may sound odd for an author to say, but having your nose buried in a book, even this book, is not the way to travel. And it certainly isn't the way to go looking for exactly that intersection or department store or luxury hotel you always see in the cop shows.

To experience New York fully, you need to give it the full attention of your eyes and your heart. This city is a romance, a record of both the finest moments and the darkest hours of our history. You need to respond to it, not just react to it. Start with our book, but don't stick to it. Admire the Empire State Building, but don't spend your whole day there. Join the crowds on the street, grab a coffee, see a show. Otherwise, you might just as well have stayed home.

Many guidebooks will tell you that New York is not for the faint-hearted; we would say that it is not for the unimaginative. Part of its fascination is its complexity: all the accents, the rhythms, the smells. For so famous a melting pot, New York has yet to produce a truly creole society; minorities here are not so much assimilated as incorporated. That means food, gifts, clothes, and "roots" of a hundred cultures. It's a permanent World's Fair, free for the strolling. Diversity isn't just a souvenir of Ellis Island or dim sum in Chinatown; it's daily life, the greatest attraction of them all.

New York is also the great silent witness to American culture. There is not a single block in the city, whether residential, renovated, commercial, or even crumbling, that does not speak of its restless and often reckless history: expansionist, extravagant, fickle, fashionable. All you have to do is look. Broadway or off-Broadway, here all the world truly is a stage.

And a stage set: If there had not been such a thing as a skyline, New York would have had to invent it. As it is, New York reconceived the horizon beyond the dreams of even the greatest medieval builders. Skyscrapers are the true cathedrals of Manhattan's private religion—not that there aren't exquisite churches and temples galore. You can almost relive the evolution of the city by glancing around at the architecture, from the 18th-century purity of St. Paul's Chapel to the 19th-century neoclassicism of Federal Hall, the French Renaissance of the Jewish Museum, and the Gothic Revival of St. Patrick's; from the Beaux Arts Grand Central Terminal (with staircases copied from the Paris Opéra) and the Art Deco Chrysler Building to the Wright-stuff Guggenheim and the Bauhaus Seagram Building.

Even "ordinary" office buildings have extraordinary features: friezes, carvings, gilding, capitals, cornice pieces, decorative sills—all the showy elements of European palaces, only bigger and brasher and designed to make aristocrats out of merchants. For these are the great palaces of trade, tributes to the variety and vitality of American industry. New York was one of the first cities to abandon class distinction, at least as far as the purveyors were concerned, between the carriage trade and the merchant class, between the custom-tailored and the store-fitted. It was the natural preserve of the department store, with its abundance of luxuries (which gradually became, by long acquaintance and by the nature of human ambition, necessities), and it fostered the democratization of service.

unofficial **TIP**
Don't miss the "outdoors" of New York. Every borough has a large public park—and no, Central Park is not the largest—and four have botanical gardens. There are five zoos and an aquarium, a wildlife refuge, and beaches and marinas.

Just as the great merchant princes of old New York—the Rockefellers, Guggenheims, Fricks, and Morgans—amassed great art collections and libraries that became public treasures, today's corporate equivalents often act the patron role for the public: There are Lichtenstein and Thomas Hart Benton murals in the lobby of the Equitable Center (Seventh at 51st); a mini-museum in the PaineWebber Building (Sixth and 52nd); an Alexander Calder sculpture outside IBM (Madison and West 57th); and a branch of the Whitney Museum of Modern Art in the Philip Morris Building (on Park Avenue, just across from the 42nd Street entrance to Grand Central).

This book is about seeing New York. Not just Midtown Manhattan, but the whole city. It's about shopping and art-gazing and theatergoing, of course, but mostly it's about looking past the sales pitches to the piers, beyond the boutiques to the brownstones, outside Times Square to Washington Square. It's about relaxing in the green spaces as well as the grand hotels, about going off-Broadway as far as Brooklyn and seeing as far back as its founding. If you want a top-ten list of tourist attractions, you can find them on any corner and any souvenir stand; but if you want to know ten lovely things to do for yourself, ten splendors to share with your children, or ten places where beauty really is truth, read on.

ABOUT *this* GUIDE

HOW COME "UNOFFICIAL"?

MOST GUIDES TO NEW YORK TOUT THE WELL-KNOWN SIGHTS, promote the local restaurants and hotels indiscriminately, and leave out a lot of good stuff. This one is different.

Instead of pandering to the tourist industry, we'll tell you if the food is bad at a well-known restaurant, we'll complain loudly about high prices, and we'll guide you away from the crowds and traffic for a break now and then.

Visiting New York requires wily strategies not unlike those used in the sacking of Troy. We've sent in a team of evaluators who toured each site, ate in the city's best restaurants, performed critical evaluations of its hotels, and visited New York's wide variety of nightclubs. If a museum is boring, or standing in line for two hours to view a famous attraction is a waste of time, we say so—and, in the process, hopefully we will make your visit more fun, efficient, and economical.

CREATING A GUIDEBOOK

WE GOT INTO THE GUIDEBOOK BUSINESS BECAUSE we were unhappy with the way travel guides make the reader work to get any usable information. Wouldn't it be nice, we thought, if we were to make guides that are easy to use?

Most guidebooks are compilations of lists. This is true regardless of whether the information is presented in list form or artfully distributed through pages of prose. There is insufficient detail in a list, and prose can present tedious helpings of nonessential or marginally useful information. Not enough wheat, so to speak, for nourishment in one instance, and too much chaff in the other. Either way, these types of guides provide little more than departure points from which readers initiate their own quests.

Many guides are readable and well researched, but they tend to be difficult to use. To select a hotel, for example, a reader must study several pages of descriptions with only the boldfaced hotel names breaking up large blocks of text. Because each description essentially deals with the same variables, it is difficult to recall what was said concerning a particular hotel. Readers generally must work through all the write-ups before beginning to narrow their choices. The presentation of restaurants, nightclubs, and attractions is similar except that even more reading is usually required. To use such a guide is to undertake an exhaustive research process that requires examining nearly as many options and possibilities as starting from scratch. Recommendations, if any, lack depth and conviction. These guides compound rather than solve problems by failing to narrow travelers' choices down to a thoughtfully considered, well-distilled, and manageable few.

HOW *UNOFFICIAL GUIDES* ARE DIFFERENT

READERS CARE ABOUT THE AUTHORS' OPINIONS. The authors, after all, are supposed to know what they are talking about. This, coupled with the fact that the traveler wants quick answers (as opposed to endless alternatives), dictates that authors should be explicit, prescriptive, and above all, direct. The authors of the *Unofficial Guide* try to do just that. They spell out alternatives and recommend specific courses of action. They simplify complicated destinations and attractions and allow the traveler to feel in control in the most unfamiliar environments. The objective of the *Unofficial Guide* authors is not to give the most information or all of the information but to offer the most accessible, useful information.

An *Unofficial Guide* is a critical reference work; it focuses on a travel destination that appears to be especially complex. Our authors and research team are completely independent from the attractions, restaurants, and hotels we describe. *The Unofficial Guide to New York* is designed for individuals and families traveling for the fun of it, as well as for business travelers and conventioneers, especially those visiting the Big Apple for the first time. The guide is directed at value-conscious, consumer-oriented adults who seek a cost-effective, though not spartan, travel style.

Special Features

The *Unofficial Guide* offers the following special features:

- Friendly introductions to New York's most fascinating neighborhoods.
- "Best of" listings giving our well-qualified opinions on things ranging from raw oysters to blackened snapper and five-star hotels to 12-story views.
- Listings that are keyed to your interests, so you can pick and choose.
- Advice to sightseers on how to avoid the worst of the crowds; advice to business travelers on how to avoid traffic and excessive costs.
- Recommendations for lesser-known sights that are away from Times Square but are no less worthwhile.
- Maps to make it easy to find places you want to go to and avoid places you don't.
- Expert advice on avoiding New York's notorious street crime.
- A hotel chart that helps you narrow down your choices fast, according to your needs.
- Shorter listings that include only those restaurants, clubs, and hotels we think are worth considering.
- A table of contents and detailed index to help you find things fast.
- Insider advice on best times of day (or night) to go places.

What You Won't Get

- Long, useless lists where everything looks the same.
- Information that gets you to your destination at the worst possible time.
- Information without advice on how to use it.

HOW THIS GUIDE WAS RESEARCHED AND WRITTEN

ALTHOUGH MANY GUIDEBOOKS HAVE BEEN WRITTEN about New York, very few have been evaluative. Some guides come close to regurgitating the hotels' and tourist offices' own promotional material. In preparing this work, we took nothing for granted. Each hotel, restaurant, shop, and attraction was visited by a team of trained observers who conducted detailed evaluations and rated each according to formal criteria. Team members conducted interviews with tourists of all ages to determine what they enjoyed most and least during their New York visit.

While our observers are independent and impartial, they did not claim to have special expertise. Like you, they visited New York as tourists or business travelers, noting their satisfaction or dissatisfaction.

The primary difference between the average tourist and the trained evaluator is the evaluator's skills in organization, preparation, and observation. The trained evaluator is responsible for much more than simply observing and cataloging. Observer teams use detailed checklists to analyze hotel rooms, restaurants, nightclubs, and attractions. Finally, evaluator ratings and observations are integrated with tourist reactions and the opinions of patrons for a comprehensive quality profile of each feature and service.

In compiling this guide, we recognize that a tourist's age, background, and interests will strongly influence his or her taste in New York's wide array of attractions and will account for a preference for one sight or museum over another. Our sole objective is to provide the reader with sufficient description, critical evaluation, and pertinent data to make knowledgeable decisions according to individual tastes.

LETTERS, COMMENTS, AND QUESTIONS FROM READERS

WE EXPECT TO LEARN FROM OUR MISTAKES, as well as from the input of our readers, and to improve with each new book and edition. Many of those who use the *Unofficial Guides* write to us asking questions, making comments, or sharing their own discoveries or lessons learned in New York. We appreciate all such input, both positive and critical, and encourage our readers to continue writing. Readers' comments and observations will be frequently incorporated in revised editions of the *Unofficial Guide* and will contribute immeasurably to its improvement.

How to Write the Authors:

Eve and Bob
The Unofficial Guide to New York City
P.O. Box 43673
Birmingham, AL 35243
unofficialguides@menasharidge.com

When you write, be sure to put your return address on your letter as well as on the envelope—sometimes envelopes and letters get separated. And remember, our work takes us out of the office for long periods of time, so forgive us if our response is delayed.

Reader Survey

At the back of the guide you will find a short questionnaire that you can use to express opinions about your New York visit. Clip the questionnaire out along the dotted line and mail it to this address.

"INSIDE" NEW YORK
for OUTSIDERS

IT'S A FUNNY THING ABOUT NEW YORK TRAVEL GUIDES: Most of them tell you too much, and a few tell you too little. This is because New York is such a complex city, so ornate and enveloping and layered with history and happenstance that it's hard to stop acquiring good stories and passing them on. And it's an endless voyage: The more time you spend there, the more you realize you don't know.

But the fact is, statistics show that the majority of visitors to New York stay only three or four days—and even that average span frequently includes time spent in business meetings or conventions. How much can you squeeze into a long weekend? How much do you want to see? This city's attractions are among the most frequently photographed in the world, yet packaged tours often haul you about the city as relentlessly as if you didn't already know what the Statue of Liberty or the horse-drawn carriages of Central Park looked like. Some tour books either skimp on shopping or endorse every dealer in town; some overlook any collection smaller than five stories tall. Some short-change any fine arts or theater productions outside Lincoln Center or Broadway, as if Midtown were the whole of Manhattan and restaurants were the sole form of nightlife. Some are too uncritical, some too "insider." Some have all the right stuff, but are poorly organized; some are easy to read, but oversimplified and boring.

Not only that, but most guidebook writers seem so attached to the modern stereotype of the city—the New York of loudmouthed cabbies, TV cop shows, the "if I can make it there" rat race, and Wall Street shark pool—that they don't express the great romance of this rich, inimitable, and electrifying metropolis. It's an asphalt wonder, sure, but there are cobblestones still to be seen; a world-famous skyline, yes, but an architectural creation, not just a higher-rent district. It's a magnet for immigration, but that also means it's a tapestry of ethnic revival. And in an era when the Statue of Liberty is animated for a deodorant commercial, it's too easy to forget what an icon it really is and has been to millions of Americans and would-be Americans. Okay, call us sentimentalists, but it's true: We do love New York, just not the one the hype artists are selling.

So as hard and heartbreaking as it is to limit a book like this, we have done so, by doubling up whenever possible. The neighborhood profiles in Part One, Understanding the City, are partly geographical descriptions and partly historical romances: They're designed to help you get your bearings, but they include enough sights and stories to give you the community's true flavor. In Part Seven, Sightseeing, Tours, and Attractions, we've listed some attractions by type—family style, theatrical, genealogical, and so on—to help you customize your visit.

Particular museums and entertainments in each neighborhood are explored in more detail and rated for interest by age group. We've also listed some personal favorites that may not get as much publicity but that we think are first-rate. In Part Nine, Shopping, we've combined best bets with do-it-yourself walking tours so you can see the sights and fill out your wish list at the same time. The maps are designed to help you with the logistics of arranging accommodations, dining, and sightseeing.

As for the hundreds of tourist attractions, well, we've tried to sort them into first-rate, special interest, and hype jobs, and we spend space on only the best. The truth is, even if you visit New York a dozen times, you won't be able to see even as much as we've described for you, and by then you'll have discovered your own favorite side to the city. But certainly we don't want you to waste any of that time, either. We take things easy, the way we think you will want to; but we don't forgive exploitation or boost unworthy distractions. If it isn't fun, if it isn't informative, if it isn't accurate, we don't want you to go. If there's a better alternative, we want you to know. We hope to keep the quality of your visit high and the irritation quotient low. And if we'd known that would turn into a poem, we'd have let you know.

unofficial **TIP**
Remember that prices and hours change constantly. We have listed the most up-to-date information we can get, but you should double-check times in particular (if prices of attractions change, it is generally not by much). And remember, this is one of the busiest tourist towns in the world, drawing more than 30 million visitors a year, so make your reservations early and reconfirm at least once.

We've covered these attractions in these various ways, often overlapping, because we want to make sure you can pick out the ones you'd most enjoy. And for those who don't wish to do it yourself at all, we have listed a number of commercial and customized tours that you can take tailored to almost any interest, also in Part Seven.

Even granting that your time will be tight, we have included a list of opportunities for exercise or play. That's partly because we at the *Unofficial Guides* try to keep up with our workouts when we're on the road; and also because you may be visiting old friends, old teammates, and tennis players. Beyond that, although you may not think you'll want to make time for a run or ride, experience has taught us that sightseeing and shopping can be exhausting, make you stiff, make you long for a little outdoors—or at least a little calorie countering.

HOW INFORMATION IS ORGANIZED

In order to give you fast access to information about the best of New York, we've organized material in several formats.

HOTELS Since most people visiting New York stay in one hotel for the duration of their trip, we have summarized our coverage of hotels in charts, maps, ratings, and rankings that allow you to quickly focus your decision-making process. We do not go on, page after page, describing lobbies and rooms that, in the final analysis, sound much the same. Instead, we concentrate on the specific variables that differentiate one hotel from another: location, size, room quality, services, amenities, and cost.

RESTAURANTS We provide plenty of detail when it comes to restaurants. Since you will probably eat a dozen or more restaurant meals during your stay, and since not even you can predict what you might be in the mood for on Saturday night, we provide detailed profiles of the best restaurants in and around New York.

ENTERTAINMENT AND NIGHTLIFE Visitors frequently try several different clubs or nightspots during their stay. Since clubs and nightspots, like restaurants, are usually selected spontaneously after arriving in New York, we believe detailed descriptions are warranted. The best nightspots and lounges in New York are profiled by category in Part Eleven, Entertainment and Nightlife.

SPECIAL TIPS In addition to singling out attractions ideally suited to younger tourists and not-to-be-missed sites in the city, we've marked some insider tips and shortcuts throughout the book.

new york metropolitan area

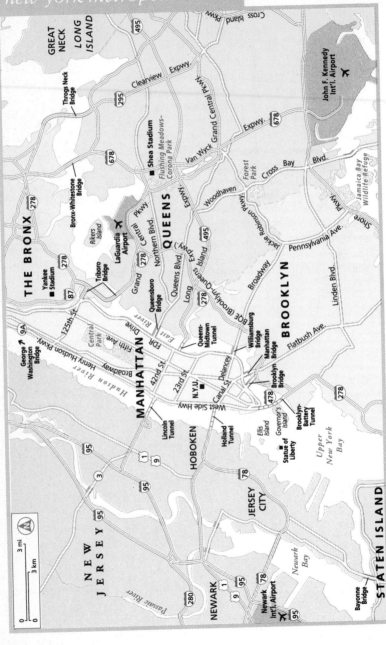

PART ONE

UNDERSTANDING
the CITY

BOROUGHS, NEIGHBOR-HOODS, *and* "DISTRICTS"

"New York, New York, it's a helluva town /The Bronx is up and the Battery's down /And the people ride in a hole in the ground." It's true, it's easy to remember . . . and you can dance to it. But it's only a little bit of the story.

WHEN WE SAY "NEW YORK," MOST OF THE TIME we really mean the island of **Manhattan,** and so does almost everybody else. Even those who live in other areas talk about going into "the city" when they mean going to Manhattan. In fact, however, Manhattan is just one of New York's five "boroughs," which are the equivalent of counties. The others are the **Bronx** to the north across the Harlem River, **Brooklyn** and **Queens** to the east on Long Island across the East River, and **Staten Island** to the south of the harbor. (Manhattanites, incidentally, refer to the other four jurisdictions as "the outer boroughs.")

Within all five boroughs are areas that have nicknames or historic designations, such as Prospect Park, the Theater District, the Garment District, the Meatpacking District, and Union Square. And with the usual shifts of time and trend, some neighborhoods have merged with others, or upscaled, or run down, and so forth. The old distinctions between Chinatown, Little Italy, and Soho are beginning to blur, and a handful of new neighborhood abbreviations—"Dumbo," short for Down Under the Manhattan Bridge Overpass, for example—demonstrate how quickly an area can shift from dilapidated to date central.

We recommend that you also read, or at least skim, Part Six, New York's Neighborhoods, once before your visit; these profiles will not only help you frame your itinerary but also will give you a sense of the historical evolution of New York—how succeeding generations of immigrants, merchants, and millionaires gradually spread up from the southern tip of the island to the top of Central Park, each generation pushing the last before it, moving the less fortunate or simply less picturesque elements up and out away from the prow of prosperity; and how in the early 21st century, the process is repeating itself, so that areas once abandoned in the wake of this northward expansion are once again gathering strength and vitality.

TAKE THE A TRAIN . . . CAREFULLY

MOST OF MANHATTAN IS LAID OUT ON A GRID, which is easy to master, but there are some irregular rules to remember. Occasionally streets change names as well, at least on the maps and signs. Sixth Avenue is officially dubbed "Avenue of the Americas," but you never hear anybody call it that except perhaps a city promoter. Where 59th Street runs along the south border of Central Park, it is called, not surprisingly, Central Park South; and when Eighth Avenue passes 59th/Central Park South on its way north along the western edge of the park, it becomes Central Park West. (Above that, in the Heights, it's officially named Frederick Douglass Boulevard, but it's more often still called Eighth Avenue.) East 110th Street, which runs along the top of Central Park on the Upper East Side, is called Central Park North along the park itself and Cathedral Parkway on the Upper West Side.

However—and these are the ones that can be more confusing—Fifth Avenue, which is the eastern border of Central Park, does not change its name; and Park Avenue, which a visitor might assume was a form of "Central Park East," is two blocks east of that. Columbus Avenue, which one might assume originated in Columbus Circle, is actually an avenue away; it is the extension of Ninth Avenue, whereas Columbus Circle is on Eighth. And West Street, which is over by the Hudson River in Lower Manhattan, Greenwich Village, and Chelsea, eventually runs over into Twelfth Avenue and becomes the West Side Expressway; don't confuse that with West End Avenue, which is the extension of Eleventh Avenue on the Upper West Side.

There is a Broad Street not far from Broadway in the Financial District, but it's less than half a mile long and a couple of blocks east of the real thing. On the other hand, there is a West Broadway that runs parallel to the "big" Broadway from Washington Square Park south to Battery Park, so Soho and Tribeca addresses can be tricky. In the East Village, it is possible to find yourself at such confusing intersections as 2nd and Second, meaning East 2nd Street and Second Avenue, but such addresses are fortunately rare.

Most of the avenues with "names"—Park, Lexington, and Madison—are on the East Side between Third and Fifth Avenues (Park was once Fourth). However, there are some places on the island that are farther east than First Avenue, namely York on the Upper East Side and Avenues A, B, C, and D—in order as they go toward the East River—in the East Village. Tenth Avenue becomes Amsterdam Avenue above West 72nd Street.

As for specific addresses, there are various ornate and unmemorizable mathematical equations for pinpointing the nearest cross street, but even these aren't always exactly the same. We suggest you either pick up one of the various pocket maps that have this formula, or just call ahead and ask; most businesses automatically supply the "between such and such" information.

unofficial **TIP**
Be careful about subway names: The Sixth Avenue subway does generally go below Sixth Avenue, but the famous A Train is on the West Side, a world (almost literally) away from Avenue A on the Lower East Side.

For more tips see, Part Four, Arriving and Getting Oriented.

"AND THE BATTERY'S DOWN"

THE SENSE OF MANHATTAN'S VARIOUS NEIGHBORHOODS as distinct "towns" with unique histories and characteristics is so strong that almost every part of that island in particular has a sobriquet (or two). (Each of the other four boroughs has their own as well, of course.) Although they sound complicated, they block off into fairly obvious pieces; see the street borders in "How Information Is Organized" in the Introduction if you'd like to mark off a map.

However, it helps to have some general notion of up and down—meaning uptown and downtown, not that hole in the ground. If you think of the island of Manhattan as running north-south, which it very nearly does, you can fix it in your head as a sort of skinny, slightly bottom-heavy watch, a Salvador Dalí affair with an oversized stem, a squiggly right edge, and Central Park more or less at the center of the dial.

The northernmost part of Manhattan, which sticks up like the extra-long clock stem, is called the **Heights,** shorthand for the series of areas called Morningside Heights, Hamilton Heights, and Washington Heights. These are divided from New Jersey on the west by the Hudson River and across the top and east by the Spuyten-Duyvil Creek. The lower eastern bulge of this area, from about 12 to 1 o'clock, is **Harlem.**

On either side of Central Park and matching it top and bottom are, logically, the **Upper East Side** and **East Side,** a long two o'clock hour, and the **Upper West Side** and **West Side** at ten. (Remember, the clock face is stretched out a little, so it's longer at the bottom.)

From the southern edge of Central Park (59th Street) it gets a little trickier, but if you imagine a line running down the middle of the rest of Manhattan—generally along Sixth Avenue and Broadway—then you can place **Midtown** at three o'clock, **Gramercy Park/Madison Square** at four, with the **East Village** and then the combined **China-**

town/Little Italy/Lower East Side filling up from around 4:30 almost to 6, where **Lower Manhattan** and the **Battery** hang at the very tip.

Swinging back around from the bottom from about 6:30 toward 8 are **Soho/Tribeca** and **Greenwich Village,** then **Chelsea** at 8, **Midtown West/the Theater District** at 9, and back to the West Side.

The **Bronx** is indeed "up"—it curves alongside the Heights above Harlem. In fact, if Manhattan were a pocket watch, the Bronx would be the fob it hung from. **Queens** is opposite the East and Upper East Side, **Brooklyn** a little southeast (4 to 5:30-ish), and **Staten Island** drops off almost directly below Manhattan, as if the tip of Lower Manhattan had let go a teardrop. Having these vague compass points in mind is especially helpful when you are trying to figure out which subway platform you want to be standing on, as most signs include "uptown," "downtown" or a borough name as a general direction. Of the five boroughs, only the Bronx is attached to the continental United States; and though most of the island's waterside culture has been almost obscured by modern development, it was integral to many areas of New York—and it also means that boats, and occasionally intrepid swimmers, can actually circumnavigate Manhattan.

A VERY SHORT HISTORY *of an* EXTREMELY COMPLEX CITY

NEW YORK IS ONE OF THE OLDEST CITIES in the United States, the nation's first capital and still one of the financial and cultural capitals of the world, and as such it has all the ingredients of a rousing history: founding fathers, first brokers, big money, political corruption, cultural diversity, ethnic riots, artistic enterprise, struggling immigrants. It was the site of many of the legendary "firsts" of America: Robert Fulton's first steamboat was launched on the Hudson River in 1807; Samuel Morse sent the first telegraph message from New York in 1837; the first organized baseball team, the New York Knickerbockers, was organized in 1845; and the first World's Fair was held in Manhattan in 1853. The first real battles of the American Revolution were fought there. Even the first antitax uprising took place in Manhattan, led by merchant Jacob Leisler more than 300 years ago.

New York has always welcomed the iconoclast: It was not the first city to have a fine church built with the donations of a retired pirate (in this case, William Kidd, who contributed much toward the construction of Trinity Church), but colonial governor Lord Cornbury, who was appointed just after the turn of the 18th century, was surely the first public official in America to appear in drag.

New York is still the great melting pot; it only covers 300 square miles—Manhattan a mere 22—but it has a population of about 9 million, speaking between 90 and 100 languages. Some schools in the outer boroughs, especially in Queens and Brooklyn, report having students who speak three dozen languages at home. Sixty percent of city residents place their city of origin outside the United States. Add the parts of Connecticut, New Jersey, Pennsylvania, Long Island, and the upstate region considered within the greater metropolitan area, and New York becomes a nation of more than 20 million speaking some 160 languages.

COLONIALISM AND CAPITALISM

IF IT WEREN'T FOR A DETERMINED JAG OF GEOGRAPHY (or, rather, political arm-twisting), New York City might not even connect with the rest of the state. It's like the little tail on a stylized comma, or the pointed throat of some vulturous bird cutting down the Hudson River toward the Atlantic.

Before the arrival of the Europeans, the region was inhabited by two groups of related native tribes: the Algonquians (which included the Canarsie, who lent their name to a section of eastern Brooklyn, and the Delaware as well as the "Mohegans" or "Mahicans," immortalized by James Fenimore Cooper) along the Hudson and on Long Island; and the Iroquois Confederacy, among them the Mohawks and Seneca, who roamed to the west and upstate. Some historians theorize that the colony reportedly established in the year 1010 by Greenlander Thorfinn Karlsfensi was in fact on the island of Manhattan, but if so, the three years of his village's existence left no trace.

As was common in the 16th and 17th centuries, the explorers who sailed for one European empire were often citizens of another, so fascinated by the prospect of travel that they accepted commissions from rival powers. So John Cabot of Genoa became a citizen of Venice, then moved to Bristol and sailed for England; he landed in Newfoundland in 1497 and returned to the region in 1498. His son Sebastian, who may have reached the Hudson Bay a decade later, sailed for the Spanish. Venetian Giovanni da Verrazano, who sailed into New York Bay in 1524, was in the pay of the French. Esteban Gomez, who sighted Manhattan a year later, was a Portuguese Moor flying the Spanish flag. Henry Hudson, who was English, was working for the Dutch. At least Samuel de Champlain, who was also carrying the French flag when he mapped eastern Canada, was working in his own language.

With its fine natural port, access to Canada via the Hudson River, and the agricultural wealth of the surrounding territory—not to mention European dreams of a vast paradise of gold in the land beyond and a marine shortcut to the Asian trade—New York was destined to be the target of political and colonial struggles. Champlain and Hudson worked their way into almost the same area at the same time, in 1609, and left their names behind as a handy reminder:

The Frenchman sailed south from Canada along what is now known as Lake Champlain to its tip, while the Englishman sailed north along the route, ever after called the Hudson River, nearly as far as modern Albany.

The French, who had earlier allied themselves with the Huron in Canada, immediately became embroiled in trade and territorial struggles with the tribes of the Iroquois, a strategy that would haunt them for more than a century. The Dutch, on the other hand, went right for the open water: In 1624, representatives of the newly created Dutch West Indies Company famously acquired the land at the south end of the island of Manhattan from the easy-going Manates tribe for trinkets worth less than $25, naming the settlement New Amsterdam. They were sometimes referred to as the Manhattan Indians, as they called the area Man-a-hatt-ta. However, that may have been a bad omen: One other possible interpretation of the word derives from "island of drunkenness," because Hudson's landing apparently turned into quite a party. Under a series of practical-minded Dutch administrators, the port prospered and expanded, and they almost certainly got their money's worth in the next 40 years. Workers, whether voluntary or involuntary, were highly desirable: the first African slaves were imported in 1625, and the first Jewish settlers arrived in 1664. By the 1660s, there were about 300 permanent homes listed in the records.

But during the Second Dutch War, England redeclared its right to the region, basing its claim on the voyages of John Cabot; in 1664, when the English fleet sailed into New York Harbor, then-governor Peter Stuyvesant struck his colors and quietly surrendered. (Actually, his constituents surrendered for him; a puritanical tyrant with a wooden leg, Stuyvesant ordered every tavern in the city to close by 9 p.m., which clearly proves he was in the wrong place.) He left behind the names of Wall Street (so called because a protective wall was raised there); Broadway (originally Breede Wegh), a cobbled route that ran the entire length of the island; the Bowery (from his own country home or "bouwerie") in the farmland a mile north and east of the city; Harlem; and of course, Stuyvesant Square. With one very brief resurgence of the Dutch in 1673, New York—now renamed in honor of King Charles's brother, the Duke of York (later James II)—was firmly in the hands of the British.

Back in Europe, the imperial and often internecine struggles between Britain and France only intermittently gave way to peace. So the colonial governor, Thomas Donegan, increasingly wary of French expansionism from the Canadian border, assiduously cultivated friendly relationships with the Iroquois. It was a good strategy, and the tribes were an invaluable ally during the decades of the French and Indian Wars that stretched from the late 17th century into the mid-18th. The Battery got its name early in those wars, when nearly a hundred cannon were lined up along the waterfront to prevent an attack on the harbor. The Treaty of Paris in 1763 confirmed the British domination of the North American territories, and the long and bitter campaigns gave way to a burst of settlement and expansion.

There was a brief period of self-satisfied prosperity. The area was covered in wheat fields and farms, like the one in the Bronx on which the Van Courtland House, now a museum, was built in 1748. King's College (now Columbia) was founded in 1754; St. Paul's Chapel was dedicated in 1766.

Then, in one of those ironies history is made of, the British crown tried to pay off its war debts by levying huge taxes on the very American colonies it had fought so hard to retain. With the passage of the Stamp Act in 1765, the resentment of many formerly loyal colonists reached a crisis. Shippers and "bolters" (millers) turned to smuggling and tariff-dodging. Fledgling Sons of Liberty took on the British authorities in the "Battle of Golden Hill" as early as 1770, and in 1774 they threw a "tea party" of their own in New York Harbor. Tensions increased to the point that many older landowners returned to England. William Tryon, the popular colonial governor of North Carolina, was transferred to New York in an attempt to contain the troubles, but he was forced out in 1775. Rebellion-minded New Yorkers—notably including English-born but radical-hearted Thomas Paine and 19-year-old Alexander Hamilton, whose eloquence would later be turned to persuading the colonies to ratify the Constitution—published scathing denunciations of the Crown's policies toward the colonies. With the capture of Fort Ticonderoga later that year, war was all but declared.

This was the crucial region of the American Revolution. Fully a third of all battles were fought in the state, including the tide-turning Battle of Saratoga. New York produced both America's first martyr, Nathan Hale, who was hanged in the city, and its most infamous hero-turned-traitor, Benedict Arnold.

But for all its cathartic rhetoric, New York City's active role in the Revolution was very short and not too sweet. General Washington suffered a series of defeats in the fall of 1776, including the battles of Long Island, Harlem Heights, and White Plains, and though the Americans held onto most of the upper and western part of the state, they eventually had to abandon the city to the British forces, who sailed into the harbor in a fleet of 500 ships and occupied it for the full seven years until the end of the war.

During the British occupation, unfortunately, the city was swept by two massive and somewhat suspicious fires, one right after the occupation that destroyed a thousand homes and Trinity Church, and the second in 1778. Consequently, there are few buildings from the colonial period visible outside Historic Richmondtown and the Alice Austen House, both on Staten Island; even the Fraunces Tavern, site of Washington's famous farewell to the troops in 1783, is a partial re-creation of the original.

THE EMPIRE STATE

ALMOST FROM THE MOMENT PEACE WAS PRONOUNCED, New York boomed—and bickered. From 1785 until 1790, New York served as the nation's capital; it was here that Washington was sworn in as the first president; and it was from here that Hamilton, John Jay, and Virginian James Madison published the so-called Federalist Papers, which eventually persuaded the states to ratify the Constitution. Hamilton, who had married the governor's daughter, served as Washington's secretary of the treasury and founded both the Bank of New York and the *New York Post*. But he and John Adams opposed the French Revolution, which widened the gap between the Federalists and the Jeffersonians, among whom were Hamilton's former collaborator Madison and the brilliant young senator Aaron Burr, strongman of the Tammany Society. (For an explanation of the Tammany Society, see the section on The Upper West Side in Part Six, New York's Neighborhoods.) Burr succeeded in becoming Jefferson's vice president, but Hamilton's jealous maneuvering prevented Burr's becoming president instead; and when Hamilton later blocked Burr's election as governor, Burr challenged him to a duel. The 1804 shootout left both Hamilton and Burr's political career fatally wounded.

About the time that political power shifted, first to Philadelphia and then to the new capital at Washington, the New York Stock Exchange opened, and New York's indefinite term as a financial capital began. The agricultural order gradually began to yield to an industrial and shipping society. Staten Island ferry boy Cornelius Vanderbilt gradually bought up the local freight lines and built his shipping force into an empire, becoming a millionaire while still in his teens. German-born John Jacob Astor, whose China trading, land sales, and fur trade companies enjoyed comfortable monopolies in the nation, was the first in New York's long line of millionaire tycoons (and first to establish the city's philanthropic tradition by leaving money for what became the New York Public Library). Confident of its own importance as early as 1804, the city established the New York Historical Society collection.

Already it was the largest city in the country, with more than 33,000 residents; ten years later the population had nearly doubled. In 1811, city planners tried to impose some order on the labyrinth of haphazard roads by laying out the famous Manhattan "grid" above 14th Street. A series of virulent epidemics—yellow fever, cholera, typhoid, smallpox—gradually drove residents from the old downtown area into what is now Greenwich Village. Another huge fire in 1835 and a third in 1845 again destroyed most of lower Manhattan and cleared the way for ever more ambitious construction. They also inspired the creation of Croton Reservoir in 1842, in the heart of Midtown where the New York Public Library is now; this project marked the beginning of fresh public water and a city-wide sewer system.

The Erie Canal was completed in 1825, drawing even more trade, and immigrants as well, through its already booming port. The great potato famine forced a huge influx of Irish immigrants—at least 200,000—in the 1840s and 1850s. A wave of German immigrants followed in the 1860s; the Chinese began arriving in the 1870s; and in the 1880s, an estimated 1.5 million Eastern European Jews flooded the Lower East Side. They were accompanied by thousands of Italians, Irish, and displaced Southern blacks, and by 1900 the city held an astonishing 3.4 million people. That would double again, to 7 million, in just 30 years. And those were just the ones who settled down; an estimated 17 million more transient immigrants passed through the city between 1880 and 1910.

The widespread poverty and incredibly unsanitary living conditions of the underclass produced not only disease, but rampant and almost institutional crime—that is, street gangs at one level, and political machines at the other. The Five Points neighborhood, recreated by Martin Scorcese in his 2002 epic *Gangs of New York,* was only blocks from Cherry Street, where William "Boss" Tweed held court. Tweed and his Tammany Hall organization looted the city of more than $160 million over the years, though they did do the immigrants the favor of registering them as Democrats by way of maintaining control.

New York took on the role of intellectual capital as well. The rest of the state might be known to have a sort of wild and bucolic beauty, thanks to the efforts of such writers as Washington Irving, James Fenimore Cooper, and William Cullen Bryant, and the Hudson River School artists, including Thomas Cole and Frederick Church; but New York City was determined that everything be modern and smart.

Horace Greeley's *New York Tribune,* the most influential newspaper before and during the Civil War, was founded in 1841; the *New York Times* followed in 1851. The University of the City of New York was chartered in 1831; the Philharmonic Society of New York gave its first concert in 1842. The Crystal Palace, modeled on the pavilion erected for London's Great Exposition of 1851, hosted the first World's Fair in 1853 (and later burned to the ground, just as the London palace had). Numerous progressive and reformist movements made New York their headquarters, including the suffragettes (the first women's rights convention was held in Seneca Falls in 1848); Greeley's *Tribune* editorialized in favor of organized labor, profit sharing (both of which he instituted at his paper), abolition, and women's suffrage. The California gold rush electrified Wall Street in 1849; a scheme by Jay Gould to corner the gold market 20 years later would nearly bankrupt it.

And in 1858, one of New York's most beloved landmarks, Central Park, opened its gates, ensuring that even the poorest sweatshop employee in the city would always have a place to walk like a prince.

CIVIL WAR AND THE "SECOND EMPIRE"

NEW YORK WAS NO STRANGER TO SLAVERY. The first slaves had been imported by the Dutch in 1625, and in fact it was slave labor that built the original fortress, including the "wall" that was Wall Street. With painful irony, Wall Street also featured the first slave market, a mercenary operation that predated the Stock Exchange by nearly a century. But New York was also in the vanguard of the abolitionist movement, outlawing slavery in the city as early as 1799 (phasing it out over 30 years) and increasingly agitating for nationwide abolition. Frederick Douglass's influential *North Star* newspaper was headquartered in Rochester; Greeley's *Tribune* was the country's most vociferous antislavery mainstream paper (though originally a passivist one). It was the growing split between the outspoken antislavery and laissez-faire elements within the long-dominant Democratic Party that helped swing New York to the Republicans and Abraham Lincoln in 1860.

Nevertheless, while the progressive intellectual element in New York favored abolition, not even all of them—and even fewer members of the laboring class and immigrant communities, who could not hope to raise the $300 "replacement fee" that was the rich man's alternative to active service—supported a war to free the Southern slaves. With the passage of the Conscription Act, draft riots broke out all over the country; those in New York City, which lasted four days in July 1863 and resulted in the death of 120 men, nearly all black, and the displacement of close to a thousand more, were the most serious. It required the mobilization of the police, navy forces, militia, and even West Point cadets, along with the troops already in the field, to restore order.

In general, however, New York vigorously supported the war effort, especially as the need for continual military supplies and transportation fueled the city's industries: battleships (including the ironclad *Monitor*) and freighters, textiles for uniforms and supplies, provisions, and, most important, the railroads that carried them. And for all the occasional Wall Street panics, the momentum never really slackened: the end of the war was for New York the beginning of what Mark Twain christened the "Gilded Age."

Luxury hotels such as the (original) Waldorf-Astoria and the Plaza opened their doors; so did the Metropolitan Museum of Art and the Metropolitan Opera House on Broadway. Fifth Avenue became known as "Mansion Row." Henry Villard, publisher of the *New York Evening Post* and founder of the Northern

Pacific Railroad, began his gilded palace (now the New York Palace) at 50th Street in 1881; W. K. Vanderbilt built an Italianate mansion at 51st and Fifth, just one of a long line—or avenue—of Vanderbilt family extravagances leading up to his cousin Cornelius II's fantastic French Renaissance chateau at the foot of Central Park (the house seen in the painting in the Plaza Hotel's Oak Bar).

Elevated railroads, or "Els," running above Second, Third, Sixth, and Ninth avenues suddenly made it easier to get uptown, and newly electrified streetlights made it safer. Telephone and telegraph wires crisscrossed the city, at least until the blizzard of 1888 ripped them down and launched the city on a buried-cable program. The first great luxury apartment building, the Dakota, designed by the architect of the Plaza, staked out a new frontier on Central Park West at 72nd Street. Henry Frick constructed his mansion on the east side of the park at 70th, within easy reach of the new Metropolitan Museum of Art. The Statue of Liberty, St. Patrick's Cathedral, the Brooklyn Bridge, Carnegie Hall—all these monuments to the New York spirit were in place within a quarter century of war's end.

And the city was stretching in other directions, too, especially to the southeast. The Brooklyn Academy of Music had been founded in 1858; Brooklyn's Prospect Park, designed by Central Park architects Frederick Olmsted and Calvert Vaux (and considered by many to be superior to the Manhattan park), was finished in 1867; the Brooklyn Museum of Art opened in 1897. In fact, Brooklyn was the third largest city in the country on its own—it would still be the fourth largest today—but in 1898, the modern city of New York, the combined five boroughs, was officially consolidated.

No economy—and no underground economy—benefited more than New York's during the postwar period. Shipping, trade, industry, government contracts, and, inevitably, corruption in the awarding of them, made millionaires out of manufacturers, mob bosses, political influence-peddlers, and sweatshop operators alike. Samuel Tilden became an early example of New York's periodic hero, the crusading reformer, when he prosecuted Boss Tweed of the Tammany Hall ring, but he made little real dent in the power of Tammany itself. (A few years later, city police commissioner Theodore Roosevelt would build a more successful political career on his reformist reputation.) The Republicans were not much cleaner, and the semi-underground power struggle led to a more overt political distance between the city's Democrats and the Republicans upstate.

The hundreds of thousands of immigrants who arrived near the end of the 19th century were herded into warehouses, mills, and industrial sweatshops, while labor leaders fought to establish minimal hour and wage (and age) standards. The tenement, the flophouse, the drug den, and the gang took up permanent positions in the city structure. Despite periodic catastrophes—most famously the Triangle Shirtwaist Factory fire of 1911, which killed 140—and the increase of institutionalized poverty, most New Yorkers were intoxicated by the flow of commercial goods and boastfully smug about the prosperity of the city.

To a great extent, both this vast prosperity and the narrowness of its beneficiaries are exemplified by the spread of the railroads and the great fortunes their owners made from them. And one way or another, most of the rail barons had New York connections. The gold rush of 1849 may have lured Collis Huntington from Oneonta, New York, to California; but he quickly realized that the real money was to be made in railroads stretching to the West Coast. The fortunes of Andrew Carnegie and his partner-turned-rival Henry Frick were forged in steel and railroading. "Commodore" Cornelius Vanderbilt expanded into railroads as well and became lord of the New York–Chicago routes. Jay Gould was forced out of the Erie Railroad and other state rails, but he merely headed west and wound up with four more.

New York stockbroker E. H. Harriman took over the Union Pacific, Southern Pacific, and Central Pacific railroads. J. Pierpont Morgan, already extremely wealthy thanks to his financier father, J. S. Morgan, took a lesson from all of these preceding examples, wresting away control of Gould's eastern railway holdings, founding U.S. Steel with Frick, and lending gold to the federal government at usurious rates during the Panic of 1895. These families, along with the Astors and Villards and their financial rivals, built lavish mansions on the East Side, establishing Midtown and Central Park as the social center of Manhattan and defining what came to be known as the "Four Hundred," the city's social elite. (It may be worth remembering that the life of luxury need not be a safe one, however: John Jacob Astor went down on the *Titanic,* and a Vanderbilt, who had originally planned to journey on the same ship, died on the *Lusitania.*)

Of course, there was nonsteel money. John D. Rockefeller's fortune, grounded in the oil-refining business, was almost incalculable, well into the hundreds of millions by the turn of the century. And he was not alone. By 1900, 70% of the nation's corporations were headquartered in Manhattan, and 65% of all import trade passed through the harbor.

THE EARLY 20TH CENTURY

IN CHARACTERISTIC FASHION, NEW YORK was too impatient to wait for the calendar to announce a new era. The age of American imperialism, such as it was, was hastened by New York newspaper tycoons William Randolph Hearst and Joseph Pulitzer, whose respective (if not entirely respectable) dailies the *Journal* and *World* so twisted coverage of Cuban-Spanish tensions that the United States was eventually lured into the Spanish-American War, from which it gained the Philippines, Guam, and Puerto Rico, not to mention the toothy New York–born hero Teddy Roosevelt.

Even so, 1900 was a landmark year. Ground for the first subway was broken in 1900; when it was completed, it was suddenly possible to cross the nine miles from City Hall to 145th Street in a little over 20 minutes. (A steam-driven version, a single car that rocketed about 300 feet along Broadway between Warren and Murray streets and then was sucked backward, was constructed in 1870, but it made little impression.)

The city of the future had already been forged from the five boroughs in 1898. New Yorkers were so confident of their home's position as First City that the Vanderbilts launched a railroad line that ran back and forth between Manhattan and Chicago, the "Second City"; it was described as the overland version of a luxury liner, and it was grandly titled *The Twentieth Century*. The "new" Grand Central Station, the Beaux Arts beauty now restored to its original glory, was begun in 1903; Pennsylvania Station (the original, not the existing building) would follow only a few years later. The Staten Island Ferry made its first crossing in 1905; the first metered taxi challenged the old omnibus system in 1907.

The scramble for the skyline began with the construction of the 300-foot Flatiron Building at Broadway, Fifth, and 23rd streets in 1902; skeptics confidently predicted its collapse, though it stands proudly today as the symbol of its own "district." At 30 stories, the 1913 Gothic Woolworth Building at Broadway and Park reigned for 17 years, until the construction of the 77-story Chrysler Building in 1930, and that topped the city for only a few months, until the 102-story Empire State Building opened in 1931. It was getting so dark above that the city finally passed an ordinance restricting the height and size of buildings in 1931. (The limits were rescinded in 1961, hence the MetLife building that hovers over Grand Central Terminal.)

The early years of the 20th century were a golden age for songwriters, playwrights, musicians, and vaudeville performers. Publishing firms crowded into the dilapidated 28th Street neighborhood, giving use to the term Tin Pan Alley.

The Apollo Theater in Harlem opened in 1913. Blacks and Hispanics settled on the West Side, in an area of the 60s then called San Juan Hill (possibly in reference to Roosevelt's great victory in Cuba), and on the north side of Manhattan in Harlem. That had been a prosperous Jewish neighborhood, but it gradually became a center for black art, literature, and music during a period called the Harlem Renaissance. In the 1920s alone, Harlem's population increased from 83,000 to more than 200,000.

World War I only boosted the city's economy, which went into overdrive to supply the troops; stocks continued to rise throughout the 1920s, which roared in New York as nowhere else. Prohibition became the law in 1920, but just as war boosted profits, so did the relatively genteel, or at least socially tolerated, crime of bootlegging. Smart, brittle, and literary characters went hand in hand with Follies. American women were not only emancipated, in the phrase of the time, but were also finally enfranchised. (Women got the vote; movies found a voice.) The *New Yorker* debuted in 1925, with its quintessential Gilded Age fop of a symbol, Eustace Tilley, on the cover. Charles Lindbergh crossed over the Atlantic Ocean in the *Spirit of St. Louis* while New Yorkers drove under the Hudson River through the brand-new Holland Tunnel. Big bands and Broadway filled the airways; so did Babe Ruth, who in 1927 hit 60 home runs for the Yankees. The Museum of Modern Art was founded in 1929, and the Guggenheim a year later.

Everything glittered until 1929, when New York once again led the nation, this time into disaster. The crash of the stock market on October 29 turned Central Park into a shantytown and the city's greatest artists into federal employees, thanks to the Works Progress Administration (WPA). At the same time, growing political tensions in Europe, particularly in Germany, inspired a whole new generation of writers and artists to emigrate to America. During the slow reconstruction of the 1930s, Mayor Fiorella La Guardia, the "Little Flower," was able to institute a series of municipal reforms so that the poorer classes could also share in the recovery. He also persuaded President (and former New York governor) Franklin Roosevelt to provide New Deal funds to build the Triborough and Hudson bridges, the Battery Park Tunnel, and dozens of other public projects. In 1939, multimillionaire philanthropist John D. Rockefeller Jr. personally drove the final rivet into the beautiful Art Deco complex at Rockefeller Plaza, and a few months later, flush with visions of a bright new future, the New York World's Fair of 1939–1940 drew a staggering 45 million visitors to Queens.

THE MODERN ERA

ONCE AGAIN, WAR FUELED THE ECONOMY. The outbreak of World War II kicked the stock market back into high gear, and it was not to slow for nearly 30 years. With the ending of the war, America the melting pot took its place at the head of international power as well; the United Nations headquarters were established in New York in 1946. Large numbers of Puerto Ricans and other Hispanic immigrants arrived, and many of them moved to the Upper East Side, to what became known as El Barrio or Spanish Harlem; the Chinese arrived in even greater numbers throughout the 1940s and 1950s. Builder and powerbroker Robert Moses remade the face of the West Side, culturally and physically, by sweeping away the crumbling buildings in the San Juan district and designing a huge arts complex, now Lincoln Center for the Performing Arts, in its place.

The 1960s were famously feverish in New York, in the arts world and in politics. The Beatles set foot on American soil for the first time at Kennedy Airport, and they played their first U.S. concert at Shea Stadium. Queens's Flushing Meadow hosted another World's Fair, and its symbolic Unisphere still holds up its one-world promise. Columbia University students staged famous sit-ins. *Hair* opened on Broadway, and Mikhail Baryshnikov and Rudolf Nureyev led the list of Russian dancers and artists who fled to the United States. A new sense of irony, expressed in various ways—Pop art, the stereotypical "neurotic" New Yorker made famous by Woody Allen, among others, and the new Beat generation of writers and so-called bohemians—made New York City seem both exotic and depraved to many conservative Americans.

New York's black intelligentsia, from Langston Hughes and Zora Neale Hurston to James Baldwin, Richard Wright, and Ralph Ellison, had been exposing racism in scathing essays, novels, and plays throughout the 1950s; now their writings and *The Autobiography of Malcolm X* became required reading. The flamboyant lifestyle of Harlem congressman Adam Clayton Powell and the charges of corruption and political favoritism that surrounded him were reminiscent of the Prohibition-era reign of Mayor Jimmy Walker. Greenwich Village became first the symbol and center of the gay rights movement, and then the equally vivid shorthand for the burgeoning AIDS epidemic. Militant civil rights groups, antigovernment radical political parties, anti-Vietnam demonstrators, and women's groups seemed to have transformed New York society top to bottom.

And perhaps it did—but in New York, money always seems to have more pull than politics. By the early 1970s, Nixon was beginning to withdraw the troops from Southeast Asia, the hippies were on the way out, and the yuppies had arrived. A burst of luxury hotels and apartment buildings and huge, showy corporate structures jacked the skyline ever higher (and led, though too late for Stanford White's Penn Station, to a greater appreciation of historic restoration and preservation).

Moreover, the expansion of New York, specifically the exodus of Manhattanites into the suburbs, began to drain the city of vital income. And as the upper-middle class moved out, the city became a playground for the super-rich and a prison for the poor.

The pride of the 1970s nearly led to a great fall. Just as the World Trade Center was completed in 1973, the city began to spiral toward bankruptcy, a fate just barely averted with the fraternal assistance of Wall Street. The Great White Way and the entire rest of the city went dark in the Blackout of 1977. Stocks ballooned again, only to crash again in 1987. (This time even Donald Trump, symbol of conspicuous consumption, had to resort to humble refinancing.) The first terrorist attack on the World Trade Center, in 1993, killed six people;

eight years later, the death toll would be nearly 3,000. But markets never stay slow in a city that never sleeps; and downtown construction, repair, and improvement of mass transit and the restaurant and entertainment industry are stronger than ever.

Heading into the millennium, and having celebrated its own official first century as a unified city, New York seemed to be turning over its own chronometers, spiritual and literal. That great symbol Ellis Island, which reopened as the Immigration Museum in 1990, is already one of the most visited sites in New York. Chelsea Piers, the crumbling remnants of the once vital Hell's Kitchen port, reopened as a massive playground, while on the east side the South Street Seaport became a sort of historical shopping mall. Another great wave of immigration brought even greater ethnic variety to the city, especially in Brooklyn (where much of the estimated half-million recent arrivals are Caribbean) and Queens, as well as in Manhattan (the Heights and Chinatown). The city's population rebounded by 10% between 1990 and 2000. And crime, the city's long-standing shadow empire, is to a substantial degree succumbing to the police department's continual investigations into corruption both external and internal. During the administration of Mayor Rudolph Guiliani, a former federal prosecutor, crime rates plummeted and (not to mention his campaign against street vagrancy and the sort of petty panhandling that annoys out-of-towners) are now at the lowest level in a half-century. Times Square, once a byword of prostitution, gambling, and purse-snatching, began an astonishing revitalization campaign that has not only reshaped the entire area but attracted a new generation of theatrical producers and media conglomerates; it is now one of the city's most profitable tourist attractions.

There can be no question, however, that the events of September 11, 2001, have forever changed this great city, sobering its financial, cultural, and architectural hubris. Yet it displayed the city at its best—heroic, united, determined. It has also demonstrated the inherent power of the American Dream: The Statue of Liberty lifts her lamp to illuminate the many monuments of both despair and hope. At press time, the Statue is open to visitors to her feet; the new Port Authority Trans-Hudson (PATH) terminal and Vesey Street pedestrian bridge had been opened to return traffic through lower Manhattan; and a network was taking shape of a dozen public parks and green spaces around the border of the island's southern tip. Despite many delays and design changes, the neighborhood now known as Ground Zero has obviously become fixed in the minds of Americans as a critical landmark. New York may wind up with an even greater sense of its skyline than it had before 9-11.

THE FICTIONAL CITY

THERE ARE FEW CITIES THAT HAVE BEEN THE SUBJECT of more novels, plays, or stories than New York, and with the advent of television and movies, the landscape is even more familiar to nonresidents. But again, we want you to see the history beneath the surface of the city, the New York that its founders dreamed of, that its wealthy ordered, and its working class constructed. So among some personal, evocative, and decidedly not modern favorites:

The Age of Innocence and *The House of Mirth,* by Edith Wharton, both titled with heavy irony, bring the heyday of Midtown society to life; so does Henry James's masterpiece *Washington Square.* (The lavish film versions of these books are worth a look for the look, at least.)

The Last of the Mohicans, by James Fenimore Cooper, may have put you off as a child by its old-fashioned prose, but Cooper's history of the colonial state and the era of the French and Indian Wars is far more fascinating. (If you were enraptured by the equally fascinating movie, be warned: Hawkeye did not fall in love with Cora Monroe; he was old enough to be her father.)

Up in the Old Hotel, by Joseph Mitchell, is an astonishing collection of articles and stories, originally written for the *New Yorker.* Mitchell brings back to life the golden era of the oyster beds, the Fulton Fish Market, and the piers and warehouses and taverns of the West Side.

Winter's Tale, by Mark Halperin, is a mystical vision of the city as an engine of pure energy, a sort of transmitter between this world and another—and no description of New York in winter can ever be more enrapturing.

Caleb Carr's two adventure novels, *The Alienist* and *The Angel of Darkness,* take place around the turn of the century, when gangs roved the city, Teddy Roosevelt was a young reformer, and forensic evidence and psychology were new and mysterious sciences. In a similar vein is *Waterworks,* by E. L. Doctorow, with its fantastic vision of the old Croton Reservoir.

In *Time and Again,* Jack Finney manages to imprint the New York City of the late 19th century so thoroughly in his contemporary protagonist's mind that he is transported there and falls in love.

And of course, those least childish of children's books, E. B. White's *Stuart Little,* the picaresque novel of a mouse-sized Manhattanite, and the wonderful *Eloise* (by Kay Thompson), whose portrait hangs in the lobby of her beloved Plaza Hotel and in whose honor one of the authors was once allowed to ride on the back of a carriage horse in Central Park.

PART TWO

PLANNING *your* VISIT

WHEN *to* GO

NEW YORK MAY SOUND "NORTHERN" TO A LOT OF FOLKS, and in winter it can certainly scrape some low temperatures and shine up the sidewalks; but in the heart of summer, especially August, it can be as thick and muggy as any Southern city, with the temperature nudging up toward the three-figure mark and sudden, sweeping rains that leave the asphalt steaming. Why do you think the Hamptons were invented? Of course, if you're inured to the humidity, or if business or school vacations require you to travel in July or August, you will still find a lot of free programs, indoors and out, all over town (and you can count on all the restaurants and museums cranking up the air-conditioning).

Actually, there's something to be said for almost any time of year in the Big Apple. If you go for the sidewalk show, spring and fall are absolutely gorgeous in New York; average temperatures are in the 60s and 70s, making for perfect walking weather, and there are flower shows, the ballet and opera spring seasons, and circus rings.

Summer, as we've said, is freebie heaven: opera, classical music, and Shakespeare in Central Park; Tuesday night chamber concerts in Washington Square Park, weekend concerts at South Street Seaport, and jazz in MoMA's sculpture garden; swing dance on Lincoln Center Plaza; at least one street fair every week; Fourth of July fireworks and sunbathing in Strawberry Fields.

Fall is one party after another, starting with Halloween and running through Thanksgiving; the Big Apple Circus sets up in the Lincoln Center Plaza, and Central Park is absolutely brilliant. For all its chill—the really brutal winds don't usually hit until after the New Year—New York is a city that really knows how to dress for the holidays,

unofficial **TIP**
January is a good time to visit with all those sales (including coats), Ice Capades at Madison Square Garden, perhaps an early Chinese New Year (of course there's a parade), and quiet time in the museums that are usually full of kids.

unofficial **TIP**
If you do wish to go during a major holiday or around a special event, such as Christmas, be sure to make your reservations well in advance and confirm at least once. Manhattan is a madhouse at prime time, although the excitement may be worth it. If you need your space, however, pick another time.

with musical programs, lighting displays, elaborate window settings, parades, and so on. (In fact, a parade is practically guaranteed for your visit: There are so many excuses for parading in this town, you'd have to look for a month to miss one.) Many parks, including the Bronx Zoo, light up and stay open late around the holidays; the atrium of the Citicorp Building holds a huge model train display, as does the New York Botanical Garden; the music of the Central Park and Rockefeller Center ice rinks fills the air. The South Street Seaport is a winter fantasy of lights, and the carolers—some of them puppets—are a family favorite. Department-store windows are almost worth the visit by themselves, particularly the tradition-minded Macy's and Saks and the extravagantly unpredictable Bergdorf-Goodman's (though lines to view the windows are enormous). This really is the town that never sleeps. See the final section of the chapter for a calendar of special events.

WHAT *to* PACK

PERHAPS A LITTLE SADLY, THIS ONCE MOST ELEGANT of societies has become extremely informal; you'll be unlikely to see a black tie or even a tuxedo outside of a wedding party unless you are fortunate enough to be invited to a serious social event. Even the old established restaurants rarely require a tie for lunch; most only "recommend" a jacket, although it's a good idea to have a tie on hand at night. (See the dress code advisories in our restaurant profiles.) However, the great majority of Manhattanites are dressed either for success or to impress, in classic style or not, so if you like to blend in with the shopping or art crowd, go for the reasonably neat look. All those gold- and silver-glittered sweatshirts just make you look as if you spent your adolescence in Atlantic City.

If you're simply sightseeing, you can pretty much do as you please; streetwear is every-wear, especially during the day. Shorts, T-shirts, or polo shirts (athletic-logo sportswear for kids) are common well into autumn, and a casual dress or reasonably neat pair of khakis will make you look downright respectable. The one "touristy" craze we do not recommend is the fanny pack. Not only does it mark you as an outsider, it can be more easily cut off and stolen than wallets or even purses.

As for outerwear, try to get something with dual use. A rainproof top of some sort, a lightweight jacket you can layer, or a sweater is probably the most you'll need in the summer, just in case a breeze comes up at night. However, remember that you will probably be going in and out of air-conditioning. If you're planning to jump in and out of buses or stores or even theaters, a light jacket you can easily unbutton or remove and carry without difficulty will keep you from alternately sweating and freezing. (A medium-weight or heavy shawl, which can be both decorative and warming, is a great alternative and easy to pack.) Those small fold-up umbrellas are preferable to the traditional sort, not only because you can stash them in your bag but also because a crowd of people wielding pointed implements or hanging them on chair backs and such can be dangerous (they're available on the street if you lose or forget one).

Something along the lines of a trenchcoat with zip-in lining or a wool walking coat with a sweater will usually do in winter, though it's smart to have the anti-wind accessories—gloves, earmuffs, hats, or scarves—tucked in your bag. Coming down through those "tunnels" of skyscrapers, the gusts pick up some surprising force. And if you have pull-on, thin plastic galoshes or waterproof boots of some sort, it wouldn't hurt to bring them; snowstorms can move in pretty quickly. Fur coats are no longer much of an issue in the moral sense in New York, but unless you're planning to go to the nicer hotels and restaurants, you may find your fur more trouble to worry about than it's worth. Lugging a fuzzy through the Metropolitan Museum of Art gets to be extremely sweaty. Of course, if you're sticking to the Metropolitan Opera, fur away.

Just don't overload yourself. Frankly, years of travel (and packing) have convinced us that most people carry more clothes than they really need. (And these days, with stricter limits on carry-ons and baggage weights, it's even sillier to overindulge.) As obvious as those easy-packing tips you see in travel magazines may be (pick a basic color and a few bright accessories or a change of ties, things that don't wrinkle, lots of light layers, and so on), most visitors fill up their suitcases with whole new outfits for every day and evening event. Who are you trying to impress? Plan your packing the way you'd plan everyday life at home. Unless you have a really formal event to go to, high heels are tiring and take up a lot of room (though at least nowadays there are "comfortable" heels). Similarly, men can easily wear one nice jacket and carry assorted slacks, or a suit and different shirts, perhaps a vest. A dark suit is next to formality, anyway. Besides, it is difficult to resist buying something new and fashionable when you're visiting, and then you have even more clothes to carry.

Two really important things to consider when packing are comfortable shoes—this is a culture of the streets, and what isn't asphalt is concrete—and expandable or forgiving waistlines. Even if you don't think you're going to eat much, the scent of food is constantly in the air; every bar lays out

*un*official **TIP**
A pair of shock-absorbent sole inserts can dramatically reduce foot and back pain as well.

those mixed nuts or something similar; and somehow even the most careful dieters seem to join the clean plate club when they visit one of the world's most famous restaurant centers. Seasoned travelers know that a change in schedule can often cause bloating as well as, paradoxically, dehydration. Make sure you have a change of shoes, too; this is not the place to save space, because wearing the same shoes through and after hours of walking or even standing around sightseeing is a good way to have sore feet, if not worse. The new anti-blister patches and sprays may be helpful as well. If you don't want to pack "fat day" clothes, you better be packing your running shoes. Or let them double as your walking shoes.

The other traveling "musts" are over-the-counter medications and ointments. People tend to drink more coffee and more cocktails on vacation, or even when taking important clients out, so be sure to pack headache medicines, Alka-Seltzer, and the like. If you are on prescription medicine, carry a little more of it than you actually need: You might drop some while sightseeing or find yourself staying a day or so longer than you expected for business or pleasure or even bad traveling weather. (It wouldn't hurt to photocopy the prescription or label, either, particularly if the medication contains any controlled substances.) If you are allergic to bites or stings, remember the antihistamines. For scratches and small annoyances, a small tube of Neosporin or other antiseptic ointment is helpful. You can get these things at a drugstore or the hotel shop, of course, but those little "travel sizes" are wildly overpriced; you'd be better off putting a small amount of each in your own containers. Be absolutely sure to pack bandage strips and muscle-pain antidotes as well; blisters can ruin an otherwise wonderful trip. Similarly, you might want to bring an extra pair of eyeglasses or contact lenses.

*un*official **TIP**
A good way to keep medications fresh is to use those small zip-plastic bags sold for jewelry (or even the sandwich-sized bags).

Most better hotels have small sewing kits in the rooms for quick fixes, although bigger emergencies will be better served by valets or a dry cleaner around the corner. But if you're staying in a basic hotel, a needle and thread may come in handy. So may a multitool pocket knife, though you must pack it with your checked baggage (any such implements in carry-on luggage, including corkscrews, might still be confiscated). If you find that you forgot to take your grandfather's pocket knife out of your kit bag, find the nearest express office and send it home.

We have found three other tiny items to be extremely useful: a handkerchief, mini magnifying or reading glasses, disposable stain-remover pads, and one of those tiny flashlights. We mean an old-fashioned man's handkerchief, not a pretty little showpiece. In the event of bad weather, allergies, air-conditioning, damp subway seats, and so on, a good 12-inch square is a lifesaver. Restaurant menus keep getting more ornate, the lighting dimmer, and—it seems—the type smaller. If you plan to spend time on the subways or the sidewalks, you will be in near-contact with a lot of coffee cups, snacks, and so on; if you find yourself having an even closer encounter thanks to a jerking subway ride, one of those towelette-sized spot treatments can save you a lot of heartache. And as more and more museums have to lower or narrowly focus their lighting to protect fragile canvases and textiles, we increasingly find ourselves squinting at the plaques and captions. A penlight comes in handy (but be sure to train it only on the information, not the art).

unofficial **TIP**
This is a city with a crime problem, so don't walk around flashing a lot of expensive jewelry. Leave it at home and stick to the costume stuff, or leave it in the hotel safe except for the big party. That way, even if you lose an earring, you can replace it quickly and cheaply at the next vendor cart. You might be surprised what nice-looking jewelry you can find on the street. For a more in-depth discussion on staying safe in the big city, see "How to Avoid Crime" in Part Four, Arriving and Getting Oriented.

GATHERING INFORMATION

BROCHURES, HISTORICAL BACKGROUND, and up-to-date schedules are available from the **New York Metropolitan Convention and Visitors Bureau** (NYMCVB), which updates its material quarterly. It's best to call in advance and get their information package mailed to you (call ☎ 800-NYC-VISIT) or go to the Web site (**www.nycvisit.com**), but they also have offices around Manhattan if you don't get to it beforehand (call ☎ 212-397-8222). There you can pick up lots of maps, free tickets or discounts, shopping guides, and so on. One of the NYMCVB branches is in the Embassy Theater in Times Square (Broadway between 46th and 47th streets), which also houses the Times Square Visitors Center and public transit information center. There are also visitors centers in Pennsylvania Station (34th Street side) and carts stationed inside the Empire State Building and outside (unless it's frigid) Madison Square Garden. Be sure to pick up the free subway map.

New York has a large gay and lesbian population and a great many services and attractions for the homosexual traveler. Among local publications reporting gay events are the *Village Voice* and *New York Press,* both free in the city; and the more specialized *Next* and *Blade,* a free weekly available at many bars and restaurants. The larger gay bookstores (see the relevant section in Part Nine, Shopping) are also bulletin boards for community information.

When it comes to Internet and Web sites, no city outdoes New York. Among them are the online version of the weekly *City Guide* provided to hotels (**www.cityguideny.com**); Citysearch (**www.citysearch.com**); the

unofficial **TIP**

Serious museum-goers should try to get a subscription to *Museums New York* ($20), a sort of playbill for museums with features, phone numbers, and current exhibits for even the smallest streetside collections, plus discount coupons for many of them; call ☎ 212-604-0877.

online site of the downtown monthly *Paper* (**www.papermag.com**); and the online version of New York's picture newspaper (**www.timeoutny.com**). The *Village Voice* has its own site as well (**www.villagevoice.com**).

New York magazine puts cultural events and restaurant and entertainment listings up at **www.nymag.com.** Even the booming Times Square has a Web site with info on local attractions (**www.timessquarebid.org**).

For those of you who are into the blogging game, there is only one site: **www.gothamist.com.** And while **www.gawker.com** has moved beyond blogging, the site is still reporting—as it eagerly mentions on the front page—from the center of the universe.

Once in New York, look for free publications in your hotel room (most often the *New York Visitors Guide* and weekly editions of the *City Guide*); check current issues of *New York* and *New Yorker* magazines and the daily *New York Times* for special events and performances. Many hotels put the monthly *Where New York* and *In New York* magazines in their rooms; they have extensive museum and entertainment listings. *Time Out* is a good source of entertainment and cultural opportunities, with a special gay-interest section. The Spanish language daily *El Diario* is available at most newsstands. There are also several entertainment and cultural hotlines to call for daily opportunities: see Part Eleven, Entertainment and Nightlife.

The main area code for Manhattan is still 212, though recent years have seen the addition of 646 and 917 (mostly for cell phones). Outer-borough area codes include 718, 347, and a few others. Despite the need to dial the area code when calling between boroughs, there are no additional charges for doing so.

SPECIAL CONSIDERATIONS

TRAVELING WITH CHILDREN

NEW YORK IS MOST FAMOUS AS A SORT OF ADULTS' playground, but if you're considering a family vacation here, don't worry: For all the bars and "the-ah-tuh," New York is absolutely packed with family-style attractions and hands-on, state-of-the-art children's museums both in and outside of Manhattan, not to mention the special events, such as the Macy's Thanksgiving Day Parade, holiday lights in the area zoos (four of them!) and botanical gardens, ice skating in Rockefeller Center, harbor tours, high views, antique carousels, and so on.

And sightseeing with small children can be a bargain if you use public transportation: Kids under 44 inches tall ride free on the buses and subways (there are handy-dandy lines by the bus driver's seat and toll gates for comparison). Remember that warnings about dehydration go double for small children, even in winter. For specific recommendations, see the "Best Children's Fare" list in Part Seven, Sightseeing, Tours, and Attractions. And for kid-friendly hotels and restaurants and the best museums to visit with young ones, check out **www.newyorkkids.net.**

If you do bring the kids but would like to have a little adults-only time, contact the **Baby Sitters Guild** (☎ 212-682-0227), which has bonded members who will stay in or carry out, so to speak, to Central Park or some other play spot. Also check with your hotel; most have a list of reliable sitters.

Incidentally, if your "children" have four legs, contact the **Wagging Tail** in Tribeca (354H Greenwich Street; ☎ 212-285-4900; **www.thewagging-tail.com**), a canine and feline hotel and day spa with webcam contact for "parents."

In the case of illness or medical emergencies, first call the front desk of your hotel; many have arrangements with physicians for house calls. Otherwise contact **Dial-a-Doctor** (call ☎ 212-971-9692). There are several 24-hour pharmacies in town, most run by the **Duane Reade** chain; the most centrally located are at Broadway and 57th Street (call ☎ 212-541-9708) and Lexington and 47th (call ☎ 212-682-5338).

TIPS FOR INTERNATIONAL TRAVELERS

VISITORS FROM THE UNITED KINGDOM, western Europe, and Japan need only a valid passport to enter the United States, not a visa; Canadian citizens can get by with only proof of residence (although passport requirements are being considered). Citizens of other countries must have a passport, good for at least six months beyond the projected end of the visit, and a tourist visa as well, available from any U.S. consulate. Some airlines and travel agents may also have forms available.

If you are taking prescription drugs that contain narcotics or require injection by syringe, be sure to get a doctor's signed prescription and instructions. Also check with the local consulate to see whether travelers from your country are currently required to have any inoculations; there are no set requirements to enter the United States, but if there has been any sort of epidemic in your homeland, there may be temporary restrictions.

If you arrive by air, be prepared to spend two hours or more entering the United States and getting through U.S. Customs. Every adult traveler may bring in, duty-free, up to one liter of wine or hard liquor; 200 cigarettes or 100 non-Cuban cigars or three pounds of loose tobacco; and $100 worth of gifts, as well as up to $10,000 in U.S. currency or its equivalent in foreign currency. No food or plants may be brought in.

The dollar is the basic unit of monetary exchange, and the entire system is decimal. The smaller sums are represented by coins. One hundred "cents" (or pennies, as the one-cent coins are known) equal one dollar; five cents is a nickel (20 nickels to a dollar); the ten-cent coin is called a dime (ten dimes to a dollar); and the 25-cent coin is called a quarter (four to a dollar). Beginning with one dollar, money is in currency bills (although there are some one-dollar coins around as well). Bills come in $1, $2 (rare), $5, $10, $20, $50, $100, $500, and so on, although you are unlikely to want to carry $1,000 or more.

unofficial **TIP**
Stick to $20 bills for taxicabs; drivers rarely make change for anything larger.

Banks in the United States are closed on federal holidays, including New Year's Day (January 1); Martin Luther King Jr. Day (celebrated the third Monday in January); Presidents' Day (celebrated the third Monday in February); Memorial Day (last Monday in May); Independence Day (July 4); Labor Day (first Monday in September); Columbus Day (second Monday in October); Veterans Day (November 11); Thanksgiving (the fourth Thursday in November); and Christmas (December 25).

Credit cards are by far the most common form of payment in New York, especially American Express, Visa (also known as BarclayCard in Britain), and MasterCard (Access in Britain, Eurocard in western Europe, or Chargex in Canada). Other popular cards include Diners Club, Discover/Novus, and Carte Blanche.

Traveler's checks will be accepted at most hotels and restaurants if they are in American dollars; other currencies should be changed into dollar figures. There are currency exchange booths in such major traffic areas as JFK and LaGuardia airports, Grand Central Station, Times Square, and even Macy's and Bloomingdale's.

unofficial **TIP**
If you need additional assistance, contact the **Traveler's Aid Society,** which has booths in JFK and Newark airports (call ☎ 718-656-4870).

Public telephones require 35 cents; although area codes must be dialed for all calls inside or between boroughs, there is no additional charge. Throughout the United States, if you have a medical, police, or fire emergency, dial 911, even on a pay telephone, and an ambulance or police cruiser will be dispatched to help you.

Incidentally, New York has one of the most stringent antismoking programs in the country, something international visitors might need to consider in advance. Smoking is prohibited on buses, on subways, and in taxicabs; in public buildings or the lobbies of office buildings; in all but designated areas in theaters; in most shops and all museums; and in all restaurants and bars.

TIPS FOR THE DISABLED

NEW YORK IS FAR MORE RECEPTIVE to the disabled tourist than its tough reputation might lead you to believe. City buses are equipped with wheelchair lifts and "kneeling" steps (though admittedly they don't always work), and disabled riders with a reduced-fare Metro-Card pay half-fare ($1). Gray Line Tours has acquired a whole fleet of wheelchair-accessible double-decker touring buses. An increasing number of subway stops are wheelchair accessible as well; for a list, contact the **Transit Authority's Customer Service Department** (370 J Street, Suite 702, Brooklyn, NY 11201; ☎ 718-330-3322). Visually impaired travelers can get a Braille subway map and other materials from the **Lighthouse** (call ☎ 800-334-5497). The hearing-impaired traveler can get similar help from the **New York Society for the Deaf** (817 Broadway, Seventh Floor; TDD ☎ 212-777-3900).

A list of wheelchair-accessible museums, hotels, and restaurants is available from the **Society for Accessible Travel and Hospitality** (347 Fifth Avenue, New York, NY 10016; ☎ 212-447-7284). A similar guidebook, "Audiences for All: A Guide for People with Disabilities to New York City Cultural Institutions," is available from **Hospital Audiences** for $5 (548 Broadway, Third Floor; ☎ 212-284-4100 or 212-575-7660). And many members of the volunteer **Big Apple Greeters,** warmly recommended in Part Seven, will partner handicapped visitors around town, but you should call at least several days in advance (☎ 212-669-2896; **www.bigapplegreeters.org**).

Visitors who use walking aids should be warned that only the larger museums and the newer shopping areas can be counted on to be wheelchair accessible. Many individual stores and smaller art collections are housed in what were once private homes with stairs, and even those at sidewalk level are unlikely to have wider aisles or specially equipped bathrooms. The restaurants that we profile later in the book all have a disabled access rating, as do most of the major attractions, but you need to call any other eatery or any store in advance. (In fact, you might check with some restaurants that were listed as not accessible at press time, as it's possible they've renovated their facilities since.) Similarly, you need to call any stores you're particularly interested in.

CALENDAR of SPECIAL EVENTS

HERE ARE THE MAJOR CELEBRATIONS AND A SAMPLING of the less well-known but unique events around New York and their approximate dates (specific ones where possible). Remember, if the event requires tickets, it's best to try to arrange them before leaving home; otherwise you may find yourself paying extra or being locked out entirely. Tickets for the U.S. Open Tennis Championships in August, for instance, go on sale in May, and the scalping fees are astonishingly high by the opening rounds.

Please note that many festivals, especially in the summer, move around from year to year, and that some close down or are replaced by others; so if you are interested, contact organizers as soon as possible. For many of the municipal functions, you may call **NYC and Company** at ☎ 212-397-8222 or check the Web at **www.nycvisit.com.** Parade routes and times will be listed in the *New York Times* on the appropriate days. The local newspapers (listed earlier) will also have numerous street fairs, art shows, and concerts to tempt you, particularly in summer.

In addition to the contacts listed in the following section, **Ticket-Master** may be able to supply tickets to particular events, although there will be an additional handling charge. Call ☎ 212-307-1212.

January

WINTER ANTIQUES SHOW AT THE ARMORY Third week in January. One of the largest and most prestigious (read: expensive) antiques gatherings in the city, this is held in the historic Seventh Regiment Armory on Park Avenue at 66th Street. Over the first weekend of the big collection, a sort of counter-show, featuring less established or edgier collectors, is held at the 26th Street Armory at Lexington Avenue, and shuttle buses run between the two. For information call ☎ 212-452-3067.

CHINESE NEW YEAR PARADE At the new moon in late January or early February. A fortnight of fireworks, street fairs, and food festivals leads toward the big dragon parade through Chinatown. Call ☎ 212-619-4785.

NATIONAL BOAT SHOW Mid-January. Sailing vessels, yachts, cruisers, and powerboats fill the Jacob Javits Convention Center; call ☎ 212-216-2000 or visit **www.javitscenter.com.**

February

BLACK HISTORY MONTH Watch the newspapers and guides for cultural events, concerts, and lectures scheduled around the city.

EMPIRE STATE BUILDING RUN Early February. Hundreds of athletes race not horizontally but vertically: 1,575 steps from the lobby to the 86th-floor observation deck. The best make it in about 11 minutes. Contact the New York Road Runners at ☎ 212-860-4455.

WESTMINSTER CLUB DOG SHOW Mid-month. This most prestigious of canine parades brings thousands of familiar, unusual, and downright rare dogs, all blow-dried and ribboned for judging, to Madison Square Garden. Heck, this dog show's so big it's on cable TV. Call ☎ 800-455-3647 or ☎ 212-465-6741.

VALENTINE'S DAY February 14. A huge vow-one, vow-all mass wedding ceremony is performed at the wedding chapel in the Empire State Building; call ☎ 212-736-3100.

COLISEUM ANTIQUES SHOW Not as elite as the Armory show, but huge and convenient: more than 100 dealers in the arena on Columbus Circle (late February or early March). For information, contact NYC and Company at ☎ 800-NYC-VISIT.

March

NEW YORK FLOWER SHOW One of the big stops on the flower circuit is the Horticultural Society of New York's annual competition/exhibition in the Coliseum on Columbus Circle; contact HSNY at ☎ 212-757-0915.

ART EXPO Early or mid-March. This huge affair at the Javits Convention Center specializes in what dealers call popular art, and that means anything from nice lithographs to the stuff you get on the sidewalk or see in chain motels. Good for a laugh and a possible find; call ☎ 212-328-8926 or visit **www.artexpos.com.**

ST. PATRICK'S DAY PARADE On March 17, everyone is Irish, so pack something green or get out of the way. The parade, at age 200 one of the oldest anywhere, includes an estimated 150,000 marchers; the route is along Fifth Avenue (of course) from 44th to 86th, with the thickest crowd around St. Patrick's Cathedral (of course).

GREEK INDEPENDENCE DAY PARADE March 25. Zorba-style food and dance along Fifth Avenue from 61st to 79th.

TRIPLE PIER EXPO Last two weekends in March. Vast antiques exhibit and sale on Piers 88, 90, and 92 (along the Hudson River). Call ☎ 212-255-0020.

RINGLING BROS. AND BARNUM & BAILEY CIRCUS PARADE Late March. Another great traditional procession, this one is now (thanks to animal protests) a semisecret wee-hours train of elephants and lions and tigers making their way from Long Island City through the Queens-Midtown Tunnel to Madison Square Garden. For information call ☎ 212- 465-6741 or visit **www.ringling.com.**

CIRQUE DU SOLEIL Late March. On alternate years watch for the appearance of the strange and fantastic Canadian one-tent circus; all acrobats and astonishing contortionists and eerie music, no animals; call ☎ 800-678-5440.

EASTER PARADE Late March to mid-April. A parade so famous they made a Fred Astaire–Judy Garland movie about it. Don that bonnet—the bigger the better—and promenade along (what else?) Fifth Avenue from 49th to 57th. Macy's flower show is scheduled for the week leading up to Easter Sunday; for information call ☎ 212-397-8222.

EASTER EGG ROLL Saturday before Easter. In the East Meadow of Central Park; call ☎ 212-360-3456 or ☎ 888-NYPARKS.

April

INTERNATIONAL ASIAN ART FAIR Early April. Increasingly, the premier Asian antiques showcase on the East Coast. At the Seventh Regiment Armory on Park Avenue at 66th Street. Call ☎ 212-877-0202.

BASEBALL SEASON OPENING DAY Mid-April. If you're a pin-striper, or just an American Leaguer at heart, you can try for tickets by calling TicketMaster or Yankee Stadium box office at ☎ 718-293-6000. For fans of the senior league, those heartbreaking Mets are at Shea Stadium (call ☎ 718-507-8499).

ROCKEFELLER CENTER FLOWER SHOW Early–mid-April. One of the nicest free shows in town. Gardening companies and landscape designers fill the plaza between 48th and 51st streets with fantasy getaways, Japanese rock gardens, arbors, and urban meadows. Call ☎ 800-NYC-VISIT.

ANTIQUARIAN BOOK FAIR Mid–late-April. First editions, rare titles, and autographed copies fill the Seventh Regiment Armory on Park at 66th Street. Call ☎ 212-944-8291.

CHERRY BLOSSOM FESTIVAL Late April–early May. A celebration of the Japanese, or flowering Kwanzan, cherry trees of the Brooklyn Botanic Garden; call ☎ 718-623-7200.

May

BIKE NEW YORK Early May. This ever-larger 41-mile for-fun bike race—it draws more than 35,000 wheelers and dealers—links all five boroughs, with the kickoff downtown and the finish line in Staten Island. Picnic at the end of pedaling. Call ☎ 212-932-2453 or check **www.bikenewyork.org.**

BROOKLYN BRIDGE DAY Second Sunday in May. Walk the bridge, admire its stunning structure, and enjoy a sort of street fair at the same time. For information, contact NYC and Company at ☎ 800-NYC-VISIT.

INTERNATIONAL FINE ARTS FAIR Mid-May. European and American artists are featured in this young but prestigious show at the Seventh Regiment Armory. For information, contact NYC and Company at ☎ 212-397-8222.

FLEET WEEK Mid-May. Ships ahoy! Naval and Coast Guard vessels of all sizes set up for tours and exhibitions. Call ☎ 212-642-8572.

MARTIN LUTHER KING JR. DAY PARADE Third Sunday in May. A salute to the civil rights leader starts on Fifth Avenue at 44th and streams up to 86th. Contact NYC and Company at ☎ 212-397-8222.

SALUTE TO ISRAEL PARADE May. Along Fifth northward from 59th

Street. Also, fashion sharks may find much to savor at the United Jewish Appeal's annual fundraiser; call ☎ 646-472-5388.

WASHINGTON SQUARE ART EXHIBITION The last two weekends in May and the first two weekends of September. An old and revered Greenwich Village gathering, this huge outdoor art show is a giant block party, with easels (and food carts) in the streets all around the park. Call ☎ 212-982-6255.

NINTH AVENUE FOOD FESTIVAL Third weekend in May. This was, and to a lesser extent still is, the international grocery strip of New York. A combination street fair and ethnic fare showcase, it stretches from 37th to 57th streets. For information, call ☎ 800-NYC-VISIT.

LOWER EAST SIDE JEWISH FESTIVAL Third or fourth Sunday in May. Combination historical tour and street party. Call ☎ 212-254-1109.

June

SHAKESPEARE IN THE PARK From June to August, this now famous, free, and star-studded series (call ☎ 212-539-8750) takes over the Delacorte Theater stage in Central Park. There are fewer than 2,000 seats, and the box office opens at 1 p.m. every day, but the line forms much earlier. (See "Ticket Tips" in Part Eleven, Entertainment and Nightlife.)

CONCERTS IN THE PARK June to August. Some concerts in Central Park, Prospect Park, and other city greens are put on by the New York Philharmonic (call ☎ 212-875-5700 or visit **www.newyorkphil harmonic.org**) and the great Metropolitan Opera (call ☎ 212-362-6000).

SUMMERSTAGE Similarly, there are free or nominally priced pop, rock, country, folk, reggae, and jazz concerts throughout the summer in Central Park: Remember Simon & Garfunkle? Garth Brooks? It's big, but it's fun. Call ☎ 212-360-2777, or look up **www.summerstage.com.**

PUERTO RICAN DAY PARADE First Sunday in June. A lively, musical march along Fifth Avenue from 44th to 86th Street. Call ☎ 800-NYC-VISIT.

BELMONT STAKES The second (occasionally the first) Saturday in June. The final leg of thoroughbred two-year-old racing's Triple Crown, and many warm-up races, go off at Belmont Park on Long Island; call ☎ 516-488-6000 or visit **www.nyracing.com.**

RESTAURANT WEEK Usually the third week in June. A sit-down Taste of the Town event, when some of the biggest-name restaurants offer special cut-price meals. As soon as you see the ads in the *New York Times* or elsewhere, listing the participating establishments, get on the phone or you'll be out of luck. Call ☎ 212-397-8222.

FEAST OF ST. ANTHONY Mid-June. Restaurant week or no, the saint of Padua must still be hungry: His street fair in Little Italy lasts two weeks.

GAY AND LESBIAN PRIDE DAY PARADE Late June. A week-long series of public and private events culminates in the parade, commemorating the Stonewall Riot of June 27, 1969, that struts down (rather than up) Fifth Avenue from 53rd to the West Village. Call ☎ 212-807-7433 or visit **www.nycpride.org.**

MERMAID PARADE Late June. A sort of pre-Halloween bash along the Coney Island–Brighton Beach Boardwalk. A few years ago, the Grand Merman, uh, Marshall, was former Talking Head David Byrne. Call ☎ 718-372-5159 for information.

JVC JAZZ FESTIVAL Late June–early July. A series of top-name concerts in Bryant Park and venues around the city; watch the papers for schedules, or call ☎ 212-219-3006 or ☎ 800-NYC-VISIT.

July

FOURTH OF JULY FESTIVAL July 4. Independence Day celebrations include street fairs, the annual sailing of the Tall Ships in the harbor, and after dark, the famous Macy's fireworks over the East River. For information, call ☎ 212-494-4495. All-day festivities in downtown around Battery Park climax with fireworks over the harbor.

LINCOLN CENTER FESTIVAL A dizzying array of dance, drama, ballet, children's shows, and multimedia and performance art that involves both the repertory companies and special guests and that moves through the indoor venues and sometimes outdoors as well, through July and August. Call ☎ 212-875-5928 or visit **www.lincolncenter.org.** There are also big-band dances (free lessons included) on weekends by the Lincoln Center fountain. And the Lincoln Center Plaza on Columbus is home territory to the two-week American Crafts Festival.

August

LINCOLN CENTER PLAZA CONCERTS Throughout the month. Some of the outdoor series taper off in August, but the music on the plaza (information at ☎ 212-875-5400) or **www.lincolncenter.org**), along with another big crafts show late in the month keeps the joint jumpin'.

DRAGON BOAT RACES First two weekends in August. Some 50 teams of 22 rowers, plus drummer and helmsman, race Chinese-style 40-foot teak boats on the lake at Flushing Meadow–Corona Park in Queens; the winners travel to Hong Kong for the international trials. Call ☎ 201-536-1311.

HARLEM HERITAGE WEEK Mid-August. Films, art exhibits, concerts, exhibition games, and street fairs celebrating the neighborhood's rich cultural history build up to the climax of Uptown Saturday Night, a combination block party and black arts expo along 125th Street between Lenox and Seventh avenues. Call ☎ 212-280-7888.

MOSTLY MOZART A famous phrase, and one of the most famous renditions (two weeks in mid- to late August) is in the Lincoln Center's Avery Fisher Hall; call ☎ 212-875-5030.

U.S. OPEN TENNIS TOURNAMENT Late August. In its expanded digs at Flushing Meadow, this Grand Slam event is one of the sport's hottest tickets—literally. Don't forget the water and the sunblock, if you can get in. For information call ☎ 888-673-6849 or visit **www.usopen.org.**

NEW YORK INTERNATIONAL FRINGE FESTIVAL Last week of August to Labor Day. Round-the-clock multimedia, dance, theater, street and musical performances, many of them free, at venues around the Lower East Side and East Village. The "Fringe" has even spanned a farther fringe—the Pure Pop Theater Festival, which runs concurrently. Check local papers for listings. Call ☎ 212-279-4488 or visit **www.fringenyc.org.**

September

WIGSTOCK PARADE Labor Day weekend. Although this parade isn't as old as the Easter or Thanksgiving Day marathons, it's catching up fast in the fame department. The wildest and most royal drag event in the city, due to growth, it has moved a couple of times from its original East Village park space, most recently to the 11th Street Pier; contact the Lesbian and Gay Community Services Center for information at ☎ 212-807-7433.

BROADWAY ON BROADWAY Early September. For one enchanted day and evening in Times Square—where else?—the casts of the big Broadway shows sing and step out in public; call ☎ 212-563-2929.

WEST INDIAN FESTIVAL AND PARADE Labor Day Weekend. It's big, it's loud, it's delicious, and it's relatively underpublicized (perhaps because it's in Brooklyn); but fans of world or Caribbean music, food, and dance won't mind the short trip to Crown Heights. For information call the Caribbean American Center of New York at ☎ 718-625-1515.

CLOISTERS MEDIEVAL FESTIVAL Early–mid September. Falconry, food, tomfoolery, jousting and feasting, all with a Middle Ages flavor. Call the Parks Department at ☎ 212-360-2777.

NEW YORK IS BOOK COUNTRY Third Sunday in September. A great indoor–outdoor book "mall" along Fifth Avenue from 48th to 59th streets, with booths and racks of old, new, used, privately published, and rare volumes. Call ☎ 212-207-7242.

ONE WORLD FESTIVAL Mid-September. International food, crafts, antiques, and street performances in a block party on East 35th between First and Second avenues.

INTERNATIONAL FESTIVAL OF PUPPET THEATER Mid-September. On alternate years (including 2004), Muppet mavens Jim Henson

Productions hosts this Manhattan family attraction. Call ☎ 212-794-2400 or visit **www.henson.com.**

FEAST OF SAN GENNARO Mid-September. This Little Italy street fest is pretty famous, probably because it lasts a long (two-weekend) week, although its rumored "family" connections have gotten a lot of publicity; along Mulberry Street. Call ☎ 212-768-9320.

BROADWAY CARES/EQUITY FIGHTS AIDS ANNUAL FLEA MARKET AND ANTIQUE SALE Last weekend of September. The theatrical garage sale, memento scuffle, and costume clearinghouse of the year. Shubert Alley and West 44th Street. Call ☎ 212-840-0770 or see local listings for date.

NEW YORK FILM FESTIVAL Late September to early October. Not so avant-garde as the New Films series, this prestigious series in Lincoln Center's Alice Tully Hall lasts two weeks and usually has a big-name premiere or two on the schedule; call ☎ 212-875-5610.

NEW DIRECTORS/NEW FILMS FESTIVAL Late September–early October. A cutting-edge cinematic collaboration between the Museum of Modern Art, which hosts the screenings, and the Lincoln Center Film Society. For more information call ☎ 212-721-6500.

October

BIG APPLE CIRCUS October to January. You might have forgotten how this cheery little one-ring operation got its name; but watch the little big top go up in the park outside Lincoln Center and then try to resist; call ☎ 212-268-2500.

FEAST OF ST. FRANCIS OF ASSISI Early October. The Francis-like blessing of the animals at St. John the Divine used to be a fairly sedate affair, but nowadays it's a sort of well-bred circus, with snakes, rabbits, ferrets, exotic birds, and, yes, even elephants being offered for prayer. Call ☎ 212-662-2133.

CHILE PEPPER FIESTA Early October. The Brooklyn Botanical Garden puts its mouth where its money is, so to speak, hosting a festival that showcases the hundreds of types of the American spice that conquered the world's cuisines. Guacamole, Jamaican jerk chicken, chili, wraps—it's hot, hot, hot. Call ☎ 718-623-7200.

GRAMERCY PARK ANTIQUES SHOW October and March. 17th-, 18th- and 19th-century porcelain, art glass, furniture, and fine art at the 69th Regiment Armory at Lexington and 26th Street; call ☎ 212-255-0020.

NBA AND NHL AT MSG Season openers. If you're a sports fan, you can read this. If not, it means that pro basketball (the Knicks) and ice hockey (the Rangers) are back in town at Madison Square Garden. Call ☎ 212-465-6741 for information on both teams.

PULASKI DAY PARADE Sunday nearest October 5. Polish-American festival, sometimes called Polish Day, marches Fifth from 26th to 52nd. Call ☎ 877-4-PULASKI.

COLUMBUS DAY PARADE Second Monday in October. A combination Founder's Day, Italian pride, and star-spangled celebration down Fifth Avenue from 44th to 86th. Call ☎ 212-249-9932 or ☎ 800-NYC-VISIT.

SOHO ARTS FESTIVAL Mid-October. This originally one-day event is up to nearly a fortnight now, with street theater, performance art, dance, and music indoors and out.

INTERNATIONAL FINE ARTS AND ANTIQUES DEALERS SHOW Mid- to late October. The last (actually, the first, as dealers consider the season) of New York's major shows comes just in time for holiday shopping, if you can afford it. At least you can look. At the Seventh Regiment Armory; call ☎ 212-642-8572.

FRAGRANCE WEEK Mid–late-October. If your nose knows, this is your week: walking–shopping tours, "fragrance lovers' breakfasts," and lots of samples. Call ☎ 212-725-2755 or visit **www.fragrance.org**.

THE NEW YORK CABARET CONVENTION Late October. For a week, more than 100 classic crooners work their way through the American popular songbook at the Rose Theater in the Time Warner Center. Call ☎ 212-721-6500.

GREENWICH VILLAGE HALLOWEEN PARADE October 31. Yet another over-the-top and inimitable dress function, this annual party-on-legs (and some wheels) circles the Village; check local papers for the exact route. Walk-ups welcome; gather at Sixth Avenue just above Houston at dusk. Call ☎ 845-758-5519 or visit **www.halloween-nyc.com.**

HULAWEEN October 31. Bette Midler and various of her superstar friends (Elton John, Sting, and so on) dress up, get down, and raise money for the New York Restoration Fund at the Waldorf-Astoria. For more information visit **www.nyrp.org.**

NEXT WAVE FESTIVAL October to December. The Brooklyn Academy of Music showcases avant-garde, experimental, and new music, dance, and performance; call ☎ 718-636-4100 or visit **www.bam.org.**

NEW YORK CITY MARATHON Last Sunday in October or first Sunday in November. One of the big races—not counting the 2.5 million cheering onlookers and volunteers—and with one of the most scenic courses, which includes the Verrazano Narrows Bridge, stretches of Fifth Avenue, and a finish line at Tavern on the Green in Central Park. Call ☎ 212-860-4455 for information.

November

CHRISTMAS EXTRAVAGANZA AT RADIO CITY MUSIC HALL Early November to January. Traditional family favorite featuring the Rockettes in their toy soldier kick line, music, costumes, and so on. Call ☎ 212-247-4777.

WTA TOUR CHAMPIONSHIPS Mid-November. Madison Square Garden lays the courts for the old Virginia Slims women's tennis tourney; call ☎ 212-465-6741.

THE CHOCOLATE SHOW Mid-November. Cooking demonstrations, tastings, cooking classes, even chocolate couture. At the Metropolitan Pavilion, 125 West 18th Street. Call ☎ 212-889-5112.

MACY'S THANKSGIVING DAY PARADE Late November. Well, how else would Santa Claus—not to mention Snoopy and Woodstock and Garfield and Bullwinkle and half of Broadway—make it to Herald Square on time? The parade begins at Central Park West and 77th and works down Broadway to the store at 34th Street. Santa takes up his station in Macy's beginning the next day. Call ☎ 212-494-4495.

December

LIGHTING OF THE CHRISTMAS TREE AT ROCKEFELLER CENTER The first Monday evening in December, the mayor pulls the switch, and people sing, ice skate, make wishes, you name it; the tree will be lit throughout the month. Call ☎ 212-332-7654.

LIGHTING OF THE HANUKKAH MENORAH AT GRAND ARMY PLAZA Sometime in December, the first "candle" on this giant (32-foot) menorah at the corner of Fifth and 59th opens the Jewish holiday season; other candles are lit every night for the next week.

ANTIQUES SHOW AT THE SEVENTH REGIMENT ARMORY Around the second weekend in December. Another blockbuster sale drawing 100 dealers in serious 17th-, 18th-, and 19th-century American, European, and Asian furniture and art. Call ☎ 212-452-3067.

NUTCRACKER BALLET The Sugar Plum Fairy is absolutely everywhere, including the IMAX in Times Square. The American Ballet Theater version, for sentimentalists, is in the New York State Theater in Lincoln Center (call ☎ 212-870-5570), but the local papers will list many others.

MESSIAH SING-ALONG AT LINCOLN CENTER Mid-December. Huge public performance of Handel's popular oratorio in Avery Fisher Hall, with rehearsals and coaching beforehand; call ☎ 212-875-5030. Dozens of other sing-alongs, carolings, and family performances will be listed in the local papers.

KWANZAA CELEBRATIONS Watch for listings of African-American ethnic festivities around town.

NEW YEAR'S EVE December 31. Times Square must be one of the most famous addresses in New Year's folklore. It's a heck of a street party, complete with countdown and lighted ball. However, for those more intrigued by culture than alcohol, Manhattan's First Night celebration is one of the largest and finest progressive parties in the country, winding up with such old-fashioned touches as a dance in Grand Central Station and fireworks over the Tavern on the Green in Central Park; call ☎ 212-873-3200. Or for those who have made their resolutions a day early, there's a midnight run through the park; call ☎ 212-360-3456 or ☎ 888-NYPARKS or visit **www.tavernonthegreen.com.**

PART THREE

ACCOMMODATIONS

NEW ROOMS *in the* SKY

BAD NEWS: NEW YORK CITY HOTEL ROOM RATES remain the highest in the country—averaging about $200 a night. Good news (sort of): With ho-hum two-bedroom condos in Manhattan costing over a million bucks, a $200 room doesn't seem so steep. In fact, if you're savvy (and if you're reading this, you are indeed), you can find rooms well under that average.

New York hotel rooms numbered almost 70,000 in 2005, a drop of about 3,000 rooms. Demolitions include the Mayflower and residential and mixed-used conversions, entirely or in part, including The Plaza, the Regent Wall Street, the Stanhope, and the St. Regis.

New properties tend to be small, reconverted, and/or niche-oriented, including **Blue Moon,** the first high-end kosher hotel. This type of lodging can be found in areas long neglected, room-wise and otherwise—including downtown, Harlem (check out **Harlem Landmark Guest House,** a restored townhouse), and the outer boroughs (**Harbor House Bed & Breakfast,** near the Staten Island ferry). Lower-priced hotel groups such as Apple Core, offer clean, budget accommodations, and bed-and-breakfasts continue to emerge throughout the five boroughs.

To experience the city over the long term, extended-stay lodgings such as the Affinia properties (formerly Manhattan East, ☎ 866-AFFINIA; **www.affinia.com**), with kitchens and maid and shopping services, have been a long-time staple. But add on the newish luxury apartment-hotels and luxury hotels with kitchenette amenities, and you have excellent options in all price ranges. Indeed, the hotel scene continues to be tough but appealing—a melting pot worthy of New York, New York.

uptown accommodations

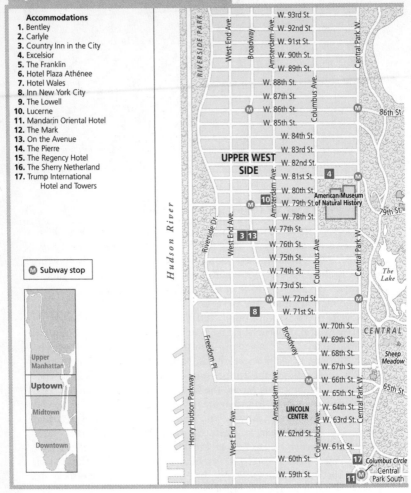

Accommodations
1. Bentley
2. Carlyle
3. Country Inn in the City
4. Excelsior
5. The Franklin
6. Hotel Plaza Athénee
7. Hotel Wales
8. Inn New York City
9. The Lowell
10. Lucerne
11. Mandarin Oriental Hotel
12. The Mark
13. On the Avenue
14. The Pierre
15. The Regency Hotel
16. The Sherry Netherland
17. Trump International
      Hotel and Towers

Ⓜ Subway stop

Upper
Manhattan

Uptown

Midtown

Downtown

RIVERSIDE PARK

West End Ave.
Broadway
Amsterdam Ave.
Columbus Ave.
Central Park W.

W. 93rd St.
W. 92nd St.
W. 91st St.
W. 90th St.
W. 89th St.
W. 88th St.
W. 87th St.
W. 86th St.
W. 85th St.
W. 84th St.
W. 83rd St.
W. 82nd St.
W. 81st St.
W. 80th St.
W. 79th St.
W. 78th St.
W. 77th St.
W. 76th St.
W. 75th St.
W. 74th St.
W. 73rd St.
W. 72nd St.
W. 71st St.
W. 70th St.
W. 69th St.
W. 68th St.
W. 67th St.
W. 66th St.
W. 65th St.
W. 64th St.
W. 63rd St.
W. 62nd St.
W. 61st St.
W. 60th St.
W. 59th St.

UPPER WEST SIDE

American Museum of Natural History

86th St.

79th St.

The Lake

CENTRAL

Sheep Meadow

65th St.

Hudson River

Riverside Dr.
West End Ave.
Amsterdam Ave.
Columbus Ave.
Central Park W.

Henry Hudson Parkway

Freedom Pl.

Broadway

West End Ave.

Amsterdam Ave.

Columbus Ave.

LINCOLN CENTER

17 Columbus Circle
Central Park South

11

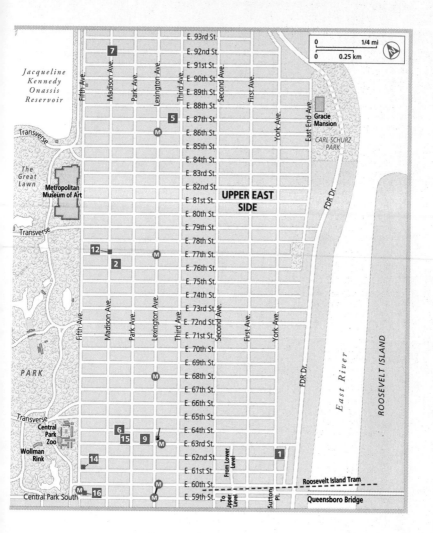

midtown accommodations

Accommodations
1. The Alex Hotel
2. The Algonquin Hotel
3. Ameritania Hotel
4. Avalon
5. Barclay New York
6. Beekman Tower Hotel
7. Benjamin Hotel
8. Blakely
9. Bryant Park Hotel
10. The Carlton
11. Chambers–a Hotel
12. Chelsea Savoy
13. City Club Hotel
14. Clarion Fifth Avenue
15. Courtyard by Marriott Manhattan Times Square South
16. Crowne Plaza Manhattan
17. Crowne Plaza United Nations
18. DoubleTree Guest Suites Times Square
19. DoubleTree Metropolitan
20. The Drake Swissôtel
21. Dream
22. Dylan Hotel
23. Essex House Hotel Nikko New York
24. Fitzpatrick Grand Central
25. Fitzpatrick Manhattan Hotel
26. Flatotel International
27. Four Points by Sheraton Manhattan Chelsea
28. Four Seasons Hotel
29. Grand Hyatt New York
30. Hilton Times Square
31. Hotel Bedford
32. Hotel Casablanca
33. Hotel Chandler
34. Hotel Elysee
35. Hotel 57
36. Hotel 41
37. Hotel Giraffe
38. Hotel Metro
39. Hotel QT New York
40. Hotel 31
41. Hudson Hotel
42. The Inn at Irving Place
43. Inn on 23rd Street
44. Iroquois New York
45. Jolly Hotel Madison Towers
46. The Kitano New York
47. La Quinta Inn Manhattan
48. Le Parker Meridien New York
49. Library Hotel
50. The Lombardy
51. The Mansfield
52. Maritime Hotel
53. The Michelangelo
54. Millennium Broadway
55. Millennium U.N. Plaza
56. Morgans
57. The Muse
58. The New York Hilton and Towers
59. New York Marriott Marquis
60. The New York Palace

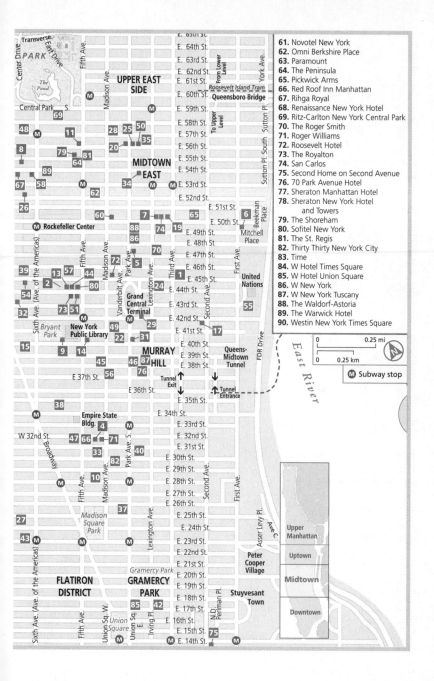

61. Novotel New York
62. Omni Berkshire Place
63. Paramount
64. The Peninsula
65. Pickwick Arms
66. Red Roof Inn Manhattan
67. Rihga Royal
68. Renaissance New York Hotel
69. Ritz-Carlton New York Central Park
70. The Roger Smith
71. Roger Williams
72. Roosevelt Hotel
73. The Royalton
74. San Carlos
75. Second Home on Second Avenue
76. 70 Park Avenue Hotel
77. Sheraton Manhattan Hotel
78. Sheraton New York Hotel
      and Towers
79. The Shoreham
80. Sofitel New York
81. The St. Regis
82. Thirty Thirty New York City
83. Time
84. W Hotel Times Square
85. W Hotel Union Square
86. W New York
87. W New York Tuscany
88. The Waldorf-Astoria
89. The Warwick Hotel
90. Westin New York Times Square

downtown accommodations

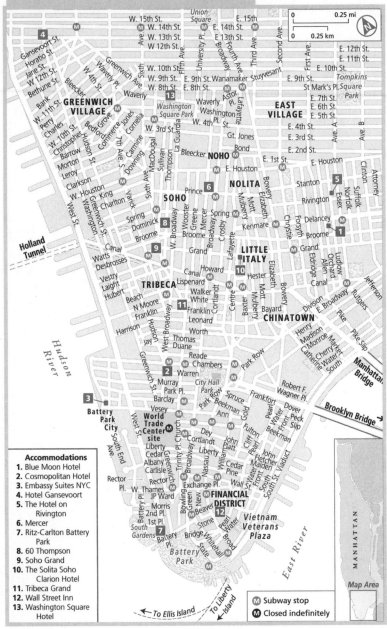

Accommodations

1. Blue Moon Hotel
2. Cosmopolitan Hotel
3. Embassy Suites NYC
4. Hotel Gansevoort
5. The Hotel on Rivington
6. Mercer
7. Ritz-Carlton Battery Park
8. 60 Thompson
9. Soho Grand
10. The Solita Soho Clarion Hotel
11. Tribeca Grand
12. Wall Street Inn
13. Washington Square Hotel

Ⓜ Subway stop
Ⓜ Closed indefinitely

ALL THINGS CONSIDERED

NEW YORK HOTELS FLAUNT BREATHTAKING VIEWS and grand
lobbies, business services and concierges, superb restaurants and
trendy bars. But even in luxury establishments, guest rooms are often
miniscule, and recreational facilities will not match those in most
major cities.

Why? Cost per square foot to build in Manhattan is outrageous, so
to turn a profit, hotels opt for creating more guest rooms and appealing watering holes where payback is high. Thus, rather than health
clubs, pools, and tennis courts, most otherwise great hotels offer only
small fitness centers or passes to health clubs in the neighborhood.

The hotel scene here is different in other ways as well, since New
York is as much a world city as an American one. Because about a
quarter of the Big Apple's visitors come here from around the globe,
hotels must deal with a decidedly international aspect: Front-desk
people speak many languages, translation services are easy to obtain,
concierges abound even at small hotels, shops sell international
goods familiar to overseas customers, and of course, many bathrooms have bidets.

Luxury—at least the illusion of it—is important, so uniformed
doormen (these greeters are almost exclusively men), standard per-
sonnel at upscale city apartments, are also a tradition at top hotels,
even if there is a revolving door. These people exist as much for show
and small services as for security: giving a friendly greeting, hailing
cabs, holding umbrellas, and bringing luggage into the lobby.

Crime rates may be down, but terrorism remains a factor in these
uncertain times, and as many guests are wealthy and/or famous,
high-profile security is the norm. Elevator operators are a thing of
the past, but especially for women traveling alone, this would be a
welcome bonus late at night. New York hotels usually provide key
cards rather than keys and maintain regular floor checks by in-house
guards. Loitering does not go unnoticed. Most upscale hotels have in-
room safes, and all comply with strict city fire codes. The safest
element of city hotels is that even in the wee hours of the morning,
staff will be at the front desk, and usually you
will find other guests in the lobby—New York
does, after all, go on around the clock.

So which hotel should you stay in? Consider
the following factors when choosing, and check
availability before booking. Our hotel chart at
the end of the chapter will help in your selection,
or you could call, peruse brochures, or access
computer information.

unofficial **TIP**
If you use a travel agent,
explain carefully what
matters most to you in
selecting a hotel, and
have the agent write
those requests down.

PURPOSE OF STAY If you know why you're traveling, you'll know
which hotel services and amenities are vital and what location is best.

- **On business?** You might need special services, meeting space, banquet rooms, translation services, and extensive room facilities. Most big hotels are well equipped in these areas. But if you're a leisure traveler, why pay for them? Major chains such as **Marriott, Hilton, Hyatt,** and **Sheraton** will have the business facilities of course, but nowadays upscale independents often have state-of-the-art room facilities—such as cell phones—even if they lack meeting space. Hotels with excellent, updated meeting space include **Mandarin Oriental New York, Ritz-Carlton New York Central Park, Flatotel International, Grand Hyatt New York,** and **Jolly Hotel Madison Towers.**

- **Out to impress?** Then concentrate on location, location, location. But different parts of Manhattan impress in different ways. The Upper East Side is the luxury address, but the Village and downtown are cutting-edge and creative. Public space and décor may be especially important if you're entertaining or on business, so you should scan brochures and Internet sites carefully. The **St. Regis, Four Seasons, Pierre, Carlyle, Mark, Waldorf-Astoria, Essex House, Lowell, Elysee, Soho Grand, Mercer,** and **W New York** are among the most impressive hotels for New York style of differing kinds.

- **Spending lots of time in your room?** Then size, view, and amenities will matter more than if you're on the town 24/7. But everyone appreciates a VCR or DVD player, CD player, big windows, and good lighting. Again, check out our chapter, chart, or hotel brochures, and have your travel agent ask about these aforementioned features.

- **Want to weave a romantic spell?** Smaller, specialized hotels can add to the mood, and around-the-clock room service, king-sized beds, whirlpool tubs, and soft lighting will help. The **Elysee,** the **Inn at Irving Place,** and the **Hotel Casablanca** are oases of romance in this tough and hectic city.

CONVENIENCE Time is perhaps your most precious commodity when traveling, especially in a city where crossing against the light to save a minute is a code of conduct. So think in terms of what you will be doing and where you will be doing it, then choose a hotel from our maps, in close proximity to your needs.

unofficial **TIP**
Check the hotel information charts to see which hotels are closest to public transportation lines—safe, affordable, and efficient ways to get around. You can save big money if you don't have to spend it on long cab rides or parking fees.

For ultimate convenience, if you'll be spending a weekend seeing Broadway shows, stay at a nearby hotel such as the **Time, Westin Times Square,** or **Marriott Marquis.** Like to jog and enjoy the country? Stay as close to country as Manhattan gets—across from Central Park at the **Essex House.** If you plan on lining up to get tickets for *The Late Show with David Letterman,* the **Ameritania** is around the corner. The **Excelsior** is near the Museum of Natural History. If you're strolling in Soho, check out the **Mercer.** The **Blakely** is directly across from City

Center, with its many entertainment productions. When visiting your cousin in Westchester, you'll appreciate the **Grand Hyatt,** connected to Grand Central, and if your cousin is on Long Island, the **Metro Hotel** is near Penn Station. The time and money saved by being able to walk or take public transportation to your destination will make your stay more special.

VIEW What NYC lacks in horizontal space it makes up for in height, and a stunning by-product is the view. Whether a favorite landmark, river, or park, a hotel somewhere in this city is sure to overlook it. Our maps will help you locate which hotels are closest to whatever it is that you may want to overlook; these are the hotels that will offer your choicest views.

For example, if you like to watch the tugboats and water traffic and bridges of the East River, hotels along First Avenue, such as the **Beekman Tower** and **Regal U.N. Plaza**, overlook that watery scene (and the bonus of the United Nations complex). Hotels that rim the Park on Fifth Avenue, Central Park South, and Central Park West offer bucolic views in this hyper-urban environment. Midtown-east hotels in the 30s and 40s are most likely to include views of such landmarks as the Chrysler Building or Empire State Building. Hotels closest to the tip of Manhattan have rooms overlooking New York Harbor and the Statue of Liberty. Hotels near Broadway, such as **Novotel New York,** the **New York Marriott Marquis,** the **Renaissance New York Hotel,** and the **Crowne Plaza Manhattan** have blazingly colorful neon vistas. And the tallest (read: largest) hotels throughout the city provide panoramas that include huge sections of dramatic skyscrapers, rivers, and parks. When reservations are made, request a high floor and the best view possible, or, even more specifically, ask for a view of whatever it is that you want to see.

NOISE To a New Yorker the sounds of silence or a twittering bird can be off-putting, but the noise of a garbage truck grinding away, a wailing, piercing ambulance, or a car alarm at 3 a.m. is standard. You learn to live with it.

The city may never sleep, but you probably want to. Downtown (especially the financial district, at night) and Uptown are quieter than Midtown, which according to traffic experts has more vehicles per square mile than anywhere else in the country—some 700,000 motorists daily.

If noise is a primary concern to you, stay away from hotels near hospitals, police stations, firehouses, or nightclubs. Major hospitals are at First Avenue and 16th Street, First Avenue and 32nd Street, York Avenue and 68th Street, East End Avenue and 88th Street, Park Avenue and 77th Street, Seventh Avenue and West 11th Street, and

unofficial **TIP**
Streets are generally less noisy than avenues—and avenues closer to the rivers than to Midtown are often quietest, although West Side Drive along the Hudson and FDR Drive along the East River are heavily trafficked and often have emergency vehicles.

Tenth Avenue and West 59th Street. Ask for a room away from street noise (or elevator noise, if that matters). High up is better, but surprisingly, not all that much, as sound seems to echo against the skyscrapers. Older hotels, built before World War II, usually have the thickest walls, but most luxury hotels are exceptionally well insulated. Check our survey to make sure your hotel's windows are at least double-glazed; triple-glazing is even better and keeps most street noise out. Hotels on heavily trafficked routes, such as the **Kitano New York** on Park Avenue, are well soundproofed because of this. And some hotels, such as the **Hotel Casablanca,** have quadruple-glazed windows!

unofficial **TIP**
Relatively quiet hotels include the **San Carlos, Omni Berkshire Place,** and the **Drake Swissôtel.**

AMENITIES New York City is the quintessential urban environment—culture, all-night action, superb restaurants, clubs, bars—and as a result many hotels offer only basic amenities. If you have special needs, mention them when booking. Physically challenged guests should clarify whether rooms designated for handicapped guests just have handrails in bathrooms or have made-to-order furnishings and complete wheelchair access. If you have a car, a garage is a major convenience, and free parking a big bonus. If you are with your family or are planning a longer stay, a suite situation or a kitchenette can be a wonderful addition. Most New York hotels offer dataports, fax and copying services, and e-mail retrieval, and big hotels have conference rooms of all sizes, with state-of-the-art facilities. Some have kitchenettes.

The **Regal U.N. Plaza** offers both an indoor pool and tennis courts—a rarity in the city. But there are more unusual amenities as well. The **Four Seasons** provides toys for kids and food for pets. The **New York Palace** sets out personalized stationery and business cards in its Towers section. The **Benjamin Hotel** has ten types of pillows. The **Mark** offers cordless phones. **Trump International Hotel & Towers** provides magnifying glasses and telescopes (presumably to look at Central Park vistas, not into other windows). The **Premier at the Millennium Broadway** offers champagne popsicles, and the **Algonquin Hotel** presents dinner and a cabaret show for guests. We have investigated to find other hotels with amenities that might appeal, so check out our hotel information chart at the end of the chapter.

FOOD AND DRINK If you enjoy the convenience of dining en suite or a mere elevator ride from your room, check our charts at the end of the chapter for hotels that include restaurants. Most hotels in the city have at least a coffee shop or an adjacent restaurant, and you can otherwise count on minibars and coffeemakers to tide you over. If there's a restaurant, room service is also often available, especially at larger establishments. A pleasant trend, especially at smaller hotels, is a continental breakfast included in the price. Among hotels offering this are the **Avalon, Bentley, Franklin, Iroquois New York, Mansfield, Roger Smith, Roger Williams, Shoreham,** and **Millennium Broadway.**

Hotel dining establishments have become among the best in the city, with star chefs, luxury décor, and multicourse tasting menus. Count on a three-course dinner at a top hotel restaurant costing at least $60 per person with a glass of wine, tax, and tip. Lunches are a better deal, and pretheater dinners or prix-fixe special meals are also good values.

As for watering holes where you can drink, nibble, and schmooze day and night, New York hotels have superb examples—and they may include

unofficial **TIP**
When you book your hotel, ask for restaurant reservations at the same time; although hotel guests have priority, some of these restaurants are booked months in advance.

light meals, sophisticated entertainment, or at least live piano music. The décor is often dramatic, as are the patrons—many of them power brokers or stylish singles. You can people-watch in style.

SERVICE The level of service in hotels here varies from world-class polished and refined to straightforward, no-nonsense Noo Yawk–style, which can border on rude. The city is used to assertive people, and to hold your own in this competitive atmosphere, hang tough, as New Yorkers do. Good manners are essential anywhere, but here you can ask a little louder or longer if there's something you'd like, or like changed. (Around here, that's called "chutzpah.") Although the service may vary from one front desk person to the next, good management ensures an atmosphere where "the guest is always right"—or at least starts out that way. The goals should be pleasing you and encouraging return visits.

Smaller hotels that cater to independent travelers are more likely to give better service, as they can't compete in terms of physical plant and amenities and focus instead on making guests feel special. So if you like to be pampered, luxury hotels and small independents will be your best bets. Word of mouth based on the actual experience of travel agents, friends, or coworkers is a great indicator. Otherwise, note:

- Is there a service desk or service representative, such as a concierge? These show that a hotel is at least aware of the importance of service. (And if there isn't one, you can still get concierge service. Check out **www.lushlifeconcierge.com** or **www.newyorkguest.com**.)
- How are you greeted? Is there a doorman? Are you taken to your room by a hotel representative? Are you provided with clear information and asked if you need anything?
- If you make a request, are your needs fulfilled promptly and courteously?
- What services are offered as standard—secretarial, translators, goods, babysitters, concierges, luggage handlers, valet parking?
- Is your bed turned down at night, and towels replaced?
- Is there 24-hour room service?

Most luxury hotels pride themselves on service, which translates into luxury and in the final analysis is what often makes a hotel great. For example, the **Michelangelo** offers a kit with everything from dental floss to condoms, and the **St. Regis** provides 24-hour butler service. Other hotels with a rep for great service include the **Four Seasons,** the **Mark,** the **Lowell,** the **Carlyle,** the **Pierre,** and the **Peninsula.**

SIZE Size-wise, most New York hotels, even the finest, have smaller rooms than in other major cities. But in a few cases, hotels such as **Flatotel International,** which have been converted from apartment houses (flat = apartment, get it?), offer huge units. Check our hotel information chart if bigger is better for you.

kids **Families** Fictional Eloise and that *Home Alone* boy may be the most famous ones, but kids regularly stay and play in New York hotels. Suites, especially with kitchenettes, are a real cost-saver and a good idea. And many hotels offer free lodging to kids staying in their parents' room. Some of New York's best hotels are surprisingly kid-friendly, with many family amenities, playrooms, increasingly lavish kids' programs, and in some cases, big discounts. Check when you reserve to make sure.

Some specifics: **Le Parker Meredien New York** has a family-friendly "Smart Aleck" service, which includes cartoons in the elevator to the rooftop pool. The **Westin New York Times Square** hosts a Kids Club; members receive a sports bottle, toys, coloring books, and a bedtime story. Toddlers get their own thing: an amenity box including step stool and potty seat. **DoubleTree Guest Suites Times Square** dedicates a playroom. The **Barclay New York** offers a backpack filled with goodies, including night-lights, a baseball cap, and a guidebook of kid events. **Novotel New York** provides a Kid's Corner, where the hotel's mascot, Dolfie, entertains. And the **Ritz-Carlton Battery Park** includes a toy menu from FAO Schwarz, a telescope for viewing the Statue of Liberty, and bikes to tour Battery Park. Ritz Kids also have their own butler to prepare a bubble bath and leave a teddy bear on their pillow.

Other kid innovations? The **Waldorf-Astoria** hosts a children's tea, featuring etiquette tips. **Loews** hotels offer several packages specifically for grandparents and grandkids.

PETS Can't bear to leave your four-legged family at home? Most hotels will only accept service animals, but a few choice properties allow pets under 20 pounds; be sure to mention your situation when booking. Hotels that may accept small animals include the **Michelangelo, New York Marriott Marquis,** and **Soho Grand. Loews** hotels provide a welcome kit, a pet menu, and a Puppy Pager, to get in touch in an emergency.

unofficial **TIP**
When staying in a large hotel, insist on a floor where no tour group is booked.

TOUR AND CONVENTION GROUPS Some New York hotels specialize in hosting convention or tour groups. For individual travelers, trying to compete with large groups can be time-consuming and frustrating. Even more maddening is to find yourself on the same floor with a tour group of 100 high-school seniors running up and down the corridor in the middle of the night, partying, and slamming doors. (We've been there.)

BE HOTEL WISE

NEW YORKERS LEARN TO USE WHAT'S AVAILABLE and make do with what isn't. Here are some general tips to help:

- Check out rooms ahead of time if possible, by Internet or brochure. Try **www.hotres.com, www.hoteldiscounts.com,** or **www.quikbook.com.**
- Request a renovated room (even if you aren't sure there are any). New York hotels are constantly renovating, often floor by floor, and newest is usually best, often at the same price. Even if the hotel has not recently renovated, asking shows that you want the best available room for the price.
- If in doubt, visit the room before committing your luggage to it, and if you are not satisfied, ask for a better one. This is a common action in Europe, but New York hoteliers are not surprised by it. If you have a specific and legitimate gripe, such as size, poor housekeeping, lack of view, or noise, chances are you will get results and a better room.
- Maximize the concierge. The best NYC hotels have extensively trained professionals who can book anything and advise about everything in the city. You can often acquire hard-to-get tickets this way, even at the last minute—if you're willing to pay the top fee for them; a good concierge has the savvy and connections needed. Even if a hotel just has a front-desk staff that goes out of its way, use their expertise. Book restaurants through concierges to get better tables, better service, and more re-sponse to complaints, as the restaurant doesn't want to offend the concierge and lose future business. If the meal was memorable and the reservation hard to get, factor part of your tip for the concierge.
- If you reserve in the hotel restaurant, be sure to mention if you are staying at the hotel. You'll probably get better attention.
- Be assertive. Don't accept the first "no" for major requests if you really want something.
- When you're on business, select a room with at least a portion of a sitting area. If you meet there, you'll save time, money, and hassle, and it will be more appropriate than sitting on a bed.
- Check in early and out late. Often you can extend your stay by several hours. If you arrive around noon for a 3 p.m. check-in, your room may already be made up. At worst, you can leave your bags in a locked room and return later. If you ask politely for a late check-out on your last day, you can often get it. But 2 p.m. check-out is usually the latest hotels are willing to give.
- If you're an independent traveler, small hotels will more often go out of their way for your business and to make you feel like a VIP. It's preferable to getting lost in the shuffle of larger groups.

- If you have a great view, open the curtains all the way! The greater your sense of place here in New York, the more you get for your money.

HOTEL NEIGHBORHOODS

UNLESS BUSINESS OR FRIENDS AND FAMILY TAKE YOU to one of the outer boroughs, or you can't get a room otherwise, the place to stay is Manhattan. Within the narrow island are hundreds of choices—from the finest in the world to faded but acceptable structures.

But where in Manhattan? Most New York hotels are clustered in the Midtown area, from 42nd Street to 59th. However, with the city on the upswing, fine new and refurbished hotels are turning up from the 90s, down to the Battery, from Soho and Chelsea to Chinatown, the Village, and the West Side. Generally, Downtown is trendy, Uptown is quiet, and Midtown is bustling, but anywhere in the city is exciting.

DOWNTOWN AND LOWER MANHATTAN

HERE PETER MINUIT BOUGHT MANHATTAN ISLAND from the Indians for the equivalent of $25, so the story goes. Today, in this pricey area, that hardly covers a room-service snack. Among the concrete canyons of the bulls and bears of Wall Street and the sightseers at a rising Ground Zero are several modern hotels, geared to the business and leisure traveler. Because many visitors are on work assignments, most hotels in this area are large and offer complete business services. But visitors also flock to Battery Park, the Statue of Liberty and Ellis Island, the new Jewish Heritage Museum, South Street Seaport, Chinatown, and Little Italy. New restaurants and shops and recreational areas and bike paths—even water sports like parasailing on the Hudson River—make this an increasingly appealing part of the city. Many hotels are converting from existing buildings in the next five years to add to their room inventory. Downtown is relatively quiet at night, with fewer nightspots than in the rest of the island. Also, although subways are convenient, bus service is erratic, and cab fares to Midtown are expensive. But the Staten Island ferry, with its great views, is free. New hotels such as **The Hotel on Rivington** and **Blue Moon** (a kosher hotel built from within an old tenement) reflect the historic character of the area.

GREENWICH VILLAGE, SOHO, AND TRIBECA

RESTAURANTS, GALLERIES, SHOPS, AND THEATERS abound, and New York University (NYU) and the New School offer courses and cultural delights. Because of students and creative types, both the East and West Village remain undeniably hip. But surprisingly, until a few years ago you'd have to go elsewhere to sleep, and there are still only a few hotels here, including the **Washington Square Hotel** and the **Soho Grand.** Nearby Tribeca and the neighboring Meatpacking District are superb artsy, boutique areas to browse in, with great new restaurants and action most of the night. Subway lines link you swiftly to other areas. Hotels remain scarce, and aside from bed-and-breakfasts and reconversions of small properties, the hotel scene has lagged behind the street scene. But this is changing. **Tribeca Grand, 60 Thompson, Soho Grand,** and **Solita Soho Clarion** are among the stylish newbies.

14TH TO 30TH STREETS: MEAT MARKET AND CHELSEA

CHELSEA IS ARTSY, AND THE COMPACT MEAT MARKET District (the northern boundary is 14th Street) is hot, hot, hot. Galleries, boutiques, and restaurants galore open daily. The 30-acre Chelsea Piers sports complex on the Hudson River offers everything from bowling to volleyball to indoor golf. Artists are converting old buildings into studios and galleries. But for the most part, good hotels are few and far between. Visitors to the Chelsea Market and the Joyce, the city's modern dance theater, will like the **Chelsea Savoy** on the West Side. Trendy hotels include the **Maritime** and the **Hotel Gansevoort.** The **Inn at Irving Place** is a tiny, choice place near leafy and quiet Gramercy Park on the East Side.

31ST TO 41ST STREETS

THIS BUSTLING AREA OF OFFICES, SPORTS COMPLEXES, the Garment District, Macy's, the Jacob Javits Convention Center, and transportation terminals is no-nonsense, and large. Midrange hotels reflect the group clientele and convention needs. Visitors to Madison Square Garden, by Penn Station, can stay at the small **Hotel Metro.** The ribbon of greenery along the Hudson, with its bicycle paths and benches, improves the West Side hotel scene. On the East Side, quiet Murray Hill, with its many historic townhouses, is home to the J. P. Morgan Library and nearby small hotels, such as the stylish **Morgans,** the **Avalon,** the spiffy **Roger Williams,** and the Japanese-influenced **Kitano.**

42ND TO 59TH STREETS: THE EAST SIDE

MIDTOWN DRAWS DELEGATES AND VISITORS to the United Nations, Carnegie Hall, Fifth Avenue shoppers, NBC and CBS sidewalk-studio gawkers, Rockefeller Center ice skaters, business travelers at corporate headquarters, and those who like being at the center of the city's energy. Some of the best hotels in the world offer great East River and landmark-building views. A beautifully refurbished Grand Central Station provides easy access to the northern suburbs and Connecticut. Among the dozens and dozens of fine skyscraper hotels clustered here are the classic Art Deco **Waldorf-Astoria** and the **Fitzpatrick Grand Central.**

42ND TO 59TH STREETS: THE WEST SIDE

IN TIMES SQUARE THE NEON IS BRIGHTER THAN EVER, and so is the spirit. Neighborhoods are cleaner and safer. Broadway, Carnegie Hall, theme restaurants, TV studios, and the office buildings along Columbus Circle and the Avenue of the Americas all draw visitors. Moderate chains, such as **Holiday Inn, Marriott, Howard Johnson,** and **Days Inn,** and older, slightly seedy hotels abound, catering to tour groups. But the **Michelangelo** and the great hotels rimming the southern end of Central Park, including the **Essex House,** are among the best in the city. And the **Peninsula,** just a hop west of Fifth Avenue, is grander than ever. Two outstanding newbies are that comet-topped **Westin New York Times Square** at E-walk, just off Times Square, and the elegant **Mandarin Oriental** on Columbus Circle.

60TH STREET AND ABOVE

UPTOWN—REFINED, FASHIONABLE, EXCLUSIVE, CULTURAL. Central Park is the oasis of this area, but it also has world-famous museums and top hospitals. Two-storied Madison Avenue is one of the most fascinating shopping areas of the world, and Lincoln Center is a renowned cultural focal point. Great views of the park and the rivers abound. Not surprisingly, some of the fanciest hotels are here, including the **Carlyle,** the **Lowell,** and the **Mark.**

OTHER BOROUGHS

IF YOU DON'T MIND NOT BEING IN "THE CITY" (and don't mind saving some big bucks), commute into Manhattan by subway, bus, ferry, or splurge on a taxi, and check out the wonders of the outer boroughs and the following hotels: In Brooklyn, the **Best Western Gregory** and **New York Marriott at the Brooklyn Bridge**; in Queens, **Comfort Inn Long Island City** and **Holiday Inn Express Queens**; in Staten Island, **Hilton Garden Inn.**

CAN YOU *even* GET IN?

EVEN WITH INCREASING NUMBERS OF HOTEL ROOMS in New York City, with apologies to songwriters Kander and Ebb, if you can make a reservation (t)here, you can make one anywhere. It's up to you—and your resourcefulness—to get a room in NY, NY.

- Try **NYC & Company's** online reservation system (**www.nycvisit.com**) to check out almost 200 New York hotels. It's powered by **www.1800-USAHOTELS.COM** and features day-to-day changes.
- Check out the **Peak Season Hotel Hotline.** It provides access to rooms at over 80 hotels in all price categories from September 1 to December 31. As a last resort, on nights when travel agents and consumers believe the city is "sold out," the hotline can find rooms. Call ☎ 800-846-7666. And note the other reservations services listed later in the chapter.

- Book as far in advance as possible. Holidays are always busy, but even when occupancy is down in many parts of the country, rooms often are fully booked here, as huge conferences reserve blocks of hotel rooms years in advance, frequently at odd times. Check with the **NYCVB** at ☎ 800-846-7666. Traditionally, the easiest time to get a room is during January and February. And Sunday is traditionally the slowest day of the week.
- Call just after 6 p.m. on the day you want to stay. That is when most properties cancel reservations not guaranteed with a credit card on the day of arrival. (In the industry, these nonguaranteed reservations are called "timers.")
- Try the Web. **www.hotres.com** has blocks of reserved rooms at 30 midtown hotels, so lodging may be available even if a hotel says it's "sold out." Sites are always expanding and new ones popping up, so use a search engine like Yahoo! or Google to find a selection.
- Use travel and tour agencies that do lots of NYC convention business. They often have the clout to find a room, even when you're on your own. Usually the major agencies will do the most convention business; otherwise, inquire from friends or business associates who have traveled on business to New York, or ask around locally. As for tour operators, five who frequently handle New York City are **ATI** (American Tour International), **Allied Tours, T-Pro, CAUSA,** and **City Tours.** Your travel agent will help you reserve through tour operators.
- Be flexible. The more rigid your requests, the harder it may be to fill them. Ask what's available. Management may not have many standard rooms but can sometimes offer luxury suites or relatively unappealing rooms—poor view, low floor, not yet refurbished. If you're willing, you can often negotiate a deal for these white elephants.
- Think small. Hotels with few rooms are least likely to host huge groups, and surprisingly, you can often find a room at small places even at busy times.
- Think independent. When rooms are scarce, non-chain hotels often have availability, as they are less well known and have smaller advertising and marketing budgets than chains.

Because many working New Yorkers live outside the city, the metro and tri-state transportation network is the biggest in the country, and you can get to almost any borough or to the suburbs by public transport until the wee hours of the morning. So if you don't mind commuting, you can find a variety of accommodations outside Manhattan.

Queens, Brooklyn, Staten Island, and the Bronx have some chain hotels, and around Kennedy, LaGuardia, and Newark airports you will find many midlevel choices (see our hotel listings). But nearby Westchester County, southern Connecticut, and Long Island have a varied selection of luxury hotels, inns, resorts, and bed-and-breakfasts, with more recreational space at generally lower cost than comparable accommodations in the city. You may miss out on urban excitement, but you're more likely to get a room.

The following notable accommodations are in the suburbs within an hour or so of the city. All are near subway or train lines (taxis usually meet trains), are in safe neighborhoods, and they offer free parking, outstanding settings and décor, and excellent on-site or nearby restaurants.

Westchester County, NY

The Castle at Tarrytown Benedict Avenue, Tarrytown;
☎ 914-631-1980; fax ☎ 914-631-4612

Crabtree's Kittle House 11 Kittle Road, Chappaqua;
☎ 914-666-8044; fax ☎ 914-666-2684

Doral Arrowwood Anderson Hill Road, Rye Brook;
☎ 800-633-6569; fax ☎ 914-323-5500

Long Island

Garden City Hotel 45 Seventh Street, Garden City;
☎ 516-747-3000; fax ☎ 516-747-1414

The Inn at Great Neck 30 Cutter Mill Road, Great Neck;
☎ 516-773-2000; fax ☎ 516-773-2020

Southern Connecticut

The Homestead Inn 420 Fieldpoint Road, Greenwich;
☎ 203-869-7500; fax ☎ 203-869–7502

Hyatt Regency Greenwich 1800 East Putnam, Old Greenwich;
☎ 203-637-1234; fax ☎ 203-637-2940

The Inn at National Hall 2 Post Road W, Westport;
☎ 800-628-4255, ☎ 203-221-1351; fax ☎ 203-221-0276

SLICE *the* PRICE *of* ROOMS *in the* APPLE

THE BAD NEWS: AVERAGE ROOM RATES ARE ABOUT $200 a night, and at top luxury hotels, standard rooms go for $400 or so—the highest rate in America. Tourists from around the world, it seems, will pay any price to visit New York.

The good news: Compared to many other great international cities, New York is a relative bargain. Remember that as you plunk down your plastic, signing off on what seems like the GNP of Honduras. Here are some helpful ideas for lowering costs:

- **Check out the Internet.** Last-minute bargains are now available online at sites such as **priceline.com, expedia.com,** and **travelocity.com.** You

can judge comparative value for money by seeing a listing of hotels—
what they offer, where they are located, and what they charge.

- **Choose a less-than-fashionable neighborhood.** New York is made up
  of many distinct enclaves, and this emphasis on address reflects itself
  in pricing. Unless you need to be there for convenience, it may not be
  worth it to you to stay on the Upper East Side when the same quality
  room on the Lower West Side may be half the cost. The East Side is
  priciest; Midtown and up to 96th Street is the fanciest area. The good
  deals are on the Upper West Side. You will occasionally find a budget
  hotel in pricey areas, such as the **Pickwick Arms,** in the 50s on the
  East Side. Some other word-of-mouth recommendations for budget
  accommodations are **Habitat** and the **Lucerne.**

- **Leave your car at home.** Garaging a car overnight in New York can cost
  as much as a motel room off the highway (with donuts and coffee). And
  you really don't need a car here; most New Yorkers—even big spenders—
  don't bother with wheels, and many can't even drive. Taxis are abundant
  and public transportation is exceptional. Manhattan is a walkers' paradise, and most of the city is divided into simple grids. If you must drive,
  try for a rare hotel with free parking. See our survey.

- **For longer stays, try an apartment hotel.** These typically offer daily
  maid service, kitchen, and laundry facilities. Several upscale hotels offer
  an apartment option, including the **Waldorf-Astoria.** These hybrids
  combine hotel services with a kitchen and a residential feel and are wonderful for entertaining, or as an alternative to getting an apartment.

- **Seek a suite, which offers the potential of whole families in one
  room.** And if there's a kitchenette, even better. Several hotels, such as
  Trump International Hotel & Towers, offer kitchenettes even in standard rooms.

- **Stay at the worst room at a good hotel, rather than the best at a
  lesser one.** The cost differential can be considerable, although the
  rest of the hotel services, amenities, and public rooms remain available
  for your pleasure. You're getting the biggest bang for your buck when
  you ask for the low-priced smallest room with the worst view on the
  lowest floor—at an otherwise good hotel.

- **Avoid room service and minibars.** Bring food up from delis, take-out
  groceries (which usually have salad bars), or sidewalk vendors, which
  purvey fresh fruits as well as hot dogs, falafel, and other ethnic
  delights. Most will provide utensils if needed, as New Yorkers are
  known for eating on the run. Or, if possible, make like a resident and
  have a restaurant deliver (frowned at by some hotels—check first).
  Neighborhood restaurants, especially the old-fashioned coffee shops
  and "ethnics," are good and surprisingly reasonable. If you eat like a
  local rather than a tourist, you can save big-time.

- **Accept shared baths.** Some hotels, such as the **Pickwick Arms,** are
  set up with some shared facilities, at around $100 a night. If price
  means more than privacy, you'll enjoy the savings.

- **Go really basic.** **YMCAs** and youth hostels are available in the city. Bare-bones, but cheap. There are Ys on the East Side (☎ 212-756-9600) and West Side (phone ☎ 212-875-4100). **Hostelling International** offers a hostel on the Upper West Side (☎ 800-909-4776; **www.hinewyork.org**). Also try **NY Hostel** (☎ 212-932-2300). For dormitory accommodations, check with universities in the city, including New York University. Judith Glynn's **Manhattan Getaways** (phone ☎ 212-956-2010; **manhattangetaways.com**) is a great source for home-style getaways, such as reconverted apartments and guesthouses.
- **Find a discounted rate.** Check out deals through ads, agents, special events, and openings. These include weekend and convention deals, frequent mileage clubs, automobile or other travel clubs, senior rates (some require ages as low as 50), military or government discounts, corporate or shareholder rates, packages, long-stay rates (usually at least five nights), and travel industry rates. Some hotels might even give lower rates if you are visiting because of bereavement or medical care.

Special Weekend Rates

Most hotels that cater to business, government, and convention travelers offer special weekend discount rates ranging 15–40% below normal weekday rates. Find out about weekend specials by calling individual hotels or by consulting your travel agent.

Corporate Rates

Many hotels offer discounted corporate rates (5–20% off rack rate). Usually you don't need to work for a large company or have a special relationship with the hotel—simply ask for this discount. Some will guarantee the discounted rate on the phone when you reserve.

Others may make the rate conditional on your providing some sort of bona fides—for instance, a fax on your company's letterhead requesting the rate, or a company credit card or business card on check-in. Generally, the screening is not rigorous.

Half-Price Programs

Larger discounts on rooms (35–60%), in New York or anywhere else, are available through half-price hotel programs, often called travel clubs. Program operators contract with an individual hotel to provide rooms at deep discounts, usually 50% off rack rate, on a "space available" basis. You can usually reserve a discounted room whenever the hotel expects less than 80% occupancy. A little calendar sleuthing to avoid city-wide conventions and special events increases your chance of finding this kind of discount.

Most half-price programs charge an annual membership fee or directory subscription charge of $25 to $125. You get a membership card and a directory listing participating hotels. But note the restrictions and exceptions. Some hotels "black out" certain dates or times of year. Others may only offer the discount certain days of the week or require you to stay a certain number of nights. Still others may offer a much smaller discount than 50% off rack rate.

Programs specialize in domestic travel, international travel, or both. More established operators offer members thousands of hotels to choose from in the United States. All of the following programs have a heavy concentration of hotels in California and Florida, and most have a limited selection in New York City.

Encore	☎ 800-444-9800
Entertainment Publications	☎ 800-445-4137
ITC-50	☎ 800-987-6216
Quest	☎ 800-638-9819

One caveat: If something seems too good to be true, it usually is, and some hotels figure the discount on an exaggerated rack rate. A few may deduct the discount from a supposed "superior" or "upgraded" room rate, even though the room you get is standard.

But the majority of participating properties base discounts on the published rate in the Hotel and Travel Index (a quarterly reference work used by travel agents) and work within the spirit of their agreement with the program operator.

unofficial **TIP**
As a rule, if you travel several times a year, your room rate savings will easily compensate for membership fees in half-price programs.

Deeply discounted rooms through half-price programs are not commissionable to travel agents, so you'll probably have to make your own calls and reservations. But if you travel frequently, your agent will probably do your legwork anyway.

Preferred Rates

This discount helps travel agents stimulate booking activity or attract a certain class of traveler. Most preferred rates are promoted through travel industry publications and are often accessible only through an agent. Sound out your travel agent about possible deals, but note that the rates shown on travel agents' computerized reservations systems are not always the lowest rates obtainable. Zero in on a couple of hotels that fill your needs in terms of location and quality of accommodations, then have your agent call the hotel for the latest rates and specials. A personal appeal from your agent to the hotel's director of sales and marketing will often get you a room.

unofficial **TIP**
Hotel reps respond positively to travel agents because they represent a source of additional business. There are certain specials that hotel reps will disclose only to travel agents.

Consolidators, Wholesalers, and Reservation Services

The discount available (if any) from a reservation service depends on whether the service functions as a consolidator or as a wholesaler.

Consolidators are strictly sales agents who do not own or control the room inventory they are trying to sell. Discounts offered by consolidators are determined by the hotels with rooms to fill. Consolidator discounts vary enormously depending on how desperate the hotel is to unload the rooms. When you deal with a room reservation service that operates as a consolidator, you pay for your room as usual when you check out of the hotel.

Wholesalers have longstanding contracts with hotels to purchase rooms at an established deep discount. Some wholesalers hold purchase options on blocks of rooms, whereas others actually pay for rooms and own the inventory, so they can offer whatever discount is consistent with current demand. Most discounts fall in the 10–40% range, and you'll usually pay for your entire stay in advance with your credit card. The service then sends you a written confirmation and usually a voucher (indicating prepayment) to present at the hotel.

Reservation services are probably more useful when availability is scarce than to obtain deep discounts. Calling the hotels ourselves, we were often able to beat the reservation services' rates (when rooms were available). When the city was booked, however, the reservation services were able to find rooms at a fair price.

Ask for a rate quote for a particular hotel, or for their best available deal, in your preferred area. If you say you're on a budget, the service might even shave a bit off their profit.

Services that frequently offer substantial discounts include:

Accommodations Express	☎ 800-444-7666
Central Reservation Service	☎ 800-548-3311
Express Reservations	☎ 800-356-1123
Hotel Reservations Network	☎ 800-964-6835
Quikbook	☎ 800-789-9887

HOW TO EVALUATE A TRAVEL PACKAGE

PACKAGE VACATIONS CAN BE WIN–WIN. The buyer only has to make one phone call and deal with a single salesperson to set up the whole vacation: transportation, lodging, meals, guided tours, and Broadway shows. The seller eliminates separate sales, confirmations, and billing. Some packagers also buy hotel rooms and airfares in bulk on contract, like a broker playing the commodities market, which can mean a significant savings from posted fares.

Choose a package with features you are sure to use; you will be paying for them. If cost is more important than convenience, make a few calls to price individual components (airfare, lodging, shows, etc.). If the costs are about the same, the package is probably worth buying just for the convenience. If your package includes a choice of rental car or airport transfers (transportation to and from the airport), take the transfers. Driving in the city is difficult, and parking in a garage is expensive, often up to $50 for a 24-hour period. During the weekend, with most businesses closed and commuters and second-home types out of town, it's relatively easier to get around, and parking spaces may be available, if you want to chance it; but during the week, forget it. (If you do take the car, find a package that includes free parking at your hotel.)

Buyer beware. You're dealing with a lot of money and trust here, and alas, a packager could cash in on discounts without passing them on, or load packages with extras that cost next to nothing but inflate the retail price higher than the Empire State Building; a real New York–style con game. So if something seems "off," check with a supervisor or a major travel agency, and be sure you're with a reputable company.

IS *your* TRAVEL AGENT NYC SAVVY?

THE CITY HOTEL SCENE IS COMPLEX and constantly changing. Has your travel agent recently been to New York? And does the agency keep up-to-the-minute info?

Some travel agents unfamiliar with the Apple may try to plug you into a tour operator's or wholesaler's preset package, allowing the agent to set up your whole trip up with a single phone call—and still collect an 8–10% commission. And many agents will place almost all their New York business with only one or two wholesalers or tour operators, which doesn't provide much choice for you.

Agents will often use wholesalers who run packages in conjunction with airlines, like Delta Vacations or American's Fly Away Vacations, and because of the wholesaler's exclusive relationship with the carrier, these trips are easy to book. However, they can be more expensive than a package offered by a high-volume wholesaler who works with airlines in a primary New York City market.

To help your travel agent get you the best possible hotel deal, follow these five steps:

1. Determine which area is best for you and, if possible, choose a specific hotel. Review the hotel information provided in this guide, and contact hotels that interest you, if necessary.

2. Check out the hotel deals and package vacations advertised on the Internet and in the Sunday travel sections of major newspapers such as the *New York Times, New York Daily News, Philadelphia Inquirer,* or *Boston Globe.* They often advertise deals that undercut anything offered in your local paper. See if you can find specials that fit your plans and include a hotel you like.

3. Call the hotels, wholesalers, or tour operators whose ads you have collected. Ask any questions you have concerning their packages, but do not book your trip with them directly.

4. Ask if your travel agent can get you something better. The deals in the paper will serve as a benchmark.

5. Choose from the options, then have your travel agent book the best one. Even if you go with one of the packages in the newspaper, it will probably be commissionable (at no additional cost to you) and will provide the agent some return on the time invested on your behalf. Also, as a travel professional, your agent should be able to verify the quality and integrity of the deal.

IF YOU MAKE YOUR OWN RESERVATION

CHECK OUT THE INTERNET. A GREAT TOOL in the hotel-hunting arsenal is **www.travelaxe.com.** Travelaxe offers free software you can download to your PC (won't run on Macs) that will scan an assortment of hotel-discount sites and find the cheapest rate for each of over 200 New York hotels. The site offers filters such as price, quality rating, and proximity to a specific location (midtown, the convention center, airport, and so on) to allow you to narrow your search. The same software also scans for the best rates in cities throughout the United States and the world. Also call the specific hotel (as opposed to the hotel chain's national toll-free number where operators are usually unaware of local specials). Always ask about specials before inquiring about corporate rates—and don't be afraid to bargain. If you're buying a hotel's weekend package, for example, and want to extend your stay into the following week, you can often obtain at least the corporate rate for the extra days. However, do your bargaining before you check in, preferably when you make your reservations.

ARE YOU COMING TO NYC ON BUSINESS?

IDENTIFY THE NEIGHBORHOOD(S) WHERE YOUR BUSINESS will take you, then use the hotel chart to cross-reference the hotels located in that area. Once you have developed a short list of possible hotels that fit your budget and offer the standards you require, you (or your travel agent) can apply the cost-saving suggestions discussed earlier to obtain the lowest rate.

Convention Rates: How They Work and How to Do Better

If you're attending a major convention or trade show, your group has probably negotiated convention rates, and hotels have booked rooms at an agreed-on price, sometimes city-wide.

Because the convention sponsor brings big business to New York and reserves many rooms, often annually, it usually can negotiate volume discounts substantially below rack rate. You may get a housing list that includes the special rates, and you can compare them with the rates using the strategies covered in the previous section.

If the negotiated convention rate doesn't sound like a good deal, try to reserve a room using an Internet bargain, a half-price club, a consolidator, or a tour operator. Remember, however, that deep discounts are usually available only when the hotel expects to be at less than 80% occupancy, a rarity when a big convention is in town.

STRATEGIES FOR BEATING CONVENTION RATES: EASY AS 1-2-3

1. Reserve early. Most big conventions and trade shows announce meeting sites one to three years in advance. If you book well ahead of the time the convention sponsor sends out the housing list, chances are good that the hotel will accept your reservation.

2. Compare your convention's housing list with the list of hotels presented in this guide. You may be able to find a suitable hotel not on the housing list.

3. Use a local reservations agency or consolidator. This is also a good strategy if you need to make reservations at the last minute. Local reservations agencies and consolidators almost always control some rooms, even during a huge convention or trade show.

HOTELS RATED *and* RANKED

WHAT'S IN A ROOM?

UNFORTUNATELY, IN NEW YORK, SOME BEAUTIFULLY appointed rooms are cramped and poorly designed. *Unofficial Guide* researchers are aware of this and spend many weeks inspecting hotel rooms. Here are a few of the things we check.

ROOM SIZE Spacious rooms are preferable, but New York's hotel rooms are generally smaller than those in other major cities, and the trend is high-style and cramped. Note the other luxuries, and if it will be a problem, ask about size when booking. (Smaller rooms can be cozy, but not if you bump your shins in the middle of the night trying to maneuver between the walls and the bed.) If a room is well designed, with big windows, mirrored walls, nooks and alcoves, it can compensate for lack of space.

unofficial **TIP**
If size really matters, rooms at the Four Seasons, at 600 square feet, are among the largest in the city—as large as many New York one-bedroom apartments—and are reputed to have cost about a million dollars each to design and furnish.

TEMPERATURE CONTROL, VENTILATION, AND ODOR Hotel rooms should be odor-free and smoke-free and not feel stuffy or damp. The most quiet and responsive system is central heating and air-conditioning, controlled by the room's own thermostat. Next best is a room module heater and air conditioner, preferably controlled by an automatic thermostat, but usually by manually operated button controls. Central heating and air without any sort of room thermostat can leave you sweltering or shivering in the changeable New York climate, without much control.

Most hotel rooms have windows or balcony doors that have been permanently sealed. Though there are legitimate safety and liability issues involved, we prefer windows and balcony doors that can be opened. A room with a view is preferable, and a balcony or terrace is especially exciting (and rare) in New York City, not just because you can step outside but because of the full-length windows—and the "fresh" NYC air.

ROOM SECURITY We'll start with front desk staffers, who need to be discreet about calling out your room number. Better rooms have locks that require a plastic card instead of the traditional lock and key; card-and-slot systems allow the hotel to change the combination or entry code of the lock with each new guest. Though larger hotels and hotel chains with lock-and-key systems usually rotate their locks once each year, they remain vulnerable to hotel thieves much of the time, and many smaller or independent properties rarely rotate their locks.

In addition to the entry-lock system, the door should have a deadbolt, and perhaps a chain that can be locked from the inside, but a chain by itself is not sufficient. Peepholes allow you to check out visitors. Any windows and balcony doors should have secure locks. Room safes are becoming standard security devices, and the bigger the better, so that technical devices, cameras, and other large items can also be stored.

SAFETY New York codes are tough. Fire or smoke alarm, clear fire instructions, and sprinkler systems are musts for rooms. Bathtubs should have a nonskid surface, and shower stall doors are safest if they either open outward or slide side-to-side. Bathroom electrical outlets high on the wall and not too close to the sink are best. Balconies should have sturdy, high rails.

NOISE As we mentioned earlier, if traffic and street noises are around-the-clock problems, make sure windows are double- or triple-glazed. In better hotels, wall and ceiling construction effectively screen routine noise, carpets and drapes absorb and muffle sounds, and mattresses mounted on stable platforms or sturdy bed frames don't squeak much, even when challenged by the most acrobatic lovers. Televisions enclosed in cabinets, and with volume governors, rarely disturb guests in adjacent rooms.

unofficial **TIP**
If you are easily disturbed by noise, ask for a room on a higher floor, off main thoroughfares, and away from elevators and ice and vending machines.

Optimally, the air-conditioning and heating system operates without noise or vibration. Likewise, plumbing is quiet and positioned away from the sleeping area. Doors to the hall, and to adjoining rooms, are thick and well fitted to better block out noise.

DARKNESS CONTROL Ever wake up at sunrise in a hotel room where the curtains would not quite meet in the middle? Thick, lined curtains that close completely in the center and extend beyond the edges of the window or door frame are ideal. In a well-planned room, the curtains, shades, or blinds should almost totally block light at any time of day.

LIGHTING Poor lighting is a problem in American hotel rooms, and New York, sorry to say, is no exception. Lighting may be dramatic, and adequate for dressing, relaxing, or watching television, but not for reading or working. Light needs to be bright over tables and desks, and beside couches or easy chairs. Since many people read in bed, best is a separate light for each person, high enough to shed light on books, but illuminating a small area so that a sleeper will not be bothered by their roommate's light. A bedside console that controls most lights and electronics is especially desirable. The worst situation is a single bedside lamp, sometimes compounded by weak light bulbs.

Closet areas should be well lit, with a switch near the door that turns on room lights when you enter. Bathroom lighting should be adequate for grooming purposes—and a heat lamp is a nice bonus.

FURNISHINGS Minimum sleep requirements are top-grade mattresses, pillows with nonallergenic fillers, warm blankets, and bed linens changed daily. Better hotels usually provide extra blankets and pillows in the room or on request, and they sometimes use a second top sheet between blanket and spread. Duvets over down comforters, once a European luxury, are the New York standard of cleanliness and comfort. Better headboards are padded for comfortable reading in bed, and a nightstand or table on each side of the bed(s) is standard.

Dressers should be large enough to hold clothes for two people during a long stay, and a luggage rack and full-length mirror are useful. As for electronics, televisions today are expected to be large as well as cable-connected—ideally, with volume governors and remote controls, and, preferably, enclosed. A local TV program guide helps. In-room movies and VCR capabilities are nice options. CD/DVD players and top-grade clock radios are pluses.

Telephones should be touch-tone, capable of international direct dialing, and conveniently situated, with easy-to-understand dialing instructions and a rate card. Local white and yellow pages should be provided. Better hotels install phones in the bathroom and furnish portable phones or equip room phones with long cords. Two lines, dataports for fax and laptop computers, and cell and mobile phones are offered at luxury and business-oriented hotels.

A table with chairs, or a desk, and a sitting area—perhaps with screens or French doors to block off work and sleep areas—are important elements. Well-designed hotel rooms usually have armchairs and sometimes a sleeper sofa for lounging and reading. Nice extras in any hotel room include small refrigerators or minibars, irons and ironing boards, coffeemakers, and trouser presses.

BATHROOM Marble, granite, and tile look best and are easy to keep clean. Two sinks are better than one, and you cannot have too much counter space. A sink outside the bath is a great convenience when one person bathes as another dresses, a separate toilet area is nice for privacy, and bidets are important options, especially for international travelers. Better bathrooms have both a tub and shower with a non-slip bottom. Tub and shower controls should be easy to operate; adjustable shower heads are preferred, and whirlpool tubs and separate shower stalls are a plus. The bath needs to be well lit and should have an exhaust fan and a guest-controlled bathroom heater. Towels and washcloths should be large, thick, and generously supplied. An electrical outlet for each sink, conveniently and safely placed, is a big convenience when you're shaving or drying hair.

Magnifying mirrors, scales, bathrobes and slippers, phones, hair dryers, lines for TVs or extra speakers, and amenities such as fine soaps, shampoos, and lotions all add to the luxury of the bathroom.

VENDING If there is no minibar, a complimentary ice machine and a drink machine should be conveniently located, or nibbles and drinks easily available from room service. Welcome additions at midrange properties include access to snacks and sundries (combs, toothpaste, etc.) in restaurants and shops. Luxury hotels will provide sundries in the room or on request.

MAINTENANCE Your eyes, nose, and fingers will tell you how your room is maintained, and even if a room is large and luxurious, if it isn't clean it isn't habitable. On the other hand, a basic but clean room may be just fine. Check out whether the hotel offers daily maid service. Luxury hotels offer turndown service (and that nice chocolate—or more—on the pillow).

"YOU'RE THE GREATEST": OUR FAVORITE NEW YORK HOTELS

WITH APOLOGIES TO NEW YORK'S OWN RALPH KRAMDEN (of the classic TV series *The Honeymooners*), here's our totally subjective listing of superlative New York hotels. Some of these listings are not rated, but since they have special reputations for one particular aspect, we include them here.

Boutique Hotels	
The Alex	The Hotel on Rivington
Bryant Park Hotel	Hudson Hotel
City Club	Le Marquis
Dream	Library Hotel
Dylan Hotel	Maritime Hotel
Hotel Chandler	Mercer
Hotel Gansevoort	The Muse
	The Solita Soho Clarion

Large Rooms

Beekman Tower
Flatotel International
Four Seasons Hotel

Fun Themes

Dream
Hotel Casablanca
Library Hotel
The Muse

NYC Icons

Algonquin Hotel
The Carlyle
The Pierre
The St. Regis
The Sherry Netherland
The Waldorf-Astoria

Bargains Under $200

Cosmopolitan Hotel
Habitat Hotel
Hotel 31
Hotel 41
Hotel QT New York
On the Avenue
Pickwick Arms Hotel
Tribeca Grand

Bed-and-Breakfasts/ Under a Dozen Rooms

Akwaaba Mansion
Country Inn the City
Harbor House (Staten Island)
Harlem Landmark Guest House
Holmes Bed-and-Breakfast
The Inn at Irving Place
Inn New York City
Inn on 23rd Street
Le Refuge Inn (Bronx)
Second Home on Second Ave.

Classic Hotel Bars

The Bull & Bear at the
  Waldorf-Astoria

Fantino at Central Park
  Intercontinental
5757 at the Four Seasons
King Cole Bar at the St. Regis
  Hotel
Mark's Bar at the Mark

Trendy Hotel Bars and Lounges

C3 Lounge at Washington Square
  Hotel
The Grand Bar at the Soho Grand
The Grotto at the Michelangelo
Hudson Bar (with library and purple
  pool table) at Hudson Hotel
Jack's Bar at Le Parker Meridien
  Hotel
Lobby Lounge, Mandarin Oriental
Morgan's Bar at Morgans
Oak Room at the Algonquin
Oasis at W New York
Subconscious
The Ws

Gay-comfortable Hotels

Chelsea Savoy
Hotel Gansevoort
Maritime
Mercer
SoHo Grand
Tribeca Grand
The Ws
Washington Square Hotel

Complimentary Breakfast

Avalon
Bentley
Hotel Giraffe
Hotel QT New York
Iroquois New York
The Roger Smith
Washington Square Hotel

Brunch

Ambassador Grill at Regal U.N.
  Plaza

Brunch *(continued)*

Halcyon's Penthouse at
  J. W. Marriott Hotel
Heartbeat at W New York
Norma's at Le Parker Meridien
  Hotel
Restaurant Charlotte at
  Millennium Broadway

High Tea

The Pierre
The Ritz-Carlton New York
  Battery Park
The St. Regis
The Waldorf-Astoria

Hotel Restaurants

Abbogado at the Blakely
Adrienne at the Peninsula
Asiate at Mandarin Oriental
C3 at Washington Square Hotel
The Coach House at Avalon
District at the Muse
Heartbeat at W New York
Ilo at Bryant Park Hotel
Jean Georges at Trump
  International Hotel & Towers
Moda at Flatotel
Nadaman Hakubai at the
  Kitano New York
Riingo at the Alex Hotel
Thom at 60 Thompson
Town at Chambers—a Hotel
Triomphe at the Iroquois New York
Virot at Dylan Hotel

Drop-dead Elegant Hotels

The Four Seasons
Mandarin Oriental
The Peninsula
St. Regis Hotel
The Waldorf-Astoria

Public Rooms and
Meeting Space

18th floor at the Waldorf-Astoria
The Hilton New York

Mandarin Oriental
The New York Marriott Marquis
St. Regis Hotel rooftop
The Sheraton New York Hotel and
  Towers

Fitness Clubs and Spas

The Drake Swissôtel
Dream
Le Parker Meridien Hotel
Mandarin Oriental
New York Palace
The Peninsula
Regal U.N. Plaza
Ritz-Carlton New York Central Park
St. Regis Hotel
W New York

Romantic

The Dylan
The Inn at Irving Place
The Lowell
The Mark
The Peninsula
The Royalton
St. Regis Hotel
60 Thompson
The Waldorf-Astoria

People-watching

Any downtown hotel less than a
  year old
Any hotel lobby where the lowest
  rates are more than $300 a night
King Cole Bar at the St. Regis Hotel
Lobby of the Royalton
Peacock Alley at the
  Waldorf-Astoria
The Regency at breakfast
Whiskey Blue at W New York

Views

Any east-side Manhattan hotel
Apartment-hotels or clubs
Beekman Tower Hotel
DoubleTree Guest Suites Times
  Square

Views *(continued)*

The Four Seasons
Hotels fronting Central Park and
  New York Harbor
Long Stays
On the Avenue
Regal U. N. Plaza
Ritz-Carlton New York Battery Park
Soho Grand (looking north)
Solita Soho Clarion
Trump International Hotel &
  Towers
The Waldorf-Astoria towers

Kid-Friendly Hotels

The Barclay New York
Essex House
Le Parker Meridien Hotel
The Lucerne
Novotel New York
Ritz-Carlton New York Battery Park
The Waldorf-Astoria

Pet-Friendly Hotels

Any Loews hotel, such as the Re-
  gency *(puppy pagers provided)*
Many Sheraton, Westin, and
  W hotels
The Muse *(doggy room service and
  pooch package)*
On the Avenue
*Check ahead—most New York hotels
  now welcome small pets*

Computer-and-Internet-friendly

Benjamin Hotel
The Drake Swissôtel
The Muse
St. Regis
Time
*(and most hotels built or rehabbed
  post-2003)*

Balconies and Terraces

Central Park Intercontinental
The Drake Swissôtel

Hotel Gansevoort
The Hotel on Rivington
The Lombardy
On the Avenue
The Warwick Hotel

Quirky Hotels

Blue Moon
The Box Tree
Chambers—a Hotel
Hudson Hotel
The Inn at Irving Place
Inn on 23rd Street
Maritime
The Roger Smith
The Sherry Netherland Hotel
Washington Square Hotel
Westin New York Times Square
The Wyndham Hotel

Notable Amenities

Benjamin Hotel *(pillow menu)*
The Four Seasons *(tubs that fill in 60
  seconds)*
Hotel Gansevoort *(45-foot outdoor
  rooftop pool)*
The Hotel on Rivington *(glass shower
  walls on building exterior)*
J. W. Marriott Hotel *(heated toilet
  seats)*
Le Parker Meridien Hotel *(home-
  made chocolate chip cookies)*
The Mark *(phones on either side of
  king bed, comp shuttle, Chinese tea
  classes)*
The New York Palace *(customized sta-
  tionery and business cards)*
Regal U.N. Plaza *(tennis court)*
The Royalton *("intimacy kit")*
Soho Grand *(goldfish)*
Trump International Hotel &
  Towers *(telescope, personal chef,
  laptop computer)*

HOTEL RATINGS

OVERALL QUALITY To distinguish properties according to relative quality, tastefulness, state of repair, cleanliness, and size of standard rooms, we have grouped the hotels and motels into classifications denoted by stars. Star ratings in this guide apply to New York–area properties only and do not necessarily correspond to stars awarded by Mobil, AAA, or other travel critics. Because stars carry little weight when awarded in the absence of common standards of comparison, we have linked our ratings to expected levels of quality established by specific American hotel corporations.

★★★★★	SUPERIOR	Tasteful and luxurious by any standard
★★★★	EXTREMELY NICE	What you would expect at a Hyatt Regency or Marriott
★★★	NICE	Holiday Inn or comparable quality
★★	ADEQUATE	Clean, comfortable, and functional without frills—like a Motel 6
★	BUDGET	Spartan, not aesthetically pleasing, but clean

Star ratings describe the property's standard accommodations. For most hotels, a "standard accommodation" is a room with either one king bed or two queen beds. In an all-suite property, the standard accommodation is either a one- or two-room suite. In addition to standard accommodations, many hotels offer luxury rooms and special suites not rated here. Star ratings are assigned without regard to whether a property has restaurant(s), recreational facilities, entertainment, or other extras.

ROOM QUALITY In addition to stars (which delineate broad categories), we also employ a numerical rating system. Our rating scale is 0 to 100, with 100 as the best possible rating and zero (0) as the worst. Numerical ratings are presented to show the difference we perceive between one property and another. Rooms at the Sheraton New York, the Maritime, and the Avalon are all rated as four-star (★★★★). In the supplemental numerical ratings, the Sheraton is rated an 89, the Maritime an 88, and the Avalon an 84. This means that within the four-star category, the Sheraton and the Maritime are comparable, and both have slightly nicer rooms than the Avalon.

COST Cost estimates are based on the hotel's published rack rates for standard rooms. Each "$" represents $80. Thus, a cost symbol of "$$$" means a room (or suite) at that hotel will cost about $240 a night.

HOW THE HOTELS COMPARE

BELOW IS A HIT PARADE OF THE NICEST ROOMS in town. We've focused strictly on room quality and excluded any consideration of location, services, recreation, or amenities. In some instances, a one- or two-room suite can be had for the same price or less than a hotel room.

How the Hotels Compare

HOTEL RATING	OVERALL RATING	ROOM QUALITY	COST ($=$80)
Mandarin Oriental Hotel	★★★★★	98	$$$$$$$$$
The Peninsula	★★★★★	98	$$$$$$$$
Ritz-Carlton Battery Park	★★★★★	98	$$$$$$
The St. Regis	★★★★★	98	$$$$$$$$
Four Seasons Hotel	★★★★★	97	$$$$$$$$$$+
Trump International Hotel & Towers	★★★★★	97	$$$$$$$$+
The Carlyle	★★★★★	96	$$$$$$$$
Essex House Hotel Nikko New York	★★★★★	96	$$$$$
The Lowell	★★★★★	96	$$$$$$$
The Mark	★★★★★	96	$$$$$$+
The New York Palace	★★★★★	96	$$$$$+
The Pierre	★★★★★	96	$$$$$$$+
Benjamin Hotel	★★★★½	95	$$$$+
Bryant Park Hotel	★★★★½	95	$$$$$–
Le Parker Meridien New York	★★★★½	95	$$$$$+
Omni Berkshire Place	★★★★½	95	$$$$
The Regency Hotel	★★★★½	95	$$$$$$$$
W Hotel Times Square	★★★★½	95	$$$$+
The Waldorf-Astoria	★★★★½	95	$$$+
The Inn at Irving Place	★★★★½	94	$$$$
Inn New York City	★★★★½	94	$$$$–
The Kitano New York	★★★★½	94	$$$
Mercer	★★★★½	94	$$$$$$–
Ritz-Carlton New York Central Park	★★★★½	94	$$$$$$$$
City Club Hotel	★★★★½	93	$$
Flatotel International	★★★★½	93	$$$$–
The Lombardy	★★★★½	93	$$$$
The Michelangelo	★★★★½	93	$$$$$
Morgans	★★★★½	93	$$$$+
Rihga Royal	★★★★½	93	$$$
The Sherry Netherland	★★★★½	93	$$$$$$–
Soho Grand	★★★★½	93	$$$+
Tribeca Grand	★★★★½	93	$$$$
The Drake Swissôtel	★★★★½	92	$$$$+
Hotel Gansevoort	★★★★½	92	$$$$$$+
Millennium Broadway	★★★★½	92	$$$$–
Sheraton Manhattan Hotel	★★★★½	92	$$$+

How the Hotels Compare (continued)

HOTEL RATING	OVERALL RATING	ROOM QUALITY	COST ($=$80)
W New York	★★★★½	92	$$$$
Blakely	★★★★½	91	$$$+
Dream	★★★★½	91	$$$$–
Hotel Elysee	★★★★½	91	$$$$$–
Renaissance New York Hotel	★★★★½	91	$$$$
The Royalton	★★★★½	91	$$$$$–
San Carlos	★★★★½	91	$$$$+
The Alex Hotel	★★★★½	90	$$$$$+
The Algonquin Hotel	★★★★½	90	$$$$+
Barclay New York	★★★★½	90	$$$$$
Embassy Suites NYC	★★★★½	90	$$$$–
Hotel Chandler	★★★★½	90	$$$+
Hotel Plaza Athenee	★★★★½	90	$$$$$–
The Muse	★★★★½	90	$$$$
70 Park Avenue Hotel	★★★★½	90	$$$$$$$$$–
W New York Tuscany	★★★★½	90	$$$$
The Carlton	★★★★	89	$$$+
Chambers–a Hotel	★★★★	89	$$$$$+
Hudson Hotel	★★★★	89	$$$+
Millennium U.N. Plaza	★★★★	89	$$$$$+
The New York Hilton and Towers	★★★★	89	$$$$–
Sheraton New York Hotel and Towers	★★★★	89	$$$+
The Shoreham	★★★★	89	$$$$
The Solita Soho Clarion Hotel	★★★★	89	$$$+
Time	★★★★	89	$$$
The Warwick Hotel	★★★★	89	$$$+
Bed-and-Breakfast on the Park	★★★★	88	$$$
Bentley	★★★★	88	$$$$+
Courtyard by Marriott Manhattan Times Square South	★★★★	88	$$$+
Fitzpatrick Manhattan Hotel	★★★★	88	$$$$
Hilton Times Square	★★★★	88	$$$$–
Hotel Giraffe	★★★★	88	$$$$+
The Hotel on Rivington	★★★★	88	$$$$+
Maritime Hotel	★★★★	88	$$$$
Novotel New York	★★★★	88	$$$
Paramount	★★★★	88	$$$$–

HOTEL	OVERALL RATING	ROOM QUALITY	COST ($=$80)
60 Thompson	★★★★	88	$$$$$+
Sofitel New York	★★★★	88	$$$$
Westin New York Times Square	★★★★	88	$$$$$$$
Crowne Plaza United Nations	★★★★	87	$$$$
New York Marriott Marquis	★★★★	87	$$$$+
W Hotel Union Square	★★★★	87	$$$$$+
Beekman Tower Hotel	★★★★	86	$$$+
Crowne Plaza Manhattan	★★★★	86	$$$$
Grand Hyatt New York	★★★★	86	$$$$$
Hotel Casablanca	★★★★	86	$$$$–
Iroquois New York	★★★★	86	$$$$–
Library Hotel	★★★★	86	$$$$
Roger Williams	★★★★	86	$$$$
Wall Street Inn	★★★★	86	$$$+
Dylan Hotel	★★★★	85	$$$$+
Excelsior	★★★★	85	$$$$–
Fitzpatrick Grand Central	★★★★	85	$$$$
Avalon	★★★★	84	$$$–
Blue Moon Hotel	★★★★	84	$$$+
Double Tree Metropolitan	★★★★	84	$$$+
Hotel Bedford	★★★★	84	$$$
Hotel Wales	★★★★	84	$$$$$
The Mansfield	★★★★	84	$$$
Four Points by Sheraton Manhattan Chelsea	★★★½	83	$$$
Hotel 41	★★★½	83	$$$$+
Red Roof Inn Manhattan	★★★½	83	$$
Thirty Thirty New York City	★★★½	83	$$
Ameritania Hotel	★★★½	82	$$$
Clarion Fifth Avenue	★★★½	82	$$
Hotel Metro	★★★½	81	$$$
La Quinta Inn Manhattan	★★★½	81	$$
Country Inn the City	★★★½	80	$$
DoubleTree Guest Suites Times Square	★★★½	80	$$$+
The Franklin	★★★½	80	$$$$$–
Hotel QT New York	★★★½	80	$$$$–
Jolly Hotel Madison Towers	★★★½	80	$$$
Le Refuge Inn	★★★½	80	$$–

How the Hotels Compare (continued)

HOTEL RATING	OVERALL RATING	ROOM QUALITY	COST ($=$80)
On the Avenue	★★★½	80	$$$
The Roger Smith	★★★½	80	$$$$
Roosevelt Hotel	★★★½	80	$$$$$$
Lucerne	★★★½	79	$$$+
Washington Square Hotel	★★★½	78	$$$−
Chelsea Savoy	★★★½	77	$$$
Second Home on Second Avenue	★★★½	77	$$
Inn on 23rd Street	★★★	76	$$$
Cosmopolitan Hotel	★★★	75	$$
Hotel 31	★★★	75	$$
Hotel 57	★★★	75	$$$+
Akwaaba Mansion	★★★	70	$$
Harbor House	★★★	68	$$−
Pickwick Arms	★★½	60	$$

If you use subsequent editions of this guide, you will notice that many of the ratings and rankings have changed. In addition to the inclusion of new properties, these changes also consider guest room renovations or improved maintenance and housekeeping. A failure to properly maintain guest rooms or a lapse in housekeeping standards can negatively affect the ratings.

Finally, before you begin to shop for a hotel, take a hard look at this letter we received from a couple in Hot Springs, Arkansas:

> We cancelled our room reservations to follow the advice in your book [and reserved a hotel room highly ranked by the Unofficial Guide]. We wanted inexpensive, but clean and cheerful. We got inexpensive, but [also] dirty, grim, and depressing. I really felt disappointed in your advice and the room. It was the pits. That was the one real piece of information I needed from your book! The room spoiled the holiday for me aside from our touring.

Needless to say, this letter was as unsettling to us as the bad room was to our reader. Our integrity as travel journalists, after all, is based on the quality of the information we provide our readers. Even with the best of intentions and the most conscientious research, however, we cannot inspect every room in every hotel. What we do, in statistical terms, is take a sample: We check out several rooms selected at random in each hotel and base our ratings and rankings on those rooms. The inspections are conducted anonymously and without the knowledge of management.

New York Hotels by Neighborhood

DOWNTOWN
Blue Moon Hotel
Cosmopolitan Hotel
Embassy Suites NYC
Hotel Gansevoort
The Hotel on Rivington
Mercer
Ritz-Carlton Battery Park
60 Thompson
Soho Grand
The Solita Soho Clarion Hotel
Tribeca Grand
Wall Street Inn
Washington Square Hotel

**CHELSEA, GRAMERCY PARK,
AND MIDTOWN**
The Alex Hotel
The Algonquin Hotel
Ameritania Hotel
Avalon
Barclay New York
Beekman Tower Hotel
Benjamin Hotel
Bryant Park Hotel
The Carlton
Chambers–a Hotel
Chelsea Savoy
City Club Hotel
Clarion Fifth Avenue
Courtyard by Marriott Manhattan
   Times Square South
Crowne Plaza Manhattan
Crowne Plaza United Nations
DoubleTree Guest Suites Times Square
DoubleTree Metropolitan
The Drake Swissôtel
Dylan Hotel
Essex House Hotel Nikko New York
Fitzpatrick Grand Central
Fitzpatrick Manhattan Hotel
Flatotel International
Four Points by Sheraton Manhattan
   Chelsea

Four Seasons Hotel
Grand Hyatt New York
Hilton Times Square
Hotel Bedford
Hotel Casablanca
Hotel Chandler
Hotel Elysee
Hotel 57
Hotel 41
Hotel Giraffe
Hotel Metro
Hotel QT New York
Hotel 31
Hudson Hotel
The Inn at Irving Place
Inn on 23rd Street
Iroquois New York
J. W. Marriott
Jolly Hotel Madison Towers
The Kitano New York
La Quinta Inn Manhattan
Le Parker Meridien New York
Library Hotel
The Mansfield
Maritime Hotel
The Michelangelo
Millennium Broadway
Millennium U.N. Plaza
Morgans
The Muse
The New York Hilton and Towers
New York Marriott Marquis
The New York Palace
Novotel New York
Omni Berkshire Place
Paramount
The Peninsula
Pickwick Arms
Red Roof Inn Manhattan
Renaissance New York Hotel
Rihga Royal
Ritz-Carlton New York Central Park

New York Hotels by Neighborhood (continued)

CHELSEA, GRAMERCY PARK, AND MIDTOWN (CONTINUED)

The Roger Smith
Roger Williams
Roosevelt Hotel
The Royalton
San Carlos
Second Home on Second Avenue
70 Doral Park Avenue Hotel
Sheraton Manhattan Hotel
Sheraton New York Hotel and Towers
The Shoreham
Sofitel New York
The St. Regis
Thirty Thirty New York City
Time
W Hotel Times Square
W Hotel Union Square
W New York
W New York Tuscany
The Waldorf-Astoria
The Warwick Hotel
Westin New York Times Square

UPTOWN

Bentley
Blakely

UPTOWN (CONTINUED)

The Carlyle
Country Inn the City
Dream
Excelsior
The Franklin
Hotel Plaza Athenee
Hotel Wales
Inn New York City
The Lombardy
The Lowell
Lucerne
Mandarin Oriental Hotel
The Mark
The Melrose Hotel
On the Avenue
The Pierre
The Regency Hotel
The Sherry Netherland
Trump International Hotel & Towers

BROOKLYN

Akwaaba Mansion
Bed-and-Breakfast on the Park

HARLEM AND UPPER MANHATTAN

Le Refuge Inn

Although unusual, it is certainly possible that the rooms we randomly inspect are not representative of the majority of rooms at a particular hotel. Another possibility is that the rooms we inspect in a given hotel are representative but that by bad luck a reader is assigned a room that is inferior. When we rechecked the hotel our reader disliked, we discovered that our rating was correctly representative but that he and his wife had unfortunately been assigned to one of a small number of threadbare rooms scheduled for renovation.

The key to avoiding disappointment is to snoop around in advance. We recommend that you search the Web, ask for a photo of a hotel's standard guest room before you book, or at least get a copy of the hotel's promotional brochure. Alas, some hotel chains use the same guest room photo in their promotional literature for all their properties; a specific guest room may not resemble the brochure photo. Find out how old the property is and when your guest room was last renovated. If you arrive and are assigned an inferior room, demand to be moved.

TOP 30 BEST DEALS IN NEW YORK

HAVING LISTED THE NICEST ROOMS IN TOWN, let's reorder the list to rank the best combinations of quality and value in a room. As before, the rankings are made without consideration of location or the availability of restaurant(s), recreational facilities, entertainment, and/or amenities. Remember that a ★★★ room at $120 may rank closely with a ★★★★ room at $240, but that does not mean the rooms will be of comparable quality. Regardless of whether it's a good deal or not, a ★★★ room is still a ★★★ room. These are the best room buys for the money, regardless of location or star classification, based on averaged rack rates.

Top 30 Best Deals in New York

HOTEL	OVERALL RATING	ROOM QUALITY RATING	COST ($=$80)
1. City Club Hotel	★★★★½	93	$$
2. La Quinta Inn Manhattan	★★★½	81	$$
3. Le Refuge Inn	★★★½	80	$$–
4. Country Inn the City	★★★½	80	$$
5. The Kitano New York	★★★★½	94	$$$
6. Red Roof Inn Manhattan	★★★½	83	$$
7. Clarion Fifth Avenue	★★★½	82	$$
8. Thirty Thirty New York City	★★★½	83	$$
9. Rihga Royal	★★★★½	93	$$$
10. Harbor House	★★★	68	$$–
11. Time	★★★★	89	$$$
12. Soho Grand	★★★★½	93	$$$+
13. Avalon	★★★★	84	$$$–
14. Blakely	★★★★½	91	$$$+
15. Second Home on Second Avenue	★★★½	77	$$
16. The Waldorf-Astoria	★★★★½	95	$$$+
17. Hotel 31	★★★	75	$$
18. Sheraton Manhattan Hotel	★★★★½	92	$$$+
19. Hotel Chandler	★★★★½	90	$$$+
20. Inn New York City	★★★★½	94	$$$$–
21. Novotel New York	★★★★	88	$$$
22. Millennium Broadway	★★★★½	92	$$$$–
23. Bed-and-Breakfast on the Park	★★★★	88	$$$
24. Embassy Suites NYC	★★★★½	90	$$$$–
25. Hotel Bedford	★★★★	84	$$$
26. Akwaaba Mansion	★★★	70	$$
27. Flatotel International	★★★★½	93	$$$$–
28. Dream	★★★★½	91	$$$$–
29. The Carlton	★★★★	89	$$$+
30. Washington Square Hotel	★★★½	78	$$$–

Hotel Information Chart

	Akwaaba Mansion ★★★	The Alex Hotel ★★★★½	The Algonquin Hotel ★★★★½
	347 MacDonough Street	205 East 45th Street	59 West 44th Street
	New York, NY 11213	New York, NY 10017	New York, NY 10036
	☎ 718-455-5958	☎ 212-867-5100	☎ 212-840-6800
	FAX 718-774-1744	FAX 212-867-7878	FAX 212-944-1419
	TOLL-FREE 888-INN-DULJ	TOLL-FREE 888-765-2370	TOLL-FREE 888-304-2047
	www.akwaaba.com	www.thealexhotel.com	www.algonquin.com
ROOM QUALITY	70	90	90
COST ($=$80)	$$	$$$$$+	$$$$+
DISCOUNTS	–	GOV'T	AAA, GOV'T
NO. OF ROOMS	18	203	165
ROOM SQUARE FEET	185	320	170
MEETING FACILITIES	–	•	•
POOL/SAUNA	–	–	–
EXERCISE FACILITIES	–	•	•
WINDOW GLAZE	SINGLE	–	DOUBLE
PARKING PER DAY	FREE	$37–$47	PUBLIC LOT $30
NEAREST SUBWAY	20 MINUTES	1.5 BLOCKS	1 BLOCK
BAR	–	•	•
ON-SITE DINING	AFRICAN/ CARIBBEAN/ MEDITERRANEAN	JAPANESE AMERICAN	DINNER SHOW, PUB FARE, CONTINENTAL
EXTRA AMENITIES	FREE BREAKFAST, TERRY CLOTH ROBES	CONCIERGE	–
BUSINESS AMENITIES	–	DATAPORT, 2 PHONE LINES, FAX ACCESS	DATAPORT

	Bed-and-Breakfast on the Park ★★★★	Beekman Tower Hotel ★★★★	Benjamin Hotel ★★★★½
	113 Prospect Park West	3 Mitchell Place	125 East 50th Street
	New York, NY 11215	New York, NY 10017	New York, NY 10022
	☎ 718-499-6115	☎ 212-355-7300	☎ 212-753-2700
	FAX 718-499-1385	FAX 212-753-9366	FAX 212-715-2525
	www.bbnyc.com	TOLL-FREE 800-637-8483	TOLL-FREE 800-637-8483
		www.affinia.com	www.nychotels.net
ROOM QUALITY	88	86	95
COST ($=$80)	$$$	$$$+	$$$$+
DISCOUNTS	AAA	–	AAA, GOV'T
NO. OF ROOMS	8	172	206
ROOM SQUARE FEET	140	250	N/A
MEETING FACILITIES	–	•	•
POOL/SAUNA	–	WHIRLPOOL, SAUNA	SPA
EXERCISE FACILITIES	–	•	•
WINDOW GLAZE	SINGLE	TRIPLE/DOUBLE	TRIPLE
PARKING PER DAY	FREE	$30	$35
NEAREST SUBWAY	–	5 BLOCKS	1 BLOCK
BAR	–	•	•
ON-SITE DINING	AMERICAN	AMERICAN	AMERICAN
EXTRA AMENITIES	ROOF GARDEN, FREE BREAKFAST	ALL-SUITE PROPERTY	CONCIERGE
BUSINESS AMENITIES	–	DATAPORT	DATAPORT, 2 PHONE LINES, FAX, DSL

Ameritania Hotel ★★★½
230 West 54th Street
New York, NY 10019
☎ 212-247-5000
FAX 212-247-3313
TOLL-FREE 888-664-6835
www.nychotels.net

ROOM QUALITY	82
COST ($=$80)	$$$
DISCOUNTS	GOV'T
NO. OF ROOMS	206
ROOM SQUARE FEET	210
MEETING FACILITIES	–
POOL/SAUNA	–
EXERCISE FACILITIES	• $20 ACCESS
WINDOW GLAZE	DOUBLE
PARKING PER DAY	$30
NEAREST SUBWAY	3 BLOCKS
BAR	•
ON-SITE DINING	ITALIAN
EXTRA AMENITIES	FREE CONT'L BREAKFAST
BUSINESS AMENITIES	DATAPORT

Avalon ★★★★
16 East 32nd Street
New York, NY 10016
☎ 212-299-7000
FAX 212-299-7001
TOLL-FREE 888-HI-AVALON
www.theavalonny.com

ROOM QUALITY	84
COST ($=$80)	$$$–
DISCOUNTS	AAA, GOV'T
NO. OF ROOMS	100
ROOM SQUARE FEET	200
MEETING FACILITIES	•
POOL/SAUNA	–
EXERCISE FACILITIES	• ACCESS
WINDOW GLAZE	DOUBLE
PARKING PER DAY	$29–$39
NEAREST SUBWAY	1 BLOCK
BAR	•
ON-SITE DINING	AMERICAN
EXTRA AMENITIES	CONT'L BREAKFAST, CONCIERGE
BUSINESS AMENITIES	DATAPORT, 2 PHONE LINES

Barclay New York ★★★★½
111 East 48th Street
New York, NY 10017
☎ 212-755-5900
FAX 212-644-0079
TOLL-FREE 877-660-8550
www.interconti.com

ROOM QUALITY	90
COST ($=$80)	$$$$$
DISCOUNTS	—
NO. OF ROOMS	686
ROOM SQUARE FEET	210
MEETING FACILITIES	•
POOL/SAUNA	–
EXERCISE FACILITIES	•
WINDOW GLAZE	SINGLE/DOUBLE
PARKING PER DAY	$38
NEAREST SUBWAY	½ BLOCK
BAR	•
ON-SITE DINING	AMERICAN
EXTRA AMENITIES	
BUSINESS AMENITIES	COURIER, INTERNET, BUSINESS CENTER

Bentley ★★★★
500 East 62nd Street
New York, NY 10021
☎ 212-644-6000
FAX 212-207-4800
TOLL-FREE 888-66-HOTEL
www.nychotels.net

ROOM QUALITY	88
COST ($=$80)	$$$$+
DISCOUNTS	–
NO. OF ROOMS	197
ROOM SQUARE FEET	235
MEETING FACILITIES	–
POOL/SAUNA	–
EXERCISE FACILITIES	DISCOUNT ACCESS
WINDOW GLAZE	DOUBLE
PARKING PER DAY	$20
NEAREST SUBWAY	5 BLOCKS
BAR	•
ON-SITE DINING	AMERICAN
EXTRA AMENITIES	CONT'L BREAKFAST, VALET, CAPPUCINO BAR
BUSINESS AMENITIES	DATAPORT, 2 PHONE LINES

Blakely ★★★★½
136 West 55th Street
New York, NY 10019
☎ 212-245-1800
FAX 212-582-8332
TOLL-FREE 800-735-0710
www.blakelynewyork.com

ROOM QUALITY	91
COST ($=$80)	$$$+
DISCOUNTS	AAA
NO. OF ROOMS	118
ROOM SQUARE FEET	425
MEETING FACILITIES	•
POOL/SAUNA	–
EXERCISE FACILITIES	•
WINDOW GLAZE	DOUBLE
PARKING PER DAY	$33
NEAREST SUBWAY	100 FEET
BAR	•
ON-SITE DINING	ITALIAN
EXTRA AMENITIES	–
BUSINESS AMENITIES	WIRELESS NETWORK, 2 PHONE LINES, FAX ACCESS

Blue Moon Hotel ★★★★
100 Orchard Street
New York, NY 10002
☎ 212-533-9080
FAX 212-533-9148
www.bluemoon-nyc.com

ROOM QUALITY	84
COST ($=$80)	$$$+
DISCOUNTS	–
NO. OF ROOMS	22
ROOM SQUARE FEET	N/A
MEETING FACILITIES	–
POOL/SAUNA	–
EXERCISE FACILITIES	–
WINDOW GLAZE	DOUBLE
PARKING PER DAY	–
NEAREST SUBWAY	2 BLOCKS
BAR	–
ON-SITE DINING	–
EXTRA AMENITIES	–
BUSINESS AMENITIES	WIRELESS NETWORK, 1 PHONE LINE

Hotel Information Chart (continued)

Bryant Park Hotel ★★★★½
40 West 40th Street
New York, NY 10018
☎ 212-869-0100
FAX 212-869-4446
TOLL-FREE 877-640-9300
www.bryantparkhotel.com

ROOM QUALITY	95
COST ($=$80)	$$$$$–
DISCOUNTS	–
NO. OF ROOMS	129
ROOM SQUARE FEET	300
MEETING FACILITIES	•
POOL/SAUNA	–
EXERCISE FACILITIES	•
WINDOW GLAZE	DOUBLE
PARKING PER DAY	$45
NEAREST SUBWAY	½ BLOCK
BAR	•
ON-SITE DINING	SEASONAL, EUROPEAN
EXTRA AMENITIES	CONCIERGE
BUSINESS AMENITIES	DATAPORT, 2 PHONE LINES

The Carlton ★★★★
88 Madison Avenue
New York, NY 10016
☎ 212-532-4100
FAX 212-696-9758
TOLL-FREE 800-601-8500
www.hotelcarltonnewyork.com

ROOM QUALITY	89
COST ($=$80)	$$$+
DISCOUNTS	AAA, GOV'T
NO. OF ROOMS	316
ROOM SQUARE FEET	250
MEETING FACILITIES	•
POOL/SAUNA	–
EXERCISE FACILITIES	PRIVILEGES
WINDOW GLAZE	–
PARKING PER DAY	$35
NEAREST SUBWAY	1 BLOCK
BAR	•
ON-SITE DINING	AMERICAN
EXTRA AMENITIES	CONCIERGE
BUSINESS AMENITIES	DATAPORT, 2 PHONE LINES, DSL, FAX ACCESS

The Carlyle ★★★★★
35 East 76th Street
New York, NY 10021
☎ 212-744-1600
FAX 212-717-4682
TOLL-FREE 800-227-5737
www.rosewoodhotels.com

ROOM QUALITY	96
COST ($=$80)	$$$$$$$$
DISCOUNTS	–
NO. OF ROOMS	192
ROOM SQUARE FEET	180
MEETING FACILITIES	•
POOL/SAUNA	SAUNA, STEAM ROOM
EXERCISE FACILITIES	•
WINDOW GLAZE	DOUBLE
PARKING PER DAY	$44
NEAREST SUBWAY	2 BLOCKS
BAR	•
ON-SITE DINING	DINNER CLUB, AMERICAN/FRENCH, TEA ROOM
EXTRA AMENITIES	CONT'L CAFE WITH LIVE MUSIC
BUSINESS AMENITIES	DATAPORT, 2 PHONE LINES, FAX

Clarion Fifth Avenue ★★★½
3 East 40th Street
New York, NY 10016
☎ 212-532-4860
FAX 212-213-0972
TOLL-FREE 800-668-4200
www.clarionfifthavenue.com

ROOM QUALITY	82
COST ($=$80)	$$
DISCOUNTS	AAA, AARP
NO. OF ROOMS	189
ROOM SQUARE FEET	260
MEETING FACILITIES	–
POOL/SAUNA	SAUNA
EXERCISE FACILITIES	PRIVILEGES, $15
WINDOW GLAZE	DOUBLE
PARKING PER DAY	$25
NEAREST SUBWAY	2 BLOCKS
BAR	–
ON-SITE DINING	LUNCH AND DINNER
EXTRA AMENITIES	FREE BREAKFAST
BUSINESS AMENITIES	DATAPORT, BUSINESS CENTER

Cosmopolitan Hotel ★★★
95 West Broadway
New York, NY 10007
☎ 212-566-1900
FAX 212-566-6909
TOLL-FREE 888-895-9400
www.cosmohotel.com

ROOM QUALITY	75
COST ($=$80)	$$
DISCOUNTS	–
NO. OF ROOMS	105
ROOM SQUARE FEET	160
MEETING FACILITIES	•
POOL/SAUNA	–
EXERCISE FACILITIES	–
WINDOW GLAZE	SINGLE
PARKING PER DAY	$25
NEAREST SUBWAY	1 BLOCK
BAR	–
ON-SITE DINING	–
EXTRA AMENITIES	–
BUSINESS AMENITIES	DATAPORT, FAX, STUDY DESK

Country Inn ★★★½
the City
270 West 77th Street
New York, NY 10024
☎ 212-580-4183
www.countryinnthecity.com

ROOM QUALITY	80
COST ($=$80)	$$
DISCOUNTS	–
NO. OF ROOMS	4
ROOM SQUARE FEET	550
MEETING FACILITIES	–
POOL/SAUNA	–
EXERCISE FACILITIES	–
WINDOW GLAZE	SINGLE
PARKING PER DAY	–
NEAREST SUBWAY	2 BLOCKS
BAR	–
ON-SITE DINING	–
EXTRA AMENITIES	KITCHENETTE, WELCOME BASKET
BUSINESS AMENITIES	–

Chambers–A Hotel ★★★★
15 West 56th Street
New York, NY 10019
☎ 212-974-5656
FAX 212-974-5657
TOLL-FREE 866-204-5656
www.chambersnyc.com

ROOM QUALITY	89
COST ($=$80)	$$$$$+
DISCOUNTS	–
NO. OF ROOMS	77
ROOM SQUARE FEET	300
MEETING FACILITIES	•
POOL/SAUNA	
EXERCISE FACILITIES	PRIVILEGES
WINDOW GLAZE	DOUBLE
PARKING PER DAY	$35
NEAREST SUBWAY	1 BLOCK
BAR	•
ON-SITE DINING	AMERICAN
EXTRA AMENITIES	CONCIERGE, CD, DVD, LIBRARY
BUSINESS AMENITIES	FAX

Chelsea Savoy ★★★½
204 West 23rd Street
New York, NY 10011
☎ 212-929-9353
FAX 212-741-6309
TOLL-FREE 866-929-9353
www.chelseasavoynyc.com

ROOM QUALITY	77
COST ($=$80)	$$$
DISCOUNTS	–
NO. OF ROOMS	90
ROOM SQUARE FEET	N/A
MEETING FACILITIES	–
POOL/SAUNA	–
EXERCISE FACILITIES	–
WINDOW GLAZE	DOUBLE
PARKING PER DAY	$25
NEAREST SUBWAY	1 BLOCK
BAR	•
ON-SITE DINING	CAFE
EXTRA AMENITIES	–
BUSINESS AMENITIES	–

City Club Hotel ★★★★½
55 West 44th Street
New York, NY 10036
☎ 212-921-5500
FAX 212-944-5544
TOLL-FREE 888-256-4100
www.cityclubhotel.com

ROOM QUALITY	93
COST ($=$80)	$$
DISCOUNTS	–
NO. OF ROOMS	65
ROOM SQUARE FEET	300
MEETING FACILITIES	–
POOL/SAUNA	–
EXERCISE FACILITIES	–
WINDOW GLAZE	DOUBLE
PARKING PER DAY	$20
NEAREST SUBWAY	½ BLOCK
BAR	•
ON-SITE DINING	BISTRO
EXTRA AMENITIES	–
BUSINESS AMENITIES	INTERNET, 2 PHONE LINES, BATH PHONE

Courtyard by Marriott ★★★★
Manhattan Times Square South
114 West 40th Street
New York, NY 10018
☎ 212-391-0088
FAX 212-391-6023
TOLL-FREE 800-321-2211
www.marriott.com

ROOM QUALITY	88
COST ($=$80)	$$$+
DISCOUNTS	AAA, GOV'T
NO. OF ROOMS	244
ROOM SQUARE FEET	187
MEETING FACILITIES	•
POOL/SAUNA	–
EXERCISE FACILITIES	•
WINDOW GLAZE	SINGLE
PARKING PER DAY	$37
NEAREST SUBWAY	1 BLOCK
BAR	•
ON-SITE DINING	CONTINENTAL/EURO-PEAN
EXTRA AMENITIES	CONCIERGE, VALET, DRY CLEANING
BUSINESS AMENITIES	2 PHONE LINES, IN-TERNET

Crowne Plaza ★★★★
Manhattan
1605 Broadway
New York, NY 10019
☎ 212-977-4000
FAX 212-333-7393
TOLL-FREE 800-243-6969
www.crowneplaza.com

ROOM QUALITY	86
COST ($=$80)	$$$$
DISCOUNTS	GOV'T
NO. OF ROOMS	770
ROOM SQUARE FEET	
MEETING FACILITIES	•
POOL/SAUNA	POOL, SAUNA
EXERCISE FACILITIES	•
WINDOW GLAZE	SINGLE
PARKING PER DAY	$39
NEAREST SUBWAY	2 BLOCKS
BAR	•
ON-SITE DINING	AMERICAN
EXTRA AMENITIES	CONCIERGE
BUSINESS AMENITIES	BUSINESS CENTER, IN-TERNET

Crowne Plaza ★★★★
United Nations
304 East 42nd Street
New York, NY 10017
☎ 212-986-8800
FAX 212-986-1758
TOLL-FREE 800-879-8836
www.crowneplaza.com

ROOM QUALITY	87
COST ($=$80)	$$$$
DISCOUNTS	AAA, AARP
NO. OF ROOMS	300
ROOM SQUARE FEET	248
MEETING FACILITIES	•
POOL/SAUNA	WHIRLPOOL
EXERCISE FACILITIES	•
WINDOW GLAZE	SINGLE/TRIPLE
PARKING PER DAY	$40
NEAREST SUBWAY	2 BLOCKS
BAR	•
ON-SITE DINING	BISTRO
EXTRA AMENITIES	–
BUSINESS AMENITIES	DATAPORT, 2 PHONE LINES

Hotel Information Chart (continued)

DoubleTree ★★★½
Guest Suites Times Square
1568 Broadway
New York, NY 10036
☎ 212-719-1600
FAX 212-921-5212
TOLL-FREE 800-222-TREE
www.doubletree.com

ROOM QUALITY	80
COST ($=$80)	$$$+
DISCOUNTS	AAA, AARP, GOV'T, MIL.
NO. OF ROOMS	460
ROOM SQUARE FEET	442
MEETING FACILITIES	•
POOL/SAUNA	–
EXERCISE FACILITIES	•
WINDOW GLAZE	SINGLE/DOUBLE
PARKING PER DAY	$35
NEAREST SUBWAY	½ BLOCK
BAR	•
ON-SITE DINING	AMERICAN
EXTRA AMENITIES	KITCHENETTE, TOUR DESK, ROBES
BUSINESS AMENITIES	3 PHONE LINES, INTERNET

DoubleTree ★★★★
Metropolitan
569 Lexington Avenue
New York, NY 10022
☎ 212-752-7000
FAX 212-758-6311
TOLL-FREE 800-695-8284
www.dtnewyork.com

ROOM QUALITY	84
COST ($=$80)	$$$+
DISCOUNTS	AAA, AARP
NO. OF ROOMS	722
ROOM SQUARE FEET	215
MEETING FACILITIES	•
POOL/SAUNA	–
EXERCISE FACILITIES	•
WINDOW GLAZE	DOUBLE
PARKING PER DAY	$30
NEAREST SUBWAY	2 BLOCKS
BAR	•
ON-SITE DINING	AMERICAN
EXTRA AMENITIES	BARBER/BEAUTY SHOP
BUSINESS AMENITIES	DATAPORT

The Drake Swissôtel ★★★★½
440 Park Avenue
New York, NY 10022
☎ 212-421-0900
FAX 212-371-4190
www.swissotel.com

ROOM QUALITY	92
COST ($=$80)	$$$$+
DISCOUNTS	GOV'T
NO. OF ROOMS	495
ROOM SQUARE FEET	300
MEETING FACILITIES	•
POOL/SAUNA	SAUNA
EXERCISE FACILITIES	•
WINDOW GLAZE	DOUBLE
PARKING PER DAY	$45
NEAREST SUBWAY	1 BLOCK
BAR	•
ON-SITE DINING	AMERICAN/ECLECTIC
EXTRA AMENITIES	
BUSINESS AMENITIES	DATAPORT, 2 PHONE LINES, FAX

Essex House ★★★★★
Hotel NikkoNew York
160 Central Park South
New York, NY 10019
☎ 212-247-0300
FAX 212-315-1839
TOLL-FREE 800-645-5697
www.westin.com

ROOM QUALITY	96
COST ($=$80)	$$$$$
DISCOUNTS	AAA, GOV'T
NO. OF ROOMS	597
ROOM SQUARE FEET	170
MEETING FACILITIES	•
POOL/SAUNA	SAUNA, STEAM ROOM
EXERCISE FACILITIES	•
WINDOW GLAZE	DOUBLE
PARKING PER DAY	$45
NEAREST SUBWAY	1 BLOCK
BAR	•
ON-SITE DINING	FRENCH, NOUVEAU, AMERICAN
EXTRA AMENITIES	SPA
BUSINESS AMENITIES	DATAPORT, 2 PHONE LINES, FAX

Excelsior ★★★★
45 West 81st Street
New York, NY 10024
☎ 212-362-9200
FAX 212-721-2994
TOLL-FREE 800-368-4575
www.excelsiorhotelny.com

ROOM QUALITY	85
COST ($=$80)	$$$$–
DISCOUNTS	–
NO. OF ROOMS	197
ROOM SQUARE FEET	250
MEETING FACILITIES	•
POOL/SAUNA	–
EXERCISE FACILITIES	–
WINDOW GLAZE	DOUBLE
PARKING PER DAY	$25–$35
NEAREST SUBWAY	½ BLOCK
BAR	–
ON-SITE DINING	CHARGE FOR BREAKFAST ROOM
EXTRA AMENITIES	LIBRARY
BUSINESS AMENITIES	DATAPORT, FAX, 2 PHONE LINES

Fitzpatrick ★★★★
Grand Central
141 East 44th Street
New York, NY 10017
☎ 212-351-6800
FAX 212-818-1747
TOLL-FREE 800-367-7701
www.fitzpatrickhotels.com

ROOM QUALITY	85
COST ($=$80)	$$$$
DISCOUNTS	AAA
NO. OF ROOMS	155
ROOM SQUARE FEET	500
MEETING FACILITIES	–
POOL/SAUNA	–
EXERCISE FACILITIES	PRIVILEGES
WINDOW GLAZE	DOUBLE
PARKING PER DAY	$38
NEAREST SUBWAY	ACROSS STREET
BAR	•
ON-SITE DINING	IRISH/AMERICAN
EXTRA AMENITIES	VALET
BUSINESS AMENITIES	DATAPORT, 2 PHONE LINES

Dream ★★★★½
210 West 55th Street
New York, NY 10019
☎ 212-247-2000
FAX 646-756-2099
TOLL-FREE 866-IDREAMNY
www.dreamny.com

ROOM QUALITY	91
COST ($=$80)	$$$$–
DISCOUNTS	–
NO. OF ROOMS	228
ROOM SQUARE FEET	155
MEETING FACILITIES	•
POOL/SAUNA	SAUNA
EXERCISE FACILITIES	•
WINDOW GLAZE	–
PARKING PER DAY	$40
NEAREST SUBWAY	2 BLOCKS
BAR	•
ON-SITE DINING	ITALIAN
EXTRA AMENITIES	CONCIERGE, 24-HOUR ROOM SERVICE, DEEPAK CHOPRA SPA
BUSINESS AMENITIES	DATAPORT, 2 PHONE LINES, DSL, FAX ACCESS

Dylan Hotel ★★★★
52 East 41st Street
New York, NY 10017
☎ 212-338-0500
FAX 212-338-0569
TOLL-FREE 800-553-9526
www.dylanhotel.com

ROOM QUALITY	85
COST ($=$80)	$$$$+
DISCOUNTS	–
NO. OF ROOMS	107
ROOM SQUARE FEET	210
MEETING FACILITIES	•
POOL/SAUNA	–
EXERCISE FACILITIES	–
WINDOW GLAZE	TRIPLE
PARKING PER DAY	$45
NEAREST SUBWAY	2 BLOCKS
BAR	•
ON-SITE DINING	CONTINENTAL BREAKFAST
EXTRA AMENITIES	CONCIERGE, SAFE, VALET
BUSINESS AMENITIES	DATAPORT, VOICEMAIL, 2 PHONE LINES

Embassy Suites NYC ★★★★½
102 North End Avenue
New York, NY 10282
☎ 212-945-0100
FAX 212-945-3012
TOLL-FREE 800-HILTONS
www.embassysuites.com

ROOM QUALITY	90
COST ($=$80)	$$$$–
DISCOUNTS	AAA
NO. OF ROOMS	463
ROOM SQUARE FEET	450
MEETING FACILITIES	•
POOL/SAUNA	–
EXERCISE FACILITIES	–
WINDOW GLAZE	SINGLE
PARKING PER DAY	$45
NEAREST SUBWAY	5 BLOCKS
BAR	•
ON-SITE DINING	STEAKHOUSE, AMERICAN
EXTRA AMENITIES	COCKTAILS, BREAKFAST
BUSINESS AMENITIES	FAX, INTERNET, 2 PHONE LINES

Fitzpatrick ★★★★
Manhattan Hotel
687 Lexington Avenue
New York, NY 10022
☎ 212-355-0100
FAX 212-317-0572
TOLL-FREE 800-367-7701
www.fitzpatrickhotels.com

ROOM QUALITY	88
COST ($=$80)	$$$$
DISCOUNTS	AAA, AARP
NO. OF ROOMS	92
ROOM SQUARE FEET	450
MEETING FACILITIES	•
POOL/SAUNA	PRIVILEGES
EXERCISE FACILITIES	PRIVILEGES
WINDOW GLAZE	DOUBLE
PARKING PER DAY	$45
NEAREST SUBWAY	2 BLOCKS
BAR	•
ON-SITE DINING	CONTINENTAL
EXTRA AMENITIES	IRISH THEME
BUSINESS AMENITIES	DATAPORT, FAX

Flatotel ★★★★½
International
135 West 52nd Street
New York, NY 10019
☎ 212-887-9400
FAX 212-887-9893
TOLL-FREE 800-FLATOTEL
www.flatotel.com

ROOM QUALITY	93
COST ($=$80)	$$$$–
DISCOUNTS	–
NO. OF ROOMS	168
ROOM SQUARE FEET	N/A
MEETING FACILITIES	SUITES
POOL/SAUNA	SAUNA, POOL PRIVILEGES
EXERCISE FACILITIES	•
WINDOW GLAZE	DOUBLE
PARKING PER DAY	$37
NEAREST SUBWAY	2 BLOCKS
BAR	–
ON-SITE DINING	BREAKFAST ONLY
EXTRA AMENITIES	KITCHENETTES, FREE BREAKFAST 24 HOURS
BUSINESS AMENITIES	DATAPORT, 2 PHONE LINES, BUSINESS CENTER

Four Points ★★★½
by Sheraton Manhattan Chelsea
160 West 25th Street
New York, NY 10011
☎ 212-627-1888
FAX 212-627-1611
TOLL-FREE 800-403-4176
www.fourpoints.com

ROOM QUALITY	83
COST ($=$80)	$$$
DISCOUNTS	AAA, GOV'T
NO. OF ROOMS	158
ROOM SQUARE FEET	200
MEETING FACILITIES	•
POOL/SAUNA	–
EXERCISE FACILITIES	•
WINDOW GLAZE	–
PARKING PER DAY	$20–$30
NEAREST SUBWAY	2 BLOCKS
BAR	•
ON-SITE DINING	ASIAN FUSION
EXTRA AMENITIES	
BUSINESS AMENITIES	DATAPORT, 2 PHONE LINES, FAX ACCESS

Hotel Information Chart (continued)

Four Seasons Hotel ★★★★★
57 East 57th Street
New York, NY 10022
☎ 212-758-5700
FAX 212-758-5711
TOLL-FREE 800-819-5053
www.fourseasons.com

ROOM QUALITY	97
COST ($=$80)	$$$$$$$$$$+
DISCOUNTS	—
NO. OF ROOMS	370
ROOM SQUARE FEET	600
MEETING FACILITIES	•
POOL/SAUNA	WHIRLPOOL
EXERCISE FACILITIES	•
WINDOW GLAZE	TRIPLE
PARKING PER DAY	$42
NEAREST SUBWAY	4 BLOCKS
BAR	•
ON-SITE DINING	CONTEMPORARY AMERICAN
EXTRA AMENITIES	SPA SUITE PACKAGES
BUSINESS AMENITIES	2 PHONE LINES

The Franklin ★★★½
164 East 87th Street
New York, NY 10128
☎ 212-369-1000
FAX 212-369-8000
TOLL-FREE 877-847-4444
www.boutiquehg.com

ROOM QUALITY	80
COST ($=$80)	$$$$$–
DISCOUNTS	—
NO. OF ROOMS	47
ROOM SQUARE FEET	150
MEETING FACILITIES	—
POOL/SAUNA	—
EXERCISE FACILITIES	PRIVILEGES, CHARGES VARY
WINDOW GLAZE	DOUBLE
PARKING PER DAY	$25–$35
NEAREST SUBWAY	1 BLOCK
BAR	—
ON-SITE DINING	—
EXTRA AMENITIES	FREE BREAKFAST (SOME ROOMS) 2 PHONE LINES, DATA-PORT, REQUEST AHEAD
BUSINESS AMENITIES	

Grand Hyatt New York ★★★★
Park Avenue at Grand Central
New York, NY 10017
☎ 212-883-1234
FAX 212-697-3772
TOLL-FREE 800-633-7313
www.grandnewyorkhyatt.com

ROOM QUALITY	86
COST ($=$80)	$$$$$
DISCOUNTS	AAA, SENIOR
NO. OF ROOMS	1,136
ROOM SQUARE FEET	210
MEETING FACILITIES	•
POOL/SAUNA	—
EXERCISE FACILITIES	—
WINDOW GLAZE	SINGLE/DOUBLE
PARKING PER DAY	$45
NEAREST SUBWAY	½ BLOCK
BAR	•
ON-SITE DINING	AMERICAN
EXTRA AMENITIES	THEATER DESK, FAX
BUSINESS AMENITIES	BUSINESS CENTER

Hotel 41 ★★★½
206 West 41st Street
New York, NY 10036
☎ 212-703-8600
FAX 212-302-0895
TOLL-FREE 877-847-4444
www.hotel41.com

ROOM QUALITY	83
COST ($=$80)	$$$$+
DISCOUNTS	—
NO. OF ROOMS	47
ROOM SQUARE FEET	100
MEETING FACILITIES	—
POOL/SAUNA	—
EXERCISE FACILITIES	PRIVILEGES, $10
WINDOW GLAZE	DOUBLE
PARKING PER DAY	$30
NEAREST SUBWAY	½ BLOCK
BAR	—
ON-SITE DINING	BAR FOOD
EXTRA AMENITIES	PET-FRIENDLY
BUSINESS AMENITIES	INTERNET

Hotel 57 ★★★
130 East 57th Street
New York, NY 10022
☎ 212-753-8841
FAX 212-829-9605
TOLL-FREE 800-255-0482
www.habitatny.com

ROOM QUALITY	75
COST ($=$80)	$$$+
DISCOUNTS	—
NO. OF ROOMS	300
ROOM SQUARE FEET	100
MEETING FACILITIES	—
POOL/SAUNA	—
EXERCISE FACILITIES	—
WINDOW GLAZE	—
PARKING PER DAY	$28
NEAREST SUBWAY	2 BLOCKS
BAR	—
ON-SITE DINING	CONTINENTAL BREAK-FAST
EXTRA AMENITIES	
BUSINESS AMENITIES	DATAPORT, 2 PHONE LINES

Hotel Bedford ★★★★
118 East 40th Street
New York, NY 10016
☎ 212-697-4800
FAX 212-697-1093
TOLL-FREE 800-221-6881
www.bedfordhotel.com

ROOM QUALITY	84
COST ($=$80)	$$$
DISCOUNTS	AAA
NO. OF ROOMS	136
ROOM SQUARE FEET	300
MEETING FACILITIES	—
POOL/SAUNA	—
EXERCISE FACILITIES	—
WINDOW GLAZE	SINGLE/DOUBLE
PARKING PER DAY	$22
NEAREST SUBWAY	1 BLOCK
BAR	•
ON-SITE DINING	AMERICAN/ITALIAN
EXTRA AMENITIES	KITCHENETTES, FREE BREAKFAST
BUSINESS AMENITIES	DATAPORT

Harbor House ★★★
One Hylan Boulevard
New York, NY 10305
☎ 718-876-0056
FAX 718-420-9940
www.nyharborhouse.com

ROOM QUALITY	68
COST ($=$80)	$$–
DISCOUNTS	MULTIROOM
NO. OF ROOMS	11
ROOM SQUARE FEET	60
MEETING FACILITIES	–
POOL/SAUNA	–
EXERCISE FACILITIES	–
WINDOW GLAZE	SINGLE
PARKING PER DAY	FREE
NEAREST SUBWAY	25 MINUTES
BAR	–
ON-SITE DINING	–
EXTRA AMENITIES	FREE CONT'L BREAKFAST
BUSINESS AMENITIES	–

Hilton Times Square ★★★★
234 West 42nd Street
New York, NY 10036
☎ 212-840-8222
FAX 212-840-5516
TOLL-FREE 800-HILTONS
www.hilton.com

ROOM QUALITY	88
COST ($=$80)	$$$$–
DISCOUNTS	AAA, GOV'T
NO. OF ROOMS	444
ROOM SQUARE FEET	300
MEETING FACILITIES	•
POOL/SAUNA	SAUNA
EXERCISE FACILITIES	•
WINDOW GLAZE	SINGLE
PARKING PER DAY	$34–$44
NEAREST SUBWAY	2.5 BLOCKS
BAR	•
ON-SITE DINING	AMERICAN
EXTRA AMENITIES	VALET, SAFE
BUSINESS AMENITIES	DATAPORT, LAPTOP, 2 PHONE LINES, BUSINESS CENTER

Hotel 31 ★★★
120 East 31st Street
New York, NY 10016
☎ 212-685-3060
FAX 212-532-1232
www.hotel31.com

ROOM QUALITY	75
COST ($=$80)	$$
DISCOUNTS	GOV'T
NO. OF ROOMS	70
ROOM SQUARE FEET	"VERY SMALL"
MEETING FACILITIES	–
POOL/SAUNA	–
EXERCISE FACILITIES	–
WINDOW GLAZE	–
PARKING PER DAY	$25
NEAREST SUBWAY	1.5 BLOCKS
BAR	–
ON-SITE DINING	–
EXTRA AMENITIES	CONCIERGE
BUSINESS AMENITIES	DATAPORT, 1 PHONE LINE, DSL

Hotel Casablanca ★★★★
147 West 43rd Street
New York, NY 10036
☎ 212-869-1212
FAX 212-391-7585
TOLL-FREE 888-922-7225
www.casablancahotel.com

ROOM QUALITY	86
COST ($=$80)	$$$$–
DISCOUNTS	–
NO. OF ROOMS	48
ROOM SQUARE FEET	270
MEETING FACILITIES	SMALL CONF. ROOM
POOL/SAUNA	PRIVILEGES, FREE
EXERCISE FACILITIES	PRIVILEGES
WINDOW GLAZE	TRIPLE
PARKING PER DAY	$25
NEAREST SUBWAY	½ BLOCK
BAR	–
ON-SITE DINING	–
EXTRA AMENITIES	FREE CONT'L BREAKFAST, WINE, HORS D'OEUVRES
BUSINESS AMENITIES	DATAPORT, 2 PHONE LINES

Hotel Chandler ★★★★½
12 East 31st Street
New York, NY 10016
☎ 212-889-6363
FAX 212-889-6699
TOLL-FREE 866-MARQUIS
www.lemarquisny.com

ROOM QUALITY	90
COST ($=$80)	$$$+
DISCOUNTS	AAA, AARP
NO. OF ROOMS	112
ROOM SQUARE FEET	200
MEETING FACILITIES	•
POOL/SAUNA	SAUNA
EXERCISE FACILITIES	•
WINDOW GLAZE	DOUBLE
PARKING PER DAY	$35
NEAREST SUBWAY	½ BLOCK
BAR	–
ON-SITE DINING	–
EXTRA AMENITIES	–
BUSINESS AMENITIES	DATAPORT, 2 PHONE LINES, INTERNET

Hotel Elysee ★★★★½
60 East 54th Street
New York, NY 10022
☎ 212-753-1066
FAX 212-980-9278
TOLL-FREE 800-535-9733
www.elyseehotel.com

ROOM QUALITY	91
COST ($=$80)	$$$$$–
DISCOUNTS	–
NO. OF ROOMS	99
ROOM SQUARE FEET	300
MEETING FACILITIES	• SMALL
POOL/SAUNA	–
EXERCISE FACILITIES	PRIVILEGES
WINDOW GLAZE	DOUBLE
PARKING PER DAY	$26
NEAREST SUBWAY	1 BLOCK
BAR	•
ON-SITE DINING	CONTINENTAL
EXTRA AMENITIES	WINE, SNACKS, FREE CONT'L BREAKFAST
BUSINESS AMENITIES	DATAPORT, 2 PHONE LINES

Hotel Information Chart (continued)

Hotel Gansevoort ★★★★½
18 Ninth Avenue
New York, NY 10014
☎ 212-206-6700
FAX 212-255-5850
TOLL-FREE 877-726-7386
www.hotelgansevoort.com

ROOM QUALITY	92
COST ($=$80)	$$$$$$+
DISCOUNTS	—
NO. OF ROOMS	187
ROOM SQUARE FEET	300
MEETING FACILITIES	•
POOL/SAUNA	•
EXERCISE FACILITIES	•
WINDOW GLAZE	DOUBLE/TRIPLE
PARKING PER DAY	—
NEAREST SUBWAY	1 BLOCK
BAR	•
ON-SITE DINING	JAPANESE
EXTRA AMENITIES	ROOF GARDEN, FEATHER BEDS
BUSINESS AMENITIES	INTERNET, 2 PHONE LINES

Hotel Giraffe ★★★★
365 Park Avenue South
New York, NY 10010
☎ 212-685-7700
FAX 212-685-7771
TOLL-FREE 877-296-0009
www.hotelgiraffe.com

ROOM QUALITY	88
COST ($=$80)	$$$$+
DISCOUNTS	—
NO. OF ROOMS	73
ROOM SQUARE FEET	325
MEETING FACILITIES	•
POOL/SAUNA	—
EXERCISE FACILITIES	—
WINDOW GLAZE	TRIPLE
PARKING PER DAY	$28
NEAREST SUBWAY	1 BLOCK
BAR	—
ON-SITE DINING	—
EXTRA AMENITIES	WINE/CHEESE, FREE BREAKFAST, REFRESHMENTS
BUSINESS AMENITIES	INTERNET, 2 PHONE LINES

Hotel Metro ★★★½
45 West 35th Street
New York, NY 10001
☎ 212-947-2500
FAX 212-279-1310
TOLL-FREE 800-356-3870
www.hotelmetronyc.com

ROOM QUALITY	81
COST ($=$80)	$$$
DISCOUNTS	—
NO. OF ROOMS	174
ROOM SQUARE FEET	150
MEETING FACILITIES	•
POOL/SAUNA	—
EXERCISE FACILITIES	•
WINDOW GLAZE	DOUBLE
PARKING PER DAY	$18
NEAREST SUBWAY	1 BLOCK
BAR	•
ON-SITE DINING	TUSCAN
EXTRA AMENITIES	FREE CONT'L BREAKFAST
BUSINESS AMENITIES	DATAPORT

Hotel Wales ★★★★
1295 Madison Avenue
New York, NY 10128
☎ 212-876-6000
FAX 212-860-7000
TOLL-FREE 877-847-4444
www.waleshotel.com

ROOM QUALITY	84
COST ($=$80)	$$$$$
DISCOUNTS	—
NO. OF ROOMS	86
ROOM SQUARE FEET	150
MEETING FACILITIES	—
POOL/SAUNA	PRIVILEGES
EXERCISE FACILITIES	PRIVILEGES + SMALL ON-SITE
WINDOW GLAZE	DOUBLE
PARKING PER DAY	$28
NEAREST SUBWAY	5 BLOCKS
BAR	•
ON-SITE DINING	AMERICAN
EXTRA AMENITIES	HARP MUSIC IN LOBBY, SPA, VIDEOS, CD, FREE BREAKFAST
BUSINESS AMENITIES	—

Hudson Hotel ★★★★
353 West 57th Street
New York, NY 10019
☎ 212-554-6000
FAX 212-554-6139
TOLL-FREE 800-444-4786
www.hudsonhotel.com

ROOM QUALITY	89
COST ($=$80)	$$$+
DISCOUNTS	—
NO. OF ROOMS	1,000
ROOM SQUARE FEET	150
MEETING FACILITIES	•
POOL/SAUNA	—
EXERCISE FACILITIES	•
WINDOW GLAZE	SINGLE
PARKING PER DAY	$46
NEAREST SUBWAY	1 BLOCK
BAR	•
ON-SITE DINING	INTERNATIONAL COMFORT FOOD
EXTRA AMENITIES	VALET, MUSIC
BUSINESS AMENITIES	INTERNET, 2 PHONE LINES

The Inn at Irving Place ★★★★½
56 Irving Place
New York, NY 10003
☎ 212-533-4600
FAX 212-533-4611
TOLL-FREE 800-685-1447
www.innatirving.com

ROOM QUALITY	94
COST ($=$80)	$$$$
DISCOUNTS	—
NO. OF ROOMS	12
ROOM SQUARE FEET	360
MEETING FACILITIES	•
POOL/SAUNA	—
EXERCISE FACILITIES	PRIVILEGES, $15–$20
WINDOW GLAZE	N/A
PARKING PER DAY	$28
NEAREST SUBWAY	3 BLOCKS
BAR	•
ON-SITE DINING	TEA ROOM, PUB FARE, CAFÉ
EXTRA AMENITIES	LIBRARY, CONT'L BREAKFAST
BUSINESS AMENITIES	DATAPORT, 2 PHONE LINES

Hotel Plaza Athenee ★★★★½
37 East 64th Street
New York, NY 10021
☎ 212-734-9100
FAX 212-772-0958
TOLL-FREE 800-447-8800
www.plaza-athenee.com

ROOM QUALITY	90
COST ($=$80)	$$$$$–
DISCOUNTS	–
NO. OF ROOMS	152
ROOM SQUARE FEET	300
MEETING FACILITIES	•
POOL/SAUNA	–
EXERCISE FACILITIES	•
WINDOW GLAZE	DOUBLE
PARKING PER DAY	$42
NEAREST SUBWAY	7 BLOCKS
BAR	•
ON-SITE DINING	FRENCH
EXTRA AMENITIES	–
BUSINESS AMENITIES	DATAPORT, 2 PHONE LINES

Hotel QT New York ★★★½
125 West 45th Street
New York, NY 10036
☎ 212-354-2323
FAX 212-302-8585
www.hotelqt.com

ROOM QUALITY	80
COST ($=$80)	$$$$–
DISCOUNTS	GOV'T
NO. OF ROOMS	150
ROOM SQUARE FEET	200
MEETING FACILITIES	–
POOL/SAUNA	•
EXERCISE FACILITIES	•
WINDOW GLAZE	–
PARKING PER DAY	$25
NEAREST SUBWAY	1 BLOCK
BAR	•
ON-SITE DINING	AMERICAN
EXTRA AMENITIES	CONTINENTAL BREAKFAST
BUSINESS AMENITIES	DATAPORT, 2 PHONE LINES

The Hotel on Rivington ★★★★
107 Rivington Street
New York, NY 10002
☎ 212-475-2600
FAX 212-475-5959
TOLL-FREE 800-915-1537
www.hotelonrivington.com

ROOM QUALITY	88
COST ($=$80)	$$$$+
DISCOUNTS	–
NO. OF ROOMS	111
ROOM SQUARE FEET	325
MEETING FACILITIES	•
POOL/SAUNA	•
EXERCISE FACILITIES	•
WINDOW GLAZE	SINGLE
PARKING PER DAY	$30
NEAREST SUBWAY	1 BLOCK
BAR	•
ON-SITE DINING	FRESH MARKET, AUSTRIAN
EXTRA AMENITIES	–
BUSINESS AMENITIES	DATAPORT, 3 PHONE LINES, FAX

Inn New York City ★★★★½
266 West 71st Street
New York, NY 10023
☎ 212-580-1900
FAX 212-875-9591
TOLL-FREE 866-823-9330
www.innnewyorkcity.com

ROOM QUALITY	94
COST ($=$80)	$$$$–
DISCOUNTS	–
NO. OF ROOMS	4
ROOM SQUARE FEET	800
MEETING FACILITIES	–
POOL/SAUNA	–
EXERCISE FACILITIES	–
WINDOW GLAZE	SINGLE
PARKING PER DAY	FREE
NEAREST SUBWAY	3 BLOCKS
BAR	–
ON-SITE DINING	–
EXTRA AMENITIES	KITCHENETTE
BUSINESS AMENITIES	–

Inn on 23rd Street ★★★
131 West 23rd Street
New York, NY 10011
☎ 212-463-0330
FAX 212-463-0302
TOLL-FREE 877-387-2323
www.innon23rd.com

ROOM QUALITY	76
COST ($=$80)	$$$
DISCOUNTS	–
NO. OF ROOMS	14
ROOM SQUARE FEET	215
MEETING FACILITIES	–
POOL/SAUNA	–
EXERCISE FACILITIES	–
WINDOW GLAZE	DOUBLE
PARKING PER DAY	–
NEAREST SUBWAY	2 BLOCKS
BAR	–
ON-SITE DINING	AMERICAN CREATIVE
EXTRA AMENITIES	FREE BREAKFAST
BUSINESS AMENITIES	DATAPORT, 2 PHONE LINES

Iroquois New York ★★★★
49 West 44th Street
New York, NY 10036
☎ 212-840-3080
FAX 212-398-1754
TOLL-FREE 800-332-7220
www.iroquoisny.com

ROOM QUALITY	86
COST ($=$80)	$$$$–
DISCOUNTS	–
NO. OF ROOMS	114
ROOM SQUARE FEET	275
MEETING FACILITIES	•
POOL/SAUNA	SAUNA
EXERCISE FACILITIES	•
WINDOW GLAZE	SINGLE
PARKING PER DAY	$29
NEAREST SUBWAY	2 BLOCKS
BAR	•
ON-SITE DINING	AMERICAN
EXTRA AMENITIES	CONCIERGE, SAFE, CD
BUSINESS AMENITIES	DATAPORT, 2 PHONE LINES

Hotel Information Chart (continued)

Jolly Hotel ★★★½
Madison Towers
22 East 38th Street
New York, NY 10016
☎ 212-802-0600
FAX 212-447-0747
TOLL-FREE 800-221-2626
www.jollymadison.com

ROOM QUALITY	80
COST ($=$80)	$$$
DISCOUNTS	–
NO. OF ROOMS	244
ROOM SQUARE FEET	80
MEETING FACILITIES	•
POOL/SAUNA	•
EXERCISE FACILITIES	–
WINDOW GLAZE	SINGLE
PARKING PER DAY	$30
NEAREST SUBWAY	½ BLOCK
BAR	•
ON-SITE DINING	AMERICAN, ITALIAN
EXTRA AMENITIES	–
BUSINESS AMENITIES	DATAPORT, 2 PHONE LINES, INTERNET

The Kitano ★★★★½
New York
66 Park Avenue
New York, NY 10016
☎ 212-885-7000
FAX 212-765-6530
TOLL-FREE 800-KITANO-NY
www.kitano.com

ROOM QUALITY	94
COST ($=$80)	$$$
DISCOUNTS	GOV'T
NO. OF ROOMS	500
ROOM SQUARE FEET	460
MEETING FACILITIES	•
POOL/SAUNA	PRIVILEGES
EXERCISE FACILITIES	PRIVILEGES
WINDOW GLAZE	DOUBLE
PARKING PER DAY	$32
NEAREST SUBWAY	4 BLOCKS
BAR	•
ON-SITE DINING	AMERICAN, JAPANESE
EXTRA AMENITIES	SAFE
BUSINESS AMENITIES	DATAPORT, 2 PHONE LINES, FAX

La Quinta Inn ★★★½
Manhattan
17 West 32nd Street
New York, NY 10001
☎ 212-790-2710
FAX 212-563-4007
TOLL-FREE 866-725-1661
www.lq.com

ROOM QUALITY	88
COST ($=$80)	$$
DISCOUNTS	AAA, AARP, GOV'T
NO. OF ROOMS	182
ROOM SQUARE FEET	160
MEETING FACILITIES	•
POOL/SAUNA	–
EXERCISE FACILITIES	–
WINDOW GLAZE	SINGLE
PARKING PER DAY	$25
NEAREST SUBWAY	½ BLOCK
BAR	•
ON-SITE DINING	AMERICAN, CHINESE
EXTRA AMENITIES	CONT'L BREAKFAST
BUSINESS AMENITIES	DATAPORT

The Lombardy ★★★★½
111 East 56th Street
New York, NY 10022
☎ 212-753-8600
FAX 212-832-3170
TOLL-FREE 800-223-5254
www.lombardyhotel.com

ROOM QUALITY	93
COST ($=$80)	$$$$
DISCOUNTS	–
NO. OF ROOMS	101
ROOM SQUARE FEET	470
MEETING FACILITIES	• IN RESTAURANT
POOL/SAUNA	•
EXERCISE FACILITIES	•
WINDOW GLAZE	DOUBLE
PARKING PER DAY	$21
NEAREST SUBWAY	3 BLOCKS
BAR	•
ON-SITE DINING	FRENCH
EXTRA AMENITIES	KITCHENS, LAUNDRY
BUSINESS AMENITIES	DATAPORT

The Lowell ★★★★★
28 East 63rd Street
New York, NY 10021-8088
☎ 212-838-1400
FAX 212-319-4230
TOLL-FREE 800-221-4444
www.lowellhotel.com

ROOM QUALITY	96
COST ($=$80)	$$$$$$$
DISCOUNTS	AAA
NO. OF ROOMS	65
ROOM SQUARE FEET	350
MEETING FACILITIES	• SMALL
POOL/SAUNA	–
EXERCISE FACILITIES	•
WINDOW GLAZE	DOUBLE
PARKING PER DAY	$45–$50
NEAREST SUBWAY	2 BLOCKS
BAR	•
ON-SITE DINING	TEA ROOM, STEAK-HOUSE
EXTRA AMENITIES	–
BUSINESS AMENITIES	DATAPORT, 2 PHONE LINES, FAX

Lucerne ★★★½
201 West 79th Street
New York, NY 10024
☎ 212-875-1000
FAX 212-362-7251
TOLL-FREE 800-492-8122
www.newyorkhotel.com

ROOM QUALITY	79
COST ($=$80)	$$$+
DISCOUNTS	AAA, AARP, GOV'T BLACKED OUT
NO. OF ROOMS	250
ROOM SQUARE FEET	204
MEETING FACILITIES	•
POOL/SAUNA	•
EXERCISE FACILITIES	PRIVILEGES
WINDOW GLAZE	DOUBLE
PARKING PER DAY	$25
NEAREST SUBWAY	1 BLOCK
BAR	•
ON-SITE DINING	BAR AND GRILL
EXTRA AMENITIES	CONT'L BREAKFAST
BUSINESS AMENITIES	DATAPORT, 2 PHONE LINES, FAX IN SUITES

Le Parker Meridien New York ★★★★½
118 West 57th Street
New York, NY 10019
☎ 212-245-5000
FAX 212-307-1776
TOLL-FREE 800-543-4300
www.parkermeridien.com

ROOM QUALITY	95
COST ($=$80)	$$$$$+
DISCOUNTS	AAA
NO. OF ROOMS	698
ROOM SQUARE FEET	312
MEETING FACILITIES	•
POOL/SAUNA	POOL
EXERCISE FACILITIES	•
WINDOW GLAZE	DOUBLE
PARKING PER DAY	$40
NEAREST SUBWAY	½ BLOCK
BAR	•
ON-SITE DINING	AMERICAN/CONTINENETAL, PUB FARE
EXTRA AMENITIES	TRACK, CD PLAYERS, DVDS, HEALTH CLUB
BUSINESS AMENITIES	DATAPORT, 2 PHONE LINES, FAX ON REQUEST

Le Refuge Inn ★★★½
620 City Island Avenue
New York, NY 10464
☎ 718-885-2478
www.lerefugeinn.com

ROOM QUALITY	80
COST ($=$80)	$$–
DISCOUNTS	–
NO. OF ROOMS	8
ROOM SQUARE FEET	N/A
MEETING FACILITIES	–
POOL/SAUNA	–
EXERCISE FACILITIES	–
WINDOW GLAZE	DOUBLE
PARKING PER DAY	FREE
NEAREST SUBWAY	–
BAR	–
ON-SITE DINING	COUNTRY FRENCH
EXTRA AMENITIES	CONT'L BREAKFAST
BUSINESS AMENITIES	–

Library Hotel ★★★★
299 Madison Avenue
New York, NY 10017
☎ 212-983-9653
FAX 212-499-9099
TOLL-FREE 877-793-READ
www.libraryhotel.com

ROOM QUALITY	86
COST ($=$80)	$$$$
DISCOUNTS	GOV'T
NO. OF ROOMS	60
ROOM SQUARE FEET	200
MEETING FACILITIES	•
POOL/SAUNA	–
EXERCISE FACILITIES	PRIVILEGES, $15
WINDOW GLAZE	SINGLE
PARKING PER DAY	$20
NEAREST SUBWAY	1 BLOCK
BAR	–
ON-SITE DINING	NORTHERN ITALIAN
EXTRA AMENITIES	CONT'L BREAKFAST, WINE, CD
BUSINESS AMENITIES	DATAPORT, BUSINESS CENTER, 2 PHONE LINES

Mandarin Oriental Hotel ★★★★★
80 Columbus Circle
New York, NY 10023
☎ 212-805-8800
FAX 212-805-8888
TOLL-FREE 800-526-6566
www.mandarinoriental.com

ROOM QUALITY	98
COST ($=$80)	$$$$$$$$$
DISCOUNTS	–
NO. OF ROOMS	251
ROOM SQUARE FEET	400
MEETING FACILITIES	•
POOL/SAUNA	POOL, SAUNA
EXERCISE FACILITIES	•
WINDOW GLAZE	DOUBLE
PARKING PER DAY	$55
NEAREST SUBWAY	½ BLOCK
BAR	•
ON-SITE DINING	FRENCH/JAPANESE
EXTRA AMENITIES	BATHROBES
BUSINESS AMENITIES	COMPUTER, INTERNET, CELL PHONE RENTALS

The Mansfield ★★★★
12 West 44th Street
New York, NY 10036
☎ 212-944-6050
FAX 212-764-4477
TOLL-FREE 877-847-4444
www.mansfieldhotel.com

ROOM QUALITY	84
COST ($=$80)	$$$
DISCOUNTS	–
NO. OF ROOMS	123
ROOM SQUARE FEET	150
MEETING FACILITIES	• SMALL
POOL/SAUNA	–
EXERCISE FACILITIES	PRIVILEGES, $20
WINDOW GLAZE	DOUBLE
PARKING PER DAY	$25–$45
NEAREST SUBWAY	2 BLOCKS
BAR	–
ON-SITE DINING	–
EXTRA AMENITIES	–
BUSINESS AMENITIES	DATAPORT, ACCESS TO COPY AND FAX

Maritime Hotel ★★★★
363 West 16th Street
New York, NY 10011
☎ 212-242-4300
FAX 212-242-1188
TOLL-FREE 866-601-9330
www.themaritimehotel.com

ROOM QUALITY	88
COST ($=$80)	$$$$
DISCOUNTS	–
NO. OF ROOMS	125
ROOM SQUARE FEET	300
MEETING FACILITIES	•
POOL/SAUNA	–
EXERCISE FACILITIES	•
WINDOW GLAZE	DOUBLE
PARKING PER DAY	$15–$36
NEAREST SUBWAY	1 BLOCK
BAR	•
ON-SITE DINING	ITALIAN, JAPANESE
EXTRA AMENITIES	BANQUET ROOM
BUSINESS AMENITIES	DATAPORT, 2 PHONE LINES, INTERNET

Hotel Information Chart (continued)

The Mark ★★★★★
Madison Avenue at 77th Street
New York, NY 10021
☎ 212-744-4300
FAX 212-744-2749
TOLL-FREE 800-843-6275
www.themarkhotel.com

ROOM QUALITY	96
COST ($=$80)	$$$$$$+
DISCOUNTS	–
NO. OF ROOMS	180
ROOM SQUARE FEET	400
MEETING FACILITIES	•
POOL/SAUNA	SAUNA, STEAM ROOM
EXERCISE FACILITIES	•
WINDOW GLAZE	DOUBLE
PARKING PER DAY	$45
NEAREST SUBWAY	3 BLOCKS
BAR	•
ON-SITE DINING	FRENCH-AMERICAN
EXTRA AMENITIES	–
BUSINESS AMENITIES	DATAPORT, 2 PHONE LINES, FAX

Mercer ★★★★½
147 Mercer Street
New York, NY 10012
☎ 212-966-6060
FAX 212-965-3838
TOLL-FREE 888-918-6060
www.mercerhotel.com

ROOM QUALITY	94
COST ($=$80)	$$$$$$–
DISCOUNTS	–
NO. OF ROOMS	75
ROOM SQUARE FEET	320
MEETING FACILITIES	–
POOL/SAUNA	–
EXERCISE FACILITIES	PRIVILEGES
WINDOW GLAZE	SINGLE
PARKING PER DAY	$40
NEAREST SUBWAY	1 BLOCK
BAR	•
ON-SITE DINING	AMERICAN FUSION
EXTRA AMENITIES	VALET, CD, SAFE
BUSINESS AMENITIES	DATAPORT, 2 PHONE LINES, FAX, COMPUTER

The Michelangelo ★★★★½
152 West 51st Street
New York, NY 10019
☎ 212-765-1900
FAX 212-541-6604
TOLL-FREE 800-237-0990
www.michelangelohotel.com

ROOM QUALITY	93
COST ($=$80)	$$$$$
DISCOUNTS	–
NO. OF ROOMS	178
ROOM SQUARE FEET	325
MEETING FACILITIES	•
POOL/SAUNA	–
EXERCISE FACILITIES	•
WINDOW GLAZE	DOUBLE
PARKING PER DAY	$38
NEAREST SUBWAY	2 BLOCKS
BAR	•
ON-SITE DINING	ITALIAN
EXTRA AMENITIES	FREE BREAKFAST
BUSINESS AMENITIES	DATAPORT, 2 PHONE LINES, FAX, COPY, PRINT

The Muse ★★★★½
130 West 46th Street
New York, NY 10036
☎ 212-485-2400
FAX 212-485-2900
TOLL-FREE 877-692-6873
www.themusehotel.com

ROOM QUALITY	90
COST ($=$80)	$$$$
DISCOUNTS	AAA
NO. OF ROOMS	200
ROOM SQUARE FEET	350
MEETING FACILITIES	•
POOL/SAUNA	–
EXERCISE FACILITIES	•
WINDOW GLAZE	SINGLE
PARKING PER DAY	$42
NEAREST SUBWAY	2 BLOCKS
BAR	•
ON-SITE DINING	AMERICAN
EXTRA AMENITIES	VALET, SAFE, REFRESHMENTS
BUSINESS AMENITIES	INTERNET, 2 PHONE LINES

The New York Hilton and Towers ★★★★
1335 Avenue of the Americas
New York, NY 10019
☎ 212-586-7000
FAX 212-315-1374
TOLL-FREE 800-HILTONS
www.hilton.com

ROOM QUALITY	89
COST ($=$80)	$$$$–
DISCOUNTS	AAA, AARP
NO. OF ROOMS	2,041
ROOM SQUARE FEET	320
MEETING FACILITIES	•
POOL/SAUNA	SAUNA
EXERCISE FACILITIES	•
WINDOW GLAZE	DOUBLE
PARKING PER DAY	$40
NEAREST SUBWAY	3 BLOCKS
BAR	•
ON-SITE DINING	AMERICAN, INTERNATIONAL, ITALIAN
EXTRA AMENITIES	SPA SERVICES
BUSINESS AMENITIES	DATAPORT, 2 PHONE LINES

New York Marriott Marquis ★★★★
1535 Broadway
New York, NY 10036
☎ 212-398-1900
FAX 212-704-8930
TOLL-FREE 800-228-9290
www.marriott.com

ROOM QUALITY	87
COST ($=$80)	$$$$+
DISCOUNTS	GOV'T, MIL.
NO. OF ROOMS	1,911
ROOM SQUARE FEET	570
MEETING FACILITIES	•
POOL/SAUNA	SAUNA, WHIRLPOOL
EXERCISE FACILITIES	•
WINDOW GLAZE	DOUBLE
PARKING PER DAY	$45
NEAREST SUBWAY	3 BLOCKS
BAR	•
ON-SITE DINING	CONTINENTAL, STEAKHOUSE, AMERICAN, DELI
EXTRA AMENITIES	HAIR SALON, BARBER
BUSINESS AMENITIES	–

Millennium Broadway ★★★★½

145 West 44th Street
New York, NY 10036
☎ 212-768-4400
FAX 212-768-0847
TOLL-FREE 800-622-5569
www.millennium-hotels.com

ROOM QUALITY	92
COST ($=$80)	$$$$–
DISCOUNTS	AAA, GOV'T, BLACKED OUT
NO. OF ROOMS	627
ROOM SQUARE FEET	150
MEETING FACILITIES	•
POOL/SAUNA	STEAM ROOM
EXERCISE FACILITIES	•
WINDOW GLAZE	DOUBLE
PARKING PER DAY	$45
NEAREST SUBWAY	2 BLOCKS
BAR	•
ON-SITE DINING	CONTINENTAL
EXTRA AMENITIES	–
BUSINESS AMENITIES	DATAPORT, 2 PHONE LINES

Millennium U.N. Plaza ★★★★

1 United Nations Plaza
New York, NY 10017
☎ 212-758-1234
FAX 212-702-5051
TOLL-FREE 866-866-8086
www.millenniumhotels.com

ROOM QUALITY	89
COST ($=$80)	$$$$$+
DISCOUNTS	AAA, BLACKED OUT
NO. OF ROOMS	427
ROOM SQUARE FEET	240
MEETING FACILITIES	•
POOL/SAUNA	POOL, SAUNA, WHIRLPOOL
EXERCISE FACILITIES	•
WINDOW GLAZE	DOUBLE
PARKING PER DAY	$24–$30
NEAREST SUBWAY	4 BLOCKS
BAR	•
ON-SITE DINING	NEW AMERICAN
EXTRA AMENITIES	HARPIST IN LOBBY
BUSINESS AMENITIES	DATAPORT, 2 PHONE LINES, FAX

Morgans ★★★★½

237 Madison Avenue
New York, NY 10016
☎ 212-686-0300
FAX 212-779-8352
TOLL-FREE 800-334-3408
www.morganshotelgroup.com

ROOM QUALITY	93
COST ($=$80)	$$$$+
DISCOUNTS	GOV'T
NO. OF ROOMS	113
ROOM SQUARE FEET	240
MEETING FACILITIES	•
POOL/SAUNA	–
EXERCISE FACILITIES	PRIVILEGES, FREE
WINDOW GLAZE	DOUBLE
PARKING PER DAY	$42
NEAREST SUBWAY	4 BLOCKS
BAR	•
ON-SITE DINING	JAPANESE-LATINO
EXTRA AMENITIES	FREE BREAKFAST
BUSINESS AMENITIES	DATAPORT, 2 PHONE LINES

The New York Palace ★★★★★

455 Madison Avenue
New York, NY 10022
☎ 212-888-7000
FAX 212-303-6000
TOLL-FREE 800-NYPALACE
www.nypalace.com

ROOM QUALITY	96
COST ($=$80)	$$$$$+
DISCOUNTS	AAA, GOV'T, BLACKED OUT
NO. OF ROOMS	900
ROOM SQUARE FEET	320
MEETING FACILITIES	•
POOL/SAUNA	STEAM ROOM
EXERCISE FACILITIES	•
WINDOW GLAZE	DOUBLE
PARKING PER DAY	$50
NEAREST SUBWAY	2 BLOCKS
BAR	•
ON-SITE DINING	MEDITERRANEAN, FRENCH
EXTRA AMENITIES	SPA SERVICES
BUSINESS AMENITIES	DATAPORT, 2 PHONE LINES, FAX

Novotel New York ★★★★

226 West 52nd Street
New York, NY 10019
☎ 212-315-0100
FAX 212-765-5365
TOLL-FREE 800-221-3185
www.novotel.com

ROOM QUALITY	88
COST ($=$80)	$$$
DISCOUNTS	AAA, GOV'T
NO. OF ROOMS	474
ROOM SQUARE FEET	276
MEETING FACILITIES	•
POOL/SAUNA	–
EXERCISE FACILITIES	•
WINDOW GLAZE	DOUBLE
PARKING PER DAY	$23
NEAREST SUBWAY	1 BLOCK
BAR	•
ON-SITE DINING	FRENCH
EXTRA AMENITIES	LIVE MUSIC IN LOUNGE WEEKNIGHTS
BUSINESS AMENITIES	DATAPORT, 24-HOUR BUSINESS CENTER

Omni Berkshire Place ★★★★½

21 East 52nd Street
New York, NY 10022
☎ 212-753-5800
FAX 212-754-5018
TOLL-FREE 800-843-6664
www.omnihotels.com

ROOM QUALITY	95
COST ($=$80)	$$$$
DISCOUNTS	AAA, GOV'T
NO. OF ROOMS	396
ROOM SQUARE FEET	300
MEETING FACILITIES	•
POOL/SAUNA	–
EXERCISE FACILITIES	•
WINDOW GLAZE	TRIPLE
PARKING PER DAY	$25–$35
NEAREST SUBWAY	1 BLOCK
BAR	•
ON-SITE DINING	ORIENTAL-MEDITER-RANEAN
EXTRA AMENITIES	SUNDECK, ELEC-TRONIC CONTROLS SUITE
BUSINESS AMENITIES	DATAPORT, 2 PHONE LINES, FAX

Hotel Information Chart (continued)

On the Avenue ★★★½
2178 West 77th Street
New York, NY 10023
☎ 212-362-1100
TOLL-FREE 800-509-7598
www.ontheave-nyc.com

ROOM QUALITY	80
COST ($=$80)	$$$
DISCOUNTS	AAA
NO. OF ROOMS	196
ROOM SQUARE FEET	375
MEETING FACILITIES	–
POOL/SAUNA	SAUNA PRIVILEGES
EXERCISE FACILITIES	PRIVILEGES, $20
WINDOW GLAZE	DOUBLE
PARKING PER DAY	–
NEAREST SUBWAY	2 BLOCKS
BAR	–
ON-SITE DINING	–
EXTRA AMENITIES	HAIR DRYERS, IRONS
BUSINESS AMENITIES	DATAPORT, 2 PHONE LINES, FAX

Paramount ★★★★
235 West 46th Street
New York, NY 10036
☎ 212-764-5500
FAX 212-554-6511
TOLL-FREE 800-225-7474
www.ianschragerhotels.com

ROOM QUALITY	88
COST ($=$80)	$$$$–
DISCOUNTS	AAA, GOV'T
NO. OF ROOMS	601
ROOM SQUARE FEET	150
MEETING FACILITIES	–
POOL/SAUNA	–
EXERCISE FACILITIES	–
WINDOW GLAZE	DOUBLE
PARKING PER DAY	$45
NEAREST SUBWAY	2 BLOCKS
BAR	•
ON-SITE DINING	CONTINENTAL
EXTRA AMENITIES	–
BUSINESS AMENITIES	DATAPORTS, 2 PHONE LINES, 24-HOUR BUSINESS CENTER

The Peninsula ★★★★★
700 Fifth Avenue
New York, NY 10009
☎ 212-956-2888
FAX 212-903-3949
TOLL-FREE 800-262-9467
www.peninsula.com

ROOM QUALITY	98
COST ($=$80)	$$$$$$$$
DISCOUNTS	–
NO. OF ROOMS	241
ROOM SQUARE FEET	350
MEETING FACILITIES	•
POOL/SAUNA	•
EXERCISE FACILITIES	•
WINDOW GLAZE	TRIPLE
PARKING PER DAY	$45
NEAREST SUBWAY	3 BLOCKS
BAR	•
ON-SITE DINING	AMERICAN, CONTINENTAL
EXTRA AMENITIES	MARBLE BATHS, ROBES, MINIBAR, SPA
BUSINESS AMENITIES	DATAPORT, 2 PHONE LINES, IN-ROOM FAX

The Regency Hotel ★★★★½
540 Park Avenue
New York, NY 10021
☎ 212-759-4100
FAX 212-826-5674
TOLL-FREE 800-233-2356
www.loewshotels.com

ROOM QUALITY	95
COST ($=$80)	$$$$$$$$
DISCOUNTS	–
NO. OF ROOMS	362
ROOM SQUARE FEET	220
MEETING FACILITIES	•
POOL/SAUNA	SAUNA, WHIRLPOOL
EXERCISE FACILITIES	•
WINDOW GLAZE	DOUBLE
PARKING PER DAY	$47
NEAREST SUBWAY	2 BLOCKS
BAR	•
ON-SITE DINING	LOUNGE, FRENCH-AMERICAN
EXTRA AMENITIES	HAIR SALON, CONCIERGE, MASSAGE
BUSINESS AMENITIES	DATAPORT, 2 PHONE LINES, FAX

Renaissance New York Hotel ★★★★½
714 Seventh Avenue
New York, NY 10036
☎ 212-765-7676
FAX 212-765-1962
TOLL-FREE 800-236-2427
www.marriott.com

ROOM QUALITY	91
COST ($=$80)	$$$$
DISCOUNTS	AAA, AARP, BLACKED OUT
NO. OF ROOMS	305
ROOM SQUARE FEET	340
MEETING FACILITIES	•
POOL/SAUNA	–
EXERCISE FACILITIES	•
WINDOW GLAZE	DOUBLE
PARKING PER DAY	$35–$48
NEAREST SUBWAY	BENEATH HOTEL
BAR	•
ON-SITE DINING	AMERICAN
EXTRA AMENITIES	–
BUSINESS AMENITIES	DATAPORT, 2 PHONE LINES

Rihga Royal ★★★★½
151 West 54th Street
New York, NY 10019
☎ 212-307-5000
FAX 212-533-4611
TOLL-FREE 800-937-5454
www.marriott.com

ROOM QUALITY	93
COST ($=$80)	$$$
DISCOUNTS	–
NO. OF ROOMS	12
ROOM SQUARE FEET	360
MEETING FACILITIES	•
POOL/SAUNA	WHIRLPOOL, SAUNA
EXERCISE FACILITIES	•
WINDOW GLAZE	DOUBLE
PARKING PER DAY	$42
NEAREST SUBWAY	2 BLOCKS
BAR	•
ON-SITE DINING	NEW AMERICAN
EXTRA AMENITIES	LOUNGE MUSIC
BUSINESS AMENITIES	DATAPORT, 2 PHONE LINES, FAX

Pickwick Arms ★★½
230 East 51st Street
New York, NY 10022
☎ 212-355-0300
FAX 212-755-5029
TOLL-FREE 800-742-5945
www.pickwickarms.com

ROOM QUALITY	60
COST ($=$80)	$$
DISCOUNTS	–
NO. OF ROOMS	350
ROOM SQUARE FEET	100
MEETING FACILITIES	–
POOL/SAUNA	–
EXERCISE FACILITIES	•
WINDOW GLAZE	DOUBLE
PARKING PER DAY	$35
NEAREST SUBWAY	2 BLOCKS
BAR	•
ON-SITE DINING	FRENCH, CONTINENTAL
EXTRA AMENITIES	–
BUSINESS AMENITIES	BUSINESS CENTER AT FRONT DESK, DATAPORTS

The Pierre ★★★★★
21 East 61st Street
New York, NY 10021
☎ 212-838-8000
FAX 212-940-8109
TOLL-FREE 800-743-7734
www.fourseasons.com

ROOM QUALITY	96
COST ($=$80)	$$$$$$$+
DISCOUNTS	–
NO. OF ROOMS	202
ROOM SQUARE FEET	455
MEETING FACILITIES	•
POOL/SAUNA	–
EXERCISE FACILITIES	•
WINDOW GLAZE	DOUBLE
PARKING PER DAY	$45
NEAREST SUBWAY	½ BLOCK
BAR	•
ON-SITE DINING	CONTINENTAL, TEA ROOM
EXTRA AMENITIES	PIANO MUSIC, HAIR SALON
BUSINESS AMENITIES	DATAPORT, 2 PHONE LINES

Red Roof Inn ★★★½
Manhattan
6 West 32nd Street
New York, NY 10001
☎ 212-643-7100
FAX 212-643-7101
TOLL-FREE 800-REDROOF
www.redroof.com

ROOM QUALITY	83
COST ($=$80)	$$
DISCOUNTS	AAA
NO. OF ROOMS	171
ROOM SQUARE FEET	N/A
MEETING FACILITIES	•
POOL/SAUNA	–
EXERCISE FACILITIES	•
WINDOW GLAZE	DOUBLE
PARKING PER DAY	$22
NEAREST SUBWAY	1 BLOCK
BAR	
ON-SITE DINING	–
EXTRA AMENITIES	CONCIERGE, FREE BREAKFAST, PAPER
BUSINESS AMENITIES	2 PHONE LINES

Ritz-Carlton ★★★★★
Battery Park
2 West Street
New York, NY 10004
☎ 212-344-0800
FAX 212-344-3804
TOLL-FREE 800-241-3333
www.ritzcarlton.com

ROOM QUALITY	98
COST ($=$80)	$$$$$
DISCOUNTS	AAA
NO. OF ROOMS	298
ROOM SQUARE FEET	425
MEETING FACILITIES	•
POOL/SAUNA	SPA
EXERCISE FACILITIES	•
WINDOW GLAZE	SINGLE/DOUBLE
PARKING PER DAY	$50
NEAREST SUBWAY	½ BLOCK
BAR	•
ON-SITE DINING	STEAK HOUSE, CHINESE
EXTRA AMENITIES	TELESCOPE
BUSINESS AMENITIES	DATAPORT, 2 PHONE LINES

Ritz-Carlton ★★★★½
New York Central Park
50 Central Park South
New York, NY 10017
☎ 212-308-9100
FAX 212-207-8831
TOLL-FREE 800-241-3333
www.ritzcarlton.com

ROOM QUALITY	94
COST ($=$80)	$$$$$$$
DISCOUNTS	AAA, AARP
NO. OF ROOMS	277
ROOM SQUARE FEET	425
MEETING FACILITIES	•
POOL/SAUNA	SPA
EXERCISE FACILITIES	–
WINDOW GLAZE	DOUBLE
PARKING PER DAY	$50
NEAREST SUBWAY	½ BLOCK
BAR	•
ON-SITE DINING	FRENCH/AMERICAN
EXTRA AMENITIES	TELESCOPE, ROBES, LIBRARY
BUSINESS AMENITIES	INTERNET, 2 PHONE LINES

The Roger Smith ★★★½
501 Lexington Avenue
New York, NY 10017
☎ 212-755-1400
FAX 212-319-9130
TOLL-FREE 800-445-0277
www.rogersmith.com

ROOM QUALITY	80
COST ($=$80)	$$$$
DISCOUNTS	GOV'T, AAA
NO. OF ROOMS	136
ROOM SQUARE FEET	204
MEETING FACILITIES	•
POOL/SAUNA	SAUNA PRIVILEGES
EXERCISE FACILITIES	PRIVILEGES, $20
WINDOW GLAZE	DOUBLE
PARKING PER DAY	$35
NEAREST SUBWAY	2 BLOCKS
BAR	•
ON-SITE DINING	CONTINENTAL/AMERICAN
EXTRA AMENITIES	FREE CONT'L BREAKFAST, GALLERY, VIDEOS
BUSINESS AMENITIES	DATAPORT, COMPUTER AVAILABLE

Hotel Information Chart (continued)

Roger Williams ★★★★
131 Madison Avenue
New York, NY 10016
☎ 212-448-7000
FAX 212-448-7007
TOLL-FREE 888-448-7788
www.rogerwilliamshotel.com

ROOM QUALITY	86
COST ($=$80)	$$$$
DISCOUNTS	AAA
NO. OF ROOMS	200
ROOM SQUARE FEET	300
MEETING FACILITIES	–
POOL/SAUNA	–
EXERCISE FACILITIES	–
WINDOW GLAZE	SINGLE
PARKING PER DAY	$27–$35
NEAREST SUBWAY	2 BLOCKS
BAR	–
ON-SITE DINING	–
EXTRA AMENITIES	FREE CONT'L BREAKFAST, FREE DESSERT BUFFET
BUSINESS AMENITIES	DATAPORT, SOME HAVE 2 PHONE LINES

Roosevelt Hotel ★★★½
45 East 45th Street
New York, NY 10017
☎ 212-661-9600
FAX 212-885-6161
TOLL-FREE 888-TEDDY-NY
www.theroosevelthotel.com

ROOM QUALITY	80
COST ($=$80)	$$$$$$
DISCOUNTS	AAA, GOV'T
NO. OF ROOMS	1,033
ROOM SQUARE FEET	200
MEETING FACILITIES	•
POOL/SAUNA	–
EXERCISE FACILITIES	–
WINDOW GLAZE	SINGLE/DOUBLE
PARKING PER DAY	$40
NEAREST SUBWAY	1 BLOCK
BAR	•
ON-SITE DINING	AMERICAN
EXTRA AMENITIES	CONCIERGE
BUSINESS AMENITIES	2 PHONE LINES, FAX, MODEM

The Royalton ★★★★½
44 West 44th Street
New York, NY 10036
☎ 212-869-4400
FAX 212-869-8965
TOLL-FREE 800-635-9013
www.morganshotelgroup.com

ROOM QUALITY	91
COST ($=$80)	$$$$$–
DISCOUNTS	GOV'T
NO. OF ROOMS	168
ROOM SQUARE FEET	250
MEETING FACILITIES	–
POOL/SAUNA	–
EXERCISE FACILITIES	•
WINDOW GLAZE	DOUBLE
PARKING PER DAY	$40
NEAREST SUBWAY	4 BLOCKS
BAR	•
ON-SITE DINING	AMERICAN
EXTRA AMENITIES	CONCIERGE
BUSINESS AMENITIES	DATAPORT, 2 PHONE LINES

Sheraton Manhattan Hotel ★★★★½
790 Seventh Avenue
New York, NY 10019
☎ 212-581-3300
FAX 212-541-9219
TOLL-FREE 800-325-3535
www.sheraton.com

ROOM QUALITY	92
COST ($=$80)	$$$+
DISCOUNTS	AAA, AARP, GOV'T
NO. OF ROOMS	650
ROOM SQUARE FEET	180
MEETING FACILITIES	•
POOL/SAUNA	POOL
EXERCISE FACILITIES	•
WINDOW GLAZE	DOUBLE
PARKING PER DAY	$27
NEAREST SUBWAY	2 BLOCKS
BAR	•
ON-SITE DINING	BISTRO
EXTRA AMENITIES	CONVENTION CENTER
BUSINESS AMENITIES	DATAPORT, 2 PHONE LINES, FAX SOME ROOMS

Sheraton New York Hotel and Towers ★★★★
811 Seventh Avenue
New York, NY 10019
☎ 212-581-1000
FAX 212-262-4410
TOLL-FREE 800-325-3535
www.sheraton.com

ROOM QUALITY	89
COST ($=$80)	$$$+
DISCOUNTS	AAA, AARP, GOV'T
NO. OF ROOMS	1,750
ROOM SQUARE FEET	180
MEETING FACILITIES	•
POOL/SAUNA	PRIVILEGES, $15
EXERCISE FACILITIES	•
WINDOW GLAZE	SINGLE
PARKING PER DAY	$35
NEAREST SUBWAY	BENEATH HOTEL
BAR	•
ON-SITE DINING	CAFE, AMERICAN
EXTRA AMENITIES	CONVENTION CENTER
BUSINESS AMENITIES	DATAPORT, 2 PHONE LINES, FAX

The Sherry Netherland ★★★★½
781 Fifth Avenue
New York, NY 10022
☎ 212-355-2800
FAX 212-319-4306
TOLL-FREE 800-247-4377
www.sherrynetherland.com

ROOM QUALITY	93
COST ($=$80)	$$$$$$–
DISCOUNTS	–
NO. OF ROOMS	60
ROOM SQUARE FEET	400
MEETING FACILITIES	• SMALL
POOL/SAUNA	–
EXERCISE FACILITIES	•
WINDOW GLAZE	SINGLE
PARKING PER DAY	$45
NEAREST SUBWAY	½ BLOCK
BAR	•
ON-SITE DINING	ITALIAN
EXTRA AMENITIES	CONCIERGE, BREAKFAST
BUSINESS AMENITIES	DATAPORT, 2 PHONE LINES, FAX SOME ROOMS

San Carlos ★★★★½
150 East 50th Street
New York, NY 10022
☎ 212-755-1800
FAX 212-688-9778
TOLL-FREE 800-722-2012
www.sancarloshotel.com

ROOM QUALITY	91
COST ($=$80)	$$$$+
DISCOUNTS	–
NO. OF ROOMS	147
ROOM SQUARE FEET	350
MEETING FACILITIES	•
POOL/SAUNA	–
EXERCISE FACILITIES	•
WINDOW GLAZE	DOUBLE
PARKING PER DAY	$30
NEAREST SUBWAY	1 BLOCK
BAR	•
ON-SITE DINING	INDIAN AMERICAN
EXTRA AMENITIES	CONCIERGE, CONT'L BREAKFAST, LAUNDRY SERVICE
BUSINESS AMENITIES	DATAPORT, 2 PHONE LINES, DSL, FAX ACCESS

Second Home on Second Avenue ★★★½
221 Second Avenue
New York, NY 10003
☎ 212-677-3161
FAX 212-677-3161
www.newyork.citysearch.com

ROOM QUALITY	77
COST ($=$80)	$$
DISCOUNTS	–
NO. OF ROOMS	7
ROOM SQUARE FEET	100
MEETING FACILITIES	–
POOL/SAUNA	–
EXERCISE FACILITIES	–
WINDOW GLAZE	SINGLE
PARKING PER DAY	$20
NEAREST SUBWAY	2 BLOCKS
BAR	–
ON-SITE DINING	–
EXTRA AMENITIES	–
BUSINESS AMENITIES	DATAPORT, 1 PHONE LINE

70 Park Avenue Hotel ★★★★½
70 Park Avenue
New York, NY 10016
☎ 212-687-7050
FAX 212-808-9029
TOLL-FREE 877-993-6725
www.doralparkavenue.com

ROOM QUALITY	90
COST ($=$80)	$$$$$$$$–
DISCOUNTS	–
NO. OF ROOMS	188
ROOM SQUARE FEET	270
MEETING FACILITIES	•
POOL/SAUNA	WHIRLPOOL
EXERCISE FACILITIES	PRIVILEGES
WINDOW GLAZE	DOUBLE
PARKING PER DAY	$40
NEAREST SUBWAY	3 BLOCKS
BAR	•
ON-SITE DINING	NEW AMERICAN
EXTRA AMENITIES	–
BUSINESS AMENITIES	DATAPORT

The Shoreham ★★★★
33 West 55th Street
New York, NY 10019
☎ 212-247-6700
FAX 212-765-9741
TOLL-FREE 877-847-4444
www.boutiquehg.com

ROOM QUALITY	89
COST ($=$80)	$$$$
DISCOUNTS	–
NO. OF ROOMS	178
ROOM SQUARE FEET	250
MEETING FACILITIES	
POOL/SAUNA	PRIVILEGES
EXERCISE FACILITIES	PRIVILEGES, FREE
WINDOW GLAZE	SINGLE
PARKING PER DAY	$40
NEAREST SUBWAY	1 BLOCK
BAR	•
ON-SITE DINING	FRENCH
EXTRA AMENITIES	–
BUSINESS AMENITIES	DATAPORT, 2 PHONE LINES

60 Thompson ★★★★
60 Thompson Street
New York, NY 10012
☎ 212-431-0400
FAX 212-431-0200
TOLL-FREE 800-325-3535
www.thompsonhotels.com

ROOM QUALITY	88
COST ($=$80)	$$$$$+
DISCOUNTS	AAA, AARP, GOV'T
NO. OF ROOMS	650
ROOM SQUARE FEET	180
MEETING FACILITIES	• SMALL
POOL/SAUNA	–
EXERCISE FACILITIES	PRIVILEGES
WINDOW GLAZE	SINGLE
PARKING PER DAY	$35
NEAREST SUBWAY	3 BLOCKS
BAR	•
ON-SITE DINING	AMERICAN
EXTRA AMENITIES	CONCIERGE, BREAKFAST
BUSINESS AMENITIES	INTERNET, FAX

Sofitel New York ★★★★
45 West 44th Street
New York, NY 10036
☎ 212-354-884
FAX 212-782-3002
TOLL-FREE 800-SOFITEL
www.sofitel.com

ROOM QUALITY	88
COST ($=$80)	$$$$
DISCOUNTS	–
NO. OF ROOMS	398
ROOM SQUARE FEET	N/A
MEETING FACILITIES	•
POOL/SAUNA	–
EXERCISE FACILITIES	•
WINDOW GLAZE	TRIPLE
PARKING PER DAY	$40
NEAREST SUBWAY	2 BLOCKS
BAR	•
ON-SITE DINING	FRENCH
EXTRA AMENITIES	CONCIERGE, RADIO
BUSINESS AMENITIES	DATAPORT, DSL, COMPUTER

Hotel Information Chart (continued)

Soho Grand ★★★★½
310 West Broadway
New York, NY 10013
☎ 212-965-3000
FAX 212-965-3200
TOLL-FREE 800-965-3000
www.sohogrand.com

ROOM QUALITY	93
COST ($=$80)	$$$+
DISCOUNTS	–
NO. OF ROOMS	367
ROOM SQUARE FEET	275
MEETING FACILITIES	•
POOL/SAUNA	–
EXERCISE FACILITIES	•
WINDOW GLAZE	TRIPLE
PARKING PER DAY	$34
NEAREST SUBWAY	1 BLOCK
BAR	•
ON-SITE DINING	NEW ENGLAND
EXTRA AMENITIES	GOLDFISH IN ROOM BY REQUEST
BUSINESS AMENITIES	DATAPORT, 2 PHONE LINES

The Solita Soho ★★★★
Clarion Hotel
159 Grand Street
New York, NY 10013
☎ 212-925-3600
FAX 212-925-3385
TOLL-FREE 888-SOLITA-8
www.solitasoho.com

ROOM QUALITY	89
COST ($=$80)	$$$+
DISCOUNTS	AAA, GOV'T
NO. OF ROOMS	42
ROOM SQUARE FEET	N/A
MEETING FACILITIES	–
POOL/SAUNA	–
EXERCISE FACILITIES	• $15 ACCESS
WINDOW GLAZE	–
PARKING PER DAY	$30–$40
NEAREST SUBWAY	2 BLOCKS
BAR	•
ON-SITE DINING	–
EXTRA AMENITIES	PLASMA TV, DUAL SHOWER HEADS
BUSINESS AMENITIES	DATAPORT, 2 PHONE LINES, FAX ACCESS

The St. Regis ★★★★★
2 East 55th Street
New York, NY 10022
☎ 212-753-4500
FAX 212-787-3437
TOLL-FREE 800-759-7550
www.stregis.com

ROOM QUALITY	98
COST ($=$80)	$$$$$$$$+
DISCOUNTS	–
NO. OF ROOMS	313
ROOM SQUARE FEET	425
MEETING FACILITIES	•
POOL/SAUNA	SAUNA, STEAM ROOM
EXERCISE FACILITIES	•
WINDOW GLAZE	DOUBLE
PARKING PER DAY	$45
NEAREST SUBWAY	2 BLOCKS
BAR	•
ON-SITE DINING	AMERICAN, FRENCH
EXTRA AMENITIES	LIVE PIANO AND HARP IN SALON
BUSINESS AMENITIES	DATAPORT, 2 PHONE LINES

Trump International ★★★★★
Hotel & Towers
1 Central Park West
New York, NY 10023
☎ 212-299-1000
FAX 212-299-1150
TOLL-FREE 888-448-7867
www.trumpintl.com

ROOM QUALITY	97
COST ($=$80)	$$$$$$$$+
DISCOUNTS	–
NO. OF ROOMS	167
ROOM SQUARE FEET	N/A
MEETING FACILITIES	•
POOL/SAUNA	POOL
EXERCISE FACILITIES	•
WINDOW GLAZE	SINGLE
PARKING PER DAY	$45
NEAREST SUBWAY	1 BLOCK
BAR	•
ON-SITE DINING	AMERICAN, FRENCH
EXTRA AMENITIES	CONCIERGE, CD, SAFE
BUSINESS AMENITIES	DATAPORT, 2 PHONE LINES, FAX

W Hotel ★★★★½
Times Square
1467 Broadway
New York, NY 10036
☎ 212-930-7400
FAX 212-930-7500
TOLL-FREE 877-946-8357
www.whotels.com

ROOM QUALITY	95
COST ($=$80)	$$$$+
DISCOUNTS	AAA, GOV'T, MIL.
NO. OF ROOMS	509
ROOM SQUARE FEET	210
MEETING FACILITIES	•
POOL/SAUNA	–
EXERCISE FACILITIES	•
WINDOW GLAZE	SINGLE
PARKING PER DAY	$45
NEAREST SUBWAY	½ BLOCK
BAR	•
ON-SITE DINING	SEAFOOD-SUSHI
EXTRA AMENITIES	SPA, BATHROBES, LIBRARY
BUSINESS AMENITIES	INTERNET, 2 PHONE LINES, DATAPORT

W Hotel ★★★★
Union Square
201 Park Avenue South
New York, NY 10003
☎ 212-253-9119
FAX 212-779-0148
TOLL-FREE 877-946-8357
www.whotels.com

ROOM QUALITY	87
COST ($=$80)	$$$$$+
DISCOUNTS	AAA, GOV'T
NO. OF ROOMS	286
ROOM SQUARE FEET	390
MEETING FACILITIES	•
POOL/SAUNA	–
EXERCISE FACILITIES	•
WINDOW GLAZE	TRIPLE
PARKING PER DAY	$45
NEAREST SUBWAY	½ BLOCK
BAR	•
ON-SITE DINING	ITALIAN
EXTRA AMENITIES	CONCIERGE, CD, DVD, LIBRARY
BUSINESS AMENITIES	DATAPORT, 2 PHONE LINES

Thirty Thirty ★★★½
New York City
30 East 30th Street
New York, NY 10016
☎ 212-689-1900
FAX 212-689-0023
TOLL-FREE 800-804-4480
www.thirtythirty-nyc.com

ROOM QUALITY	83
COST ($=$80)	$$
DISCOUNTS	AAA, GOV'T
NO. OF ROOMS	210
ROOM SQUARE FEET	200
MEETING FACILITIES	–
POOL/SAUNA	–
EXERCISE FACILITIES	–
WINDOW GLAZE	SINGLE
PARKING PER DAY	$25
NEAREST SUBWAY	2 BLOCKS
BAR	–
ON-SITE DINING	–
EXTRA AMENITIES	–
BUSINESS AMENITIES	2 PHONE LINES

Time ★★★★
224 West 49th Street
New York, NY 10019
☎ 212-246-5252
FAX 212-245-2305
TOLL-FREE 877-846-3692
www.thetimeny.com

ROOM QUALITY	89
COST ($=$80)	$$$
DISCOUNTS	–
NO. OF ROOMS	194
ROOM SQUARE FEET	235
MEETING FACILITIES	•
POOL/SAUNA	–
EXERCISE FACILITIES	–
WINDOW GLAZE	DOUBLE
PARKING PER DAY	$25
NEAREST SUBWAY	1 BLOCK
BAR	•
ON-SITE DINING	AMERICAN
EXTRA AMENITIES	–
BUSINESS AMENITIES	DATAPORT, 2 PHONE LINES, FAX, WEBTV

Tribeca Grand ★★★★½
25 Walker Street
New York, NY 10013
☎ 212-519-6600
FAX 212-519-6700
TOLL-FREE 877-519-6600
www.tribecagrand.com

ROOM QUALITY	93
COST ($=$80)	$$$$
DISCOUNTS	GOV'T
NO. OF ROOMS	203
ROOM SQUARE FEET	N/A
MEETING FACILITIES	•
POOL/SAUNA	POOL
EXERCISE FACILITIES	•
WINDOW GLAZE	SINGLE
PARKING PER DAY	$40
NEAREST SUBWAY	2 BLOCKS
BAR	•
ON-SITE DINING	AMERICAN
EXTRA AMENITIES	CHAMPAGNE, BREAKFAST
BUSINESS AMENITIES	2 PHONE LINES, BUSINESS CENTER

W New York ★★★★½
541 Lexington Avenue
New York, NY 10022
☎ 212-755-1200
FAX 212-644-5951
TOLL-FREE 877-946-8357
www.whotels.com

ROOM QUALITY	92
COST ($=$80)	$$$$
DISCOUNTS	GOV'T, MIL.
NO. OF ROOMS	700
ROOM SQUARE FEET	200
MEETING FACILITIES	•
POOL/SAUNA	SAUNA, WHIRLPOOL
EXERCISE FACILITIES	•
WINDOW GLAZE	DOUBLE
PARKING PER DAY	$40
NEAREST SUBWAY	1 BLOCK
BAR	•
ON-SITE DINING	–
EXTRA AMENITIES	–
BUSINESS AMENITIES	DATAPORT

W New York ★★★★½
Tuscany
130 East 39th Street
New York, NY 10016
☎ 212-685-1100
FAX 212-779-0148
TOLL-FREE 877-946-8357
www.whotels.com

ROOM QUALITY	90
COST ($=$80)	$$$$
DISCOUNTS	GOV'T, MIL.
NO. OF ROOMS	199
ROOM SQUARE FEET	400
MEETING FACILITIES	•
POOL/SAUNA	–
EXERCISE FACILITIES	–
WINDOW GLAZE	DOUBLE
PARKING PER DAY	$40
NEAREST SUBWAY	2 BLOCKS
BAR	•
ON-SITE DINING	TUSCAN
EXTRA AMENITIES	PACKAGES
BUSINESS AMENITIES	DATAPORT, 2 PHONE LINES

The Waldorf-Astoria ★★★★½
301 Park Avenue
New York, NY 10022
☎ 212-355-3000
FAX 212-872-7272
TOLL-FREE 800-WALDORF
www.hilton.com

ROOM QUALITY	95
COST ($=$80)	$$$+
DISCOUNTS	GOV'T, AAA
NO. OF ROOMS	1,138
ROOM SQUARE FEET	N/A
MEETING FACILITIES	•
POOL/SAUNA	WHIRLPOOL
EXERCISE FACILITIES	•
WINDOW GLAZE	DOUBLE
PARKING PER DAY	$45
NEAREST SUBWAY	1 BLOCK
BAR	•
ON-SITE DINING	FRENCH, AMERICAN, JAPANESE
EXTRA AMENITIES	COCKTAIL TERRACE WITH PIANIST, SALON, SPA
BUSINESS AMENITIES	DATAPORT, 2 PHONE LINES, FAX

Hotel Information Chart (continued)

Wall Street Inn ★★★★
9 South William Street
New York, NY 10004
☎ 212-747-1500
FAX 212-747-1900
TOLL-FREE 877-747-1500
www.wallstreetinn.com

ROOM QUALITY	86
COST ($=$80)	$$$+
DISCOUNTS	GOV'T
NO. OF ROOMS	46
ROOM SQUARE FEET	250
MEETING FACILITIES	•
POOL/SAUNA	SAUNA, STEAM ROOM
EXERCISE FACILITIES	• SMALL
WINDOW GLAZE	DOUBLE
PARKING PER DAY	–
NEAREST SUBWAY	3 BLOCKS
BAR	–
ON-SITE DINING	–
EXTRA AMENITIES	FREE CONT'L BREAKFAST, HAIR DRYERS
BUSINESS AMENITIES	DATAPORT, 2 PHONE LINES

The Warwick Hotel ★★★★
65 West 54th Street
New York, NY 10019
☎ 212-247-2700
FAX 212-957-8915
TOLL-FREE 800-223-4099
www.warwickhotels.com

ROOM QUALITY	89
COST ($=$80)	$$$+
DISCOUNTS	AAA, GOV'T
NO. OF ROOMS	422
ROOM SQUARE FEET	240
MEETING FACILITIES	•
POOL/SAUNA	–
EXERCISE FACILITIES	–
WINDOW GLAZE	DOUBLE
PARKING PER DAY	$25
NEAREST SUBWAY	2 BLOCKS
BAR	•
ON-SITE DINING	ITALIAN CAFE
EXTRA AMENITIES	–
BUSINESS AMENITIES	DATAPORT, 2 PHONE LINES

Washington Square Hotel ★★★½
103 Waverly Place
New York, NY 10011
☎ 212-777-9515
FAX 212-979-8373
TOLL-FREE 800-222-0418
www.washingtonsquarehotel.com

ROOM QUALITY	78
COST ($=$80)	$$$–
DISCOUNTS	–
NO. OF ROOMS	180
ROOM SQUARE FEET	120
MEETING FACILITIES	• SMALL
POOL/SAUNA	–
EXERCISE FACILITIES	•
WINDOW GLAZE	SINGLE
PARKING PER DAY	N/A
NEAREST SUBWAY	1 BLOCK
BAR	•
ON-SITE DINING	AMERICAN
EXTRA AMENITIES	FREE CONTINENTAL BREAKFAST
BUSINESS AMENITIES	DATAPORT

Westin New York ★★★★
Times Square
270 West 43rd Street
New York, NY 10036
☎ 212-201-2700
FAX 212-201-2701
TOLL-FREE 866-837-4183
www.westinny.com

ROOM QUALITY	88
COST ($=$80)	$$$$$$$
DISCOUNTS	AAA, GOV'T
NO. OF ROOMS	863
ROOM SQUARE FEET	310
MEETING FACILITIES	•
POOL/SAUNA	SPA
EXERCISE FACILITIES	•
WINDOW GLAZE	DOUBLE
PARKING PER DAY	$38
NEAREST SUBWAY	½ BLOCK
BAR	•
ON-SITE DINING	STEAK HOUSE, AMERICAN
EXTRA AMENITIES	THEATER TICKET DESK
BUSINESS AMENITIES	DATAPORT, 2 PHONE LINES

PART FOUR

ARRIVING *and* GETTING ORIENTED

GETTING INTO AND OUT OF MANHATTAN changed forever in the aftermath of the September 11th terrorist attacks. If you intend to drive a truck or van into the city, be forewarned that some bridges and tunnels may be closed to commercial vehicles. At all bridges and tunnels, all vehicles are subject to search at the discretion of the authorities. While a search itself is a minor inconvenience, the traffic backups attending such searches are not. Once arrived, be aware that there's still a lot of surface traffic congestion in lower Manhattan in the area surrounding Ground Zero.

unofficial **TIP**
Leave your vehicle outside the city and train in.

At the three area airports, you can expect the same security screenings as at other U.S. facilities, so be sure to arrive two or more hours prior to departure time. Train travel has been less affected by new security procedures than has air or automobile travel. If you had considered flying up from Washington or down from Boston on one of the air shuttles, you'll probably save time by switching from the plane to the train.

ARRIVING

MANHATTAN ISLAND AND THE OTHER BOROUGHS that compose New York City are situated near the mouth of the Hudson River off a narrow spit of land that dangles like an udder beneath the bulk of upstate New York. To the west, across the Hudson from Manhattan, is the rest of the United States, starting with New Jersey. Travel in any other direction and you will find yourself in one of New York City's boroughs. To the north of Manhattan across the Harlem River is the Bronx. Due east, on the opposite bank of the East River, is Queens. South of Queens and southeast of Manhattan is Brooklyn, and farther south and a little to the west sits Staten Island.

If you are an American, there's a good chance that your forebears entered the United States through New York, steaming west out of the Atlantic Ocean into Lower New York Bay, through the Narrows between Staten Island and Brooklyn, north into Upper New York Bay, and finally past the Statue of Liberty to docks near the southern tip of Manhattan Island. Today, it's possible to arrive in New York by just about any means imaginable, making it one of the most accessible cities in the world.

BY CAR

IF YOU ARE PLANNING TO ARRIVE VIA AUTOMOBILE, you need this guidebook more than you ever imagined. Traffic in Manhattan comes in two basic modes: nutso and gridlock. With nutso you're moving, but everybody else is moving faster and usually at an angle that presupposes an imminent collision. Gridlock is gridlock. Bring a sandwich and a pocket edition of *War and Peace* and prepare yourself for some serious downtime. Native New Yorkers will consider this a gross exaggeration, of course, but then most of them have cab-driver genes somewhere in their lineage.

If there were a driving school to prepare you for driving in Manhattan, it would emphasize the automobile as an offensive weapon and would teach you various foreign dialects so that you could converse with other drivers. The final exam would involve wedging your car on the fly into spaces too small for the average cephalopod.

And then there are parking and gas. Filling stations are rare and generally not conveniently located, while safe, off-street parking in Manhattan costs as much per night as a hotel room in most other cities.

Driving in the boroughs is somewhat less daunting but is still more challenging than motoring in most other large U.S. cities.

So, having been warned, in case you elect to bring your nice, clean, undented car into Manhattan, here's what you need to know.

- Manhattan is an island! This means that you must enter via a bridge or a tunnel.
- Rush-hour traffic clogs all the tunnels and bridges, so time your arrival for off-peak traffic times—10 a.m. to 2:30 p.m. and 7:30 p.m. to 6 a.m. on weekdays are best.
- Traffic in Manhattan is decidedly more civil on weekends, but avoid arriving during the late afternoon and early evening on Sunday.
- Fill up your gas tank before coming into Manhattan.
- If you will be lodging in Manhattan, use the hotel information chart in Part Three to find hotels with parking garages.
- Expect to pay at least $25–$50 a day for parking in addition to the room charge.

Some Specific Directions

COMING FROM SOUTH OR WEST OF NEW YORK CITY Coming from New Jersey, south of New York, you can take the Holland Tunnel into downtown Manhattan or the Lincoln Tunnel into Midtown. Both require tolls and both are accessed from Interstate 95. The Holland Tunnel is also accessible from Interstate 78. Unless you are heading for lower (downtown) Manhattan, we recommend the more northerly Lincoln Tunnel. A third option is to take Interstate 278 across Staten Island and into Brooklyn, and from there enter Manhattan via the Brooklyn–Battery Tunnel. This last is quite roundabout and should only be considered when there is a traffic advisory for the Holland Tunnel.

COMING FROM NORTH OF NEW YORK CITY Coming from north of the city and west of the Hudson River, you can choose between the Lincoln Tunnel or the George Washington Bridge, which crosses onto Manhattan at the northern end of the island.

East of the Hudson River, there's a dandy tangle of highways branching south to New York City from upper New York State, Connecticut, Rhode Island, and points farther north. Coming south on Interstate 87, pick up the Henry Hudson Parkway below Yonkers to enter Manhattan. From I-95 south you have several choices. Either stay on I-95 as it crosses the upper end of Manhattan Island, or branch off onto I-278 and enter New York City via the Triborough Bridge (toll).

unofficial **TIP**
Although it may sound less convenient, consider driving to the Metropark Station, leaving the car there ($4 a day instead of 20 times that), and buying a ticket on New Jersey Transit ($12.50 round-trip) into the city. (Amtrak also stops at Metropark, but is more expensive.) To reach Metropark, take the New Jersey Turnpike to the Garden State Parkway, then go about two miles to Exit 131 and into Metropark.

ARRIVING AND DEPARTING BY AIRPLANE

THE NEW YORK AREA IS SERVED BY THREE MAJOR AIRPORTS. LaGuardia Airport, located in Queens, is the closest airport, followed by John F. Kennedy International Airport (JFK), situated south of Queens on Jamaica Bay. To the west, in New Jersey, is Newark International Airport. LaGuardia services primarily domestic flights and carriers, while JFK and Newark handle both international and domestic air traffic.

In general, LaGuardia is closer and more convenient than JFK or Newark, though the difference is not all that great—about 20 or so additional minutes and about $10 cab fare—to most Manhattan destinations. However, there are free shuttles from JFK to the Howard Beach subway station, so you could make it into Manhattan for only $2. There is also bus service via **New York Airport Service Express Bus** (call ☎ 718-875-8200) from JFK ($15) and LaGuardia ($10).

unofficial **TIP**
You may find bargain fares to Newark (and occasionally JFK) that more than make up for the longer commute.

If you are visiting New York during the winter, we recommend flying into either Newark or JFK. These airports have

unofficial **TIP**

Flying into Baltimore/ Washington International (BWI) can be a big dollar-saver. We flew Southwest Airlines to BWI for $112 round-trip from Birmingham, Alabama, and then transferred to Amtrak. Our total cost was $238—$112 round-trip air plus $126 round-trip rail from BWI—compared with airfares to LaGuardia, JFK, or Newark ranging from an economy $398 to a full coach fare of $788. Because the train deposits you right in the heart of Manhattan, you also avoid taxi or bus fares from the airport.

longer runways and electronic instrumentation that allows them to operate in weather that might shut LaGuardia down. In addition, because they are larger than LaGuardia, Newark and JFK can perform airplane de-icing operations adjacent to the active runways. At LaGuardia, planes in need of de-icing are usually detoured to a remote staging area.

Another way to hedge your bets during the winter is to fly into Baltimore/Washington International (BWI) and then take an Amtrak train directly to New York Penn Station. There are more than 20 trains a day, and there is an Amtrak station right at the airport. Conventional trains take about three hours and a quarter, whereas the Acela Express and express Metro-Liners make the trip in two and a half hours. Also, if you can fly directly from your home airport to BWI, the plane/train combo can sometimes get you to New York faster than an air itinerary that requires a change of planes.

With the more stringent security enforced for carry-on luggage, you must be careful to pack the following items in your check-in luggage: scissors, nail files, nail clippers, pen-knives, razors or razor blades, or any other sharp object that could conceivably be used as a weapon.

PUBLIC TRANSPORTATION ROUTES FROM LAGUARDIA AIRPORT

SERVICE	TO	DEPARTS	TRAVEL TIME
Super Shuttle Fare: $15	Drop-off anywhere between Battery Park and 227th Street; also stops at certain hotels	24 hours	55–110 min. depending on destination
Cab Fare: $21–$30 plus tolls and tip	Any stop in Manhattan	At your convenience	20–35 min. depending on destination (nonrush)
Limo Cost depends on type of limo	Any stop in Manhattan	At your convenience	20–35 min. (nonrush)
New York Airport Service Fare: $12	Grand Central Station & Port Authority Terminal	Every 30 minutes from 6:45 a.m. to midnight	35–45 min. (nonrush)

TRANSPORTATION CHART

NAME	SERVICE	PHONE
Airlink	Bus service	☎ 718-560-3900
Airporter	Airport-to-airport transfers	☎ 609-587-6600
Amtrak	Train service	☎ 800-872-7245
JFK International Airport	Airport	☎ 718-244-4444
LaGuardia Airport	Airport	☎ 718-533-3400
Long Island Railroad	Commuter railroad	☎ 718-217-LIRR
Metro-North Railroad	Commuter railroad	☎ 212-532-4900
New Jersey Transit	Buses & trains to NYC	☎ 800-772-2222
NYC Bridges & Tunnels	Bridge & tunnel info	☎ 800-221-9903
NYC D.O.T.	Parking, etc.	☎ 212-639-9675
NYC Taxi & Limo Commission	New York City taxis	☎ 212-692-8294
NYC Transit Authority	Subways & buses	☎ 718-330-1234
New York Airport Service	NYC–airport bus service	☎ 718-875-8200
New York Waterway	Commuter ferry service	☎ 800-533-3779
Newark Liberty International Airport	Airport	☎ 973-961-6000
Olympia Trails Express Buses	NYC–airport bus service	☎ 877-863-9275
PATH Train	New Jersey–NYC train	☎ 800-234-7284
Port Authority Bus Terminal	Bus & subway station	☎ 212-564-8484
Road Conditions	Road condition information	☎ 800-847-8929, ☎ 212-639-9675
Super Shuttle	LaGuardia–NYC shuttle	☎ 212-315-3006

LaGuardia Airport

LaGuardia, the smallest of the New York airports, is located just off Grand Central Parkway in Queens. LaGuardia has four terminals. All airlines except Northwest, Delta, and US Airways use the Central Terminal. US Airways and Delta have their own terminals. Delta shares its main terminal with Northwest and also uses the Marine Air Terminal for its Delta Shuttle flights. Because the Delta Shuttle operates at the opposite end of the airport from Delta's other flights, make sure you know from which terminal your Delta flight departs.

If you plan to arrive by air (except during winter, as discussed earlier) from within the United States or Canada, flying into LaGuardia will usually get you to your Manhattan destination faster. How much faster depends on highway traffic conditions at the time of day you arrive. During nonrush periods it takes about 20 to 25 minutes by cab or limo and 35 to 45 minutes by bus from LaGuardia to Midtown. During rush hour, traffic flows both in and out of the city, and the convenience of flying into LaGuardia is sometimes offset by the snarled traffic of surrounding streets and highways. Although there is a water shuttle to the 34th Street Pier in Midtown, most arriving passengers commute to the city in cabs, limos, or buses. Getting into Manhattan from LaGuardia during rush hour, though a hassle (allow 35 to 60 minutes to Midtown), is doable. Going to the airport in afternoon rush-hour traffic is problematic. If you are booked on a flight that departs between 4:30 and 8 p.m. on weekdays, leave Manhattan three hours in advance if traveling by cab, three and a half hours in advance if using an airport shuttle bus.

To get from LaGuardia to Manhattan, you have your choice of cab, limo, bus, or water taxi.

John F. Kennedy International Airport

JFK is a sprawling, confusing, nine-terminal facility that most savvy travelers go out of their way to avoid. Almost 100 airlines, including most foreign carriers, use JFK. International travelers make domestic connections at JFK, and U.S. carriers daily fly in thousands of passengers bound for international destinations. To get from JFK to Manhattan you have your choice of cab, limo, bus, or subway.

PUBLIC TRANSPORTATION ROUTES FROM JFK AIRPORT

SERVICE	TO	DEPARTS	TRAVEL TIME
Super Shuttle Fare: $17–$19	Drop-off anywhere between Battery Park and 227th Street; also stops at certain hotels	24 hours; reservations required for return service	55–110 min. depending on destination
New York Airport Service Fare: $15	Grand Central Station & Port Authority Terminal	Every 30 minutes from 6 a.m. to midnight	45–65 min. (nonrush)
Subway, "A" Line Fare: $2	Manhattan—all stops from Fulton Street to 207th Street, Howard Beach Station to Midtown, plus stops in Queens and Brooklyn	24 hours	60–75 minutes
Cab Fare: $45 flat rate plus tolls and tip	Any stop in Manhattan	At your convenience	40–60 minutes
Limo Cost depends on type of limo	Any stop in Manhattan	At your convenience	40–60 minutes

Newark International Airport

Newark International Airport is located in New Jersey between Newark and Elizabeth. There are three terminals serving about 50 domestic and foreign airlines. All of the terminals and long-term parking lots are connected by monorail. Newark International is better organized and decidedly less intimidating than JFK and generally more efficient than LaGuardia. If your Manhattan destination is downtown or Midtown on the West Side, you should consider flying into Newark. Bus service, especially to downtown and to the Port Authority Terminal in Midtown, is excellent, with buses departing every 20 to 30 minutes, 24 hours a day; and Amtrak offers train service from the airport to New York Penn Station.

To get from Newark International Airport to Manhattan, you can choose from among limos, cabs, buses, trains, or a combination of bus or cab, and train.

PUBLIC TRANSPORTATION ROUTES FROM NEWARK INTERNATIONAL

SERVICE	TO	DEPARTS	TRAVEL TIME
Newark Airport Express **Bus Fare: $13**	**Port Authority Terminal at 42nd and Eighth Ave.**	**Every 20–30 minutes 24 hours a day**	**40–50 minutes**
Newark Airport Express **Bus Fare: $13**	**Grand Central Terminal or Penn Station**	**Every 20–30 minutres**	**50–70 minutes**
Airlink Bus **Fare: $15**	**Anywhere between Battery Park and 125th Street**	**On demand 24 hours**	**15 minutes**
Cab **Fare: $40–$55 rate plus tolls and tip**	**Any stop in Manhattan**	**At your convenience**	**40–60 minutes**
Limo **Cost depends on type of limo**	**Any stop in Manhattan**	**At your convenience**	**40–60 minutes**
Train New Jersey Transit **Fare: $14**	**New York Penn Station**	**Every 15–30 minutes**	**30–45 minutes**
Train Amtrak Regional **Fare: $35**	**New York Penn Station**	**Every 25–60 minutes**	**20 minutes**

Getting into Manhattan from the Airports

When it comes to getting into the city from the airport, we opt for simplicity, even if it costs a dollar or two more. The fewer times you must heft your luggage around, the better, and likewise, the fewer stops or transfers necessary, the less complicated the trip.

From LaGuardia we always take a cab or limo (see above), unless we are arriving at the Marine Air Terminal at rush hour, in which case we sometimes use the Delta Water Shuttle. From JFK we take a cab or limo. The JFK A-train subway looks good on paper and is definitely the least expensive way to get into town, but it takes forever owing to countless intermediate stops. When it comes to Newark, we usually take the Olympia Trails express bus to the Port Authority Terminal on Manhattan's West Side in Midtown. Because of preferential treatment at the Lincoln Tunnel and a direct "buses only" throughway into the Port Authority Terminal, the bus can often make it to Manhattan faster than a cab (once the bus leaves the airport). From the Port Authority Terminal you can catch a cab or, if traveling light, a subway to your destination.

As an aside, the Port Authority Terminal is a huge, generally confusing maze of a building. After you disembark from the bus, your best bet is to make your way to ground level and exit the building on 42nd Street. You will find a cab stand just outside the door. If you plan to return to the airport via the terminal, locate the Airport Transportation Lobby on the first floor of the northern (42nd Street) side of the terminal. Though New York has made great progress in reducing crime in public places, the Port Authority Terminal is not a great spot to hang around. Unless, as we Southerners say, "you're fixin' to explode," wait until you reach your hotel to use the restroom. If you are considering a taxi, fares from Newark International to Midtown run about $45 plus tolls and tip—a bit pricey unless there are three or more in your party.

Amtrak opened a train station at Newark International in the fall of 2001. From the terminal, catch an AirTran monorail to the airport train station. The monorail is free if you have a prepurchased Amtrak ticket, or $5 if you don't. Trains from the airport station depart every 25–60 minutes, depending on time of day, and they stop at Newark Penn Station enroute. The commute via Amtrak takes only about 20 minutes, making it the fastest way into the city. It is also, however, the most expensive option short of a private cab, costing about $35 one way, not including any monorail charges. If you book your Amtrak itinerary on the Amtrak Web site, be aware that you must

unofficial **TIP**
New Jersey Transit trains run almost the same route from Newark as their faster Amtrak counterparts, and they are much cheaper. At the entrance to the AirTran monorail, vending machines sell NJ Transit tickets. Follow the on-screen directions and buy a ticket for New York Penn Station (about $14). Use this ticket to get through the AirTran turnstiles; the monorail will take you to the train station. Once your NJ Transit train arrives, board and find a seat. A conductor will come by to punch your ticket.

enter the airport code "EWR" rather than typing "Newark International Airport Station."

From LaGuardia and JFK, if there are two or more in your party, a cab is not much more expensive than the bus, plus it takes you right to your hotel. The New York Airport Service Express Bus from LaGuardia to Grand Central Terminal, for example, is $12 per head. A couple using the Carey bus would spend $24 to get to Grand Central and then would probably need a cab to reach their hotel. By the time you add it all up, the cost is very comparable to the price of a cab straight from the airport, including tolls and tip.

unofficial **TIP**
Do not accept a ride from any person who approaches you in the terminal or on the sidewalk. Official, licensed cabs load only at designated taxi stands, supervised by a dispatcher.

Each terminal at all three airports has a taxi queue, a designated place for arriving passengers to catch a cab. Because there are always lots of cabs at the airport awaiting fares, it usually takes only a couple of minutes in line to get a cab.

Savvy travelers have discovered limo services. For sometimes even less than a cab, a limo and driver will meet your flight and transport you into Manhattan. Rates range from $28–$35 for a trip from LaGuardia to Manhattan in a modest sedan to over $150 for a ride to Newark International in something fancy. Although you can occasionally beat the price of a cab, the big advantage to reserving a limo is having somebody there waiting for you—that is, no taxi queue. To reserve, call one of the operators listed below. Have your flight information handy, including airline, flight

unofficial **TIP**
Limos, which incidentally encompass a diverse assortment of vehicles in addition to stretch Cadillacs, can be reserved by the trip or by the hour.

number, and arrival time. The service will also ask for your Manhattan destination. Although you can request that your driver meet you in the terminal, it's customary (and sometimes cheaper) to meet him or her curbside. Most limo services will accept prepayment by credit card, or alternatively, you can pay the driver. Tolls, parking fees, and gratuities are extra.

Westchester Express	☎ 800-532-3730 or 201-997-7368
Super Saver by Carmel	☎ 800-924-9954 or 212-666-6666
Classic Limousine	☎ 800-666-4949 or 631-567-5100
Tel Aviv Car & Limo Service	☎ 800-222-9888 or 212-777-7777
Dial Car	☎ 800-DIAL-743 or 718-743-8383

Getting to the Airports from Manhattan

Essentially, you have the same options available when it's time to go to the airport for your return flight. For LaGuardia and JFK, your best bet is a cab. For Newark, take a cab to the Port Authority Terminal and then board a Newark Airport Express bus for the airport.

There is one additional option for commuting to the airports: ride-sharing services. These services offer reserved-space door-to-door transportation to the airports.

| To LaGuardia or JFK | Classic Airport Ride Share | ☎ 631-567-5100 |
| To Newark International | Super Shuttle | ☎ 212-315-3006 |

With ride-share services, you call the service and advise them of your flight time. They integrate you into their pickup schedule and tell you what time to be ready to go. If you are the first person collected, you have a bit of driving to look forward to. On the other hand, if you are the last person in the van, it's straight to the airport you go. The service to Newark is a bargain at $15 and eliminates carting all your stuff through the Port Authority Terminal or paying big bucks for a cab. Ride-share service to JFK for one person will save you about $5–$10 over the cost of a cab. Going to LaGuardia, you're better off in terms of convenience and costs to take a taxi. For the record, the same companies also provide shared-ride service from the airports to Manhattan.

BY TRAIN

NEW YORK HAS EXCELLENT TRAIN CONNECTIONS south to Baltimore and Washington, D.C.; north to upstate New York, Boston, and New England; and west to New Jersey and eastern Pennsylvania. From these areas you can commute directly to Midtown Manhattan in a time span that rivals or betters that of traveling by air. From Baltimore, for example, we departed our hotel for the 10-minute ride to the Amtrak Station, waited less than 20 minutes for the train to arrive, and then buzzed up to New York's Penn Station in about two and a half hours— a total of just under three hours for the whole trip. (Using the new high-speed Acela Express trains, you can make it even faster.) By contrast, our colleagues commuted 20 minutes to the airport, then consumed two hours and ten minutes checking in, walking to the departure gate, and boarding. The flight from gate to gate to LaGuardia took another hour. They had no checked luggage, but it took 15 minutes to unload and make it to the taxi queue, where the wait for a cab was a modest five minutes. Cabbing from LaGuardia to Midtown consumed a little over 20 minutes—for a total of four hours and ten minutes.

Amtrak's Acela high-speed service from Washington, D.C., to New York, and from Boston to New York, is on a par with Europe's bullet trains. Reaching speeds of 150 miles an hour, Acela Express trains provide first- and business-class service, while Acela Regional trains (which make more stops) offer both business and coach accommodations. Plush seating, seatside electrical outlets for computers, conference tables, and a club car are standard on all Acela trains. Acela Express trains additionally offer a "quiet" car, as well as complimentary full meal and beverage service for first-class passengers. With departures throughout the day, and business and first-class fares comparable to airfares, it's hard to figure why anyone in the Boston–New York–DC corridor would opt to fly. For additional information, check out **www.amtrak.com** or call ☎ 800-USA-RAIL.

If you are traveling from points farther afield than the cities and areas listed above, the train probably requires more time than you are prepared to invest. Sometimes, however, the longer hauls offer some unexpected benefits. Bill, traveling from Atlanta to New York, caught the Amtrak Crescent at 7:30 p.m. With first-class accommodations, he enjoyed a sleeping compartment, and his meals were included as well. He arrived in New York at 2:10 the following afternoon. Because it was easy to work on the train, Bill had plenty of time to both relax and prepare for his afternoon meeting in New York. His partner, Jane, by contrast, spent a busy morning hustling to the airport, flying to LaGuardia, cabbing into the city, and then trying to catch a bite to eat on the run. Other eastern cities with fairly attractive Amtrak schedules and fares include Richmond, Norfolk, Raleigh/Durham, Charlotte, Charleston (SC), Birmingham, Savannah, Jacksonville, Orlando, Cleveland, Pittsburgh, Chicago, and Montreal. For information, call Amtrak at ☎ 800-872-7245.

unofficial **TIP**
Unless you're still in the backpacking years, it's worth spending the extra money to get a ticket on a reserved-seating train; especially if you're traveling during a holiday or heavy convention time. (And in New York, there's never a light season.) Do it ahead of time, or it's possible you may even have to stand part of the way.

In addition to Amtrak, four commuter railroads serve the greater New York area. New Jersey Transit (call ☎ 973-762-5100 or ☎ 800-772-2222) operates two lines, using New York Penn Station along with Amtrak and the Long Island Railroad (call ☎ 718-217-LIRR). The Metro-North Commuter Railroad, serving towns north along the Hudson River, arrives and departs from Grand Central Station.

BY SHIP

IF YOU ARRIVE IN NEW YORK ON A CRUISE SHIP you will probably tie up at the Passenger Ship Terminal on the far west side of the city between West 51st and West 52nd streets. Cabs and limos provide transportation from the terminal to Manhattan and area destinations.

GETTING ORIENTED

LAID OUT IN A GRID, NEW YORK IS A VERY EASY CITY to navigate. Avenues run north–south, and streets run east–west. Though some avenues have names (Park and Madison avenues, for example) and some have names and numbers (Avenue of the Americas is also Sixth Avenue), most avenues just have numbers (First Avenue, Fifth Avenue, etc.). The numbering starts on the east side of Manhattan, with First Avenue, and ascends to Eleventh Avenue on the west side of the island.

Streets are a little trickier, but not much. Do you remember regular and irregular verbs from your English grammar studies? Well, in New York there are regular streets and irregular streets. Regular streets are numbered streets that run east–west, forming a nice grid with the avenues. Irregular streets are likely to run in just about any direction and generally have names instead of numbers. Most of the irregular streets are in the lowermost or uppermost parts of the island. In between the lower part and the upper part, in the 60% of Manhattan that composes the middle, are the regular streets. Between 191st Street way uptown (north) and 14th Street downtown (south) there is a lovely, predictable grid. The only notable irregular street in this section of Manhattan is Broadway, which carves a lazy diagonal from northwest to southeast across the grid. Another exception, though it's not a street, is Central Park, a long north–south rectangle running from 110st Street south to 59th Street.

Going south from 14th Street toward the lower part of the island, the grid system prevails all the way down to First Street and Houston Street, but *only* on the east side. On the west side below 14th Street to Houston is Greenwich Village, which contains mostly irregular streets. From Houston Street on down to Battery Park at the tip of Manhattan is a crazy patchwork of irregular streets. Some of New York's more colorful neighborhoods and districts, including Chinatown, Little Italy, the Bowery, Soho, Tribeca, and the Financial District, are packed into this confined space. City Hall and the World Trade Center site now known as Ground Zero are also located here. If you are walking or driving in this area, the best way to stay oriented is to imagine a finger pointed down with the palm toward you. Wall Street is the crease at the first knuckle from the tip. The middle crease (second knuckle) is Canal Street, and the crease where the finger joins the palm is Houston Street. If you take a pen and draw a line down the middle of the finger from your palm to the tip, bisecting all three creases, that would be Broadway. If you can keep these streets and their relationship to one another straight, you will never be lost for long in Lower Manhattan. If you use this little memory aid in public, we strongly recommend that you use your index finger (the finger located closest to the thumb).

THINGS *the* LOCALS *already* KNOW

TIPPING

AS WE'VE SAID, NEW YORK'S UNFRIENDLY REPUTATION is highly exaggerated, but the city requires a little "friendliness" on your part as well. This is a society accustomed to—one might almost say built on—

the tipping system, and you should be prepared right from the start. Cabbies generally expect 15–20% of the fare as a tip, and you should certainly be generous if traffic is as bad as it generally is. If your hotel doorman gets you the cab, it's customary, though still optional, to slip him a dollar bill (besides, you don't want to have to wait next time, do you?). However, if you pick up the cab from one of the managed taxi stands at the train stations or airports, do not tip the traffic conductor.

Once at the hotel, expect to slip the bellman a dollar per suitcase ($2 if it's really heavy or clumsy); when you check out, leave behind at least $2 a day for the maids, $3 if the room has a second visit for turndown service or extra care. Tipping the concierge is a question of letting the reward fit the service: If she merely makes dinner reservations, a warm thank-you may suffice; but if she finagles them in the hottest restaurant in town, or gets opening-night tickets to a Broadway blockbuster, go for the 20% rule.

Bartenders typically get a dollar a drink for a simple cocktail, but the elaborate ones now common—and especially the "signature" creations at the trendier bars, which may involve infusions, muddlings, or fancy garnish—get $2 or $3. Waiters generally get 15–20%, although you should look to see whether an automatic gratuity has been built into the total. If you check your coats, tip the attendant $1 per wrap when you pick them up, and perhaps another dollar for large umbrellas or briefcases. Legends to the contrary, it is rare that slipping the maitre d' a bribe will do you much good, and it makes you look like a rube unless some actual rearrangement has been necessary. If you have summoned the sommelier to consult on the wine choice, you should leave him something in the range of 10% of the cost of the bottle.

Any personal services you arrange, such as a massage, hairstyling, manicure, or the like, also require a tip of about 20%. And if you get a shoeshine—an underestimated pleasure, incidentally—you should surely throw in a similar bonus.

RADIO AND TELEVISION STATIONS

NEW YORK HAS A THOUSAND RADIO STATIONS—well, maybe it just sounds that way, getting in and out of taxis and shopping malls —but among the most useful for out-of-towners are the National Public Radio WNYC (AM 820 and FM 93.9); sports WFAN (AM 660); and the all-news WBBR (AM 1130) and WINS (AM 1010). For the runners, etc., music choices include classical WQXR (FM 96.3); jazz WBGO (FM 88.3); rock Z100 (FM 100.3); Top 40 WPLJ (FM 95.5); classic rock WAXQ (FM 104.3); dance WKTU (FM 103.5); and urban WRKS (FM 98.7).

Most hotels have cable, and if you're lucky, the list of stations in your room will more or less correspond to what you actually get. The major networks are easy to find, however: CBS on Channel 2, NBC on Channel 4, Fox on 5, ABC on 7, and PBS on 13.

PUBLIC ACCOMMODATIONS

THE *UNOFFICIAL GUIDES* ARE STARTING TO GET a reputation for worrying about restrooms or, rather, about your being able to find them. This is a, uh, tribute to the relatively short staying power of our founder, Bob Sehlinger, and someday we'll stop teasing him about it. But he has a good point; being uncomfortable doesn't help you enjoy a walking tour or a museum. And especially in summer, when New York can be so hot, it's tempting to drink a lot. (When on a vacation is it not tempting to drink a lot?)

New York is experimenting with the automated kiosks familiar to European travelers, and you will spot them—they look something like circular phone booths—in City Hall Park and other public gathering spots. However, it is best to ask yourself the same question you ask the kids—Are you sure you don't have to go?—before you go, because the good restrooms are not always easy to spot.

There are plenty of restrooms in the transportation terminals, such as Grand Central and Penn Station, which are much cleaner and safer than they used to be; the large theaters (though most lobbies will be inaccessible during the day) and museums have them, too, but the lines can be rather long. In Central Park, look for the restrooms near the Delacorte Theater at 79th Street; and there are public facilities behind the New York Public Library in Bryant Park on Sixth Avenue and 42nd Street. Castle Clinton in Battery Park is nice and not usually crowded. The nearby Robert Wagner Park facility is even better. Big tourist centers such as the Chelsea Piers development, department stores, and malls are good bets, though the quality varies with the age and general atmosphere (in the Manhattan Mall, check the seventh floor). The large hotel lobbies have restrooms, of course, although you should only take advantage of them in an emergency and when you are reasonably well dressed.

unofficial **TIP**
If you are really in a pinch for a restroom, go to a bar and at least order a soda before you hit the john.

HOW *to* AVOID CRIME *and* KEEP SAFE *in* PUBLIC PLACES

OKAY, LET'S FACE IT. NEW YORK IS NOT THE SORT OF PLACE where you can leave your door open. But you don't need a false bottom on your boot heel for your credit cards, either. All you need is a little common sense.

For many years, New York's "mean streets" were the national symbol of America's crime problem. Statistics were big; headlines were bigger. TV police shows and legal procedurals, series after series of precinct crime novels, and big-name movies played on that reputation. It wasn't organized crime that began to worry out-of-towners (although it did produce even more famous movie characters), or professional burglars, or con men; it was the independent and unpredictable punk, the street hood, the drug addict who might corner you on the subway or go "wilding" with his friends like the kids who gang-raped, beat, and left comatose a runner in Central Park.

But all of a sudden, in the last few years, the word *crime* is back on New Yorkers' lips—and they're smiling. Although analysts and politicians argue over who gets the credit, it is clear that crime has been sharply reduced in recent years. Homicide is at its lowest rate in three decades. Subway crime has been curtailed to an amazing degree: Robberies on the system, the threat of which formerly made late-night or solo travel worrisome, are down fully 80% since the beginning of the 1990s. (Intriguingly, transit police have demonstrated that one out of every six fare-evaders is either carrying a weapon or already has an outstanding warrant against him, so try to spot someone with a MetroCard and stick close.) And in one of those strange psychological victories, the renovation of many subway stations is improving users' attitudes toward the system; littering is down, on-board soliciting has nearly disappeared (except for the occasional itinerant musician or candy-seller), and the level of civility, as the president would say, has greatly increased.

One of the most obvious changes is around Times Square, once the byword for X-rated urban sleaze and now the site of a frenetic rebuilding and restoration movement. Crime is no longer much of an issue in the area, although the crowding and milling about does make some pickpocketing possible.

Similarly, many of the neighborhoods that were once a little questionable after dark, especially in the southern part of Manhattan around Tribeca or Chelsea, are now busy with restaurants and young urban dwellers. Perhaps you still don't want to hang around the northern stretch of Central Park at night, and it never hurts to carry Mace or pepper spray and a strong whistle; but a reasonable amount of street smarts should keep you in good health.

Most of Manhattan is pretty safe during the day, but after dark you should stick to the more populated streets. Don't leave a lot of money or traveler's checks in your hotel room, even though the employees are probably dependable. And if you buy any valuables of the sort that can be easily pawned, such as silver, gems, or electronics, ask the hotel to lock them in the safe.

unofficial **TIP**
Do not, repeat, *do not* carry your wallet and valuables in a fanny pack. Thieves can easily snip the belt and disappear into the crowd before you realize what's happened. Front pockets are safer than back pockets or suitcoat pockets, though with a little effort, pickpockets can get at front pockets, too. The safest place to carry valuables is under your arm in a shoulder-holster-style pouch.

RIPOFFS AND SCAMS

A LIVELY STREET SCENE IS A VERITABLE INCUBATOR for ripoffs and scams. Although pickpockets, scam artists, and tricksters work throughout Manhattan, they are particularly thick in the bus and train terminals, along Broadway and Seventh Avenue near Times Square, and along 42nd Street between Grand Central Station and the Port Authority Terminal. Although some of the scams are relatively harmless, others can be costly as well as dangerous.

PART FIVE

GETTING AROUND

TAXIS

WHEN IT COMES TO TAXICABS, MANHATTAN IS THE LAND of plenty, a revelation for tourists from towns where you have to reserve one in advance. The main thoroughfares sometimes look like rivers of yellow, with four and five lanes of cabs whipping along. The New York City Taxi and Limousine Commission licenses and regulates the yellow "medallioned" taxis ("medallioned" refers to the illuminated light on top of the cab), and there are currently more than 12,000 Yellow Cabs alone. These taxis must be hailed on the street—in other words, you cannot call them on the phone to pick you up.

There is little trick to hailing one: First make sure you're not on a one-way street trying to wave somebody down on the wrong side. (This happens more often than you'd think.) Then stand at the edge of the curb—try not to walk out into traffic unless you're blocked by parked vehicles, and even then be very careful—and raise your arm high. You don't need to wave it about frantically unless you're in an emergency: Cabbies have a sort of radar. If you feel a little awkward at first pay a visit to the corner of Park Avenue and 49th Street; there you will find a J. Seward Johnson bronze of a very harried salaryman semaphoring for a cab in a sort of urban despair. It's rude to cut off someone who's already signaling by getting downstream (though it happens); however, you may approach a cab that's letting someone else out and wait by the open door.

To avoid unnecessary frustration, realize that in New York, unlike some other cities, passengers are guaranteed a private ride. That is, the cabbie cannot just veer over and see if you happen to be going in the same direction the first passenger is, and then pop you in the front seat. So don't swear at cabs with shadowy figures in the back. Of course, if there are several in your party who get in together, you can drop off some riders before others. Also note that the cab is not on duty unless

unofficial **TIP**
If you are not encumbered by luggage and the like, you can save yourself some time and money by walking to the closest one-way street heading in your direction and hailing a cab there. In a similar vein, if you find yourself gridlocked in a cab within a block or two of your destination, go ahead and pay your fare and proceed on foot.

the little light in the middle of the rooftop sign—the "medallion" that proves the cab is legit—is lit: If the yellow one in the middle that reads "off duty" is lit, he or she is headed home.

If you're staying at one of the nicer hotels, there is likely to be a doorman available to whistle a cab up for you. This also allows for a bit of cheating if you are a little timid or loaded down. You can walk into the hotel lobby from one entrance and pass through to the other side and, looking as though you just left your room, ask the doorman there to hail you one.

Many New York cabbies speak only marginal English. You can expect them to be familiar with major hotels, train and bus terminals, and major attractions. For more obscure destinations or addresses, you will do yourself (and the cabbie) a favor by writing down the exact address where you want to go.

Once inside the cab, you should make sure the driver's license with photograph and name are clearly displayed on the passenger side visor. This is required for your protection in case of disagreement (for complaints, contact the Taxi and Limousine Commission by simply dialing ☎ 311). It doesn't hurt to notice the number, either, in case you leave something behind; perhaps then you can get the dispatcher to send the cab to your hotel.

In our experience, New York cabbies usually take the most direct route to any given destination. Sometimes there is a little fudging, as when a driver circles an entire block to deliver you to a corner address on a one-way street, but in the main you can count on cabbies to keep it short and simple. If you prefer, you can specify the route you want your driver to take, and sometimes on longer fares the cabbie will actually ask if you have a preference. Still, many New York first-timers are a bit paranoid about cabbies taking them for a ride. In particular, LaGuardia Airport to Midtown via the Triborough Bridge arouses suspicions, though it is a perfectly acceptable route.

In addition to the medallion on the roof, a legitimate cab will have an automatic receipt machine mounted on the dashboard so that you can get an immediate record. (Fares begin at $2.50, and the meter ticks over $0.40 for each fifth of a mile, or $0.20 per minute of standing time; there's a dark-hours surcharge of $0.50, and passengers are responsible for tolls.)

If you are making two stops—as when you are picking someone else up at one location and proceeding somewhere else—you need to tell the cabbie this. After you get in the cab, simply say, "Two stops," and provide your destinations in order. This lets the cabbie know not to turn off the meter when you reach the first destination.

Don't be surprised if your cabbie drives fast and aggressively. More often than not, you will feel like an extra in a movie chase scene as you careen through the concrete canyons, weaving in and out of traffic. The good news is that these guys are excellent drivers. The other good news is that cabs now have seat belts in the back.

Although cabs range throughout Manhattan and the boroughs, they are most plentiful in Midtown. If you find yourself below Canal Street after business hours or on a weekend, for example, finding an empty yellow medallioned taxi cruising down the street may be a challenge. Your alternative is to phone one of the many companies listed under "Taxicab Service" in the yellow pages. Although these companies are also licensed by the Taxi and Limousine Commission, their cars will probably not be yellow or have a medallion. Some companies dispatch cars on demand 24 hours a day, seven days a week, but others require advance arrangements. Fares, as you would expect, are generally higher than those of metered, yellow, medallioned cabs. Late at night, in bad weather, and/or in isolated areas, however, phoning for a taxi is a safer and less stressful option than trusting to luck on the street. For the lowest fares ask your concierge, hotel desk clerk, or restaurant maitre d' for a recommendation before hauling out the yellow pages. When you call, tell the dispatcher where you want the car to pick you up and where you are going, and ask to be quoted a fare. Almost all of the car-on-demand companies accept credit cards. As always, tips and tolls are extra.

Now, as to illicit taxis. New York has a lot of limousines and luxury cars because of all its executives and celebrities. Consequently, it also has a lot of chauffeurs with time on their hands. So frequently, when you are standing on the street trying to hail a cab—and this is particularly true if you are a woman or if it is clearly theater-rush or dinner time and you look a little harried—a nice-looking sedan or town car may pull over and the driver offer to take you to your destination. These are sometimes referred to as gypsy cabs; although few of them pose a threat in the sense that they are unlikely to kidnap you, they will almost certainly want to charge you a very hefty fee. If it's raining or snowing or you're really late, or you really want to make an entrance, you might want to take him up on it. Just be prepared to pay the fee—and realize that you won't have any legal complaint if you're ripped off.

THE SUBWAY

ONE OF THE FIRST THINGS THAT YOU NOTICE about New York is the snarled traffic. But underground, far removed from the cursing, horn blowing, and bumper-to-bumper slog of the mean streets, is a fast, efficient subway system 250 miles in toto and carrying 3.5 million passengers 24 hours every day. Learn a little about how it operates and you will be able to get around New York quickly and affordably. The key to the city is just beneath the sidewalk, and it will set you free. For an online introduction visit **www.nycsubway.org** or **www.mta.nyc.ny.us.**

The Subway vs. Cabs

We recommend cabs whenever you are encumbered by luggage, multiple shopping bags, or anything large you must haul around. Cabs are also preferred for getting around in the evening after rush-hour traffic has abated and after 11 p.m. or so for safety reasons. If there are two or more in your party and you are heading to different destinations, sharing a cab makes more sense than taking the subway. Another good time to take a cab, provided you can find one, is when it's raining or snowing.

From 6:30 a.m. until about 8 p.m. on weekdays, New York streets and avenues are insanely congested. This is the time that the subway really shines. While cabs are stuck for three changes of the same traffic signal trying to crawl through a single intersection, the subways are zipping efficiently along. Plus, the subway is much less expensive.

Will the subway save you time? Maybe; it depends. With the subway, you must walk to the closest station, wait for the train, ride to your destination station, and then walk to wherever you're going. If you are traveling a relatively long distance, say 35 blocks or more, during business hours on a weekday, the subway will beat the cab about 60% of the time. If you are traveling a shorter distance, or if you must transfer on the subway to reach your destination, the cab will probably be faster. On weekends, when the streets are less congested and when trains run less frequently, the primary rationale for using the subway is to save money.

unofficial **TIP**
The subways do not run particularly close to the far east or the far west sides of the island. Thus, subway travel to such destinations as the Javits Center, the Passenger Ship Terminal, or the United Nations is not recommended.

This latter, saving money, is no small potatoes. With fare and tip, the shortest cab ride will cost you about $5, compared to $2 on the subway. When we work in New York, we almost always use the subway, allowing enough time between meetings to walk to and from the stations and to wait for the train.

Subway Basics

The New York subway system is one of the world's largest; almost 700 miles of track connect the four boroughs of Manhattan, the Bronx, Brooklyn, and Queens. There are close to 500 stations, so you are likely to find one near where you want to go.

The nexus of the system is the complex of stations and routes below Central Park extending to the southern tip of Manhattan Island. Though service to other areas of Manhattan and the outlying boroughs is more than adequate, this Midtown and Downtown ganglion

of routes, connections, and stops provides the most frequent and flexible level of service that you are likely to find in any American city.

Safety

Once the butt of talk-show jokes, the New York subway system is
now clean, scoured of (most) graffiti, and well policed. While not
quite as secure as Disneyland, subway travel does not represent much
of a risk. Muggings and violent crime are extremely rare these days,
though riders on crowded trains and in crowded stations should continue to be alert for pickpockets.

In recent years, many stations have been renovated to include
various kinds of artwork—murals, paintings, even mosaics—
reflecting neighborhood attractions. The station at 81st Street near
the Museum of Natural History has mosaics of reptiles, birds,
butterflies, sharks, scorpions, and the like. In the Times Square
station are murals by Jacob Lawrence and Jack
Beal. Houston Street station shows a man
sitting on a bench reading a newspaper while a
whale kibbitzes over his shoulder. Alice—she of
the "Adventures Underground"—and her Mad
company are in evidence at 50th Street. Coffee
cups and poetry come together beneath
Bloomingdales, and 100 eyes, like Argus's, peer
out at Chambers Street travelers.

From 6 a.m. until 11 p.m. or so, you can ride
the subway with no more concern for your personal safety than you feel on the streets during
business hours. After 11 p.m. it's wise to use the
special "Off-Hours Waiting Areas" that are
monitored by subway security. When the train arrives, we suggest that
you ride in the same car as the train's conductor (usually one of the
middle cars).

unofficial **TIP**
Any time of day, if you
are carrying packages, a
briefcase, or luggage, sit
as far from the doors as
possible. A favorite ploy
of thieves is to grab the
purse or package of a
person sitting near a
door and escape onto the
platform just as the doors
are closing.

Finding the Subway

An indispensable aid to locating stations and understanding the subway system is the "New York
City Transit Subway Map." The map shows all
routes and stations and offers helpful information
about fares and frequency of service, among other
things. Once you know the address of your New
York hotel, you can use the subway map to plan
your travel around town. You can arrange to have
a map mailed to you at home by calling Subway
Travel Information at ☎ 718-330-1234 (open 24 hours), or you can begin to familiarize yourself with the routes by logging onto
www.mta.nyc.ny.us. If you forget to request a map before traveling to
New York, you can usually pick one up at the airports, Penn Station,

unofficial **TIP**
The NYNEX Manhattan
Yellow Pages book
includes complete color
maps of both the subway
system and Manhattan
bus routes; you'll find
them at the beginning of
the book.

Grand Central Station, or the Port Authority Terminal. Some hotel front desks and concierges also stock a supply of maps.

If you are on the streets of Manhattan without a subway map, look for the lighted globes (about the size of bowling balls) that mark most subway entrances. A green globe means the subway entrance is open and staffed 24 hours a day. A red (or red and white) globe indicates that the entrance is open only during hours posted above the station. Some of the larger subway entrances are accessed through buildings. The majority of these have good street signage, although a few do not. Along similar lines, you may exit the subway at a station where the exits lead into a building, as opposed to directly back on the street. If this happens, simply exit the building and from there proceed to the nearest street corner to regain your orientation.

In Midtown and Downtown where various lines converge, there may be several stations located close together. The subway map will help you sort the stations out. If you don't have a map, descend into the closest station and check the system map displayed on the wall.

Reading the Subway Map

Each subway line is shown in a different color. Though some lines diverge into separate routes above Central Park in Manhattan and in the boroughs, they bear the color of the trunk (main) line. Each of the diverging routes is designated by a letter or number displayed in a circle or diamond of the same color. Terminals (ends of the line) are indicated by squares for normal service routes and diamonds for rush-hours-only routes.

The Lexington Avenue line, for example, is represented in green. Four routes—the 4-Circle, 5-Diamond, 5-Circle, and 6-Circle—originate in the Bronx and are likewise depicted in green. The routes converge in Manhattan, where all four follow Lexington Avenue (from which the line takes its name). The end of the line for 6-Circle is City Hall, and the end for 5-Circle is Bowling Green, both in the Downtown tip of the island. 4-Circle and 5-Diamond cross out of Manhattan and head east into Brooklyn. 4-Circle terminates at Utica Avenue, and 5-Diamond ends at Flatbush Avenue. In this example we followed the routes south (downtown) from the Bronx. If we boarded the 5-Diamond subway at Flatbush Avenue and headed north (uptown), we would converge with the other green lines in lower Manhattan, follow Lexington Avenue north, and diverge at 138th Street to cross into the Bronx. If we stayed on to the end of the line, we would wind up at 241st Street in the Bronx.

Each station's name is shown in bold type. Station names are usually streets or avenues—for example, the Houston Street Station on the Red Line is shown on the map as **Houston St.** Some stations, however, have place names, such as **Penn Station** or **Times Square.**

Stations are represented on the map by:

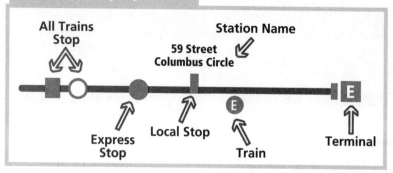

Underneath the station name, the map shows which routes stop at that particular station. If the station is wheelchair accessible, the visual wheelchair graphic will be printed alongside the station name.

The 23rd Street Station on the Eighth Avenue (because the line follows Eighth Avenue) Blue Line looks like this on the map:

23 Street

C-E

This means that the C-Circle Train and the E-Circle Train both stop at this station. The A-Circle Train, which also runs on the Blue Line, does not stop here. If it did, the station would look like this:

23 Street

A-C-E

You might see a station where some of the routes are not depicted in bold, such as:

72 Street

1-2-3-9

This means that the 1-Circle, 2-Circle, and 3-Circle trains offer regular service but that the 9-Circle train only provides part-time service, in this case during rush hours Monday through Friday (you need the subway route chart for this last piece of information).

Where certain lines meet or come close to meeting, you will see little symbols that look like this:

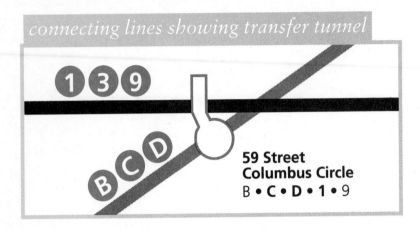

connecting lines showing transfer tunnel

**59 Street
Columbus Circle**
B • **C** • **D** • **1** • 9

This means that there is a pedestrian walkway or tunnel that connects two or more stations, thus allowing riders to transfer to other lines without exiting and reentering the subway system.

Fares

It costs $2 to ride the subway. (There is no charge for children under 44 inches in height.) Tokens are no longer accepted; you must buy a MetroCard. A MetroCard looks like a credit card. Available at subway stations and at over 2,000 neighborhood stores, the MetroCard can be purchased in any amount from $2 (a single ride) to $80. Each time you ride the subway you swipe your card—back to front, with the stripe facing you—through a little electronic reader on the right side of the turnstile. The electronic reader reads the amount of credit you have on the card and deducts $2 for every ride. When you use your card, your balance is displayed on the turnstile. All the accounting is maintained electronically, so there's no way to tell the fare credit remaining by looking at the card. If you want to check your balance, there are "reader" machines at most stations that will show the card's current balance without deducting anything. It is not necessary to get a new card when your balance gets low: All you have to do is take the card to a fare booth or to one of the automated machines inside the station and pay to have your balance increased. MetroCards expire after one

unofficial **TIP**
When you buy a card or pay to increase your balance, always run your card through the reader (before you leave the fare window) to make sure your purchase was properly recorded.

year, but any amount remaining on the card can be transferred to a new card. For additional information on the MetroCard, call ☎ 212-METROCARD.

It's more economical to get at least $10 on your MetroCard at a time; each five rides come with a free bonus sixth. An even better bargain is the one-day, unlimited-ride MetroCard, which costs $7 (so after only four rides in a day you're already ahead); and which is good until 3 a.m. the morning after it's activated, so you can really see the town. Seven-day, unlimited-ride MetroCards cost $24, and if you're in town for the long haul, 30-day cards cost $76. In addition to being available anywhere regular MetroCards are sold, you can also buy these prepackaged cards at Hudson News and many drugstores.

unofficial TIP
Unlimited-ride Metro-Cards are bargains, as they can be used for the buses all day as well as the subway.

Admittedly, we are not great fans of New York City buses, but you should know that with MetroCard you can transfer free from subway to bus, bus to subway, or bus to bus. You must use your MetroCard to start your trip and must make your transfer within two hours. Transfers from subway to subway are also free, with or without the MetroCard, as long as you do not exit the system.

Finally, be aware that the card was designed for New Yorkers, who, of course, are always in a hurry. In practical terms, this means you have to swipe your card fast! If you ease it through the turnstile device at a more leisurely tempo, it won't work. When in Rome . . .

Riding the Subway: A Primer

Looking at your subway map (or at one of the large poster-sized subway maps on display in the stations), try to locate the stations closest to your starting point and to your destination. If the station closest to your starting point does not offer service in the general direction you'll be going, check to see whether there are any other stations reasonably close by that do. Try to find a subway route that requires no transfers. It is generally faster to get within a few blocks of your destination on the subway and then cover the remaining distance on foot than it is to make a transfer. As a rule of thumb, it takes less than two minutes to walk the short blocks between streets. Walking crosstown, you can cover the long blocks between avenues in four to five minutes each.

Check to see which trains stop at stations you have identified. In general, the more trains, the better. Make sure that trains that stop at your departure station also stop at your destination station.

Almost all trains except the 7-Circle Flushing Local and the L-Circle 14th Street Canarsie Local (crosstown trains) travel generally north–south, or, in subway-speak, uptown (north) and downtown (south). Traveling on the subway is immensely simplified if you can determine whether you are traveling uptown or downtown.

If you want to go crosstown (east or west), you may need to know where the train terminates. Let's say you want to go from the west side to the east side on the E-Circle train. The signs for this train will not say "crosstown"; they will say "Jamaica/Queens," indicating the train's final destination. If you know (or learn by looking at the subway map) that this train travels crosstown en route to the borough of Queens, you will know to board in the direction of "Jamaica/Queens" to reach your crosstown destination. Incidentally, most trains that run crosstown also run part of their route north–south. Thus, signs for the E-Circle train may read "Uptown–Jamaica/Queens" or "Downtown–World Trade Center."

When you approach the station, there may be one or multiple entrances. If there is only one entrance, proceed inside and follow the signs directing you to the Uptown or Downtown train platforms, whichever applies. If you are standing at a street intersection and there is a subway entrance on all four corners, or on both sides of an avenue, the entrance(s) on the west side of the avenue will lead to Downtown platforms, and the entrance(s) on the east side of the street will lead to Uptown platforms. Normally there is good signage at the entrances identifying the line, trains (routes), and direction that the particular entrance serves. Usually, because you do not have to swipe your MetroCard until you are within spitting distance of the platform, you can verify that you have chosen the correct entrance by checking the signage on the platform. If you want to travel uptown and you descend to a platform that reads "Downtown," do not pass through the turnstiles. Instead, return to the street, cross the avenue, and descend to the Uptown platform.

unofficial **TIP**
If you start your trip at a station served by several lines, locate the system map near the entrance and determine which line you need and which direction you want to go. Armed with this knowledge, follow the signs to the correct platform.

Though most stations are served by only one line, there are a number of stations, particularly in Midtown and Downtown, that are served by several lines. What you have here, essentially, is a sort of double- or even triple-decker station. With these stations it's a little more complicated than understanding uptown versus downtown. At these multiline stations you may have a choice of lines going uptown and downtown as well as, possibly, some crosstown lines.

Be aware that in the larger stations you may have to pay and go through the turnstiles before you get anywhere near the train platforms. Don't worry. The inside signage is good, and there are interior passages that will allow you to correct your mistake if you end up on the wrong platform.

Once on the platform, double-check the signs, and if necessary recheck the system map. The platform sign will show the trains that stop at that platform, indicate their direction (usually uptown or downtown), and specify the terminal (end of the line) for each route.

Sometimes a single waiting platform will serve two tracks. Trains arriving on one side of the platform will go in one direction, and trains on the other side will go in the opposite direction. If you descended a long way or had to navigate a spiraling stairwell, you may arrive on the platform somewhat disoriented. Check the signage to determine the correct direction for your travel. If the signs don't help, simply ask another waiting passenger.

If there are several trains that stop at both your departure and destination stations, you can take your choice. If you are going a relatively short distance (30 blocks or less), go ahead and hop on the first train that comes along. If it's a "local," it will make a lot of stops, but you will still probably arrive sooner than if you waited for an express.

unofficial **TIP**
If you are going a long way, you may want to hold out for an express train.

When the train comes into the station, it will be well marked. The A-Circle train on the Eighth Avenue Blue Line, for example, will sport big blue circles with the letter A inside. The conductor usually rides in the middle of the train and will usually stick his head out of the window when the train stops. If you are really confused, ask him if the train goes to your destination station.

You've probably seen film footage of people crowding on and battling off subways. Although this does sometimes occur at the height of rush hour in the larger stations, usually things are much more civil. When the train stops, approach the door and wait for it to open. Allow passengers getting off to disembark, then step into the car. The conductor observes the loading process, so unless you're trying to leap on or off at the last second (not recommended), you shouldn't have to worry about getting caught in a closing door.

unofficial **TIP**
If you have mistakenly boarded the right train in the wrong direction, wait until the train stops at one of the larger stations where transfers are optional. These larger stations have internal passages that will allow you to cross over to the right platform without leaving the system and having to pay again to reenter.

Once inside, take a seat if there is one available. If you are still a little confused, you will find a system map displayed on the wall of the car. Check the next scheduled stop for the direction you wish to travel. When the train pulls in, verify by the signs on the platform that you are traveling in the right direction.

BUSES

IN ADDITION TO BEING SUBJECT TO ALL THE PROBLEMS that afflict Manhattan surface traffic, buses are slow, make innumerable stops, and have difficulty maneuvering. Even so, there are several good reasons to use public bus service. After 11 p.m. buses are safer than walking if you are not up to springing for a cab. Though subways excel in north–south, uptown–downtown service, there is less crosstown (east–west) subway service than one would hope (especially since no subways cross beneath Central Park). Buses fill this public transportation gap, running a goodly number of crosstown routes. You can get a vague idea of the bus's destination by noticing the initial that precedes the route number: "M" for Manhattan, "Q" for Queens, "B" for Brooklyn, and "Bx" for the Bronx. That's "up," remember? Finally, of course, buses are inexpensive to ride, especially with the MetroCard, which allows bus-to-bus, bus-to-subway, and subway-to-bus transfers. Maps of Manhattan bus routes can be found in the front of the NYNEX Manhattan Yellow Pages book. MTA buses cost $2 and require either exact change or a MetroCard. For more information, check out **www.mta.nyc.ny.us.**

WALKING

NEW YORK IS A GREAT TOWN FOR WALKING. Like most cities, it has neighborhoods that are not ideally suited for an evening stroll, but these are easily avoided. If you observe a few precautions and exercise some common sense, you will find the sidewalks of New York not only interesting and exhilarating but also quite hospitable.

As you begin to explore, you will find that the blocks between the east/west streets are quite short. Thus, walking south (toward Downtown) on Seventh Avenue, most folks will be able to cover the blocks from 59th Street to 49th Street in about 12 minutes, even assuming a wait for traffic at several intersections. Crossing town from east to west (or vice versa), the blocks are much longer. A walk from First Avenue to Tenth Avenue along 42nd Street is a real hike, requiring more than 30 minutes for most people.

If you want to try a restaurant eight blocks away, and the address is north or south of where you are, you won't even need a cab. If the restaurant is eight blocks away across town (east–west), take a subway or hail a taxi.

If you become disoriented during a walk, proceed to the nearest street corner and see what the street is (as opposed to an avenue). Then walk one additional short block in either direction. If the next cross street is higher in number, you are heading north (uptown). East will be to your right, and west to your left. If the next cross street is lower in number, then you are walking south. East will be to your left, and west to your right.

Let's say, for example, that you just emerged from a subway station on the Avenue of the Americas (also called Sixth Avenue) and are not sure which way's which. Walking to the nearest corner, you discover that you are at the intersection of 24th Street and the Avenue of the Americas. You continue one more block on Avenue of the Americas and reach 23rd Street. You now know that you are going south and that First through Fifth avenues are to your left (east) and that Seventh through Eleventh avenues are to your right (west).

Or you can go by the traffic: Fifth, Park, and Lexington avenues are one-way streets going south; Park, Madison, and Third go north. Seventh and Broadway go south; Eighth goes north until it becomes Central Park West, when it is two-way (but of course, you can see the park from there anyway), and so on.

Because there is no better or more direct way to experience New York than to explore it on foot, we recommend that you do as much hoofing as your time and stamina permit. To help you organize your walking, we include several walking tours (guided and self-guided) in Part Seven, Sightseeing, Tours, and Attractions.

PART SIX

NEW YORK'S NEIGHBORHOODS

THE SIDEWALKS *of* NEW YORK

NOW THAT YOU'VE DECIDED WHICH PARTS OF THE CITY you're most interested in seeing, it's time to hit the road. Actually, you can use the following neighborhood descriptions as armchair tours, and if you don't have time to see more than a little of the city this time, you might enjoy reading about the rest to see how all the pieces fit together.

The profiles in this chapter are designed to convey a little of the geographical layout, historical relevance, tourist attractions, chronological development, and general character of the neighborhoods—they're overviews to help you grasp the spirit of the area. We have included some phone numbers, but not all. Most of the buildings mentioned here are public structures, important for their exteriors; if they have particularly stunning lobbies, they will probably be open to the public during general office hours. Similarly, most churches welcome visitors, but a few smaller or older churches (or those with valuable antiques) may ask that you make an appointment to visit. In any case, apply common sense and courtesy; be quiet for the sake of those using the premises for its original purposes, and try not to interrupt religious services.

Some museums or collections may charge admission or ask for donations. Most will be closed on major holidays. (Remember, too, that Jewish museums and houses will probably be closed at least half a day Friday and all day Saturday.) A few of the most important historical buildings, museums, and landmarks in each neighborhood are described in detail in Part Seven, Sightseeing, Tours, and Attractions.

LOWER MANHATTAN, WALL STREET, AND THE BATTERY

 ALWAYS A MAJOR TOURIST AREA BECAUSE OF THE **Statue of Liberty,** lower Manhattan has become an even more emotionally powerful destination since the World Trade Centers

manhattan neighborhoods

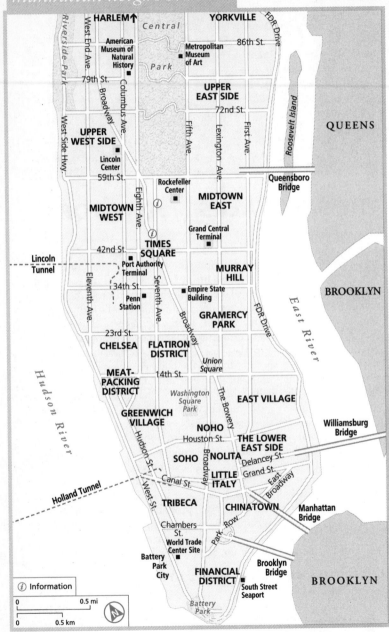

were blasted off the skyline by the hijacked jetliners. And that is entirely appropriate, as New York's historical and spiritual footprint is at the tip of the island. The area below Chambers Street is the original New York—Nieuw Amsterdam, the port "bought" from the natives, and the village occupied by the British for virtually the entire Revolutionary War. The colonial administrators lived in the mansion on **Governors Island** out in the harbor; **Castle Clinton** (☎ 212-344-7220) on the west side of the Battery, which was then 300 feet offshore, raised 28 cannon against the threat of invaders in 1811 (and a few years later became an entertainment venue). A recently uncovered wall, unearthed during subway construction at the South Ferry stop, is at least 260 years old, and may even be from around 1700—part of the original Battery. The Declaration of Independence was read aloud on the **Bowling Green** on July 9, 1776; the crowd then pulled down the statue of King George III that had stood there for almost half a century and melted it down into ammunition. George Washington prayed here, in the simplicity of **St. Paul's Chapel** on Broadway (profiled in depth in Part Seven); he bade farewell to his officers here, on the site of the **Fraunces Tavern Museum** at Pearl and Broad streets (☎ 212-425-1778); he was sworn in as the first president here as well, on the site of what is now the Greek Revival **Federal Hall National Memorial** at 26 Wall Street (☎ 212-825-6888), probably just as the bronze statue on the steps there suggests.

The other thing to remember, though, is just how very small that original city was, not nearly so large even as this one area. Nearly a third of it—including the entire **Battery Park** area and the eastern strip from Pearl Street to the East River, including the Franklin Roosevelt Drive and South Street Seaport areas—was actually constructed from landfill after the War of 1812. **Wall Street,** literally a wooden wall built in 1653, was the northern border of Nieuw Amsterdam. Even in colonial times the town (population 20,000) was only ten blocks square, counting the Bowling Green—which in those days really was one. Although it won't quite adjoin the original "green," the proposed **National Sports Museum,** in the landmark Standard Oil building at 26 Broadway, will be very near.

It wasn't until the early decades of the 19th century that the lawyers and stockbrokers had so taken hold of what is now known as the Financial District that residences began to be built farther north. In fact, when **City Hall** was constructed in 1811, a little more than half a mile up Broadway, it was considered so far out of town that the north face was covered in brownstone instead of marble because city officials never expected anyone to view it from that side. (For more on Battery Park, see "Other Green Corners of the City" at the end of this chapter.)

Nowadays, Lower Manhattan is one of the most fascinating areas of the city, still the financial capital of the nation—the **Federal Reserve Bank** (☎ 212-720-6130) on Liberty Street, the **New York Stock Exchange**

(☎ 212-656-5165) at Broad and Wall streets, the **American Stock Exchange** on Trinity Place (☎ 212-306-1000), and the **Mercantile Exchange** (1 North End Avenue; ☎ 212-299-2000)—and, for so relatively young a city, very nearly the financial capital of the world. The various bank buildings along Wall Street and around the Exchange are New York's version of the Forum in Rome, veritable temples of finance.

If you're of a bearish temperament, the **Museum of American Financial History** (28 Broadway; ☎ 212-908-4110), a one-room office formerly occupied by Alexander Hamilton, later secretary of the Treasury, exhibits various bits of Wall Street exotica, including the only remaining bit of ticker tape from the infamous "Black Tuesday" crash of 1929. If, on the other hand, you prefer your assets in a more tangible form, you can tour the vaults of gold and museum exhibits at the **Federal Reserve Bank,** but you'll have to reserve at least two weeks in advance.

From City Hall Park and the courthouse complex at the "north pole" of the neighborhood to Battery Park on the south, the **South Street Seaport** (☎ 212-748-8600) on the east, and the glorious **Trinity Church** (☎ 212-602-0872) going eye-to-eye with Wall Street—God and mammon in daily competition—it covers far and away the greatest range of New York history of any single region. (Many of these attractions are profiled in detail in Part Seven.) From here the soaring **Brooklyn Bridge** joins Manhattan to one sibling borough; the **Staten Island Ferry** to a second; and Broadway, which runs all the way from Bowling Green to the Bronx, to a third. The gloriously Gothic **Woolworth Building** at 233 Broadway may no longer seem so huge—although until the construction of the Chrysler Building in 1930, it stood for nearly 20 years as the unchallenged lord of the skyline—but its tiered crown, gargoyles, mosaics, and caricatures (including some of architect Cass Gilbert and nickle-and-dime tycoon F. W. Woolworth) make it a fitting tribute to New York's unabashed mercantile spirit.

The good thing about riding the **Staten Island Ferry** (☎ 718-390-5253) is that you can do it anytime, whenever your schedule is open for about an hour (or a little more, if you have to wait in line). You can choose to see Manhattan by dawn or sunset or even moonlight. It's a very cooling trip in summer and picturesque in the snow. And astonishingly, it's now free.

As befits the original Manhattan, the Battery contains memorials ranging through New York's history, from its first sighting (the **Verrazano Monument** in the southwest corner of Battery Park) to its military heroes (the **New York Korean War Veterans Memorial** and **Coast Guard** tribute, both on the Battery along with a tribute to the wireless operators lost at sea and the Marines, and the **Vietnam Veterans Plaza,** a simple glass-block fountain between Water and South streets). The **New York City Police Museum,** with its collection of badges and weapons dating to 1658 and its third-floor tribute to 9/11 heroics, has moved into the old First Precinct station on Old Slip Street (☎ 212-480-3100). One site even exposes 400 years of city life—the **New York Unearthed** permanent archeological exhibit at State and Water streets (☎ 212-748-8628).

unofficial **TIP**
While riding the Staten Island Ferry, once the thrill of the view of the Statue of Liberty and Lower Manhattan has paled, some children may be restless. There isn't anything else to do on board but wait for the other end, so you may want to bring small toys or snacks. Ferries leave every 20 to 30 minutes during the day, more like every 45 minutes at night.

This is also a good area to remember the melting pot of Manhattan history. The flagpole in **Peter Minuit Plaza,** a sort of corner of Battery Park near the ferry building, salutes the courage of New York's first Jewish immigrants, who had been caught up in the Portuguese-Dutch wars and were harried back and forth between Europe and Brazil, attacked by pirates, and finally carried to Nieuw Amsterdam, where they were allowed to settle in 1626. Another plaque salutes the 32 Belgian Huguenots who were turned away by the virulently anti-Catholic British in Virginia but allowed to land by the Dutch East India Company in 1724. The sculpture near Castle Clinton, with its eager arms and hopeful postures, is a tribute to the spirit of the millions of immigrants who landed here. (Before they were diverted to the Ellis Island complex, immigrants entered America through Castle Garden, an estimated 8 million of them between 1855 and 1890.)

The pair of circa-1800 townhouses at State and Water streets were the family home of, and are now a shrine to, **"Mother" Elizabeth Ann Seton** (☎ 212-269-6865), the first American-born saint of the Catholic Church; it was also, appropriately, a home for immigrant Irish women, sheltering as many as 170,000 after the Civil War. Just north of North Cove, at the foot of Vesey Street, is the **Irish Hunger Memorial,** dedicated in 2002. The little fieldstone cottage is a real one, brought over from Ireland and reconstructed on the site; and the garden includes more than 60 species of wildflowers and plants native to Ireland—along with, as a quiet reminder of the great famine, rows of potato vines. And the recently discovered **African Burial Ground** near Broadway and Chambers streets dates back at least to the 18th century and, archeologists say, quite likely to the 17th, a reminder that the labor of slaves, as well as so many others, built this city.

Another stop on this mini-tour of New York history is the battered "world sphere" sculpture rescued from the ruins of the

World Trade Center, that originally (ironically) represented global peace. The sculpture's temporary home here is also marked by an eternal flame.

Two less celebrated but entertaining sidelights are very near Ground Zero: the 1907 neo-Gothic building at 90 West Street, where a $140-million restoration has renewed the mansard roof and terra-cotta gargoyles; and the Verizon building at 140 West Street, where the restoration of the lobby also meant restoring the 1926 ceiling murals illustrating the history of human communications. The former was designed by architect Cass Gilbert, whose next project was the Woolworth Building.

Two museums remind us to remember the "forgotten peoples": the **National Museum of the American Indian** within the fine Beaux Arts **U.S. Custom House** (☎ 212-514-3700) at Broadway and Bowling Green; and the **Museum of Jewish Heritage—A Living Memorial to the Holocaust** in Battery Park City (☎ 212-968-1800). And it is from here, of course, that most visitors look to the **Statue of Liberty** (☎ 212-363-3200) and the **Ellis Island Museum of Immigration** (☎ 212-363-3200), perhaps the most lasting memorials to the American spirit anywhere. (All four attractions are profiled in depth in Part Seven.)

Also out in the harbor is the 172-acre **Governors Island,** site of the 1988 Reagan-Gorbachev meetings, which has recently been returned to New York's possession after having been sold to the federal government for $1 in 1800. Summertime tours are available from Ferry Slip 7, visit **www.governorsislandnationalmonument.org** for information.

The new **Skyscraper Museum,** at 39 Battery Place in Battery Park City (☎ 212-945-6324), offers a fascinating glimpse into the creation of New York and its famous "profile." It's a small, sleek, mirror-floored museum, easily viewed, but the models of the proposed Twin Towers memorials alone are worth a trip.

One of the best views, though not yet widely known, is from the newly renovated elevated plaza at **55 Water Street.** From 30 feet up, it looks out across the East River toward Brooklyn Heights and the Brooklyn Bridge, with a boardwalk, a series of terraces and overlooks, even a seven-tier amphitheater where the city will sponsor movies and entertainment. The 50-foot translucent glass "lantern" is in part a memorial as well: It stands where the Titanic Memorial Lighthouse, now at South Street Seaport, originally marked the Seamen's Church.

If you are interested in monumental views in architectural terms, be sure to walk up Broadway to **City Hall Park** and admire the elegant municipal buildings, including the French Renaissance **City Hall,** with its lobby murals, double-hanging staircase, and exhibits of official gifts to the city; **Surrogate's Court** at Chambers and Centre, inspired by the Paris Opéra and arrayed with a pageant of sculpture and a neo-Egyptian mosaic ceiling in the lobby that, like Grand Central's, reproduces the zodiac; and the nearby court buildings of the **Civic**

Center, especially the rotunda of 60 Centre Street, with its restored 1930s murals. Grab a snack from the park vendors while you're there. The statue of Benjamin Franklin at the south end of the park recalls a time when this stretch of Park Row was filled with newspaper presses, like London's Fleet Street.

SOHO AND TRIBECA

NOW THAT POPULAR MUSIC AND HIP-INDUSTRY logos have made odd capitalizations common, the names "Soho" and "Tribeca" don't stand out the way they used to. Both are purely physical descriptions, only in shorthand: Soho is SOuth of HOuston Street—it has nothing to do with the Soho of London—and Tribeca is an anagram for the TRIangle BElow CAnal, though it more closely resembles a slightly bottom-heavy diamond.

unofficial **TIP**
Note that Houston is pronounced *"house-*ton," not like the Texas city.

In some ways, Soho gave rise to Tribeca, in that as the former evolved from rundown warehouse neighborhood to chic loft space to ultra-chic shopping central, the trendy but less prosperous loft-dwellers, artists, and restaurateurs were pushed south.

Though it's now one of the two main art neighborhoods in the city, Soho was largely rural until well after the turn of the 19th century. Remnants of the old Canarsie–Manate Indian tribe continued to live here throughout the Dutch and early British colonial eras. In the 18th century, it was largely farmland (like much of Manhattan) and country estates of the more prosperous residents. It was gradually consumed by townhouses after the turn of the 19th century; there is a four-block area at the north-central corner, bordered by Sixth Avenue, West Houston, and Varick and Vandam streets, that is a historic district of its own; developed by John Jacob Astor in the late 1820s, it contains the city's largest concentration of Federal-style row houses.

But Soho came into its own in the mid-18th century, when the architectural movement sometimes called American Industrial—large, almost warehouse-sized spaces covered with pseudo-classical columns and cornices made of cast iron—swept in and transformed it into the light industrial and retail center of the city. It is still home to the largest concentration of cast-iron ornamentation in the city; and many of those oversized buildings have been transformed into art galleries, furniture display rooms, and even museums. The five cobblestone blocks of Greene Street from Canal to Houston are the centerpiece of the **Cast-Iron Historic District,** with more than 50 intact 19th-century buildings with façades in the neoclassical, Renaissance Revival, and Corinthian styles. The one at 72–76 Greene, a sort of duplex with a five-story Second Empire façade, is called the **"King of Greene Street."** The **"Queen of Greene,"** built by the same developer, Isaac Duckworth, is the mansard-roofed building at 28–30 Greene. (For more on this area, see "Great Neighborhoods for Shopping" in

Part Nine.) The **New York City Fire Museum** at 278 Spring Street
(☎ 212-691-1303) is the largest collection of antique firefighting
equipment, engines, pumps, bells, and hydrants in the country.

unofficial **TIP**
While you're in Tribeca, check out the 14-story clock tower at Leonard Street and Broadway; you can actually climb the stairs and look out through the giant works.

Like Soho, Tribeca is a treasure trove of
late–19th century commercial and industrial
architecture: The cast iron and marble buildings along White, Franklin and Walker streets
between Broadway and Church offer a quick
tour, and the **Carey Building** at 105 Chambers
Street is considered one of the finest examples
of cast iron anywhere. Another can be found at
85 Leonard Street, which was designed by cast-
iron innovator James Bogardus.

Tribeca is increasingly "hot," although it affects a kind of gritty
urban chic, and the shops are a little funkier still. It has been getting
a reputation (with good reason) as a restaurant and nightlife haven,
possibly because of the many old and family-owned food-import
businesses around. And thanks to the well-advertised presence of
actor Robert De Niro, part-owner of such hotspots as the **Tribeca Grill**
and **Nobu,** as well as restaurants from chefs David Bouley and David
Waltuck, Tribeca is developing a certain celebrity population.

CHINATOWN, LITTLE ITALY, AND THE LOWER EAST SIDE

TIME WAS WHEN THESE THREE ETHNIC NEIGHBORHOODS were
not just distinct, they were rigorously segregated. More recently, however, the outlines of the three have blurred and overlapped, and Little
Italy in particular is being subsumed as Chinese businesses spill north
of Canal Street and up alongside the long strip of **Sara Delano Roosevelt
Park.** Chinese immigrants have been one of the fastest-growing communities in the city for several decades, and an estimated 175,000 now
live in Chinatown alone. In addition, Chinatown is now far more
broadly Asian. The signs and sounds of Vietnamese, Thai, and Indonesian society are almost as common as Chinese. Hence, the entire
area is now frequently referred to simply as the Lower East Side.

At the same time, the eastward gradual expansion of Soho chic,
and even some neo-1960s-style hippie culture from the East Village to
the north, is turning parts of even **Orchard Street,** the heart of Lower
East Side bargain territory, into the latest bohemian and art-ware-
house hangout. Hence the latest "neighborhood" nicknames,
Nolita—North of Little Italy—and Noho, for the blocks north of
Houston and between the East and West (Greenwich) Villages.

The first Chinese residents arrived on Mott Street in the mid–19th
century, and Chinatown's history is as convoluted (or as romantic,
depending on your outlook) as any Manhattan neighborhood's,
dominated by family networks, community associations, and more

serious criminal gangs, but all operating in so closed a circle as to be nearly invisible to outsiders. It has little architectural style in comparison to, say, San Francisco's Grant Avenue area; but it is full of street vendors (most selling cheap knockoffs, but highly popular in themselves), produce and fish markets, restaurants, and import shops. More popular in recent years are the herbal apothecaries—herbal pharmacies with remedies dating back thousands of years.

The **Museum of Chinese in the Americas** at Mulberry and Bayard streets (☎ 212-619-4785) is small, but its collection of old photographs, business leases, and oral histories is first-class; you might also be able to piggyback onto one of the walking tours the museum sometimes arranges. The **Eastern States Buddhist Temple** on Mott near Canal houses more than 100 golden statues of the Enlightened One (☎ 212-966-6229), and Confucius stands in monumental contemplation in **Confucius Plaza** on the Bowery near Pell Street. Ironically, the nearby block of **Doyers Street,** which takes a sharp turn between the Bowery and Pell, is what was known as Chinatown's "Bloody Angle," back when the opium dealers lured rivals into ambush. Pell Street was also a center of Italian crime, apparently: A waiter and hopeful entertainer named Irving Berlin, who worked in a bar at 12 Pell Street, complained to his manager about the clientele and was promptly fired.

Columbus Park, a small green oasis south of Bayard Street more or less at the juncture of Little Italy and Chinatown, was once the heart of the Five Points slum, one of the city's largest gang havens and red-light districts. The jagged Art Moderne **Criminal Courts Building** nearby used to be the jail, the last one built before Riker's Island.

As indicated earlier, Little Italy is a shadow of its former self, except perhaps during the Feast of San Gennaro in the fall and when the old-timers gather to play bocce in Roosevelt Park. Its most famous address is **Mulberry Street.** (Its most infamous address is probably the Bowery, thanks to that street's role in the *Bowery Boys* serials.) Although they are now intermixed with Asian and Hispanic businesses, there are still blocks of delis and family restaurants stoop to stoop. **Old St. Patrick's Cathedral** at Mott and Prince (☎ 212-226-8075), begun in 1809, is still the parish church, although the big St. Patrick's uptown is now the archdiocesan seat.

Especially if you loved those old *Untouchables* shows, you must stop at **Ratner's** at Delancey and Norfolk (☎ 212-677-5588). The restaurant's back room, now the neo-cocktail Prohibition-swank **Lansky Lounge,** is where gangster Meyer Lansky used to have breakfast, sometimes with childhood pal Lucky Luciano; Bugsy Siegel made his first hit on the corner outside the door, and there's an alley entrance to the bar that rumor has it was the old speakeasy slip-in. And the sidewalk in front of **Umberto's Clam House** at Broome and Mulberry (☎ 212-431-7545) was the scene of "Crazy" Joey Gallo's last meal—and last breath—in 1973.

To give equal time to the "coppers," walk by the luxury apartment building at Grand and Centre streets, with its Baroque clock-tower dome, stone friezes, and guardian lions; it used to be the police head-quarters, and gazing up the front steps at the guard's desk, you can just imagine how impressive it must have been to be hauled up in front of the sergeant in the heyday of New York's Irish finest. And at Lafayette and Hester streets is the **Engine Co. No. 31,** an 1895 gem that looks more like a French country castle than a firehouse (it's now a community TV and film center).

The Lower East Side, generally on the south side of East Houston from the Bowery east, was not particularly desirable land in the early decades of New York development because it was largely wetlands. It had served as temporary quarters for a series of the poorest immi-grants, first Irish victims of the potato famine and then German farmers whose own potato crops were gradually infected, followed by periodic influxes of Turkish and Greek families.

It held on to the name Kleindeutschland, or Little Germany, for decades; it was the site of literally hundreds of burials in 1904, when the burning and then sinking of the paddlewheel steamboat *General Slocum,* carrying a load of mostly German immigrant women and children on a Sunday picnic excursion up the East River, killed an estimated 1,300—the city's deadliest disaster prior to 9/11.

However, the most famous and lasting immigration began in the late 19th century, when as many as 1.6 million Eastern European Jews arrived, creating the neighborhood famous from photographs of tenement houses, sidewalk carts, and orthodox scholars. It was both a slum and a cultural haven (not an unusual paradox for a peo-ple used to ghettos), filled with synagogues, debating clubs, and community banks as well as vendors and sweatshops. At its height, New York provided jobs for more than 5,000 kosher butchers and 1,000 ritual slaughterers. (For more on this area, see "Great Neigh-borhoods for Shopping" in Part Nine.)

In recent years, the Lower East Side has made a concerted effort to turn itself into a historical as well as retail tourist attraction. The irony is that many of the Jewish families have moved up-island to the wealthier areas on either side of the park and out to Brooklyn, and large numbers of Hispanic, black, and Asian families have replaced them. Nevertheless, the creation of the **Lower East Side Tenement Museum** on Orchard Street (profiled in depth in Part Seven, Sightsee-ing, Tours, and Attractions), in addition to the more organized promotion of the many family-owned clothing stores in that neigh-borhood (hearkening back to its merchant origins), has brought it a certain revived prosperity. The 1887 Moorish Revival **Eldridge Street Synagogue** on Eldridge at Bayard Street (☎ 212-219-0888), with its lavish stained glass, carved detailing, and chandeliers, is being restored to its full beauty; oral histories are welcome, and there is also a mini-museum of Jewish life in America in the building. **Schapiro's House of Kosher and Sacramental Wines** at 126 Rivington Street is the last winery still in operation in the city; you can tour it (by appointment) or purchase consecrated wine.

 Incidentally, this is a good area for bridge enthusiasts. Only about a mile separates three of New York's major interborough spans: the Brooklyn, Manhattan, and Williamsburg bridges. (Going from the Battery north, think BMW.) The **Brooklyn Bridge,** the oldest of the three, bears traffic away from near City Hall Park just south of Chinatown. The **Manhattan Bridge,** which has lost its allegorical sculptures to the Brooklyn Museum of Art but still has its triumphal arch, takes off from Canal Street, and the **Williamsburg Bridge** from Delancey Street.

GREENWICH VILLAGE

THIS IS PROBABLY THE MOST FAMOUS NEIGHBORHOOD in New York, known even to outsiders as "the Village" and symbol of the city's artistic and literary history. It had originally been covered with largish "country houses" belonging to the businessmen from downtown and smaller homes along the riverfront built by marine craftsmen and merchants before it was sold off and subdivided.

Herman Melville lived here as a child, working around the docks before shipping off with whalers, being shipwrecked, and thinking twice about his choice of career.

Because it was largely developed in the late 19th century before the grid system was put in place—the regular grid actually begins at 14th Street, the northern border of the Village—it has a number of diagonals, triangles, and bends that newcomers sometimes find confusing. The part of Greenwich Village east of Sixth Avenue more regularly ascribes to the numbered-street system, but on the west side, most streets have names rather than numbers, and even those few numbers don't behave very predictably: West 4th Street, for example, seems to move in the usual cross-island direction beneath Washington Square, but almost immediately begins making a series of elbow shifts north, and by the time it gets to the top of the Village, it's nearly gone perpendicular.

Think of the Village map as the left half of an opened fan: The area between Broadway and Sixth Avenue would be the fan's center, with the avenues as fairly upright spines. Seventh Avenue spreads out a little, and beyond that, the main avenues—Hudson Street, Washington Street, and West Street along the Hudson River—all bend a little farther out. (Greenwich Street squiggles a little, like a bent feather, between Washington and Hudson.) By the time the side streets are filled in, you have a series of trapezoids and triangles; it may be hard to negotiate at first, but it gives the area a true village atmosphere.

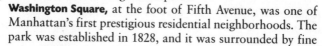 **Washington Square,** at the foot of Fifth Avenue, was one of Manhattan's first prestigious residential neighborhoods. The park was established in 1828, and it was surrounded by fine

Greek Revival townhouses; several of the oldest are still standing, as is the Stanford White–designed archway. Even the mayor's official residence was here, at No. 8 (the façade is real, but the rest is not). Brothers Henry and William James grew up in the neighborhood; Henry James's *Washington Square* was set at No. 18, where his grandmother lived. James himself, Edith Wharton, and William Dean Howells all lived at various times at No. 1; John Dos Passos was living at No. 3 when he wrote *Manhattan Transfer*. All of those structures have been razed. (The so-called **Hanging Elm** in the northwest corner, a last reminder of the public executions of the early 19th century, is still hanging in there, though.) Nowadays, the park is alive with New York University (NYU) students, aspiring musicians, chess players, dogs on playdates, kids on playground dates, and, on summer evenings, the legendary free Shakespeare performances of the Gorilla Repertory Company.

Patchin Place on West 10th Street just west of Sixth Avenue, a little cluster of rooming houses built in 1848, eventually housed such writers as e. e. cummings, Theodore Dreiser, and Djuna Barnes. The **Jefferson Market Public Library** on Sixth Avenue at West 10th Street, built in 1877, was modeled on one of Mad King Ludwig of Bavaria's castles, hiked up at one end with a clock tower and positively pockmarked with arched windows and pointed gables. It was actually a courthouse—and of all things, it was voted the country's fifth most beautiful building when it was completed.

As the money moved north, the Village became a more middle-class though still very desirable area, until the sprawling commercial development of the riverfront and the repeated waves of immigration threatened to pinch it between Hell's Kitchen (the area from Ninth Avenue west from the 30s to the 50s and once the territory of the Irish gang of the same name) and Little Italy. Townhouses were divided up into apartments, studio space became cheap, and the Village began to attract a second generation of writers and painters, either poorer or more naturally bohemian in outlook, among them Edna St. Vincent Millay, Walt Whitman, Mark Twain, Edgar Allan Poe, O. Henry, Louisa May Alcott, Albert Bierstadt, Gertrude Vanderbilt Whitney, Winslow Homer, and Edward Hopper.

The Village was also one of the first centers of theatrical experimentation (a tradition honored by the many street performers in Washington Square). The **Provincetown Playhouse** on MacDougal was Eugene O'Neill's first showcase, and the **Sullivan Street Playhouse** was home for more than 40 years and 16,000 performances of the quintessential off-Broadway hit *The Fantastics*. Dylan Thomas famously drank himself to death in the **White Horse Tavern** on Hudson at West 11th Street (☎ 212-243-9260), and the ghost of Aaron Burr is said to haunt the **One if by Land, Two if by Sea** restaurant at 17 Barrow Street, not because he was poisoned by anyone's cooking (except perhaps his wife—see mention of the Morris-Jumel House under Washington Heights) but because he lived in a house on that site.

Louisa May Alcott wrote *Little Women* while living at **130 Mac-Dougal.** Ruth McKenney, and her sister Eileen, whose exploits eventually inspired the musical *On the Town,* lived at **14 Gay Street.** O. Henry supposedly modeled the scene of "The Last Leaf" on the gate at **10 Grove Street.** Hart Crane lived at **45 Grove,** and there was a tavern called Marie's Crises at **59 Grove** where Thomas Paine reportedly drafted "Common Sense." James Fenimore Cooper lived at **45 Bleeker Street,** and both Willa Cather and Richard Wright occupied **82 Washington Place.** There was a gentlemen's club at **83 West Third** where Poe worked on "The Raven."

The third and fourth generations, beats and bohemians, moved in after World War II, followed by the flower children and finally the retro-radicals. The **New York University** campus sprawls around Washington Square, and the **New School for Social Research** and **Parsons School of Design** are also here. The earlier artists left their mark by way of the dozens of off-Broadway theaters and jazz clubs, the later by way of the **New York Studio School of Drawing, Painting, and Sculpture** (the original home of the Whitney Museum)

unofficial TIP
This is a great spot for just walking, because of the mix of 18th- and 19th-century architecture (look for cobblestones on the west side), the ethnic assortment, and the mingling of social classes.

and **Parsons,** which combines art design and philosophy. Most appropriate of all might be the presence of the **Malcolm Forbes Gallery** on Fifth Avenue at West 12th (profiled in depth in Part Seven, Sightseeing, Tours, and Attractions), the palace of playthings from the prince of capitalism.

The Village is a famous refuge for gay and lesbian residents, though in recent years many gays have moved north into Chelsea and left the Village to the women. The gay scene centers around **Christopher Street;** the **Stonewall Tavern,** site of the infamous 1969 police–gay standoff, has moved about a little, but is now at 53 Christopher. (Gay Street, as it happens, was named after a family.)

Even if you only have a few minutes, the tiny area around Bedford Street from Christopher to Commerce is especially worth seeing. At 102 Bedford is the house called **Twin Peaks,** which looks a little like a Tudor cottage with a Hessian helmet on it; the original 1830 cottage was "done up" by architect Clifford Reed Daily to put a little more fun into the artists' community. The mansard-topped twins at **39** and **41 Commerce Street** around the corner were supposedly built in 1831 by a sea captain for his spinster daughters, who did not speak to each other; the central garden apparently did not bring them closer together, either. On Grove Street just off Bedford is a row of Federal townhouses, and in between **Nos. 10** and **12 Grove** is an alley of mid–19th-century workingmen's cottages.

The brick-covered clapboard house at No. 77 Bedford, the **Isaacs-Hendricks House,** is the oldest in the Village, built in 1800. And the house next door, the 1873 building at **75½ Bedford Street,** was Edna St. Vincent Millay's last New York home and was later home to John Barrymore and Cary Grant; only 9.5 feet wide, it is the narrowest building in the city, built in what was once a passageway.

The very northwest corner of the Village, a sort of trapezoid inside Gansevoort, West 14th, Hudson, and Washington streets, has begun to shape its own identity as the Meatpacking District. Centered on the site of the late 19th-century landmark Gansvoort Market, it's suddenly chock-a-block with boutique hotels, designer shops and spas, and chic cafes so chic and so tiny it's hard to score a reservation. Even the venerable Balducci's market has moved here, into a 25,000-square-foot 1897 Beaux Arts bank building at West 14th and Eighth Avenue.

THE EAST VILLAGE

THE EAST VILLAGE—WHICH, LOGICALLY, EXTENDS EAST of Greenwich Village from Broadway to the East River—is topographically far more regular than its sibling: the avenues (here including Avenues A, B, C, and D, known as "Alphabet City," beyond First Avenue) run longitudinally, and the obediently numbered streets, from East First to East 14th, crisscross them more or less latitudinally.

Socially the population of the East Village is all over the map: a mix of Indian and Italian restaurateurs, Ukrainian boutiques, art students, street performers, and proto-punks. It's a hot club scene, studded with preserved churches and monuments to art movements of earlier days; it is also still a stronghold of the drug culture, though that is much less visible than in the 1970s. But it has many beautiful buildings and important cultural sites, and its history goes back to the days of Nieuw Amsterdam.

Peter Stuyvesant once owned the lion's share of what is now the East Village, and a fair amount of the island north of there as well (see the section on Gramercy Park and Madison Square). The western border of the "bouwerie" was Fourth Avenue, which explains why that street becomes known as Bowery to the south. His country home was near 10th and Stuyvesant, and he had his own chapel, too, on the site of what is now **St. Mark's-in-the-Bowery** on East 10th at Second Avenue (☎ 212-674-6377), which itself goes back to 1799; he was buried in the ground beneath it. Poet W. H. Auden is memorialized there because he lived for many years at **77 St. Mark's Place.**

Astor Place, like Washington Square, was inhabited by the richest of the rich in the early 19th century. The Astor Place Opera House, actually the second famous theater in that park, was the site of what is known as the Astor Place Riots of 1849; it started as a quarrel between the paid adherents of two rival actors and ended in the death of several dozen people. In the same area are the **Public Theater,** originally the Astor Library building donated by John Jacob Astor and now best known as home of the year-round Shakespeare Festival founded by Joseph Papp; and **Cooper Union,** the famous free adult educational institution that was the first to accept women and students of all races and religions. Its columned Great Hall, where Lincoln delivered his "Right Makes Might" speech, is still the site of popular public debates. **Colonnade Row,** the homes from 428 to 434 Lafayette off Astor Place, was also known as "LaGrange Terrace" when the Astors themselves and the Vanderbilts and Delanos lived there, along with such temporary celebrity residents as Charles Dickens and William Makepeace Thackeray; but only four of the original nine buildings, and just the façades, survive.

The **Old Merchant's House** (☎ 212-777-1089), just south of the Public Theater at 29 East 4th Street, is an intact 1830s Greek Revival home with all its furnishings, paintings, and even books just the way they were when merchant Seabury Tredwell forbade his daughter Gertrude to marry a man he disapproved of. Gertrude then decided never to marry at all. Sex also used to be an issue at **McSorley's Old Ale House,** which from its founding in 1854 until the 1970s admitted only men; other than that, it's still the same old saloon—complete with a "wanted" poster for John Wilkes Booth, a pair of Houdini's handcuffs, and a legendary array of old wishbones (East 7th and Cooper streets; phone ☎ 212-473-9148).

On East 2nd Street between Second Avenue and the Bowery is the **New York Marble Cemetery,** founded in 1830, where many famous New York names are represented (and where one recently discovered unused vault in the middle of the cemetery is on the market for a six-figure sum). If you go into the alley on the other side of Second Avenue, you'll find its sister institution, the **New York City Marble Cemetery,** founded 18 months later—or, rather, the marble plaques above the underground vaults.

An odd little spire seems to poke up above Broadway, where it makes a funny little quirk around what was then an apple orchard; the spire leads down to the lovely Gothic Revival Grace Church at 802 Broadway (☎ 212-254-2000), designed by St. Patrick's architect James Renwick when he was 23 years old. It has particularly beautiful stained glass in the pre-Raphaelite style, and its moment in the celebrity sun occurred in 1863 when P. T. Barnum staged General Tom Thumb's wedding there.

unofficial **TIP**
If you hear the designation "Noho," it means "north of Houston," the area around Broadway and Lafayette whose commercial spirit has more in common with the West Village these days than the East.

CHELSEA

WHEN CAPTAIN THOMAS CLARKE ACQUIRED THE LAND from Eighth Avenue to the Hudson River between West 14th and 25th

unofficial **TIP**
If you've ever longed to lounge in one of those huge ornate public baths, here's your chance—the Russian and Turkish baths at 268 East Tenth (☎ 212-674-9250). Do call ahead: Some days are men-only, some women-only, and some coed.

streets, he named it, in what must have seemed a rather ambitious flight of fancy, after a neighborhood in London famed for its high fashion and literary and artistic life. As it turned out, it was prophetic. Chelsea was the first Broadway, the original Hollywood, and over the years it has been home to dozens of artists and writers. It was an early fashion center and is still home to the **Fashion Institute of Technology** and the **"Fur District"** (between Sixth and Eighth avenues and West 27th and 30th streets), though the serious retail boutiques have long since moved farther uptown.

As noted in Part One, Understanding the City, most of Clarke's property was inherited by his grandson, Clement Clarke Moore of (disputed) "'Twas the Night before Christmas" fame. Among his gifts, the public-good component of his commercial development was the land for the **Theological Seminary** on Ninth Avenue between West 20th and 21st (☎ 212-243-5150). St. Mark's Library now has what is believed to be the largest collection of Latin Bibles in the world; the West Building is the oldest example of Gothic Revival architecture in the city.

But that is only one of several important religious-studies centers in the neighborhood: **The New Center for Jewish History** (15 West 16th Street; ☎ 212-294-8301) incorporates the libraries of five major organizations, including **Yeshiva University** and the **American Jewish Historical Society,** as well as the publicly accessible **Genealogy Institute** and performance spaces for concerts and lectures. Across Ninth Avenue is **St. Peter's Episcopal Church** (346 West 20th Street); Moore insisted that it should be built in the style of a classical Greek temple, and the foundation was, but in midconstruction church officials shifted to the Gothic style then sweeping England.

The **New Museum of Contemporary Art,** which is sharing space at West 22nd and Eleventh Avenue with the **Chelsea Art Museum** until its new home is complete, has some of the area's most significant cutting-edge shows (☎ 212-219-1222). (The **Dia Art Museum,** which had planned to renovate its spaces nearby, will instead move to Washington Street.)

The home at **Ninth and West 21st Street,** with the ornate peaked roof, is the oldest home in the neighborhood, built in the 1820s. When Moore subdivided the property in 1830, he required the residential developers to put gardens in front of the homes and trees along the street; the exteriors of the townhouses along **West 21st between Ninth and Tenth** are nearly intact, though many of the buildings are now apartments or shops. The Greek Revival row houses along **West 20th Street** in the same block were originally constructed as middle-class rental units in the late 1930s; notice the cast-iron detailing and the brownstone door frames that became a synonym for Manhattan homes.

The 19-story **Starrett-Lehigh Building,** which occupies the block between Eleventh and Twelfth avenues and 26th and 27th streets, was constructed in 1930 as a warehouse and freight terminal for the railroads; it is now a combination fashion mall and high-tech office campus (the old truck-sized elevator now carries occupants like Martha Stewart—and her car—directly to these nifty ninth-floor parking spaces.

The block bounded by West 23rd and 24th and Ninth and Tenth is taken up by the **London Terrace Apartments.** During the Depression, for some speculative reason, developers tried to play on the name by razing the mid–19th-century Greek Revival complex there and replacing it with this Mayfair-wannabe block with a garden in the middle and doormen dressed as London "bobbies." Across Tenth at 519 West 23rd Street is the **WPA Theatre,** one of the best-known off-off-Broadway venues; *Little Shop of Horrors* and *Steel Magnolias* began here, among others.

The **Chelsea Hotel,** which at various times was home or hotel to O. Henry, Mark Twain, Thomas Wolfe, Arthur Miller, Tennessee Williams, Brendan Behan, Vladimir Nabokov, Sarah Bernhardt, Dylan Thomas, Virgil Thomson, Jack Kerouac, and assorted touring rock stars, is on West 23rd between Seventh and Eighth avenues (☎ 212-243-3700).

What is now the **Serbian Orthodox Church of St. Sava** at 15 West 25th Street was built as Trinity Chapel; in 1885, Edith, or "Miss Pussy" Jones, as she was known, was married here and emerged as Mrs. Edward Robbins Wharton.

The Gothic Revival **Marble Collegiate Church** at Broadway and West 29th Street (☎ 212-686-2770) is famous for its Tiffany windows and former pastor Norman Vincent Peale (*The Power of Positive Thinking*). **St. John the Baptist** (☎ 212-564-9070) on West 31st Street just west of Seventh Avenue is like a geode—nearly obscured by the development around it, but glorious within.

Chelsea went through a long decline before urban renewal moved in, but nowadays, from its vantage point between the modern Theater District and Greenwich Village, it is at once a target for upwardly mobile young families, art and antiques dealers who have shifted north from the high-rent Soho, and (increasingly) a wealthy gay population. And with **Madison Square Garden** at one corner and the huge, renovated **Chelsea Piers** playground–tourist draw at the other, the famous Chelsea loft spaces are once again getting hard to find. (The original Pennsylvania Station was twin to the great Beaux Arts **Post Office** across Eighth Avenue, the one emblazoned with the famous "Neither snow nor rain . . ." slogan.)

If you're interested in fashion and design, you should stop by the free galleries at the **Fashion Institute of Technology** on Seventh Avenue at 27th Street (☎ 212-217-5779), which, like the better-known **Costume Institute at the Metropolitan,** assembles special exhibits that either trace a style through history or showcase designers or collectors and that sometimes detail a technique or material. One other Chelsea neighborhood worth noting is the **"Flower District"** along Sixth Avenue in the upper 20s.

GRAMERCY PARK AND MADISON SQUARE

THIS OLD AND IN MANY CASES WELL-PRESERVED SECTION of Manhattan, which faces Chelsea across Sixth Avenue, is punctuated by squares and parks and white-collar firms. It is also the area that symbolized the commercial ambitions of the Gilded Age, home to the **Flatiron Building** in the triangle of Fifth Avenue, Broadway, and 23rd Street by Madison Square Park, which was the world's largest building when it was completed in 1903; the **Metropolitan Life Insurance Building** at Madison and 23rd, which topped it by adding a tower in 1909; and the **Empire State Building** (profiled in depth in Part Seven, Sightseeing, Tours, and Attractions), which beat them both in 1931.

kids In late 2006, the huge collection of vintage comic book, cartoon, and animation art from the old International Museum of Cartoon Art is scheduled to open as the **National Cartoon Museum** in the Empire State Building.

What was sometimes called "Ladies' Mile," a cluster of the first department stores—notably, the original Lord & Taylor and Tiffany stores—and custom shops catering to the carriage trade, ran along Broadway from Union Square to Madison Square—the heart of what is also sometimes known as the Flatiron District. ("Ladies" was a trifle sarcastic, as it had previously been a neighborhood of prominent brothels.) The Flatiron Building was actually named the Fuller Building, but its shape, something like the prow of a great ocean liner or an old press, inspired the nickname. (More recently, the streets around it have picked up the phrase "Flat-iron District" as a moniker for its newly renovated buildings and influx of restaurants.)

Society figures and politicians made their homes here (Union Square was the home of Tammany Hall), and it was near enough to the theater district to attract the most important actors and writers as well. Edwin Booth, whose statue stands in the park, founded the famous **Players Club** on the south side. The **"Little Church around the Corner"** (also known as the Church of the Transfiguration) at East 29th and Fifth Avenue (☎ 212-684-6770), which became famous because it buried actors when some more "respectable" churches wouldn't, has a collection of theatrically inspired stained glass.

Before the Empire State Building was erected, the block of Fifth Avenue between West 33rd and West 34th streets held two of the many Astor mansions, one belonging to William Waldorf Astor and the other to his aunt, Mrs. William Astor. An argument led to his moving out and putting up a hotel on the site called the Waldorf; almost immediately she moved out and built a connecting hotel, the Astoria. The two operated as a single company—though with the provision that she could block off the connection at any time—until 1929, when the Park Avenue hotel of that name was built and the Empire State Building begun.

Gramercy Park, the neighborhood centered on Gramercy Park at the foot of Lexington Avenue between West 20th and West 21st, was one of the first "gated communities," as we would call them now. In the 1830s, developer Samuel Ruggles bought a large chunk of the old Stuyvesant estate that included a creek shaped like a "crooked little knife," or "Crommessie." Ruggles wanted to entice a wealthy patronage, so he filled in the marshy creek area and laid out a London-style park in the heart of his territory, with one adjoining avenue named for the famous Revolutionary victory and one on the south side called Irving Place after writer Washington Irving. Astonishingly, it is still a private park, the only one in the city—area residents have keys to the lock—and the entire area is a historic district. Teddy Roosevelt was born on East 20th Street between Park and Broadway. The **Theodore Roosevelt Birthplace Museum** (☎ 212-260-1616) had to be reconstructed because the actual building was demolished during World War II, but the five rooms of period furniture, memorabilia, teddy bears, and campaign memorabilia are real enough.

Madison Square Park, between Fifth and Madison avenues and between West 23rd and West 26th streets, was part of the original grid plan of 1811, though only well into the mid–19th century did it become much more than a commons and parade ground (and "potter's field" or pauper's cemetery). This was the site of the second Madison Square Garden, the palatial exhibition hall/entertainment complex designed by Sanford White; its rooftop garden was also the place where White was shot to death in 1906 by millionaire socialite Harry Thaw, who believed White was having an affair with his showgirl wife, Evelyn Nesbit. The original New York Knickerbockers, the nation's first organized baseball team, played here; and before it was permanently hoisted into harbor-lighting position, the torch and upraised arm of the Statue of Liberty was exhibited here as well.

Overlooking Madison Square is the clock tower of the **Metropolitan Life Insurance Building,** nearly five feet taller than London's Big Ben. In the lobby are a series of historical murals painted by famed children's illustrator N. C. Wyeth. On the other corner, at Madison and East 25th, is the **New York State Supreme Court's Appellate Division,** believed to be the busiest appellate court in the world (among the former plaintiffs here: Babe Ruth, Charlie Chaplin, Edgar Allan Poe, and Harry Houdini). The many fine sculptures outside are matched by stained glass, murals, and carving inside, which you can see unless court is in session.

This neighborhood is also home to three small and particularly special-interest collections, the **Museum of Sex** (27th Street and Fifth Avenue; ☎ 212-689-6337); **Tibet House** (22 West 15th Street; ☎ 212-807-0563); and the new **Rubin Museum of Himalayan Art** (profiled in detail in Part Seven). The first is a quintessentially American institution, with exhibits that range from the curious and even quaint (flyers for patent medicines, antique underwear, and nickelodeon-style film of pioneering ecdysiasts) to the X-tremely graphic (clips of hard-core films on repeating loops). Not surprisingly, no one under 18 is admitted. Tibet House, on the other hand, is a museum in exile, some 350 pieces of art that staffers hope to return to Tibet when that nation achieves independence.

Among other old neighborhood names sometimes used by city residents or prestige-savvy developers are **Rose Hill,** a residential area north of Stuyvesant Square, and **Kips Bay,** for the area between Gramercy and Murray Hill north of 34th Street. Both names go back to old farming estates. The Kip family established their farm almost as soon as the Canarsie had sold Manhattan, and Rose Hill was sold off the Stuyvesant estate in the mid–18th century. **Murray Hill** itself gets its name from colonial merchant Robert Murray, whose country estate it was: It ranges from Madison to Lexington avenues between 33rd and 39th streets. Legend has it that Mary Murray invited General Howe to tea in 1776, knowing he would be far too polite to refuse, and thus bought Washington time to escape up the island to Fort Tryon. It's worth a stroll: Of the 100 original residences listed in the 1892 Social Register, more than 60 survive. On the east side of Third Avenue is **Sniffen Court,** a beautifully preserved mews of ten Romanesque Revival houses, built about 1850, at 150–160 East 36th Street. The **"Block Beautiful"** is simply a well-preserved row of houses along East 19th Street between Irving Place and Third Avenue; theater great Mrs. Patrick Campbell and movie vamp Theda Bara both lived (at various times, of course) in **No. 132 19th Street.**

Union Square describes the area just north of the East Village between the actual Union Square Park and Stuyvesant Square. The rather stolid **St. George's Episcopal Church** overlooking Stuyvesant Square is where J. P. Morgan attended what one must imagine were safely conservative services. The night-lit clock tower that looks down from Irving Street at East 14th is part of the **Consolidated Edison** (ConEd) headquarters, but at various times this site held Tammany Hall and the Academy of Music. **Union Square** itself, at the intersection of Broadway and Park between West 14th and West 17th streets, is the first of a series of squares marking the diagonal northward progress of Broadway. Like the East Village, it had become a famous drug market, but the influx of boutique hotels and restaurants and the success of the open-air green market have revived it considerably.

Incidentally, this entire section of Manhattan was the "turf" of the original Gashouse Gang, so called because many of the factories that supplied the city's lights were located along the East River.

MIDTOWN WEST, TIMES SQUARE, AND THE THEATER DISTRICT

WHEN PEOPLE TALK ABOUT BROADWAY, they rarely mean the street; they mean the **Theater District**—an area that ranges along both sides of Broadway from Times Square at West 42nd up to about 47th Street and between Ninth and Sixth avenues. Nearby are many of the more important off-Broadway venues: the Shriner–Moorish Revival **City Center Theater of Music and Drama** on West 55th at 1212 Broadway (☎ 212-581-1212), **Carnegie Hall** on West 57th around the corner of Broadway (☎ 212-903-9600), and even the **Brill Building,** the one-time "Broadway" of pop music and the heart of Tin Pan Alley (between West 49th and West 50th streets).

This is also the so-called **Garment District,** which began on the Lower East Side and gradually followed the department stores up Broadway. However, the most influential merchants decided that the showroom and the sweatshop shouldn't be so close together, and in cooperation they constructed large warehouses on Seventh Avenue at West 37th Street, which is why some of the Seventh Street signs have subtitles reading **Fashion Avenue.**

Among the most famous areas in this neighborhood is **Times Square,** which, until the paper's headquarters moved there in 1905, had been called Long Acre Square, home to stables and blacksmiths and the occasional thief. This is where the famous ball drops to mark the New Year as it has every year since 1905; and although it had become notoriously seedy, studded with porn shops and cheap bars, the neighborhood underwent one of the most sweeping renovations in city history, perhaps second only to the development of Lincoln Center in place of the West Side

unofficial **TIP**
Enjoying the street theater too much to watch TV? Catch Jay Leno's monologue (subtitled) on the NBC Astrovision.

slums. Times Square now draws an estimated 20 million visitors a year, making it one of the major tourist attractions in itself (not to mention a gridlock of pedestrian and vehicular traffic). In fact, things are opening so fast that you may want to pick up a copy of the neighborhood guide at the **Times Square Visitors Center** in the old Embassy Theatre on Broadway between 46th and 47th streets; it offers full-scale tourist services, ATMs, tickets, Internet access, and handicapped-accessible bathrooms. Or you can take a tour to explore the myriad attractions—some historical, some hilarious, and not a few strictly commercial—by showing up at the visitors center at noon on Friday. (Not all Times

Square visuals are outdoors: Look for the newly expanded **International Center of Photography** on Sixth at 94th; ☎ 212-857-0000.)

New theaters and renovated ones, trendy restaurants, comedy and music clubs, high-tech virtual playgrounds and megastores—plus those famous huge billboards and the *Times's* running-lights headline service—are bursting almost daily out from behind construction fences. The Disney Company restored the historic **New Amsterdam** on 42nd Street at Seventh Avenue as a showcase for its extraordinary adaptation of *The Lion King*. (It's just behind the Disney superstore, but frankly, the theater lobby is the more fantastic of the two.) The **New Victory** across the street is a throwback to the golden age of children's theater. Two historic but aging theaters, the 1903 Lyric and the 1920 Apollo, have been replaced at a cost of $30 million by the single **Ford Center for the Performing Arts,** which will be the second-largest auditorium on Broadway.

The *New York Times* itself long ago had to move out of the old tower on the square to larger digs on West 43rd Street, but it is having an extraordinary 650-foot-tall glass tower constructed back in the "old neighborhood," and Reuters plans to follow suit. The Condé Nast magazine group, Viacom, Bertelsman (the German publisher that has acquired Random House and others), and MTV have moved into the "new" Times Square, along with the huge Ernst & Young advertising corporation. Other entertainments include the huge **Warner Bros., Virgin,** and **Disney** megastores, the **World Wrestling Federation** restaurant, a **Rain Forest Café,** a **Hard Rock Cafe, B.B. King's Blues Room** and **Lucille's Café,** another **NBA/WNBA** store, the **Madame Tussaud's Wax Museum,** the sports-celebrity **All-Star Café,** the **ESPN Zone,** a

> ✱ *unofficial* **TIP**
> If you hang around the **MTV Studios,** whose mezzanine-level offices overlook the square from 44th to 46th, or watch the marquee outside **Cinema Ride,** one of those 3-D shows, you may see yourself among the models and billboards; there are hidden video cameras around the sidewalk.

Hershey's Chocolate super-store, and the retro 1950s **Ellen's Stardust Diner.** A magic-theme restaurant from David Copperfield is in the works off and on (now you see it . . .). Another famous "running clock" is the **National Debt Clock** above Sixth Avenue between West 42nd and West 43rd; watch how fast it mounts up. And the **Times Square Brewery** offers pizza bagels and house-brewed beer.

Notice the sudden boom in old-fashioned moving "headline" signs known as "zippers," named for the first running signboard installed at 1 Times Square in 1928. In addition to the *Times* news board, there are stock market quotation runners of the sort you might more reasonably expect down near Wall Street; the first one outside the **Dow Jones** offices at 1 Times Square, a **Morgan-Stanley** zipper on 1585 Broadway, and an even more astonishing **NASDAQ** board—$15 million worth and 125 feet high—on the Condé Nast building at 42nd and Broadway.

Reuters News Service has a competing headline sign at 42nd and Seventh, just like the Fox News sign at 47th and Sixth and the NBC versions in Times Square and Rockefeller Plaza. And ABC—which, you may remember now belongs to the Disney company—has a sidewalk-view studio at 1500 Broadway for *Good Morning America* like the *Today Show* peek-in that packs Rockefeller Plaza every weekday at 7 Times Square. The same thing goes for CBS's *Early Show* at Fifth Avenue and 59th, across from the Plaza Hotel and Central Park.

Herald Square is named for the *New York Herald* newspaper building at West 34th, just as Times Square was named for the *New York Times*. And just as Times Square isn't really square, Herald Square is actually a triangle. (You could call it the Daily District: Greeley Square, another triangle one block south at West 33rd, was named for *New York Tribune* founder Horace Greeley.) Herald Square was the very center of the venomous **Tenderloin,** a thriving red-light and speakeasy district. It was partly the arrival of **Macy's Department Store** in 1901 that gave this area new respectability, and nowadays Herald Square is most famous for serving as the finale stage for Macy's annual Thanksgiving Day Parade and the arrival of Santa Claus.

The west side of this area also has a florid past, though not much of it is left to be seen. From Ninth Avenue west from the 30s to the 50s is what is most often known as **Hell's Kitchen,** the territory of the Irish gang of the same name, but also sometimes called Paddy's Market or **Clinton,** the name now coming back into style. Nowadays the strip along Eleventh and Twelfth avenues is mostly reduced to autobody shops and a few X-rated theaters playing off (or off-off) the Broadway name. **Ninth Avenue,** however, particularly through the 40s, is a bazaar of small ethnic restaurants—Brazilian, Jamaican, Afghani, Peruvian, Greek, Turkish, Thai, Morroccan, Japanese, and even Burmese, as well as the relatively tame Italian and Mexican. Not only are these some of the better restaurants in the Theater District, they're much

> *unofficial* **TIP**
> There is a Hell's Kitchen Flea Market on 39th between Ninth and Tenth avenues every weekend, when the block is closed to vehicular traffic.

hipper (where do you think the actors eat?) and a lot less expensive. But for pretheater class, try **Restaurant Row,** the block on West 46th Street between Eighth and Ninth avenues, home to the **Firebird, Orso,** celeb-spot **Joe Allen,** and **Becco,** among others.

Times Square is sometimes called "The Crossroads of the World," and it's also one of the major transportation crossroads of Manhattan: Several of the large subway transfer points, including 34th Street, Penn Station, Times Square, Rockefeller Center, 42nd Street, 49th Street, and Columbus Circle are in this area, and so is the Port Authority Bus Terminal. The Lincoln Tunnel runs west from West 38th. And the western edge of the neighborhood is the unlovely but essential West Side Expressway.

North of the Javits Convention Center and Lincoln Tunnel, near Pier 86 at the foot of West 46th Street, is the popular **Intrepid Sea-Air-Space Museum** (profiled in depth in Part Seven, Sightseeing, Tours, and Attractions). And at 237 West 51st Street is the baroquely extravagant **Times Square Church,** built as the Warner Hollywood movie palace in 1930 but quickly transformed into a playhouse (*Jesus Christ Superstar* was housed here, appropriately). The building opens at 5 p.m. Tuesdays and Fridays and 8 a.m. on Sundays; call ☎ 212-541-6300 for more information.

MIDTOWN EAST

THIS NEIGHBORHOOD IS FOR MANY TOURISTS the heart of Manhattan: It includes **Rockefeller Center** (☎ 212-632-3975), **Radio City Music Hall** (☎ 212-247-4777), and the great shopping boulevard of Fifth Avenue; many of the city's most famous restaurants and such famous hotels as the **Waldorf-Astoria, New York Palace, St. Regis, Algonquin** (where you can still have a drink in the Rose Room and imagine the wits of the 1920s gathered around you), **Four Seasons,** and **Plaza.** The newly (and extravagantly) renovated **Museum of Modern Art** is on West 53rd between Fifth and Sixth (☎ 212-708-9480), across from the **Museum of Art and Design** (☎ 212-956-3535) and the new, eight-level **American Folk Art Museum** (☎ 212-265-1040), and a block from the **Museum of Television and Radio** on West 52nd (☎ 212-621-6600). (All four are profiled in depth in Part Seven, Sightseeing, Tours, and Attractions.) CBS Inc., the infamous **"Black Rock,"** is that monolith overshadowing the museum at Fifth and 52nd. The small but often uniquely satisfying **Dahesh Museum** has relocated to larger quarters at 580 Madison Avenue between 56th and 57th (☎ 212-759-0606). The **Sony Wonder Technology Lab** (☎ 212-833-8100) on Madison between 55th and 56th has become the city's hippest hands-on playground for both children (who talk with a robot, view the inner workings of the body, and surf the web) and electronic-trend fashion victims. There is even a miniature free branch of the **Whitney Museum of American Art** in the Philip Morris building on Park Avenue across from Grand Central with a sculpture garden and rotating exhibits from the main collection (☎ 917-663-2453).

*un*official **TIP**
At Grand Central Terminal, be sure to peek into the **Campbell Apartment** above the West Balcony, a 13th-century Florentine-style hall that was once a luxury office and is now a trendy lounge.

This is also a living coffee-table book of monumental architecture. Among its landmarks are the lavishly restored Beaux Arts **Grand Central Terminal** at 42nd and Park Avenue (look up at the constellations winking in the ceiling); the gleaming, Buck Rogers–ish, Art Deco **Chrysler Building,** with its stainless steel "grill" crown and hood-ornament gargoyles saluting the spirit of the automotive age (Lexington at 42nd); the Mies van der Rohe–designed **Seagram Building** on Park Avenue between East 52nd and East 53rd streets, elegant in its bronze and glass; the equally startling glass razor of the **Lever House** on Park at 54th; the literally gilded palace—now part of the **New York Palace** and Le Cirque 2000 restaurant—that was the **Villard House** on Madison between 50th and 51st streets; the almost Disneyesque Gothic Revival **St. Patrick's Cathedral** on Fifth at 50th, the largest Catholic cathedral in this country (profiled in Part Seven); and the reserved but powerful **United Nations** complex, a perfect architectural metaphor (and one that is scheduled to begin a massive refurbishing and rehabbing in 2007), on the East River at 43rd Street (☎ 212-906-5000).

You don't need permission to stroll around **Grand Central Terminal** at East 42nd and Park Avenue, but if you'd like to know more about the classical sculptures and so on, contact the Municipal Arts Society (☎ 212-935-3960; **www.mas.org**), which leads free tours Wednesdays at 12:30 p.m. (For more on Grand Central, see Part Nine, Shopping.)

The same is true of the **New York Public Library** on Fifth Avenue at 42nd, another civic treasure, with its nearly 100-year-old and newly restored signature lions (representing Patience and Fortitude) at the entrance, twin fountains (Beauty and Truth, which would please Keats), interior murals, paintings, documents (Jefferson's copy of the Declaration of Independence), and so on. The newly rededicated ceiling of the Guttesman Exhibition Hall sometimes outshines the exhibits. It's a 300-foot-long trompe d'oeil mural that seems to open the room to a classical sky inhabited by angels. And the glories of the great manuscripts and first-editions collection in Room 320 are primarily intellectual. But if you like, free tours leave from the front desk every day at 11 a.m. and 2 p.m.

Rockefeller Center itself is a landmark, a total of 19 Art Deco buildings between Fifth and Seventh avenues and 48th and 51st streets, clustered around the famous plaza-cum–ice rink and including the eternally youthful Radio City Music Hall, with its Rockettes and classic revivals. Its façades are virtual museums of sculpture, bas-relief, gilding, mosaics, carvings, and molding; during the Great Depression, construction of the original 14 buildings kept a quarter of a million laborers and artists busy. The **Diamond District** is right next door, along West 47th Street between Sixth and Fifth, with wall-to-wall and mall-to-mall shops hawking earrings, rings, and pins. The Diamond District dates from almost the same era as Rockefeller Center, when the Jewish merchants of Europe began fleeing the increasingly restrictive anti-Semitic laws.

unofficial **TIP**
The **Rainbow Room** (☎ 212-632-5000) offers a sheltered bird's-eye view of the skyline from the 65th floor of the tallest building of Rockefeller Center. But the newly reopened observation deck on the 69th floor, and its even higher walk-up platform, are open to the air in all directions.

The **Church of the Incarnation** (☎ 212-689-6350) on Madison Avenue at East 35th is modest on the outside, but its art collection—Louis Comfort Tiffany, William Morris, and Edward Burne Jones stained-glass windows; Saint-Gaudens and Daniel French sculptures; and so on—is anything but modest. More obvious, perhaps, is the gold-leaf dome atop **St. Vartan Cathedral** on Second Avenue between East 34th and East 35th, but then it is the seat of the Armenian Orthodox Church in the United States. The Byzantine **St. Bartholomew's** on Park at East 50th is truly byzantine: part James Renwick, part Stanford White. St. Patrick's is the Gothic giant, but **St. Thomas's** just up the street at Fifth and 53rd is stubborn as a little David (☎ 212-757-7013). It's worth stopping in to admire its fantastic stone redos, a wall of 60 figures behind the altar that represent Jesus and his apostles and family, saints, martyrs, prophets, and missionaries. And at the foot of the gallery stairs, to the right as you enter, is an "Adoration of the Magi" believed to be the work of Peter Paul Rubens.

The **New York Daily News Building** on 42nd and Second Avenue was used as the scene for the *Daily Planet* in the *Superman* movies, and there's an inside joke to that: The building has its own "planet," a huge revolving globe, in the lobby. Across the street is **Tudor City,** Henry VIII–style apartments, restaurants, shops, and services built in the 1920s as a sort of early urban renewal project.

unofficial **TIP**
Be sure to step into the meditation garden of **Holy Family Church** a few doors west of the Japan Society.

The **Japan Society** on East 47th between First and Second avenues (☎ 212-832-1155) offers changing exhibits of antique scroll paintings, textiles, ceramics, arms, and antiques as well as lectures and exhibitions; it also has a traditional Japanese garden.

This wasn't really "good" territory until well into the 20th century. From Fourth Avenue (before it was called Park) east to the river lay stockyards and slums; there were railroad yards between Lexington and Madison, where Grand Central is now, and the gashouse, glue factories, prisons, workhouses, and asylums were all on what is now Roosevelt Island in the East River. In fact, what seems to be a pretty series of gardens down the center of Park Avenue actually covers the remnants of the railroad tracks.

Consequently, there aren't a lot of old neighborhood names attached to this part of the island. **Beekman Place** is a two-block enclave that has been home to such theatrical greats as Lunt and Fontanne, Ethel Barrymore, Irving Berlin, and "Auntie Mame"; climb the steps on 51st Street to the East River Promenade between 49th and 51st. **Sutton Place,** the southernmost section of York Avenue that runs between East 54th and 59th, was yet another, though later, London-style development aimed at the first families, and various of the Morgans and Vanderbilts in their turn lived here. The residence of the U.N. secretary general is there now. In the park between 58th and 59th is a statue of a boar, which may seem strange unless you know that it's a copy of *Il Porcallino,* which stands in the market in Florence, Italy; pat its head for luck. And yes, Simon and Garfunkle fans, that is the 59th Street Bridge immortalized in "Feelin' Groovy," officially named the **Queensboro Bridge.**

On the other hand, Fifth Avenue along the 40s and 50s was the site of huge palaces during the Gilded Age, half a dozen belonging to the Vanderbilts alone and nearly as many to the Astors. One of the greatest of those old mansions is now a fine museum: the magnificent **J. Pierpont Morgan Library** at 36th and Madison (also profiled in Part Seven), which houses an unparalleled collection of illuminated medieval manuscripts, rare books, etchings, musical scores, and prints. Fifth Avenue may not be "Millionaire's Mile" anymore (unless you're paying the American Express bill after a shopping tour of the 50s), but you can stroll up the avenue feeling like a million.

THE UPPER WEST SIDE

THE WEST SIDE JUST ABOVE THE THEATER DISTRICT had never had much identity of its own until fairly recently. There was some port trade—the big cruise ships and liners still use piers in the lower 50s— and some hotel and theater spillover, but not of the better sort. In the early part of the 20th century it was a respectable if not particularly fashionable district, populated first by Jewish immigrants who prospered and moved out of the Lower East Side and later by middle-class blacks, who began to be pushed out again by Puerto Rican immigrants and blue-collar white families from Hell's Kitchen. But with the creation of **Lincoln Center for the Performing Arts** (which involved the demolition of San Juan Hill, the Hispanic neighborhood in the West 60s, and the degenerating middle-class houses around it, exactly the area portrayed in *West Side Story*), businesses began to return.

The southwest corner of the area is **Columbus Circle,** where Broadway, Eighth Avenue, and West 59th/Central Park South come together, and where the eponymous **Christopher** stares out from his 77-foot-high vantage. The gold figure of a goddess on a seashell drawn by three seahorses is a monument to the sailors who died in the explosion of the USS *Maine,* which launched the Spanish-American War. The circle is dominated by the two glass spires of the new **Time Warner Center** and the **Shops at Columbus Circle,** home of numerous upscale apartments, restaurants, bars, shops, and the **Mandarin Oriental Hotel.** It's not only the new luxury center of Manhattan, it's literally the epicenter of New York—the place from which all those mileposts reading "425 miles to New York" are measured. The massively renovated **Trump International Hotel & Towers** (a.k.a. the Paramount Building, née Gulf & Western), with its minimal and chic eateries, is another tourist attraction in its own right. And the circa 1964 Gallery of Modern Art, with its curved facade, is scheduled to be renovated as the **Museum of Arts and Design.**

Meanwhile, the artsiest bit of this whole theatrical scene is the **Prow Sculpture,** a constantly changing light construction 150 feet tall that tells the time by changing color.

Lincoln Center and its associated plazas and annexes pretty much take up the area from Columbus Avenue (the extension of Ninth Avenue, remember, not Eighth) and very nearly Broadway to Tenth Avenue between West 62nd and West 66th streets. The law-school campus of **Fordham University** is just to its south, and the **School of American Ballet** and **Juilliard School of Music** are associated with the Lincoln Center complex, so the neighborhood is spotted with small cafes and shops that attract students and culture-lovers, as well as several health clubs and gymnasiums. On Thursdays and Fridays, the cobblestone area at 66th Street is an open-air farmers' market.

An offshoot gallery of the **American Folk Art Museum** (☎ 212-595-9533) is in what is called Lincoln Square on Columbus Avenue between West 65th and 66th. It specializes in textiles, furniture, and decorative arts from the 18th century, with particularly nice quilts and frequent lectures and demonstrations.

And if you ever wondered what "Tammany" really was, it, or rather he, was actually Tamanend, an Indian chief who supposedly befriended William Penn. The New York Tammany society, incorporated in 1789, was originally a Masonic-style fraternity with a Native American twist: 13 "tribes"—for the 13 colonies—with pseudo-Indian ceremonies and titles. If you look up at the weathervane in the museum atrium, you will see old Tamanend, looking sadly into the future, which would only associate his name with corruption.

The new **Museum of Biblical Art** (Broadway at 61st Street; ☎ 212-408-1500) mounts rather surprisingly wide-ranging exhibits of religious art, from traditional to faux and folk, and a vast collection of Bibles and scriptural publications.

No tourist-savvy city would be complete without an **IMAX theater** these days, and one of New York's is here, at Broadway and 68th. The screen is "seven elephants high" (☎ 212-336-5000).

There's plenty of streetside sightseeing around these parts as well. **Alwyn Court** (58th Street and Seventh Avenue) has one of the most fantastic terra-cotta facades in the entire city—designed by the same men who created the Gothic cathedral–look midblock highrise on **77th off Central Park West** and the **Loire Valley castle at 350 West 85th Street.** The darkly Art Deco apartment building at 55 Central Park West (between 65th and 66th) served as the battleground between the demon Gozur and the Ghostbusters. The **Hotel des Artistes** on West 67th Street at Central Park West was actually constructed as artists' studios, with its two-story spaces designed to take advantage of the daylight (and exterior sculptures for inspiration), but now these are highly prized apartments. Noel Coward, Rudolph Valentino, Alexander Woollcott, Norman Rockwell, Isadora Duncan, and Howard Chandler Christy all lived there; Christy did the murals of romantic nudes in the popular **Café des Artists** (☎ 212-877-3500) in the lobby.

The towered apartment buildings along Central Park West mostly date to the 1920s, when building regulations allowed greater height in return for at least partial light (which is why so many New York skyscrapers have those angled or pointed tops). The pretty Art Nouveau building at West 64th and Central Park West is the home of the **New York Society for Ethical Culture** (☎ 212-874-5210). The **Spanish and Portuguese Synagogue** on the corner of West 70th Street at Central Park West, though built (with Tiffany windows) only in 1897, is home to the oldest Jewish congregation in the city, dating to the arrival in 1654 of fugitives from the Inquisition; it still adheres rigorously to Sephardic ritual (by appointment; ☎ 212-873-0300).

As suggested in the "Very Short History" section of Part One, development of the West Side was the stepchild of the Gilded Age. It required the daring of a few developers and the construction of the El up Ninth Avenue to persuade middle-class and professional Manhattanites that it was worth living above Midtown. On the other hand, because the land was a better bargain, many of the apartment buildings and brownstones were more gracious and seemed to have more elbow room. Broadway, in particular, has a European boulevardlike spaciousness in this area. Nowadays, it is a popular area for relatively affluent professionals, studded with restaurants, especially along Columbus Avenue.

In its heyday, Riverside Drive was the Fifth Avenue of the West Side, with mansions gazing out over their own Frederick Olmsted greenery, Riverside Park, instead of Central Park and with the Hudson River beyond that. Only a few of the old buildings remain; look for the turn-of-the-century **Yeshiva Chofetz Chaim,** the former Isaac Rice home, at West 89th for an example.

It was the construction of the **Dakota** on Central Park West at 72nd Street, the first luxury apartment building on the Upper West Side, in the 1880s that sparked a development boom. Designed by Plaza Hotel architect Henry Hardenberg for Singer Company heir Edward Clark, it is still probably the most famous apartment building in the city, used as the movie setting of *Rosemary's Baby* (Boris Karloff is said to haunt the building) and now, unfortunately, best known as the home and assassination spot of John Lennon.

Once the Dakota was in place, other developers hastened to get in on the act, and this resulted in such other extravagances as the Beaux Arts **Dorilton** at West 71st and Broadway; the **Alexandria** on West 70th, with its hieroglyphic detailing, monsters, and rooftop pharaohs; and the Belle Epoque **Ansonia Hotel** on Broadway at West 74th, which attracted such musical eminences as Arturo Toscanini, Enrico Caruso, and Leopold Stokowski. William Randolph Hearst was originally satisfied with the view from the top three floors of the 12-story **Clarendon** on Riverside Drive and West 86th, but after a few years he decided he needed the whole thing and bought it out.

The stretch of **Central Park West** between West 75th and West 77th is a historical district, dating from the turn of the 19th century. The double-towered **St. Remo** between 74th and 75th is a little younger, finished in 1930, but it has its pride; this is the co-op that turned down Madonna, though several other famous actors and musicians do live here. The same architect, Emery Roth, topped himself by giving the **Beresford** at West 81st Street three turrets a few years later.

One of the oddest corners is a little gated mews off West 94th Street near West End Avenue known as **Pomander Walk;** though built in 1921, it looks just like a movie set of old London—and in fact, it was modeled after the stage set of a popular play of the time called *Pomander Walk.* So it sentimentally attracted such tenants as Lillian and Dorothy Gish and Humphrey Bogart.

Although the Upper West Side can't rival the East Side's "Museum Mile," it does have some popular attractions. The **New York Historical Society** building on Central Park West between West 76th and West 77th houses an eclectic collection ranging from American-made fine silver and decorative arts to original prints for John J. Audubon's *Birds of America,* Hudson River School painters, furniture that marches through the building in chronological order, and Gilbert Stuart's portrait of Washington.

The **American Museum of Natural History** annex, newly refurbished and riding the crest of dinosaur fever, and the stunning **Rose Center** and **Hayden Planetarium** face Central Park from West 77th Street to 81st (profiled in depth in Part Seven). The **Children's Museum of Manhattan,** one of the city's first institutions to go heavily into interactive exhibits, is on West 83rd Street between Broadway and Amsterdam Avenue.

Symphony Space, which is a cult location both for its Bloomsday marathon readings of *Ulysses* every June 16 and its 12-hour free spring musical marathon, is on Broadway at West 94th Street.

And should you venture up to the little park at Broadway and 106th, you'll see a bronze called *Memory* looking into a wave-shaped pool and inscribed, "In their death they were not divided" (II Samuel). It was erected by Macy's employees after the death of store owner Isdaor Straus and his wife, Ida, on the *Titanic.*

THE UPPER EAST SIDE

THIS IS ARGUABLY THE MOST BEAUTIFUL AREA OF MANHATTAN, fashionable and prosperous almost from the very beginning, and like the dowager of a good family, remarkably well preserved. It is an area of apartment houses open only to true millionaires (and not always open to them, either) and of the most expensive of boutiques, art and antiques houses, elegant hotels, private clubs, and old-line restaurants, churches, and educational institutions.

The riverfront was the original draw; it was an in-town "beach" and resort area in the early 19th century before bridges made travel to the outer boroughs common. The wealthy (who still lived firmly downtown) built summer homes all the way up the East River to what is now Harlem, boating up- and downtown, taking carriages along the Boston Post Road (Third Avenue) and later the El. A huge complex called Jones's Wood filled the whole stretch east of the Post Road from near what is now the **Rockefeller University/Cornell University Medical Center** neighborhood in the 60s north to John Jay Park at East 76th; it offered genteel bathing facilities, theatrical entertainments, a beer garden, and parade grounds.

The apartment buildings on the East Side broke ground in several ways; they were so large that even families with whole staffs of servants might share them. (And nowadays, several families can fit within the various subdivisions of one formerly palatial apartment.) The new luxury townhouses had elaborate bathrooms, not just water closets. They were fully electrified, not just refitted. And of course they had the immense swath of Central Park for their front yard. Those that had to settle for views of Madison Avenue or Park Avenue offered elaborate lobbies and exterior detail instead: look at the outside of the building on the corner of **East 66th Street and Madison.**

Once Caroline Schermerhorn Astor—the same Mrs. William Astor whose feuding with her nephew produced the Waldorf-Astoria Hotel—actually moved all the way up Fifth Avenue as far as 65th Street, the last great millionaires' migration began. Several of their mansions are still visible, including the **Frick Collection,** home of steel boss Henry Clay Frick, on Fifth at East 70th Street (profiled in depth in Part Seven, Sightseeing, Tours, and Attractions); the extravagant Second Empire **Lotos Club** on East 66th just off Fifth Avenue, former home of pharmaceutical tycoon and civil rights activist William Schieffelin; and the onetime **George T. Bliss House** on East 68th just off Fifth Avenue, which has four giant columns for just one little overlook. No wonder Fifth Avenue became the semi-official parade route, with its blocks of balconies like reviewing stands along one side and the peoples' park on the other.

The Beaux Arts home of banker Henri Wertheim on East 67th just off Fifth is now the **Japanese consul general's residence.** The side-by-side 1890s French Renaissance homes of Oliver Gould Jennings and Henry T. Sloane are now the **Lycée Français** on East 72nd Street between Fifth and Madison avenues. What is now the **Explorer's Club** on East 70th between Madison and Park was built for Stephen Clark, owner of the Singer Sewing Machine Company and founder of the Baseball Hall of Fame in Cooperstown. The Venetian Revival home of Edwin Berwin, who had the coal monopoly for American warships, is now an apartment building at **Fifth and East 64th.** And the neo-Tudor **Lenox School** on East 70th between Lexington and Third avenues was originally the home of Stephen Brown, head of the New York Stock Exchange. Astor's own home was torn down to make room for the partially Romanesque, partially Byzantine, and Astorially opulent **Temple Emanu-El.**

Hunter College has one of the most enviable locations in town, around Park Avenue between East 68th and 69th streets. Hunter's community center is the **Sarah Delano Roosevelt Memorial House**—or, rather, houses—on East 65th between Park and Madison. FDR's mother famously commissioned these twin townhouses, one for herself and one for the newly married Franklin and Eleanor, with a single entrance and various connecting doors. It was in the fourth-floor front bedroom that FDR endured his long bout with polio, and Eleanor the almost equally paralyzing domination of her mother-in-law.

Among smaller museums of note in this area are the **Queen Sofía Spanish Institute** on Park at 68th Street (☎ 212-628-0420), which showcases great Spanish art in limited exhibits, and easy hour's visit; and the **Abigail Adams Smith Museum** on East 61st Street between York and First avenues, named for—but never occupied by—the daughter of John Quincy Adams. She and her husband were the landowners, at least; they originally planned to build a country estate there called Mount Vernon in honor of George Washington, under whom William Smith had been a colonel. But they had to sell the land in 1799 without getting much further than building the stone stable (later an inn) that is now the museum. It has been furnished in the Federal style, given a period garden, and stocked with antiques; and especially for children, the tour (by costumed members of the Colonial Dames of America, which maintains the house) is pretty interesting.

The **Asia Society** (☎ 212-288-6400), housing the collection of John D. Rockefeller III, is on Park Avenue at East 70th Street; the space has been renovated, and a garden cafe installed. If you enjoy more commercial art, the **Society of Illustrators** at 128 East 63rd east of Park Avenue exhibits graphic arts, illustrations, and award-winning book jackets. The **New York Women's Exchange** on Third Avenue above East 64th is more than a century old, one of those cooperatives designed to help women make money from their handicrafts; it's still an interesting source of crafts and gifts.

The **Seventh Regiment Armory** on Park between East 66th and 67th, where many of the city's major art and antiques exhibits are held, looks like an oversized sand castle, but the inside, if you can see past the wares of the fairs, was furnished by Louis Comfort Tiffany.

This is still where the wealthy gather: The 17-story Art Deco building known both as **740 Park Avenue** and 71 East 71st Street was the childhood home of Jacqueline Bouvier, whose grandfather built it, and the final residence of John D. Rockefeller Jr., who lived in a 24-

room, 12-bathroom apartment from 1938 to 1960. At various times it has been home to philanthropist Enid Haupt, corporate buyout king Henry Kravitz, Saul Steinberg, Seagrams founder Edgar Bronfman, Steven Ross (who built a 24-room, 11-bath of his own), Greek shipping tycoon Spyros Niarchos, Ronald Lauder of Estee Lauder, Ronald Perelman of Revlon, heads of banana and sugar conglomerates, actor Gary Cooper, and a few diplomats as well.

Among other buildings with strange histories is the one at **131 East 71st Street** between Park and Lexington; it was built during the Civil War, but designer Elsie de Wolfe redid the façade in 1910 as a sort of silent advertisement of her own style. The **Knickerbocker Club** building on East 62nd at Fifth Avenue used to have a twin next door; it was famous as the home of Mrs. Marcellus Hartley Dodge, a Rockefeller cousin, who filled her five-story mansion with all the stray dogs she could rescue. Next to it is the **810 Fifth Avenue** building, onetime home to William Randolph Hearst, Richard Nixon, and Nelson Rockefeller—penthouse, bomb shelter, and all.

Madison Avenue is now more commercial than residential, but oh, what commercialism! (For more on Madison Avenue shopping, see "Great Neighborhoods for Shopping" in Part Nine.)

kids For fans of Ludwig Bemelmans' *Madeline* children's books, the **Carlyle Hotel's Bemelmans' Bar,** which the author decorated, prepares special dishes for proper young ladies, Wednesday through Sunday at lunch and tea time (East 76th Street and Madison Avenue; ☎ 212-744-1600).

Although **Roosevelt Island** in the East River is now a residential community, it once held a rather exotic assortment of institutions—lunatic asylums, smallpox hospitals, workhouses, poorhouses, and prisons; it was almost the dark reflection of the wealth of the East Side. (It was once called Welfare Island, as a matter of fact, but of course that word isn't P.C. anymore.) There are a few historical buildings left, including a lighthouse; and the **Roosevelt Island Aerial Tramway,** a 250-foot-high sky ride, crosses over from Second Avenue and 60th Street about every 15 minutes (☎ 212-832-4543).

unofficial **TIP** Roosevelt Island is a particularly great place to watch the Fourth of July fireworks.

Starting at about 70th Street, Fifth Avenue is the heart of "Museum Mile," that fantastic array of museums and collections ranging more than 20 blocks—more nearly a mile and a half—from the **Metropolitan Museum of Art** at 82nd Street (☎ 212-535-7710) and the **Neue Gallerie** of German and Austrian decorative arts across the street (☎ 212-628-6200) past the **Guggenheim** (☎ 212-423-3500), the **Museum of the City of New York** (☎ 212-534-1672), the **National Academy Museum** (☎ 212-369-4880), and the **Cooper-Hewitt National Museum of Design** (☎ 212-849-8300) to **El Museo del Barrio** at 104th (☎ 212-831-7272). (Many of these museums are profiled in depth in Part Seven.)

Like the rest of the East Side, Fifth Avenue didn't really hit its stride until about a century ago, when the Fourth Avenue railroad track became Park Avenue and the Met, as the Metropolitan Museum is almost universally known, had acquired a reputation rivaling the great collections of Europe (and when conditions in Midtown, increasingly crowded, middle-class, and noisy, made these "inner suburbs" more desirable). Like the area to the south, it is studded with the onetime homes of the wealthy; the French Renaissance **Jewish Museum** on Fifth Avenue at East 92nd (☎ 212-423-3200) was once the homestead of financier Felix Warburg, and the **Cooper-Hewitt** on East 91st at Fifth Avenue was originally Andrew Carnegie's home (he asked for something "modest and plain"). The **National Academy Museum** at 89th was railroad magnate Archer Huntingdon's home.

The shortest of strolls will be enough to show you what real wealth bought a hundred years ago. The current headquarters of the **Commonwealth Fund** at East 75th and Fifth was built for an heir to a Standard Oil fortune; the Renaissance Revival mansion at **25 East 78th Street** and Madison Avenue was built for a railroad president. New York University's **Institute of Fine Arts,** down the block on 78th at Fifth, is housed in what was once the home of American Tobacco founder James Duke and was copied from a chateau in Bordeaux. At **111 East 77th Street** is the stable used by Edith Wharton when she lived on Park between 78th and 79th streets. And also on Fifth Avenue between 78th and 79th streets is the **French Embassy,** once the home of finance icon Payne Whitney, and more recently the site of an apparent Michelangelo sighting, although the Cupid in question has been removed from the lobby and consigned to experts' debates.

Consider the single block of East 91st Street between Fifth and Madison avenues. Facing the Cooper-Hewitt at **No. 1 East 91st** is the last palace of **"Millionaire's Row,"** built for banker Otto Kahn and now a convent school; at No. 7 is the **Burden House,** the home of a Vanderbilt shipping heiress who married a Burden steel scion and of a prominent society rental site (the spiral staircase, centered under a stained-glass dome, was known as "the stairway to heaven"). And next to that, at **No. 9,** is the house where jazz record producer John Hammond was "set up" by his wife's old-society family.

One of the ex–Mrs. Vanderbilts commissioned the French Revival mansion at **60 East 93rd Street** between Park and Madison. Flashy Broadway figure and party boy Billy Rose was a millionaire of a lesser sort, perhaps best known as Mr. Fanny Brice, but he lived well enough to build a great Scottish-romantic mansion of his own across the street at **No. 56** (now an alcoholism treatment facility). Even the **Synod of Bishops of the Russian Orthodox Church outside Russia** across the street was once a private home, the mansion of banker George Baker; its collection of icons is a must-see for devotees of Byzantine and Eastern Orthodox art (by appointment only; ☎ 212-534-1601).

The block of East 80th Street between Lexington and Park also has three mansions lined up one after another, built for a Whitney (**No. 120**), a Dillon (**No. 124**), and another Astor (**No. 130**).

If these mansions start to overwhelm you, go east. **Gracie Mansion** (☎ 212-570-4751), the official residence of the mayor of New York and original home of the Museum of the City of New York, is in **Carl Schurz Park** overlooking the East River at East 88th Street. Its name salutes Scottish immigrant Archibald Gracie, who built a summer home here back in 1799, although an earlier house is known to have been destroyed during the American Revolution. It has only been the mayor's residence since the days of Fiorello La Guardia—like Lincoln Center, it was the brainchild of Parks Commissioner Robert Moses.

The newly repolished **Whitney Museum of American Art** (profiled in detail in Part Seven), too aggressively modern for Museum Mile, juts out in an inverse pyramid over Madison Avenue at East 75th Street. The **92nd Street Y** (☎ 212-996-1100), as the Young Men and Women's Hebrew Association there is commonly known, is famous for its concerts, readings, and lectures by national and international as well as local artists and writers. The original **Playhouse 91,** home of the Jewish Repertory Theater, is on East 91st between First and Second (☎ 212-831-2000).

The **Russian Orthodox Cathedral of St. Nicholas** at East 97th and Fifth is like the whole Kremlin squashed together, with five onion domes and multicolored tile detailing—Moscow on, if not the Hudson, at least the East River (by appointment only; phone ☎ 212-289-1915). It is also the repository of 34 icons that had been smuggled out and were about to be sold on the black market when customs officials rescued them; they are estimated to be worth more than $3 million and date to the mid-18th and 19th centuries. The **Islamic Center of New York** on Third at East 96th Street is the spiritual home to the city's Moslems of whom there may be as many as half a million; it was computer-measured to ensure that it faces directly toward Mecca.

A few old-time neighborhood nicknames persist. **Yorkville** is what used to be New York's Germantown but is now just as much black and Hispanic as European, running nearly the length of the Upper East Side from Lexington Avenue over to the river. Carl Schurz, for whom the park surrounding Gracie Mansion is named, was a German immigrant who became editor of the *New York Post* and *Harper's Weekly* and, after the Civil War, secretary of the interior. **Hell Gate** was not a gang hangout but the spot where the Harlem River and Long Island Sound converge into New York Harbor—perhaps a hellish spot for river pilots. **Carnegie Hill,** which ranges from the Cooper-Hewitt (formerly the Carnegie mansion) at 91st Street north to the boutique and cafe area of Madison Avenue, is a rapidly upscaling residential neighborhood. And the area north of 96th Street and east of Fifth Avenue is still commonly known as Spanish Harlem or East Harlem.

MORNINGSIDE HEIGHTS, HAMILTON HEIGHTS, AND HARLEM

THOUGH OFTEN OVERLOOKED BY TOURISTS, Upper Manhattan is filled with important educational institutions, historical sites, and beautiful churches, museums, and 19th-century houses. And Harlem, of course, is both New York's proudest and poorest black neighborhood: rich in architecture, onetime center of a cultural renaissance and on the verge of becoming one again, but also the area with the highest death rate among young black men in the nation. East Harlem runs with an almost official harshness into the Upper East Side at 97th Street, despite the extension of Museum Mile up to **El Museo del Barrio** on 104th. Whole rooms from John D. Rockefeller's onetime mansion at Fifth and 51st Street have been moved to the **Museum of the City of New York** on Fifth at 103rd (both are profiled in Part Seven). But walk across 103rd to the east, and you'll find yourself in an area Rockefeller wouldn't have stabled horses in.

There are real "heights," or at least ranges of hills, that stand between the Upper West Side and such western neighborhoods as Morningside Heights (between about West 110th and Martin Luther King Boulevard); Hamilton Heights, also known as Harlem Heights, centered on City College of New York (CCNY) and running up to around Trinity Cemetery at West 155th Street; and Washington Heights above that. The Heights run about four blocks west from the long green of Riverside Park; Harlem (and East Harlem, as the area beyond Fifth Avenue is called) runs to the East River and up alongside the Harlem River, an area of nearly six square miles.

Morningside Park, a sort of comma between Central Park and Riverside Park, opened in the late 19th century and almost immediately became an enclave of scholars and theologians. **Columbia University**, whose campus ranges from about 116th Street to 124th from Morningside to Riverside Drive, is the heart of this neighborhood, with **Barnard College**, the **Union Theological Seminary,** and massive **Riverside Church** on its western flank and the extraordinary and still-growing **Cathedral Church of St. John the Divine** on Amsterdam at 112th (profiled in depth in Part Seven, Sightseeing, Tours, and Attractions).

Riverside Church, at 122nd Street, was another of John D. Rockefeller Jr.'s gifts to the city, a 21-story Gothic beauty inspired by the cathedral at Chartres; its carillon of 74 bells is the largest in the world (one weighs 20 tons by itself), and the 22,000-pipe organ is one of the largest. Free tours are offered following Sunday services, about 12:30 p.m. (☎ 212-870-6700).

*un*official **TIP**
Riverside Church offers a spectacular view of the river and a 360-degree view of the city from the observation deck off the bell tower, nearly 400 feet high.

And if you want to know who's buried in **Grant's Tomb,** walk through Riverside Park to that mausoleum on the hill. (The answer, incidentally, is both Grant and his wife.)

On Morningside Drive at West 114th Street is a more intimate chapel, the **Eglise de Notre Dame.** It contains a replica of the grotto of Lourdes where young girls saw visions of the Virgin Mary; a woman who believed her son was healed there had the replica constructed in thanks.

If you drew a line extending Central Park West (Eighth Avenue) past Cathedral Parkway, which runs along the northern border of Central Park, and on up into the Heights where Eighth Avenue is called Frederick Douglass Boulevard, it would be a very rough estimate of the western edge of Harlem. In fact, **Hamilton Heights,** which has several beautiful blocks of row houses along Convent Avenue between about 141st and 145th streets, was a highly desirable neighborhood for both turn-of-the-19th-century white and early-20th-century black residents, when it was nicknamed **Sugar Hill** and housed such jazz celebrities as Cab Calloway, Duke Ellington, and Count Basie; writers including Langston Hughes, Zora Neale Hurston, and Ralph Ellison; and such prominent blacks as Sugar Ray Robinson, Paul Robeson, and Thurgood Marshall. It was also home to Richard Rodgers, Lorenz Hart, and Milton Berle, among others. The current **Hamilton Heights–Sugar Hill Historic District**—so named because the area was once the country estate of Alexander Hamilton—is centered on four blocks of finely preserved row houses, many of them now residences of City College (CCNY) faculty and administrators. (Hamilton's 1802 house, the Grange, has been moved to 287 Convent Avenue.) The watchtower just south of CCNY on Amsterdam at 135th Street and the gatehouses at 113th and 119th streets are remnants of the old aqueduct system. More intriguingly, the three-level cast-iron tower in **Marcus Garvey Park** (East 120th to 124th and Madison) is a survivor of the Revolutionary Battle of Harlem Heights.

And speaking of remnants: **Our Lady of Lourdes Church** at 142nd Street and Amsterdam is a true miracle of salvage, having been put together in 1904 from bits of the old National Academy of Design at Park and East 23rd Street, the A. T. Stewart department store on the old Ladies' Mile, and the former Madison Avenue apse of St. Patrick's Cathedral, removed to make room for what is now the Lady Chapel.

At the top of Hamilton Heights are **Trinity Cemetery** and **Audubon Terrace,** which face each other across Broadway between West 153rd and 155th streets. This whole area was once part of the estate of John James Audubon, and the naturalist himself, along with many of those whose names appear repeatedly in these pages—Astors, Schermerhorns, Van Burens, and Clement Clarke Moore—are buried at Trinity Cemetery. (Audubon's gravestone is, appropriately, carved with birds.)

Several institutions of more specialized interest are gathered at Audubon Terrace, including the **American Numismatic Society** (☎ 212-234-3130) and the **Hispanic Society of America** (☎ 212-926-2234), a little-known museum with a fantastic collection of Spanish art by

Goya, El Greco, Velázquez, etc. The **American Academy of Arts and Letters,** which mounts periodic exhibitions featuring the works of members, is also here (☎ 212-368-5900). Audubon Terrace is a sort of family affair itself; Architect Charles Pratt Huntington designed the buildings, his philanthropist cousin Archer Huntington donated most of the money and the bulk of the Spanish art collection, and Charles's wife, Anna Hyatt Huntington, sculpted the Cid memorial. (This isn't even the only Huntington museum. Archer Huntington donated his private home on Fifth Avenue for the National Academy Museum and School of Fine Arts.)

Although Harlem is generally thought of as a black area, it is actually a mix of African American, Caribbean, and Hispanic (particularly Puerto Rican) families. East Harlem is often referred to as **El Barrio,** Spanish for "the neighborhood," or **Spanish Harlem.** However, in recent years, a growing Cuban/Caribbean community has flourished along Broadway north of Hamilton Heights as well.

In any case, Harlem certainly began as a black neighborhood; it was the first African slaves, in fact, imported by the Dutch, who blazed the original Broadway by moving up the island to Nieuw Haarlem in 1658. And though most of the area was taken up by the large farms and country estates, the East and Harlem riverfronts were an inevitable ramshackle assortment of immigrants and watermen. It was a popular upper-middle-class suburb for most of the 19th century, with its own commuter rail system, the New York and Harlem Railroad, to carry businessmen back downtown; but around the turn of the century, things began to go sour. Businesses went bankrupt, buildings emptied, and the continual northward press of development from the wealthier sections of Manhattan drove black and immigrant families into many of the poorer areas.

By the early 20th century, Harlem was the major community for blacks with all levels of income. The famous Harlem Renaissance of literature, music, and philosophy had a powerful effect on both high art and popular culture, raising Harlem's profile and giving greater force to the growing civil rights debate.

Despite the predations of time, poverty, and unimaginative urban renewal, many old brownstones are still visible in such areas as the **Mount Morris Park Historical District,** a Victorian enclave that was dominated by German-Jewish families "moving up" from the Lower East Side. It covers about five blocks between Lenox Avenue and Marcus Garvey Park (formerly Mount Morris Park) between West 119th and 124th streets, and there are several proposals for renovating buildings for boutique hotels or bed-and-breakfasts here. The fire tower in the park dates from 1856. **St. Martin's Episcopal Church** at Lenox and 122nd has a fine carillon of its own, about 40 bells strong.

A couple of blocks northwest of the park are the **Studio Museum of Harlem,** west of Lenox Avenue on 125th Street (☎ 212-864-4500), a small (but expanding) select collection of African, African American, and Caribbean fine arts that also offers lectures and educational programs; and the famed **Apollo Theater** on West 125th between Adam Clayton Powell and Frederick Douglass boulevards (☎ 212-531-5305), founded as a vaudeville house in 1914 and the major showcase of black talent well into the 1960s. It has been revived, and the Wednesday Amateur Night tradition is as strong and lively as ever.

From here it's only a block's walk to **Sylvia's,** a soul-food restaurant so famous that its gospel brunch is on many Harlem tours; it's located on Lenox between West 126th and 127th streets (☎ 212-996-0660). Then head straight up Lenox to West 135th and the **Schomburg Center for Research in Black Culture,** the largest library of African and African American cultural and sociological materials in this country (☎ 212-491-2200).

On West 138th Street between Lenox and Adam Clayton Powell Avenue is the **Abyssinian Baptist Church,** equally famous as the one-time pastoral seat of Powell himself and for its gospel choir; its Sunday services draw busloads of tourists from all around the world (☎ 212-862-7474). The blocks of West 138th and 139th from Adam Clayton Powell Avenue over to Frederick Douglass constitute the **St. Nicholas Historic District,** another group of late–19th-century homes designed by several different prominent architects of the day. The neighborhood is also known as **Striver's Row** because it drew a pre-yuppie-era group of ambitious young professionals.

At the top of St. Nicholas Park at West 141st Street is the famous **Harlem School of the Arts,** which has come to rival the New York High School for the Performing Arts (the model for the school in *Fame*) with its music, dance, and theater classes (☎ 212-926-4100).

If you are particularly interested in contemporary black theater, you may also wish to contact the **Frank Silvera Writers' Workshop** at West 125th and St. Nicholas (☎ 212-281-8832) and the small but prestigious **National Black Theater** at Fifth and East 125th Street (☎ 212-722-3800).

> *unofficial* **TIP**
> If you like walking, you can fairly easily follow the path we've laid out from Marcus Garvey Park back to Harlem Heights. Sadly, although conditions are improving, we still cannot recommend that you wander other parts of Harlem by yourself, especially after dark; it's best to stick to the most famous sites, take cabs, or hook up with a tour group.

WASHINGTON HEIGHTS

THE AREA NORTH OF TRINITY CEMETERY and Audubon Terrace, called Washington Heights, was the area to which Washington's troops retreated—the Morris-Jumel Mansion served as his headquarters—during the early battles of the American Revolution, and it centers on Fort Tryon Park. While the park's official highlights are the remaining defiant bulwark and its overlook, the 62-acre park offers a far finer overview of Manhattan's original beauty, the Hudson River, and the fine woods and animal life; and it serves as a natural approach to the stunning Cloisters collection of the Met.

The **Morris-Jumel Mansion** at West 160th Street and Edgecrombe (☎ 212-923-8008), which dates from 1765, is one of the very few colonial buildings still standing in New York. It was a summer estate—its grounds stretched from Harlem to the Hudson—belonging to Roger Morris, a prominent Loyalist who had served as aide to General Braddock. Morris refused to act against his former colleague (and rumored rival for the hand of the wealthy Mrs. Morris) Washington, but even so, his estates were confiscated by the revolutionary state government, and the Morrises returned to England. Washington did in fact sleep here and briefly used it as a headquarters; so, ironically, did Sir Henry Clinton, the British commander. More amazingly, Washington, Jefferson, Hamilton, John Adams and his son John Quincy Adams met here for lunch in 1790. The "Jumel" part is equally intriguing: French-Caribbean Creole merchant Stephen Jumel bought it in 1810 and lavishly remodeled it with the help of his socially ambitious wife, Eliza; she allegedly slept her way through much of New York society, let her husband bleed to death so as to make her a very rich widow, and then married the ruined, aging Aaron Burr—only to divorce him on his deathbed. Her reputation for cold-bloodedness and the house's reputation for reproachful spirits led to its having been "cleansed" by a Haitian exorcist a few decades later. Among her furniture is a dolphin chair said to have been purchased from Napoleon.

The new five-acre **Swindler Cove Park,** where Dykeman Street meets the Harlem River, owes its existence in great part to singer Bette Midler and her New York Restoration Project; it is the home of a new rowing program intended to provide underpriviledged kids with experience and perhaps scholarships.

Fort Tryon Park, which runs from Broadway to Riverside Drive between West 192nd and Dykeman streets, is only part of the original Billings estate; the massive series of arches on Riverside Drive was the "driveway." It was landscaped, like most of New York's great parks, by Frederick Law Olmsted, and it has an incredible assortment of views and gardens. The effect is immediately visible and almost shocking as you get off the "A" train at 190th Street; although they have not yet been fully restored, the stone terraces down the hillside and the arched entrance to the park seem to bound a different world, a medieval one; it couldn't be a better setting for the **Cloisters.** Its various paths and roadways (watch out for buses) are popular with joggers and exercise walkers, but are rarely crowded. There is a marker, a bit of remaining battlement, on the hilltop of the park that recalls the defense of Fort Washington from the British. (A little gatehouse, down the slope from the marker, has been turned into a nice little cafe, good for a break.)

The Cloisters (profiled in depth in Part Seven, Sightseeing, Tours, and Attractions) is actually the medieval collection arm of the Metropolitan Museum of Art (you can use the same admission badge to enter both on a single day), and it was constructed from wings of several medieval French and Spanish cloisters. This is one of New York's premier attractions, gloriously evocative and frequently nearly deserted. Astonishingly, the estate that is now Fort Tryon Park, the Cloisters buildings—painstakingly transported from Europe and reassembled here—as well as the Palisades across the Hudson River and the art and manuscripts of the collection itself were all gifts of philanthropist John D. Rockefeller Jr.

Almost at the other end of the spectrum is the **Shrine of St. Frances X. Cabrini** on Fort Washington Avenue at 190th. Mother Cabrini, as she is usually called, is the patron saint of immigrants, and her remains (with the exception of her head, which is in Rome) are encased within the altar. The miraculous story here is that shortly after her death in 1917, a blind child was touched with a lock of her hair and received sight; naturally, he entered the priesthood. Mother Cabrini was the first American citizen to be canonized, but since she was Italian by birth, Mother Elizabeth Seton can honestly claim to be the first American-born saint (see the section on Lower Manhattan, Wall Street, and the Battery).

A few blocks from the Cloisters at Broadway and West 204th Street (☎ 212-304-9422) is the **Dyckman House,** the only surviving 18th-century Dutch farmhouse (circa 1783) on the island, authentically fitted out and surrounded by a smokehouse and garden.

Other sites of interest in Washington Heights include **Yeshiva University,** the oldest Jewish seminary in the country, founded in 1886 (at West 186th Street and Amsterdam Avenue); the old **Loews 175th Street Theatre** at Broadway, another of those fantastic movie palaces-turned-churches (it was called a "Wonder Palace," which seems appropriate); and the **High Bridge,** the oldest footbridge (and sometime aqueduct) between Manhattan and the mainland. Begun in 1839, it stretches across the Harlem River from Highbridge Park at West 174th Street to West 170th in the Bronx.

If your children have read *The Little Red Lighthouse and the Great Gray Bridge,* head to Fort Washington Park at about West 178th Street and you'll see the lighthouse just below the eastern tower of the George Washington Bridge.

kids

BROOKLYN

BROOKLYNITES HAVE GOOD REASON TO RESENT all those jokes about accents and Coney Island culture. Even if it seceded from the rest of New York City, Brooklyn (from "Breukelen," Dutch for "Broken Land") would be the nation's fourth largest city, with enough famous landmarks, museums, and resorts to make it a long weekend's destination of its own.

Start by walking across the Brooklyn Bridge itself, which offers one of New York's best viewpoints in all directions. Fulton Ferry Landing is the site of Bargemusic, and beyond that is the **Brooklyn Heights Historic District.** Ranging from the riverfront Expressway to about Atlantic Avenue, this area is an amazing pre–Civil War enclave of more than 600 churches and homes (including those of Walt Whitman, Arthur Miller, W. H. Auden, Thomas Wolfe, and Truman Capote). **The Promenade,** along the East River, has a spectacular view of Manhattan, an almost idyllic grid of community gardens and playgrounds, and a marker for Four Chimneys, where George Washington billeted during the War of Long Island. **Park Slope,** the stretch of Fifth Avenue between Ninth Street and Bergen Street, and **Smith Street** near Carroll Garden are among the hottest new restaurant and boutique enclaves in any of the five boroughs. The **Brooklyn Historical Society,** which spotlights local heroes ranging from the Brooklyn Dodgers to *The Honeymooners,* is in the historic district at Pierrepont and Clinton streets (☎ 718-222-4111 or visit **www.brooklyn history.org**). **St. Ann and the Holy Trinity Episcopal Church** at Montague and Clinton is in need of repair, but its extremely fine stained-glass windows by William Jay Bolton are the oldest set of figural windows made in the United States.

A little to the north is the neighborhood now known as **DUMBO**— Down Under the Manhattan Bridge Overpass—which is threatening to supplant Chelsea as the artists' hangout, just as Chelsea once supplanted Soho. Around the area where the footings of the Manhattan and Brooklyn bridges nearly meet, an estimated 1,000 artists and performers fill 700 lofts in 15 square blocks. And plans are underway to renovate the huge **Empire Stores** warehouse into a state-of-the-art restaurant, retail, and performance space.

Brooklyn's population has always been a vital ethnic mix, but these days it has replaced Manhattan as the real melting pot. Its many distinct communities include Caribbean (especially Jamaican and Haitian), African (Nigerian, Senegalese, Ghanian), Spanish, Middle Eastern and Arabic, Turkish and Georgian, Scandinavian, Russian, Polish, Orthodox Jewish, and Italian. Many famous neighborhoods and destinations—not just Coney Island but also Brighton Beach and Rockaway Beach, Flatbush, Brooklyn Heights, Prospect Park, and Jamaica Bay—are in this 75-square-mile borough. (Incidentally, be careful not to confuse the Broadway in Brooklyn with the Broadway in Manhattan; Brooklyn's runs southeast from the Williamsburg Bridge.)

It has also become a sort of second Harlem, in that it is developing a group of black cultural and social centers that could easily become another "Renaissance." The Fort Greene area in particular has a number of cafes that sponsor poetry readings, art galleries, and performance spaces. The most prestigious are the **Paul Robeson Theater** (40

Greene Avenue; ☎ 718-783-9794) and **BAM Café** (30 Lafayette; ☎ 718-636-4139), an outreach project of the Brooklyn Museum. Fort Greene may become even more popular if plans go through for the New Jersey Nets to move to a huge new arena complex there.

One of the most important neighborhoods for first-time visitors is the area around **Prospect Park,** at the junction of Eastern Parkway and Flatbush Avenue (☎ 718-965-8900). This, the Central Park of Brooklyn (designed by the same men, Frederick Olmsted and Calvert Vaux, and with similar facilities and features), includes a children's zoo, officially the **Prospect Park Wildlife Conservation Center** (☎ 718-399-7339), that is even larger than the more famous Bronx facility; an **antique carousel** as fine as Central Park's and rescued from Coney Island; a mid–19th-century Italianate villa; and a skating rink and croquet shed designed by Stanford White. It even has its own cemetery, a Friends (Quaker) burial ground where Montgomery Clift is interred.

The northern boundary of the park adjoins the **Brooklyn Botanic Garden** grounds, which then lead over to the **Brooklyn Museum,** a collection nearly as comprehensive as the Metropolitan's but far more comprehensible. On weekends and holidays, a free trolley links these three major attractions. And serving as a grand foyer to it all is **Grand Army Plaza** at Plaza Street and Flatbush Avenue: Olmsted and Vaux's grand oval, with its triumphal Soldier's and Sailor's Arch and a monument bust of JFK.

kids   In addition to these sites, Brooklyn has several other attractions of particular interest to families. At the closer end are the **Brooklyn Children's Museum** (☎ 718-735-4402), actually only another few blocks away from the parks we just discussed; and the newly renovated **New York Transit Museum** (☎ 718-694-1600), a little east of the Brooklyn Heights Historic District at Schermerhorn Street between Court Street and Boerum Place. A former subway station, it now houses a fine collection of vintage cars, signal equipment and signs, old photos, drawings, and subway mosaics that served as directions for the illiterate and non-English-speaking immigrants.

The other most intriguing area is the Brighton Beach–Coney Island area at the southern end of the borough. The famous **Coney Island** amusement park, somewhat less lustrous than in its heyday as "the world's largest playground" but still good for a stroll along the boardwalk, a ride on the teeth-rattling wooden Cyclone roller coaster (the skeletal remains of its predecessor, the Tornado, are almost scary), and an original Nathan's "foot-long" hot dog; the **New York Aquarium** (☎ 718-265-3474), with its shark tank, SeaWorld–style whale and dolphin "theater," and hands-on Discovery Cove is just alongside the park, and so is the new **Brooklyn Cyclones** (aka "Baby Mets") stadium; the Miami Beach–like Borscht Boardwalk of **Brighton Beach** is perhaps another mile down the way. Eat in the melting pot; have a hot dog at the game and a knish later. Or sushi—advertised in Cyrillic letters. Now you know why they call it "Little Odessa by the Sea." Even farther east is **Jamaica Bay Wildlife Refuge Center,** a ten-mile stretch of beach near Rockaway that is a migratory marker for more than 300 species of birds. Park rangers lead hikes on weekends (☎ 718-318-4340). The park even has its own subway stop at Broad Channel.

The **Brooklyn Academy of Music** (BAM) on Lafayette near Fulton Street (☎ 718-636-4100), as mentioned in Part Eleven, is not only a respected concert venue and home of the Brooklyn Philharmonic but also has its own opera house, the restored and aptly named Majestic Theater a block down Fulton Street, and several smaller performance spaces. As the BAM boosters like to point out, its history is every bit as lustrous as Broadway's: Sarah Bernhardt, Edwin Booth, Anna Pavlova, Sergei Rachmaninoff, Carl Sandburg, Winston Churchill, and Enrico Caruso all performed here. Its October Next Wave Festival is extremely popular.

QUEENS

QUEENS, PARTICULARLY THE AREA CALLED **Long Island City,** is suddenly being rediscovered. Here you'll find the recently renovated **Isamu Noguchi Museum** (32–37 Vernon Boulevard; ☎ 718-204-7088), **P.S. 1 Contemporary Art Center** (Jackson Avenue at 46th Street; ☎ 718-784-2084), and the **Museum for African Art** (43rd Avenue and 36th Street; ☎ 718-784-7700). All this art has in turn sparked a flurry of neighborhood eateries. The Noguchi home is one of the few collections in the world devoted to one man's work, filling 12 galleries with his celebrated lamps and theatrical sets, and a gorgeous sculpture garden displays his larger pieces. The adjoining **Museum for African Art** is small but first-rate, exhibiting both traditional and contemporary arts.

Queens offers another example of a fine day's sightseeing, since most of what a visitor is likely to want to see is at **Flushing Meadows–Corona Park,** especially if you figure in the Mets' **Shea Stadium,** also used as a concert venue, and the **U.S. Tennis Association's** complex, where the U.S. Open is held. This is Queens's main public park, with its own zoo, rowboat lake, ice rink, dual-stage theater in the park, bike rentals, and so on, and frequent special events (☎ 718-520-5900); it was the site of two World's Fairs (1939–1940 and 1964–1965) and is still home of the **New York Hall of Science,** the **Queens Wildlife Center** (☎ 718-271-1500), and the **Queens Museum of Art.** It's a world unto itself—that is, the 140-foot, 350-ton Unisphere globe, created for the 1964 World's Fair, still stands at the entrance. And this world, too, we owe to Robert Moses, who dredged out what had been a notorious swamp and rubbish pile to make a place worthy of an international exhibition.

Restored and renovated a couple of years ago, the park is now a sort of Disney Futurama of the past—what New Yorkers of 60 years ago expected of the 21st century. The "skyscape" is almost a spacescape, full of rocket ships and planets. And like Disney World's backwards glimpse at "progress," it reminds us that such marvels as robots, color film, synthetic fabrics, FM radio, and dishwashers were brand new in 1939. Space vehicles, elevated superhighways, and heliports were the hottest draws in 1964. Many of these exhibits have been preserved, along with time capsules, one from each fair, not to be opened for 5,000 years.

unofficial TIP
Friday through Sunday, trolleys circulate among the park attractions and the Willets Point–Shea Stadium subway; $1 buys you all-day access.

The **New York Hall of Science** (☎ 718-699-0005) was originally constructed as the Hall of Education for the 1964–65 World's Fair (and has recently been provided with a 55,000-square-foot addition), but is scrupulously and often astonishingly up to date; it has interactive video stations that store outer-space transmissions, super-TV-sized microscope displays, and scores of hands-on demonstrations of light, music, color, and physical properties—not to mention the 3-D spiderweb.

If Brooklyn's Museum of Art is like a miniature Metropolitan, the **Queens Museum of Art** (☎ 718-592-9700) is like a miniature New York: It was the original New York City Building of the fair. It houses a huge and detailed scale model (1 inch to 100 feet) of New York called the Panorama that was also constructed for the World's Fair and is regularly updated to reflect changes in the New York skyline (including the destruction of the Twin Towers, represented by beams of light). It includes all five boroughs, almost 900,000 individual buildings, a 15-inch Empire State Building, 35 bridges, and airplanes that actually "take off" from LaGuardia. The museum also has hundreds of bits of World's fair memorabilia, such as guidebooks, souvenir plates and pins, board games, and banners. It also has a fine collection of Tiffany glass, reflecting the time when Tiffany's studios were in Queens.

For history buffs, this building also has special significance: It served as the temporary headquarters of the United Nations from 1946 to 1951, and it was here that the nation of Israel was voted into existence.

Queens has recently opened an attraction that might seem more suited to Harlem, but that is completely at home here: **Louis Armstrong's** longtime home, extravagantly decorated in high 1940s style by his fourth wife, Walle Wilson. They lived here together until his death—in his beloved "wall-to-wall" bed (which is very nearly that wide)—in 1971; she lived there until her death in 1983. Highlights include the custom-built turquoise kitchen appliances, the gold-foil master bathroom, and the portrait of Armstrong by Tony Bennett. The house is located on 107th Street between 34th and 37th avenues, in Corona (☎ 718-997-3670).

For foodies, the stretch of **Roosevelt Avenue** from about 60th Street to 90th Street is a famous world's fare, so to speak. Here you can sample Indian, Pakistani, Mexican, Korean, Cuban, Uruguayan, Filipino, Chinese, Thai, and even Texan cooking. **Flushing** has become a multi-regional Chinatown. Be sure to carry that Alka-Seltzer.

If you love over-the-top architecture, it might be worth ending the day with a side trip to Jamaica (to either the Parsons Boulevard or Jamaica Center subway stops, accessible from the Forest Hills station at the east end of the park or the 74th Street station at the west side) to visit the **Tabernacle of Prayer for All People** at Jamaica and Merrick Boulevard. Constructed in the late 1920s as a movie palace, it is a rococo Spanish extravaganza of gold, enamel, cobalt, inlay, and even stars above. Open to visitors Friday evenings and Sundays; call ☎ 718-657-4210 for information.

Astoria, the northwest part of Queens (the part that faces the Upper East Side across the East River), is home to the **American Museum of the Moving Image** at 35th Avenue and 36th Street (☎ 718-784-4520) and **PS 1** (Jackson Avenue at 46th Avenue; ☎ 718-784-2084), one of the largest and most influential contemporary art centers. The "PS 1" name is short for Public School No. 1, which is what it originally was; now, it's an affiliate of the Museum of Modern Art.

In recent years, Queens has become a trendy destination for food-lovers as well. Flushing is flush with inexpensive Asian delights, and Corona is King of the Brazilian churrascaria. And Astoria's famous Greek ethnic community is second in size only to that in Athens itself; it is packed with restaurants, delicatessens, bakeries, and gift shops. Just stroll Broadway in the 30s and follow your nose.

THE BRONX

THERE WAS A TIME WHEN THIS WAS RICH WOODLANDS, then farmland (it was the 17th-century estate of retired sailor Jonas Bronck); it was genteel country estate territory in the 19th century; and even into the early 20th century it was a prestigious address. (Many neighborhoods, particularly Riverdale, still are.) Sadly, at this point in history those northward waves and ripples of alternating prosperity and decay have left the South Bronx in a slough. However, there is revived interest in the area, and some philanthropic and government funding is coming in for restoration.

Its most famous attractions, of course, are the **Bronx Zoo** (formally, the International Wildlife Conservation Park), the **New York Botanical Garden,** and **Yankee Stadium,** the House that Ruth Built—and when you come out of the subway at 161st Street, you'll see why the old Yankees-Dodgers contests were called "subway series": You can see right into the stands from the tracks. And it's here that you'll find the city's largest public green space, Pelham Bay Park, which is three times as large as Central Park.

The Grand Concourse, which is the great boulevard of the Bronx, runs from the Harlem River right up toward the botanical garden. The garden and the Bronx Zoo are neighbors, more or less, although there is a bit of a walk between the respective entrances. Both are near the campus of **Fordham University.**

The **Edgar Allan Poe Cottage** (☎ 718-881-8900) at Grand Concourse and East Kingsbridge Road is where Poe and the dying Virginia lived from 1846 to 1848, and it houses many of his manuscripts and memorabilia.

Toward the northern edge of the Bronx (and of the subway lines) are several historical estates, most notably the **Van Cortlandt House Museum** in Van Cortlandt Park (☎ 718-543-3344), a restored mid–18th-century mansion used by Washington as one of his headquarters (there was skirmish fire in the yard) and furnished with authentic period Dutch and American pieces as well as Delft ceramics. On the east side, Van Cortlandt Park adjoins **Woodlawn Cemetery** (☎ 718-920-0500), where the wealthy (Woolworths, Macys, Goulds, Belmonts, Armours, etc.) built eternal homes as elaborate as their temporal ones; get a map at the Webster Street entrance.

A few blocks west of Van Cortlandt Park is **Wave Hill,** the former estate of financier/conservationist George Perkins and at various points home to Theodore Roosevelt, Mark Twain, Arturo Toscanini, and so on. Take one glimpse of its view, over the Hudson River toward the Palisades, and you'll see why. The mansion is now used for concerts (in the vaulted Armor Hall), art exhibits ranging from sculpture to topiary, and demonstrations; the gardens and grounds are also open; call ☎ 718-549-3200.

unofficial **TIP**
Although it requires a little more planning, those interested in sailing and whaling might want to visit **City Island** just off the northeast shore of the Bronx, a community of sailing vessels, boatyards (including the manufacturers of several America's Cup champs), marinas, and old-fashioned waterside eateries. Take the 6 subway to Pelham Bay and transfer to the Bx29 bus.

STATEN ISLAND

"I'LL TAKE MANHATTAN/THE BRONX and Staten Island, too . . ." Staten Islanders could be forgiven for sometimes feeling as if they were an afterthought, famous primarily as the turnaround point for the Staten Island Ferry. In fact, Staten Island would still be part of New Jersey if the Duke of York hadn't put it up as a prize in a sailing contest in 1687. It wasn't even connected to any other borough until 1964, when the Verrazano Narrows Bridge between Staten Island and Brooklyn opened; it's the world's longest suspension bridge and still the only actual point of contact. And Staten Islanders have repeatedly voiced enthusiasm for breaking away from the rest of New York; a 1993 referendum on secession passed by a two-to-one vote.

Despite this apparent sense of independence, or perhaps because of it (too much progress can be a short-sighted thing), Staten Island is the site of several very old structures that might be worth an excursion, especially for families interested in American history. (For information on the ferry, see the section on Lower Manhattan, Wall Street, and the Battery.) And though it's a little farther south than most tourists usually get, the **Greenbelt** (☎ 718-667-2165), or more formally High Rock Park, is nearly three times the size of Central Park—an outdoor paradise one could scarcely envision from the rusty environs of the ferry terminal.

The 28-building **Snug Harbor Cultural Center** at Richmond Terrace and Tysons Street (☎ 718-448-2500) was founded in 1801 as a home for aging sailors and served as one, at least in part, for nearly 150 years. Now converted to an arts center (the visitors center has a listing of current exhibitions), it still has several fine Greek Revival structures dating to the 1830s. The oldest, Main Hall, with its seafaring-themed stained glass, is now the **Newhouse Center for Contemporary Art** (☎ 718-448-2500). Snug Harbor is also the site of the **Staten Island Children's Museum** (☎ 718-273-2060), which emphasizes performances as well as science, and the **Staten Island Botanical Garden,** with its lush orchid greenhouse and the brand-new traditional Chinese scholar's garden, built by local contractors with the assistance of 40 craftsmen from Suzhou (☎ 718-273-8200).

Overlooking the Narrows a little north of the Verrazano Bridge is the **Alice Austen House Museum** on Hylan Boulevard at the Bay (☎ 718-816-4506), a long, low, gracious cottage built in 1710. The prominent 19th-century photographer lived most of her life here and took more than 7,500 photographs of the evolution of New York life, but they went almost unnoticed, and at the age of 84, having lost everything in the stock market crash, she had to move into the poorhouse. But only a year later, she and her work were "discovered" by *Life* magazine, and she was able to spend her last years in a nursing home. Her photos are exhibited in the house on a rotating basis.

Historic Richmond Town (☎ 718-351-1611) on Clarke Avenue south of the Staten Island Expressway is even older, at least in part. It includes 29 buildings, about half of them open to the public, in a restored "village" something like a Williamsburg of the north. Among the open structures is the 1695 Voorlezer House, the oldest elementary school in the country; the 1839 Bennet House, now called the Museum of Childhood (see the toy room); and the 1840 General Store–cum–post office. Like Williamsburg, it is populated by costumed craftsmen and artisans who give demonstrations and sell reproductions as souvenirs in the Historical Museum gift store.

Thanks to a recent spate of movies and celebrity campaigns, there is increasing interest in Tibetan culture, and one of the few museums of Tibetan art is the **Jacques Marchais Center** (☎ 718-987-3500) at 338 Lighthouse Avenue, not far from Historic Richmond Town. "Marchais" was actually Asian art dealer Mrs. Harry Klauber, who built this replica of a Himalayan temple to house her private collection of Buddhas, religious artifacts, and other contemplative figurines. There are even life-sized stone Buddhas in the garden, and its visitors have included the Dalai Lama.

In addition, plans are underway to construct a national lighthouse museum a short walk from the ferry terminal, but it has had funding troubles.

▌ CENTRAL PARK

AS GREAT CITIES GO, NEW YORK IS STILL YOUNG: brash, mercurial, simultaneously bursting out of its seams and shooting its cuffs. But that it early on considered itself the equal of any European capital is evident from its sweeping avenues and the long rise of Central Park, a project whose design and construction fascinated and eventually captured the imagination of people from every social class in the city. In fact, an early proposal to put it on the old Jones's Wood site (see the section under the Upper East Side) was furiously shouted down as being too niggardly and peripheral.

Ultimately, the construction of the park—the original construction, setting aside later additions—took 16 years. It covered almost 850 acres and required 5 million tons of fill dirt and rock (not counting the glacial rocks and schist that already stick up all over the park) and another 5 million trees, increasing the number of hardwood species from about 40 to more than 600, and more than 800 kinds of shrubs and bushes.

Nowadays, the park is an internationally recognized symbol of the city, attracting more than 20 million tourists every year, not to mention the thousands of residents who are drawn here every day. Its recreational facilities are particularly rich, including 22 separate playgrounds as well as the famous skating rink, and so on (for more information, see Part Ten, Exercise and Recreation). It has concessions stands and real restaurants, but there is an almost inexhaustible supply of other family attractions, plus long stretches of theme gardens, performance venues, and many miniparks, within the overall park.

When Central Park was begun, or rather, when the first attempts were made to clear out the squatters and renderers, Frederick Law Olmsted wasn't even a landscape designer; he was a journalist. But he was fascinated by the concept of a European-style commons, or "greensward," and backed by fellow writers Horace Greeley, William Cullen Bryant (who had been one of the first to inveigle against consuming development), and Washington Irving, he successfully applied to become superintendent of the park. A year later, in partnership with his friend Calvert Vaux, who was an architect and landscape professional, he secured the designer's position as well.

They did not always agree. Olmsted wanted no reservoirs or museums or structures of any sort beyond arches and bridges; Vaux himself designed most of the bridges, as well as the original Metropolitan Museum of Art building. Olmsted tried to block the

central park

Attractions

1. *Alice in Wonderland* Statue
2. *Balto* Statue
3. The Bandshell
4. Belvedere Castle
5. Bethesda Terrace & Bethesda Fountain
6. Boathouse Cafe
7. Bow Bridge
8. Carousel
9. Central Park Zoo
10. Charles A. Dana Discovery Center
11. Cleopatra's Needle (The Obelisk)
12. Conservatory
13. Conservatory Garden
14. The Dairy Information Center
15. Delacorte Clock
16. Delacorte Theater
17. Diana Ross Playground
18. *Hans Christian Andersen* Statue
19. Harlem Meer
20. Hecksher Ball Fields
21. Hecksher Playground
22. Henry Luce Nature Observatory
23. *Imagine* Mosaic
24. Jacqueline Kennedy Onassis Reservoir
25. Lasker Rink and Pool
26. Loeb Boathouse
27. The Mall
28. North Meadow Ball Fields
29. Pat Hoffman Friedman Playground
30. The Pool
31. Rustic Playground
32. Shakespeare Garden
33. Spector Playground
34. Swedish Cottage Marionette Theatre
35. Tavern on the Green
36. Tisch Children's Zoo
37. Wollman Rink

ⓘ Information
Ⓜ Subway stop

0   0.2 mi
0   0.2 km

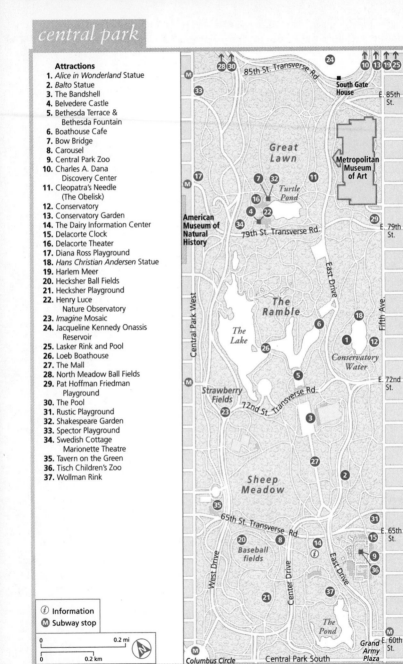

construction of the Sheepfold, a haven for the flock that grazed in what is still called the Sheep Meadow, but it was pushed through by Tammany Hall's Boss Tweed (it's now the Tavern on the Green restaurant). Nor did Olmsted and Vaux like the idea of monuments, though the park now has close to 100 busts, plaques, statues, and memorial gardens. What they would have said about the World War I–era proposal to put an airfield in, one can only imagine.

"NEW YORK'S BACKYARD"

CENTRAL PARK RANGES NEARLY 50 BLOCKS, from Central Park South (59th Street) to Central Park North (110th), and fills three avenues, from Fifth to Eighth. It is crossed from east to west in only five places, at roughly 65th, 72nd, 79th, 85th, and 99th streets—"roughly" both because most of the transverse roads have pleasant curves rather than gridlike rigidity and because vehicular traffic is prohibited during the middle of the day and all weekend.

Several of the most famous children's attractions are in the southernmost segment of the park, including **Wollman skating rink** (restored by Donald Trump), the **Zoo** (officially the Central Park Wildlife Conservation Center), and the **Carousel.** The Carousel (☎ 212-879-0244), a 1908 model with 58 hand-carved horses just south of the 65th Street transverse, was moved to Central Park from Coney Island in 1951, replacing a far less attractive merry-go-round. Back in the 19th century, real horses, on a treadmill beneath the carousel gazebo, pulled little carriages around.

Looking north, the **Dairy** is to the right of the Carousel, closer to Fifth Avenue. The twin-peaked shed is now the main Visitors Center (☎ 212-794-6564), and Urban Park Rangers (☎ 212-360-2774) sometimes lead tours of the park from here. The **Chess and Checkers House,** a gift of financier Bernard Baruch, is on a rock just southwest of the Dairy. And beyond that, across Center Drive, are **Heckscher Playground** and the **softball fields,** which pretty much fill up the southeast part of this section to Columbus Circle.

The Pond, a reed-edged sanctuary filled with ducks and other wildlife, is curled up near Grand Army Plaza in the literal shadow of the St. Moritz and Helmsley Park Lane hotels.

The frontispiece of the zoo, near where East 64th Street runs into Fifth Avenue, is the **Arsenal** building (☎ 212-360-1311), which originally earned its cannon, but in the years since it was built in 1851, it has been a weather station, a police station, a menagerie, the original Museum of Natural History, and finally, headquarters of the Parks and Recreation Department. The original Olmsted-Vaux plans for the park are exhibited here. The **Zoo** itself (☎ 212-439-6500) was renovated in the late 1980s; the parks department found new homes for the animals that were too large for such a crowded facility, and it constructed more contemporary, eco-sensitive settings for the animals that were kept. The monkey house is now a real jungle gym, the bats have an eternally nocturnal home, and the reptiles have a swamp that is almost a pre-Olmsted joke. There are free tours daily at 2:30 p.m. and weekends at 10:30 a.m. as well.

(Don't just check your watch; check out the **Delacorte clock** by the zoo entrance. Every 30 minutes, a bronze menagerie of musical animals appears to peal out nursery rhymes.)

Just above the 65th Street transverse, almost to Central Park West, is the elaborate **Tavern on the Green** restaurant, with its famous conservatory style Crystal Room and the quainter upstairs dining rooms and lounge, still reminiscent of a sheepfold's loft. The **Sheep Meadow** is the 15-acre green alongside the Tavern (which has a new cafe; ☎ 212-873-3200), and nearby is the **Bowling Green,** where top-ranked competitive collegiate and professional croquet teams still play.

Just to the right of the Sheep Meadow and Bowling Green, running just about down the middle of this second rung of the park's ladder, is a popular rollerblading strip. And on the other side of that is **the Mall,** a formal promenade of elms that formed a sight line of ten blocks all the way up to Belvedere Castle atop Vista Rock. The bandshell there, the second on the site, is no longer used; summer concerts are now held on the adjoining playground, **Rumsey Field,** which, in case you need a good meeting point, is the one with the statue of Mother Goose.

Facing the old bandshell across Terrace Drive (the 72nd Street transverse) is **Bethesda Terrace,** a fountain setting at the edge of the lake that offers a grand view of the Ramble on the other side. The statue atop the fountain represents "The Angel of the Waters," from a story in the Gospel of John that says the touch of an angel gave healing powers to a Bethesda pool in Jerusalem. **The Lake,** which is about one-third of the way up the park, is the second largest body of water in the park, pinched together in the middle and crossed by Vaux's 60-foot-high cast-iron **Bow Bridge.**

unofficial **TIP**
In the northeast corner of the Lake is **Loeb Boathouse** (☎ 212-517-2233), with its Venetian gondola and rowboat rentals—you can take a 30-minute ride from an Italian-trained gondolier for about $30.

Nearby is the **Boat House,** one of Manhattan's most popular scenic eateries for tourists. A little beyond Loeb toward Fifth Avenue is an unconnected, smaller lake called **Conservatory Water,** where the Kerbs Model Boathouse houses the miniature yachts that race every Saturday afternoon in summer. Nearby are the statues of the **Mad Tea Party** from *Alice's Adventures in Wonderland* **and Hans Christian Andersen;** Andersen's only permanent audience is a bronze bird, but his memorial is the gathering place for storytime on Saturdays at 11 a.m.

To the west of Bethesda Terrace is the **Cherry Hill** overlook, which offers a view of the Mall, the Lake, and the Ramble; beyond that, between the southernmost little finger of the Lake and the West 72nd Street entrance, is **Strawberry Fields,** Yoko Ono's memorial to John Lennon; it's across from the Dakota apartments, where he was assassinated. The mosaic, reading "Imagine," was a gift from the city of Naples, Italy; and the "peace garden" includes plants from 161 nations.

North of the Lake is **the Ramble,** 37 acres of woods and wildflower gardens and a haven for birds and bird-watchers alike; more than 250 species have been spotted here, many of which migrate along the Atlantic flyway. On the western shore of the lake at about 77th Street is the **Ladies Pavilion.**

Across from the Ramble, in the middle of the 79th Street transverse, is **Vista Rock** and its crowning glory, **Belvedere Castle,** a somewhat smaller but impressive replica of a Scottish stone castle—turrets, terraces, and all—that was just meant to be part of the décor back in Olmsted and Vaux's day. Today it houses the **Henry Luce Nature Observatory,** which arranges lots of family tours and programs (☎ 212-772-0210) and a branch of the National Weather Service that has information on wildlife and whose roof offers a splendid view of the park. West of the castle near Winter Drive are the **Swedish Cottage** (☎ 212-988-9093), a marionette theater originally built for the Philadelphia Exposition of 1876, and the **Shakespeare Garden,** a sort of bard-lover's botanical Bartlett's; all the trees and flowers planted around the pools are mentioned in his works.

Visible across Belvedere Lake to the northwest is the **Delacorte Theater,** the 2,000-seat site of the popular summer Shakespeare in the Park shows, named for publisher George Delacorte, who also donated the animal fair clock at the zoo and the Mad Tea Party sculpture. In fact, he is said to have been the model, somewhat exaggerated, for the Mad Hatter himself.

Visible to the northeast is **Cleopatra's needle,** actually built by Thutmos III in 1600 BCE, despite its popular nickname. The obelisk and its twin were presented by the Khedive of Egypt to the city of New York and to Queen Victoria in 1881. Translations of the hieroglyphs, which have been nearly eradicated by modern air pollution, are engraved on plaques donated by that Cleopatra lover, moviemaker Cecil B. DeMille. Beyond Cleopatra's needle, along Fifth Avenue from East 81st to 84th, is the **Metropolitan Museum of Art.** And the great green oval in the center of the park from Belvedere Lake nearly to the 85th Street transverse is the 55-acre **Great Lawn,** with the brilliant Green Oval at its heart.

At least, now it's a lawn. It started out as a reservoir; it was the site of Central Park's Hooverville, as the Depression-era shantytowns were called, and later was used as an athletic field until the mid-1930s when Robert Moses, the great public works developer, created the great lawn. Most recently, resodded and regraded, it has been the venue for several famous concerts, including Simon and Garfunkle's

1981 concert, which drew a crowd of half a million; the even larger "No Nukes" show a year later; and Pavarotti's recital in 1993. It is also where the Metropolitan Opera and the New York Philharmonic stage their summer concerts.

The 85th Street transverse is geographically the waistline of the park. Above it is the 106-acre **Reservoir,** by far the largest of the park's half-dozen bodies of water, which takes up most of the area between the 85th and 97th Street transverses. It dates back to the original Croton reservoir system of 1862 and was in active use until only a couple of years ago. Now a popular jogging route, the trail around the reservoir has been named in honor of one of its most faithful visitors, Jacqueline Kennedy Onassis. The remaining corner of this section, northwest of the reservoir, is where the tennis courts are.

North of the 97th Street transverse are the large **North Meadow** and smaller **East Meadow,** which even for some city dwellers seems to be the end of the park. However, there are more gardens and even some historic sites above about 105th Street. The **Conservatory Garden,** actually three formal gardens (and no conservatory building) that were once part of the Cornelius Vanderbilt mansion in Midtown, includes a "secret garden," with an appropriate statue of Dickon and Mary; the entrance gate, also from the Vanderbilt estate, is on Fifth Avenue between 104th and 105th.

Behind the Conservatory Garden is **the Mount,** which is now bare but once held a tavern (later a convent!) from which Washington's men held off the British. It looks down on **McGowan's Pass** at East 106th Street and beyond the pass to the former site of a pair of 1812 forts (now identified by markers only). Look for the blockhouse below East Drive (about West 109th Street) south or the Adam Clayton Powell Boulevard entrance.

At the opposite end of the park from Wollman Rink is **Lasker Rink,** another ice-skating rink—a wading pool in summer. Due to its location, this rink is cheaper and generally less crowded than Wollman.

Finally, at the top of the park beyond the **Harlem Meer** lake is **Charles A. Dana Discovery Center** (☎ 212-860-1370), once the boathouse and now an outpost of the Urban Park Rangers, dedicated to environmental issues.

OTHER GREEN CORNERS
of the CITY

PERHAPS ONLY CITIES WITH ELBOW-CRUNCHING CROWDS really value open spaces. Like the most densely populated capitals of Europe and Asia, New York has, with revived resolution, maintained its squares and even established newer parks to give its residents and visitors respite from the noise and strife.

Perhaps the most under-rated public space in Manhattan is **Battery Park,** which, in addition to the numerous statues and memorials mentioned earlier in this chapter, offers some of the most beautiful and evocative views, walkways and bikeways, shopping and dining, sailing slips, and even fishing piers. From May to October, it is also the site of bird-watching and garden tours, musical and dramatic performances, childrens' activities, tai chi and casting lessons, backgammon and chess instruction, art shows and storytelling, singalongs and drum jams, ethnic festivals, and even occasional Hudson River swims. Visit **www.bpcpc.org** for more information.

From the shiny new Staten Island Ferry terminal, you can stroll waterside for a mile or so to the renovated **Battery Park City,** with its 120-foot-high Winter Garden atrium and name-brand shopping mall; along the way enjoy ever-shifting vistas of Governors' Island, Ellis Island and the Statue of Liberty, and the Jersey City skyline (which rivals pre-9/11 Manhattan's). There are elevated views as well, from the top of the cafe in **Robert Wagner Park** and from the splendid Asian-style **South Cove,** with its observation deck that resembles a high Chinese garden bridge. (If you go through the **Museum of Jewish Heritage,** you'll find that the newer wing has a living tree-sculpture garden on its roof as well.)

The Esplanade itself, which meanders along the Hudson, is a broad brick expanse with benches, separate lanes for bikes and blades, little niches of park, and a playground. When you turn the corner to see the **North Cove,** home to yachts and sailboats, you may be surprised to see a huge sail streaking up the yards.

Among the most popular smaller hideaways is **Bryant Park,** behind the New York Public Library between Fifth and Sixth avenues and 40th and 42nd streets (that's poet and *Evening Sun* publisher William Cullen Bryant in bronze and Gertrude Stein in stone). It has its own restaurant, the Bryant Park Grill, and an ice cream parlor in season, public restrooms, wireless computer access, public chess tables, frequent art exhibits, occasional movie screenings, and a half-price/same-day music and dance tickets booth.

Union Square, which is at the heart of one of the city's fastest-growing restaurant scenes, plays host every September to the free **Manhattan Short Film festival.** Year-round, it offers statues of Washington, Lincoln, and Lafayette—and Mondays, Wednesdays, Fridays, and Saturdays, a famous green and farmers' market.

Washington Square Park at the foot of Fifth Avenue in Greenwich Village is street theater (and dog society central) even when the summer troupes aren't out in force. Some of those game boards are for chess. A similar hideaway is **Washington Market Park,** once the premiere green market, between Harrison and Chambers streets and Greenwich and West Street at the foot of Tribeca. It even has a view of the Hudson. There are community gardens behind the Jefferson Market Library in Greenwich Village (see page 148) and on the West

Side between Amsterdam and Columbus avenues from 89th to 90th streets.

There are very urban sculpture gardens, such as the **Abby Aldrich Rockefeller Sculpture Garden** at the rear of the Museum of Modern Art and the **Iris and G. Gerald Cantor Roof Garden** atop the Metropolitan Museum of Art. And a host of midtown nooks and crannies hold fountains and noise-curtaining waterfalls, including the two neighboring piazzas on the north side of 52nd between Fifth and Sixth.

The city also has several pass-throughs, such as **Fisher Park,** a precisely arranged connection of 54th and 55th streets between Sixth and Seventh avenues. It has a fountain, kite-like awnings, and benchlike pedestals around its trees.

Such mansion-turned-museums as the **J. Pierpont Morgan Library** and the **Frick Collection** have internal gardens.

When in doubt, however, head for the water. Just as you can walk the western periphery of Lower Manhattan from **Hudson River Park** at the south end of TriBeCa down the Esplanade to **Battery Park,** you can follow **East Side Park** from the Lower East Side up through the East Village to **Gramercy Park;** the **United Nations gardens** on First Avenue range from 42nd to 48th streets.

Riverside Park is the anchor of a green swatch that goes up the Hudson riverfront from West 72nd Street with little interruption all the way to the Spuyten-Duyvil Creek.

And lest we seem to neglect the outer boroughs, as so many people do, we suggest you look up those neighborhood descriptions found earlier in this chapter; no borough in New York is without a substantial public park and/or botanical garden, several of which rival Central Park in beauty and wealth of facilities.

PART SEVEN

SIGHTSEEING, TOURS *and* ATTRACTIONS

LET *your* FINGERS *do* *the* WALKING . . . FIRST

THE NICE THING ABOUT SIGHTSEEING is that you can do it at your own pace, looking closely at what intrigues you, gazing appreciatively at what only pleases you, and pushing right on past what stirs not a flicker of interest. In New York, you can tour by land, sea, air, horse-drawn carriage, and even parasail. You can see historic spots or literary haunts, cathedrals or courts, authentic remnants or virtual realities. (And you can pay nothing or, well, something.)

You can see them all best if you get right down to street level. New York is particularly well suited to walking tours, and that's what we recommend. (Skylines are lovely, but you have to be at a distance to see them.) We want you to get up close and personal here. Keep your eyes open and your schedule a little loose: Several office buildings around town have minimuseums and free galleries on the street level; some technology firms such as Sony have informal try-out rooms.

But it's a little smarter to consider your preferences before you start off—before you leave home, if you have time, or maybe on the plane. New York offers so much that it can be confusing if not downright intimidating. So we've outlined some categories of special interest, suggested some specialized tours you might be interested in, and even sketched out a few starting points and highlights in Part Six, New York's Neighborhoods.

In Part Nine, Shopping, we've combined souveniring with introductory walks around the most important neighborhoods (to visitors, at least), with a little background flavor and a few landmarks for orientation. Some of the most important museums, historic houses, and buildings are described in more detail in the attraction profiles at the end of this chapter.

unofficial **TIP**
If you're worried about a teenager getting completely wound up in whatever museum or exhibit he's into and losing track of the time, schedule this separate tour session just before lunch; there are few things that can override a kid's stomach alarm, even a *T. rex* skeleton.

On the other hand, we know that not everybody prefers do-it-yourself tours. Some people find it a bit distracting to try to read directions and anecdotes while walking, and others use packaged tours as a way of getting a mental map of the area. So we've also listed some of the most reputable guided tours available. (These are surely not all of them; tourism is a boom industry in New York, and you'll see flyers for new tours every month. If you do want to take a guided tour, check through the material at the information desks and visitors centers or even your hotel lobby; you may find a discount coupon lurking.) And on Fridays, the *New York Times* lists special-interest tours scheduled that weekend, often remarkably eccentric (the homes of famous salsa musicians, for instance).

We also realize that New York is not one-size-fits-all. Walking is wonderful if you're young and fit, but if your party includes children or seniors, make sure to pace yourself. Build in a timely stop in a park; split the touring day into "shifts" so that, if necessary, those with less stamina can head back to the hotel for a rest while the others continue; or lay out the schedule on the democratic scheme—that is, put the attractions everyone wants to see first, the could-be-missed intermediate ones later, and the only-for-fanatics excursions last. That way, whoever wants to drop out can. If each member of the party has his or her own must-sees, then set a particular hour to split up and a clearly understood place to regroup.

The former World Trade Center and environs, now known as Ground Zero after the terrorist attacks of 9/11, are the hub of a complicated and sometimes dangerous recovery effort. The roughly rectangular area (bounded by Barclay Street on the north, Church Street on the east, Albany Street on the south, and West Street on the west) is off-limits to everyone except recovery workers. For your own safety and that of workers (as well as out of respect for those who lost loved ones), sightseeing in this area is discouraged.

unofficial **TIP**
Because the food and beverage lures are everywhere, especially around major tourist attractions, avoid stomach overload or whining children by carrying a supply of snacks in plastic bags. And don't forget water or soda: It's easy to become dehydrated when you're doing a lot of walking.

However, recognizing the worldwide interest in Ground Zero, the City of New York has constructed a viewing platform to allow the public to see the area safely and without interfering with recovery work. The platform is at the south side of the site at Church and Maiden streets, and it's open daily, 9 a.m.–8 p.m. Tickets are no longer required, though security officers may limit access during heavy crowding. The pedestrian bridge at Liberty Street to the World Financial Center (and many neighboring buildings) also offer views of the area.

CATEGORIES AND RECOMMENDATIONS

Best Children's Fare

Abigail Adams Smith Museum (Upper East Side)

American Museum of Natural History (Upper West Side)

Bronx Zoo (The Bronx)

Central Park

Coney Island and the Brooklyn Aquarium (Brooklyn)

Forbes Magazine Galleries (Greenwich Village)

Hayden Planetarium (Upper West Side)

IMAX Theater (Upper West Side)

Intrepid Sea-Air-Space Museum (Midtown West)

Museum of the City of New York (Upper East Side)

Museum of Television and Radio (Midtown East)

New York City Fire Museum (Soho and Tribeca)

New York City Police Museum (Lower Manhattan)

New York Hall of Science (Queens)

New York Transit Museum (Brooklyn)

Roosevelt Island Aerial Tramway (Upper East Side)

Sony Wonder Technology Lab (Midtown East)

Best Views

Empire State Building (Gramercy Park)

Marriott-Marquis View Restaurant (Midtown West)

Metropolitan Museum of Art Roof Garden (Upper East Side)

Rise Bar, Ritz-Carlton Battery Park (Lower Manhattan)

River Cafe (Brooklyn)

Riverside Church (Heights/Harlem)

Rockefeller Center's rooftop observation deck (Midtown East)

Terrace on the Park (Queens)

Ethnic and "Roots" Exhibits

Ellis Island Immigration Museum (Lower Manhattan)

Japan Society (Midtown East)

The Jewish Museum (Upper East Side)

Lower East Side Tenement Museum (Lower East Side)

El Museo del Barrio (Upper East Side)

The Museum for African Art (Soho and Tribeca)

Museum of Chinese in the Americas (Lower East Side)

The Museum of Jewish Heritage/ Holocaust (Lower Manhattan)

National Museum of the American Indian (Lower Manhattan)

Rubin Museum of Art (Chelsea)

Schomberg Center for Research in Black Culture (Heights/Harlem)

Smaller, Less-crowded Museums of Note

The Asia Society (Upper East Side)

The Cloisters (Washington Heights)

Dahesh Museum (Midtown East)

The Frick Collection (Upper East Side)

Hispanic Society of America (Upper West Side)

CATEGORIES AND RECOMMENDATIONS (CONTINUED)

Smaller, Less-crowded Museums of Note (continued)

Isamu Noguchi Garden Museum (Queens)

Museum of the City of New York (Upper East Side)

New York City Police Museum (Lower Manhattan)

New York Historical Society (Upper West Side)

Rubin Museum of Art

Free (or pay what you wish) Museum Hours

American Folk Art Museum, Friday 6–8 p.m.

American Museum of the Moving Image, Friday 4–8 p.m.

The Asia Society, Friday 6–9 p.m.

Bronx Museum of the Arts, Wednesday 3–9 p.m.

Bronx Zoo, Wednesday 10 a.m.– 4:30 p.m.

Brooklyn Museum, first Saturday of the month 5–11 p.m.

Cooper-Hewitt National Design Museum, Tuesday 5–9 p.m.

Guggenheim Museum, Friday 6–8 p.m. (pay what you wish)

International Center of Photography, Friday 5–8 p.m. (pay what you wish)

Jewish Museum, Tuesday 5–8 p.m.

Metropolitan Museum of Art, Friday 4–8:45 p.m.

Museum of Art and Design, Thursday 6–8 p.m. (pay what you wish)

Museum of Chinese in the Americas, Friday noon–7 p.m.

Museum of Jewish Heritage, Wednesday 4–8 p.m.

Museum of Modern Art, Friday 4–8 p.m. (pay what you wish)

New Museum of Contemporary Art, Thursday 6–8 p.m.

New York Botanical Garden, Wednesday 10 a.m.–6 p.m.

New York Hall of Science, Thursday and Friday (except July and August) 2–5 p.m.

Whitney Museum of American Art, Friday 6–9 p.m.

TOURING OPTIONS

PACKAGED TOURS

THERE ARE WELL OVER 1,000 LICENSED TOUR GUIDES in New York, and many more unlicensed ones. And no wonder: The city draws 30 million visitors every year, and the numbers keep going up. That's good news and bad—good because you as a tourist have a huge number of tours and guides to choose from, and bad because it can be difficult to differentiate between the worthwhile and the time-consuming.

Frankly, we're not so enthusiastic about most packaged mass tours. We think it's more rewarding to select the attractions you're truly interested in and go on your own or with a more intimate group. After all, most of the "sights" on those sightseeing tours are so famous you already know what the outside looks like, and a lot of the time that's all you see out the window, anyway. And you're a lot more likely to end the day feeling, just as you did in the morning, that Manhattan is a large, crowded, and loud place.

Besides, there are several drawbacks to taking these overview tours. For one thing, simply loading and off-loading passengers at every stop—not to mention dealing with traffic— takes up a substantial portion of the time you are supposedly sightseeing. And a more recent twist is that more and more of the neighbor-

unofficial **TIP**
If you're not wedded to a guide, go online at **citypass.com** (☎ 707-256-0490) or **newyorkpass.com** (☎ 877-714-1999) and see what discount packages you can get on the classic attractions such as the Empire State Building, Statue of Liberty, and various museums.

hoods, from Soho to Harlem, are complaining about tour bus traffic and the noise and pollution created by idling vehicles. Commercial traffic is banned around some important historical areas, most notably Washington Square.

On the favorable side, you are apt to be swept around enough to get an idea of the island's layout, and if you plan to return frequently, that might be an advantage. Many of the longer tours have lunch or dinner and even a little entertainment scheduled right along with the ride, which may be a relief for those with sticker or map shock. Those with limited walking power might prefer to stay on the bus, in any case. Those shy of sidewalk adventures may find security in numbers. And you can hear a lot of history and humor in a single dose, if that's what you like. Note that prices frequently change; you might want to ask whether the tour company has discounts for members of AARP, AAA, and such.

Gray Line Tours, which has conventional buses, a newer fleet of eco-friendly (low-emission) and wheelchair-accessible double-decker buses, and trolleys, remains one of the most reliable packaged tour operators. You can spend from two hours to the whole day in the tour company's care, see the whole island or just a district or two, and get picked up from many major hotels as well as its headquarters at the side entrance to the Port Authority Bus Terminal on 42nd Street near Eighth Avenue and the Times Square pickup (☎ 800-669-0051 or 212-445-0848). A nice feature is that hop-on, hop-off tickets are good for two days, so you can spread it out if you don't want to make the whole circuit at once. Gray Line has tour guides who speak French, German, Italian, Spanish, and Portuguese as well as English. If you want to be picked up from the airport as well, call ☎ 212-315-3006.

Harbor cruises lasting about 90 minutes and offering views of the Statue of Liberty and the downtown skyline are offered by **NY Waterways Tours** (call ☎ 800-533-3779); cruises leave from Pier 78 (West 38th Street), but there's free bus pickup from various sites around town. Even more intriguing is the *Yankee Clipper* cruise to Yankee Stadium or the dinner-theater ride to Broadway. **World Yacht** leaves from Pier 81 (41st Street) and goes down the west side of the island each night for dinner and weekends and Wednesdays for brunch (☎ 212-630-8100). **Seaport Music Cruises** swing around the Statue of Liberty and Ellis Island from the South Street Seaport in about an hour; they also offer two-hour jazz cruises on Thursday evenings and blues cruises on Wednesdays ($40–$55; ☎ 212-630-8888).

A somewhat more "exciting" version of the harbor tour, for the amusement-park thrill ride generation, is on the **"Beast,"** which uses 145-seat speed boats painted with Jaws-style grins and rock 'n' roll music to spice up a 30-minute, wet, and (fairly) wild tour available daily, April to October ($15; ☎ 212-563-3200). For sailing buffs, the *Schooner Adirondack* goes the windy route with a "Champagne City Lights" after-dark tour (Pier 62 at Chelsea Piers; ☎ 646-336-5270).

For a bird's-eye view, take a helicopter tour: The **Gray Line** office sells no-reservation tickets for flights leaving continually from 9 a.m. to 6 p.m. weekdays (☎ 212-397-2620). **Liberty Helicopters** take off from 30th Street at Twelfth Avenue and from Pier G on the East River for a variety of customized tours; call ☎ 212-465-8905 or 800-542-9933.

More fun than a simple harbor cruise is the **Circle Line** tour, a surprisingly entertaining three-hour, 39-mile circumnavigation of Manhattan entirely by water. The ships, all former Coast Guard cutters or navy landing craft, head down the Hudson past the Statue of Liberty, back up the East River along the old Upper East Side, and through Spuyten-Duyvil Creek. In addition to the full three-hour tour ($28 adults, $23 seniors, $15 children), they also offer a two-hour Harbor Lights tour ($23 adults, $19 seniors, $12 children). The headquarters are at Pier 16 in the South Street Seaport; three tours plus various shorter and evening tours leave daily April through mid-December (☎ 212-563-3200). The Circle Line has its own "beast," the *Shark*, and the somewhat more gentle cruiser, the *Zephyr*.

GUIDED WALKING (MOSTLY) TOURS

AS WE'VE SAID, WE THINK WALKING TOURS, either independent or guided, are the way to really see New York. Just use a little common sense. Many walking tours are weather-dependent, so be sure to ask how to confirm whether the tour is on if the skies darken. The big tour companies are full-time, but many of the smaller tour groups (or personal guides) have more limited schedules. Most walking tours offered through museums or other groups are on weekends, as are most of the specialty tours, though you can often arrange for a weekday tour if you get in touch with the company in advance. Tips are appreciated by some but declined by others, particularly those arranged by nonprofit agencies; you can ask when you call.

Some of the best things really are free, even in New York. The **Urban Park Rangers** offer green-minded weekend walking tours through Central Park and other green areas in all five boroughs, and the guides are as family-friendly as the price. Call ☎ 718-430-1832. The **Times Square Tours** have great guides, too—professional actors, in fact. The free tour starts at noon on Fridays, rain or shine, at the Times Square Visitors Center (☎ 212-768-1560) at 226 West 42nd Street or 1560 Broadway. And the Friday "Weekend" section of the *New York Times* often mentions special-interest tours arranged through nonprofit organizations or museums.

If you want to set up a more personalized tour, or one with a specialized focus, contact **Big Apple Greeters,** who can put you in contact with an expert in your field if you give them a few days' notice (☎ 212-669-8159 or visit **www.bigapplegreeters.com**). The tour guides are volunteers, and the buddy-system tour, arranged though the Manhattan borough president's office, is free (though it would be nice if you offered to buy lunch or something). Similarly, you can start putting together a customized itinerary by calling **Signature Tours** (☎ 212-517-4306).

Of course, most tour guides are trying to make a paid living at this. Especially if you're interested in authentic flavor (as opposed to memorized brochure stuff), the neighborhood walking tours are the way to go.

Among the very best such tours are the **Big Onion Walking Tours** ("Long before it was dubbed the Big Apple, those who knew New York City called it the Big Onion," announces the brochure). Most of the Big Onion tours cover the historically polyglot region of Little Italy, Chinatown, the Bowery, and the Lower East Side, but they have expanded their staff to cover Gramercy Park and Union Square, Historic Harlem, the East Village, Brooklyn Heights and the Brooklyn Bridge, gay and lesbian New York, "Revolutionary New York," Tribeca, and so forth.

Big Onion is the brainchild of two history scholars, Seth Kamil and Ed O'Donnell, and they and a staff of graduate students from New York University (NYU) and Columbia University bring to life the eras of Tammany Hall, tenements, sweatshops and flophouses, and ethnic gang struggles. You can either take a sort of two-hour overview tour that covers the waterfront, so to speak, or sign up for the more in-depth walks titled "Before Stonewall: A Gay and Lesbian History Tour," "The Bowery," "Historic Harlem," "Immigrant New York," or "Jewish Lower East Side." And speaking of authentic flavors, you can even sign up for the "Multiethnic Eating Tours," in which you nosh a pickle, swipe a dumpling, and savor fresh mozzarella as you go. Tours range from $12 to $18 for adults (depending on whether food or museum admissions are involved) and from $10 to $16 for students and seniors; call ☎ 212-439-1090 or visit **www.bigonion.com** for a schedule of tours or reservations.

Similarly evocative tours are the specialty of the **Adventure on a Shoestring** folks, who put together itineraries such as "The World of Edith Wharton" and "Hell's Kitchen Hike" ($5; ☎ 212-265-2663).

Native New Yawker **Michael Kaback** sponsors tours of such historic areas as the Garment District and "Bizarre and Eccentric" East Village ($15; 212-370-4214); **Beyond Times Square** is a taste-and-tour company ranging over 20 neighborhoods (800-999-8160); and **The Dorothy Parker Society** leads literary-legend tours (646-435-2799). Linda Sarrell of **Rent A New Yorker Tours** offers both public and private itineraries by request (from $10; 212-982-9445). For the exercise and history buff, Kaback also leads six eight-mile hikes around Manhattan, and **Bike the Big Apple** works the outer boroughs (201-837-1133).

Georgette Blau's "Scene on TV" tours leads channel surfers past such buildings as the Jeffersons' high-rise, the West Village site of *Friends,* the Huxatables' Brooklyn brownstone—actually in Greenwich Village—and the Soup Nazi's kitchen, along with some very familiar-looking courthouses. The 90-minute bus tour leaves from the Times Square Visitors Center Saturdays and Sundays at 10 a.m., noon, 2 p.m., and 4 p.m. ($20 for adults, $10 children ages 6 to 12; 800-669-0051). **On Location Tours** takes a similar TV tack, with tours ranging from $30 to $40 (212-209-3370).

Some of the most hilarious tours are actually scavenger hunts: **Watson Adventure Scavenger Hunts** range from famous TV and movie location sites to Warhol studios; for information call 212-726-1529 or log onto **www.watsonadventures.com. Great Central Park Treasure Hunts** are grown-up versions of the favorite childhood game, complete with treasure map (845-225-2539). If you don't know what the **Kramer's Reality Tour for Seinfeld Fans** is, you don't need to call (800-KRAMERS; three hours for $37.50).

If you're interested in historical sites in Harlem and African American culture, particularly jazz, gospel, and soul (as in food), contact **Harlem Spirituals** ($30 to $95, depending on whether food is included, etc.; 212-391-0900 or 888-340-6400), which offers tours in a half-dozen languages—hey, gospel is hot! **A La Carte New York** also specializes in the neighborhood ($125 an hour; 646-265-8923). Or check out **Harlem Your Way** (212-690-1687; **www.harlem yourwaytours.com**) for the $25 "Sights and Sounds" tour, Monday through Saturday at 10 a.m., which meets at 129 West 130th; and the Gospel Tour, Sunday at 10:30 a.m., also $25; visit their Web site for details on champagne safari specials.

If architecture and design or cultural history are of interest, try the **Municipal Art Society,** which offers a variety of tours around town for $25 (212-439-1049; **www.mas.org**); or **NYC Cultural Walking Tours** (212-979-2388; **www.nycwalk.com**).

NYU New School for Society Research professor **Joyce Gold** has been leading her walking tours of Manhattan neighborhoods for more than 20 years; the group tours are $12, but you can also arrange a private tour (212-242-5762). Queens College history professor **Harriet Davis-Kramm** offers a theme tour related to labor called "Manhattan Memories" (212-628-9517). Former high school teacher (academics are big in the tour biz these days!) **Ruth Alscher-Green** can lead you "River to River" downtown ($35 for one person or $50 for two; group rates can be arranged; ☎ 212-321-2823; river2nyc@aol.com). Self-described "radical historian" **Bruce Kayton** arranges his "radical walk-ing" tours off the beaten track on the beaten tracks. That is, his Green-wich Village tour points out sites of murder, riots, and general mayhem, and his Harlem tour is as much about the Black Panthers as it is the black arts scene ($12; ☎ 718-492-0069). As for **Strange Tours,** well, ask 'em yourself (☎ 646-523-5337).

Other highly regarded walking tours include the **New York City Cul-tural Tours,** either the Sunday public ones ($10) or customized private ones ($20 to $30 an hour; ☎ 212-979-2388); **Landmark West!,** a non-profit group working to preserve the Upper West Side's architectural treasures (☎ 212-496-8110), and **Bravo New York** (☎ 718-834-8655).

Some tours are, unfortunately, available only in warm weather (that is, high tourist season). **The New York Historical Society** sponsors sum-mer walking tours through Central Park highlighting its history and evolution; tours are at 2 p.m. Fridays, Saturdays, and Sundays (☎ 212-873-3400; **www.nyhistory.org**). The occasional but fascinating tours of-fered by the **Museum of the City of New York** cover "Historic Harlem" and arts-oriented tours (but again, these are mostly good-weather op-tions) every other Sunday from April to October ($12; ☎ 212-534-1672 x206; **www.mcny.org**). You might also check the **Cooper-Hewitt National Design Museum** (☎ 212-849-8300) or the **92nd Street Y** (☎ 212-415-5500).

SELF-GUIDED WALKING TOURS

THERE ARE SEVERAL BOOKS IN PRINT with in-depth walking tours of New York, but frankly, we're confident that what we've pointed out in Part Six, New York's Neighborhoods, will tell you most of what you want to know. However, in some neighborhoods, you can easily pick up additional guides as you go. Some of the very best are the **Heritage Trails/New York** maps of downtown pre-pared by a nonprofit state foundation and full of first-class historical information. If you are mostly interested in direc-tions, there is a free map with highlights marked, but for $4 you can get a brochure with quite a lot of info; call ☎ 212-825-6888.

> *uno*fficial **TIP**
> Many neighborhoods supply do-it-yourself walking tour guides for a few dollars at most; **the Chinatown History Project** at 70 Mulberry Street has one for $1 (☎ 212-619-4785) and also offers occasional guided tours of the neighborhood.

BACKSTAGE AND BEHIND THE SCENES

THERE ARE ACTUALLY FOUR SEPARATE TOURS of facilities at Lin-coln Center, but the two finest—which are also two of the finest in town—are the backstage tours of the **Metropolitan Opera House,** led by members of the Opera Guild from October through June ($12 and reservations required; ☎ 212-769-7020), and a general **Lincoln Center** tour that explores three theaters in the complex and comes with enthusiastic background info and the nicest kind of gossip ($12.50, $9 seniors and students, and $6 under age 12; tours at 10:30 a.m. and 12:30, 2:30, and 4:30 p.m. Venues toured depend on rehearsal, matinee, and set-construction schedules, so call ahead if you want to know which theaters are going to be included (☎ 212-875-5350).

Tours of **Carnegie Hall** are $6 ($5 for seniors and students), offered at 11:30 a.m., 2 p.m., and 3 p.m. Mondays, Tuesdays, Thursdays, and Fridays; for more information call ☎ 212-247-7800. Members of the Municipal Arts Society lead free tours of **Grand Central Terminal** every Wednesday and Friday at 12:30 p.m. (☎ 212-935-3960). Tours of the **New York Public Library,** like its neighbor Grand Central, a gem of Beaux Arts design, are free at 11 a.m. and 2 p.m. (☎ 212-869-8089; **www.nypl.org**).

Not only are there tours of Times Square, as mentioned in Part Six, but also the magnificently Disney-restored **New Amsterdam Theater,** den of "The Lion King" ($14 adults, $7 under age 12).

The **Radio City Music Hall** tour lasts about an hour, shows off the theater's wonderful Art Deco interior, and usually includes an up-close-and-personal appearance by at least one Rockette. Tours are Monday through Saturday from 10 a.m. to 5 p.m. and Sundays 11 a.m. to 5 p.m.; adult admission $18, children ages 12 and under $12. For information call ☎ 212-307-7171. While you're in the neighborhood, ask about the **NBC Studio Tour** and see what Conan O'Brien sees (☎ 212-664-7174; $19 for adults, $16 for children ages 6 to 16 or seniors ages 65 and older; no children under age 6); or the **Broadway Open House Theatre Tours,** which last about two hours and spotlight some very fine old venues (☎ 888-BROADWAY). **Rockefeller Center,** that landmark of Deco idealism, offers an hour-long tour that includes glimpses of **Rockefeller Plaza, Radio City Music Hall,** and its many vintage murals, mosaics, and statuary. Tours begin on the hour at the NBC Experience Store at Rockefeller Plaza and 49th Street ($10; ☎ 212-664-3700.) The NBC Studio Tour goes where only Katie and Conan dare to tread ($17.95; ☎ 212-664-3700). Or you can just focus on **Radio City Music Hall** from the stage-door angle (tours every 30 minutes between 11 a.m. and 3 p.m.; $17 adults, $14 seniors and students, and $10 children under age 12; ☎ 212-307-7171).

CNN's insider tours are more hands-on and interactive, which might make them more appealing to kids ($15 adults, $13 students and seniors, $11 ages 3 to 6; ☎ 866-426-6692).

Several of the museums, especially the larger ones, offer highlights tours that give you an overview of the exhibits. The **American Museum of Natural History** (☎ 212-769-5100) offers highlights tours at 10:15 and 11:15 a.m., and 1:15, 2:15, and 3:15 p.m.; meet on the second floor in the Hall of African Mammals. The **Metropolitan Museum of Art** highlights tours are conducted in Italian, Spanish, French, Japanese, Korean, Portuguese, Russian, and German as well as English, at 10:15 and 11:15 a.m. and 1, 2, and 3:15 p.m.; tours leave from the great front hall (☎ 212-535-7710; **www.metmuseum.org**).

Madison Square Garden is both a famous sports arena—home to the Knicks, the Rangers, and the Liberty—and a famous rock arena, not to mention the site of circuses, tournaments, and general craziness. Go behind the scenes and play star ($17 adults, $12 students and seniors; ☎ 212-465-5800).

AN ABUNDANCE *of* RICHES

OKAY, YOU'VE AT LEAST SKIMMED the neighborhood profiles in Part Six and the lists of sightseeing recommendations earlier in this chapter, and hopefully you've settled on a few areas of special interest to you or your group. The following are more in-depth descriptions of a few of the most important attractions in each neighborhood, to add to your enjoyment of each or perhaps help you winnow down the selection even further. After all, if you're faced with only a few hours, choosing among the museums in the Upper East Side alone might come down to whether you prefer Asian, European, or American art—or even ancient, medieval, or modern.

We try to estimate how long it will take to see, in any reasonable sense, the extent of the collection or building, although of course you must factor in both the extent of your own interest and your stamina when sketching out your schedule. We've also tried to convey the degree to which a particular museum or church might interest visitors of different ages and backgrounds so that you might be able to set up a tag-team plan allowing members of your group to divide up within a neighborhood and see things to their particular liking, and then reunite. In that case, however, be sure to calculate not only the time involved in seeing an attraction but also the possible extra time required to stand in line. Again, if a particular teenager is boat- or book-crazy, she may score an otherwise two-star attraction a four.

Below, you'll find charts and maps that organize New York's attractions by type and neighborhood. After that are profiles of individual New York attractions, arranged alphabetically by attraction name.

ATTRACTION PROFILES
American Museum of the Moving Images

APPEAL BY AGE	PRESCHOOL ★½	GRADE SCHOOL ★★	TEENS ★★★½
YOUNG ADULTS ★★★★		OVER 30 ★★★½	SENIORS ★★★

35th Avenue and 36th Street, Queens; ☎ **718-784-0077; www.ammi.org**

Type of attraction Entertainment history as entertainment. **Nearest subway station** Steinway Street. **Admission** $8.50 adults; $5.50 seniors and college

New York City Attractions by Type

TYPE AND NAME	NEIGHBORHOOD	AUTHOR'S RATING
CHURCHES		
Cathedral Church of St. John the Divine	Heights/Harlem	★★★
St. Patrick's Cathedral	Midtown East	★★
St. Paul's Chapel	Lower Manhattan	★★★★
Trinity Church	Lower Manhattan	★★★
FAMOUS BUILDINGS		
Empire State Building	Gramercy Park	½
Lower East Side Tenement Museum	Lower East Side	★★★
LIBRARY		
J. Pierpont Morgan Library	Upper East Side	★★★★
MONUMENTS		
Ellis Island National Monument	Lower Manhattan	★★★★★
Statue of Liberty/Liberty Island	Lower Manhattan	★★★
MUSEUMS		
American Museum of the Moving Image	Queens	★★★½
American Museum of Natural History	Upper West Side	★★★★
Brooklyn Museum	Brooklyn	★★★★½
The Cloisters	Washington Heights	★★★★★
Cooper-Hewitt National Design Museum	Upper East Side	★★★
Forbes Magazine Galleries	Gramercy Park	★★★½

students with ID; $4.50 children ages 5–18; children ages 4 and under free. **Hours** Tuesday–Friday, noon–5 p.m.; Saturday and Sunday, 11 a.m.–6 p.m.; closed Monday. **When to go** Weekends for film programs. **Special comments** Admission includes screenings. **Author's rating** Intriguing look at not only cinematic techniques but also the integration of "science" and "art," and the selling of both. ★★★½. **How much time to allow** 1½–4 hours.

DESCRIPTION AND COMMENTS The museum is actually part of a larger movie-making complex—the restored historic Astoria Studios, where Valentino, the Marx Brothers, and Gloria Swanson worked in the 1920s and Woody Allen and Martin Scorsese have worked in the 1990s. In between it was used for army training films. Only the museum building is open to the

TYPE AND NAME	NEIGHBORHOOD	AUTHOR'S RATING
MUSEUMS (CONTINUED)		
The Frick Collection	Upper East Side	★★★★★
Guggenheim Museum	Upper East Side	★★★★
Intrepid Sea-Air-Space Museum	Midtown West	★★★
Jewish Museum	Upper East Side	★★★½
Metropolitan Museum of Art	Upper East Side	★★★★★
El Museo del Barrio	Upper East Side	★★★
Museum of the City of New York	Upper East Side	★★★
Museum of Jewish Heritage	Lower Manhattan	★★★★
Museum of Modern Art	Midtown East	★★★★★
Museum of Television and Radio	Midtown East	★★★
National Museum of the American Indian	Lower Manhattan	★★★
Rubin Museum of Art	Gramercy Park	★★★★½
South Street Seaport and Museum	Lower Manhattan	★★
Whitney Museum of American Art	Upper East Side	★★★★
PARKS AND GARDENS		
Bronx Zoo/International Wildlife Conservation Park	Bronx	★★★½
Brooklyn Botanic Garden	Brooklyn	★★★
New York Botanical Garden	Bronx	★★★½

public. It's a combination of memorabilia, costumes, props, posters, oddities (à la Planet Hollywood), reconstructed sets, and screening rooms. Smaller kids will get a kick out of exhibits that let them "enter" the set—speak through actors' mouths, put their heads on other bodies, and so on. The major exhibit, "Behind the Scenes," is an interactive explanation of the technology and history of the music biz, which allows visitors to make computer-animated shorts, step into the set of *The Glass Menagerie,* compare the tedious manual film-splicing process of yesteryear with modern digital editing, and the like. Screenings range from vintage rarities (silents are shown with music) to cutting-edge art films, and lectures are often lively and celebrity-studded; call for schedule.

New York City Attractions by Neighborhood

NAME	DESCRIPTION	AUTHOR'S RATING
LOWER MANHATTAN, WALL STREET, AND THE BATTERY		
Battery Park/Esplanade	Monument park and public gardens	★★★★★
Ellis Island National Monument	Re-creation of immigrants' first contact with America	★★★★★
Museum of Jewish Heritage	Re-creation of Jewish culture of the last century	★★★★
National Museum of the American Indian	Part art collection, part anthropology lesson	★★★
St. Paul's Chapel	Small pre-Revolutionary church	★★★★
South Street Seaport and Museum	Historic district and maritime museum	★★
Statue of Liberty/Liberty Island	America's symbol of freedom	★★★
Trinity Church	Gothic Revival church from mid-19th century	★★★
CHINATOWN, LITTLE ITALY, AND THE LOWER EAST SIDE		
Lower East Side Tenement Museum	Reconstructed early 20th-century slum	★★★
GREENWICH VILLAGE		
Forbes Magazine Galleries	Fantastic collection of toys (for both kids and adults)	★★★½
GRAMERCY PARK AND MADISON SQUARE		
Empire State Building	Landmark tower with famous view	½
Rubin Museum of Art	First-rate collection of Himalayan art and icons	★★★★½
MIDTOWN WEST, TIMES SQUARE, AND THE THEATER DISTRICT		
Intrepid Sea-Air-Space Museum	Minifleet of retired military vessels	★★★
MIDTOWN EAST		
J. Pierpont Morgan Library	Medieval and Renaissance books and drawings	★★★★
Museum of Modern Art	Premier collection of modern and contemporary art and design	★★★★★
Museum of Television and Radio	Combination archives and rerun haven	★★★
St. Patrick's Cathedral	Largest Catholic cathedral in U.S.	★★

NAME	DESCRIPTION	AUTHOR'S RATING
UPPER WEST SIDE		
American Museum of Natural History	Popular and scientific collection	★★★★
UPPER EAST SIDE		
Cooper-Hewitt National Design Museum	International design and design art	★★★
The Frick Collection	18th- and 19th-century art in mansion	★★★★★
Guggenheim Museum	20th-century European art	★★★★
Jewish Museum	Ancient Judaica and Jewish art	★★★½
Metropolitan Museum of Art	One of greatest museums in the world	★★★★★
El Museo del Barrio	Pan-American Hispanic art and culture	★★★
Museum of the City of New York	Specific and often unusual collection of city history	★★★
Whitney Museum of American Art	20th-century American art	★★★★
MORNINGSIDE HEIGHTS, HAMILTON HEIGHTS, AND HARLEM		
Cathedral Church of St. John the Divine	Vast Episcopal cathedral	★★★
WASHINGTON HEIGHTS		
The Cloisters	Premier medieval art collection	★★★★★
BROOKLYN		
Brooklyn Botanic Garden	Landscaped park with Japanese garden and greenhouse	★★★
Brooklyn Museum of Art	Cultural artifacts and fine art	★★★★½
QUEENS		
American Museum of the Moving Image	Entertainment history	★★★½
THE BRONX		
Bronx Zoo/International Wildlife Conservation Park	Famous old-fashioned zoo	★★★½
New York Botanical Garden	Gardens and greenhouse complex	★★★½

uptown attractions

Attractions
1. American Museum of Natural History
2. Cathedral of St. John the Divine
3. Cooper-Hewitt National Design Museum
4. El Museo del Barrio
5. The Frick Collection
6. Guggenheim Museum
7. Jewish Museum
8. Metropolitan Museum of Art
9. Museum of the City of New York
10. Whitney Museum of American Art

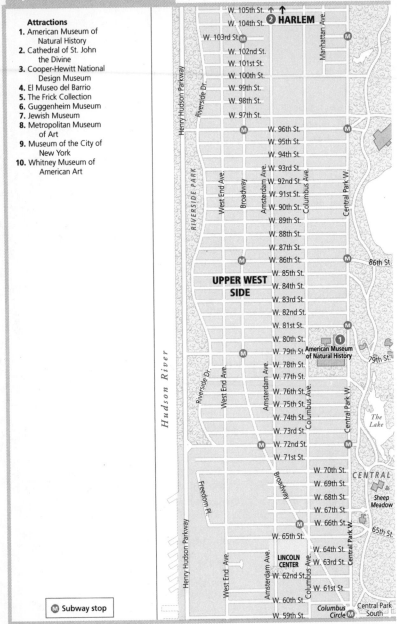

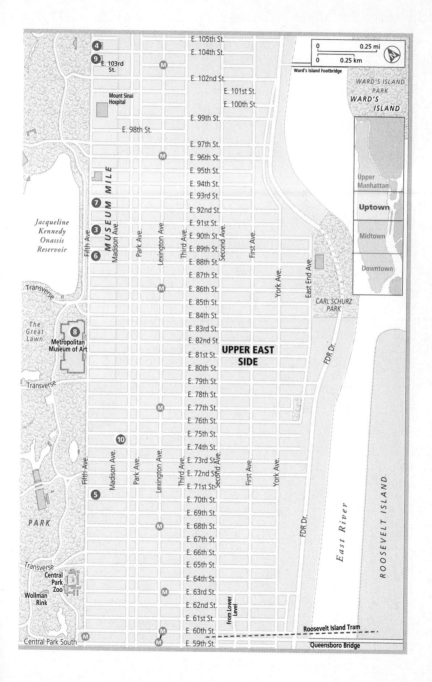

midtown attractions

Attractions
1. Bryant Park
2. Carnegie Hall
3. Central Park Zoo
4. Chelsea Piers Sports
   and Entertainment
   Complex
5. Chrysler Building
6. Empire State building
7. Inrepid Sea-Air-Space
   Museum
8. J. Pierpont Morgan
   Library
9. Lincoln Center
10. Museum of Modern Art
11. Museum of Television
    and Radio
12. Radio city Music Hall
13. Rubin Museum of Art
14. St. Patrick's Cathedral

UPPER WEST
SIDE

CENTRAL

W. 64th St.
W. 63rd St.
W. 62nd St.
W. 61st St.
W. 60th St.
West Drive

West End Ave.
Amsterdam Ave.
Columbus Ave.
Central Park W.

W. 59th St.
Columbus
Circle

Central Park S.

W. 58th St.
W. 57th St.
W. 56th St.
W. 55th St.
W. 54th St.
W. 53rd St.
W. 52nd St.
W. 51st St.

DeWitt
Clinton
Park

Tenth Ave.
Ninth Ave.

Broadway

THEATER
DISTRICT

W. 50th St.
W. 49th St.
W. 48th St.
W. 47th St.
W. 46th St.
W. 45th St.
W. 44th St.
W. 43rd St.
W. 42nd St.

MIDTOWN
WEST

TIMES
SQUARE

Twelfth Ave.
Eleventh Ave.
Tenth Ave.
Eighth Ave.
Seventh Ave.

W. 41st St.
W. 40th St.
W. 39th St.
W. 38th St.
W. 37th St.
W. 36th St.
W. 35th St.
W. 34th St.
W. 33rd St.

Port
Authority

Lincoln
Tunnel

Javits
Convention
Center

GARMENT
DISTRICT

W 32nd St.

Penn Station/
Madison Square
Garden

Tunnel
Entrance

W. 31st St.
W. 30th St.
W. 29th St.
W. 28th St.

Ninth Ave.

Chelsea Park

W. 27th St.
W. 26th St.
W. 25th St.
W. 24th St.

West Side HWY.
Eleventh Ave.
Tenth Ave.

W. 23rd St.

CHELSEA

W. 22nd St.
W. 21st St.
W. 20th St.
W. 19th St.

Chelsea Piers

Hudson River

W. 18th St.
W. 17th St.
W. 16th St.
W. 15th St.
W. 14th St.

Eighth Ave.
Ninth Ave.
Seventh Ave.

MEAT-PACKING
DISTRICT

downtown attractions

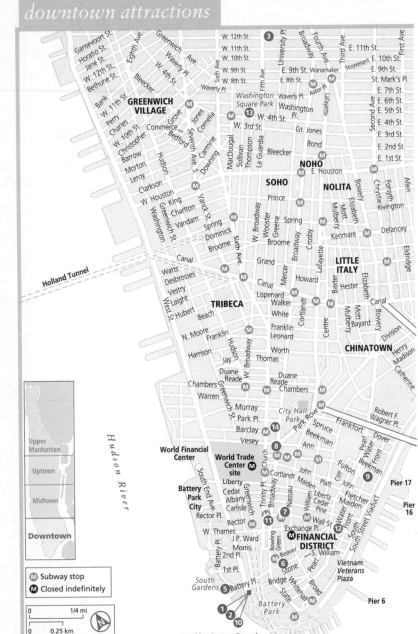

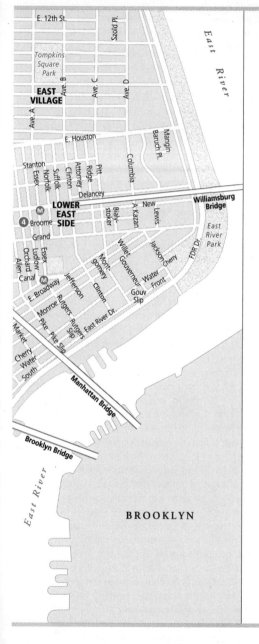

Attractions
1. Battery Park/Esplanade
2. Ellis Island National Monument
3. Forbes Magazine Galleries
4. Lower East Side Tenement Museum
5. Museum of Jewish Heritage
6. National Museum of the American Indian
7. New York Stock Exchange
8. St. Paul's Chapel
9. South Street Seaport and Museum
10. Statue of Liberty/ Liberty Island
11. Trinity Church
12. Wall Street
13. Washington Square Park
14. Wodworth Building

kids American Museum of Natural History

APPEAL BY AGE	PRESCHOOL ★★	GRADE SCHOOL ★★★½	TEENS ★★★½
YOUNG ADULTS ★★★★		OVER 30 ★★★	SENIORS ★★½

Central Park West at 79th Street, Upper West Side; ☎ 212-769-5100; IMAX, ☎ 212-769-5200; www.amnh.org

Type of attraction Popular and wide-ranging scientific and research collection. **Nearest subway station** 81st Street–Museum of Natural History or 79th Street. **Admission** "Suggested" $13 adults, $10 seniors and students, $7.50 children ages 12 and under; additional charge for some special exhibits; IMAX: $15 adults, $11 seniors and students, and $10 children (includes museum admission). **Hours** Sunday–Thursday, 10 a.m.–5:45 p.m.; Friday and Saturday, 10 a.m.–8:45 p.m.; closed Thanksgiving and Christmas. **When to go** Weekdays. **Special comments** The standing exhibits at the Rose Center/Hayden Planetarium are included in museum admission, but Space Show (planetarium) admission is extra. **Author's rating** Thanks to the museum's careful combination of adult and family-style exhibits, this will keep a whole group occupied really as long as you want. ★★★★. **How much time to allow** 2–4 hours.

DESCRIPTION AND COMMENTS This is a museum that inspires affection and frequently a kind of nostalgia; its dioramas of Africa and the evolutionary progress of humans and its gemstones (worth an estimated $50 million and including the famous Star of India sapphire) are perennial favorites, and they're the sort of exhibits we all seem to remember. The famous dinosaur skeletons are far more convincing since their cleaning and reconfiguration; the new exhibit halls are airy and the captioning first-rate. The museum's special exhibits have been headline-chasers, perhaps, focusing on the newly renovated dinosaur floor (and plugging into *Jurassic Park* fever) and the endless fascination of oversized diamonds, but they have certainly been blockbuster successes. There are several new hands-on and interactive exhibits, including the huge dinosaur of the Cultural African Republic rain forest, and a children's Discovery Room opens on weekends from noon to 4 p.m. It has a couple of gift shops, but the one in the midst of the big cats is the most fun.

The stunning Rose Center of Earth and Space is a visible "universe"— a 95-foot glass cube enclosing a "floating" sphere that is the planetarium itself. The computer-assisted effects are as far beyond old star-light projections as *Star Wars* EFX were to *King Kong*. A Guggenheim-style ramp holds interactive displays, models, etc. Adjoining exhibits discuss the evolution of the universe and the liklihood of extraterrestrial life.

The four statues atop the columns outside on Central Park West represent Lewis and Clark, Daniel Boone, and John J. Audubon. Walk around to the West 77th Street side or Columbus Avenue to try to see the museum as it looked at the turn of the century, with its Romanesque Revival structure already once expanded.

TOURING TIPS The museum offers highlights tours at 10:15 and 11:15 a.m. and 12:15, 1:15, 2:15, and 3:15 p.m.; meet on the second floor in the

Hall of African Mammals. The museum has a cafeteria, cocktail bar, and restaurant. Even if you just walk by, be sure to see the Rose Center building; it's even more breathtaking at night.

kids Bronx Zoo/International Wildlife Conservation Park

APPEAL BY AGE	PRESCHOOL ★★★	GRADE SCHOOL ★★★★	TEENS ★★★½
YOUNG ADULTS ★★★	OVER 30 ★★★		SENIORS ★★

Bronx River Parkway at Fordham Road; ☎ 718-367-1010; www.bronxzoo.com

Type of attraction Famous old-fashioned zoo in transformation to modern times. **Nearest subway station** Pelham Parkway. **Admission** $16 adults, $8 ages 2–12 and 65+. **Hours** Monday–Friday, 10 a.m.–5 p.m.; weekends and holidays until 5:30 p.m.; November to March, until 4:30 p.m. every day. **When to go** Wednesday; weekdays. **Special comments** Wednesday free; parking $7. **Author's rating** Although several of the older facilities badly need upgrading (particularly the monkey house), the endangered snow leopards and Mexican wolves alone are worth the visit. ★★★½. **How much time to allow** 1½–4 hours.

DESCRIPTION AND COMMENTS The main buildings date from the turn of the 19th century and for that reason are both wonderful (the monkey house has playful animals around the roof edge, the former big-cat house has lions and tigers around the frieze, etc.) and in some places looking a little sad. However, the zoo is moving quickly toward replacing all the old-fashioned cage-type enclosures with naturalistic ones, divided up by "continent," and some of these, including the wildlife marsh and savannah areas, are quite fine. The Wild Asia minizoo (with its glass-enclosed tropical rain forest, elephant plain, tiger hillside, and encircling monorail), the bat house, and the hands-on petting zoo are extremely popular. There are more than 4,300 creatures living here, representing 775 species.

The Congo Gorilla Forest is a park in itself—six-and-a-half acres that houses 300 primates and 75 species of smaller animals and birds such as okapi, red river hogs, and hornbills; 1,500 plants (400 varieties) that took a decade of greenhouse cultivation; 11 waterfalls; 55 artificial trees; mist machines; sound effects; and so on. It cost $43 million and is only open about eight months of the year. Its most popular resident is Pattycake, a New York native: She was born at the Central Park Zoo in 1972.

Like the nearby Botanical Gardens, the zoo goes all-out for kids from Thanksgiving past New Year's, staying open until 9 p.m. and filling the park with animal-shaped light "trees" and sculptures, with a special focus on reindeer and other seasonal topics. The hands-on Children's Zoo is great, but it may be a madhouse on weekends.

TOURING TIPS Frankly, the zoo is not a whole lot closer to the subway than the botanical gardens are (see "TOURING TIPS" in the Garden's description just below), and for out-of-towners, the route is a little confusing. It would be easier to use Metro North to the Botanic Garden stop and do a combination day (and perhaps even if you aren't stopping by the gardens, although you really should). The grounds adjoin, but the entrances don't; there's about a half-mile walk from the garden's main gate to the zoo, but at least it's a fairly straight shot. Or take a Liberty Line bus ($3 one way, $6 round-trip; ☎ 718-652-8400). There is a full-service cafe, plus seasonal concessions, stalls, and smaller cafes.

Brooklyn Botanic Garden

APPEAL BY AGE	PRESCHOOL ½	GRADE SCHOOL ★★	TEENS ★★
YOUNG ADULTS ★★	OVER 30 ★★★		SENIORS ★★★

Washington Avenue at Eastern Parkway, Brooklyn; ☎ 718-623-7200; www.bbg.org

Type of attraction Landscaped park with Japanese garden and greenhouse complex. **Nearest subway station** Prospect Park or Eastern Parkway–Brooklyn Museum. **Admission** $4 adults, $2 seniors and students with ID; free for children ages 16 and under; free for seniors on Friday. **Hours** October–March: Tuesday–Friday, 8 a.m.–4:30 p.m.; weekends and holidays, 10 a.m.–4:30 p.m.; closed Monday. April–September: Tuesday–Friday, 8 a.m.–6 p.m.; weekends and holidays, 10 a.m.–6 p.m. Free admission on Tuesday and Saturday until noon. **When to go** Anytime. **Author's rating** ★★★. **How much time to allow** 1–1½ hours.

DESCRIPTION AND COMMENTS Even if you only walk through the grounds on your way from Prospect Park or the subway to the Brooklyn Museum of Art, it's worth a few minutes to look into the greenhouses, particularly the lily-pond room, the mini–rain forest (which includes several promising medicinal trees), and the bonsai garden; and it's absolutely essential to see the Japanese Tea Garden, with its many small pleasures and twists. If possible, see this in late April or May, when the thousands of Japanese cherry trees blossom (as they do more famously in Washington, D.C.), along with nearly 80 magnolias. Among other popular areas is the fragrance garden, which is heavily perfumed and has Braille labeling.

TOURING TIPS On weekends and holidays, a free trolley circles among the Botanic Garden, the Brooklyn Museum of Art, and the Prospect Park zoo; call ☎ 718-965-8967.

Brooklyn Museum

APPEAL BY AGE	PRESCHOOL ½	GRADE SCHOOL ★★	TEENS ★★½
YOUNG ADULTS ★★★★	OVER 30 ★★★★		SENIORS ★★★

Eastern Parkway at Washington Avenue, Brooklyn; ☎ 718-638-5000; www.brooklynart.org

Type of attraction World-class collection of cultural artifacts and fine art. **Nearest subway station** Eastern Parkway. **Admission** $8 adults, $4 students and seniors (some special exhibits extra); free to children under 12. **Hours** Wednesday–Friday, 10 a.m.–5 p.m.; first Saturday of every month except September, 11 a.m.–11 p.m.; all other Saturdays, 11 a.m.–6 p.m.; Sunday, 11 a.m.–6 p.m.; closed Monday and Tuesday. **When to go** Anytime. **Special comments** Strollers are permitted in only a few areas on weekends. **Author's rating** In some ways, a more user-friendly mirror of the Met. ★★★★½. **How much time to allow** 2–4 hours.

DESCRIPTION AND COMMENTS Probably only in a city that already boasted the Metropolitan Museum of Art could the Brooklyn Museum (BMA) be so often overlooked. (And if Brooklyn hadn't been absorbed into New York City, the original plans for the museum might have been fulfilled, which would have made it the largest in the world.) Its collections may be a little smaller, but they're no less well exhibited; in fact, the Met can be so overwhelming that the Brooklyn Museum is almost nicer (and it's certainly less crowded). Its Egyptian and African holdings and the 19th-century American and European (particularly French) collections are world-renowned, and it has its own complex of 28 reconstructed rooms from the New York area going back to the 17th century and up to the Gilded Age (more Rockefeller Moorish-ness); but it has particular strengths in less familiar areas as well, including the art of Native American peoples, spectacular Persian paintings, and a smallish but exquisite gallery of Korean art. BMA's definition of "prints" should set a new dictionary standard: from Dürer woodblocks to Whistler lithographs, from Toulouse-Lautrec posters to Cassatt portraits, Winslow Homer engravings, and Picasso line drawings. In the past few years, the museum has also hosted several blockbuster exhibits, including "Monet in the Mediterranean" and "In the Light of Italy: Corot and Early Open-Air Painting."

TOURING TIPS There is a nice little cafe on the ground floor. First Saturday of each month offers late-night music and wine. Also, check the schedule of the **Brooklyn Academy of Music** (call ☎ 718-636-4100 or visit **bam.org**), which is only a pleasant walk or a couple of subway stops back toward Manhattan; you might be able to top off your day with a concert.

Cathedral Church of St. John the Divine

APPEAL BY AGE	PRESCHOOL ★	GRADE SCHOOL ★★	TEENS ★★
YOUNG ADULTS ★★★	OVER 30 ★★★		SENIORS ★★★

Amsterdam Avenue at 112th Street, Heights/Harlem; ☎ 212-316-7540; www.stjohndivine.org

Type of attraction Vast (though unfinished) Episcopal cathedral. **Nearest subway station** Cathedral Parkway (110th Street). **Admission** Suggested donation, $3. **Hours** Monday–Saturday, 7 a.m.–6 p.m.; Sunday, 7 a.m.–8 p.m. unless there's a concert. **When to go** Weekdays midmorning or afternoon to avoid disrupting services. **Special comments** Try to hook up with one of the tours; there's so much going on. **Author's rating** The continued ambitions (or is that aspirations?) of the builders are somehow moving, the adherence to traditional building methods even more so. ★★★. **How much time to allow** 1½–2 hours.

DESCRIPTION AND COMMENTS After more than a century, this almost symbolically style-embracing cathedral is still only two-thirds complete, and it may take most of a second century and half a billion dollars to finish it. But already it is a wonder, part Romanesque and part Gothic; a little Spanish, a little French, a little Italian. When finished, it will be the largest cathedral in the world—as large as Notre Dame and Chartres put together, with 300-foot towers and a 600-foot nave. There's a scale model in the gift shop that shows how at least the front half, from tower to tower, will look. Builders are trying to stick to real medieval methods. Up until recently, the stone blocks were being carved out just as they had been centuries ago (some Harlem students apprenticed under imported British master masons), and there are no steel supports. The portals were cast by the man who cast the Statue of Liberty; the so-called temporary dome has lasted nearly 90 years. Be sure to look closely at the stone carvings atop the columns and friezes. They're not all solemn; some feature famous New York landmarks and creatures.

Inside, the "melting pot" philosophy has been extended to religion: The various chapels salute other major religions and ethnic groups, and the justly famous concerts and lectures are as often secular as sacred. One of the most popular events of the year is the annual Memorial Day concert by the New York Philharmonic; another is the famous blessing of the animals on the feast of St. Francis, the first Sunday in October, which each year attracts hundreds of not only dogs and cats but exotic birds, snakes, and even a zoo animal or two.

TOURING TIPS Tours are offered Tuesday through Saturday at 11 a.m. and 12:30 p.m.

The Cloisters

APPEAL BY AGE	PRESCHOOL ★	GRADE SCHOOL ★★	TEENS ★★½
YOUNG ADULTS ★★★	OVER 30 ★★★		SENIORS ★★½

Fort Tryon Park, Washington Heights; ☎ 212-923-3700; www.metmuseum.org

Type of attraction Premier medieval art collection in evocative historical setting. **Nearest subway station** 190th Street. **Admission** "Suggested" $12 adults, $7 seniors and students; children ages 11 and under (with adult) free. **Hours** Tuesday–Sunday, 9:30 a.m.–5:15 p.m. (9:30 a.m.–4:45 p.m. November though February); closed Monday. **When to go** Weekdays. **Special comments** One ticket covers both the Metropolitan Museum of Art (includes main building) and the Cloisters on the same day. **Author's rating** It was a stroke of genius (and immeasurable philanthropy) to build a period home for part of the Metropolitan's medieval art collection. ★★★★★. **How much time to allow** 1½–2 hours.

DESCRIPTION AND COMMENTS This fantastic assemblage of stone, with its serenely beautiful and stylistically otherworldly saints, stained glass, prayer-eroded blocks, and entombed crusaders, is like a dream. You're not even surprised to find, hanging on one wall, the frequently reproduced pictures of the hunting of the unicorn. Or the almost-as-familiar illuminated *Belles Heures* of the Duc de Berry. The cloisters of the title—five of them, taken from the ruins of French monasteries dating from the 12th through the 15th centuries, plus a 12th-century Spanish apse and a Romanesque chapel—have been fitted together on two levels, so that you can actually stroll through them as the residents did. (They are actually organized chronologically, so you sort of circle from the Romanesque period, about 1000, to the Gothic era, circa 1500.) The stone block benches of the chapter house are curved with the long erosion of centuries of use. One of the cloister gardens has been planted to match the courtyard garden seen in one of the huge tapestries, another with the herbs and medicinal plants of the Middle Ages. There is an air- and light-conditioned room of jewels, enamels, reliquaries, and manuscripts (this is one of those museums where a penlight might be helpful). There are also sculptures and altarpieces and a rare and extremely fine early 15th-century triptych of the *Annunciation* by Robert Campin of Tournai.

The Cloisters frequently offers lectures, some of them aimed at students, and wonderfully atmospheric concerts; call for schedules.

TOURING TIPS The museum itself is at least in part wheelchair accessible (there is an elevator down by the security desk), but handicapped patrons would be well advised to spring for a cab, at least from the 175th Street subway station, which is accessible. Or take the M4 bus, which, though notoriously slow, stops right at the museum entrance.

Cooper-Hewitt National Design Museum

APPEAL BY AGE	PRESCHOOL ½	GRADE SCHOOL ★★	TEENS ★★
YOUNG ADULTS ★★★		OVER 30 ★★★	SENIORS ★★

East 91st Street and Fifth Avenue, Upper East Side; ☎ 212-849-8300

Type of attraction Collection of international design and design art. **Nearest subway station** 96th Street or 86th Street. **Admission** $10 adults, $7 seniors and students; children ages 11 and under free. **Hours** Tuesday, 10 a.m.–9 p.m.; Wednesday–Saturday, 10 a.m.–6 p.m.; Sunday, noon–6 p.m.; closed Monday and federal holidays. **When to go** Midafternoon. **Special comments** This is a branch of the Smithsonian Institution; members get in free. Everyone gets in free Tuesday, 5–9 p.m. **Author's rating** The strength of the museum's appeal to younger visitors depends heavily on the special exhibits on view at the time, but adults will probably always find something to like. ★★★. **How much time to allow** 1–1½ hours.

DESCRIPTION AND COMMENTS This was originally the "modest" home of Andrew Carnegie (the first private establishment in the city with an elevator, incidentally); the two families whose names are linked in the title collected textiles, jewelry, glassware, silver, furniture, and artisan paper from all over the world. Although the museum's collection as a whole is quite large, only a small fraction is on view at one time, but there may be several different exhibits coexisting; for example, most of one whole room may be given over to a lineup of six or eight intriguing chairs, while the library and the hallway may serve as a "rogue's gallery" of lettering styles. (Additional gallery space was created in the mid-1990s.)

Incidentally, this has one of the most intriguing museum shops in the city, with a lot of clever, attractive, and convenient writing implements, clocks and calculators, and other utensils.

TOURING TIPS If you are a member of the Smithsonian System, ask for your discount.

Ellis Island National Monument

APPEAL BY AGE	PRESCHOOL ½	GRADE SCHOOL ★★★	TEENS ★★★
YOUNG ADULTS ★★★★★		OVER 30 ★★★★★	SENIORS ★★★★

New York Harbor, Lower Manhattan; ☎ 212-269-5755

Type of attraction Re-creation of immigrants' first contact with America. **Nearest subway station** Bowling Green or South Ferry. **Admission** $10 adults, $8 seniors, $4 children; ages 3 and under free (ticket covers ferry transport and admission to Liberty Island); $7 each for groups of 25+. **Hours** Daily, 9 a.m.–5:15 p.m. (last ferry at 4 p.m.); extended hours during summer months and on some holidays; closed Christmas. **When to go** Weekdays. **Special comments** The museum is wheelchair accessible and offers other disability assistance. **Author's rating** ★★★★★. **How much time to allow** 1½–2 hours.

DESCRIPTION AND COMMENTS Few museums can have an association for as many Americans as this one; by some estimates, half of the nation's population has roots here. From 1892 to 1954, when the processing center was abandoned, as many as 10,000 immigrants per day, a total of more than 12 million, stumbled off often wretched boats into the waiting lines of Ellis Island, where they were examined, cross-examined (whether or not they could speak English), quarantined, frequently rechristened, and just as frequently turned away. And that total would be higher if the station hadn't been used to house German POWs during World War II. Many of the arrivals were children or orphans; the very first immigrant to set foot on the island, on New Year's Day, was 15-year-old Annie Moore.

Visitors follow the immigrants' route, entering through the main baggage room and up to the high-vaulted and intentionally intimidating Registry and then the bluntly named Staircase of Separation. Astonishing, these historic rooms can be rented out for catered events. Exhibits include the stark dormitories and baggage, dozens of rooms full of poignant photos and oral histories, video clips and dramatic presentations, and a thousand individual remembrances of home—crucifixes, jewelry, clothing, family heirlooms—donated by the families of those who passed through. The 1898 main building has been magnificently restored at a cost of more than $150 million, from the copper roofing to the rail-station-like glass and wrought-iron entranceway; plans for the other buildings are uncertain. The Immigrant Wall of Fame lists half a million names, including the grandfathers of presidents from Washington to Kennedy, whose descendants contributed to the restoration. Except for the very youngest, who may get tired in the long lines, almost everyone will be taken with this experience—not only the older visitors, who remember the melting-pot era best, but also those school-age visitors for whom multiculturalism is a daily affair. First- and second-generation Americans will be especially affected.

kids Empire State Building

| APPEAL BY AGE | PRESCHOOL ★ | GRADE SCHOOL ★★½ | TEENS ★★★ |
| YOUNG ADULTS ★★★ | OVER 30 ★★½ | | SENIORS ★★½ |

350 Fifth Avenue (at 34th Street), Midtown West; ☎ 212-736-3100; www.esbnyc.com

Type of attraction Landmark tower with famous view. **Nearest subway station** 34th Street. **Admission** $13 adults, $12 military and seniors, $8 for children ages 6–11 p.m.; free for children ages 5 and under. **Hours** Daily, 9:30 a.m.–midnight (last elevator ascends at 11:15 p.m.). **When to go** After dark. **Special comments** Some small children may find this rather scary. **Author's rating** A nice view, but not the only choice. And since this is squarely on many bus tour routes, it can be very crowded. ½. **How much time to allow** 30–45 minutes.

DESCRIPTION AND COMMENTS There are two observation decks: one on the 86th floor, which is a glass-enclosed viewing area surrounded on all sides by open-air decks (from which, promoters say, you can see ships 40 miles out at sea); and an entirely enclosed one on the 102nd level, near the top of the spire, whose range, on the legendary clear day, is supposed to be 80 miles. The decks are open until midnight, when the view is even nicer and, oddly, less vertiginous. Its pride of reputation is shown in the lobby paintings, which picture the seven wonders of the ancient world and the "Eighth Wonder of the Modern World"–the Empire State Building. Currently the tallest building in the city, it's 1,454 feet tall (counting the transmitters and all; the 102nd-floor observatory is 1,250 feet up), and it took six months to build, required 10 million bricks, and weighs 360,000 tons. There are 1,860 steps, as veterans of the annual race up can attest, and 73 elevators. King Kong wasn't really here, of course; but the tower was struck by a fog-bound bomber back in 1945 just above the 78th floor, and it's still struck by lightning as many as 500 times a year. It has hosted more than 90 million visitors in its time, over 3.5 million every year. The exterior lights—always on, to avoid a second plane crash—are color-coded on holidays and special occasions: red, white, and blue on Independence Day; green for St. Patrick's; pink for Gay Liberation Day, and so on. Once it was lit blue to honor Frank "Ol' Blue Eyes" Sinatra.

The building now includes some more commercial tourist attractions as well. On the concourse, where the ticket booth is located, there's a Guinness World Records Exhibit Hall with dioramas and photos of some strange human endeavors. There are several other smaller simulated adventures, something like IMAX movies with motion, located in the building as well.

TOURING TIPS There's a snack bar at the 86th-floor level. Tickets are sold on the concourse level below the main lobby; you don't have to use the tickets on the same day you buy them. The ticket office closes at 11:30 p.m.

kids *Forbes* Magazine Galleries

APPEAL BY AGE	PRESCHOOL ★★★	GRADE SCHOOL ★★★★	TEENS ★★★
YOUNG ADULTS ★★★		OVER 30 ★★★	SENIORS ★★½

62 Fifth Avenue (at 12th Street), Gramercy Park; ☎ 212-206-5548

Type of attraction Fantastic collection of toys, both children's (tin soldiers, model boats) and adults (Fabergé) collected by Malcolm Forbes Sr. **Nearest subway station** 14th Street–Union Square. **Admission** Free, but limited numbers admitted per day. **Hours** Tuesday, Wednesday, Friday, Saturday, 10 a.m.–4 p.m.; closed Sunday, Monday, and Thursday. **When to go** Before lunch if there are children in the party, after if not. **Special comments** Children ages 15 and under must be accompanied by an adult, and no more than four children per adult are allowed. **Author's rating** This says something about how some adults, particularly unrealistically wealthy ones (meaning both Forbes and the Romanovs), never have to outgrow childhood. Quite the escape even now. ★★★½. **How much time to allow** 1–1½ hours.

DESCRIPTION AND COMMENTS If you think you've seen toy soldiers before, think again. The more than 12,000 flat and 3-D tin figures arranged in dioramas here—not just soldiers of every historical period and nation, but cowboys and Indians, Aztecs and Spaniards, knights and ladies, and so on—are only about one-tenth of Forbes's collection. The room built to match the famous "counterpane" illustration from Robert Louis Stevenson's *Child's Garden of Verse* has a glass bubble above the dummy figure allowing visitors to become the "child" in the picture. This labyrinth of galleries begins with a series of cases holding more than 500 vintage toy boats (not model boats, an interesting distinction) arranged in flotillas against a background of etched-glass Art Deco panels from the *Normandie;* it continues with a collection of period and special-edition Monopoly sets, trophies, sporting awards, and rotating exhibits of presidential memorabilia, including Nixon's letter of resignation and models of Washington's headquarters at Yorktown and Jefferson's bedroom at Monticello.

   The grand finale is a collection of 300-plus Fabergé eggs, personal accessories, jewelry, and household items formerly belonging to the Romanovs of Russia, including the imperial diadem of diamonds, platinum, gold, and cobalt enamel. Forbes's collection of the famous eggs, 12 of the surviving 43, includes such spectacular examples as the Coronation Egg, presented by Nicholas II to Alexandria in 1899, which opens to reveal a tiny replica of the coronation coach. Finally, there is a gallery with changing selections of the paintings, prints, and autographs from the collection.

TOURING TIPS This can be so exhilarating for kids that they get a little loud, and the space is very small. Older adults may want to go at lunchtime to avoid the competition. The tight space and highly focused lighting can make this tiring for some older visitors. Also note that the galleries are occasionally closed on regular viewing days; it wouldn't hurt to call ahead.

The Frick Collection

APPEAL BY AGE	PRESCHOOL ★½	GRADE SCHOOL ★½	TEENS ★★
YOUNG ADULTS ★★★½		OVER 30 ★★★★	SENIORS ★★★★

1 East 70th Street (at Fifth Avenue), Upper East Side; ☎ 212-288-0700; www.frick.org

Type of attraction Collection of 18th- and 19th-century art in a gracious mansion. **Nearest subway station** 68th Street–Hunter College. **Admission** $12 adults, $8 seniors, $5 students; children under 16 must be accompanied by an adult; under 10 not admitted. **Hours** Tuesday–Saturday, 10 a.m.–6 p.m.; Sunday, 1–6 p.m. **When to go** Weekdays. **Special comments** Children under age 10 are not admitted. **Author's rating** A personal favorite, glorious in both setting and collection. ★★★★★. **How much time to allow** 1½–3 hours.

DESCRIPTION AND COMMENTS Maybe this betrays a Western romantic or even DWM-nostalgic mindset, but this is to our taste the perfect philanthropic collection, small by Met standards but studded with exquisite portraits (Whistler, Goya, El Greco, Titian, Vermeer, Sargeant, Holbein, Rembrandt), landscapes (Turner, Constable), and allegories (Fragonard and an entire boudoir's worth of Boucher panels painted for Madame de Pompadour). Then there's the enamel Limoges miniatures, the garden court with its lily pond, the ghost of the pipe organ (the pipes are still there, in the hallway, though the works are gone), all those Oriental rugs (you are looking down, aren't you?), and just a smattering of fine furniture left from the days when steel magnate Henry Clay Frick and his family lived here.

TOURING TIPS This is only two blocks from the Asia Society collection at 70th and Park, which is a fine match in terms of temperament and pacing even if it is a world, or half a world, away in art.

Guggenheim Museum

APPEAL BY AGE	PRESCHOOL ½	GRADE SCHOOL ★★	TEENS ★★
YOUNG ADULTS ★★★½		OVER 30 ★★★	SENIORS ★★★

Fifth Avenue at 88th Street, Upper East Side; ☎ 212-423-3500; www.guggenheim.org

Type of attraction Fine collection of 20th-century European art. **Nearest subway station** 86th Street. **Admission** $15 adults, $10 seniors and students; children ages 11 and under free. **Hours** Saturday–Wednesday, 10 a.m.–5:45 p.m.; Friday, 10 a.m.–8 p.m.; closed Thursday. **When to go** Anytime. **Special comments** Fridays, 6–8 p.m., pay what you wish. Though the spiral ramp seems good for wheelchairs and keeping kids interested, it can be hard on the legs. **Author's rating** ★★★½. **How much time to allow** 1½–3 hours.

DESCRIPTION AND COMMENTS This is one of those museums more famous for its architecture than for its collection. Frank Lloyd Wright's upwardly expanding six-floor spiral, like a squared-off chambered nautilus (it's been called ruder things), frames the Great Rotunda and looks up to an often brilliantly lit glass dome; the exhibits fill the walls of the long ramp and lead off into the chambers. Among the permanent exhibits are major pieces by Klee, Picasso, Kandinsky, Chagall, and Modigliani; the museum also has a fine selection of French Impressionists, including Monet, Renoir, and Van Gogh.

Though in the shadow of the giant Museum of Modern Art collection, the Guggenheim, which has more European works, forms a strong duet with the Whitney Museum of American Art. (Also, it reaches back a little farther into the 19th century.) Guggenheim himself was aggressive in collecting avant-garde and new talent, and that was the reputation the museum was supposed to have, although it has been criticized for "maturing." Its new Soho branch (and the vast new branch in Bilbao, Spain) may give it new vitality.

kids Intrepid Sea-Air-Space Museum

APPEAL BY AGE	PRESCHOOL ★½	GRADE SCHOOL ★★★	TEENS ★★½
YOUNG ADULTS ★★½	OVER 30 ★★★	YOUNG ADULTS ★★½	SENIORS ★★★

Pier 86, West 46th Street at 12th Avenue, Midtown West;
☎ **212-245-0072,** ☎ **877-957-7447; www.intrepidmuseum.org**

Type of attraction Minifleet of retired navy and coast guard vessels, including the World War II aircraft carrier *Intrepid*. **Nearest subway station** 42nd Street or 50th Street. **Admission** $16.50 adults, $12.50 veterans, seniors, and students, $11.50 children ages 6–11, $4.50 children ages 2–5; free for children under 2 and active military and travel professionals; half-price for disabled visitors. **Hours** Summer: Monday–Friday, 10 a.m.–5 p.m.; Saturday–Sunday, 10 a.m.–6 p.m.; winter: Tuesday–Sunday 10 a.m.–5 p.m.; last admission one hour before closing. **When to go** Early or immediately after lunch. **Special comments** Only limited areas of some of the six vessels, and the exhibit halls, are wheelchair accessible, and other areas (particularly staircases) may be difficult for older visitors, small children, or the claustrophobic. In addition, these are not generally air-conditioned or heated facilities; dress accordingly. Note that the ticket office closes at 4 p.m. **Author's rating** This is really a sort of amusement park–cum–elephant graveyard, and for those with a real interest (or experience) in naval history, it's a four- or even five-star attraction. But don't underestimate this. If you add up the time recommended for touring the various vessels, it totals nearly five hours, and there are two exhibit halls as well. And there can be waiting lines for the guided tours. Better pick your spots. ★★★. **How much time to allow** 2–5 hours.

DESCRIPTION AND COMMENTS This complex includes half a dozen vessels and a mix of guided and self-guided tours. The centerpiece is, of course, the *Intrepid,* which has a 900-foot flight deck on which sit 40 real planes dating from the 1940s to the 1990s (including an A12 Blackbird spy plane). Visitors can wander through the bridge and most of the corridors and may well spend, as staffers estimate, three hours on the carrier alone. Only guided tours of specific areas are offered of the guided-missile submarine *Growler* (17 minutes), the Vietnam-era destroyer escort *Slater* (22 minutes), the coast guard lightship *Nantucket* (10 minutes), and the *S.S. Elizabeth* research ship; both (partial) guided and self-guided tours cross the fleet destroyer *Edson* (40 minutes). Pioneers Hall uses antique equipment, mock-ups, and some video to trace the history of flight; Technologies Hall showcases modern and futuristic methods of space and underwater exploration, including rockets, robots, and even some weapons.

TOURING TIPS As noted, this is almost a whole day's outing; it's best to pack snacks and water, particularly if there are children in your party.

J. Pierpont Morgan Library

APPEAL BY AGE	PRESCHOOL ★	GRADE SCHOOL ★★	TEENS ★★½
YOUNG ADULTS ★★★	OVER 30 ★★★★		SENIORS ★★★

29 East 36th Street (at Madison Avenue), Midtown East;
☎ **212-685-0008; www.morganlibrary.org**

Type of attraction World-class collection of medieval and Renaissance illuminated manuscripts, rare books, and master drawings. **Nearest subway station** 33rd Street. **Admission** $9 adults, $7 students and seniors; children ages 12 and under free when with an adult. **Hours** Tuesday–Thursday, 10:30 a.m.–5 p.m.; Friday, 10:30 a.m–8 p.m.; Saturday, 10:30 a.m.–6 p.m.; Sunday, noon–6 p.m.; closed Mondays and holidays. **When to go** Weekdays; late afternoon. **Special comments** There are child-friendly areas, but some special exhibits, say of children's books and illustrations, might have even higher appeal for young visitors. **Author's rating** As admitted medieval history freaks and bibliophiles to boot, we think this is an incredible collection, and usually not very crowded. ★★★★. **How much time to allow** 1½–3½ hours.

DESCRIPTION AND COMMENTS Legendary financier J. P. Morgan may have been giving himself aristocratic airs when he built this Renaissance palace of a home, but he and his collection must have been a perfect fit for this warm, otherworldly complex. Gold and full-color manuscripts, the most delicate of red-chalk sketches, the almost illegibly tiny handwriting of the Brontë children, Mozart's own scores, Gutenberg's *Bible,* Voltaire's briefcase, Dickens's cigar case—the rotating pleasures of this museum are perhaps specialized, but they are certainly superior. The sheer number of books will fill you with envy, and the glorious murals, woodwork, and plaster detailing will do the same.

TOURING TIPS There is a pretty little cafe on site that serves breakfast, lunch, and even, appropriately, tea, so true book-lovers can make quite a day of it.

Jewish Museum

APPEAL BY AGE	PRESCHOOL ½	GRADE SCHOOL ★★	TEENS ★★★
YOUNG ADULTS ★★★½	OVER 30 ★★★½		SENIORS ★★★★

Fifth Avenue at 92nd Street, Upper East Side; ☎ 212-423-3200;
www.jewishmuseum.org

Type of attraction Surprisingly rich collection of ancient Judaica and Jewish art. **Nearest subway station** 96th Street. **Admission** $10 adults, $7.50 seniors and students; children ages 11 and under free. **Hours** Sunday, Monday, Wednesday, and Thursday, 11 a.m.–5:45 p.m.; Tuesday, 11 a.m.–8 p.m.; closed major legal and

Jewish holidays. **When to go** Anytime. **Special comments** "Pay what you wish" on Tuesday, 5–8 p.m. **Author's rating** One becomes so accustomed to seeing Christian relics and even Asian religious art that the age and variety of these ruins and sacred objects are startling. ★★★½. **How much time to allow** 1–2 hours.

DESCRIPTION AND COMMENTS This fine collection, now moving toward its centennial, centers around a permanent exhibition on the Jewish experience—religious and secular—that ranges back 4,000 years. Among its works are temple facades from Sumeria, wall paintings of biblical battles, *Torah* covers and crowns, fine art and sculpture, candelabras, flatware, manuscripts, ceremonial cups, and a gripping three-dimensional installation by Eleanor Antin and George Segal. The collection also includes many fine portraits of Jewish Americans and a computer/video library. Downstairs is a gallery used for special exhibitions.

Like many of the fine specialized museums in the city, this was originally a mansion, and the two-level wood-paneled library, which is filled with fine arks and altars and ceremonial items and holds an almost pulpitlike spiral staircase, is a beauty. There is also a family exhibit area designed for children and parents to visit together. Incidentally, the stonework in the rear extension was done by the same masons who are working on the Cathedral of St. John the Divine (see profile).

TOURING TIPS This museum is extremely accessible for wheelchair users; but if you can use the stairs, be sure to come down stairwell No. 1, a glass-brick turret with a plaintively beautiful audio installation. There is a cafe in the basement.

Lower East Side Tenement Museum

APPEAL BY AGE	PRESCHOOL ½	GRADE SCHOOL ★½	TEENS ★★
YOUNG ADULTS ★★★	OVER 30 ★★★		SENIORS ★★★

**90 Orchard Street (the actual tenement building is 97 Orchard),
Lower East Side; ☎ 212-431-0233; www.tenement.org**

Type of attraction Reconstructed early-20th-century slum. **Nearest subway station** Delancey or Grand Street. **Admission** $15 adults, $11 seniors and students. **Hours** Gallery 90, the office/shop, is open Tuesday–Sunday, 11 a.m.–6 p.m.; tours are offered during summer, Thursday evening only. **When to go** Weekdays. **Special comments** Only guided tours are available; reserve in advance if possible. **Author's rating** The only way to understand 12 people living in one room is to see it. ★★★. **How much time to allow** 1–1½ hours.

DESCRIPTION AND COMMENTS In 1903, city officials reported that there were at least 2,200 people, most of them immigrants, packed into the single block bounded by Orchard, Delancey, Broome, and Allen streets, in buildings like this 1863 tenement, restored in the main to turn-of-the-century conditions (it had no water, heat, or toilets until 1905). One apartment was left just as it was found in 1988, having been abandoned for about 50 years; another was restored to the (relatively) comfortable state it was in when the Gumpertz family lived there in 1878. The museum puts together changing exhibits portraying life of the neighborhood. Incidentally, this is not, as some people may think, a "Jewish museum"—it's very hybridized.

TOURING TIPS The museum also offers hour-long neighborhood heritage tours weekends at 1 and 2:30 p.m., which leave from Gallery 90; you can buy either tickets for tours alone (also $10 and $8) or a combination ticket for a tenement tour and walking tour ($14 for adults and $12 for seniors and students).

A block north at 89 Rivington Street is the Roumanian Shul, a continuously active 1881 Romanesque structure with handsome windows that, like the Eldridge Street Synagogue, is undergoing a thorough facelift.

Metropolitan Museum of Art

APPEAL BY AGE	PRESCHOOL ★	GRADE SCHOOL ★★	TEENS ★★½
YOUNG ADULTS ★★★★		OVER 30 ★★★★	SENIORS ★★★★

Fifth Avenue between 80th and 84th streets (entrance at 82nd), Upper East Side; ☎ 212-535-7710; www.metmuseum.org

Type of attraction One of the greatest museum collections in the world. **Nearest subway station** 86th Street. **Admission** "Suggested" $15 adults, $10 seniors; $7 students; children ages 11 and under free. **Hours** Sunday and Tuesday–Thursday, 9:30 a.m.–5:30 p.m.; Friday and Saturday, 9:30 a.m.–9 p.m.; closed Monday. **When to go** Friday and Saturday evenings for dining and music; call ☎ 212-570-3949 for special events schedule. **Special comments** No strollers allowed on Sundays. **Author's rating** We could visit this every time we were in New York and never feel as if we had seen it all. ★★★★★. **How much time to allow** 1½–5 hours.

DESCRIPTION AND COMMENTS The figures are almost unbelievable: 3.5 million pieces of art, some dating back more than 5,000 years, and representing every culture in the world; 32 acres of exhibit space; 5 million visitors a year. It was founded in 1870 by New York's leading philanthropists and city boosters, who intended it to rival the great museums of Europe and prove New York the equal of any Old World center—and they were willing to pony up to make it happen. It worked, too.

You can't see it all, so pick a century, a style, or a special exhibit and start there. Or pick a centerpiece. For example, the American wing gently spirals down past Tiffany glass and Arts and Crafts pieces to the neoclassical sculpture in the garden court; the Temple of Dendur, which was erected by Augustus, has been reconstructed in a chamber of glass at the end of the Egyptian wing (a thank-you from the nation of Egypt for the United States' help in rescuing monuments threatened by the Aswan Dam); and the Astor Court, a replica of a Ming Dynasty–era scholar's garden created by artisans from Souzhou, China, using traditional techniques, is the jewel at the heart of the Asian art department on the second floor. Or you could luxuriate in medieval art, including ornately carved altarpieces and icons; all-American painting; or entirely reinstalled rooms—art, furniture, and all—from the Lehman townhouse on West 54th Street. And these are just the permanent exhibits. The Metropolitan continually hosts or initiates special collections of block-buster art from other countries or by great masters.

Despite the museum's seeming austerity, there are several areas that even small children seem to like: the classical statues, the Egyptian mummies, and the reconstructed Temple of Dendur; the armor; the musical instruments; the furnished rooms, and so on. Depending on the exhibit, they may also get a kick out of the Costume Institute downstairs, which owns 45,000 pieces of clothing dating back to the 17th century. And there's a playground just outside, to the south, for emergencies.

As if it weren't impressive enough, the Met is also adding a huge new expanse along the south end facing Central Park, including a Roman Court.

TOURING TIPS There are several places to eat in the museum: the classical-looking but often loud full-service restaurant on the ground floor (☎ 212-570-3964); the sponsors' dining room on the second floor, open to the public on weekends; and the good-weather wine bar on the roof in the sculpture garden. The gift shop is famous. The Metropolitan also administers the Cloisters in the Heights (see profile); admission to one includes admission to the other on the same day. Across the street on Fifth between 83rd and 84th streets is the small and specialized Goethe House German Cultural Center (☎ 212-439-8700), which often has exhibits of contemporary German art, films, and concerts.

El Museo del Barrio

APPEAL BY AGE	PRESCHOOL ★	GRADE SCHOOL ★★	TEENS ★★★
YOUNG ADULTS ★★★½		OVER 30 ★★★★	SENIORS ★★★½

Fifth Avenue at 104th Street, Upper East Side; ☎ 212-831-7272; www.elmuseo.org

Type of attraction Smallish but distinguished collection of Pan-American Hispanic art and culture. **Nearest subway station** 103rd Street. **Admission** "Suggested" $5 adults; $3 seniors and students; children ages 11 and under free. **Hours** Wednesday–Sunday, 11 a.m.–5 p.m.; closed Monday and Tuesday. **When to go** Midafternoon. **Author's rating** Its cultural message is pointed without being at all preachy. ★★★. **How much time to allow** 1–1½ hours.

DESCRIPTION AND COMMENTS This is not an especially large facility, and it shares its space with a training center, but its exhibits are well considered and well displayed, and the hands-on children's room, though small, is a good place to park the youngest members of the group. The collection includes religious carvings, textiles, prints, paintings, vintage photographs, pre-Columbian artifacts, and contemporary art; the exhibits often focus on thematic issues, such as dream symbols or regional developments.

kids   Museum of the City of New York

APPEAL BY AGE	PRESCHOOL ★★½	GRADE SCHOOL ★★★	TEENS ★★
YOUNG ADULTS ★★★		OVER 30 ★★★	SENIORS ★★★

Fifth Avenue at 103rd Street, Upper East Side; ☎ **212-534-1672; www.mcny.org**

Type of attraction Historical collection that shines specific and often unusual lights on city history. **Nearest subway station** 103rd Street. **Admission** "Suggested" $7 adults, $4 seniors and children; $12 for families. **Hours** Wednesday–Saturday, 10 a.m.–5 p.m.; Sunday, noon–5 p.m. **When to go** Anytime. **Author's rating** ★★★. **How much time to allow** 1½–2 hours.

DESCRIPTION AND COMMENTS   This might be the sort of museum in which families could split up to see different wings and then regroup—say, at the huge mezzanine-level model of what the museum will look like once its vast wing-addition is built in the 21st century. The rotating exhibits are often quirky and fascinating, focusing on such topics as the long tradition of circuses in New York (the theme music included a snatch from *Washington Week in Review,* perhaps a joke on media circuses!); the building of the Empire State Building and some of the art it has inspired; and the Broadway tradition with posters and recordings. And there are some fine examples of native craftsmanship, furniture, household items, and the like. In the basement is a mini–fire museum and a selection of antique city maps. But the two best exhibits are the toys—including novelty banks, fire trucks and trains, tin soldiers and animals, and a series of dollhouses from the 18th, 19th, and even early 20th centuries—and the reconstructed Moorish-fantasy bedroom and dressing room from John D. Rockefeller's demolished mansion at Fifth and 51st. (You'll spot a matching room in the Brooklyn Museum of Art.) Just look at the stenciled canvas ceiling over the sleigh bed; or the woodwork in the dressing room, decorated with appropriate implements such as scissors and combs and mirrors worked in mother-of-pearl. There are other restored rooms and a display of custom Spode, Royal Doulton, Crown Derby, and Minton porcelain belonging to another prominent household. These rooms are up on the fifth floor and are quite frequently overlooked.

Museum of Jewish Heritage

APPEAL BY AGE	PRESCHOOL ½	GRADE SCHOOL ★★★	TEENS ★★★
YOUNG ADULTS ★★★★		OVER 30 ★★★★	SENIORS ★★★★★

18 First Place, Battery Park City, Lower Manhattan; ☎ **212-786-0820 for information; for tickets call TicketMaster at** ☎ **212-945-0039**

Type of attraction Re-creation of Jewish culture over the last century—that is, before, during, and after the Holocaust. **Nearest subway station** Bowling Green or South Ferry. **Admission** $10 adults, $7 seniors, $5 students; children ages 5 and under free. **Hours** Sunday–Wednesday, 9 a.m.–5 p.m.; Thursday, 9 a.m.–8 p.m.; Friday, 9 a.m.–5 p.m.; closed Saturdays and Jewish holidays (museum closes at 4 p.m. the afternoon before Jewish holidays) and Thanksgiving. **When to go** Anytime; tickets are timed and numbers restricted. **Special comments** The museum is wheelchair accessible. The third-floor reception room, with its panoramic view of the harbor, is available for rental. **Author's rating** This seems to hit seniors (who remember the bad times) and teenagers (who may not previously have really understood the Holocaust) the hardest. ★★★★. **How much time to allow** 2–3½ hours.

DESCRIPTION AND COMMENTS This carefully orchestrated collection, which begins in a subtle key, crashes into the Holocaust, and climaxes in a visual paean to the future and specifically to the United States, is subtitled "A Living Memorial to the Holocaust," with emphasis on the "Living," and it has a gentler, more affirmative, and in some ways more objective tone than the larger U.S. Holocaust Memorial Museum in Washington, D.C.. Instead of placing visitors in the character of victims, as the Washington site does with its "passports," the New York museum tries to make all visitors, Jewish and not, feel included in the story by emphasizing the importance of tradition and faith. And although the Washington memorial is almost entirely focused on the Holocaust itself, this collection also speaks to the recovery of Judaism, the state of Israel—a happier present and future. The key to its mission is in the dual message carved in the wall of the foyer: "Remember . . . NEVER FORGET." And right next to it, "There is hope for the future."

The lower floor (one moves from the bottom up) spotlights the richness of Jewish family life in the late 19th and early 20th centuries, with clothing and artifacts from holidays and special occasions, such as a gorgeous silver and silk bride's headdress and belt, as well as simpler reminders of Sabbath and toys. (Wherever possible, the photograph of the item's owner—victim or survivor—is shown with it.) One of the most spectacular items is a handpainted Sukkah mural, almost Byzantine in its detail, showing life in Budapest in the 1920s and 1930s, along with biblical scenes and family portraits created by an untrained kosher butcher.

The second story tells the story of the Holocaust itself, with thousands of photos of the executed (posted on the stall-like wooden slabs that symbolize the boxcars that carried Jews to the concentration camps); toys and mementos of both escapees and victims; and a salute to those who, like Raoul Wallenberg and the now famous Oskar Schindler, helped Jews escape the Nazis. (Notice how many of the smaller interior gallery spaces are six-sided, like the building itself.) The third floor, which spotlights the post-Holocaust era, is a bit of a letdown until one reaches the last gallery, a glass-walled expanse, almost blinding after all that granite darkness, that looks directly out upon the icons of Jewish freedom: the Statue of Liberty, Ellis Island, and the lesser-known but equally important railroad terminal on the Jersey shore, from which many immigrants began their new lives.

There are two dozen videos in the museum (many of the witnesses are part of Steven Spielberg's Shoah project). Intriguingly, the bulk of the museum's thousands of photographs and personal items are in storage so secret that most staff members don't know their location.

The museum's second wing has an outdoor balcony with a living-tree installation on the roof.

TOURING TIPS There is no cafeteria in the museum, but just outside its parking lot is the new and understated Robert Wagner Park, a two-story brick structure that offers a fine view of the harbor and has clean public restrooms as well as (from about April to mid-December) a nice little cafe.

Museum of Modern Art

APPEAL BY AGE	PRESCHOOL ½	GRADE SCHOOL ★★	TEENS ★★
YOUNG ADULTS ★★★	OVER 30 ★★★★		SENIORS ★★★

11 West 53rd Street, Midtown East; ☎ 212-708-9400; www.moma.org

Type of attraction Premier collection of modern and contemporary art and design. **Nearest subway station** Fifth Avenue–53rd Street. **Admission** $20 adults, $16 seniors; $12 students; children ages 16 and under free. **Hours** Monday, Wednesday–Sunday, 10 a.m.–5 p.m.; Friday, 10 a.m.–7:45 p.m.; closed Tuesday, Thanksgiving, and Christmas Day. **When to go** Weekdays; Friday afternoons. **Special comments** Friday 4–8 p.m. admission is "pay what you please." **Author's rating** Challenging and often difficult, but fascinating—clearly the world's leading modern art collection, just as advertised. As at many really first-rate museums, you can't really see it all in a few hours, but you can only take so much in at a time, anyway. ★★★★★. **How much time to allow** 2–4 hours.

DESCRIPTION AND COMMENTS Following its $850-million renovation (and admission ticket prices to match), this icon of American art and design is bigger—630,000 square feet over six floors—brasher, and more breathtaking than ever. First-timers may be surprised at how many of these great paintings and prints they already "know," because so many of the most famous and frequently reproduced 20th-century works hang here, from those by the Impressionists to those by the Cubists to the Pop Artists and so on. (Stop by the main desk and ask for the self-guided tour; it points up many of these "greatest hits," including Van Gogh's *Starry Night,* Monet's *Water Lilies,* and Picasso's *Demoiselles d'Avignon.*) A soaring, six-floor glass atrium and repeated glimpses of the sculpture garden blurs the line between art and nature-as-art, and even art as nature. As might be guessed by the sight of the 1945 Bell "bug-eyed" helicopter suspended over a walkway, MoMA is also famous for its vetting of industrial and commercial design, from automobile bodies to typewriters, architectural models to appliances, even watches; one of Movado's most famous faces, the one with a single dot at the 12, is called "the Museum Watch" because MoMA approved of it so highly. The shop also has many disabled-friendly utensils.

TOURING TIPS Every Friday is Jazz Night in the Garden Cafe, and in good weather it's out in the Sculpture Garden. Also call and ask about film screenings, or check the local press; the museum's collection of films tops 10,000. Food is art here as well. The main restaurant, the Modern, is a full-fledged member of Danny Meyer's group (Gramercy Tavern,

Union Square Cafe, etc.). There's a busy area and a more casual second-floor cafe.

Museum of Television and Radio

APPEAL BY AGE	PRESCHOOL ★½	GRADE SCHOOL ★★★	TEENS ★★★
YOUNG ADULTS ★★★	OVER 30 ★★★½		SENIORS ★★½

25 West 52nd Street, Midtown East; ☎ 212-621-6600 for information; ☎ 212-621-6800 for schedule; www.mtr.org

Type of attraction A combination archives and rerun haven. **Nearest subway station** 47th–50th Street/Rockefeller Center or Fifth Avenue–53rd Street. **Admission** $10 adults, $8 seniors and students, $5 for children ages 12 and under; members free. **Hours** Tuesday–Sunday, noon–6 p.m.; theaters only, Thursday until 8 p.m.; closed Monday, New Year's Day, Independence Day, Thanksgiving Day, and Christmas Day. **When to go** Early, at least to check schedule. **Special comments** If you want to use the archives, add at least another hour, but the kids will be happy parked in one of the theaters. Note that the age group appeal may vary depending on the day's screenings. **Author's rating** Although the computerized files are still being organized, meaning that it can be laborious to look some topics or subjects up, it's fascinating; and the rare films shown are a delight. ★★★. **How much time to allow** 1–2½ hours.

DESCRIPTION AND COMMENTS A handsome if simple building, with five floors of exhibits, various-sized screening theaters, and radio listening room, all fully wheelchair accessible and with listening-assist devices at the front counter and closed-captioning decoders in the library.

Not so famous as most of New York's older museums, this is nevertheless a fine attraction, and one with strong interest for all ages. In fact, with its ongoing screenings on various floors, through which visitors are welcome to sit for as long or as short a time as they like, this is channel surfing to the max. In a single afternoon, for example, you might be able to see rare footage of Sinatra's "Rat Pack" in action, a segment of *The George Burns and Gracie Allen Show,* Jackie Kennedy taking CBS for a tour of the White House, a full-length *Wallace and Gromit* claymation adventure, bits of *Sesame Street* and *Fraggle Rock,* some *Beakman* science, a semiserious documentary on the evolution of sci-fi TV, and so on. The hallways are filled with changing photographic exhibits on such topics as journalists and special-effects makeup. The museum also produces salutes and series featuring the works of specific actors or directors, and many of these are shown in the evenings, making this an all-day bargain. Screenings begin at noon each day, and the full schedules are available at the counter, along with six months' advance schedules of the special exhibitions and series. There are special screenings of children's programming on weekends, but there is plenty of kid-vid all week long, too.

You can take a guided tour of the museum if you're curious about its history and collection (offered only a couple of times a day), but it's easily negotiated alone. The real treasure trove is the library, for which

you need time-specific tickets (available at the front counter). You cruise the museum's library on computer, picking segments from 75,000 radio and TV programs and even TV and radio advertising, and then are sent to a private booth to screen (or hear) your selections. If you're not sure what you'd like to see, skim the category of 400 highlights, which are the segments most frequently requested by visitors—the final episode of *The Mary Tyler Moore Show,* for example.
TOURING TIPS There is no cafeteria on the premises.

kids National Museum of the American Indian

APPEAL BY AGE	PRESCHOOL ★½	GRADE SCHOOL ★★★	TEENS ★★★
YOUNG ADULTS ★★½		OVER 30 ★★★	SENIORS ★★½

Old U.S. Custom House, 1 Bowling Green (near State and Whitehall streets), Lower Manhattan; ☎ 212-514-3700; www.nmai.si.edu

Type of attraction Part art collection, part anthropology lesson. **Nearest subway station** Bowling Green or South Ferry. **Admission** Free. **Hours** Daily, 10 a.m.–5 p.m. **When to go** Anytime. **Author's rating** There is beautiful work here, and surprising (to many Americans) diversity, but it may run into a generational guilt gap; it captures many children's attention faster than their parents'. ★★★. **How much time to allow** 1–1½ hours.

DESCRIPTION AND COMMENTS This is a branch of the Smithsonian Institution, and not surprisingly, its captions and clarity of information are first-rate. It includes artifacts not only from the more familiar (from TV and movies) Plains Indians but also from the Aztec, Olmec, Mayan, northwestern, and even Siberian tribes. Voiceover narratives and mini–oral histories run into and over one another as you pass through various exhibits. There are often demonstrations of weaving or music in the center area, which children will enjoy.
TOURING TIPS Don't overlook the Beaux Arts Custom House itself, with its exterior sculptures of metaphoric goddesses by Daniel Chester French representing Asia (the meditative one), America (the optimistic one), Europe (with the vestiges of her empire), and Africa (unawakened). Well, it was pre-PC. Also, good and reasonable items are available in the gift shop.

New York Botanical Garden

APPEAL BY AGE	PRESCHOOL ★★★	GRADE SCHOOL ★★★★	TEENS ★★½
YOUNG ADULTS ★★★		OVER 30 ★★★	SENIORS ★★★★

200th Street and Southern Boulevard, Bronx; ☎ 718-817-8700; www.nybg.org

Type of attraction Half "natural," half formal array of gardens with dazzling greenhouse complex. **Nearest subway station** Bedford Park Boulevard. **Admission** Grounds: $5 adults, $4 seniors and students, $2 children ages 2–17; greenhouse and tram tours additional. **Hours** October–April only: Tuesday–Sunday, 10 a.m.–6 p.m.; closed Monday, except holidays. **When to go** Midweek.

Special comments Free admission on Wednesday. **Author's rating** Restful and restorative, and particularly family-friendly; four-star attraction for gardeners. ★★★½. **How much time to allow** 1½–4 hours.

DESCRIPTION AND COMMENTS Within this 250-acre spread are a 40-acre forest with a variety of shortish but pretty trails through the sorts of hard-woods New York state had in abundance back in the last days of the Mohicans; and more than two dozen specialty gardens: a seasonal rose garden, a cherry valley, a picnic area, a giant water lily pond, a rock garden, orchid houses, a mini-maze, an herb garden, and so on. The star is the Enid A. Haupt Conservatory, the glorious Crystal Exposition–style greenhouse complex, which recently completed a four-year, $25 million restoration and now encloses both upland and lowland rain forests (with mezzanine-level walkway), deserts from the Americas and Africa, and special collections. The garden's children's fare is first-rate, with special "treasure map" guides to the conservatory gardens, a hands-on adventure garden, family plant-your-own areas, and the like, plus there are a wide variety of special programs, children's walking tours, and demonstrations.

Incidentally, the gardens make a surprisingly buoyant addition to a holiday trip. The plants inside the conservatory are covered in lights, along with many outdoor trees; a huge model train exhibition winds through both imaginary and real miniature New York landscapes; special family concerts and performances are scheduled, and so on.

TOURING TIPS The garden is actually about eight blocks from the Bedford Park subway stop, and though it's downhill on your way there, it's a hard uphill return. However, Metro North commuter trains (☎ 212-532-4900) run from Grand Central right to a Botanic Garden stop a stone's throw from the side entrance in about 20 minutes. Also, during summer months, a shuttle operates among the American Museum of Natural History, the Metropolitan Museum of Art, and the botanical garden; call the garden's main number for information.

There is a full-service cafe between the conservatory and the train-side gate.

Rubin Museum of Art

APPEAL BY AGE	PRESCHOOL ★★½	GRADE SCHOOL ★★½	TEENS ★★★
YOUNG ADULTS ★★★		OVER 30 ★★★★	SENIORS ★★★★

150 West 17th Street; ☎ 212-620-5000; www.rmanyc.org

Type of attraction Collection of fine Himalayan secular and religious art. **Nearest subway station** 18th Street (1,9), 14th Street (1,2,3,9), or 14th Street (F). **Admission** $7 adults, $5 seniors, students, artists, and neighborhood residents. **Hours** Tuesday, 11 a.m.–7 p.m.; Wednesday, 11 a.m.–5 p.m.; Thursday and Friday, 11 a.m.–9 p.m.; Saturday, 11 a.m.–7 p.m.; Sunday, 11 a.m.–5 p.m.; closed Monday and major holidays. **When to go** Anytime. **Special comments** The museum has established two on-line projects, including the Himalayan Art Web site (**www.himalayanart.org**), which has scanned some 1,700 images and is intended to become a digital repository of all known Himalayan art objects; and the Tibetan Buddhist Resource Center (**www.tbrc.org**), a similar catalogue of texts. **Author's rating** The appeal of this collection to individual visitors may be influenced by the growing interest in Tibetan and Buddhist culture, and in the particular special exhibits mounted at the time, but the quality of the art is uniformly high. ★★★★½. **How much time to allow** 1½–2 hours.

DESCRIPTION AND COMMENTS This astonishing collection of more than 1,700 paintings, sculptures, and textiles from the mountainous tribes of Tibet, Nepal, Bhutan, Mongolia, China, India, and Pakistan was assembled over 30 years by New Yorkers Donald and Shelley Rubin, who fell in love with a painting of White Tara, guide of pilgrims, that they saw in a window. (Astonishingly, they made their first actual trip to Tibet in 2002.) The museum, six years and $160 million in the renovation, is housed in the old Barney's department store, and the spiral staircase design has been retained; but now, open and airy, it reflects the Buddhist concept of rising through stages of enlightenment to the Nirvana of the fifth-floor gallery. There is also a basement exhibition space for temporary exhibits of more modern art, photographs of the region, etc.

Exhibits tend to emphasize paintings of Buddhas, demons, avatars, and protectors, many of them brilliantly colored, which may entice younger children who see them as cartoons or anime art. (A step-by-step "coloring" exhibit explains how the ritualized paintings are created.) A few children may find some of the demons a little scary, but most will be fascinated by the exotic mask-like features. The museum has many tours and sketching programs aimed at the under-15 crowd.

The cafe offers light Asian-fusion fare and a menu of boutique teas. The gift shop is unusually intriguing, with belts, beaded skullcaps, gumball-sized turquoise bead necklaces, ring boxes, carpets, and even cabinets. The museum also houses a 150-seat theater, which is used for film series, live concerts and performances, poetry, lectures, and family activities.

TOURING TIPS For those particularly interested in this field, Tibet House, which has its own galleries of art and sculpture and a small bookshop, is an easy walk away at 22 West 15th Street.

St. Patrick's Cathedral

APPEAL BY AGE	PRESCHOOL ½	GRADE SCHOOL ★★	TEENS ★★
YOUNG ADULTS ★★½	OVER 30 ★★★		SENIORS ★★★

Fifth Avenue between 50th and 51st streets, Midtown East;
☎ **212-753-2261**

Type of attraction The largest Catholic cathedral in the country. Nearest subway station 47th–50th Street/Rockefeller Center or 51st Street. Admission Free. Hours Monday, 7 a.m.–9:30 p.m.; Saturday 7 a.m.–8 p.m. When to go Late morning or mid-afternoon to avoid interrupting services. Author's rating Although this clearly has greater resonance for Catholic visitors, it is quite beautiful and well worth a visit, if only as a rest between other attractions. ★★. **How much time to allow** 30–45 minutes.

DESCRIPTION AND COMMENTS   This cathedral was designed by James Renwick at the request of John Hughes, the first archbishop of New York, shortly before the Civil War; it was not until 1889 that the 330-foot spires were raised in the religious art competition at the 1893 Chicago World's Fair. This looks almost as much like a fairy-tale castle as a cathedral, it's so busy with spires and arches and stained glass. Among the highlights are its huge and transporting organ (nearly 8,000 pipes) and the 26-foot Rose Window, both right over the main Fifth Avenue entrance; the Pietà in the rear near the Lady Chapel, which has its own set of gorgeous stained-glass windows; and the all-bronze baldachin that protects the high altar. (In the crypt below are the remains of Pierre Toussaint, a onetime Haitian slave who is likely to become the fourth American saint and the first black one.) Altogether there are 70 stained-glass windows, more than half from Chartres and Nantes.

TOURING TIPS   So much of the cathedral's power comes from the windows that sunlight (or reflected snow) really makes a difference; try to avoid going on a rainy day.

St. Paul's Chapel

APPEAL BY AGE	PRESCHOOL ½	GRADE SCHOOL ★★	TEENS ★★
YOUNG ADULTS ★★★	OVER 30 ★★★		SENIORS ★★★

Broadway at Fulton Street, Lower Manhattan; ☎ 212-602-0872

Type of attraction Small, remarkably peaceful pre-Revolutionary church. **Nearest subway station** Cortlandt or Fulton Street. **Admission** Free; donations requested for concerts. **Hours** Monday–Friday, 9 a.m.–3 p.m.; Sunday, 8 a.m.–3 p.m.; closed Saturday. **When to go** Anytime. **Special comments** George Washington's private pew and a few artifacts are preserved here. **Author's rating** ★★★★. **How much time to allow** 30 minutes.

DESCRIPTION AND COMMENTS   You might almost walk right by this little church without noticing it, it seems so beleaguered by development. But it's a blessing in its own right—warmly though simply painted, the wood lit by Waterford crystal chandeliers, and with President Washington's box unobtrusively roped off. It dates from the mid-1760s, and in one of those ironies of history, is purely Georgian—the style named for the kings New Yorkers would shortly renounce. More specifically, it is modeled on St.-Martin-in-the-Fields in London's Trafalgar Square and, like St. Martin's, is renowned for the quality of its concerts (noon, usually Monday and Thursday). It's one of the very few buildings to have survived the great fire of 1776, not to mention 9/11. In fact, it became a special sanctuary for rescue workers and support staff in the horrific days following the attacks.

TOURING TIPS   Don't enter, as most people do, right off Broadway; that's actually the altar end. Walk around the yard (the cemetery once reached all the way to the river, providing a much grander setting) and come in at the "rear"; the effect is much more dramatic.

Also, from here go north a block to the Gothic Woolworth Building at 233 Broadway and walk into the elaborate and often hysterically funny interior; kids will go wild over the gargoyles, including caricatures of architect Cass Gilbert clutching a model of the building and F. W. Woolworth himself counting out coins—"fives and dimes," in fact.

Note that at press time, the Woolworth's lobby was closed for security reasons.

kids South Street Seaport and Museum

APPEAL BY AGE	PRESCHOOL ★	GRADE SCHOOL ★★	TEENS ★★
YOUNG ADULTS ★★★★	OVER 30 ★★★		SENIORS ★★

Water Street between John Street and Peck Slip, Lower Manhattan; General information, ☎ 212-748-8600; www.southstseaport.org

Type of attraction Combination historic district, shopping mall, and maritime museum. **Nearest subway station** Fulton Street. **Admission** Museum: $8 adults, $5 seniors and students, $3 children 11 and under. **Hours** October 1–March 31: 10 a.m.–5 p.m. (closed Tuesdays); April 1–September 30: 10 a.m.– 6 p.m. (open until 8 p.m. Thursdays). **When to go** Anytime. **Special comments** The hours given above are retail area hours; restaurants may be open later. **Author's rating** ★★. **How much time to allow** 1½–4 hours.

DESCRIPTION AND COMMENTS   This is sort of a miniature theme park, covering 11 square blocks (some of them cobblestone) of real and reproduced seafaring New York. (It's a Rouse development, like Boston's Faneuil Hall and Baltimore's Harborplace.) In its heyday, the first half of the 19th century, it was so busy that South Street was nicknamed the "street of sails." But once steamships took over, the deeper-water piers on the Hudson River side gradually drew ship traffic away from this area. It wasn't until the early 1980s that its commercial potential was understood. From the Visitors Center in the former Pilothouse, where you pick up the free guide maps, you look right to the main food stand and shopping mall of Pier 17 and beyond that to the very real, 150-year-old Fulton Fish Market. One of the nicest stretches, in terms of architectural preservation, is Schermerhorn Row, Federal-style warehouses on the south side of Fulton Street between Front and South streets dating from the very early 19th century (that's how far back the Schermerhorn money goes); they were later used as hotels and shops and are now boutiques and restaurants. A $21 million expansion has already uncovered such unique artifacts as Gaelic graffitti.

Quite frankly, most of the good stuff here is free: the view from Pier 17 (one of the most evocative and least publicized views of the harbor); craftsmen building and restoring small boats; and the view of the Brooklyn Bridge, which took 16 years to build and the lives of 20 of the 600 workers—many from the bends because they emerged too quickly from underwater assignments. (John Roebling, who designed it, had his foot crushed in a freak accident on the pier just before construction was to begin in 1869 and died three weeks later. His son took over, but repeated bouts of the bends left him partially paralyzed; finally Roebling's widow replaced him as supervisor.) The best reason to buy the museum ticket is to tour the tall ships anchored there: the 1991 *Peking*, the second largest sailing ship ever built, and the three-masted *Wavertree* of 1885. If you want to take a harbor tour from here, on the schooner *Pioneer* (March to November only), you can either make reservations up to two weeks in advance (☎ 212-748-8590) or take a chance on unreserved tickets at 10 a.m. Other commercial cruises also leave from here.

TOURING TIPS Walk past Fulton Fish Market to the corner of Peck Slip and Front Street and look at the mural on the ConEd substation; it's a trompe d'oeil painting of the Brooklyn Bridge (which in reality rises just beyond it), designed to make the station less obtrusive. Also look for the lighthouse at the intersection of Fulton and Water streets. A memorial to the 1,500 passengers of the *Titanic* who perished in the 1912 catastrophe, it originally overlooked the harbor from the Seamen's Church near the current Vietnam Veterans Memorial but was moved here in 1976.

Statue of Liberty/Liberty Island

APPEAL BY AGE	PRESCHOOL ½	GRADE SCHOOL ★★	TEENS ★★½
YOUNG ADULTS ★★★	OVER 30 ★★★		SENIORS ★★½

New York Harbor, Lower Manhattan; ☎ 212-363-3200; ticket and ferry information, ☎ 212-269-5755; www.statueofliberty.org

Type of attraction America's premier symbol of freedom. **Nearest subway station** Bowling Green or South Ferry. **Admission** $10 adults, $8 seniors, $4 children ages 3–17; children under age 3 free (combination ticket covers ferry transport and admission to Liberty Island). **Hours** Daily, 9:30 a.m.–5 p.m. (last ferry at 4 p.m.); extended hours during summer months and on some holidays; closed Christmas. **When to go** Weekdays. **Special comments** Wheelchair access extends only to the observation deck at pedestal height; only stairs ascend to the crown. **Author's rating** For all its very real emotional appeal, the actual impact of this attraction close-up may depend on the length of time you have to stand in line, making it problematic for small children. ★★★. **How much time to allow** 1½–4 hours.

DESCRIPTION AND COMMENTS This most famous symbol of liberty is also a reminder of the revolutionary fervor often required to obtain it. It was a gift from the republic of France, a massive feat of both art (sculpted by visionary Frederic-Auguste Bartholdi, who used his mother as the model for that stern yet merciful face) and engineering (erected by Gustave Eiffel, whose own eventual monument would be the landmark tower in Paris). It was formally unveiled on October 28, 1896, and restored for its centennial at a cost of $70 million plus $2 million for the fireworks. However, the torch had corroded so badly that a replica, covered in 24-carat gold, was put in its place; the original is in the lobby.

There are four stations, so to speak: the outside of the base, engraved with Emma Lazarus's "New Prometheus" ("Give me your tired, your poor

. . ."); the exhibit hall inside the base, with its record of Bartholdi's 17-year struggle and the many patriotic and commercial uses his figure has been put to; the observation decks at the top of the pedestal; and the view from the crown—the crowning touch, so to speak. Bartholdi's title for the massive sculpture was "Enlightening the World," and the crown's seven rays represent the seven continents and the seven seas.

While you're waiting, you can ponder the numbers: The statue itself is a little over 150 feet tall, twice that counting the pedestal and base; and it weighs 225 tons—100 tons of which represent the copper sheeting that covers the frame. There are 354 steps from the pedestal up into the crown, the equivalent of 22 stories. And don't feel bad about your own nose; hers is four-and-a-half feet long.

Note that although discussions on reopening it were underway, the statue has been closed to visitors since 9/11. Only the pedestal and plaza are open.

TOURING TIPS If temperatures are predicted to go above 100°, only passengers from the first ferry of the day will be allowed to go all the way into the crown because of the even greater heat up there. All others will have to stop on the tenth floor pedestal level. That means you need to be among the first 600 people in line for the 8:30 a.m. ferry, so expect to be there at 7:30 a.m. And if the lines are very long, the staff may close them off early. Note also that the last ferries leave Lower Manhattan in mid-afternoon; call for exact times. (The only consolation for having to wait until late is that in winter you'll see the Manhattan skyline begin to light up.) Note again that tours are currently limited to the outside area following the events of 9/11; call for updates.

Trinity Church

| APPEAL BY AGE | PRESCHOOL ½ | GRADE SCHOOL ★ | TEENS ★★ |
| YOUNG ADULTS ★★½ | OVER 30 ★★★ | | SENIORS ★★★ |

Broadway at Wall Street, Lower Manhattan; ☎ 212-602-0872; www.trinitywallstreet.org

Type of attraction Fine Gothic Revival church from the mid-19th century. **Nearest subway station** Wall Street (4, 5) or Rector Street (N, R). **Admission** Free. **Hours** Monday–Friday, 9 a.m.–1:45 p.m., 1–3:45 p.m; Saturday, 10 a.m.–3:45 p.m.; Sunday, 1–3:45 p.m.; free tours daily at 2 p.m. and Sunday after the 11:15 a.m. service. For group tours, call ☎ 212-602-0872. **When to go** Mid-afternoon **Special comments** Hearing-impaired services at 2 p.m. **Author's rating** ★★★. **How much time to allow** 30 minutes.

DESCRIPTION AND COMMENTS This church, as much as any other single edifice, is responsible for the Gothic Revival craze of the 19th century; its balance of interior extravagance (carved wood, stained glass, and ornate stone) and exterior restraint (itself a metaphor for religious faith) is striking. Actually, this is the third church on this site: The first one was built in 1698 and burned in the conflagration of 1776; the second was razed in 1839. There's a small museum behind the altar with records of the congregation's homes. The brass doors are a tribute to Ghiberti's

Doors of Paradise at the Duomo in Florence. Thanks to painstaking efforts by restorationists, who removed a supposedly protective layer of paraffin, the sandstone's original cherry tone is back. The 280-foot steeple pointed unrivaled to heaven until the late 19th century, and even surrounded by the towers of international finance, it has a certain obdurate confidence.

Romantics take note: This is where founding Federalist and dueling victim Alexander Hamilton is buried, along with inventor Robert Fulton and other luminaries.

TOURING TIPS This is a wonderful place to hear music, either choral or concert. Come Sundays or check local listings for special events.

Whitney Museum of American Art

APPEAL BY AGE	PRESCHOOL ½	GRADE SCHOOL ★★½	TEENS ★★★
YOUNG ADULTS ★★★	OVER 30 ★★★½		SENIORS ★★★½

Madison Avenue at 75th Street, Upper East Side; ☎ 212-570-3676; www.whitney.org

Type of attraction World-class collection of 20th-century American art. **Nearest subway station** 77th Street. **Admission** $12 adults, $9.50 seniors and students; children ages 11 and under free. **Hours** Wednesday–Thursday, 11 a.m.–6 p.m.; Friday, 1–9 p.m.; Saturday and Sunday, 11 a.m.–6 p.m.; closed Monday and Tuesday. **When to go** Anytime. **Special comments** "Pay what you wish" Friday 6–9 p.m. **Author's rating** ★★★★. **How much time to allow** 1½–3 hours.

DESCRIPTION AND COMMENTS There is much to be said for an insider's eye, and since the Whitney was founded by sculptor Gertrude Vanderbilt Whitney, its collection of modern American art in many opinions rivals the international collection of the Museum of Modern Art. (She founded a new museum when the prestigious and no doubt somewhat pompous Metropolitan turned down her offer to donate the whole collection.)

Since its recent expansion and extensive exterior cleaning, this inverted concrete pyramid seems less forbidding and more quirky, though still mysterious; instead of seeming to lower, it seems to be playing at reticence, hiding its goods behind the drawbridge like a castle. It's a collection with a great deal of humor; and though it has many serious and dark pieces as well, it may surprise you how interested younger patrons may be in the cartoonlike Lichtensteins or robust Thomas Hart Bentons, the boxing art of George Bellows, Warhol's post-advertising art and other familiar elements of Pop Art, O'Keeffe's flowers, or the super-realistic Hopper paintings—or even many of the brilliantly colored abstracts. The famous Calder assemblage called "Circus" that used to be mounted just inside the main entrance has been moved upstairs; it is still the only piece on permanent display.

TOURING TIPS There is a cafe in the museum, a branch of the Upper East Side home-style restaurants called Sarabeth's (☎ 212-570-3670).

PART EIGHT

DINING *and* RESTAURANTS

NYC EATS: *Everything, Anything, All the Time*

EVEN IF YOU LOVE COOKING AT HOME, the culinary adventures offered in NYC warrant eating out at least twice a week, and that's a conservative number when you consider that you can eat any conceivable type of meal or snack from breakfast to post-clubbing munchies outside of the house. With food on offer from every part of the globe presented on paper plates to porcelain platters, New York boasts a plethora of culinary delights that takes months to fully digest. The longer you are here, the more adventurous and discerning your taste buds become. Trying the new, vying for reservations at the trendy, or simply sharing a meal at a neighborhood favorite is recreation, sport and entertainment for thousands of New Yorkers. When you get to the stage of knowing the differences between chorizo and andouille, discerning between a Roquefort and a Stilton, or arguing where to find a decent dosa, the quest for insider information is insatiable and thus begins the NY obsession with food and the places that serve it. You're hooked before you realize it. Therefore, it's best to know the **guidelines:**

- **Don't judge** an establishment by its tabletop. Some of the tastiest food can be served on formica whilst mediocrity can be hidden superficially on an expanse of starched linen. Price doesn't necessarily reflect quality, and we've found that many midrange restaurants tend to be the weakest link in the dining spectrum.
- **Understand** the difference between fad and revolutionary gastrodelights: Tasti-D-Lite yogurt, baby vegetables of all kinds, and cosmopolitans were fads; sushi, although admittedly trendy for a long time, is here to stay and is currently opening the door for various other types of Japanese fare to be appreciated. Similarly, tapas is currently an *it* dining

experience but will probably manage to survive once the wave of fashion subsides; the food itself is innovative for light meals. The point is that diners should beware of overdressed and overhyped menu items, unless the chef is known for being particularly experimental and opts to serve anchovy sorbet with flaming, barbecued sweetbreads.

- **Remember** that 'less is (very often) more.' Some of the finest food doesn't need to get intricate, it just needs to be served with the freshest of ingredients with a creative flair for taste and presentation.

- **Know** the playing field: Manhattan alone has over 4,000 restaurants, and the range of food and flavors is exhilarating. The array of indigenous kitchens testify to the range of people who have chosen to settle on the New York shores. Feel safe in the knowledge that if you have a yearning for artichokes or crave a zucchini pie you'll find your dish and please your taste buds somewhere in the metropolis.

- **Make** the effort to go the extra mile to find the best dim sum (Flushing, Queens) an amazing falafel (Atlantic Avenue, Brooklyn) or real pierogies (Greenpoint, Brooklyn). For a quick culinary tour, we'll fill you in on just a few neighborhoods worth visiting for dining explorations: Sunset Park, Brooklyn—for Chinese, Vietnamese, and Mexican. If you're in town between May and September, visit the soccer fields in Red Hook, Brooklyn, on the weekend to savor some of the best homecooked Honduran, Mexican, and other Latin American–inspired dishes. Bedford-Stuyvesant has soul food and renowned roti (**Ali's Roti Shop,** 1267 Fulton Street). Indian food can be found not just on East Sixth Street, but also in the "Curry Hill" area between 33rd and 26th streets, between Third, Lexington, and Park avenues in Manhattan, and in Jackson Heights in Queens. Contrary to tourist belief, Little Italy is no longer the place to sample some of the best Italian fare on offer. You can find tasty Italian throughout the city, but Staten Island, not generally a mecca for discerning gourmets, is considered by natives to have a few exceptional Southern Italian establishments; the same can be said for areas in the Bronx, including Arthur Avenue.

- **Experience** the interesting variety of food in the outer boroughs firsthand. Be adventurous—make use of the NYC public transportation system, visit some of our suggestions, and talk to the locals.

- Above all: **Enjoy** your food, and come back to New York for seconds.

unofficial **TIP**
For specific advice on far-flung underground dining and opinions on every type of food imaginable, visit sites like www.chowhound.com and www.addyourown.com.

This chapter provides some insight and reviews a few highlights, but if you'd like more information check the *Village Voice, Time Out* reviews, or the Dining Out section in the Wednesday edition of the *New York Times.* Also search the Web (**www. citysearch.com**).

PICKLES *or* PANACHE

A TRIP TO THE BIG APPLE ISN'T COMPLETE without tasting quintessential New York fare, such as a bagel, a slice of pizza, or a hot dog, as well as reserving a table at a fashionable and/or established kitchen. Our definition of "fashionable" doesn't include the spots that survive purely on the whim of the fickle. Rather it encompasses the enviable combination of excellent food, ambience, and a steady flow of people, many who may be famous, which gives the place an added mystique. People wait months to get a reservation at renowned chef Thomas Keller's **Per Se** (10 Columbus Circle; ☎ 212-823-9335), and it's only been open since 2004, but the food is sublime, creative, and impeccably presented. Although not as difficult to get a seat, **Le Perigord** (405 East 52nd Street; ☎ 212-755-6244), one of the last bastions in New York City of traditional French culinary restaurants, has maintained its level of food and service for years. As for New York landmarks, restaurants that have stood the test of time include the **Four Seasons** (99 East 52nd Street; ☎ 212-754-9494), **21 Club** (21 West 52nd Street; ☎ 212-582-7200; www.21club.com) and **Café des Artistes** (1 West 67th Street; ☎ 212-877-3500; www.cafenyc.com).

At the other end of the spectrum, but just as important, are the staples of New York snacks, light meals, or brunches. If you can, try a New York bagel. **H & H Bagels,** a perennial NY favorite, is great, as is **Murray's Bagels** (500 Sixth Avenue; ☎ 212-462-2830), offering delicious, hand-rolled bagels from plain to "everything," with cream cheese and lox, otherwise known as smoked salmon. Hot dogs can be had at many a stand, but traditionalists like to go to **Nathan's Famous Hot Dogs** on the pier at Coney Island in Brooklyn. Many of these typical New York selections have heavy influences from Italy (pizza and calzones), and Eastern Europe. Besides bagels, some of the Eastern European selections include knishes, that is, potato pies (**Yonah Schimmel's,** 137 East Houston Street; ☎ 212-477-2858), pickles (**Gus's Pickles,** 85/87 Orchard Street; ☎ 516-569-0909), and whitefish salad (**Sable's Smoked Fish,** 1489 Second Avenue; ☎ 212-249-6177; and **Russ & Daughters,** 179 East Houston Street; ☎ 212-475-4880). For another New York dining experience, have lunch at a coffee shop and order anything in the realm of eggs, burgers, salads, sandwiches, and grilled cheese, and wash it down with a milkshake or chocolate egg cream (seltzer, milk, and chocolate syrup). You'll feel the fast New York pace, and if you're lucky, you'll get a pleasantly churlish New Yorker as a waiter. If the bill is more than $27 for two people, then it's not a typical coffee shop.

HOT SPOTS

FASHIONABLE, AS DEFINED ABOVE, CAN SOMETIMES mix with hot spot, but we find that some New York hot spots are more about the hype and the clientele than the food. That said, as the NY restaurant business is very competitive, an experienced and/or famous chef does wonders to the reservation line. Whereas Jean-Georges Vongerichten's restaurant **66** was very *it* in 2003 and 2004, its hip factor has cooled, but the food is still a constant, which ensures a loyal following. Chef Vongerichtens' more recent venture, **Spice Market** (403 West 13th Street; ☎ 212-675-2322) is now an *it* place, but even after the embers smolder, it will last because of its innovative Vietnamese cuisine and appealing décor. Another place that will most likely outlive its current magnetic appeal is **The Modern,** chef and restaurateur Danny Meyer's dining gem at the Museum of Modern Art (9 West 53rd Street; ☎ 212-333-1220). If you'd like to dine in hotels, we can recommend dinner at **Asia de Cuba** at the Morgan Hotel (237 Madison Avenue; ☎ 212-726-7755) and **Riingo** at the Alex Hotel (205 East 45th Street; ☎ 212-867-4200). For a very pricey but memorable meal, try **Alain Ducasse at the Essex House** (155 West 58th Street; ☎ 212-265-7300).

unofficial **TIP**
Brunch is a fun affair at **Café Botanica** in the Essex House (160 Central Park South; ☎ 212-484-5120), and for a festive and filling brunch at Christmas time try **Mark's Restaurant** at the Mark Hotel (25 East 77th Street; ☎ 212-744-4300).

WHERE'S THE BEEF?

THE POPULARITY OF THE ATKINS DIET MAY HAVE waned, but protein, although in smaller doses, is still on the menu, and steak houses are still enjoying the renaissance period that Atkins helped kindle. **Peter Luger** (see profile) is a top steak house favorite with a no-nonsense wait staff serving some of the best porterhouse in the country. That said, Wolfgang Zweiner, former headwaiter at Peter Luger's, has opened his own place, simply called **Wolfgang's Steakhouse** (4 Park Avenue; ☎ 212-889-3369). The meat, food, and ambience is outstanding, causing ripples of dissent amongst PL aficionados. Another meat institution is **Old Homestead Steakhouse** (56 Ninth Avenue; ☎ 212-242-9040), where the jury is still out whether it deserves or surpasses its meaty merits, but it *is* the place to get a Kobe beef hamburger. After renovating, **Patroon** (160 East 46th Street; ☎ 212-883-7373) altered the menu to add more than just steak, but it still has a good meaty base and a rooftop terrace for cigar smokers. For a very masculine midtown chop house, try **Ben Benson's** (123 West 52nd Street; ☎ 212-581-8888). And for meat with a South American flavor, try Brazilian rodizio at **Churrascaria Plataforma** (see profile).

THE DRESS CODE: SILK OR SNEAKERS

IT'S SAID THAT ANYTHING GOES IN NEW YORK, and in many cases this is true. However, there are some establishments that expect people to abide by a certain decorum that requires a jacket; we've noted where this is the case. Also, some places have jackets and occasionally ties on hand to loan, so as not to turn business away. Some pricey places will not require a jacket, merely a sense of chic, all black, or cockiness to get you through the door. If that's the case, chances are that the food isn't as important as the scene. Business casual to casual and/or funky are usually the norm for most of our profiled restaurants. However, should you be dining in one of these places on business, then your own sense of the importance of the meeting should dictate your clothing. Common sense and an air of confidence will go a long way.

GREEN TIP

WE'RE NOT HERE TO PREACH NOR TO MAKE YOU eat your vegetables, but in the light of recent food debates discussing genetically modified (GM) food and "organic" counterparts, these issues have become more prominent for many New Yorkers. Directives of the Slow Food Movement are moving to the fore, which is why restaurants, meat and vegetarian alike, providing "GM free" ingredients and organic alternatives have been gaining support over the past few years. Sustainably raised fish is a factor to consider, so before you tuck into a bowl of caviar, a medallion of monkfish, or order the Chilean seabass, consider whether the produce has been obtained from a legal and ecologically sound source. You may be pleased to know that Arctic Char, the salmon-like fish, is currently in abundance and has graced many of the top restaurant menus—in part due to its good taste and ready availability.

WHERE TO FIND A DEAL FOR A MEAL

TRUE TO ENTREPRENEURIAL SPIRIT, MANY NY restaurants, eager to attract a hungry crowd, offer some super deals at lunch or dinner for pre-theater and prix-fixe meals. Not all prix-fixe menus are cheap, but specials exist in restaurants covering all price ranges. Two of the best lunch prix fixe in town are at **Jean-Georges** (1 Central Park West; ☎ 212-299-3900), offering a superb dining experience for $20 in the Nougatine dining area, and a $5.95 lunch buffet at **Chennai Garden** (129 East 27th Street; ☎ 212-689-1999) for wonderfully fresh and tasty kosher vegetarian Indian food. During June many top restaurants sign up to be part of the annual city-wide Summer Restaurant Week, which allows lucky diners to eat at first-rate restaurants for a fixed price. Each place gets to choose whether the deal will be valid for either lunch or dinner, or both. Sometimes these offers last through Labor Day, but that tends to be the exception rather than the rule. Summer Restaurant Week 2005 offered prix-fixe lunch menus for $20.12 and dinner menus for $35. Participating restaurants included **Café Boulud, davidburke & donatella, Aquavit, Nobu, Café Boulud, Artisanal, Union Square Cafe,** and many others. Winter Restaurant Week has started more recently and usually takes place in late January. Look out for ads and check the **www.nycvisit.com** Web site for more info.

THE RESTAURANTS

OUR FAVORITE NEW YORK RESTAURANTS

THIS SURVEY OF OVER 100 OF NEW YORK'S NIFTIEST nosheries covers a wide spectrum of price categories, global origins, and New York neighborhoods, including tried and true oldies, popular trendies, offbeat ethnics, and local favorites. We give an overall impression of food and mood and what it will cost. Don't be surprised if some of our menu recommendations are not available on a particular day; many New York restaurants change their menus often to take advantage of ultra-fresh seasonal offerings. And though we've worked overtime to ensure the freshness of our opinions (places were checked at the very last minute before publication), do bear in mind that restaurants are works in progress. They're not static and are essentially a moving target. The only opinion that's 100% timely is your own, of your own meal as you eat it. Chefs change . . . or call in sick . . . or have bad days . . . or simply get bored and lose their edge. So . . . caveat eater!

We have developed detailed profiles for the best and most interesting restaurants in town. Each profile features an easily scanned heading that allows you to check out the restaurant's name, cuisine, star rating, cost, quality rating, and value rating.

CUISINE The more entrenched imported cuisines are fragmenting— French into bistro fare and even Provençal, "new continental" into regional American and "eclectic"—while others have broadened and fused: Middle Eastern and Provençal into Mediterranean, Spanish and South American into nuevo Latino, and so on. In some cases, we have used the broader terms (that is, "French") but added descriptions to give a clearer idea of the fare. Remember that experimentation and "fusion" are ever more common, so don't hold us or the chefs to too strict a style.

OVERALL RATING The star rating encompasses the entire dining experience, including style, service, and ambience, in addition to the taste, presentation, and quality of the food. Five stars is the highest rating possible and connote the best of everything. Four-star restaurants are exceptional and three-star restaurants are well above average. Two-star restaurants are good. One star is used to indicate an average restaurant that demonstrates an unusual capability in some area of specialization—for example, an otherwise unmemorable place that has great barbecue chicken.

PRICE This is an expense description that provides a comparative sense of how much a complete meal will cost. A complete meal for our purposes consists of an entrée with vegetable or side dish and choice of soup or salad. Appetizers, desserts, drinks, and tips are excluded.

Inexpensive	$20 and less per person
Moderate	$21–$40 per person
Expensive	Over $41 per person

QUALITY RATING The food quality is rated on a scale of one to five stars, five being the best rating attainable. The quality rating is based expressly on the taste, freshness of ingredients, preparation, presentation, and creativity of food served. There is no consideration of price. If you are a person who wants the best food available, and cost is not an issue, you need look no further than the quality ratings.

VALUE RATING If, on the other hand, you are looking for both quality and value, then you should check the value rating. The value ratings are defined as follows:

★★★★★	Exceptional value; a real bargain
★★★★	Good value
★★★	Fair value; you get exactly what you pay for
★★	Somewhat overpriced
★	Significantly overpriced

NEIGHBORHOOD This designation will give you a general idea of where each profiled restaurant is located. We've divided New York into the following neighborhoods:

Lower Manhattan, Wall Street, and the Battery
Soho and Tribeca
Chinatown, Little Italy, and the Lower East Side
Greenwich Village
The East Village

Chelsea
Gramercy Park and Madison Square
Midtown West, Times Square, and the Theater District
Midtown East
Upper West Side
Upper East Side

Morningside Heights, Hamilton Heights, and Harlem
Washington Heights
Brooklyn
Queens
The Bronx
Staten Island

PAYMENT We've listed the type of payment accepted at each restaurant using the following code: AE equals American Express (Optima), CB equals Carte Blanche, D equals Discover, DC equals Diners Club, MC equals MasterCard, and V equals VISA.

WHO'S INCLUDED Restaurants in New York open and close at an alarming rate. So, for the most part, we have tried to confine our list to establishments with a proven track record over a substantial period of time. The exceptions here are the newer offspring of the demigods of the culinary world—these places are destined to last, at least until our next update. Newer or changed establishments that demonstrate staying power and consistency will be profiled in subsequent editions. Also, the list is highly selective. Failure to include a particular place does not necessarily indicate that the restaurant is not good, only that it was not ranked by us to be among the best in its genre.

The Best New York Restaurants

TYPE AND NAME	OVERALL RATING	PRICE	QUALITY RATING	VALUE RATING
AMERICAN				
Gramercy Tavern	★★★½	Exp	★★★★	★★★
Blue Water Grill	★★★	Mod	★★★★	★★★★
Parsonage	★★★	Mod/Exp	★★★★	★★★★
Blue Ribbon	★★★	Mod	★★★½	★★★★
EJ's Luncheonette	★★	Inexp	★★★½	★★★½
Gray's Papaya	★★	Inexp	★★★½	★★★★★
The Pink Teacup	★½	Inexp	★★★½	★★★½
AMERICAN SOUTHWEST				
Mesa Grill	★★★	Exp	★★★½	★★★
ARGENTINEAN				
Old San Juan	★★½	Inexp	★★★★	★★★★
ASIAN				
Cendrillon	★★★	Mod	★★★★	★★★★
Zen Palate	★★½	Inexp	★★★½	★★★★
ASIAN FUSION				
Rain	★★★	Mod	★★★★	★★★
Rice	★★★	Inexp	★★★½	★★★★★
AUSTRIAN				
Café Sabarsky	★★★★	Mod/Exp	★★★½	★★★
BELGIAN				
BXL Café	★★★	Mod	★★★	★★★
Petite Abeille	★★½	Inexp	★★★★	★★★★½
BISTRO				
Artisanal	★★★½	Mod/Exp	★★★★	★★★
Florent	★★½	Mod	★★★½	★★★★
Pastis	★★½	Mod	★★★½	★★★½
Tartine	★★½	Inexp	★★★★	★★★★

Detailed profiles of individual restaurants follow in alphabetical order at the end of this chapter.

TYPE AND NAME	OVERALL RATING	PRICE	QUALITY RATING	VALUE RATING
BRAZILIAN				
Churrascaria Plataforma	★★★	Mod	★★★★	★★★★
Cabana Carioca	★★½	Inexp	★★★★	★★★★★
BRITISH				
Tea & Sympathy	★★★	Inexp/Mod	★★★½	★★★
CANTONESE				
The Nice Restaurant	★★★½	Mod	★★★★½	★★★★
CHINESE (SEE ALSO DIM SUM)				
Ping's	★★★★	Mod	★★★★½	★★★★½
Shun Lee West, Shun Lee Café	★★★½	Mod/Exp	★★★★	★★★
66	★★★	Exp	★★★★	★★½
Joe's Shanghai	★★★	Mod	★★★★½	★★★★★
Grand Sichuan International	★★★	Mod	★★★★	★★★★★
Kam Chueh	★★★	Mod	★★★★	★★★★½
CREOLE				
Stan's Place	★★★	Inexp/Mod	★★★	★★★
CUBAN				
Margon Restaurant	★★	Inexp	★★★½	★★★★★
DIM SUM (SEE ALSO CHINESE)				
Ping's	★★★★	Mod	★★★★½	★★★★½
The Nice Restaurant	★★★½	Mod	★★★★½	★★★★
ETHIOPIAN				
Meskerem	★★★	Inexp/Mod	★★★½	★★★½
FRENCH				
Le Bernardin	★★★★½	Very Exp	★★★★★	★★★
Chanterelle	★★★★	Very Exp	★★★★½	★★★★
Jean-Georges	★★★★	Exp	★★★★½	★★★
Il Buco	★★★★	Exp	★★★★½	★★★
Café Boulud	★★★½	Exp	★★★★½	★★★½

The Best New York Restaurants (continued)

TYPE AND NAME	OVERALL RATING	PRICE	QUALITY RATING	VALUE RATING
FRENCH (CONTINUED)				
Montrachet	★★★½	Exp	★★★★	★★★½
Balthazar	★★★½	Mod/Exp	★★★★	★★★★
Les Halles	★★½	Exp	★★★½	★★★
La Boite en Bois	★★½	Mod	★★★½	★★★★
GREEK				
Molyvos	★★★½	Exp	★★★★	★★★★
Symposium	★★★	Inexp/Mod	★★★½	★★★★
INDIAN				
Tabla	★★★★	Exp	★★★★½	★★★★
Tamarind	★★★½	Exp	★★★★	★★★
Chennai Garden	★★★	Inexp	★★★½	★★★★
Jackson Diner	★★	Inexp/Mod	★★★½	★★★★★
INDONESIAN				
Borobudur Café	★★	Inexp	★★½	★★★
IRISH				
Molly's	★★½	Mod	★★★★	★★★★
ITALIAN				
Il Buco	★★★★	Exp	★★★★½	★★★
Piccola Venezia	★★★★	Exp	★★★★½	★★★
Noodle Pudding	★★★★	Mod	★★★★	★★★½
Mulino	★★★½	Exp	★★★★½	★★★½
Babbo	★★★½	Exp	★★★★	★★★★
Pó	★★★½	Mod	★★★★	★★★★
Osteria Del Circo	★★★	Exp	★★★★	★★★
Paola's	★★★	Mod/Exp	★★★★	★★★★
Piccolo Angolo	★★★	Mod	★★★★	★★★★
Orso	★★★	Mod	★★★½	★★★½
Iammo Bello	★★½	Inexp	★★★★	★★★★★
Becco	★★½	Mod	★★★½	★★★★★
Gigino	★★½	Mod	★★★	★★★½
JAPANESE				
Nobu	★★★★	Exp	★★★★½	★★★
Sachiko's on Clinton	★★★★	Mod/Exp	★★★½	★★★
Tomoe	★★★½	Mod	★★★★½	★★★★

TYPE AND NAME	OVERALL RATING	PRICE	QUALITY RATING	VALUE RATING
JAPANESE (CONTINUED)				
Soba-ya	★★★½	Inexp/Mod	★★★½	★★★★
Sushi-Ann	★★★½	Exp	★★★★	★★★★
Honmura An	★★★	Exp	★★★★	★★★
Menchanko-Tei	★★	Inexp	★★★½	★★★★
JEWISH DELI				
Mr.Broadway Kosher Deli	★★★	Mod	★★★★	★★★★★
Second Avenue Deli	★★½	Mod	★★★½	★★★
KOREAN				
Woo Chon	★★★	Mod	★★★★	★★★★
LATIN AMERICAN				
Calle Ocho	★★★	Mod	★★★★	★★★
Café con Leche	★★½	Inexp	★★★★	★★★★★
El Papasito	★★	Inexp	★★★½	★★★★★
MALAYSIAN				
Penang	★★½	Mod	★★★½	★★★
Jaya Malaysian	★★	Inexp	★★★½	★★★★½
MEDITERRANEAN				
Picholine	★★★★	Exp	★★★★½	★★★
The Tree House	★★	Inexp/Mod	★★★½	★★★½
MEXICAN				
Rosa Mexicano	★★★	Mod	★★★★	★★★★
MIDDLE EASTERN				
Sahara East	★★½	Mod	★★★★	★★★★
MOROCCAN				
Café Mogador	★★½	Mod	★★★★	★★★★★
NEW AMERICAN				
The River Café	★★★★★	Very Exp	★★★★★	★★★★½
Veritas	★★★★	Very Exp	★★★★½	★★★★
Union Square Café	★★★★	Exp	★★★★½	★★★★
Gotham Bar & Grill	★★★½	Exp	★★★★	★★★
PASTA				
Tre Pomodori	★★½	Mod	★★★★	★★★★★

The Best New York Restaurants (continued)

TYPE AND NAME	OVERALL RATING	PRICE	QUALITY RATING	VALUE RATING
PERUVIAN				
Rinconcito Peruano	★★★	Inexp	★★★★	★★★★★
PIZZA				
Patsy's Pizza	★★★	Inexp	★★★★½	★★★★★
PORTUGUESE				
Cabana Carioca	★★½	Inexp	★★★★	★★★★★
PUERTO RICAN				
Old San Juan	★★★	Inexp	★★★★	★★★★
RUSSIAN				
Firebird	★★★	Exp	★★★★	★★★★
Petrossian	★★★	Exp	★★★★	★★★
SCANDINAVIAN				
Aquavit	★★★★½	Very Exp	★★★★★	★★★½
SEAFOOD				
Le Bernardin	★★★★	Very Exp	★★★★★	★★★★
Atlantic Grill	★★★★	Exp	★★★★	★★★½
Oceana	★★★½	Exp	★★★★½	★★★
Blue Water Grill	★★★	Mod	★★★★	★★★★
Mary's Fish Camp	★★★	Mod	★★★½	★★★
SOUL FOOD				
Soul Fixin's	★★★	Inexp	★★★★	★★★★★
Jezebel	★★★	Exp	★★★★	★★★

New York Restaurants by Neighborhood

LOWER MANHATTAN, WALL STREET, AND THE BATTERY
Gigino

SOHO AND TRIBECA
Balthazar
Blue Ribbon
Cendrillon

Chanterelle
Honmura An
Montrachet
Nobu
Penang
Petite Abeille
66

CHINATOWN, LITTLE ITALY, AND THE LOWER EAST SIDE
Jaya Malaysian
Joe's Shanghai
Kam Chueh
New Pasteur
The Nice Restaurant

TYPE AND NAME	OVERALL RATING	PRICE	QUALITY RATING	VALUE RATING
SPANISH				
Il Buco	★★★★	Exp	★★★★½	★★★
Xunta	★★★	Mod	★★★★	★★★★
STEAK				
Peter Luger	★★★	Exp	★★★★	★★★★
Les Halles	★★½	Exp	★★★½	★★★
TEAROOM				
Lady Mendl's Tea Salon	★★★	Mod	★★★★½	★★★
THAI				
My Thai	★★★★	Inexp	★★★★½	★★★★★
Sea	★★★	Inexp/Mod	★★★	★★★½
Jasmine	★★½	Mod	★★★	★★★
VEGETARIAN				
Candle Café	★★★½	Inexp/Mod	★★★★	★★★½
Gobo	★★★½	Mod	★★★½	★★★
Kate's Joint	★★½	Mod	★★★★	★★★★
Zen Palate	★★½	Inexp	★★★½	★★★★
VIETNAMESE				
New Pasteur	★★★½	Inexp	★★★★	★★★★★
Saigon Grill	★★★	Inexp	★★★★½	★★★★★

Rice
Sachiko's on Clinton
GREENWICH VILLAGE
Babbo
EJ's Luncheonette
Florent
Gobo
Gotham Bar & Grill

Il Mulino
Mary's Fish Camp
Meskerem
Otto
Pastis
Petite Abeille
Piccolo Angolo
The Pink Teacup

Pó
Tartine
Tea & Sympathy
Tomoe

THE EAST VILLAGE
Borobudur Café
Café Mogador

New York Restaurants by Neighborhood *(continued)*

THE EAST VILLAGE (CONTINUED)
Il Buco
Kate's Joint
Sahara East
Second Avenue Deli
Soba-ya
Xunta

CHELSEA
Grand Sichuan
Petite Abeille
Soul Fixin's

GRAMERCY PARK AND MADISON SQUARE
Artisanal
Blue Water Grill
Chennai Garden
Gramercy Tavern
Lady Mendl's Tea Salon
Les Halles
Mesa Grill
Molly's
Tabla
Tamarind
Tre Pomodori
Union Square Café
Veritas
Zen Palate

MIDTOWN WEST, TIMES SQUARE, AND THE THEATER DISTRICT
Aquavit
Becco
BXL Café
Cabana Carioca

Churrascaria Plataforma
El Papasito
Firebird
Jezebel
Le Bernardin
Margon Restaurant
Menchanko-Tei
Meskerem
Molyvos
Mr. Broadway
Old San Juan
Orso
Osteria Del Circo
Petrossian
Rinconcito Peruano
Zen Palate

MIDTOWN EAST
Menchanko-Tei
Oceana
Rosa Mexicano
Sushi-Ann
Woo Chon

UPPER WEST SIDE
Café con Leche
Calle Ocho
EJ's Luncheonette
Gray's Papaya
Jean-Georges
La Boite en Bois
Penang
Picholine
Rain
Saigon Grill
Shun Lee West, Shun Lee Café
Zen Palate

UPPER EAST SIDE
Atlantic Grill
Café Boulud
Café Sabarsky
Candle Café
EJ's Luncheonette
Gobo
Iammo Bello
Jasmine
Paola's
Rain
Saigon Grill

MORNINGSIDE HEIGHTS, HAMILTON HEIGHTS, AND HARLEM
Patsy's Pizza
Symposium

BROOKLYN
Blue Ribbon
Noodle Pudding
Peter Luger
Rice
The River Café
Sea
Stan's Place

QUEENS
Jackson Diner
Joe's Shanghai
My Thai
Piccola Venezia
Ping's

THE BRONX
The Tree House

STATEN ISLAND
Parsonage

MORE RECOMMENDATIONS

The Best Brunch

- **Bistro St. Mark's** 76 St. Mark's Avenue, Brooklyn; ☎ 718-857-8600
- **Café des Artistes** 1 West 67th Street; ☎ 212-877-3500
- **Café Botanica** Essex House, 160 Central Park South; ☎ 212-484-5120
- **Danal** 90 East Tenth Street; ☎ 212-982-6930
- **Good Enough to Eat** 483 Amsterdam Avenue; ☎ 212-496-0163
- **Tartine** (see profile)
- **Zoe** 90 Prince Street; ☎ 212-966-6722

The Best Burgers

- **Corner Bistro** 331 West Fourth Street; ☎ 212-242-9502
- **Cozy Soup & Burger** 739 Broadway; ☎ 212-477-5566
- **Gotham Bar & Grill** (see profile)
- **Joe Allen** 326 West 46th Street; ☎ 212-581-6464
- **Molly's** (see profile)
- **P. J. Clarke's** 915 Third Avenue; ☎ 212-759-1650
- **Pop Burger** 58–60 Ninth Avenue; ☎ 212-414-8686

The Best Cappuccino

- **Joe** 141 Waverly Place; ☎ 212-924-6750
- **Mudspot** 307 East Ninth Street; ☎ 212-228-9074
- **Sant Ambroeus** 1000 Madison Avenue; ☎ 212-570-2211
- **Via Quadronno** 25 East 73rd Street; ☎ 212-650-9880

The Best Chinatown Restaurants

- **Grand Sichuan** 125 Canal Street; ☎ 212-625-9212
- **Joe's Ginger** 113 Mott Street; ☎ 212-966-6613
- **Joe's Shanghai** (see profile)
- **Kam Chueh** 40 Bowery; ☎ 212-791-6868
- **Mandarin Court** 61 Mott Street; ☎ 212-608-3838
- **New Pasteur** (see profile)
- **Nha Trang** 87 Baxter; ☎ 212-233-5948
- **The Nice Restaurant** (see profile)
- **NY Noodle Town** 28 Bowery; ☎ 212-349-0923
- **Sweet and Tart Café** 76 Mott Street; ☎ 212-334-8088

The Best Cozy Tearooms

- **Cha An, Japanese Tea Room** 230 East Ninth Street; ☎ 212-228-8030
- **Lady Mendl's Tea Room** (see profile)
- **The Rotunda** At the Pierre, 2 East 61st Street; ☎ 212-838-8000
- **Tea & Sympathy** (see profile)

- **Wild Lily Tea Room** 511-A West 22nd Street; ☎ 212-691-2258

The Best Delis

- **Barney Greengrass** 541 Amsterdam Avenue; ☎ 212-724-4707
- **Ben's Best** 96–40 Queens Boulevard, Rego Park, Queens; ☎ 718-897-1700
- **Carnegie Deli** 854 Seventh Avenue at 54th Street; ☎ 212-757-2245
- **Fine and Schapiro** 138 West 72nd; ☎ 212-877-2874
- **Katz's Deli** 205 East Houston; ☎ 212-254-2246
- **Mr. Broadway Kosher Deli** (see profile)
- **Second Avenue Deli** (see profile)

The Best Family Dining

- **Barking Dog** 1453 York Avenue; ☎ 212-861-3600
- **Bright Food Shop** 218 Eighth Avenue; ☎ 212-243-4433
- **Churrascaria Plataforma** (see profile)
- **City Crab** 235 Park Avenue South; ☎ 212-529-3800
- **Popover Café** 551 Amsterdam Avenue; ☎ 212-595-8555

The Best Fireplaces

- **The Black Sheep** 583 Third Avenue at 39th; ☎ 212-599-3476
- **I Trulli** 122 East 27th Street; ☎ 212-481-7372
- **La Ripaille** 605 Hudson Street; ☎ 212-255-4406
- **Molly's** (see profile)
- **Savoy** 70 Prince Street; ☎ 212-219-8570
- **Vivolo** 140 East 74th Street; ☎ 212-737-3533

The Best Gardens

- **Barbetta** 321 West 46th Street; ☎ 212-246-9171
- **Barolo** 398 West Broadway; ☎ 212-226-1102
- **Boathouse Café** Central Park Lake, East Park Drive at 72nd Street; ☎ 212-517-2233
- **Cloisters Café** 238 East Ninth Street; ☎ 212-777-9128
- **Gascogne** 158 Eighth Avenue (between 17th and 18th streets); ☎ 212-675-6564
- **Le Jardin Bistro** 25 Cleveland Place (between Kenmare and Spring); ☎ 212-343-9599
- **Le Refuge** 166 East 82nd Street; ☎ 212-861-4505
- **Sahara East** (see profile)
- **Shake Shack** Madison Square Park (at 23rd Street); ☎ 212-889-6600

The Best Legends and Landmarks

- **Algonquin Hotel** 59 West 44th Street; ☎ 212-840-6800 (stick to the lobby bar)
- **Chumley's** 86 Bedford Street; ☎ 212-675-4449 (former speakeasy)

- **Grand Ticino** 228 Thompson Street; ☎ 212-777-5922 (*Moonstruck* set)
- **Oyster Bar** Grand Central Station, Lower Level; ☎ 212-490-6650
- **PJ Clarke's** 915 Third Avenue; ☎ 212-317-1616
- **Peter Luger Steakhouse** (see profile)
- **Pete's Tavern** 129 East 18th Street; ☎ 212-473-7676
- **Rao's** 455 East 114th Street; ☎ 212-722-6709
- **White Horse Tavern** 567 Hudson Street; ☎ 212-243-9260

The Best Night-owl Prowls

- **Blue Ribbon** Closes 4 a.m. (see profile)
- **Café Noir** 32 Grand Street; ☎ 212-431-7910; closes 4 a.m.
- **Cafeteria** 119 Seventh Avenue; ☎ 212-414-1717; 24 hours
- **Corner Bistro** 331 West Fourth Street; ☎ 212-242-9502; closes 3:30 a.m.
- **Florent** 24 hours (see profile)
- **Lucky Strike** 59 Grand Street; ☎ 212-941-0479; closes 2:30 a.m. on weekends
- **The Odeon** 145 West Broadway; ☎ 212-233-0507; closes 2 a.m.
- **Sahara East** Closes 2 a.m. (see profile)
- **Veselka** 144 Second Avenue (corner of Ninth Street); ☎ 212-228-9682 24 hours
- **Woo Chon** 24 hours (see profile)

The Best Pizza

- **Arturo's** 106 West Houston; ☎ 212-677-3820
- **DiFara's Pizza** 1424 Avenue J, Brooklyn; ☎ 212-258-1367
- **Grimaldi's** 19 Old Fulton Street, Brooklyn; ☎ 718-858-4300
- **John's of Bleecker Street** 278 Bleecker Street; ☎ 212-243-1680
- **La Pizza Fresca** 31 East 20th Street; ☎ 212-598-0141
- **Lombardi's** 32 Spring Street; ☎ 212-941-7994
- **Patsy's Pizza** Spanish Harlem (see profile)
- **Sal and Carmine's Pizza** 2671 Broadway; ☎ 212-663-7651
- **Two Boots** 44 Avenue A; ☎ 212-254-1919; 74 Bleecker; ☎ 212-777-1033; 75 Greenwich Avenue; ☎ 212-633-9096

The Best Raw Bars

- **Aquagrill** 210 Spring Street; ☎ 212-274-0505
- **Atlantic Grill** 1341 Third Avenue; ☎ 212-988-9200
- **Blue Ribbon** (see profile)
- **Blue Water Grill** 31 Union Square West; ☎ 212-675-9500
- **Docks Oyster Bar & Grill** 633 Third Avenue; ☎ 212-986-8080; Uptown, 2427 Broadway; ☎ 212-724-5588
- **Oyster Bar** Grand Central Station, Lower Level; ☎ 212-490-6650
- **Redeye Grill** 890 Seventh Avenue; ☎ 212-541-9000

The Best Romantic Dining

- **The Box Tree** 250 East 49th Street; ☎ 212-758-8320
- **Café des Artistes** 1 West 67th Street; ☎ 212-877-3500
- **King's Carriage House** 251 East 82nd Street; ☎ 212-734-5490
- **March** 405 East 58th Street; ☎ 212-754-6272
- **Mas** 39 Downing Street; ☎ 212-255-1790
- **One if by Land, Two if by Sea** 17 Barrow Street; ☎ 212-228-0822
- **The River Café** (see profile)

The Best Steak Houses

- **Churrascaria Plataforma** (see profile)
- **Palm** 837 Second Avenue; ☎ 212-687-2953
- **Pampa** 768 Amsterdam Avenue, near 98th Street; ☎ 212-865-2929
- **Peter Luger Steakhouse** (see profile)
- **Sparks Steakhouse** 210 East 46th Street; ☎ 212-687-4855
- **Wolfgang's Steakhouse** 4 Park Avenue; ☎ 212-889-3369

The Best Sushi

- **Japonica** 100 University Place; ☎ 212-243-7752
- **Sushi of Gari** 402 East 78th Street; ☎ 212-517-5340
- **Tomoe Sushi** 172 Thompson Street; ☎ 212-777-9346

The Best Ultracheap Meals (under $10)

- **Bao Noodles** 391 Second Avenue (between 22nd and 23rd streets); ☎ 212-725-7770
- **Cosmic Cantina** 101 Third Avenue; ☎ 212-420-0975
- **Excellent Dumpling House** 111 Lafayette Street; ☎ 212-219-0212
- **Gray's Papaya** (see profile)
- **Momofuku Noodle Bar** 163 First Avenue; ☎ 212-475-7899
- **Soul Fixin's** (see profile)
- **Zozo's Juice and Grille** 172 Orchard Street; ☎ 212-228-0009

The Best Vegetarian

- **Angelica Kitchen** 300 East 12th Street; ☎ 212-228-2909
- **Candle Café** (see profile)
- **Caravan of Dreams** 405 East Sixth Street; ☎ 212-254-1613
- **Gobo** (see profile)
- **Hangawi** 12 East 32nd Street (between Fifth and Madison avenues); ☎ 212-213-0077

The Best Views

- **Gigino** (see profile)
- **Rainbow Room** 30 Rockefeller Plaza, 65th floor; ☎ 212-632-5100
- **The River Café** (see profile)

- **Terrace in the Sky** 400 West 119th Street; ☎ 212-666-9490
- **Top of the Tower at Beekman Tower Hotel** 49th Street and First Avenue;
  ☎ 212-980-4796

So You Won't Drop while You Shop

- **Bodum Café and Homestore** 413–415 West 14th Street (near Jeffrey, Stella McCartney, and other hot shops); ☎ 212-367-9125
- **Café S.F.A.** Sak's Fifth Avenue, 611 Fifth Avenue, Eighth floor;
  ☎ 212-940-4080
- **Fred's at Barney's** Lower level, 660 Madison Avenue at 61st Street;
  ☎ 212-833-2200
- **Le Train Blue** 10 East 61st Street; ☎ 212-705-2100
- **The Tea Box** Takashimaya, 693 Fifth Avenue; ☎ 212-350-0180

RESTAURANT PROFILES

Aquavit ★★★★½

SCANDINAVIAN	VERY EXPENSIVE	QUALITY ★★★★★	VALUE ★★★½

65 East 55th Street, Midtown East; ☎ 212-307-7311; www.aquavit.org

Reservations Necessary. **When to go** Anytime. **Entrée range** Prix-fixe dinner, three-course menu, $78 per person; seven-course chef's tasting menu, $100 per person; vegetarian seven-course tasting menu, $90 per person; "Aquavit Bite" multicourse tasting menu, $125 per person; prix-fixe lunch (in cafe) $20, five-course tasting menu, $55; à la carte lunch, $22–$28. Note that cafe is cheaper (see below). **Payment** All major credit cards. **Service rating** ★★★★ **Friendliness rating** ★★★★½ **Bar** Full service, many housemade aquavits. **Wine selection** Very Good. **Dress** Dressy casual to business and elegant. **Disabled access** Yes. **Customers** Business, curious foodies without a budget, New York elite. **Hours** Monday–Friday, noon–2:30 p.m. and 5:30–10:30 p.m.; Saturday, 5:30–10:30 p.m.; Sunday, noon–2:30 p.m. (brunch) and 5:30–10:30 p.m. Chef's tasting menus served until 10 p.m.; multicourse menu served until 9:30 p.m.

SETTING AND ATMOSPHERE Giving up the lovely atrium space and waterfall when Aquavit moved in 2004 must not have been easy, but the advantages of the new space, for the chefs, include a bigger and more user-friendly kitchen that makes the creation of superb food easier. The main dining room is simple and clean in its Scandinavian décor, with a muted cream, brown, and wood color scheme, plus fresh orchids. No natural light. Some argue that tables are a bit too close together, but the food far surpasses any décor faux pas or masterful stroke. The cafe is naturally brighter, as it's close to the front of the restaurant and has windows. Private dining available.

HOUSE SPECIALTIES Herring plate (various herring preparations served with Carlsberg beer and aquavit); lobster roll; gravlax; hot smoked trout; seafood stew.

midtown, chelsea, flatiron district, and

◆ **Dining**
1. Aquavit
2. Artisanal
3. Becco
4. Blue Water Grill
5. BXL
6. Cabana Carioca
7. Chennai Garden
8. Churrascaria Plataforma
9. El Papasito
10. Firebird
11. Grand Sichuan International
12. Gramercy Tavern
13. Jean-Georges
14. Jezebel
15. Lady Mendl's Tea Salon
16. Le Bernardin
17. Les Halles
18. Margon Restaurant
19. Menchanko-Tei
20. Mesa Grill
21. Meskerem
22. Molly's
23. Molyvos
24. Mr. Broadway Kosher Deli
25. Oceana
26. Old San Juan
27. Orso
28. Osteria Del Circo
29. Petite Abeille
30. Petrossian
31. Picholine
32. Rinconcito Peruano
33. Rosa Mexicano
34. Soul Fixin's
35. Sushi-Ann
36. Tamarind
37. Tabla
38. Tre Pomodori
39. Union Square Café
40. Veritas
41. Woo Chon
42. Zen Palate

● **Nightclubs**
43. Bongo
44. Campbell Apartment
45. Carolines
46. Flatiron Lounge
47. Hudson Bar
48. O'Flaherty's Ale House
49. Pen-Top Bar at the Peninsula Hotel
50. PJ Clarke's
51. Rodeo Bar
52. Saka Gura
53. Swing 46
54. The Ginger Man
55. Top of the Tower
56. Town

gramercy park dining and nightlife

PARK

Transverse

Center Drive

East Drive

Fifth Ave.

The Pond

Central Park S.

Madison Ave.

UPPER EAST SIDE

E. 65th St.
E. 64th St.
E. 63rd St.
E. 62nd St.
E. 61st St.
E. 60th St.
E. 59th St.
E. 58th St.
E. 57th St.
E. 56th St.
E. 55th St.
E. 54th St.
E. 53rd St.
E. 52nd St.
E. 51st St.
E. 50th St.
E. 49th St.
E. 48th St
E. 47th St.
E. 46th St.
E. 45th St.
E. 44th St.
E. 43rd St.
E. 42nd St.
E. 41st St.
E. 40th St.
E. 39th St.
E. 38th St.
E. 37th St.
E. 36th St.
E. 35th St.
E. 34th St.
E. 33rd St.
E. 32nd St.
E. 31st St.
E. 30th St.
E. 29th St.
E. 28th St.
E. 27th St.
E. 26th St.
E. 25th St.
E. 24th St.
E. 23rd St.
E. 22nd St.
E. 21st St.
E. 20th St.
E. 19th St.
E. 18th St.
E. 17th St.
E. 16th St.
E. 15th St.
E. 14th St.

From Lower Level

Roosevelt Island Tram

Queensboro Bridge

To Upper Level

Queens

York Ave.

Sutton Pl. South

Sutton Pl.

Beekman Place

Mitchell Place

First Ave.

Third Ave.

Second Ave.

United Nations

Queens–Midtown Tunnel

East River

FDR Drive

MIDTOWN EAST

Rockefeller Center

Fifth Ave.

Madison Ave.

Vanderbilt Ave.

Park Ave.

Lexington Ave.

Grand Central Terminal

Sixth Ave. (Ave. of the Americas)

Bryant Park

New York Public Library

MURRAY HILL

Tunnel Exit

Tunnel Entrance

Empire State Bldg.

W 32nd St.

Broadway

Madison Ave.

Park Ave. S.

Lexington Ave.

Fifth Ave.

Madison Square Park

Asser Levy Pl.

Ave. C

Upper Manhattan

Uptown

Midtown

Downtown

Peter Cooper Village

Stuyvesant Town

N.D. Perlman Pl.

FLATIRON DISTRICT

Sixth Ave. (Ave. of the Americas)

Fifth Ave.

GRAMERCY PARK

Gramercy Park

Union Sq. W.

Union Square

Union Sq. E.

Irving Pl.

0 _____ 0.25 mi
0 _____ 0.25 km

Ⓜ Subway stop

uptown dining and nightlife

◆ Dining
1. Atlantic Grill
2. Café Boulud
3. Café con Leche
4. Café Sabarsky
5. Calle Ocho
6. Candle Café
7. EJ's Luncheonette
8. Gobo
9. Gray's Papaya
10. Iammo Bello
11. Jasmine
12. La Boite en Bois
13. Paola's
14. Penang
15. Rain
16. Saigon Grill
17. Shun Lee West,
    Shun Lee Café
18. Zen Palate

● Nightclubs
19. Café Carlyle
20. Club Macanudo
21. Lenox Room
22. Smoke

Ⓜ Subway stop

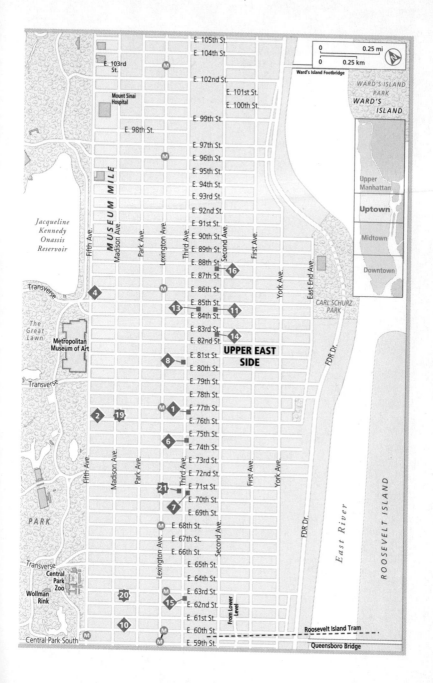

E. 105th St.
E. 104th St.
E. 103rd St.
E. 102nd St.
E. 101st St.
E. 100th St.
E. 99th St.
E. 98th St.
E. 97th St.
E. 96th St.
E. 95th St.
E. 94th St.
E. 93rd St.
E. 92nd St.
E. 91st St.
E. 90th St.
E. 89th St.
E. 88th St.
E. 87th St.
E. 86th St.
E. 85th St.
E. 84th St.
E. 83rd St.
E. 82nd St.
E. 81st St.
E. 80th St.
E. 79th St.
E. 78th St.
E. 77th St.
E. 76th St.
E. 75th St.
E. 74th St.
E. 73rd St.
E. 72nd St.
E. 71st St.
E. 70th St.
E. 69th St.
E. 68th St.
E. 67th St.
E. 66th St.
E. 65th St.
E. 64th St.
E. 63rd St.
E. 62nd St.
E. 61st St.
E. 60th St.
E. 59th St.

Ward's Island Footbridge

WARD'S ISLAND PARK
WARD'S ISLAND

Upper Manhattan
Uptown
Midtown
Downtown

Mount Sinai Hospital

Jacqueline Kennedy Onassis Reservoir

MUSEUM MILE

Fifth Ave.
Madison Ave.
Park Ave.
Lexington Ave.
Third Ave.
Second Ave.
First Ave.
York Ave.
East End Ave.

Transverse

The Great Lawn

Metropolitan Museum of Art

Transverse

UPPER EAST SIDE

CARL SCHURZ PARK

FDR Dr.

East River

ROOSEVELT ISLAND

PARK

Transverse

Central Park Zoo

Wollman Rink

Central Park South

From Lower Level

Roosevelt Island Tram
Queensboro Bridge

0   0.25 mi
0   0.25 km

financial district, tribeca, chinatown, and little italy dining

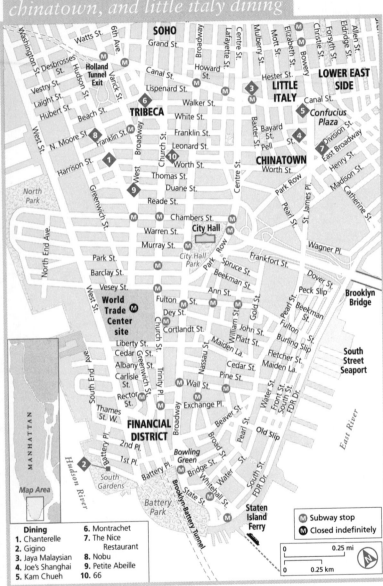

SOHO
Grand St.

Washington St.
Watts St.
6th Ave.
Broadway
Lafayette St.
Centre St.
Mulberry St.
Mott St.
Elizabeth St.
Bowery
Christie St.
Forsyth St.
Eldridge St.
Allen St.

Desbrosses St.
Hudson St.
Varick St.
Canal St.
Howard St.
Hester St.
LITTLE ITALY

Holland Tunnel Exit

Vestry St.
Lispenard St.
Canal St.
LOWER EAST SIDE

Laight St.
Walker St.
Confucius Plaza

Hubert St.
TRIBECA
White St.
Bayard St.
Division St.
East Broadway

Beach St.
Franklin St.
Pell
Henry St.

N. Moore St.
Franklin St.
Broadway
Leonard St.
Baxter St.
CHINATOWN
Worth St.
Madison St.

Harrison St.
Church St.
Worth St.
Park Row
Catherine St.

West St.
Greenwich St.
Thomas St.
Centre St.
St. James Pl.

North Park
Duane St.
Pearl St.

Reade St.

Chambers St.

North End Ave.
Warren St.
City Hall
Wagner Pl.

Murray St.

City Hall Park
Park Row
Frankfort St.
Dover St.
Brooklyn Bridge

Park St.
Spruce St.
Peck Slip

Barclay St.
Beekman St.

Vesey St.
Ann St.
Gold St.
Pearl St.
Beekman St.
South Street Seaport

West St.
World Trade Center site
Fulton St.
Dey St.
William St.
John St.
Platt St.
Fulton St.
Burling Slip

Church St.
Cortlandt St.
Maiden La.
Fletcher St.
Maiden La.

Liberty St.
Cedar St.
Greenwich St.
Nassau St.
Cedar St.

Albany St.
Trinity Pl.
Pine St.
Water St.
Front St.
South St.
FDR Dr.

Carlisle St.
South End Ave.
Wall St.
East River

Rector St.
Broadway
Exchange Pl.

Thames St. W.
MANHATTAN
FINANCIAL DISTRICT
Beaver St.
Pearl St.
Old Slip

2nd Pl.
Bowling Green
Broad St.
Water St.
South St.
FDR Dr.

1st Pl.
Battery Pl.
Bridge St.
Whitehall St.
State St.

Map Area
Hudson River
South Gardens
Battery Park
Brooklyn-Battery Tunnel
Staten Island Ferry

Dining	
1. Chanterelle	6. Montrachet
2. Gigino	7. The Nice Restaurant
3. Jaya Malaysian	8. Nobu
4. Joe's Shanghai	9. Petite Abeille
5. Kam Chueh	10. 66

Ⓜ Subway stop
Ⓜ Closed indefinitely

0   0.25 mi
0   0.25 km

lower east side, soho, nolita, and east village dining and nightlife

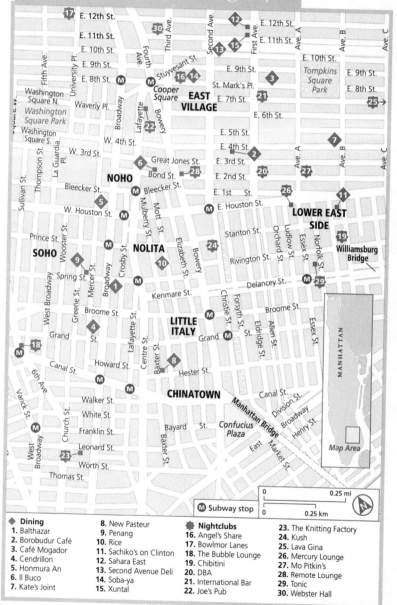

E. 12th St. · E. 11th St. · E. 10th St. · E. 9th St. · E. 8th St. · Stuyvesant St. · Third Ave. · Second Ave. · First Ave. · Ave. A · Ave. B · Ave. C

E. 12th St. · E. 11th St. · E. 10th St. · E. 9th St. · E. 8th St. · E. 7th St. · E. 6th St. · E. 5th St. · E. 4th St. · E. 3rd St. · E. 2nd St. · E. 1st St.

Fifth Ave. · University Pl. · Fourth Ave. · Broadway · Lafayette · Bowery · Mulberry St. · Mott St. · Elizabeth St. · Bowery

Washington Square N. · Washington Square Park · Washington Square S. · Waverly Pl. · W. 4th St. · W. 3rd St. · La Guardia Pl. · Thompson St. · Sullivan St.

Cooper Square · St. Mark's Pl. · **EAST VILLAGE**

Tompkins Square Park

NOHO · Great Jones St. · Bond St. · Bleecker St. · W. Houston St. · E. Houston St.

Bleecker St. · Prince St. · Spring St. · Broome St. · Grand St.

SOHO · Wooster St. · Greene St. · Mercer St. · West Broadway · Broadway · Crosby St.

NOLITA · Lafayette St. · Centre St. · Baxter St. · Kenmare St. · Christie St. · Forsyth St.

Stanton St. · Rivington St. · Delancey St. · Broome St. · Grand St.

Ludlow St. · Orchard St. · Essex St. · Norfolk St. · Allen St. · Eldridge St. · Essex St.

LOWER EAST SIDE · Williamsburg Bridge

LITTLE ITALY · Hester St. · Howard St. · Canal St. · Walker St. · White St. · Franklin St. · Leonard St. · Worth St. · Thomas St.

CHINATOWN · Bayard St. · Canal St. · Confucius Plaza · Manhattan Bridge · Division St. · Broadway · Henry St. · East Market St.

6th Ave. · Varick St. · Church St. · West Broadway · 6th Ave.

MANHATTAN · Map Area

Ⓜ Subway stop

0 — 0.25 mi
0 — 0.25 km

◆ Dining
1. Balthazar
2. Borobudur Café
3. Café Mogador
4. Cendrillon
5. Honmura An
6. Il Buco
7. Kate's Joint
8. New Pasteur
9. Penang
10. Rice
11. Sachiko's on Clinton
12. Sahara East
13. Second Avenue Deli
14. Soba-ya
15. Xuntal

✿ Nightclubs
16. Angel's Share
17. Bowlmor Lanes
18. The Bubble Lounge
19. Chibitini
20. DBA
21. International Bar
22. Joe's Pub
23. The Knitting Factory
24. Kush
25. Lava Gina
26. Mercury Lounge
27. Mo Pitkin's
28. Remote Lounge
29. Tonic
30. Webster Hall

greenwich village dining and nightlife

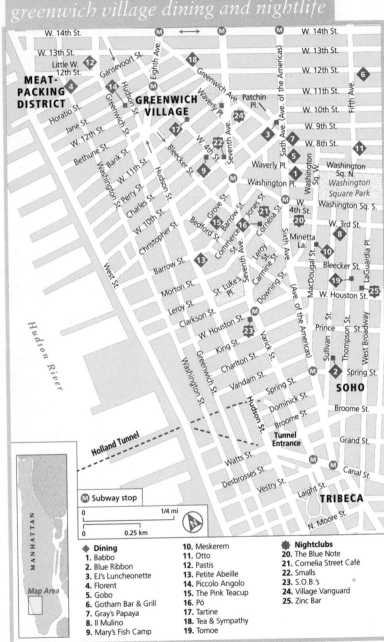

Dining
1. Babbo
2. Blue Ribbon
3. EJ's Luncheonette
4. Florent
5. Gobo
6. Gotham Bar & Grill
7. Gray's Papaya
8. Il Mulino
9. Mary's Fish Camp
10. Meskerem
11. Otto
12. Pastis
13. Petite Abeille
14. Piccolo Angolo
15. The Pink Teacup
16. Pó
17. Tartine
18. Tea & Sympathy
19. Tomoe

Nightclubs
20. The Blue Note
21. Cornelia Street Café
22. Smalls
23. S.O.B.'s
24. Village Vanguard
25. Zinc Bar

OTHER RECOMMENDATIONS Brioche-wrapped salmon; sautéed halibut; Wagyu carpaccio; salsify noodles in a Vasterbotten cheese, mustard, and mushroom sauce.

SUMMARY AND COMMENTS Swedish chef Marcus Samuelsson, who won the James Beard Foundation accolade of "Best Chef in New York City for 2003," has taken Aquavit to new levels of culinary prowess. If it weren't for the prices, we'd recommend a few return visits to try the tasting menu as well as some of the selections from the prix fixe. Housemade aquavits can accompany the fish appetizers perfectly; selections include pear, vanilla and black peppercorn, cloudberry, and citrus flavors. Presentation of all dishes is creative. The cafe is cheaper and worth a try. Keep in mind, though, that the cafe kitchen is separate from that of the main dining room; it is supervised by the executive chef and a little bit of overlap can be found. If you want Swedish meatballs, you can only get them in the cafe.

Artisanal ★★★½

BISTRO/FROMAGERIE   MODERATE/EXPENSIVE   QUALITY ★★★★   VALUE ★★★

2 Park Avenue (entrance on 32nd Street), Gramercy Park and Madison Square; ☎ 212-725-8585

Reservations Recommended, but first come, first served at few tables by bar. **When to go** Anytime. **Entrée range** $17–$32; prix-fixe lunch and dinners available. **Payment** AE, MC, V. **Service rating** ★★★ **Friendliness rating** ★★★ **Bar** Full service. **Wine selection** Extensive. **Dress** Business casual. **Disabled access** Yes. **Customers** Regulars, couples, professionals. **Hours** Monday–Thursday, noon–11 p.m.; Friday, noon–midnight; Saturday, 11 a.m.–3 p.m. (brunch) and 5 p.m.–midnight; Sunday, 11 a.m.–3 p.m. (brunch) and 5–10 p.m.

SETTING AND ATMOSPHERE A large, bustling dining room with high ceilings, large windows, and happy diners. There's an upscale bistro/brasserie ambience and a buzz in the air, which can often be almost too loud. If you're looking for intimacy, go somewhere else. That said, there's something quite romantic about sharing fondue for an entrée and dessert.

HOUSE SPECIALTIES Cheese, fondue, and wine.

OTHER RECOMMENDATIONS Chocolate fondue; cassoulet; side of creamed spinach with parmesan; three-cheese onion soup; "chicken under brick"; tarte tatin.

SUMMARY AND COMMENTS The great thing about Artisanal is that you don't need to have a full meal to enjoy and sample some of their specialties. Apart from lunch, dinner, brunch, and a late-night menu on offer after 9:30 p.m., you can come in and have a cheese and wine flight combination that offers three wines paired with three specific cheeses. Some of these preselected flight combinations include three choices from categories like International, Champagne, Italian, Alsatian, and Spanish; prices range from $29–$32. If you decide on the full-meal option, go crazy with cheese, but make sure you have time for a walk afterwards. Fried fish and chips at $17.50 is hardly worth it, so opt for other dishes.

Even if you are already cheese savvy, take advantage of the fromager to ask him or her questions about their selection of over 200 cheeses. A cheese plate takes on new meaning after you discuss your options and realize that a good way to go about selecting a five-cheese platter is to include "a goat, a cow, a sheep, a blue, and a cheddar." Fondue can be ordered in two sizes and a choice of varying cheese, herb, and oil infusion combinations. There's always a fondue of the day. If you need something sweet besides a cheese plate, try the chocolate fondue or the tarte tatin with the cheddar cheese crust.

Atlantic Grill ★★★★

SEAFOOD	EXPENSIVE	QUALITY ★★★★	VALUE ★★★½

1341 Third Avenue (between 76th and 77th streets), Upper East Side; ☎ **212-988-9200; www.brguestrestaurants.com**

Reservations Highly recommended. **When to go** Anytime. **Entrée range** $22–$26. **Payment** All major credit cards. **Service rating** ★★★★½ **Friendliness rating** ★★★½ **Bar** Full service. **Wine selection** Decent. **Dress** Business, casual chic. **Disabled access** Yes. **Customers** Local, fish and raw bar lovers, professionals. **Hours** Monday–Thursday, 11:30 a.m.–4 p.m. and 5 p.m.–midnight; Friday, 11:30 a.m.–4 p.m. and 5 p.m.–12:30 a.m.; Saturday, 11:30 a.m.–4 p.m. and 4:30 p.m.–12:30 a.m.; Sunday, 10:30 a.m.–4 p.m. (brunch) and 4:30–11 p.m.

SETTING AND ATMOSPHERE Stylish yet unimposing. An entrance through the front bar makes way for two adjacent spaces. The first space feels roomier, with banquettes along the walls and tables in the center. The second space is through the banquette area and is narrower and full of tables along either side of the wall. There is a pervasive positive buzz of activity and conversation in the air.

HOUSE SPECIALTIES Oysters and clams from the raw bar; nori-wrapped tuna; barbecue-glazed mahi mahi.

OTHER RECOMMENDATIONS Anything from the sushi bar; green market salad; shrimp-and-lobster spring roll; organic salmon.

SUMMARY AND COMMENTS An Upper East Side favorite and perennially consistent for fresh fish and enjoyable dining. That said, if you're interested in eating in a quiet setting this is not the place. Banquettes can be intimate, but the restaurant is usually full, so noise levels are high. The sushi rolls are scrumptious, and the daily special roll is often worth trying. Efficient wait staff aim to please, but be mindful of the zealous wine and water pouring, which results in over-filled glasses and what appears to be a need for another bottle before the main course arrives. Sidewalk dining available when weather allows.

Babbo ★★★½

ITALIAN	EXPENSIVE	QUALITY ★★★★	VALUE ★★★★

110 Waverly Place (between MacDougal and Sixth Avenue), Greenwich Village; ☎ **212-777-0303; www.babbony.com**

Reservations A must. **When to go** Anytime you can get a reservation. **Entrée range** $17–$33; seven-course pasta-tasting menu, $64; seven-course traditional tasting menu, $70. **Payment** All major credit cards. **Service rating** ★★½ **Friendliness rating** ★★★ **Bar** Full service. **Wine selection** Lots of Italian; ask for recommendations; fairly priced. **Dress** Casual to dressy. **Disabled access** Main dining room and restrooms. **Customers** Locals, professionals, celebrities. **Hours** Sunday, 5–10:45 p.m.; Monday–Saturday, 5:30–11:15 p.m.

SETTING AND ATMOSPHERE Formerly home to James Beard's classic Coach House, this Greenwich Village bi-level space has been thoroughly updated to house Mario Batali's innovative Italian cooking. The main room is dressed comfortably in soft yellow, with banquettes running along the walls and a center table proudly displaying a beautiful bouquet of flowers. A majestic staircase splits the back of the room and leads up to a more serene second floor with white walls and a grand skylight. The main room brims with energy and resultant noise, and upstairs tends to be more relaxed and civilized.

HOUSE SPECIALTIES Marinated fresh sardines; warm tripe parmigiana; mint love letters; pappardelle Bolognese; grilled lamb chops with eggplant; saffron panna cotta with poached peaches.

OTHER RECOMMENDATIONS Mackerel tartare; beef-cheek ravioli with crushed squab livers; two-minute calamari, Sicilian lifeguard style; whole roasted fish with lemon-oregano jam; assortment of gelati and sorbetti; cheesecake with raspberries and figs.

SUMMARY AND COMMENTS Power team Molto Mario Batali (Po) and Joseph Bastianich (Felidia, Becco, Frico) have opened one of New York's most ambitious and most successful Italian restaurants. The room is raucous, and an open table comes up about as often as Halley's Comet, but it's worth the wait for Batali's fearless food. Batali pushes the limits of traditional Italian cooking, using ingredients most diners shun, like anchovies, calf's brains, and beef cheeks. More of it works than doesn't, but figuring it out is all the fun. For starters, Batali smartly tempers fresh silvery anchovies with dusky summer beans, softening the fish's sharper edges, and normally bland tripe gets a healthy dose of character from a spicy, hot tomato sauce. The surprisingly tender bites please almost instantly, and it's almost enough to make you a lifelong fan of this unusual delicacy. But certain pastas can be disappointing. Avoid overly rich preparations like duck liver ravioli, buried in an overly sweet, overbearing hoisin-like sauce, and beef-cheek ravioli, which may be too much for some. As for entrées, two-minute calamari is very good, but would work better as an appetizer. Stick with fish or the grilled lamb chops.

Balthazar ★★★½

| FRENCH | MODERATELY EXPENSIVE | QUALITY ★★★★ | VALUE ★★★★ |

80 Spring Street, Soho; ☎ **212-965-1785; www.balthazarny.com**

Reservations Recommended. **When to go** Anytime. **Entrée range** $16–$36. **Payment** All major credit cards. **Service rating** ★★★ **Friendliness rating** ★★★

Bar Full service and usually full. **Wine selection** Good and not overpriced; heavy on French options; house wine by the carafe is drinkable and inexpensive. **Dress** Chic—upscale or down. **Disabled access** Yes. **Customers** The "trendetti," celebrities, locals. **Hours** Monday–Friday, 7:30–11:30 a.m., noon–5 p.m.; and 5:45 p.m.–midnight; Saturday, 7:30–11:30 a.m., 11:30 a.m.–4 p.m. (brunch), and 5:45 p.m.–midnight; Sunday, 8–10 a.m., 11:30 a.m.–4 p.m. (brunch) and 5:30–11 p.m.

SETTING AND ATMOSPHERE Keith McNally, his advisors, and a fortune in francs (or dollars) turned what had been a leather store into a fabulous facsimile of a timeworn Paris brasserie that looks as though it has nestled on this East Soho street for years. Outside, red awnings mark the spot; inside, uneven old-gold-ocher walls, slightly scuffed and stained, peeling mirrors, a tiled floor, an old bar with a pewter top, and paper-covered wooden bistro tables set the trendy stage.

HOUSE SPECIALTIES Balthazar salad; steak au poivre; steak frites; beef short ribs; brandade de morue (puréed salt cod); warm goat cheese and caramelized onion tart; whole roast chicken.

OTHER RECOMMENDATIONS Duck and pistachio terrine; roasted halibut with crushed potatoes and warm tomato-almond vinaigrette; duck shepherd's pie; caramelized banana tart.

SUMMARY AND COMMENTS Though not quite the place to see and be seen as when it first opened, Balthazar has more than held its own as a New York hot spot thanks to its laid-back, lively atmosphere and solid bistro fare. Bistro classics like steak frites and steak au poivre remain stellar, and garlicky brandade will have you coming back for more. Prices are surprisingly reasonable, but reservations are still hard to come by, so try to go for an upbeat and satisfying late lunch. If you can stand the wait, go for a super brunch. If you're on the go, the adjacent Balthazar Bakery offers an excellent selection of tasty breads, pastries, and sandwiches.

Becco ★★★

ITALIAN	MODERATE	QUALITY ★★★½	VALUE ★★★★★

355 West 46th Street (between Eighth and Ninth avenues),
Midtown West, Times Square, and the Theater District;
☎ **212-397-7597; www.becconyc.com**

Reservations Recommended; a must before theater. **When to go** Anytime. **Entrée range** $18–$29; prix-fixe lunch, $16.95; prix-fixe dinner, $21.95. **Payment** All major credit cards. **Service rating** ★★★ **Friendliness rating** ★★★ **Bar** Full service. **Wine selection** Good; there's a sizable list for only $25. **Dress** Casual, theater. **Disabled access** No. **Customers** Pre- and post-theater, tourists, locals. **Hours** Monday–Saturday, noon–3 p.m. and 5 p.m.–midnight; Sunday, noon–3 p.m. and 5–10 p.m.

SETTING AND ATMOSPHERE This thriving Restaurant Row-er is thronged with theatergoers. The narrow dining area in the front, with its beamed ceilings, has a few touches that suggest a country inn, but tables are so close together that the happy din can become daunting. The upstairs dining room, away from the noise and constant bustle, is a much better bet for a civilized dining experience, and the cute but smaller back room can be a pleasant diversion as well.

HOUSE SPECIALTIES Sinfonia di pasta, unlimited servings of three pastas that change daily; antipasto of grilled, marinated veggies and fish; home-made fruit sorbets; ricotta tart with orange caramel sauce.

OTHER RECOMMENDATIONS Osso buco with barley risotto; grilled swordfish with balsamic sauce; Italian stuffed peppers; rack of lamb.

SUMMARY AND COMMENTS You get a lot for your lire at this popular Theater District trattoria run by the Bastianich family, who also run the famed **Felidia** (243 East 58th; ☎ 212-758-1479). For $29.50, you get a choice of several selections, including chicken breast with lemon-caper sauce, pan-seared salmon, or fresh veal, plus a choice of dessert and coffee or tea. The pastas are almost always homemade and usually surprisingly good; you'd be hard-pressed to find a better deal in the city. Entrées are good but for the most part unspectacular. Stick with the all-you-can-eat pastas and use the money you save on entrées to order a couple of extra bottles from their wine list. This way you're guaranteed to leave both happy and satisfied.

Blue Ribbon ★★★

ECLECTIC AMERICAN   MODERATE   QUALITY ★★★½   VALUE ★★★★

97 Sullivan Street (near Spring Street), Soho; ☎ 212-274-0404; 280 Fifth Avenue (between First Street and Garfield Place), Brooklyn; ☎ 718-840-0404; www.blueribbonrestaurants.com

Reservations Only for parties of five to eight. **When to go** Dinner only. **Entrée range** $14–$102. **Payment** All major credit cards. **Service rating** ★★★ **Friendliness rating** ★★★ **Bar** Full service. **Wine selection** Interesting. **Dress** Anything goes. **Disabled access** Yes, but very crowded. **Customers** Locals, trendies, night owls. **Hours** Daily, 4 p.m.–4 a.m.

SETTING AND ATMOSPHERE A smallish, square, very dark room that seems to be a magnet for young and not-so-young trendies. It's not the décor that does it. If you can see through the throng at the bar, you'll find a wall of painted dark red brick, dark red plush banquettes, and one large semicircular enclosure seating five or more, with a few interestingly odd paintings above and closely spaced tables. It's noisy.

HOUSE SPECIALTIES Fried chicken with collard greens and mashed potatoes; whole steamed flounder; anything from the raw bar; chocolate Bruno; banana split.

OTHER RECOMMENDATIONS Roast duck; sweet and spicy catfish; hanger steak with wild mushrooms and onion rings; french fries; crème brûlée. Skip "favorites" like the pu-pu platter and paella.

SUMMARY AND COMMENTS This is the happening place in the happening Soho scene. Open until 4 a.m., it attracts a late-night crowd, local chefs included, but it's jammed from 8 p.m. on. Expect to wait at least one hour, and very possibly more, to sample chef Eric Bromberg's eclectic menu. Hanging out here is fun; the crowd is anything but dowdy. But if the waiting game is not for you, go north up Sullivan Street and see if you can get into **Blue Ribbon Sushi** (119 Sullivan Street; ☎ 212-343-0404), Blue Ribbon's hip Japanese sibling restaurant. Or keep on going to **Jean Claude** (137 Sullivan Street; ☎ 212-475-9232), another perfect Parisian transplant from St. Germain or Montparnasse—noisy, smoky, good bistro food, and not too expensive (cash only).

Blue Water Grill ★★★

AMERICAN/SEAFOOD	MODERATE	QUALITY ★★★★	VALUE ★★★★

31 Union Square West (at 16th Street), Gramercy Park and Madison Square; ☎ 212-675-9500; www.brguestrestaurants.com

Reservations Recommended. **When to go** Anytime. **Entrée range** $14–$32. **Payment** All major credit cards. **Service rating** ★★★ **Friendliness rating** ★★★ **Bar** Full service. **Wine selection** Not particularly exciting, but not bad either. **Dress** Casual. **Disabled access** In main dining room. **Customers** Professionals, locals, celebs, tourists. **Hours** Monday–Thursday, 11:30 a.m.–4 p.m. and 5 p.m.–midnight; Friday and Saturday, 11:30 a.m.–4 p.m. and 5 p.m.–12:30 a.m.; Sunday, 10:30 a.m.–4 p.m. (brunch) and 5–11:30 p.m.

SETTING AND ATMOSPHERE Big, breezy, and beautiful, this converted bank built in 1904 features vaulted marble ceilings and marble walls, high columns and old-fashioned architectural details. Perfect-for-warm-weather seating is available outside just above street level, and during dinner you can listen to jazz while you eat downstairs. But the best seats in the house are the banquettes in the balcony of the main dining room. The epitome of laid-back and casual, the atmosphere at Blue Water Grill cannot be described as anything other than pleasant.

HOUSE SPECIALTIES Maryland crab cakes with lobster mashed potatoes; ginger-crusted tuna with potato pot stickers, shitake mushrooms, and white soy vinaigrette; blackened swordfish; grilled fish; warm chocolate cake.

OTHER RECOMMENDATIONS Jumbo sea scallops; tartare sampler; warm lobster salad; sweet potato–crabmeat hash; crème brûlée with fresh berries and ginger snaps.

SUMMARY AND COMMENTS People love Blue Water Grill. Whenever out-of-towners visit, New Yorkers invariably take them here. Not surprisingly, talk to anyone outside New York and they've all been here. And for one simple reason: Blue Water Grill knows how to make people happy. With its cool setting, casual atmosphere, friendly service, and something-for-everyone menu at prices that won't empty your wallet, Blue Water executes the game plan for success to perfection. And the food is always good enough to ensure return trips. At the fresh raw bar, choose from the extensive and user-friendly list of oysters, each with a quick description and those for beginners marked conveniently with asterisks. Owner Steve Hanson has repeated his formula for success at uptown sibling **Ocean Grill** on the Upper West Side (384 Columbus Avenue; ☎ 212-579-2300), and **Atlantic Grill** on the Upper East (1341 Third Avenue; ☎ 212-988-9200) deserves an honorable mention for its fish and seafood menu.

Borobudur Café ★★

| INDONESIAN | INEXPENSIVE | QUALITY ★★½ | VALUE ★★★ |

128 East Fourth Street (between First and Second avenues), The East Village; ☎ 212-614-9079

Reservations Not necessary. **When to go** Anytime. **Entrée range** $9–$15. **Payment** MC, V. Service Rating ★★★ **Friendliness rating** ★★★ **Bar** None. **Wine selection** None–beer available. **Dress** Casual. **Disabled access** Yes. **Customers** Ethnic, locals, regulars. **Hours** Sunday–Thursday, noon–10:30 p.m.; Friday and Saturday, noon–midnight.

SETTING AND ATMOSPHERE Small, simply designed, no-frills décor. Single-bulb lighting is softened with candlelight on each table in the evening. The exposed brick wall provides a sense of warmth.

HOUSE SPECIALTIES Special rice dinners, offering a selection of Indonesian specialties; gulai kambing (lamb cooked with curry, vegetables, and onions); martabak borobudur (fried phyllo dough with ground beef, onion, and eggs with curry).

OTHER RECOMMENDATIONS Pempek (fried fish cake); balacan chilli sauce, sayur lodeh (a soup with vegetables in coconut milk); spiced iced tea with cinnamon and cloves. The gado-gado (light salad with peanut sauce) isn't what it could be.

SUMMARY AND COMMENTS Apparently known in certain Indonesian circles, this unassuming restaurant serves consistently tasty Indonesian fare. The low prices may account for why the food lacks in presentation, but this has no effect on taste. The service is friendly, and they are eager to please and explain anything on the menu that may appear puzzling.

BXL Café ★★★

| BELGIAN BISTRO & BEER BAR | MODERATE | QUALITY ★★★ | VALUE ★★★ |

125 West 43rd Street (between 6th and 7th avenues), Midtown West, Times Square, and the Theater District; ☎ 212-768-0200; www.bxlcafe.com

Reservations Recommended. **When to go** Anytime. **Entrée range** $10–$17 (lunch); $12–$24 (dinner). **Payment** All major credit cards. **Service rating** ★★★. **Friendliness rating** ★★★. **Bar** Full service. **Wine selection** Small. **Dress** Casual. **Disabled access** Good. **Customers** Expat Belgians, theater crowd, business. **Hours** Daily, 11:30 a.m.–11.30 p.m.; brunch: weekends, 11.30 a.m.–4 p.m.; bar open most nights until 2 a.m.

SETTING AND ATMOSPHERE Small, cozy bistro and bar. The décor reflects the authenticity and ambience of a Belgian bistro in a small town. The decoration—huge pictures of the Belgian kings from Leopold I all the way to present-day King Albert II. The only lady joining the illustrious group is Queen Astrid, surnamed the "Snow Princess." This Swedish Princess's death in 1935 triggered a Princess Diana–like mourning in Belgium.

HOUSE SPECIALTIES Steamed mussels and frites; Flemish stew cooked with beer (Leffe brown); croquettes with grey north sea shrimps; classic steak tartare.

OTHER RECOMMENDATIONS Near Times Square, this is a great place for a preshow dinner. The bar features 10 Belgian beers on tap and another 20 in bottles. On the must-try list: Delirium tremens and a triple fermented Chimay cinq cents. Both are available on draft. Among the bottled goodies: Westmalle Triple and Rochefort 10.

SUMMARY AND COMMENTS Good brasserie fare combined with decent prices at a top location. The restaurant is small, and lunch can be a noisy affair. The all-you-can-eat mussels night every Monday ($17 includes 1 Stella Artois) is a steal.

Cabana Carioca ★★½

BRAZILIAN/PORTUGUESE	INEXP	QUALITY ★★★★	VALUE ★★★★★

123 West 45th Street, Midtown West, Times Square, and the Theater District; ☎ 212-581-8088

Reservations None accepted for lunch; dinner only for four or more. **When to go** Lunch for buffet, dinner for bar specials. **Entrée range** $12.95–$19.95. **Payment** All major credit cards; cash only at the bar. **Service rating** ★★★ **Friendliness rating** ★★★ **Bar** Full service. **Wine selection** Small. **Dress** Casual. **Disabled access** Fair. **Customers** Professionals at lunch; tourists, theater workers, ethnic at dinner. **Hours** Monday–Thursday, 11:30 a.m.–11 p.m.; Friday and Saturday, 11:30 a.m.–midnight; Sunday, 11:30 a.m.–10 p.m.

SETTING AND ATMOSPHERE Service is offered on three levels, connected by steep steps (painted in garish happy colors). With tables close together and sound levels high, this is not the place for lingering or romance. Management tries for a fun, colorful, tropical look, but it's been a while since the last makeover, and things are starting to get just a tad seedy at the edges. Don't look too closely; just enjoy.

HOUSE SPECIALTIES These change daily. Examples include roast chicken, shrimp gumbo, pot roast, shell steak, caipirinhas.

OTHER RECOMMENDATIONS Caldo verdhe (potato soup with kale and chorizo sausage) is satisfying, almost a meal in itself for $20. Ask for some homemade hot sauce—vinegary and terrific (shake the bottle!)—and don't forget to spoon farofa (toasted yucca flour) over the beans.

SUMMARY AND COMMENTS The buffet lunch is an astounding bargain: $10 buys you unlimited access to a large array of meat, salad, and vegetable dishes, as well as desserts (come early; the steam tables are less frequently replenished later on). But there's an even better deal: daily dinner specials, available only at the bars—and the tables near them—on all three levels, such as a crunchy, garlicky half roast chicken; homey pot roast; a huge mound of garlicky, spicy baby shrimp gumbo (not really gumbo, but tasty); or a pretty serviceable garlic-marinated steak. Each includes a heap of rice, excellent black beans, and lots of homemade thick-cut potato chips, plus unlimited access to the salad bar, all for well under $12. Amazing. But if you're here for a bargain, be wary of drinks; ordering beer or cocktails will almost double your tab (but they make good caipirinhas—Brazilian cocktails of distilled sugar cane and tons of limes). The spotty regular menu is not particularly recommended, nor is the feijoada (Brazilian black bean stew); stick with the bar and the buffet.

Numerological oddity: An address you'll never forget: 1-2-3 West 4-5 Street between 6th and 7th avenues.

Café Boulud ★★★½

FRENCH	EXPENSIVE	QUALITY ★★★★½	VALUE ★★★½

20 East 76th Street, Upper East Side; ☎ 212-772-2600; www.danielnyc.com

Reservations Required. **When to go** Anytime. **Entrée range** $18–$40. **Payment** All major credit cards. **Service rating** ★★★★½ **Friendliness rating** ★★★★ **Bar** Full service. **Wine selection** Extensive and reasonably priced. **Dress** Nice casual–dressy. **Disabled access** Yes. **Customers** Business, locals. **Hours** Tuesday–Friday, noon–2:30 p.m. and 5:45–11 p.m.; Saturday–Monday, 5:45–11 p.m.

SETTING AND ATMOSPHERE On entering the restaurant you are met by a small sea of white linen–dressed tables, elegant ochre walls with muted pastel-toned oil paintings, and a few large mirrors. Black-and-white photographs line part of a wall leading to the well-appointed yet not over-the-top bathrooms. The atmosphere is more at ease than you might expect from such an Upper East Side establishment. There's an almost hushed sanctity within the restaurant, which allows diners to talk in low to normal decibels and yet not be heard at the next table. It's possible to eat outside during warm weather.

HOUSE SPECIALTIES The menu is divided into four sections: La Tradition, La Saison, Le Potager, and Le Voyage. La Tradition focuses on classic French dishes, La Saison concentrates on what's fresh in the market, Le Potager celebrates the vegetable (good choices for vegetarians), and Le Voyage highlights a chosen world cuisine and creates dishes within the genre. Le Voyage selections change monthly, and the others alter depending on the market and the chef. Some specialties have included lobster and seafood bisque; Peeky Toe crab salad; roasted beet and pear salad; roasted chicken with potatoes and bacon; and steamed wild striped bass.

OTHER RECOMMENDATIONS Poached pear; warmed madeleines; raw and cooked tuna with beans, potatoes, and quail egg; roasted monkfish.

SUMMARY AND COMMENTS Formerly housing Daniel Boulud's restaurant Daniel, Café Boulud took over when Boulud moved to a larger space and he decided to open another project. Café Boulud is designed to be more casual than its predecessor, yet created with the intent to maintain high-quality offerings. The food is clearly fresh and undoubtedly delicious, but not superb. The chefs seem to excel when working with fish, seafood, or vegetables. Meat dishes are a little disappointing. However, with each month bringing a new variation on a dish or a different flavor inspired by a new destination, the meat or chicken could be transformed into something very special. The choice of breads—such as sourdough, pumpkin seed, and olive—also varies depending on the chef's whim and the availability of ingredients. Service is well-paced and professional. Desserts are a little overly sweet except for the poached pear in wine sauce. The fresh, hot madeleines served at the table in a linen funnel at the end of the meal are a lovely treat. Take advantage of the prix-fixe lunch menu before you commit to a hefty bill at dinner. If the season is right, though, you might find that dinner will be well worth the cost.

Café con Leche ★★½

DOMINICAN	INEXPENSIVE	QUALITY ★★★★	VALUE ★★★★★

424 Amsterdam Avenue (between 80th and 81st streets), Upper West Side; ☎ 212-595-7000; www.cafeconlechenyc.com

Reservations Accepted Monday–Wednesday only. **When to go** Anytime; especially for bargain weekday lunch specials. **Entrée range** $10–$30. **Payment** All major credit cards. **Service rating** ★★½ **Friendliness rating** ★★★ **Bar** Full service. **Wine selection** Limited. **Dress** Casual. **Disabled access** Small step up; restrooms not accessible. **Customers** Locals. **Hours** Daily, 8 a.m.–11 p.m.; weekend and holiday brunch, 8 a.m.–4 p.m.

SETTING AND ATMOSPHERE This sunny cafe looks like any old joint from outside, but the interior is a pleasant surprise: a pizazzy, updated coffee shop with a colorful, tropical (carnival masks, silver trim on bright yellow walls) look.

HOUSE SPECIALTIES The pernil asado (roast pork) is intense, amazingly rich stuff; delicious, revisionist chicharrones de pollo (chunks of on-bone chicken) are herbacious and expertly deep fried with a batter that's more St. Louis than San Juan. Black bean soup is awesome, with good, crunchy onions, and sancocho (a ubiquitous, thick Dominican soup), often a special, is even better—an intense golden brown broth, clearly the product of long, careful cooking, with lovingly cooked root vegetables and a few chunks of pork. Beans and rice, served in appealing decorative bowls, are quite good (the rice is never dry here), and both tostones (starchy green plantains) and maduros (sweet ripe plantains) are skillfully fried.

OTHER RECOMMENDATIONS The condiments almost steal the show; there's a sensational hot sauce with incendiary flecks of black, green, and red and an innocent-looking thick white dressing that looks like sour cream but is actually potent garlic sauce . . . great on bread toasts. Not all the clever touches work: surprisingly light and greaseless mofongo (fried mash of plantains, pork, and garlic) comes with a fatally overwrought gravy, and the Cuban sandwiches taste too cleaned-up—not compressed, greasy, or garlicky enough for the flavors to come together.

SUMMARY AND COMMENTS Café con Leche is the diametrical opposite of those trendy, Pan-Latino fusion places. The latter tend to start with $4 million and a publicist and try to graft Latino flavors onto the kitchen's carefully designed Product. Café con Leche has solid Dominican coffeeshop credentials: the salsa recordings are what the staff wants to hear, not "Latin atmosphere"; the roast pork is rich and garlicky; and they shmoosh the bread slices when they toast them. Their innovative touches—for example, that frothy purée of a garlic sauce replacing the standard emulsion of garlic chunks and oil—have grown organically from serious tradition. There's a second Café con Leche farther up Amsterdam Avenue (at #726), but it's nowhere near as good.

Café Mogador ★★½

MOROCCAN   MODERATE   QUALITY ★★★★   VALUE ★★★★★

101 St. Marks Place, East Village; ☎ **212-677-2226;**
www.cafemogador.com

Reservations Accepted (necessary Wednesdays). **When to go** Anytime (arrive by 8 p.m. for the Wednesday night belly dancing). **Entrée range** $9–$16. **Payment** All major credit cards. **Service rating** ★★★ **Friendliness rating** ★★ **Bar** Beer and wine only. **Wine selection** House. **Dress** Casual. **Disabled access** Very poor. **Customers** Local. **Hours** Daily, 9 a.m.–1 a.m.; weekend brunch, 11 a.m.–4 p.m.

SETTING AND ATMOSPHERE Mogador looks less Moroccan than a standard-issue East Village bohemian cafe. It's a casual space below street level with tiny tables, faux oil lamps, and ceiling fans.

HOUSE SPECIALTIES Several flavors of tagine (a thick, complex stew made with chicken or lamb, served over rice or couscous), bastilla (an exotic dish of sweet and savory chopped chicken in flaky pastry) containing real saffron, homemade baklava (very sweet and cinnamony), and great fresh-squeezed pulpy lemonade, served with a mint leaf.

SUMMARY AND COMMENTS If you're a fan of Moroccan cooking—or are looking for an authentic experience—stay away. This leisurely East Village cafe doesn't purport to serve the Real Deal. But it's not fake tourist fodder, either—they do honest Moroccan American food, as if made from hand-me-down recipes from someone's great-grandmother. The little appetizer plates (you'll be shown a trayful of selections) are tempting simple things like spicy sliced carrots, peppery garlic potatoes, and long-stewed chicken livers. As with the rest of the menu, all are pleasing but none attention-grabbing; this is more everyday food than a special occasion eat. The cafe's relaxing (the busboys are too relaxed; you must beg and whimper for water), a rare Manhattan place where you can eat an exotic (but not too exotic) bite, look out the window, sigh, and daydream.

Café Sabarsky ★★★★

AUSTRIAN   MODERATE/EXPENSIVE   QUALITY ★★★½   VALUE ★★★

1048 Fifth Avenue, Upper East Side; ☎ **212-288-0665; www.wallse.com**

Reservations Not necessary. **When to go** Mid-to-late afternoon. **Entrée range** $10–$25. **Payment** All major credit cards. **Service rating** ★★★½ **Friendliness rating** ★★★ **Bar** Beer only. **Wine selection** Very small. **Disabled access** Yes. **Dress** Casual chic. **Customers** Locals, ladies who lunch, gallery viewers. **Hours**

Monday and Wednesday, 9 a.m.–6 p.m.; Thursday–Sunday, 9 a.m.–9 p.m.; breakfast served 9–11 a.m.; closed Tuesday.

SETTING AND ATMOSPHERE A perfect place to have either a late lunch or a coffee and dessert break on an autumnal or winter afternoon. The cafe has a typical Viennese coffeehouse feel, with newspapers on wooden sticks, marble-topped tables, dark wood, and an impressive selection of cakes displayed on one side of the space.

HOUSE SPECIALTIES Spring pea soup; spatzle with mushrooms and sweet corn; sausage with sauerkraut; sachertorte; apple streudel

OTHER RECOMMENDATIONS Matjes herring sandwich; trout crêpes; guglhupf (marble cake).

SUMMARY AND COMMENTS Set in a beautiful stone building that is part of the Neue Galerie, a gallery dedicated to German and Austrian art, the cafe exudes refinement. Even when the space is full, which is often, it never seems noisy. While the savory lunch dishes conceived by chef Kurt Gutenbrunner are delicious, the main attractions are his sweet pastries, which pair wonderfully with a coffee of one's preference. The presentation of the coffee on a silver tray with accompanying glass of water is as much true to Viennese style as is the décor. If you try to go before or after the lunch rush (noon–1:45 p.m.), you'll be less likely to have to wait for a table. Cabaret evenings combined with a prix-fixe dinner sometimes occur—call for information. If you'd like to try more of Chef Gutenbrunner's dishes, check out **Wallse** (344 West 11th Street; ☎ 212-352-2300). Keep in mind that **Café Fledermaus** is a recent addition to the Neue Galerie and is downstairs from Café Sabarsky—same food, different ambience.

Calle Ocho ★★★

NUEVO LATINO	MODERATE	QUALITY ★★★★	VALUE ★★★½

446 Columbus Avenue (between 81st and 82nd streets), Upper West Side; ☎ 212-873-5025; www.calleochonyc.com

Reservations Recommended. When to go Anytime. Entrée range $17–$30. Payment All major credit cards. Service rating ★★★ Friendliness rating ★★★ Bar Full service. Wine selection Heavy on Spanish, Argentinean, and Chilean. Dress Casual, hip. Disabled access Dining room, yes; restrooms, no. Customers Locals, trendies. Hours Monday–Thursday, 6–11 p.m.; Friday, 6 p.m.–midnight; Saturday, 5 p.m.–midnight; Sunday, 11 a.m.–3 p.m. (brunch) and 5–10 p.m.

SETTING AND ATMOSPHERE Formerly home to Main Street, the front area has been transformed into a colorful bar/lounge, complete with its own singles scene and highlighted by a technicolor wall of brightly lit circles. The cavernous main dining room has the look and feel of a fancy airplane hangar, and may be just as loud. Bottom line: Downtown is uptown at this happening spot. Cool and fun are the operative words.

HOUSE SPECIALTIES Puerto Rican rum-glazed jumbo shrimp with crispy onions and avocado salsa; Caribbean lobster ceviche in a passion fruit mojo; Jamacian jerk chicken; mango bread pudding.

OTHER RECOMMENDATIONS Sweet corn arepa with braised short ribs and spicy radish salad; lobster empanada; spicy oxtail stew; black beans and rick; yucca fries; Spanish chocolate fritters.

SUMMARY AND COMMENTS Brought to you by the owners of Rain, Calle Ocho brings sass and style to the Upper West Side restaurant scene. Chef Alex Garcia comes from Patria, and the pedigree shows in the lively presentation and brash blending of flavors. Appetizers are clearly the highlight here. Lobster ceviche comes heaped on top of fresh mangoes with passion fruit and a splash of hot sauce. Puerto Rican rum–glazed shrimp, the best of the lot, are big, bold, and fantastic. And fragrant arepa warms the soul. You may find yourself chewing longer than you normally would, as each sultry bite reveals a new layer of flavor. Entrées lack the same impact, though spicy adobo-rubbed pork loin is more than respectable, and carnivores will savor the Argentine hanger steak. Salt lovers will appreciate the chef's heavy-handedness. Fish entrées like the red snapper try too hard and come up short. The churros (elongated donut-type desserts) are made to order, making them a prime dessert choice. This is a super place for a date.

kids Candle Café ★★★½

VEGETARIAN/VEGAN   INEXPENSIVE/MODERATE   QUALITY ★★★★   VALUE ★★★½

**1307 Third Avenue (between 74th and 75th streets), Upper East Side;
☎ 212-472-0970; www.candlecafe.com.**

Reservations Not necessary. When to go Anytime. Entrée range $8–$18. Payment All major credit cards. Service rating ★★★½ Friendliness rating ★★★★ Bar Only juice bar. Wine selection A few choices of organic reds and whites. Dress Casual and/or funky. Disabled access Yes. Customers Regulars, locals, vegans, herbivores, and even closeted carnivores. Hours Monday–Saturday, 11:30 a.m.–10:30 p.m.; Sunday, 11:30 a.m.–9:30 p.m.

SETTING AND ATMOSPHERE Except for off-peak times, Candle Café is often full of people and good vibes. The juice bar, with a good view of the vast selection of ripe fruits and veggies on offer and a bright chalkboard listing the drinks, dominates the entrance. Wooden tables line the walls along a medium-sized, rectangular space. Pro-veggie reading material is available at the bar. This is a popular spot for prams at lunchtime, but keep in mind that it's often incredibly busy. Kids who like their greens will find plenty here to satisfy.

HOUSE SPECIALTIES Anything from the juice bar; Aztec salad (barbequed seitan, pumpkin seeds, mixed greens, quinoa, black beans, corn, and red onions); soba noodle salad, ginger-miso stir-fry; macrobiotic life platter.

OTHER RECOMMENDATIONS Carrot-ginger dressing; cornbread; chocolate cake; daily wraps; many of their daily specials; tofu club.

SUMMARY AND COMMENTS Don't let the vegetarian label scare you away. The food here is well prepared and often so well executed that you might not even miss the taste of meat. Daily specials include combinations such as lemon parsley ravioli with artichoke filling served with spinach in a roasted tomato truffle sauce; and cumin seed–crusted tofu with eggplant and chickpea masala, coconut brown basmati rice, and lemon-date chutney. Call beforehand or check the web for their daily specials. You can also stop here for a quick smoothie or fresh fruit or vegetable juice. Staff are knowledgeable and not militant about their food predilections, which makes for a calm dining experience, even when the place is packed. Candle Café has been so successful that they opened another, slightly more formal space, **Candle 79,** not far away at 154 East 79th Street (corner of Lexington Avenue).

Cendrillon ★★★

FILIPINO/ASIAN	MODERATE	QUALITY ★★★★	VALUE ★★★★

45 Mercer Street (between Broome and Grand streets), Soho;
☎ **212-343-9012; www.cendrillon.com**

Reservations Recommended. **When to go** Anytime. **Entrée range** $16–$23; appetizers $5.50–$11. **Payment** AE, MC, V. **Service rating** ★★★ **Friendliness rating** ★★★ **Wine selection** Good, and good range of prices. **Dress** Casual. **Disabled access** Yes. **Customers** Ethnic, local. **Hours** Tuesday–Friday, 11 a.m.–4 p.m. and 6–11 p.m.; Saturday and Sunday, 11 a.m.–4 p.m. (brunch) and 6–11 p.m.

SETTING AND ATMOSPHERE A few twinkling lights on a relatively quiet street mark the entry to this unusually shaped but inviting Soho establishment. Comfortable booths with carved wooden tables front the open kitchen and lead to an airy, high-ceilinged back dining room. Exposed brick walls throughout, accented with touches of carved wood, hold changing exhibits of contemporary paintings.

HOUSE SPECIALTIES Amy's spring roll; grilled squid salad with eggplant fritter; chicken adobo; Romy's spareribs; black rice paella with crab, shrimp, and Manila clams; banana crêpe with banana, rum, and cashew ice cream; blueberry and purple yam tart with young coconut sorbet.

OTHER RECOMMENDATIONS Grilled oxtail kare-kare; Balinese lamb shank with tomatillo and mango chutney; salt-roasted duck with cellophane noodles; warm chocolate cake with passion fruit sorbet.

SUMMARY AND COMMENTS Chef/owner Romy Doroton offers fine Filipino fare and enhances his menu with a few "fusion" features that showcase his flare with Asian ingredients. Doroton and his staff are wonderfully helpful and friendly and make this an excellent place to try a new cuisine—still of the Asian persuasion, but different enough to make it fun and intriguing. Remember to leave room for one of the fine desserts and cleanse your palate with one of Cendrillon's rare exotic teas, brought directly from China. You can also buy Southeast Asian products and gifts.

Chanterelle ★★★★

FRENCH	VERY EXPENSIVE	QUALITY ★★★★½	VALUE ★★★★

2 Harrison Street (at Hudson Street), Tribeca; ☎ **212-966-6960;**
www.chanterellenyc.com

Reservations A must. **When to go** Anytime. **Entrée range** $22–$30; prix-fixe lunch, $42; prix-fixe dinner, $85, $95, and $115. **Payment** All major credit cards. **Service rating** ★★★★ **Friendliness rating** ★★★ **Bar** Full service. **Wine selection** Excellent. **Dress** Dressy. **Disabled access** Yes. **Customers** Local. **Hours** Tuesday–Saturday, noon–2:30 p.m. and 5:30–11 p.m.; Monday, 5:30–11 p.m.

SETTING AND ATMOSPHERE Elegance prevails; peachy, sort of chanterelle-colored walls are punctuated with dark, carved wood panels. Polished brass chandeliers light the room warmly, and well-spaced tables make intimate dining more than a possibility.

HOUSE SPECIALTIES Grilled seafood sausage; loin of lamb with cumin salt crust; bacon-wrapped roast leg of red venison; grilled turbot with celery root and white truffle coulis.

OTHER RECOMMENDATIONS Fennel-marinated salmon; Maine sea scallops sautéed with winter vegetables; seared duck breast; five-spice chocolate crème brûlée with banana milk chocolate roll.

SUMMARY AND COMMENTS Chanterelle is one of only a handful of restaurants to garner four stars from the *New York Times,* yet it isn't content to simply rest on its laurels. Chef David Waltuck changes the menu every six weeks, and every six weeks patrons will find creative, daring, and delicious food. One constant is the seafood sausage, always grilled to perfection and intensely satisfying. Though Chanterelle is well worth every penny and is a grand place to celebrate a special occasion, you might try it for lunch ($42 prix fixe) if your pennies are otherwise allocated.

Chennai Garden ★★★

INDIAN/KOSHER/VEGETARIAN   INEXPENSIVE   QUALITY ★★★½   VALUE ★★★★

129 East 27th Street, Gramercy Park and Madison Square;
☎ **212-689-1999; www.chennaigarden.com**

Reservations Not necessary. **When to go** Lunch. **Entrée range** $7–$15. **Payment** All major credit cards. **Service rating** ★★★½ **Friendliness rating** ★★★ **Bar** Beer only. **Wine selection** Very small. **Dress** Casual. **Disabled access** No. **Customers** Locals, ethnic, regulars, vegetarians. **Hours** Tuesday–Sunday, 11:30 a.m.–3 p.m. and 5–10 p.m.

SETTING AND ATMOSPHERE Perhaps the lack of atmosphere is what enables the food to be sold at such low prices. It's not that there's anything wrong with the décor, it's simply not a factor. The space is modestly sized and filled with tables both in the middle and lined along the walls. Everything is clean, but nothing catches the eye—but that's okay, because the focus is definitely the food.

HOUSE SPECIALTIES Dosai (also known as dosa—rice and lentil flour crepe) of various descriptions, including one with onions and potatoes, masala, and butter; chana saag curry (spinach and chickpea).

OTHER RECOMMENDATIONS Buffet lunch; lassi; coconut chutney; samosa.

SUMMARY AND COMMENTS Chennai Garden caught the attention of the *New York Times* within months of its opening and has gained a steady following ever since. How it manages to produce freshly prepared, natural and/or organic and flavorful South Indian fare at such low prices is both a mystery and a blessing. The buffet lunch is so popular that there's no danger of food sitting too long in a pan or becoming stale. The fare is so tasty that one forgets there's not a hint of meat. The food is kosher as well!

Churrascaria Plataforma ★★★

BRAZILIAN	MODERATE	QUALITY ★★★★	VALUE ★★★★

316 West 49th Street, Midtown West, Times Square, and the Theater District; ☎ 212-245-0505; www.churrascariaplataforma.com

Reservations Recommended. **When to go** Avoid weekend dinner rush; probably too heavy for lunch. **Entrée range** Prix fixe $40 ($9 for lunch); children under 5 years, free; ages 5–10 years, half-price. **Payment** All major credit cards. **Service rating** ★ **Friendliness rating** ★★★ **Bar** Full. **Wine selection** Decent. **Dress** Casual. **Disabled access** Restrooms not accessible. **Customers** Tourists, professionals (at lunch), pretheater. **Hours** Daily, noon–midnight.

SETTING AND ATMOSPHERE Enormous space, dominated by a monster salad bar at center. Desserts and cocktails are dispensed by beautiful young waitresses wheeling carts. The place is brightly lit, with refined, understated décor, but amid all the swirling meat and trips to the salad bar, who's paying attention? Sound level is high at peak times.

HOUSE SPECIALTIES All-you-can-eat meat, with all the trimmings (including gigunda Brazilian salad bar and good fried stuff).

OTHER RECOMMENDATIONS Caipirinhas are the traditional accompaniment; they're a cocktail of cachaça (a spirit similar to rum) and lots of fresh lime. Here, they also make them with passion fruit for an extra-tropical flavor.

ENTERTAINMENT AND AMENITIES Live Brazilian music Wednesday through Sunday nights.

SUMMARY AND COMMENTS Rodizio is a Brazilian tradition where all-you-can-eat roast meats are brought to your table by skewer-bearing waiters. It's all very ritualized in Brazil, and this is the only one of a rash of local rodizios that observes all the rituals (it's also the only one that's Brazilian-owned and -run). You're served the traditional plates of fried yucca, french fries, batter-fried bananas, and particularly good fried polenta. Management hopes you'll fill up on this cheap stuff, as well as the extensive salad bar (vegetarians will be more than sated: tons of salads, vegetables, and even a few entrées in their own rights, like the good shrimp moqueca, a peppery stew with coconut milk), but savvy diners hold out for the meat. Pace yourself carefully as more than a dozen cuts come around. The best thing of all doesn't come unless you ask for it, though: unbelievably delicious black beans, made from specially imported small and silky beans. Spoon farofa (garlicky toasted yucca flour) over them. If all the meat doesn't give you a coronary, the service will; confused and incompetent waiters take their cue from the managers, who pompously stroll through in suit and ties, scanning the room for trouble spots and summarily ignoring your desperate pleas for service, dessert, or the check. Bad service also extends to the reservations line; call three times and you'll get three different answers regarding table availability.

EJ's Luncheonette ★★

AMERICAN	INEXPENSIVE	QUALITY ★★★	VALUE ★★★½

432 Sixth Avenue (Ninth and Tenth streets), Greenwich Village;
☎ **212-473-5555; 447 Amsterdam Avenue (81st and 82nd streets),**
Upper West Side; ☎ **212-873-3444;**
1271 Third Avenue (at 73rd Street), Upper East Side; ☎ **212-472-0600**

Reservations Not accepted. **When to go** Anytime. **Entrée range** $9–$12; appetizers, $5–$9. **Payment** Cash only. **Service rating** ★★★ **Friendliness rating** ★★★ **Wine selection** Limited; three house wines. **Dress** Casual. **Disabled access** All on one level. **Customers** Locals and local children. **Hours** Daily, 8 a.m.–11 p.m., but hours vary slightly by location.

SETTING AND ATMOSPHERE Think *Happy Days*. This luncheonette could just as well be on Main Street in Small Town, U.S.A. It's straight-up 1950s "Dinersville" all the way from the blue-and-white vinyl booths with Formica tables to the counter with blue-topped stools. The separate locations differ in detail only.

HOUSE SPECIALTIES Buttermilk or multigrain flapjacks with a dozen different toppings; ditto for the buttermilk or bran Belgian waffles; Caesar salad; EJ's club sandwich; salami and eggs, pancake-style; great home fries; Stewart's root beer float.

OTHER RECOMMENDATIONS Macaroni and cheese; grilled tuna club with wasabi; Thai chicken salad; EJ's chicken Reuben. Check the daily specials and the special kid's menu.

SUMMARY AND COMMENTS This New York standby packs it in with people of all ages, solo diners, couples, and families small and large. They come for the large portions, kid-friendly atmosphere, and good, familiar food. There may be a wait, but service is so fast that once you sit down you'll be out before you can sing "Blueberry Hill." Great place for breakfast or weekend brunch, but watch out for those weekend crowds.

El Papasito ★★

DOMINICAN	INEXPENSIVE	QUALITY ★★★½	VALUE ★★★★★

346 West 53rd (near Ninth Avenue), Midtown West, Times Square, and the Theater District; ☎ **212-265-2225 or 212-265-2227**

Reservations Not required. **When to go** Anytime. **Entrée range** $7–$22. **Payment** All major credit cards. **Service rating** ★½ **Friendliness rating** ★★ **Bar** Beer and wine only. **Wine selection** Minimal. **Dress** Casual. **Disabled access** Small step up; restroom doors narrow. **Customers** Local Latinos. **Hours** Daily, 7 a.m.–11 p.m.

SETTING AND ATMOSPHERE Narrow space allowing for simple square tables and wooden backed chairs with a few colorful paintings on the walls. If the space is too crowded, you can order to go. Not much of an atmosphere, but authentic music is often played in the background.

HOUSE SPECIALTIES New York is shockingly bean deprived, quality-wise, but El Papasito is legume heaven; several dishes (possibilities include white, pink, red, and black beans, chick/pigeon peas, etc.) are made daily, each accorded the respect of its own recipe (silky, intense black beans have a hit of vinegar, pink beans are more starkly elemental). Mofungo—a fried mash of starchy plantains, garlic, and pork that's one of the heaviest dishes on earth (and easy to miss under the "side orders" heading)— here somehow manages to taste light and greaseless, served with a cup of delicious intense gravy that's instantly absorbed. Chicharrones are crunchy pieces of on-bone pork or chicken, not just fried skin (as the dish is often mistranslated); squirt lime over them. Asopado is a thick, intensely garlicky rice soup; one order is easily enough for three. Don't miss stewed goat when it's a special or the off-menu silky yucca (a yam-ish vegetable elsewhere cooked to death), served with great marinated onions that enhance the sweetness of the tuber. Chicken in any form (ubiquitous on the daily specials menu) is dependably good, and flan (caramel custard) is downright fantastic—just the right balance of ultra-eggy richness and lightness, with a non-cloying intense caramel sauce.

SUMMARY AND COMMENTS This is the class act for Dominican cooking in lower Manhattan. El Papasito serves—in a jazzy, approachable ambience—great, fresh plates with all the soulful authenticity of a Spanish Harlem hole-in-the-wall. Surprisingly, the café con leche is mediocre. Servers are very friendly but utterly unprofessional; they speak decent English, but you'll ask twice for silverware, and the check is a major production (also, beware of the dreaded pre-dessert Windex tabletop spray-down). Perhaps the waiters figure that with food so good at such low prices, they don't need to do much more than carry plates . . . and they may be right.

Firebird ★★★

RUSSIAN	EXPENSIVE	QUALITY ★★★★	VALUE ★★★★

365 West 46th Street (between Eighth and Ninth avenues), Midtown West, Times Square, and the Theater District; ☎ 212-586-0244; www.firebirdrestaurant.com

Reservations Recommended. **When to go** Anytime. **Entrée range** $20–$38 (lower range includes hefty appetizer prices); $38 prix fixe. **Payment** All major credit cards. **Service rating** ★★★ **Friendliness rating** ★★★ **Bar** Full service, with a selection of 14 vodkas. **Wine selection** Good, with some surprisingly low-priced choices. **Dress** Upscale casual, Theater District dressy. **Disabled access** Yes. **Customers** Theatergoers, locals, tourists. **Hours** Wednesday, 11:15 a.m.–2:30 p.m. and 5:15–11:15 p.m.; Tuesday, Thursday, and Friday, 5:15–11:15 p.m.; Saturday, 11:15 a.m.–2:30 p.m. and 5:15–11:15 p.m.; Sunday, 5:15–8:15 p.m.

SETTING AND ATMOSPHERE Two spruced-up brownstones stand behind gilt-edged gates manned by a Cossack-costumed sentry. No, you're not really in imperial St. Petersburg, but you're close. The fabulously over-done, charmingly ornate interior, with eight rooms and two pretty bars, is decorated with chandeliers, lushly patterned carpets, Fabergé-ish objects, Russian wall hangings, ballet costumes, and ancient books. Despite the pomp, the greeting is gracious and the atmosphere not at all forbidding.

HOUSE SPECIALTIES Wild mushroom and three-grain soup; buckwheat blini with sour cream; lightly smoked salmon with cucumber salad and five-grain bread; crab and rice croquettes with mâche; grilled marinated sturgeon; Uzbek skewered quail; pelmeni Siberian.

OTHER RECOMMENDATIONS Kasha wild mushroom salad; roasted eggplant caviar; Karsky shashlik; roast chicken with bulgur-okra salad; Armenian yogurt-spiced lamb.

SUMMARY AND COMMENTS Firebird prides itself on detail—the china was spe-cially designed, the waitstaff garbed by Oleg Cassini—and on serving the authentic cuisine of czarist Russia in the ambience of equal authen-ticity. Best of all, it's fun; you actually hear people say "Wow!" when they walk in. The seven-course "Taste of the Tsars" menu is $80 per per-son. It's a wonderfully theatrical addition to Theater District dining.

Florent ★★½

DINER/BISTRO	MODERATE	QUALITY ★★★½	VALUE ★★★★

69 Gansevoort Street (between Washington and Hudson streets), Greenwich Village; ☎ 212-989-5779; www.restaurantflorent.com

Reservations Not accepted. **When to go** Anytime. **Entrée range** $10–$24. **Pay-ment** Cash only. **Service rating** ★★★ **Friendliness rating** ★★★ **Bar** Full service. **Wine selection** Minimal. **Dress** Anything goes. **Disabled access** Yes. **Customers** Anything goes. **Hours** Daily, 24 hours.

SETTING AND ATMOSPHERE Turn the corner of Hudson Street and you leave the bistro-fied West Village for Manhattan's gentrified former meat market. Florent, an elongated ur-diner, sits in the middle of the block and fits in perfectly. There's not a frill in sight, unless you count the late-night/early-morning clientele and the occasional paper streamers and strings of pearls festooning the interior. (Or as a charming waiter put it, "We're always decorating with something tacky.") The atmosphere is set by the crowd that ranges from debs and celebs to ordinary and extraordinary New Yorkers of every hue and persuasion. Opened in 1985, Florent was hip way before the meatpacking district "packed up" and became the new place to be seen.

HOUSE SPECIALTIES Check daily specials; dry aged New York sirloin au poivre; meat loaf with mashed potatoes; boudin noir with apples and onions; omelet with smoked salmon and arugula (brunch); crème caramel; moules frites.

OTHER RECOMMENDATIONS Homemade rillettes with roasted garlic; moules frites; steak (aged rib-eye) frites; chicken breast stuffed with wild mush-rooms; many of the soups du jour.

SUMMARY AND COMMENTS This is a great after-hours spot—supper and break-fast are served from midnight on—and it's just as good at other times. The food, a balance of bistro and diner dishes, is hearty and plentiful, and the people-watching may not be hearty, but it certainly is an eyeful. The waitstaff, young and ebullient, seems to be having as good a time as the customers. The board over the bar always has some interesting, amusing, and/or cryptic messages.

Gigino ★★½

ITALIAN	MODERATE	QUALITY ★★★	VALUE ★★★½

20 Battery Place, Lower Manhattan; ☎ 212-528-2228;
www.gigino-wagnerpark.com

Reservations Suggested. When to go On a sunny day. Entrée range $15–$27. Payment All major credit cards. Service rating ★★★½ Friendliness rating ★★★½ Bar Full service. Wine selection Not bad. Dress Business casual. Disabled access Yes. Customers Locals, business, tourists. Hours Monday–Thursday, 11:30 a.m.–10:30 p.m.; Friday, 11:30 a.m.–1 a.m.; Saturday and Sunday, 11:30 a.m.–11 p.m.

SETTING AND ATMOSPHERE There aren't many ground-level dining establish-ments in New York that boast fantastic views at such reasonable prices. In spite of feeling as if you're bound to go subterranean once you enter, the narrow entrance opens up to a medium-sized space with a huge window overlooking New York Harbor and the Statue of Liberty. For those who think they are unlucky to be seated with their backs to the window, a mirror (positioned just above eye level so you won't need to see your own face with your mouth full) will provide you with a similar view. During warmer weather, parts of the window open up onto a patio where al fresco dining takes place.

HOUSE SPECIALTIES Gazpacho; grilled calamari; homemade chicken sausage.

OTHER RECOMMENDATIONS Angel hair pasta with shrimp, broccoli, and pep-pers; penna alla Norma; Esotica salad; calamari fritti.

SUMMARY AND COMMENTS This eatery has been chosen for it's super views and location. The food, although certainly tasty, is not the best Italian available, but you should make allowances for the trade-off of a lovely vista. If it's too cold to dine outside, be sure to get a table against the wall opposite the big window. Once you're fed and watered, take a stroll up the West Side along the Hudson River Park path, or, if you're not keen to go far, walk down to the tip of Manhattan to Battery Park.

Gobo ★★½

VEGAN/VEGETARIAN	MODERATE	QUALITY ★★★½	VALUE ★★★

1426 Third Avenue, Upper East Side; ☎ 212-288-5099;
401 Avenue of the Americas, Greenwich Village; ☎ 212-255-3902;
www.goborestaurant.com

Reservations Not necessary. When to go Anytime. Entrée range $8–$17. Payment All major credit cards. Service rating ★★★½ Friendliness rating ★★★ Bar Fine selection of organic wines and beer. Wine selection Limited. Dress

Casual chic. **Disabled access** Yes. **Customers** Locals, vegans, vegetarians, and the carnivore curious. **Hours** Daily, noon–11 p.m.

SETTING AND ATMOSPHERE   The atmosphere is decidedly non-crunchy and not tie-dyed; rather it attracts health-conscious and eco-aware types that can afford stylish organic cotton and French lentil truffle soup. The interior includes well-lit square-shaped space with tables both in the center and along the sides of the walls and windows, and fresh décor in hues of light green, cream, and pale wood. The focal point on the main wall is a beautifully polished portion of a tree trunk.

HOUSE SPECIALTIES   Green tea noodle with smoked seitan, teriyaki sauce, and pickled papaya; creamy corn polenta with roasted mushrooms; nori wrapped tofu in red Thai curry sauce.

OTHER RECOMMENDATIONS   Anything from the juice bar; five-spice tofu rolls with mango puree; scallion pancakes; creamed spinach gratin with prunes and cognac.

SUMMARY AND COMMENTS   Gone are the days when meatless food was equated with tasteless cubes of tofu thrown over a bowl of overcooked vegetables. In fact, with each update of this guide, we can't ignore the increase of meat-free kitchens providing new and innovative fare. The newer Upper East Side location for Gobo opened in 2004 and the chef de cuisine, Yuki Chen—creator of many of the **Zen Palate** (see profile) dishes—has extended the food influences to include Pan-Asian tastes of Malaysia, Japan, Thailand, India, and Vietnam. The fresh juice and herbal drink list is useful for knowing which elixir will ease which malaise. The vegan chocolate cake dusted with green tea is surprisingly tasty considering it contains no butter. To finish off food of this caliber, it would be a bonus to have the option of organic and fair-trade espresso on the menu—but perhaps that wouldn't be healthy . . . .

Gotham Bar & Grill   ★★★½

NEW AMERICAN   EXPENSIVE   QUALITY ★★★★   VALUE ★★★

12 East 12th Street (between University Place and Fifth Avenue), Greenwich Village; ☎ **212-620-4020; www.gothambarandgrill.com**

Reservations Recommended. **When to go** Anytime. **Entrée range** $15–$37; three-course prix-fixe lunch; $25. **Payment** AE, MC, V. **Service rating** ★★ **Friendliness rating** ★★ **Bar** Full service. **Wine selection** Very good. **Dress** Business, dressy, casual chic. **Disabled access** No. **Customers** Business, local. **Hours** Monday–Thursday, noon–2 p.m. and 5:30–10 p.m.; Friday, noon–2 p.m. and 5:30–11 p.m.; Saturday, 5–11 p.m.; Sunday, 5–10 p.m.

SETTING AND ATMOSPHERE   This lofty space has been tamed by sophisticated alterations: grand, fabric-draped overhead lighting fixtures, tables on varying levels, ocher columns, teal trim, bountiful bouquets of flowers on pedestals and on the imposing bar. All is dimly lit and austerely opulent.

HOUSE SPECIALTIES   Soft-shell crab; seafood salad; seared yellowfin tuna; rack of lamb with garlic mashed potatoes; caramelized banana cake filled with bitter chocolate custard.

OTHER RECOMMENDATIONS Ricotta cheese ravioli; Chinese spiced duck breast with seared foie gras; red snapper in shellfish broth; lemon tart with warm blueberry compote.

SUMMARY AND COMMENTS Chef Alfred Portale, a major influence on New American cuisine and mentor to many of its now successful practitioners, continues to turn out reliable and memorable food. His soaring, structured presentations seem perfectly suited to the impressive room in which they are served. Gotham keeps its standing as a perennial favorite, both for the food and the welcoming predictability of it all.

Gramercy Tavern ★★★½

AMERICAN	EXPENSIVE	QUALITY ★★★★	VALUE ★★★

42 East 20th Street (between Broadway and Park Avenue South), Gramercy Park; ☎ 212-477-0777; www.gramercytavern.com

Reservations Essential in the main dining room. **When to go** Anytime. **Entrée range** $36 and $55 prix-fixe lunch; $76, $80, and $95 prix-fixe dinner. **Payment** All major credit cards. **Service rating** ★★★ **Friendliness rating** ★★ **Bar** Full service. **Wine selection** Excellent, many available by the glass or a three-ounce tasting glass; $25 corkage fee. **Dress** Anything goes; jacket suggested in the main dining room. **Disabled access** Yes. **Customers** Business, locals, celebs. **Hours** Monday–Thursday, noon–2 p.m. and 5:30–10 p.m.; Friday, noon–2 p.m. and 5:30–11 p.m.; Saturday, 5:30–11 p.m.; Sunday, 5:30–10 p.m.

SETTING AND ATMOSPHERE Lovely and inviting—flowers in profusion deck the entry, spill over a table near the open grill, ornament the dining spaces, even bloom in the restrooms. Floor-to-ceiling windows front the tavern room, with its big, black-topped bar, and boldly colored paintings of fruits and vegetables brighten the upper walls. The lighting in the more formal, cathedral-ceilinged dining rooms goes from early American to trendy glass buckets; the decorations follow suit with a few American primitive portraits, a quilt, and large metal starfish. Somehow it all works well together.

HOUSE SPECIALTIES Fondue of Maine crabmeat with sweet pea sauce, smoked bacon, and pink peppercorns; tuna tartare with cucumber vinaigrette; roasted sirloin and braised beef cheeks with farro, morels, and red wine; individual nectarine tatin.

OTHER RECOMMENDATIONS Marinated hamachi; roasted cod; salt-baked salmon; chocolate pudding; selection of cheeses.

SUMMARY AND COMMENTS Danny Meyer, the man who brought you Union Square Café (and Eleven Madison Park and Tabla), teamed up with chef Tom Colicchio to open this Gramercy-area winner in 1994. Gramercy has the same comfortable atmosphere and agreeable service that makes Union Square Café such a hit; the surprise lies in the food, which is more adventurous than that of its older sibling. The seafood fondues, a running theme at Gramercy, consistently please beyond expectation, and the meat entrées shine, especially the recently added roasted sirloin. Desserts are good but not memorable, so a selection of fine cheeses may be the way to go here. For a more informal and less expensive alternative, try the equally pleasing Tavern Room up front.

Grand Sichuan International ★★★

| CHINESE | MODERATE | QUALITY ★★★★ | VALUE ★★★★★ |

229 Ninth Avenue at 24th, Chelsea; ☎ 212-620-5200

Reservations Accepted. **When to go** Anytime. **Entrée range** $10–$16.95. **Payment** All major credit cards. **Service rating** ★★ **Friendliness rating** ★ **Bar** Beer and wine only. **Wine selection** Small. **Dress** Casual. **Disabled access** Good, but tight path to restrooms. **Customers** Locals. **Hours** Daily, 11:30 a.m.–11 p.m.

SETTING AND ATMOSPHERE To all appearances a generic, "nice" Midtown Chinese place, with track lighting, elegant shiny little black chairs, and nice tablecloths. Only the huge informational pamphlet-cum-textbook, unfurled across the length of the front window, tells you that this is not just another mediocre joint for gringo moo-shoo. Foodie passersby stop and gape at the menu as if it were a Christmas window at Macy's.

HOUSE SPECIALTIES Terrific spicy Szechuan cuisine, with some other hard-to-find (and good) regional dishes from Hunan, Shanghai, and even a small selection of "Mao's Home Cooking," culled from the former leader's little black book of favorite recipes (he had good taste; they're mostly winners). You can't go wrong if you stick with hot and spicy stuff and the fancier exotic specialties (borrow the informational pamphlet and choose from the more extolled items); avoid duller-sounding and more clichéd offerings (chow fun or egg rolls, for example, are wrong orders, and your taste buds will be punished accordingly). Don't miss tea-smoked duck (so smoky, so addictive), the spicy double-cooked pork, or any of the Shanghai "red cooking" dishes (none of which, peculiarly, appear on Mao's list of faves). Dan dan noodles with chili sauce is a popular starter that will get the peppery fires going.

OTHER RECOMMENDATIONS Beware: Grand Sichuan looks like a neighborhood generic Chinese restaurant, and it really does serve that function for the area. Don't be tempted by the cheap lunch and dinner specials (pepper steak, chicken with broccoli, etc). Sit down and pay a few more bucks for what this place does well.

SUMMARY AND COMMENTS Be warned: Sichuan (also known as Szechuan) cuisine is spicy, hearty, and oily. Complaining about the greasiness of, say, Sichuan twice-cooked pork is like objecting to the wetness of soup; it's a raison d'être. So . . . don't come here if you're on a diet. The aforementioned pamphlet—a thick swath of information written in great enthusiastic detail—makes a super guide to the restaurant's offerings. Unfortunately you won't have much time to read it—despite Grand Sichuan's relatively upscale Midtown décor, the rushed service is strictly Chinatown style. Despite endless ownership infighting and debate on the rights to the name, GSI has five other nominal locations: 125 Canal Street, ☎ 212-625-9212; 227 Lexington Avenue, ☎ 212-679-9770; 745 Ninth Avenue, ☎ 212-582-2288; 1049 Second Avenue,

☎ 212-355-5855; and 19–23 St. Mark's Place (at E. Eighth Street), ☎ 212-529-4800. Different owners and styles, but good food all around.

kids Gray's Papaya ★½

AMERICAN	INEXPENSIVE	QUALITY ★★★½	VALUE ★★★★★

2090 Broadway (at 72nd Street), Upper West Side; ☎ 212-799-0243
402 Sixth Avenue (at Eighth Street), Greenwich Village; ☎ 212-260-3532

Reservations Not necessary. **When to go** Anytime. **Entrée range** Less than $15. **Payment** Some loose change. **Service rating** ★ **Friendliness rating** ★½ **Bar** None. **Wine selection** Only if grape juice counts. **Dress** Pretty much anything, or nothing at all. **Disabled access** Drive-through accessibility. **Customers** Anybody and everybody (except vegetarians). **Hours** Daily, 24 hours.

SETTING AND ATMOSPHERE Cheery and cheap old-school orange counters, white tile, paper fruits hanging from the ceiling; décor is not exactly a priority here. Although it's not a place to bring kids for a sit-down meal, the food here is cheap and cheerful enough to satisfy a child who needs a quick fix and is prepared to nosh either standing up or al fresco.

HOUSE SPECIALTIES Hot dog; hot dog with mustard; hot dog with sauerkraut; hot dog with sautéed onions; hot dog with mustard, sauerkraut, and sautéed onions. They toast their buns for a crispier hot-dog experience.

OTHER RECOMMENDATIONS Hot dog with ketchup; hot dog with ketchup and mustard; hot dog with ketchup, mustard, sauerkraut, and sautéed onions. You get the idea.

SUMMARY AND COMMENTS New York wouldn't be New York without hot dogs, and Gray's is a New York institution. Although prices may have gone up by 50%, hot dogs are still only 75 cents a pop, and the recession special is by far the best deal in town at $2.45 for two dogs and a drink. The franks are grilled to perfection, leaving the skin crisp and locking in the flavor, and like all good wieners, come regular or well done. Everyone has a favorite, but all the fruity tropical drinks provide the perfect refreshment to wash down the best dogs in town.

Honmura An ★★★

JAPANESE (SOBA)	EXPENSIVE	QUALITY ★★★★	VALUE ★★★

170 Mercer Street, Soho; ☎ 212-334-5253

Reservations Recommended for dinner. **When to go** Anytime. **Entrée range** $10–$25. **Payment** All major credit cards. **Service rating** ★★★ **Friendliness rating** ★★★ **Bar** Wine, beer, and sake. **Wine selection** Fair. **Dress** Casual. **Disabled access** No. **Customers** Ethnic, local, Soho celebs. **Hours** Wednesday–Friday, noon–2:30 p.m. and 6–10:30 p.m.; Tuesday, Saturday, and Sunday, 6–10:30 p.m.

SETTING AND ATMOSPHERE Plain wooden stairs with a few distinctly Japanese flower arrangements lead to a serene second-floor space that's the epitome of elegant understatement. Large pieces of plain white rice paper hang on the high brick walls, and polished wooden tables and dark green banquettes circle the room. A glass-enclosed corner is dedicated to the in-house production of the soba (buckwheat) noodles used in most of the main dishes.

HOUSE SPECIALTIES Hot soba with sliced duck; anything soba; tempura, with rice in a lacquer box—and giant prawns specially shipped from a fish market in Tokyo; soba sushi, a sushi thick roll made of soba (what else!) with mashed prawns that must be ordered in advance.

OTHER RECOMMENDATIONS Seiro soba (cold soba noodles with dipping sauce) and zaru soba (the same thing except the noodles are topped with nori, chopped dried seaweed).

SUMMARY AND COMMENTS The soba specialties, uncommon and superb, plus the tranquil setting and unobtrusive service make this an extremely popular Soho spot. Most of the appetizers tend to be disappointing, so stick with what this place does best, and that's soba. Though prices are a bit high for the portions, you won't find much better soba in the city. Zaru soba is a great snack in the summer, and you're likely to crave it throughout the year. This is a subtle cuisine that could fast become a healthy addiction. The $18–$24 prix-fixe lunch makes a great intro, but the pricier $50 prix-fixe soba dinner may not be worth it.

Iammo Bello ★★½

ITALIAN CAFETERIA	INEXPENSIVE	QUALITY ★★★★	VALUE ★★★★★

39 East 60th Street, Upper East Side; ☎ 212-935-9418

Reservations Not accepted. **When to go** Early or late to miss the crowds, but queues move quickly even at peak hours. **Entrée range** $5.25–$8.50. **Payment** Major credit cards. **Service rating** ★★★½ **Friendliness rating** ★★★ **Bar** None. **Wine selection** None. **Dress** Casual. **Disabled access** No. **Customers** Locals, business. **Hours** Monday–Friday, 11:30 a.m.–4:30 p.m.; Saturday, 11:30 a.m.– 3 p.m.; closed Sunday.

SETTING AND ATMOSPHERE A quick-moving queue snakes through this subterranean cafeteria, past myriad steam tables manned by hyperkinetic servers. All remaining space is crammed with long tables full of harried, ravenous eaters, forks and jaws working at a prodigious pace. It's all so fast-paced that you feel as if a request to pass the salt might elicit a hail of shakers flung at you from all directions.

HOUSE SPECIALTIES Wonderful heroes like chicken, veal, eggplant, or meatball parmigiana (with good, funky Parmesan cheese rather than the usual clots of bad mozzarella); zesty chicken francese (hot only on Thursdays, other days available cold at the antipasto bar); delicious homey lasagna; soups; well-fried calamari (Fridays only). Skip the deftly flavored pastas if you demand al dente (impossible to achieve in a steam table), but you'll be missing a pretty good alfredo sauce.

OTHER RECOMMENDATIONS There are various fancy pizzas (including one with nicely grilled vegetables) as well as regular slices (intriguingly different from the usual Gotham slice) available from a separate concession in the back. Up front, the abundantly stocked self-service antipasto bar costs $5.75 a pound (don't miss the rice with vegetables).

SUMMARY AND COMMENTS Iammo Bello means "come here, handsome," in Italian, but this no-frills bustling cafeteria depends more on its cooking than its looks to attract. Chicken francese is downright scrumptious, and even rough, unsubtle dishes like lasagna taste soulful. There's a certain satisfaction that comes from having eaten a really good $8 meal in a neighborhood filled with mediocre $30 lunches. It's centrally located, and the food is certainly worlds above the heros, pastas, and salads served in local pizzerias.

Il Buco ★★★★

| FRENCH/SPANISH/ITALIAN | EXPENSIVE | QUALITY ★★★★½ | VALUE ★★★ |

47 Bond Street; ☎ 212-533-1932, The East Village; www.ilbuco.com

Reservations A must. **When to go** Anytime. **Entrée range** $16–$27. **Payment** AE, MC, V. **Service rating** ★★★ **Friendliness rating** ★★ **Bar** Full service. **Wine selection** Carefully selected collection of unusual (but savvy) choices. **Dress** Expensive informal. **Disabled access** Good. **Customers** Local. **Hours** Tuesday–Saturday, noon–4 p.m. and 6 p.m.–midnight; Sunday, 5–10 p.m.

SETTING AND ATMOSPHERE Antique store by day, restaurant by night, woody, atmospheric Il Buco has an old European farmhouse feeling quite unlike that of any other spot in the city. You eat at rough, candlelit tables surrounded by old furnishings and knickknacks, all for sale. It's tremendously romantic in its rustic way.

HOUSE SPECIALTIES Changing seasonal menu, but risottos, grilled octopus, homemade sausages, pastas, flourless chocolate cake, and plum cake are delicious fixtures.

ENTERTAINMENT AND AMENITIES The wine cellar allegedly was the inspiration for Edgar Allan Poe's story "The Cask of Amontillado," and it's got atmosphere galore; have a peek.

SUMMARY AND COMMENTS Il Buco's cooking incorporates French, Italian, and Spanish influences, and the chef shows considerable command in all three culinary languages; the risotto is creamy, peasanty, and completely unpretentious; the octopus tastes like first-hand Mediterranean rather than a cooking school grad working from a recipe. This rogue kitchen has its own distinctive style; it follows no trends. Though not widely known, Il Buco is much loved by a discerning few, and the smallish place fills up most nights. This is an especially good locale for special occasions—long tables can be reserved either in the middle of the main room or in a rear alcove.

Il Mulino ★★★½

| ITALIAN | EXPENSIVE | QUALITY ★★★★½ | VALUE ★★★★½ |

86 West Third Street (between Sullivan and Thompson), Greenwich Village; ☎ 212-673-3783

Reservations Highly recommended. **When to go** Anytime. **Entrée range** $22–$35. **Payment** All major credit cards. **Service rating** ★★★ **Friendliness rat-**

ing ★★★ **Bar** Full service. **Wine selection** Good. **Dress** Upscale, business suits. **Disabled access** Yes. **Customers** Business, local. **Hours** Monday–Friday, noon–2:30 p.m. and 5–11 p.m.; Saturday, 5–11 p.m.; closed Sunday.

SETTING AND ATMOSPHERE There's no mistaking this for a Village trattoria; low-key elegance and low-key lighting prevail from the small, pretty bar in the front to the single perfect rose and heavy white cloths on each table. Tall potted plants separate the dining room from the entrance; the ceiling is mercifully soundproofed, though this is hardly the place for a raucous crowd; and the walls that are not exposed brick are covered in soft, feathery wallpaper. The service is unobtrusively attentive.

HOUSE SPECIALTIES Check the daily specials; carpaccio; spaghettini carbonara; fillet of beef with caper sauce; rolled veal braised in wine, cream, and wild mushrooms; veal chop.

OTHER RECOMMENDATIONS Spaghettini with clams; spicy veal with anchovies, capers, and mushrooms; chicken and sausage in white wine; capellini Il Mulino; minestrone.

SUMMARY AND COMMENTS Most New Yorkers consider Il Mulino the best Italian in the the city, and with good reason. Complimentary appetizers, including delicious fried zucchini, superb salami, spicy bruschetta, and scrumptious chunks off the biggest slab of Parmigiano-Reggiano you've ever seen, will have your stomach running up the white flag before you've even ordered. The pastas prove addictive, like the rich capellini Il Mulino and perfect spaghettini carbonara, and the veal, in any of its multitude of preparations, is excellent. Portions are more than generous and one thing's certain—you won't leave here hungry. Finish your meal with a bang by taking in a glass of the potent homemade grappa.

Jackson Diner ★★½

| INDIAN | INEXPENSIVE/MODERATE | QUALITY ★★★½ | VALUE ★★★★★ |

37–47 74th Street, Jackson Heights; ☎ 718-672-1232

Reservations Not necessary. **When to go** Anytime. **Entrée range** $8–$21. **Payment** Cash only. **Service rating** ★★½ **Friendliness rating** ★★★ **Bar** Good Indian beer only. **Wine selection** None. **Dress** Casual. **Disabled access** Two steps into restaurant; none for restrooms. **Customers** Locals, ethnic, spice lovers. **Hours** Sunday–Thursday, 11:30 a.m.–10 p.m.; Friday and Saturday, 11:30 a.m.–10:30 p.m.

SETTING AND ATMOSPHERE A large, high-ceilinged room filled with no-nonsense tables and chairs ready to house the crowds of regulars and soon-to-be converted. To be brief: There is no atmosphere! Banquet hall also available.

HOUSE SPECIALTIES Shrimp curry with coconut and spices; lentil cakes (iddly) and other variations of Southern Indian pancakes and crêpes; sag paneer (spicy spinach and homemade cheese cubes); murg lajwab (chicken cooked with tomatoes, ginger, and cilantro).

OTHER RECOMMENDATIONS Lentil soup (mulligatawny); baignan bhurta (eggplant with onions, ginger, and tomatoes); dal diwan (yellow lentils with coriander and cumin); tandoori mix grill.

SUMMARY AND COMMENTS So many of the dishes here hit the spot and tantalize the taste buds—assuming you appreciate Indian spice blends. This is not a place for the weak-hearted, although you're allowed to choose from mild, medium to hot; it seems that the chef feels a lot more comfortable farther up the spicy scale. Hardly a surprise when the food is so authentic. The main concern here is delivering good food at incredibly reasonable prices, so the atmosphere isn't given much attention. Jackson Diner has received its fair share of awards for its food, and no doubt it will continue to take home a few more accolades. From the chutney to the lassi and everything in between, you won't be disappointed.

Jasmine ★★½

THAI	MODERATE	QUALITY ★★★	VALUE ★★★

1619 Second Avenue (at 84th Street), Upper East Side;
☎ **212-517-8854**

Reservations Not accepted. **When to go** Anytime. **Entrée range** $9.50–$17.50. **Payment** All major credit cards. **Service rating** ★★½ **Friendliness rating** ★★½ **Bar** Beer only. **Wine selection** Limited. **Dress** Casual. **Disabled access** Yes. **Customers** Locals. **Hours** Monday–Saturday, noon–10 p.m.; Sunday, 1–10 p.m.

SETTING AND ATMOSPHERE Dark, candlelit with lots of dark red wood and wooden tables and chairs. Clean, new, and comfortable with some Southeast Asian touches like potted palms and bamboo wall hangings. Nicer than most neighborhood Thai places, but certainly no Vong when it comes to décor.

HOUSE SPECIALTIES Steamed shrimp dumplings with garlic-ginger sauce; pad see yu (chow fun noodles with chicken or beef, Chinese broccoli, and eggs); spicy basil chicken with peppers, onions, and chili paste; gaeng penang (Thai red curry with beef or chicken, basil, coriander, pepper, and coconut milk).

OTHER RECOMMENDATIONS Po pia (spring rolls); tom kha gai (spicy Thai coconut milk soup); pad thai noodles; khao pad supparot (coconut fried rice with chicken topped with ground peanuts and fried onions); goong phao (grilled jumbo prawns with house special chili sauce); green curry chicken; Thai iced tea or iced coffee.

SUMMARY AND COMMENTS The best Thai on the Upper East Side, this neighborhood favorite draws crowds for its well-prepared food and spicy change of pace. Though its menu is small, there's enough to choose from, and the things they do, they do very well. Start with one of the soups or excellent steamed shrimp dumplings. Of particular note are the spicy and fragrant Thai curries, tempered with coconut milk and a real treat. You can't miss with either gaeng penang with beef or green curry with chicken. Pahd thai and other noodle and rice dishes are above average, and to douse the flames in your mouth there's nothing better than soothing Thai iced tea or yummy Thai iced coffee.

Jaya Malaysian ★★

MALAYSIAN	INEXPENSIVE	QUALITY ★★★½	VALUE ★★★★½

90 Baxter Street, Chinatown; ☎ 212-219-3331

Reservations Not necessary. **When to go** Anytime. **Entrée range** $5–$18. **Payment** All major credit cards. **Service rating** ★★½ **Friendliness rating** ★★½ **Bar** Beer only. **Wine selection** None. **Dress** Casual. **Disabled access** No. **Customers** Ethnic, locals. **Hours** Daily, 11 a.m.–10:30 p.m.

SETTING AND ATMOSPHERE The storefront looks a little tacky, and it hardly convinces you that you've arrived at a place that serves authentic Malaysian food. Don't let the outside deter you; the restaurant is a fair size and can easily seat large groups. The décor consists of bamboo light fixtures, a wooden mesh ceiling, and one wall of painted plaster with seashells, rocks, dried sea creatures and vegetation, and other ocean motifs. The interior simply exists; it's neither offensive nor stimulating, and it certainly won't affect your enjoyment of the meal.

HOUSE SPECIALTIES Stingray in lotus leaf; shrimp with dried chili paste; various laksas (noodles in curried broth with either chicken, shrimp, seafood, or tofu); chendor (shaved ice with coconut, red beans, and green jelly).

OTHER RECOMMENDATIONS Thai-style fish cake; bean curd stuffed with cucumber and bean sprouts; lemongrass jumbo shrimp; carp with ginger-garlic sauce; Malaysian iced coffee; lychee iced tea.

SUMMARY AND COMMENTS If possible, try to get here early because the place is full by 7:30 p.m., and the noise level can really rise. The menu is extensive, and there's everything from standard fried rice to more adventurous dishes such as crispy pork intestines. If this cuisine is new to you, try a shrimp, squid, or fish dish with curry, chili, and/or garlic. The stingray in lotus leaf is incredibly succulent, but it has a weird smell attributed to the leaf. It's also worth trying a selection of appetizers. Ask your waiter for some suggestions. If you need a shot of caffeine, don't forget to end the meal with an iced coffee—the condensed milk makes it heavenly. Jaya has another branch on the Upper West Side, but that location has a limited menu without the true spicy variety of this one in Chinatown.

Jean-Georges ★★★★

FRENCH	EXPENSIVE	QUALITY ★★★★½	VALUE ★★★

1 Central Park West (at 60th Street) in Trump Tower, Upper West Side; ☎ 212-299-3900; www.jean-georges.com

Reservations Required. **When to go** Anytime. **Entrée range** $29–$35 entrées, $45 prix-fixe lunch; $85 prix-fixe dinner. **Payment** Most major credit cards. **Service rating** ★★★★ **Friendliness rating** ★★★ **Bar** Full service. **Wine selection** Excellent, good range of prices from $22 to $1,000. **Dress** Jacket required for men; dressy. **Disabled access** Yes. **Customers** Local. **Hours** Monday–Thursday, noon–3 p.m. and 5:30–11 p.m.; Friday, noon–3 p.m. and 5:30–11:30 p.m.; Saturday, 5:30–11:30 p.m.

SETTING AND ATMOSPHERE   Restaurant designer Adam Tihany has kept this large dining room simple and spare with subdued tones of beige and gray. The huge windows let in sun and sky and views of Central Park during the day; at night the lights of Columbus Circle and Central Park South twinkle in the distance, and the gargantuan globe that sits outside the Trump International Tower takes on extra prominence. The overall feeling is more cool than cozy, but definitely elegant.

HOUSE SPECIALTIES   Foie gras and duck prosciutto roulade; asparagus with morel mushrooms; lobster tartine; baked arctic char; chocolate soufflé with warm raspberries and vanilla ice cream.

OTHER RECOMMENDATIONS   Sea scallops in caper-raisin emulsion with caramelized cauliflower; broiled squab with corn pancake and foie gras; turbot uba Chateau Chalon sauce; rhubarb tart with rhubarb crème glacée.

SUMMARY AND COMMENTS   Jean-Georges, given four stars by the *New York Times*, is the eponymous jewel in Jean-Georges Vongerichten's culinary crown—he also owns JoJo, Vong, 66, and Mercer Kitchen. This is where Vongerichten concentrates on his signature French cuisine, the innovative, intensely flavored dishes that made his Restaurant Lafayette, now closed, a four-star hit. The food is superb, as is the service; each dish is finished at your table, and this kind of attention is rare indeed. Jean-Georges was a New York sensation from the moment it opened, and reservations are hard to come by, but try. The sleeker Nougatine Café, the front room and bar of the restaurant, serves breakfast as well as lunch and dinner. Entrées are less expensive there, and the atmosphere is somewhat less formal. The outdoor Mistral Terrace is open seasonally.

Jezebel ★★★

SOUL FOOD	EXPENSIVE	QUALITY ★★★★	VALUE ★★★

630 Ninth Avenue (corner of 45th Street, entrance on 45th), Theater District; ☎ 212-582-1045; www.jezebelny.com

Reservations Recommended. **When to go** Anytime. **Entrée range** $20–$30. **Payment** All major credit cards. **Service rating** ★★★ **Friendliness rating** ★★★ **Bar** Full service. **Wine selection** Not extensive. **Dress** Casual to dressy. **Disabled access** Yes. **Customers** Locals, tourists. **Hours** Tuesday–Thursday, 5–10 p.m.; Friday and Saturday, 5 p.m.–midnight.

SETTING AND ATMOSPHERE   It's easy to miss the low-key entrance, but open the door and it's the Vieux Carré, sultry and seductive all the way. Fringed shawls hang from the ceiling like Spanish moss; large potted palms, camellias, and vases of lilies bloom all around the room; Oriental carpets accent the polished floors; and the walls are covered in posters—authentic French Art Nouveau, authentic American Andy Warhol, and a few Josephine Baker biggies. Mirrored columns, white wooden swings, crystal chandeliers, glass-topped tables with lace-bottomed clothes, wicker screens, and wrought-iron chairs all add to the lushly romantic effect.

HOUSE SPECIALTIES   She-crab soup; Gula curried goat; smothered pork chops; shrimp Creole; barbecue spareribs.

OTHER RECOMMENDATIONS Smothered garlic shrimp; Jezebel's green pea soup; coconut sweet potato pie; pecan pie.

SUMMARY AND COMMENTS "Down-home" goes upscale here, and all is overseen by Alberta Wright—the sophisticated yet soothingly savory soul food that comes out of the kitchen and the fabulous festoonery of the dimly lit dining room. This is an unexpected wow of a Theater District restaurant, a performance in itself, and worth the trip even if a show is not on the evening's schedule.

Joe's Shanghai ★★★

CHINESE	MODERATE	QUALITY ★★★★½	VALUE ★★★★★

9 Pell Street (between Mott and Bowery), Chinatown; ☎ 212-233-8894
136–21 37th Avenue, Flushing; ☎ 718-539-4429

Reservations Only for parties of ten or more. **When to go** Off hours (between 2:30 and 5:30 p.m., or after 9:30 p.m.), to avoid wait. **Entrée range** $9.95–$12.95. **Payment** Cash only. **Service rating** ★★★ **Friendliness rating** ★★★ **Bar** Beer only, and a limited variety. **Wine selection** BYOB. **Dress** Casual. **Disabled access** Queens good, Manhattan fair (one step to dining room). **Customers** Locals, foodies. **Hours** Daily, 11 a.m.–11 p.m.

SETTING AND ATMOSPHERE Several notches up from a Chinatown-style no-frills cafe, always busy but comfortable. The big tables are shared, but that's part of the ritual.

HOUSE SPECIALTIES Crabmeat steamed buns, stewed pork balls, shredded pork with pickled cabbage soup, anything with mushrooms, shrimp-fried rice cake, hot and sour soup, pork shoulder (with honey glaze), Shanghai fried flat noodles, shredded turnip shortcakes, soya (mock) duck.

SUMMARY AND COMMENTS By all means, start with the crabmeat steamed buns, amazing soup-filled dumplings that New Yorkers have been going wild over. Wait for them to cool a bit, then delicately (don't puncture—you'll lose the soup!) transfer a dumpling to a spoon into which you've pooled a bit of soy-ginger sauce and a dab of hot sauce. Nibble a hole in the skin, suck the soup, then down the dumpling. The shiitake mushrooms are great here, and the stewed pork balls are the lightest meatballs you've ever tasted, in a succulent sauce. Don't order typical Chinese restaurant fare, though—try to stick with the Shanghai specialties. Ask the harried but affable waiters for tips, or ask about good-looking dishes passing by. You can also check out **Joe's Ginger** (same owners) at 113 Mott Street, ☎ 212-966-6613.

Kam Chueh ★★★

CHINESE	MODERATE	QUALITY ★★★★	VALUE ★★★★½

40 Bowery #1 (South of Canal Street), Chinatown;
☎ 212-791-6868 or 212-791-6866

Reservations Large groups only. **When to go** Late. **Entrée range** $4–$22. **Payment** Cash only. **Service rating** ★★★½ **Friendliness rating** ★★½ **Bar** Beer only. **Wine selection** None. **Dress** Casual. **Disabled access** Small step up; restrooms not accessible. **Customers** Good blend of Chinese and serious aficionados. **Hours** Daily, 11 a.m.–4 a.m.

SETTING AND ATMOSPHERE   Contented fish swim spunkily through crystal clear water in front-window display tanks. Humans are accommodated in an only slightly less congenial habitat; the brightly lit dining room goes for an upscale look, with faux marble tiles and glittery cheap chandeliers.

HOUSE SPECIALTIES   Razor clams (or jumbo shrimp) in superb black bean sauce; salt-and-pepper squid (basically top-notch fried calamari sans dipping sauce); chunks of excellent medium-rare T-bone steak with flowering chives; sautéed mixed vegetables (order with off-menu foo yee sauce with briny fermented bean curd); super-delicate snowpea leaves; intense hot-and-sour soup; satisfying winter melon soup; flowering chives with clams; huge crabs with either ginger-scallion or black bean sauce.

OTHER RECOMMENDATIONS   You can't go wrong ordering from the smaller specials menu listing exotic baby vegetables and fancier preparations many restaurants refuse to translate into English. Don't order egg rolls and such; the menu lists a few Chinese American workhorses, but the chef is clearly not happy about it.

ENTERTAINMENT AND AMENITIES   Each table is covered with a thick wad of white plastic sheeting; don't miss the meal-end spectacle when your waiter bundles up the remains inside the topmost sheet and hauls it back to the kitchen on his back, leaving behind a new layer of clean, virgin plastic.

SUMMARY AND COMMENTS   Kam Chueh descends from Cantonese royalty; he's the estranged brother of the late, lamented Shing Kee, Chinatown favorite of many cognoscenti. Their menu is nearly identical, and the cooking comes pretty close (their black bean sauce should be declared a cultural landmark by the city). This is an after-hours scene; it's quite the hangout at 2 or 3 a.m., as gigging musicians and snazzily dressed young Chinese clubbers converge here.

Kate's Joint ★★½

VEGETARIAN	MODERATE	QUALITY ★★★★	VALUE ★★★★

58 Avenue B at Fourth Street, The East Village;
☎ **212-777-7059**

Reservations Only for parties of eight or more. **When to go** Anytime. **Entrée range** $8–$12. **Payment** Most major credit cards. **Service rating** ★★ **Friendliness rating** ★★ **Bar** Beer and wine. **Wine selection** Small. **Dress** Casual. **Disabled access** Good. **Customers** Locals. **Hours** Sunday–Thursday, 9 a.m.–midnight; Friday and Saturday, 9 a.m.–2 a.m.

SETTING AND ATMOSPHERE   Informal, mellow bohemian cafe with broodingly dark-colored walls and a good view of the East Village sidewalk parade.

HOUSE SPECIALTIES   Mock-meat dishes; chile-con-tofu carne, southern-fried tofu cutlets with mashed potatoes, un-turkey club.

SUMMARY AND COMMENTS   There are few vegetarian restaurants of merit in New York, but this is a notable exception. Chef/owner Kate Halpern cooks with a deft, knowing touch; her grilled vegetable hero is a knockout, her hummus assertively pungent and garlicky, and her mock meat dishes (made from carefully marinated tofu) both delicious and convincingly meatlike. Though the regular menu is reliable, daily specials are more hit-and-miss. Expect the usual spacy vegetarian restaurant service (it must be the meat deprivation). Kate's was a pioneer in the new restaurant row that's cropped up on formerly scary Avenue B; it's no longer a frightening area.

La Boite en Bois ★★½

FRENCH	MODERATE	QUALITY ★★★½	VALUE ★★★★

75 West 68th Street (Central Park West and Columbus Avenue), Upper West Side; ☎ 212-874-2705; www.laboitenyc.com

Reservations Recommended. **When to go** Anytime. **Entrée range** $32 per person. **Payment** All major credit cards. **Service rating** ★★★ **Friendliness rating** ★★★ **Bar** Full service. **Wine selection** Good range, good prices. **Dress** Casual. **Disabled access** No. **Customers** Loyal locals, Lincoln Center attendees. **Hours** Monday–Friday, noon–3 p.m. and 5–10:30 p.m.; Saturday, 11:30 a.m.–3 p.m. and 5–11 p.m.

SETTING AND ATMOSPHERE This cute, cozy, hole-in-the-wall bistro takes you from the sidewalks of Manhattan right into the French countryside. Only a few blocks from Lincoln Center, it's no wonder this is a preconcert favorite.

HOUSE SPECIALTIES Rack of lamb au jus; French string bean with wild mushroom salad; breast of duck with wild rice; tiny quail with lentils; seafood crêpe with tomato coulis; praline mousse.

OTHER RECOMMENDATIONS Pan-roasted chicken with herbs; pot-au-feu de poisson; côte de veau grillée au Calvados; crème brûlée.

SUMMARY AND COMMENTS Popular with concertgoers in the know, this small space can get quite crowded, but by 7:45 p.m. it clears out and quiets down. The pretheater menu runs for $29, but an even better deal is three courses of your choice for $32 with no time constraints. The bread is wonderfully warm and tasty, the service personal and attentive, but the menu needs updating and the food, though decent, could use some fresh legs or at least a kick in the rear to get it going.

Lady Mendl's Tea Salon ★★★

TEAROOM	MODERATE	QUALITY ★★★★	VALUE ★★★

56 Irving Place, Gramercy Park and Madison Square; ☎ 212-533-4466; www.ladymendls.com

Reservations Accepted. **When to go** Anytime. **Entrée range** $30 prix fixe. **Payment** All major credit cards. **Service rating** ★★ **Friendliness rating** ★★★½ **Bar** Beer, wine, champagne, port, sherry. **Wine selection** Very small. **Dress** Nice casual. **Disabled access** No. **Customers** Hotel guests, locals. **Hours** Wednesday–Friday, seatings at 3 p.m. and 5 p.m.; Saturday and Sunday, seatings at 2 p.m. and 4:30 p.m.

SETTING AND ATMOSPHERE This tearoom, located in the pricey Inn at Irving Place, aims for an upscale English boardinghouse look. Unlike some of the Midtown hotel teas, this room—equipped with a working fire-place—is whisper-quiet.

HOUSE SPECIALTIES A five-course tea, with all the usual fixtures: crustless sandwiches of cucumber and smoked salmon; pâtés; warm scones; clotted cream; jams; tarts; and chocolate mousse cake, all served with a pot of tea per guest.

ENTERTAINMENT AND AMENITIES People-watching; The Inn at Irving Place is an exclusive hotel, so high-powered and celebrity guests are common.

SUMMARY AND COMMENTS The food is nearly irreproachable; sandwiches are properly fussy, scones (perhaps the best item) taste homemade, and chocolate mousse cake is far better than the usual. There is a wide selection of teas and herbal infusions—all fancier than on-the-shelf brands—and each guest is served from one of the handsome antique pots collected by the owners. As you'd expect at a proper tea, everything's served on bone china. This is a very popular place for bridal and baby showers.

Le Bernardin ★★★★½

FISH/FRENCH	VERY EXPENSIVE	QUALITY ★★★★	VALUE ★★★

155 West 51st Street (between Sixth and Seventh avenues), Midtown West, Times Square, and the Theater District; ☎ 212-489-1515; www.le-bernardin.com

Reservations Required. **When to go** Anytime. **Entrée range** Dinner is prix-fixe only, $75; $120 for the seven-course tasting menu; prix-fixe lunch, $32–$43. **Payment** All major credit cards. **Service rating** ★★★★ **Friendliness rating** ★★★★ **Bar** Full service. **Wine selection** Excellent. **Dress** Dressy; jackets required for men. **Disabled access** Yes. **Customers** Business, local. **Hours** Monday–Thursday, noon–2:30 p.m. and 5:30–11 p.m.; Friday, noon–2:30 p.m. and 5:30–11:30 p.m.; Saturday, 5:30–11:30 p.m.

SETTING AND ATMOSPHERE Formal elegance, without arrogance, suffuses this grand space, and the clientele dress and act accordingly—this is, unmistakably, a luxurious setting for truly upscale dining. Blue-gray walls, adorned with fine classic maritime paintings in ornate frames, rise to a teak ceiling. Small roses top tables, handsomely set and graciously spaced.

HOUSE SPECIALTIES Yellowfin tuna carpaccio; lemon-splashed slivers of fluke with chives and lemon juice; warm lobster timbale in champagne-chive nage; seared, rare hamachi over sweet cherry tomato, onion, and portobello escabeche; steamed black bass with fresh coriander, ginger, and crab vermicelli in a tangy spiced citrus broth; spice-crusted cobia, duck sauce, sauté of cavaillon melon and preserved ginger; warm chocolate tarte with melting whipped cream and dark chocolate sauce.

OTHER RECOMMENDATIONS Spanish mackerel tartare topped with osetra caviar; shaved geoduck clam marinated with wasabi and soy-ginger dressing; pikytoe crab with green tomatoes and preserved lemon in a chilled gazpacho sauce; warm barbecue eel, sautéed black trumpet mushrooms, and chive blossoms; poached skate with caramelized baby fennel ragoût; lobster tail with shrimp sambal sauce and roasted mangoes; pan-roasted codfish on a bed of braised sweet peppers in their sweet and sour jus; sautéed Brazilian dorade, soft fresh corn purée, aged sherry, and portobello jus; passion fruit crêpe soufflé and Grand Marnier ice cream.

SUMMARY AND COMMENTS Flawless fish, flawless service. Another New York candidate for number one—whether restaurant, fish restaurant, or French restaurant. Only the very finest fish and celestial shellfish are accorded the honor of appearing at table here, and these stars of the sea are prepared with panache and perfection by Eric Ripert, who has reached the same glorious gastronomic heights as Gilbert Le Coze, his renowned predecessor. Trying to choose from among the wide assortment of appetizers and entrées is like trying to choose a member of the Dream Team for your fantasy basketball team—you just can't go wrong. Steamed black bass is one of the best dishes in Manhattan; with soft citrus notes and fresh coriander that gives it an Indian edge, its subtle complexity will have you shaking your head in disbelief that food could ever be this good. Le Bernardin is on another level. Even the service is eerily psychic; simply stare at the back of your waiter's head as he walks 20 feet away and he'll turn around. To ease the stress of picking your own dishes, it might be best to go with one of the tasting menus. They may be ridiculously expensive, but if there was ever a place to justify such an expense, this is it. Eric Ripert also consulted on the menu for a restaurant called **Geisha** (33 East 61st Street; ☎ 212-734-2676).

Les Halles ★★½

FRENCH BISTRO/STEAK   EXPENSIVE   QUALITY ★★★½   VALUE ★★★

411 Park Avenue South (between 28th and 29th streets), Gramercy Park;
☎ **212-679-4111; www.leshalles.net**

Reservations Recommended. **When to go** Anytime. **Entrée range** $14.50–$28. **Payment** All major credit cards. **Service rating ★★ Friendliness rating ★★★ Bar** Full service. **Wine selection** Well chosen; some good values. **Dress** Casual. **Disabled access** Yes. **Customers** Locals, professionals. **Hours** Daily, 8 a.m.–midnight.

SETTING AND ATMOSPHERE Don't expect a quiet, romantic evening for two at this boisterous, Gramercy-area French bistro/butcher shop. Patrons are packed elbow to elbow like, dare we say, cattle, and the noise quotient is high throughout most of the night. The glass-enclosed meat case at the front is a nice touch, and the room has a familiar, well-worn feel with dozens of posters and photos lining the walls. Throw in some cigarette smoke and you might as well be in Paris.

HOUSE SPECIALTIES Endive salad with apples, walnuts, and Roquefort cheese; steak frites; boudin aux pommes (blood sausage, caramelized apples); Onglet (hanger steak); warm chocolate and banana tart.

OTHER RECOMMENDATIONS Tarte Alsacienne (caramelized onion tart); homemade rillettes; steak tartare; moules marinières (mussels steamed in white wine); rib-eye steak; fresh apple tart with vanilla ice cream.

SUMMARY AND COMMENTS Les Halles proves that predictability can be a good thing. If you're in the mood for a dependable bistro menu and train terminal atmosphere, Les Halles should be your call. Appetizers are win some, lose some. A good starter is the endive and arugula salad with walnuts and a bit of cheese. Chunks of fresh apples make this a refreshing beginning and serve to get rid of some of the impending guilt that arrives with the artery-clogging meat. Steaks here may not be up to par with Peter Luger's or any of the city's other big-name establishments, but they're good for what they are, and at $16.50, the steak frites is a great deal. Frites come with every steak and are meaty and delicious.

Margon Restaurant ★★

CUBAN CAFETERIA	INEXPENSIVE	QUALITY ★★★½	VALUE ★★★★★

136 West 46th Street #1, Midtown West; ☎ 212-354-5013

Reservations Not accepted. When to go Quick lunch. Entrée range $5.25–$7.25 (breakfast, $2–$5). Payment Cash only. Service rating ★★½ Friendliness rating ★★★ Bar None. Wine selection None. Dress Casual. Disabled access No. Customers Locals, businessmen. Hours Breakfast, Monday–Friday, 6 a.m.–5 p.m.; Saturday, 6 a.m.–2:30 p.m.; closed Sunday.

SETTING AND ATMOSPHERE A harshly lit, bare-bones hustle-your-tray-through-the-line basement cafeteria.

HOUSE SPECIALTIES Roast chicken, octopus salad, rice and beans, fried plantains; all the standard-issue Latino luncheonette fare, but good!

SUMMARY AND COMMENTS If you need to catch a quick lunch in Midtown, this place will get you in and out in a jiffy (don't sweat long lines; they move quickly), but patrons' fast-shoveling forks belie the high quality of the food. Everything's very fresh and made with care. There are precious few Latin lunch counters left in this part of town, and friendly, efficient Margon is a proud bastion.

Mary's Fish Camp ★★★

SEAFOOD	MODERATE	QUALITY ★★★½	VALUE ★★★

64 Charles Street at Fourth Street, Greenwich Village; ☎ 646-486-2185; www.marysfishcamp.com

Reservations Not accepted. When to go Anytime. Entrée range $11–$25. Payment All major credit cards. Service rating ★★★ Friendliness rating ★★★ Bar Beer only. Wine selection Very small. Dress Casual. Disabled access One small step into restaurant; no access for bathroom. Customers Locals, regulars, those hankering for a lobster roll. Hours Monday–Saturday, noon–3 p.m. and 6–11 p.m.

SETTING AND ATMOSPHERE You'll either be charmed by it's Lilliputian size, cramped table positions, and cozy shack appearance, or you'll feel claustrophobic and wonder what the fuss is about. Although the orginal 'camp' is in Florida, there's a casual New England, nautical feel.

HOUSE SPECIALTIES Malpeque oysters; lobster roll; crab au gratin; clams.

OTHER RECOMMNDATIONS Lobster pot pie; fried fish sandwich; tartar sauce.

SUMMARY AND COMMENTS Unless you come for a late lunch or dinner time, chances are you'll have to wait for a table, but the wait is worth it if you have an urge for a lobster roll, scallops, or clams. Service is either no nonsense or rushed during peak periods, so the objective is eating and not loitering. The tartar sauce is homemade and very special. If you can't stand the wait or the close quarters, try ordering out and find a bench in nearby Bleecker Playground (Bleecker and West 11th streets). Note that a 'sister' branch, **Brooklyn Fish Camp** opened recently in Park Slope (162 Fifth Avenue; ☎ 718-783-3264).

Menchanko-Tei ★★

JAPANESE	INEXPENSIVE	QUALITY ★★★½	VALUE ★★★★

39 West 55th Street (between Fifth and Sixth avenues), Midtown West; ☎ 212-247-1585; 131 East 45th Street (between Lexington and Third avenues), Midtown East; ☎ 212-986-6805

Reservations *45th Street:* accepted; *55th Street:* Only for parties of five or more. **When to go** If possible, avoid the 1 p.m. rush. **Entrée range** $7.75–$13. **Payment** All major credit cards. **Service rating** ★★★★ **Friendliness rating** ★★ **Bar** Full service, with several sakes, Japanese beers, and spirits like shochu. **Wine selection** House. **Dress** Nice casual. **Disabled access** Difficult (restrooms not accessible) at both branches. **Customers** Locals and local workers. **Hours** Daily, 11:30 a.m.–12:30 a.m.

SETTING AND ATMOSPHERE Noodles are taken very seriously here, and the dignified décor immediately signals that this ain't no fooling around. The 55th Street Menchanko-Tei has stylish Midtown Japanese restaurant ambience: low ceilings, nice wood floors, halogen lights, some cursory Oriental tchotchkes, a low bar in front of an open (sparkling) kitchen, and a long line of tables for two and four (there's also a more peaceful dining room in back, painted a friendly mustard yellow). The 45th Street branch—airier and more Western—is also designed with a careful touch: higher ceilings, green carpet, potted plants, and a small dining spillover area upstairs near the restrooms. Clientele in both is mixed, but predominantly Japanese.

HOUSE SPECIALTIES Several variations on souply themes: Menchanko itself is an egg noodle soup of profound delicacy; it can also be prepared with a miso base, and additions can include hot, pickled vegetables; fish balls; or a kitchen sink version called tokusei menchanko, dominated by chunks of fresh, flaky salmon that assertively flavor the delicate broth. There are two ramen soups, both topped with a succulent slice of yakibuta pork: hakata is a white broth (gingery and simple, but with great balance), and kikuzo is soy-based (the plainest of all, but no less worthy). Zousui soups are made with plump rice rather than noodles; Kimchi Zousui is particularly good, homey, and quite spicy from the hot, pickled cabbage. Nagasaki saraudon is frizzy, thin, fried noodles with a sweetish seafood sauce; Nagasaki chanpon is the same, but in soup.

OTHER RECOMMENDATIONS There are a handful of non-noodle options, few of them in a class with the soups: onigiri (rice balls wrapped in nori seaweed, containing stuff like umeboshi, salmon, or preserved cod fish roe) are perhaps too subtle for the unaccustomed palate. Oden are small appetizer plates; check out kinchaku—a deliciously exotic cake of fried tofu stuffed with sticky rice paste in a soothing broth-sauce. There are also side orders like yakibuta (pork), menma (tender bamboo shoots with a slightly caramelized flavor), or kimchi (hot, pickled cabbage). Ask for some yuzu-kosho—a red pepper paste flavored with yuzu fruit—to spoon into the soups.

A fuller menu is served nights at the 55th Street location; 45th Street offers Onigashima, a more full-service restaurant, upstairs.

SUMMARY AND COMMENTS Fans of the film *Tampopo* will feel at home here in NYC's best Japanese noodle soup restaurant, where noodles are made with great care for a discerning clientele. These loyal customers come often; the 55th Street branch will sell regulars a full bottle of booze to keep on reserve (they have three months to drain it). Soups are served in heavy iron kettles, with a wooden ladle for transferance to your bowl. Slurp loudly (silent noodle scarfing is an insult to the chef), but get out quick; despite the deliciousness, the well-appointed décor, the polite service, and the nonbargain prices (soups run as high as $13), this type of restaurant is considered fast food, so lingering is discouraged. The oden are better at 55th Street, but the soups may be slightly more complex at 45th Street (considered by many the superior location). Another great noodle place is **Sobaya** (229 East Ninth Street; ☎ 212-533-6966).

Mesa Grill ★★★

AMERICAN/SOUTHWEST	EXPENSIVE	QUALITY ★★★½	VALUE ★★★

102 Fifth Avenue (15th and 16th streets), Gramercy Park;
☎ **212-807-7400; www.mesagrill.com**

Reservations Recommended. **When to go** Anytime. **Entrée range** $18–$34; appetizers, $7.50–$14.50. **Payment** All major credit cards. **Service rating** ★★★ **Friendliness rating** ★★ **Bar** Full service, with 20 different kinds of tequila. **Wine selection** Good. **Dress** Casual; some business at lunch; no jacket required. **Disabled access** Yes, downstairs. **Customers** Locals, business. **Hours** Monday–Thursday, noon–2:30 p.m. and 5:30–10:30 p.m.; Friday, noon–2:30 p.m. and 5:30–11 p.m.; Saturday, 11:30 a.m.–3 p.m. (brunch) and 5:30–11 p.m.; Sunday, 11:30 a.m.–3 p.m. (brunch) and 5:30–10:30 p.m.

SETTING AND ATMOSPHERE Substantial columns, painted with bands of southwestern colors, hold up the two-story high ceiling. The lime green and yellow walls sprout tin lighting fixtures, and the banquettes are covered in a kitsch-cute "Hi-ho Silver" design. All this to let you know that you're in for spicy southwestern fare. The tables are close, and the noise level can rear up and buck like a bronco. Quieter late in the evening and at brunch.

HOUSE SPECIALTIES Shrimp and roasted garlic corn tamale; spicy salmon tartare with plantain croutons and cilantro oil; blue corn tortilla–crusted red snapper; potato-corn taco and smoked red pepper–grilled onion relish.

OTHER RECOMMENDATIONS Barbecue chicken quesadilla; grilled squid and Vidalia onion salad with smoked tomatoes and green chile vinaigrette; spicy maple-glazed veal chop with red onion marmalade and blue corn–sweet potato taco; grilled striped bass with roasted corn–red pepper relish and buttermilk onion rings; miniature ice cream sandwiches.

SUMMARY AND COMMENTS Celebrity-chef Bobby Flay has pizzazz aplenty, and this smart venue is the perfect place for him to strut his southwestern stuff. Every dish has a spicy regional accent—even the romaine salad has red chile croutons, the red snapper is crusted with blue corn tortillas, and there's blue corn again in the biscotti. The appetizers are especially interesting and pretty on their Fiesta-ware plates, and the main courses are large enough to satisfy the hungry cowboys in the cookhouse, though some of the combos can be a little over the top. The clientele is trendy, the atmosphere animated.

Meskerem ★★★

ETHIOPIAN   INEXPENSIVE/MODERATE   QUALITY ★★★½   VALUE ★★★½

124 Macdougal Street (between Bleecker and West Third streets), Greenwich Village; ☎ 212-777-8111
468 West 47th Street (between Ninth and Tenth avenues), Midtown West; ☎ 212-664-0520; www.meskeremrestaurant.com

Reservations Not required, unless large group; the Village location doesn't take reservations. **When to go** Anytime. **Entrée range** $8–$13.50. **Payment** MC, V. **Service rating** ★★★½ **Friendliness rating** ★★★★ **Bar** Full service. **Wine selection** Very small, but does offer Ethiopian honey wine. **Dress** Casual. **Disabled access** No for Village, yes for Midtown. **Customers** Locals, ethnic, regulars. **Hours** Daily, noon–midnight.

SETTING AND ATMOSPHERE Cheery, casual and almost always full of happy people sharing their food and looking almost guilty for not having to use utensils. Ethiopian prints, artifacts, and cloths can be found in both locations.

HOUSE SPECIALTIES Shero wat (ground chickpeas with ground red pepper–berbere sauce); yebeg alecha (lamb with ginger, garlic, and curry); kifto (chopped beef with butter and mitmita–ground chili pepper sauce, often served rare or raw); miser wat (lentils with garlic, onions, and berbere sauce).

OTHER RECOMMENDATIONS Timatim salad (tomatoes, onions, scallions, peppers); Meskerem combo dish with beef, lamb, and vegetables prepared in various ways.

SUMMARY AND COMMENTS This is an ideal place for at least four people with clean hands. This way you can try several dishes and have them all placed before you, collectively, on a huge circular platter, and then everyone gets to dig in on one plate using the injera (slightly sour, spongy, flat, soft bread made from an Ethiopian grain called tef) as the tool to collect, scoop, and place food into your mouth (or that of a friend's). Utensils are available for those unable or unwilling to suspend their usual cultural habits. A recommended way to order is one vegetarian combo entrée plus two to three meat entrées to get a full spectrum of tastes. Individual plates aren't provided unless you ask. You can wait by the bar (although it's quite small) for your table and order an Ethiopian honey wine as an aperitif.

Mr. Broadway Kosher Deli ★★★

JEWISH DELI	MODERATE	QUALITY ★★★★	VALUE ★★★★★

1372 Broadway (between 37th and 38th streets), Midtown West; ☎ 212-921-2152

Reservations Accepted. **When to go** Anytime. **Entrée range** $4.25–$21.75. **Payment** All major credit cards. **Service rating** ★★★ **Friendliness rating** ★★★ **Bar** Beer and wine. **Wine selection** Small (kosher). **Dress** Casual. **Disabled access** Fair. **Customers** Locals, professionals. **Hours** Sunday–Friday, 11 a.m.–10 p.m.; closed Saturday.

SETTING AND ATMOSPHERE From the front, this looks like just another of the area's many kosher fast-food spots, but the rear is classic Jewish deli, a bustling cavern with darting waiters, tables crammed with pickles and cole slaw, and regulars who look like they eat a lot of pastrami trying to squeeze their way through the tight floor plan.

HOUSE SPECIALTIES Outstanding garlicky baba ghanoush (eggplant salad); potato knishes; couscous; kasha varnichkes (oniony buckwheat with bow-tie noodles); potato pancakes (deep fried, but good); homemade french fries; chicken soup with matzo balls; falafel; derma (rich spicy stuffing in sausage casing); fried "Moroccan cigars" (pastry flutes stuffed with finely minced meat); homemade gefilte fish.

OTHER RECOMMENDATIONS There's a terrific self-service Middle Eastern salad bar up front, for take-out ($3.99/pound) or to accompany falafel and shwarma sandwiches.

SUMMARY AND COMMENTS Mr. Broadway Kosher Deli & Restaurant is known by many names: it's also Me Tsu Yan Kosher Chinese Restaurant and Chez Lanu, serving North African dishes. The confluence of cuisines makes for some strange culinary juxtapositions, from customers smearing hummus on their hot dogs to the Moroccan couscous served with a homely piece of Eastern European roast chicken riding on top. For both Middle Eastern and deli specialties, Mr. Broadway is a winner. The kitchen somehow manages to turn out perfectly balanced baba ghanoush and flaky potato knishes without watering down the soulfulness of chicken soup or tender gefilte fish. Corned beef is, of course, of paramount importance in a Jewish deli; theirs is good and well cut but perhaps a bit too lean (everything's a tad lighter than usual here; perhaps it's the Sephardic influence). Chinese dishes—glatt kosher, like everything else—are handily available for those for whom real Chinese isn't an option. This place is only a few years old and unpedigreed in NYC deli history, but the more venerated delis seem grimily past their primes, while Mr. Broadway thrives.

Molly's ★★★

IRISH PUB FOOD	MODERATE	QUALITY ★★★★	VALUE ★★★★

287 Third Avenue, Gramercy Park; ☎ 212-889-3361

Reservations Limited. **When to go** Anytime. **Entrée range** $10.50–$21.50. **Payment** All major credit cards. **Service rating** ★★½ **Friendliness rating** ★★ **Bar** Full. **Wine selection** Small. **Dress** Casual. **Disabled access** Fair. **Customers** Locals. **Hours** Monday–Saturday, 11 a.m.–4 a.m.; Sunday, noon–4 a.m.

SETTING AND ATMOSPHERE Classic Irish pub; woody and snug, complete with fireplace. Lots of booths and tables (the largest, a round table seating eight, is handy for after-work get-togethers).

HOUSE SPECIALTIES Cheeseburgers, shepherd's pie and chicken pot pie, respectable steak, mashed potatoes, and most fried items.

OTHER RECOMMENDATIONS Avoid specials; stick with the main menu. Ask for fried onions on your cheeseburger (they're sensational), and request the special walnut dressing on your salad.

SUMMARY AND COMMENTS The area has plenty of anonymous Irish bar/restaurants to choose from, but this is the standout. Typical pub food is grand (best cheeseburgers and shepherd's pie in Manhattan), and they transcend type with touches like a surprisingly worthy bread basket and fresh (gasp!), not overcooked vegetable sides. Guinness stout, properly creamy and not overchilled, is among the best in town.

Molyvos ★★★½

GREEK	EXPENSIVE	QUALITY ★★★★	VALUE ★★★★

871 Seventh Avenue (between 55th and 56th streets), Midtown West; ☎ 212-582-7500; www.molyvos.com

Reservations Recommended. **When to go** Anytime. **Entrée range** $18–$34. **Payment** All major credit cards. **Service rating** ★★★ **Friendliness rating** ★★★★ **Bar** Full service; excellent ouzo selection. **Wine selection** Good; especially interesting Greek selections. **Dress** Business, casual. **Disabled access** Fair; three steps to the dining room. **Customers** Business, locals. **Hours** Monday–Thursday, noon–3 p.m. and 5:30–11:30 p.m.; Friday, noon–3 p.m. and 5:30 p.m.–midnight; Saturday, noon–3 p.m. and 5 p.m.–midnight; Sunday, noon–11 p.m.

SETTING AND ATMOSPHERE An airy, comfortable Greek taverna with a bright front room and substantial bar that lead into a large, somewhat dimmer main dining room. Greek key panels top stenciled planks, the terracotta sponged walls are dotted with black-and-white photos of Molyvos, and all is accented with Hellenic objects, plates, amphorae, glass bottles, and the capital of a marble column.

HOUSE SPECIALTIES Marinated lamb shanks; moussaka; grilled baby octopus; meze; shrimp saganaki; wood-grilled whole fish; loukoumades (dessert fritters with honey sauce); coffee crème brûlée.

OTHER RECOMMENDATIONS Cabbage dolmades; grilled jumbo prawns; steamed mussels; ocean blackfish plaki; semolina and almond cake.

SUMMARY AND COMMENTS With Molyvos, John Livanos (also owner of Oceana) pays homage to his hometown on the Greek island of Lesbos. The result is wonderful, authentic Greek cuisine and a great change of pace from more traditional New York upscale dining. The mouthwatering mezedes (little bites) such as tzatziki and grilled, marinated sardines alone can make a meal, but don't limit yourself or you could miss out on such great dishes as grilled baby octopus. Smoky and packed with flavor, the octopus needs little else to satisfy. With this dish and others, chef James Botsacos smartly chooses not to overpower the food with different flavors but instead to subtly complement it and entice the true flavors out. Simplicity never tasted so good. The superfast service and great food make this an excellent stop either before or after a concert at Carnegie Hall.

Montrachet ★★★½

FRENCH BISTRO   EXPENSIVE   QUALITY ★★★★   VALUE ★★★½

239 West Broadway (between Walker and White), Tribeca;
☎ **212-219-2777; www.myriadrestaurantgroup.com**

Reservations Necessary. When to go Anytime; Friday lunch. Entrée range $24–$36; tasting menu, $79 for four courses. Payment All major credit cards. Service rating ★★★ Friendliness rating ★★★★ Bar Full service. Wine selection One of the best in the city and top 100 in the country. Dress Dressy casual to business. Disabled access Three steps up to enter. Customers Locals, professionals, oenophiles. Hours Monday–Thursday, 5:30–10:30 p.m.; Friday, noon–2:30 p.m. and 5:30–11 p.m.; Saturday, 5:30–11 p.m.

SETTING AND ATMOSPHERE This three-room Tribeca space is subtle and at ease. The front room boasts comfy plum-colored banquettes with narrow mirrors running just on top and modern art on the walls. The two back rooms remain simple with pale blue walls offset against dark wood tables and chairs. The mood reflects this easy relaxation and laid-back comfort.

HOUSE SPECIALTIES The menu changes regularly. Examples of some of the staples include warm oysters with champagne sauce and osetra caviar; salmon with fresh dill, cucumber, and mustard; roasted chicken with potato purée and fennel; crème brûlée; and chocolate brioche with pistachio ice cream.

OTHER RECOMMENDATIONS Coriander-encrusted red snapper with red peppers; foie gras; roasted lobster salad with sweetcorn, bacon, and chanterelles; chilled rhubarb soup and Long Island Duck.

SUMMARY AND COMMENTS Often overlooked because of its hard-to-find Tribeca location, Montrachet quietly goes about its business, serving great food with an award-winning wine list in a low-key atmosphere. Chef Harold Moore has maintained the traditional French menu. The restaurant attracts a varied clientele, including the conservative business types, the glamorous, and the more casual. The food here is excellent in its own right, but the wine accompaniment and advice of the sommelier is part and parcel of the Montrachet experience. True, the wine itself can, at least, double the bill, but the assumption is that if you've decided to dine here, then you're well prepared to give your wallet a decent airing. There's no need to be intimidated. The sommelier is patient, helpful, and eager to help, advise, and explain the merits and drawbacks of any bottle. Descriptions such as "full-bodied," "oak-filled bouquet," and "fruity" have never had so many nuances. The chef is a little over-indulgent with salt, but the fresh ingredients and varied mix of herbs and spices help keep a balance. The chicken is absolutely melt-in-your-mouth succulent. Cappuccino is surprisingly disappointing, but the scrumptious petits-fours and desserts will keep you happy. Make sure to try some of the chef's complimentary preparations for tasting. Note that the lunch menu on Friday is similar to that of dinner's offerings, except the salmon is prepared differently.

My Thai ★★★★

THAI	INEXPENSIVE	QUALITY ★★★★½	VALUE ★★★★

8347 Dongan Avenue, Elmhurst; ☎ 718-476-6743

Reservations Accepted. **When to go** Anytime. **Entrée range** $6.95–$22.95. **Payment** Cash only. **Service rating** ★★★★ **Friendliness rating** ★★★★★ **Bar** None. **Wine selection** None. **Dress** Casual. **Disabled access** Small step in; tight route to accessible restroom. **Customers** Thai locals, questing aficionados. **Hours** Sunday–Thursday, noon–11 p.m.; Friday and Saturday, noon–11:30 p.m.

SETTING AND ATMOSPHERE A warm, well-lit, immaculate little dining room, with a few hard-to-find Thai products on display. Certainly not elegant, but invitingly bright and cheery in this neighborhood of inexpensive holes-in-the-walls. Comfortable seating.

HOUSE SPECIALTIES Start with larb (pronounced "lab"), ground pork with plenty of red onion, mint, lime, and pepper. All noodle dishes are beyond wonderful (pad thai is a revelation, with flavors fresh and focused, not all sweet and gunky like elsewhere). Chinese broccoli with crispy pork (really meaty cracklings) is amazing, and you can't go wrong with any other entrées (don't miss the curries, though). Specials of the day (often smoky, marinated pieces of roast chicken or Manila clams in a succulent brown sauce) are always good. Iced tea (served in a tall glass with milk) is bright orange, aromatic, and slightly smoky; Thai iced coffee is as rich and delicious as melted ice cream.

OTHER RECOMMENDATIONS Soups are good, not great (but do feature nice, fresh galangal), and skip the stuffed chicken wings. For dessert, they offer "toast": thick-cut good white bread carefully, evenly toasted and carefully, evenly spread with butter and a light sprinkling of sugar (and, optionally, a light drenching of condensed milk), which is a far cry from the stuff served with eggs in diners. There are also shaved ice desserts (choose from a large bar of toppings, including various beans, jellies, syrups, and squiggly things). Do not by any means miss the fried bananas if they have them (they'll be on a platter by the cash register). They are a peak experience.

SUMMARY AND COMMENTS   My Thai, formerly Kway Tiow Thai, alone is world-class. Not coincidentally, it's also one of the only Thai restaurants in town patronized by a largely Thai clientele. There is a battle among ethnic food devotees as to which is more important: authenticity or pure deliciousness. This place offers tons of both. Throw in friendly, sincere service by a family staff that clearly takes great pride in what they're doing, and you have an unbeatable combo. My Thai is very much worth a trip from anywhere in the city. The restaurant is a quick walk from the G/R subway (Elmhurst Avenue stop). Nearby and just as great (what a neighborhood!): **Ping's** (see profile) for Cantonese, and **Captain King** (82–39 Broadway; ☎ 718-429-2828) for Shanghai/Taiwanese (and the best dumplings in town).

New Pasteur ★★★½

VIETNAMESE	INEXPENSIVE	QUALITY ★★★★	VALUE ★★★★★

85 Baxter Street, Chinatown; ☎ 212-608-3656 or 212-608-4838

Reservations Suggested. **When to go** Avoid the peak hours of 8–10 p.m. **Entrée range** $4.75–$11. **Payment** Cash only. **Service rating** ★★★ **Friendliness rating** ★★½ **Bar** Beer and wine. **Wine selection** House. **Dress** Casual. **Disabled access** Fair. **Customers** Ethnic, locals, foodies. **Hours** Daily, 11 a.m.–10 p.m.

SETTING AND ATMOSPHERE   Spare storefront with little decoration to detract from the memorable cooking. Be prepared to share tables.

HOUSE SPECIALTIES   Any of the phos (elemental beef-based soups), barbecue beef (with vermicelli or on its own), shrimp rolls, fried spring rolls, barbecue shrimp roll on sugarcane, iced coffee.

SUMMARY AND COMMENTS   Year in and year out, homely New Pasteur (formerly Pho Pasteur) outclasses all new Vietnamese startups with no-nonsense first-class cooking. The barbecue beef is a marvel of gastronomic engineering, an entire beefy symphony compressed into each small nugget (wrap them in lettuce leaves, along with mint, cucumber slices, sprouts, and carroty fish sauce; the Vietnamese eat almost everything this way). If New Pasteur is full, as it often is, head up the block to larger and more upscale Nha Trang, whose food is nearly as good.

The Nice Restaurant ★★★½

CANTONESE/DIM SUM	MODERATE/EXPENSIVE	QUALITY ★★★★½	VALUE ★★★★

35 East Broadway, Chinatown; ☎ 212-406-9510

Reservations Suggested. **When to go** As early as possible for dim sum. **Entrée range** $10–$34 (up to $50 for specials); dim sum: $2–$6. **Payment** AE, MC, V. **Service rating** ★★★★ **Friendliness rating** ★★½ **Bar** Beer only. **Wine selection** House. **Dress** Nice casual. **Disabled access** Upstairs room not accessible; downstairs (closed Monday and Friday), one step up. **Customers** Business, families. **Hours** Daily, 9 a.m.–10:30 p.m.

SETTING AND ATMOSPHERE   Not as over-the-top as some of the more garish Hong Kong–style pavilions, the Nice is done up mostly in burgundy red (imagine a Chinese version of an upscale suburban catering hall). Noise levels run high, but it's an excited buzz, emanating from avid eaters.

HOUSE SPECIALTIES Minced conch and seafood with coconut curry sauce in conch shell; crispy seafood roll, minced squab with pine nuts in lettuce leaf; baby veal chops hot pot; tofu, minced chicken, and salted fish casserole; sautéed snow pea shoots with shredded dried scallops; stewed abalone in oyster sauce; crispy shrimp with walnuts.

OTHER RECOMMENDATIONS Dim sum: garlic har gow (garlic shrimp dumplings).

SUMMARY AND COMMENTS The top end of Cantonese cuisine recalls that of France, what with the complexities of flavor, intricate presentation, attention to aroma and aftertaste, and strikingly unusual juxtapositions. The Nice Restaurant consistently attains these lofty heights; order well and you'll taste fancy Cantonese–Hong Kong banquet cooking at its best. Anything on the above list of sensational—and largely off-menu—specialties will leave you forever convinced that Chinese food is much more than General Tso or shrimp in lobster sauce. The Nice puts on some of Chinatown's better dim sum, too, but arrive early, avoid fried things, and don't forget to special-order the amazing garlic shrimp dumplings from a manager.

Nobu ★★★★

JAPANESE	EXPENSIVE	QUALITY ★★★★½	VALUE ★★★

105 Hudson Street (at Franklin Street), Tribeca; ☎ 212-219-0500; www.myriadrestaurantgroup.com

Reservations Absolutely necessary. **When to go** Anytime. **Entrée range** $13–$31; multicourse "Omakase," chef's choice, $70 dinner, $45 lunch; sushi and sashimi à la carte, $3.50–$5. **Payment** All major credit cards. **Service rating** ★★★ **Friendliness rating** ★★★ **Bar** Full service. **Wine selection** OK, but sipping sake might be better. **Dress** Business, casual. **Disabled access** Fair; call in advance to arrange. **Customers** Locals, business, celebs, ethnic. **Hours** Monday–Friday, 11:45 a.m.–2:15 p.m. and 5:45–10:15 p.m.; Saturday and Sunday, 5:45–10:15 p.m.

SETTING AND ATMOSPHERE Birch tree columns, blond wood, high copper-leafed ceiling, plush banquettes, a wall of black river stones, and a large sushi counter are all part of the stunningly original million-dollar décor. Just as stunning are the number of well-known faces to be seen.

HOUSE SPECIALTIES The "Omakase" tasting dinner; toro tartar with caviar; black cod with miso; sea urchin in spinach; Matsushisa shrimp and caviar; yellowfin sashimi with jalapeño; squid "pasta" with garlic sauce.

OTHER RECOMMENDATIONS Broiled toro with spicy miso; shrimp and lobster with spicy lemon sauce; salmon tartar with caviar; sea urchin tempura; toro "to-ban" yaki.

SUMMARY AND COMMENTS No doubt, Nobu is one of the most exciting eateries in New York—it's not the place to order simply sushi. Chef Nobuyuki Matsushisa's brilliant, innovative menu is as stunningly original as the décor and considered by some to be the city's best Japanese food, by others to be just the city's best food. The menu is huge, with over a hundred small and medium-size dishes—a grazer's paradise. Reservations are hard to come by, but you can get the same food without the formality at **Next Door Nobu.** This spot doesn't take reservations, though you may still have to wait up to an hour to get a table. Next Door is a bit more casual than the original but has many of the same menu items, including unforgettable toro tartar with caviar and everybody's favorite blackened cod with miso. You'll even find a few noodle dishes for good measure, something big brother lacks (though you can hardly call Nobu lacking).

Noodle Pudding ★★★★

ITALIAN	MODERATE	QUALITY ★★★★	VALUE ★★★½

38 Henry Street, Brooklyn; ☎ 718-625-3737

Reservations Not accepted. **When to go** Dinner. **Entrée range** $10–$25. **Payment** Cash only. **Service rating** ★★★★ **Friendliness rating** ★★★★ **Bar** Full service. **Wine selection** Very good. **Dress** Casual. **Disabled access** Yes to space; no to bathroom. **Customers** Locals, regulars from far and wide. **Hours** Tuesday–Thursday, 5:30–10:30 p.m.; Friday and Saturday 5:30–11 p.m.; Sunday, 5–10 p.m.

SETTING AND ATMOSPHERE There's neither a number nor a sign to attest to its existence, but look hard enough and once you see happy diners, comfortably ensconced in a dark wooden interior, simply furnished with wooden tables and a bar at the front of the space, you have probably found the spot. Acoustics are poor, so when the space is crowded, it's a bit noisy, but not offensive.

HOUSE SPECIALTIES Homemade gnocchi with sage butter; osso bucco; pannacotta of varying flavors; daily fish specials.

OTHER RECOMMENDATIONS Strozzapretti with ricotta and eggplant; calamari fritti; mushroom risotto; beet salad; polenta.

SUMMARY AND COMMENTS Divulging the whereabouts and existence of Noodle Pudding is almost tantamount to admitting where you've placed a family hidden treasure: the family (read: locals) will not be happy. That said, the secret is already out and the locals may need to wait just a bit longer for a table. Service is very personable and efficient and each table is always presented with warmed ciabatta and decent olive oil. The food is consistently delicious which may explain why the place is such a local favorite. Those who move away, return especially for the food! During warm weather the front window opens up completely for a feel of al fresco dining. To walk off such a super feed, head toward the Promenade for a stroll and lovely view of the Brooklyn Bridge or walk further down Henry Street toward DUMBO (Down Under the Manhattan Bridge Overpass) and the Fulton Ferry landing.

Oceana ★★★½

FISH	EXPENSIVE	QUALITY ★★★★½	VALUE ★★★

55 East 54th Street (between Madison and Park avenues), Midtown East; ☎ 212-759-5941; www.oceanarestaurant.com

Reservations Recommended. **When to go** Anytime. **Entrée range** Prix fixe only; lunch $45, dinner $65. **Payment** All major credit cards. **Service rating** ★★★ **Friendliness rating** ★★★ **Parking** Garage complimentary after 4 p.m. **Bar** Full service. **Wine selection** Excellent. **Dress** Jacket and tie. **Disabled access** No. **Customers** Business, locals. **Hours** Monday–Friday, noon–2:30 p.m. and 5:30–10:30 p.m.; Saturday, 5–10:30 p.m.

SETTING AND ATMOSPHERE This Midtown townhouse has been transformed into a luxury yacht, the kind captains of industry—and otherwise—and their wealthy pals ply the seas in. Downstairs, diners look out of faux windows on what might be Capri, maybe Antibes, or at a vintage ocean liner sailing by. The elegant, high-ceilinged upstairs bar serves oysters and the like and welcomes cigar smokers.

HOUSE SPECIALTIES Oysters; salmon tartare wrapped with smoked salmon and topped with osetra caviar, with pea shoots and toast points; lobster ravioli in a tomato-basil broth; seared Florida grouper fillet, fingerling potatoes, watercress, arugula, and pancetta with a whole-grain mustard vinaigrette; Oceana East Coast bouillabaisse; warm chocolate tart.

OTHER RECOMMENDATIONS Grilled marinated sardines; grilled fillet of rouget and orzo salad; soft-shell crabs (in season); jumbo lump crab cakes; Chilean sea bass steamed with ginger, soy, and fresh coriander; fresh fruit Napoleon.

SUMMARY AND COMMENTS In case you couldn't tell from the name or the fact that you're basically seated inside a yacht, Oceana serves fish, and serves it well. Chef Rick Moonen turns out some of the best seafood in New York, drawing inspiration from around the globe, be it Asia, the Mediterranean, or down-home regional American. Regardless of the accents, Moonen's creations all speak the universal language of very good food. Unfortunately, the clientele mainly consists of what you would expect to find in such a yacht—men in suits—but service is impeccable and desserts are top-notch.

Old San Juan ★★½

PUERTO RICAN/ARGENTINEAN **INEXPENSIVE** **QUALITY** ★★★★ **VALUE** ★★★★

765 Ninth Avenue (51st and 52nd streets), Midtown West;
☎ **212-262-7013**

Reservations Not accepted. **When to go** Anytime. **Entrée range** $7.50–$22.95. **Payment** All major credit cards. **Service rating** ★★★ **Friendliness rating** ★★★ **Bar** Full service. **Wine selection** Limited, heavy on the Argentinean. **Dress** Pretheater, casual. **Disabled access** Everything on street level. **Customers** Pretheater, ethnic, locals. **Hours** Daily, 10:30 a.m.–11 p.m.

SETTING AND ATMOSPHERE This addition to Ninth Avenue's restaurant roster is not big on décor. There's a luncheonette-like counter to handle the take-out crowd, plus a very small bar and a larger, low-ceilinged dining room with random Puerto Rican objects on the walls. But when you're welcomed by the owner, who says, with all sincerity, "I want you to be happy," who needs designer décor?

HOUSE SPECIALTIES Cazuela de mariscos, seafood in a casserole served over yellow rice; asopaos, soupy Puerto Rican rice stews, in various flavors; mofongo, a garlicky mound of mashed plantains and pork cracklings, with crab or roast pork; churrasco Argentino, a grilled skirt steak.

OTHER RECOMMENDATIONS Pasteles puertoriquenos, a comforting, tamale-like concoction steamed in a banana leaf; clams in garlic sauce; Argentinean empanadas; mofongo; caramel-crusted bread pudding.

SUMMARY AND COMMENTS Old San Juan successfully fills a rather surprising void in Manhattan's ethnic restaurant array. With its huge Puerto Rican population, the city should have more places accessible to non-natives that feature the island's hearty, savory dishes. It's crowded, but that doesn't diminish the service, which would be more than reputable in a far more expensive establishment. The daily lunch specials, at $6.50, are truly hard to beat. Similar fare can be had at the spin-off **Old San Juan Too** (Second Avenue and 26th Street; ☎ 799-9360).

Orso ★★★

NORTHERN ITALIAN	MODERATE	QUALITY ★★★ ½	VALUE ★★★

322 West 46th Street, Theater District; ☎ 212-489-7212; www.orsorestaurant.com

Reservations Necessary at least a week in advance. **When to go** Anytime. **Entrée range** $18–$22. **Payment** MC, V. **Service rating** ★★★ **Friendliness rating** ★★★ **Bar** Full service. **Wine selection** Italian only; house wine by the carafe is serviceable and well-priced. **Dress** Casual. **Disabled access** No. **Customers** Theatergoers, theater people, locals. **Hours** Monday, Tuesday, Thursday, and Friday, noon–11:45 p.m.; Wednesday and Saturday, 11:30 a.m.–11:45 p.m.; Sunday, noon–11:45 p.m.

SETTING AND ATMOSPHERE This star of Restaurant Row occupies a narrow space with a low-ceilinged bar area that leads to a vaulted back room where an active, open kitchen is fronted by a counter topped with large flower pots heaped with bread and lemons. Modesty prevails, the lights are low, adornment is limited to framed black-and-white photos, and, grazie Dio, there is soundproofing so that you can hear your dining companions and gather snatches of theatrical gossip from your neighbors.

HOUSE SPECIALTIES This menu changes daily, but there are always wonderful thin-crusted pizzas; pasta with porcini mushrooms; grilled vegetable plate; calf's liver with onions.

OTHER RECOMMENDATIONS Ultra-thin pizza bread with oil and rosemary; arugula salad with prosciutto; bruschetta; panzanella; gelato.

SUMMARY AND COMMENTS Orso has been a winner for over 15 years, and it's still hard to get a reservation—so if this is your pretheater destination, book well in advance. The northern Italian dishes are expertly and authentically prepared, the waiters are cordial, the setting is relaxed, theater folk actually eat here, and prices are fair.

Osteria del Circo ★★★

ITALIAN	EXPENSIVE	QUALITY ★★★★	VALUE ★★★

120 West 55th Street (between Sixth and Seventh avenues), Midtown West; ☎ 212-265-3636; osteriadelcirco.com

Reservations Recommended. **When to go** Anytime. **Entrée range** $16–$45; appetizers, $8.50–$26.50. **Payment** All major credit cards. **Service rating** ★★★ **Friendliness rating** ★★★ **Bar** Full service; serves a top-notch "Negroni." **Wine selection** Very good. **Dress** Midtown melange of business and casual. **Disabled access** Yes. **Customers** Business, locals, tourists. **Hours** Monday–Saturday, 11:30 a.m.–2:30 p.m. and 5:30–11:30 p.m.; Sunday, 5:30–11:30 p.m.

SETTING AND ATMOSPHERE From the tent-like red and yellow swaths of cloth that adorn the high ceiling to the trapeze ladder with hanging monkeys over the bar, designer Adam Tihany set out to create an atmosphere of fun—and he succeeded. The bright colors bring the room to life and the wide-open space and festive aura bring a smile to the face and create childlike anticipation for the main attraction: Mama Maccioni's food.

HOUSE SPECIALTIES Egi's ravioli; fresh Maine lobster with fennel in tomato confit, pink grapefruit, arugula, and red bliss potato salad; Zuppa alla frantoiana (Tuscan 30-vegetable soup); daily risottos; crème brûlée; bomboloncini (custard-, chocolate-, and raspberry-filled doughnuts).

OTHER RECOMMENDATIONS Cacciucco (Tuscan fish soup); any of the thin-crust pizzas; tripe stew with Parmesan; warm bread pudding.

SUMMARY AND COMMENTS It's hard not to enjoy yourself at this Midtown Italian hot spot run by Sirio Maccioni's (Le Cirque) three sons. The room is spacious, the mood festive, and everyone seems happy to be there. The food, however, can be hit or miss. The lobster appetizer improves on the excellent lobster salad, which it replaced. The dish is a perfect marriage of contrasting flavors that come together on the palate. But the yellowfin tuna tartare is a flat and bland mush, held together barely by tender white beans on top. Egi's ravioli (a must-order), stuffed delicately with spinach, bitter greens, and sheep's milk ricotta, comes with a choice of sauces, but works best with the butter-sage. Unfortunately, agnolotti, half moon–shaped shrimp and corn ravioli in a curry sauce, fails miserably. Desserts, on the other hand, steal the show. The list is among the largest and best in the city, and the warm bread pudding topped with caramelized pecans is blissful and addictive. Although for now only a sideshow item that appears occasionally as a special on the menu, this scrumptious wonder deserves to be part of the big show.

Otto ★★★

PIZZERIA/ENOTECA	MODERATE	QUALITY ★★★★	VALUE ★★

One Fifth Avenue (corner of Eighth Street), Greenwich Village; ☎ 212-995-9559; www.ottopizzeria.com

Reservations Only for parties of six or more. **When to go** Off-peak so you won't have to wait too long. **Entrée range** $7–$14. **Payment** All major credit cards. **Service rating** ★★★ **Friendliness rating** ★★½ **Bar** Full service. **Wine selection** Extensive Italian. **Dress** Casual and hip. **Disabled access** Yes. **Customers** Professionals, fashionistas, locals. **Hours** Daily, 11:30 a.m.–midnight; pizza served all day.

SETTING AND ATMOSPHERE Although the space, including the bar and dining rooms, is large, the area doesn't seem cavernous, in part due to the partitions and shades of red, burgundy, and brown colors along with the wooden furniture and floor. The atmosphere is far from cozy, but it's warm and sleek. Noise levels can be overwhelming when it's packed.

HOUSE SPECIALTIES Otto lardo pizza (yep—paper-thin strips of pork fat and fresh rosemary over a pizza crust); gelato—all flavors; seasonal hot chocolate; fennel and bottarga pizza (fennel, fish roe, two cheeses, and tomato); Italian wine.

OTHER RECOMMENDATIONS Funghi misti (mixed mushrooms); ceci bottarga (fried chickpeas with fish roe); figs agrodolce.

SUMMARY AND COMMENTS Mario Batali, of Babbo fame (along with a few other eateries), opened Otto in spring 2003 and it became, instantly, a controversial hit. The controversy is not about the pizzas (although the "otto lardo" pizza reached cult status in months), but more about the antipasti and whether Otto can justify charging $4 to $21 for small to "grande" portions of various cuts of ham, preserved swordfish, cheese, olives, and various salads. We think the portion size is a bit lilliputian, but many of the dishes are well executed with subtle tastes worth trying in spite of the poor cost-size ratio. There are daily pizza and bruschetta specials, along with the regular "otto" and "classica" pizza varieties. Otto pizzas have untraditional toppings (see above for examples). The knowledgeable sommelier is on hand to discuss Italian wine accompaniments. As you wait for your table in the bar, we'd suggest indulging in a flight of wine for tasting. The gelato has already been graced with well-deserved awards; the olive oil, coffee, and hazelnut stracciatella flavors are superb.

Paola's ★★★

| NORTHERN ITALIAN | MODERATE/EXPENSIVE | QUALITY ★★★★ | VALUE ★★★★ |

245 East 84th Street, Upper East Side; ☎ 212-794-1890

Reservations Recommended. **When to go** Dinner only. **Entrée range** $17.95–$27. **Payment** All major credit cards. **Service rating** ★★★ **Friendliness rating** ★★★ **Wine selection** Good; a bit pricey. **Dress** Casual. **Disabled access** Fair. **Customers** Locals. **Hours** Monday–Saturday, noon–4 p.m. and 5–11 p.m.; Sunday, 5–10 p.m.

SETTING AND ATMOSPHERE Lovely and low-key; you could be sitting in a side-street establishment in Florence or Siena. The two rooms are small, the tables subtly lit with candles, the walls dark red with gilt-edged mirrors in a repeated pattern. When it fills up, the noise level can rise; in the warmer months, the noise spills out the windowed doors to the umbrella-topped tables of the sidewalk cafe.

HOUSE SPECIALTIES Pan-seared baby artichokes; homemade "malfatti," dumplings made of Swiss chard and ricotta; chicken and sweet sausage in wine sauce; ricotta cheesecake; cozze alla marinara (cultivated mussels sautéed in a light tomato sauce); macco (purée of fava beans over sautéed broccoli rabe with tomatoes and onions); casunsei ampezzani (beet-and-ricotta-stuffed pasta topped with poppy seeds).

OTHER RECOMMENDATIONS Mozzarella with tomatoes and basil; mixed baby greens with pears, walnuts, and shaved pecorino cheese; veal and chicken ravioli in a light tomato sauce; potato gnocchi; risotto del giorno; veal scaloppine.

SUMMARY AND COMMENTS A cut or two above a neighborhood trattoria, this intimate Upper East Side Italian restaurant is worth the trip. The service is solicitous, and the food is authentic, homey, and very comforting. Chef/owner Paola Marracino has changed the menu very little over the years, and it's obvious she knows what she's doing with appetizers like pan-seared baby artichokes and mussels marinara that are the best versions of those dishes you'll find in Manhattan. Pastas are also first-rate, especially the stuffed variety, like ravioli and tortelloni. Great for a special occasion or a romantic night out.

The Parsonage ★★★

AMERICAN/ITALIAN   MODERATE/EXPENSIVE   QUALITY ★★★★   VALUE ★★★★½

74 Arthur Kill Road (corner of Clarke), Staten Island; ☎ 718-351-7879

Reservations Recommended. **When to go** Anytime. **Entrée range** $14–$28. **Payment** All major credit cards. **Service rating** ★★★½ **Friendliness rating** ★★★★ **Wine selection** Modest, but varied and inexpensive. **Dress** Nice casual, dressy. **Disabled access** Yes. **Customers** Locals, Manhattanites in the know. **Hours** Sunday–Thursday, 11:30 a.m.–10 p.m.; Friday and Saturday, 11:30 a.m.–11 p.m.

SETTING AND ATMOSPHERE The Parsonage is in a 140-year-old colonial house in the heart of historic Richmond on Staten Island. Wooden tables and chairs are arranged in a few rooms throughout the house. Features such as a beautiful old clock on a mantlepiece are included among the décor, while a few illustrations and paintings hang on the walls. The setting is ubercozy—it's almost like being at your aunt's house for a special occasion.

HOUSE SPECIALTIES Creamy polenta with mushroom and sausage; oatmeal-crusted lamb with mint; veal osso bucco; monkfish; grilled portobella mushroom with asagi cheese.

OTHER RECOMMENDATIONS Homemade pizzas; chicken with sausage and peppers; Caesar salad; sesame-crusted salmon with mushrooms; tartuffo.

SUMMARY AND COMMENTS Proprietors Paul Montella and James McBratney really know how to make the guests feel at home. The service is unpretentious and very friendly. Their confidence and pride in both the restaurant and food are well deserved. The creamy polenta is delectably smooth and rich. Presentation isn't a high priority, but it seems like you can't go wrong whether you order a fish, chicken, meat, or pasta dish. Treat getting to the location as an adventure. If you take the ferry, simply get on the S74 bus which waits at the terminal, and ask the driver to tell you when you get to Arthur Kill Road; or simply ask for the Parsonage. Most people on the island know the place, and the bus stops directly outside the restaurant. Allow for a 25- to 30-minute bus ride.

Pastis ★★½

BISTRO/FRENCH	MODERATE	QUALITY ★★★½	VALUE ★★★½

9 Ninth Avenue (corner of Little West 12th Street), Greenwich Village;
☎ **212-929-4844; www.pastisny.com**

Reservations Recommended. **When to go** Anytime. **Entrée range** $9–$20. **Payment** All major credit cards. **Service rating** ★★★ **Friendliness rating** ★★★½ **Bar** Full service, very popular. **Wine selection** Decent. **Dress** Casual for day; chic at night. **Disabled access** Accessible in front room and bathrooms. **Customers** Locals, trendies, celebrities. **Hours** Monday–Friday, 8–11:30 a.m., noon–5 p.m., and 6 p.m.–midnight; Saturday and Sunday, 10 a.m.–4:45 p.m. and 6 p.m.–midnight.

SETTING AND ATMOSPHERE Large restaurant with an airy, crisp, bistro-French feel. Mirrors, brass, wood, and tile are the predominant materials used to decorate the expanse. Brunch and lunchtime brings a more relaxed feel to the restaurant, but come nighttime, the glitz shines in all its glory, and the front room with the bar becomes very crowded.

HOUSE SPECIALTIES Steak frites with Bearnaise sauce; onion soup, croque monsieur; croque madame; chicken sandwich with portobella and roasted peppers; crêpes suzette.

OTHER RECOMMENDATIONS Gratin dauphinois; skate; BLT with french fries; omelette.

SUMMARY AND COMMENTS Pastis is not a place noteworthy for its food (though the coffee is excellent), but it has a high glamour factor, particularly at night. Its sibling Balthazar seems to have a better grip on food but has lost its hold on celebrities who seem to be flocking here instead. Come for brunch, get a feel for the place, and then decide if you'd like to tackle dinner here in another outfit. The bar scene is extremely lively and chic, so you could always forget dinner and stick to drinks. The food is standard, but brunch is fun if you order a drink and munch on the bread basket, a croque monsieur, or an omelette. One favorite beverage is the l'orchidee verte that consists of pastis, mint, and water; the crowning touch is its bold green color. The bathrooms are stylized for an old-fashoined, continental European feel; men and women wash their hands together in a trough-like sink, but use separate rooms for the toilets. In warm weather, sit outside where it feels a bit more relaxed (but it's harder to spot a celeb). Alternatively, you could enjoy the hyped atmosphere inside and join in on the eyeballing.

Patsy's Pizza ★★★

PIZZERIA	INEXPENSIVE	QUALITY ★★★★½	VALUE ★★★★★

2287 First Avenue, Spanish Harlem; ☎ **212-534-9783**

Reservations Not necessary. **When to go** Anytime. **Entrée range** Whole pizzas, $10–$19 (that's with three toppings). **Payment** Cash only. **Service rating** ★★

Friendliness rating ★★ **Bar** None. **Wine selection** None. **Dress** Casual. **Disabled access** Good. **Customers** Locals, foodies. **Hours** Daily, 11 a.m.–midnight.

SETTING AND ATMOSPHERE The room with the oven (where you order) is harshly lit but permeated with the collective spirit of a century of great pizza, so it would be a pity to lose that atmosphere as well as the pile of coal in front of the oven. Next door, the restaurant has friendly but amateurish waiter service.

HOUSE SPECIALTIES Fantastic unpretentious brick-oven pizza by the slice from an ancient coal-burning oven.

ENTERTAINMENT AND AMENITIES A semibroken black-and-white television blasting Spanish programs (ordering area only).

SUMMARY AND COMMENTS Though this is the only top-notch brick oven pizzeria that will serve slices, you should really get a whole pie in order to experience the full grandeur (order slices—from pies that have been sitting—and you may face less crusty crust, though the taste is still tops). The neighborhood is Spanish Harlem, so taxi in after dark and remain on full alert. Across the street, open during warm weather only, Rex's is an eccentric spot serving some of the city's best Italian ices (avoid strawberry, though!). Important note: The other Patsy's Pizzas in Manhattan have merely licensed the name; they're not recommended.

Penang ★★½

MALAYSIAN	MODERATE	QUALITY ★★★ ½	VALUE ★★★

240 Columbus Avenue (71st Street), Upper West Side; ☎ 212-769-3988
109 Spring Street (between Greene and Mercer streets),
Soho; ☎ 212-274-8883
1596 Second Avenue (83rd Street), Upper East Side; ☎ 212-585-3838

Reservations Only for parties of six or more. **When to go** Anytime. **Entrée range** $11.95–$19.95. **Payment** All major credit cards. **Service rating** ★★★ **Friendliness rating** ★★★ **Bar** Full service. **Wine selection** Limited, but the beers on tap seem to be the beverage of choice. **Dress** Casual. **Disabled access** West Side: fair, no access to bathrooms; Soho: none; East Side: yes. **Customers** Locals, ethnic. **Hours** *West Side:* Monday–Thursday, noon–midnight; Friday and Saturday, noon–1 a.m.; Sunday, noon–11 p.m. *Soho:* Monday–Thursday, noon–midnight; Friday and Saturday, noon–1 a.m.; Sunday, noon–11 p.m. *East Side:* Daily, noon–11 p.m.

SETTING AND ATMOSPHERE Downtown, it's rain forest funk with a waterfall, no less. Uptown, it's wood paneling, wooden tables, windows, and bamboo with a few non–rain forest potted plants. The subterranean "lounge" is low on lights and high on decibels. There's more decoration outside—a large relief of plowing water buffalo—than in.

HOUSE SPECIALTIES Masak nenas, chicken or beef with fresh pineapple chunks and lemon grass, served in a pineapple shell; roti canai, Indian flat bread with curry dipping sauce; chicken with shredded mango and peppers served in a mango shell; spiced, deep-fried whole red snapper with a spicy sauce.

OTHER RECOMMENDATIONS Penang clay pot noodles with seafood; Malaysian nasi goreng; fried taro stuffed with seafood; beef rendang.

SUMMARY AND COMMENTS Malaysia, the crossroads of the food world, incorporates into its cooking the best culinary qualities of nearby India, China, Thailand, and Vietnam, along with some European touches from the British colonizers. Though Penang has suffered from expansion and sometimes spotty food, it remains a viable venue for Malaysian cooking in Manhattan. Appetizers outpace entrées, so load up on those, especially the roti canai, warm, ultrathin ribbony bread that you tear up and dip into positively addictive chicken and potato curry sauce. **Nyonya** (194 Grand Street between Mott and Mulberry), by the same owners, has a wider selection of more obscure and authentic Malaysian dishes (try the Hainanese chicken rice and mee siam), but for the real thing, take the 7 train to Flushing and hit the original Penang (call ☎ 718-321-2078); it's truly worth the trip.

Peter Luger ★★★½

STEAK HOUSE   **EXPENSIVE**   **QUALITY** ★★★★   **VALUE** ★★★★

178 Broadway (Driggs Avenue), Brooklyn (Williamsburg);
☎ **718-387-7400; www.peterluger.com**

Reservations Required for dinner. **When to go** Anytime. **Entrée range** $30–$60 per person. **Payment** Cash only. **Service rating** ★★★ **Friendliness rating** ★★★ **Bar** Full service, proud of its "oversized drinks." **Wine selection** Fair. **Dress** Casual. **Disabled access** Yes. **Customers** Locals, business, tourists. **Hours** Monday–Thursday, 11:45 a.m.–9:45 p.m.; Friday and Saturday, 11:45 a.m.–10:45 p.m.; Sunday, 12:45–9:45 p.m.

SETTING AND ATMOSPHERE Just over the bridge in the Williamsburg section of Brooklyn, this 110-year-old landmark steak house is as plain as its menu. Scrubbed wooden tables, scrubbed wooden floors, a few beer steins, and crusty veteran waiters (who are actually very nice) are all right at home here. This is the way a steak house should be.

HOUSE SPECIALTIES USDA prime dry-aged (on the premises) porterhouse steak; creamed spinach; Luger's German fried potatoes; apple strudel with whipped cream.

OTHER RECOMMENDATIONS Double-thick loin lamb chops; steak sandwich; french fries; thick sliced bacon; cheesecake.

SUMMARY AND COMMENTS What's a trip to New York City without a trip to the city's best steak house? Okay, so maybe Luger's isn't in the city, but it's close enough and more than worth the cab fare over to Williamsburg for the best steak in town. Why not start with a thick strip of bacon to loosen up the arteries a bit? Hey, if you're going to Luger's, you may as well go all the way. It's greasy, it's fatty, and it's good. But don't have too many strips, because you're going to need all the stomach room you can spare for that porterhouse, a huge cut of meat for two. Watch greedily as the waiter pours the excess meat juices and melted butter over the perfectly cooked slices for effect. Then take one bite of the tender, juicy meat and you'll soon know why many will never go to another steak house again. Just for fun, try ordering some chicken.

kids Petite Abeille ★★½

BELGIAN LUNCHEONETTE	INEXPENSIVE	QUALITY ★★★★	VALUE ★★★★½

134 West Broadway (at Duane Street), Tribeca, ☎ 212-791-1360; 466 Hudson Street, ☎ 212-741-6479; 401 East 20th Street, ☎ 212-727-1505; www.petiteabeille.com

Reservations Not accepted. **When to go** Anytime. **Entrée range** $10–$16.95. **Payment** All major credit cards. **Service rating** ★★ **Friendliness rating** ★★★ **Bar** None. **Wine selection** None. **Dress** Casual. **Disabled access** Good; staff helps with step. **Customers** Locals, business, expat Belgians. **Hours** Monday–Friday, 7 a.m.–7 p.m.; Saturday and Sunday, 9 a.m.–6 p.m. (brunch)

SETTING AND ATMOSPHERE Décor is different in each Petite Abeille; what is consistent is the distinctly European flair, good food, and friendly service. Full bar except Hudson Street location.

HOUSE SPECIALTIES Waffles (unadorned, as per Belgian tradition), Flemish-style carbonade (savory beef stew cooked in abbey beer), stoemp de carrote (ultra-homey carrot-flecked mashed potatoes), and mussels.

OTHER RECOMMENDATIONS Brunch omelettes are tasty and fluffy, while coffee and cappuccino tend to be spot on.

ENTERTAINMENT AND AMENITIES Every other Tuesday night at the 20th Street location is jazz night. They deliver.

SUMMARY AND COMMENTS It's hard to decide whether you're eating in a good restaurant masquerading as a cheap lunchroom or if this is simply a super-high-quality lunchroom. Don't expect gastronomic miracles, just skillfully cooked Belgian comfort food, unusual but accessible, easy to enjoy, and you can't beat the price. All locations offer some terrific specials: Monday night is half-price Belgian beer night; Wednesday is all-you-can-eat Mussels night; and Thursday is lobster night. At press time, Petite Abeille planned to close its 107 West 18th location and replace it with another full-service restaurant at 44 West 17th Street. The new location will open May 2006 and keep the same telephone number as the old 18th street location (☎ 212-604-9350). Petite Abeille is child-friendly for its bright, colorful, and casual atmosphere and selection of simple and tasty fare. However, the Hudson Street location needs a facelift. Books of Belgian comic strip hero Tintin and his adventures are at hand for the reading pleasure of young and old.

Petrossian ★★★

RUSSIAN	EXPENSIVE	QUALITY ★★★½	VALUE ★★★

182 West 58th Street (at Seventh Avenue), Theater District; ☎ 212-245-2217; www.petrossian.com

Reservations Recommended. **When to go** Anytime. **Entrée range** $27–$40. **Payment** All major credit cards. **Service rating** ★★★ **Friendliness rating** ★★★

Bar Full service. **Wine selection** Very good, especially the champagne by the glass. **Dress** Upscale; jackets and ties. **Disabled access** No. **Customers** Business, ladies who lunch, caviar cravers. **Hours** Daily, 11:30 a.m.–10:30 p.m.

SETTING AND ATMOSPHERE Only one block from Carnegie Hall, this dimly lit caviar cave is nestled in a corner of the Alwyn Court. Art Nouveau lovelies grace the mirrors behind the polished granite bar. The dining area, mirrored, small, and darkly elegant, is appointed in rose, black, and well-buffed wood.

HOUSE SPECIALTIES Caviar! Beluga, sevruga, osetra, and so on, served with toast or blini and crème fraîche; "teasers," an assortment of smoked fish appetizers with a touch of foie gras; sautéed loin of arctic venison; sea scallop soufflé with truffles.

OTHER RECOMMENDATIONS Borscht with piroshki; foie gras salad; steamed lobster; tropical fruit, vodka sorbets; Valhrona chocolate soufflé; lemon tart.

SUMMARY AND COMMENTS You can blow a big budget on the caviar, but don't be intimidated—you can also dine surprisingly well on the $24 prix-fixe lunch, which includes a glass of fine champagne or the $42 prix-fixe dinner, graciously served throughout the evening. Brunch, too, is excellent. The Boutique offers caviar and foie gras to go, as well as table service for breakfast, lunch, or snacks.

Piccola Venezia ★★★★

ITALIAN	EXPENSIVE	QUALITY	★★★★½	VALUE	★★★

4201 28th Avenue (at 42nd Street), Astoria; ☎ 718-721-8470; www.piccola-venezia.com

Reservations Necessary. **When to go** Avoid lunch (same menu, same stratospheric prices). **Entrée range** $17.95–$33.95. **Payment** All major credit cards. **Service rating** ★★★★★ **Friendliness rating** ★★★★ **Bar** Full service. **Wine selection** Extensive; mostly Italian. **Dress** Elegant casual to dressy. **Disabled access** Good. **Customers** Politicians, movie stars, and neighborhood folks who've been eating here for decades. **Hours** Monday–Friday, 11:30 a.m.–11 p.m.; Saturday, 4:30 p.m.–midnight; Sunday, 2–10:30 p.m.

SETTING AND ATMOSPHERE Spirited conviviality amid Old-World graciousness. This is a real class joint, from the quality table linens to the marble paneling and uniformed waiters, and it's filled to the rafters meal after meal with celebratory eaters (and celebrity eaters, too; there are more celeb sightings here than in nearly any Manhattan eatery). Venetian scenes decorate the walls; however, the management is actually Istrian (part of former Yugoslavia, though the region was once under Venetian rule).

HOUSE SPECIALTIES Excellent veal, especially the oversize veal porterhouse, veal chop giardiniera, or stunning veal franchaise. Don't miss fusi (a twisty Istrian pasta), with either grappa sauce or a traditional Istrian veal sauce. Fried calamari, roasted peppers, tricolor and house salad, tripe, chicken campagnola (basically chicken Marsala with mushrooms), and oniony sautéed Venetian liver are all dependably first-rate. With seafood, stick to specials (and ask your waiter for help—some days are better than others, and the waiters know). Try the terrific osso buco (get it with brown sauce if you can). Specials not to miss: venison, rabbit, seafood pasta with onions, veal valdestano, and Istrian sauerkraut soup). Avoid contadinas and other mixed grills, risotto. Pesto is best in summer (again, best when a special). Ask nicely and you may be granted some of these off-menu faves: roast loin of pork, scallops casino, stuffed artichokes, and shrimp or clams in vodka sauce.

OTHER RECOMMENDATIONS This was not always such an expensive ticket; it's a regular neighborhood restaurant that over the years has grown exorbitant. So while the plainer preparations are perfectly fine, they may not taste as sensational as their price tag. Avoid potential disappointments, such as the two lobster tail selections (whole lobster, when a special—for example, wonderful lobster fra diavolo—is much more interesting), cold antipasto plate (just the usual cast of characters), minestrone soup, and filet mignon. Some whole-fish dishes can be a bit pedestrian as well. And definitely skip the ho-hum desserts.

ENTERTAINMENT AND AMENITIES Valet parking.

SUMMARY AND COMMENTS Piccola Venezia, the most senior of several Astoria Istrian-Italians, has a fanatically devoted clientele. These folks know the waiters (old pros all) and count on them for guidance on matters of pesto freshness, seafood quality, etc. Newcomers are warmly served, but the staff may not go the extra mile for fresh faces. Unless you manage to establish a particular rapport with your waiter, stick with the above suggestions, the accumulated insights of several knowledgeable insiders.

Piccolo Angolo ★★★

ITALIAN	MODERATE	QUALITY ★★★★	VALUE ★★★½

621 Hudson Street (Jane Street), Greenwich Village; ☎ 212-229-9177

Reservations Recommended. **When to go** Dinner only. **Entrée range** $12–17; pastas, $7.95–$12.95. **Payment** MC, V. **Service rating** ★★★ **Friendliness rating** ★★★ **Wine selection** Limited, mostly Italian; hold out for the inexpensive homemade "house" wine. **Dress** Casual. **Disabled access** No. **Customers** Locals. **Hours** Tuesday–Thursday, 4–11 p.m.; Friday and Saturday, 4–midnight; Sunday, 4–9 p.m.

SETTING AND ATMOSPHERE This storefront West Village classic is small and crowded, but with good reason. The décor is limited to exposed brick with a few black-and-white prints. The tables are on top of each other and the noise level is high, but that doesn't stop regulars and a steady stream of newcomers from huddling in the doorway while they wait to be seated.

HOUSE SPECIALTIES Listen to the list of daily specials; fettucine with porcini mushrooms; linguine with white clam sauce; lobster ravioli; rack of lamb with Marsala.

OTHER RECOMMENDATIONS Hot seafood antipasto; shrimp fra diavolo; grilled portobello mushrooms; eggplant rolitini; ricotta cheesecake.

SUMMARY AND COMMENTS This place is family-run in the best sense. Renato Migliorini and his son, Peter, welcome customers and worry over the pint-sized kitchen, which somehow manages to turn out enough traditional, "home-cooked" Italian food to satisfy the full house expecting to be fed. When Papa lists the ample array of daily specials, it sounds more like a fast recitative from a Verdi opera. Listen closely; he's loathe to repeat, and these are the dishes to eat. Try to resist the irresistible garlic bread—you'll need room for the large, reasonably priced portions.

Picholine ★★★★

| MEDITERRANEAN | EXPENSIVE | QUALITY ★★★★½ | VALUE ★★★ |

35 West 64th Street (between Columbus and Central Park West), Upper West Side; ☎ 212-724-8585

Reservations Recommended. **When to go** Anytime. **Entrée range** $26.50–$36; pretheater prix fixe, $52 and $62; tasting menus, $73 and $88; lunch, $17.50–$21; three-course lunch for $28. **Payment** All major credit cards. **Service rating** ★★★ **Friendliness rating** ★★★ **Bar** Full service. **Wine selection** Interesting selections in a good range of prices. **Dress** Business, dressy, upscale casual; jacket required. **Disabled access** Yes. **Customers** Locals, business, Lincoln Center. **Hours** Monday–Wednesday, 5–10:30 p.m.; Thursday and Friday, 5–11:30 p.m.; Saturday, 11:45 a.m.–2 p.m. and 5–11:30 p.m.; Sunday, 5–9 p.m.

SETTING AND ATMOSPHERE East Side elegance on the West Side, with tapestries on the walls, lavishly framed paintings, ornate ceilings, shaded chandeliers, brocade banquettes, and some well-placed French country touches. The "picholine" (a small green olive) theme appears on the pretty plates and the warm olive green of the lower walls.

HOUSE SPECIALTIES Warm Maine lobster; foie gras, black mission figs, duck "prosciutto," and purslane; tournedos of salmon, horseradish crust, cucumbers, and salmon caviar; Jamison Farm organic loin of lamb; baked to order warm Valrhona chocolate tart; Picholine cheese cart.

OTHER RECOMMENDATIONS Tuna carpaccio; chilled white gazpacho; peekytoe crabmeat salad; wild mushroom and duck risotto; dayboat seafood selection; rabbit au Riesling; cheesecake mousse napoleon.

SUMMARY AND COMMENTS By far the best restaurant on the Upper West Side of Manhattan, Picholine would more than hold its own against its East Side counterparts as well. Chef Terrance Brennan's Mediterranean-influenced French fare sparkles with originality and substance, like the white bean gazpacho filled with little surprises like white grapes, almond slivers, and tiny bits of chopped red pepper. Warm Maine lobster is absolutely sensual, and Brennan's perfectly balanced signature dish of salmon, cucumbers, and salmon caviar with a horseradish crust is an absolute must. There's no shortage of good food here, and the truly knowledgeable and pleasant staff will be happy to steer you in the right direction. Even desserts are excellent, but who has time for dessert when you have that incredible cheese cart running around the room? Maître de fromage Max McCalman chooses about 50 cheeses from Picholine's own cheese cave and sets about the room, offering suggestions for enthralled patrons and enthusiastically describing each cheese.

For those with only a short-term memory, McCalman supplies a small index, noting the cheeses he has selected. Customers should feel welcome to stop in for cheese alone. A late-night stop for wine and cheese after a concert at Lincoln Center or even on a whim makes for a wonderful end to an evening (or maybe just a beginning).

Ping's ★★★★

| CHINESE | MODERATE | QUALITY ★★★★½ | VALUE ★★★★½ |

8302 Queens Boulevard, Elmhurst; ☎ 718-396-1238

Reservations Accepted. **When to go** Before noon for dim sum; otherwise, anytime. **Entrée range** $18.95 and up. **Payment** All major credit cards. **Service rating** ★★★★ **Friendliness rating** ★★★½ **Bar** Beer and wine only. **Wine selection** House. **Dress** Nice casual. **Disabled access** Good (if the dim sum carts can get around, so can you!). **Customers** Local Chinese and questing occidentals. **Hours** Daily, 8 a.m.–3:30 p.m. (dim sum) and 3:30 p.m.–4 a.m.

SETTING AND ATMOSPHERE Despite its bleak Queens Boulevard location, Ping's is an elegant upscale Hong Kong banquet hall, with red velvet, gold tassles, and a wall of sparkling fish tanks. In spite of the grand décor (and suavely attired staff), many patrons come quite casually dressed.

HOUSE SPECIALTIES Very skillful and schooled renditions of classic Hong Kong dishes, plus the best Peking duck in town. Try the exquisitely fresh and delicate scallops in shell, whole sea bass (prepared in a variety of ways), snow peapod leaves (ultra-delicate greens) served with egg, any of the shellfish, pretty much anything on the specials menu, and the more ambitious-sounding offerings on the regular menu. Even less ambitious dishes like humble seafood pan-fried noodles are prepared with uncommon flair and served with great pizzaz (this one on an elegant white serving plate, garnished with a seamless bouquet of broccoli heads).

OTHER RECOMMENDATIONS Outstanding dim sum each morning, perhaps the city's best (it's crowded on weekends, but the selection is also wider). Don't miss the awesome roast pork triangles (xia siu so, pronounced "Cha Sill Sew"), with ultra-flaky pastry and rich, tender barbecue filling. For dessert, buns decorated with a yellow spiral, stuffed with potent coconut-spiked egg custard.

ENTERTAINMENT AND AMENITIES Free parking (you'll need it!) in a lot just across the side street. Don't forget to have your ticket stamped by the restaurant's cashier.

SUMMARY AND COMMENTS The kitchen's elegance and flair belie the reasonable prices of many menu items. But while it's possible to make out quite well with noodles or chicken–cashew nuts here, don't waste your trip (or the kitchen's great skill) by bargain-hunting. This is a special-occasion place for exotic shellfish, rare baby vegetables, and fancy whole fish preparations. For especially special occasions, Ping's will put together a banquet meal (sky's the limit, price-wise; negotiate with a manager and be sure to carefully specify your party's squeamishness with unfamiliar ingredients). Service is excellent, with English-speaking managers in slick gray suits constantly walking the floor and offering help.

All the best action for Chinese food is happening in Queens these days, and although Flushing is a trek from Manhattan, Elmhurst—fast morphing into the city's fourth Chinatown—is much more accessible (a ten-minute ride once over the 59th Street Bridge, or take the E/F subway to Roosevelt Avenue, switch to the local G/R to the Grand Avenue stop). It's worth the trip, for dinner or dim sum; you'd have to go to Hong Kong to find much better food than this. For other superb eats in this area, see the profile for Kway Tiow Thai.

kids The Pink Teacup ★½

SOUTHERN	INEXPENSIVE	QUALITY ★★★½	VALUE ★★★½

42 Grove Street (between Bleecker and Bedford), Greenwich Village; ☎ 212-807-6755; www.thepinkteacup.com

Reservations Not accepted. **When to go** Great $7 lunch special (weekdays 11 a.m.–3 p.m.). **Entrée range** $11–$15. **Payment** Cash only. **Service rating** ★★ **Friendliness rating** ★★½ **Bar** None. **Wine selection** None. **Dress** Nice casual. **Disabled access** Good; restrooms not accessible. **Customers** Locals (mostly long-time regulars). **Hours** Daily, 8 a.m.–midnight.

SETTING AND ATMOSPHERE Simple two- to four-person glass-topped tables filling a small space with one wall full of glossy black-and-whites of below-A-list actors, and another wall with a painted piece featuring Martin Luther King Jr. It's suitably cheerful and casual for children.

HOUSE SPECIALTIES The state-of-the-art in fried pork chops; also, salmon croquettes (made with canned salmon, as per tradition); wonderful fried smoked bacon, ham, and sausage; great collard greens and black-eyed peas (stir in Tabasco). Breakfast, available at all times, is the best meal; grits and home fries are especially good. For dessert, sweet potato pie is a better choice than the cakes.

SUMMARY AND COMMENTS Lots of diners do wrong here by ordering the menu's less-distinguished offerings. Stick with breakfast; pork chops (try them with eggs and grits for breakfast), smoked meats, collard greens, and black-eyed peas are the way to go. Play some tunes on the Motown-and-funk–filled jukebox. Kids will like staples on the main menu such as macaroni and cheese.

Pó ★★★½

ITALIAN	MODERATE	QUALITY ★★★★	VALUE ★★★★

31 Cornelia Street (between Bleecker and West Fourth streets), Greenwich Village; ☎ 212-645-2189

Reservations A must. **When to go** Dinner only. **Entrée range** $14–$18. **Payment** AE. **Service rating** ★★★ **Friendliness rating** ★★★ **Wine selection** Limited, but good and fairly priced. **Dress** Casual. **Disabled access** Fair. **Cus-**

tomers Locals, aficionados from the boroughs and the burbs. **Hours** Tuesday, 5:30–11:30 p.m.; Wednesday–Sunday, 11:30 a.m.–3 p.m. and 5:30–11 p.m.

SETTING AND ATMOSPHERE A thimbleful of space (with hardly more than a dozen tables), creamy buff walls, and the patterned tin ceiling so characteristic of old Village buildings. Mirrors above the simple banquettes and discreet lighting are the sole decoration, but the feeling is warm, informal, and inviting.

HOUSE SPECIALTIES Check daily specials; grappa-cured salmon; white bean ravioli with balsamic vinegar and brown butter; marinated quail with plums and pomegranate molasses; terrine of dark chocolate, amaretti, and vin santo with espresso caramel.

OTHER RECOMMENDATIONS Coach farm goat cheese truffle with balsamic onions, roasted peppers, and tapenade; linguine with clams, pancetta, and hot chiles; cool-roasted veal breast with rucola grana and Ama oil; grilled lamb sirloin with merguez, white beans, and preserved lemons; campari-grapefruit sorbetto.

SUMMARY AND COMMENTS The décor is not the draw here—it's the very well-prepared, often inventive Italian food. The tradition began with former celeb chef Mario Batali and has since continued. Excellent white bean bruschetta, good bread, and olive oil come to the table to whet your appetite, but don't over-nibble; you'll need the room for what follows. If choosing is too taxing, try the six-course tasting menu for $40. The prices are as unpretentious as the setting; ditto for the service, helpful and friendly without fuss. Perhaps not as well kept a West Village secret as many of its repeat patrons would like: Reservations can be hard to come by, so plan ahead for this one.

Rain ★★★

ASIAN FUSION	MODERATE	QUALITY ★★★★	VALUE ★★★

100 West 82nd Street (Columbus Avenue), Upper West Side;
☎ **212-501-0776;**
1059 Third Avenue (between 62nd and 63rd streets), Upper East Side;
☎ **212-223-3669**

Reservations Recommended. **When to go** Anytime. **Entrée range** $12–$24. **Payment** All major credit cards. **Service rating** ★★★ **Friendliness rating** ★★★ **Bar** Full service. **Wine selection** Good. **Dress** Informal, casual. **Disabled access** No. **Customers** Locals. **Hours** Monday–Thursday, 6–11 p.m.; Friday, 6 p.m.–midnight; Saturday, 5 p.m.–midnight; Sunday, 5–10 p.m.

SETTING AND ATMOSPHERE With a few simple strokes, the ground floor of this Upper West Side brownstone has taken on the sultry feel of Rangoon in the rainy season. Rattan settees with boldly flowered cushions cluster around low bamboo tables in the always crowded bar area, and the large dining area is simple and comfortable—tables covered with no-nonsense white paper; plain, polished wood floors; and slowly circling ceiling fans. Its new crosstown cousin has a more modern look, with a row of wooden booths bathed in soft lighting and separated by hanging swaths of linen along the wall.

HOUSE SPECIALTIES Crispy Vietnamese spring rolls stuffed with shrimp, vegetables, and glass noodles; Thai-style fajitas, a cross-cultural knockout that combines roast duck and Asian vegetables wrapped in moo-shu pancakes; a delicate salmon fillet roasted in a banana leaf and spiced with pepper and garlic.

OTHER RECOMMENDATIONS Daily specials; Malaysian chicken satay, with the traditional cucumber salad and peanut sauce; pad thai, rice noodles with chicken, shrimp, bean sprouts, and egg; crispy whole fish served with tangy "three-flavor" sauce. And if your sweet tooth needs satisfying, the fried coconut ice cream is a must.

SUMMARY AND COMMENTS Chef Taweewat Hurapan handles this combo of Southeast Asian cuisines—Thai, Vietnamese, and the lesser-known Malaysian—with ease and elegance. Traditional dishes alternate with innovative adaptations, and the presentations have a stylish pizzazz not often found in Asian restaurants. This is a very popular spot with the trendy and the non-, so book well in advance for weekend dinners. Only half the tables can be reserved; the rest are held for walk-ins, and that can leave you lifting libations in the bar for quite a while.

Rice ★★★

ASIAN FUSION   INEXPENSIVE   QUALITY ★★★½   VALUE ★★★★★

227 Mott Street (between Prince and Spring streets), Little Italy; ☎ 212-226-5775; 81 Washington Street, Brooklyn; ☎ 718-222-9880; www.riceny.com

Reservations Not necessary. When to go Anytime. Entrée range $5–$13. Payment Cash or checks only. Service rating ★★★ Friendliness rating ★★★ Bar Beer, limited drinks. Wine selection Very small. Dress Casual or funky. Disabled access Yes. Customers Locals, regulars, hipsters on a budget or a health kick. Hours Manhattan: Daily, noon–midnight; Brooklyn: daily, noon–11 p.m.; Brooklyn offers brunch on Sunday beginning at 10 a.m.

SETTING AND ATMOSPHERE Rice manages to perfect a combined atmosphere of calm, relaxation, and stylish appeal. The background music is unobtrusive but often tastefully selected. Simple wooden-topped tables and straight-backed chairs. The Brooklyn branch has a great outdoor patio for warm weather.

HOUSE SPECIALTIES Thai black rice with edamame peas; Asian coleslaw (no mayonnaise, and flavored with a delicious carrot-ginger dressing); coconut curry shrimp; pear cider; banana leaf wrap dessert (sweet plantain rolled in sticky rice).

OTHER RECOMMENDATIONS Tea-smoked salmon salad; pad thai; eggplant maki; tamales.

SUMMARY AND COMMENTS Rice caters to vegetarians and carnivores equally successfully, which is not always an easy task; tofu steak and chicken kabobs are given the same attention. Similarly, waifs and those with heartier appetites will be satisfied with the option of ordering either a small bowl of rice and topping instead of a larger size. The options are tasty and often healthy and the prices are low. Contrary to what might be considered a confused selection, the mixture of Thai, Indian, Mexican, and Japanese influences works for the menu as there aren't too many options for the mix to go overboard. Try to get to the Brooklyn branch as it's located in that borough's DUMBO (Down Under the Manhattan Bridge Overpass), which has a super view of Manhattan and has new galleries and a funky old factory appeal. If you're early enough (before 7 p.m. Monday–Saturday), visit the **Jacques Torres Chocolate Shop** (66 Water Street).

Rinconcito Peruano ★★★

PERUVIAN	INEXPENSIVE	QUALITY ★★★★	VALUE ★★★★★

803 Ninth Avenue (between 53rd and 54th streets), Midtown West; ☎ 212-333-5685

Reservations For large parties only. **When to go** Anytime (more choices on weekends). **Entrée range** $6–$15. **Payment** MC, V. **Service rating** ★½ **Friendliness rating** ★★½ **Bar** None. **Wine selection** None. **Dress** Casual. **Disabled access** Good; restrooms not accessible. **Customers** Peruvians from all over, locals. **Hours** Sunday–Thursday, noon–9 p.m.; Friday and Saturday, noon–10 p.m.

SETTING AND ATMOSPHERE A little touch of Jackson Heights, Queens, in Manhattan, with a modest, tidy little dining room. Although they seem to have learned restaurant management from a correspondence course, the mom-and-pop owners are lovely people (food this good doesn't come from cold-hearted cooks), and the good vibes that enliven the food permeate this humble parlor. Peruvians flock here, as do in-the-know Anglos.

HOUSE SPECIALTIES Tamales are the very epitome of corn; papas à la huancaina (the Peruvian classic of cold, boiled potatoes drenched in spicy cheese sauce) luxuriate in a rich, slightly chunky yellow sauce, not chalky or bland as elsewhere; papa rellena is an ungreasy fried ball of subtly spiced mashed potatoes stuffed with tender ground meat; aji de gallina is a casserole with chunks of tender chicken and good potato (along with ground walnuts, Parmesan cheese, and mirasol peppers) afloat in a sweetish sauce that's beautifully unified of flavor. Splendid fish ceviche (raw fish cooked through acidic limey marination) is quite spicy, the flesh so rich it's almost buttery; tacu tacu is smooth, irresistible soupy rice with white beans (also available with meat). For dessert, helado de lucuma is very smooth and deep-flavored ice cream made from a popular (but untranslatable) South American fruit. Another dessert, choclo peruano, confronts you with a small ear of huge kerneled corn and a small brick of extremely mild cheese. At first you're not quite sure what to do, but nature quickly takes its course.

OTHER RECOMMENDATIONS The dynamite hot sauce contains some avocado; it's great for dunking bread in.

SUMMARY AND COMMENTS Manhattan's been sadly lacking good South American food for years, but Rinconcito Peruano has upped the ante, serving Peruvian dishes worlds tastier than you'll find in even the best places in Queens and New Jersey (the food can't possibly be much better even in Peru!). It's so homey that nothing is ever made exactly the same way twice (much to the delight of the many regulars here, who seldom grow bored). The well-meaning staff is decidedly not ready for prime time, and the kitchen gets overwhelmed when crowds peak (so go at off hours). But gawd, is it ever worth it. To find most of the menu actually available, go for lunch on a Saturday or Sunday.

The River Café ★★★★★

NEW AMERICAN	VERY EXPENSIVE	QUALITY ★★★★★	VALUE ★★★★½

1 Water Street, Brooklyn; ☎ 718-522-5200; www.therivercafe.com

Reservations Necessary, unless you wish to have drinks or order à la carte in the Terrace Room; call in advance to see if room is booked. **When to go** Anytime. **Entrée range** Prix-fixe three-course dinner, $70 per person; six-course tasting menu, $90 per person; à la carte lunch menu, $23–$27. **Payment** All major credit cards. **Service rating** ★★★★½ **Friendliness rating** ★★★★ **Bar** Full service. **Wine selection** Extensive; over 500 selections. **Dress** Dressy for women, jacket required for men in main dining room; less formal in Terrace Room. **Disabled access** Yes. **Customers** Couples, loyal and deep-pocketed regulars, professionals, anyone celebrating extra-special occasions. **Hours** Monday–Saturday, noon–3 p.m. and 6–11 p.m.; Sunday, 11:30 a.m.–3 p.m. (brunch) and 6–11 p.m.

SETTING AND ATMOSPHERE It's hard to find restaurants with better views, and there's not even any elevation involved. The restaurant is directly on the waterfront on the Brooklyn side of the East River, just south and almost under the Brooklyn Bridge. Romantic and elegant in the evening, and inspiring (and a bit cheaper) during the day. At risk of belaboring the point, this may be one of the top ten places in New York for marriage proposals, wedding celebrations, and anniversary meals. Noise levels are controlled, and couples can be seated either next to the window, so they sit across form each other, or across from it against the wall along a comfortable banquette, so they can sit next to each other, hold hands, and look at the view together.

HOUSE SPECIALTIES Roasted pear salad; roasted "Bee Gee" shrimp; Maine lobster (seasonal preparations); rack of lamb; chocolate marquise Brooklyn Bridge dessert.

OTHER RECOMMENDATIONS Venison loin; most of their daily specials, especially the creative appetizers; the roquefort cheese soufflé is a decent vegetarian option, but can sometimes err on the heavy side.

SUMMARY AND COMMENTS Tourist and locals are always in awe of the superb setting of the River Café. However, unlike other known spots, that may have great settings but mediocre food, the River Café excels in food and service—it's well worth a splurge on all levels. This is the place where several famed chefs once reigned, including Larry Forgione; Brad Steelman is currently at the helm. If the Terrace Room isn't booked, and you don't feel like paying for a full meal, enjoy some wine and an appetizer or two.

Rosa Mexicano ★★★

MEXICAN	MODERATE	QUALITY ★★★★	VALUE ★★★★

1063 First Avenue (58th Street), Midtown East; ☎ 212-753-7407; www.rosamexicano.com

Reservations Recommended. **When to go** Dinner only. **Entrée range** $17–$28. **Payment** All major credit cards. **Service rating** ★★ **Friendliness rating** ★★★ **Bar** Full service; emphasis on margaritas, especially the pomegranate variation. **Wine selection** Limited. **Dress** Casual. **Disabled access** Yes. **Customers** Locals, ethnic, tourists. **Hours** Daily, 5–11:30 p.m.

SETTING AND ATMOSPHERE It's always fiesta time here, with a boisterous bar scene in the front. Colorful cutout banners flutter from the dark rose ceilings over dusty rose adobe walls, star lighting fixtures twinkle, potted ferns add a little greenery, and traditional copper plates add a little elegance to the table settings.

HOUSE SPECIALTIES Guacamole; crepas de cuitlacoche (Mexican corn fungus— a real delicacy); enchiladas de mole poblano; posole (a stew with pork, chicken, and hominy); alambres de camarones (grilled, skewered marinated shrimp).

OTHER RECOMMENDATIONS Ceviche of bay scallops; menudo (tripe stew); enchiladas de pato (duck with a green mole sauce); crepas camarones (crêpes filled with shrimp in a chile pasilla sauce).

SUMMARY AND COMMENTS Above and beyond the usual Tex-Mex fare, this is as close to authentic, classic Mexican cuisine as you will find in New York. Be sure to order the made-to-order-at-your-table guacamole; it has become a renowned signature dish. The color and dash of the food and the setting are guaranteed to lift your spirits, even before you down a few divine margaritas. They also have another site at 61 Columbus Avenue (☎ 212-977-7700). If you'd like to continue the practice of paying a lot for Mexican fare, try **Dos Caminos** (373 Park Avenue South, between 26th and 27th streets; ☎ 212-294-1000).

Sachiko's on Clinton ★★★★

JAPANESE	MODERATE/EXPENSIVE	QUALITY ★★★½	VALUE ★★★

25 Clinton Street, Lower East Side; ☎ 212-253-2900; www.sachikosonclinton.com

Reservations Not necessary. **When to go** Anytime. **Entrée range** $12–$36. **Payment** All major credit cards. **Service rating** ★★★½ **Friendliness rating** ★★★★ **Bar** Sake, beer, special cocktails. **Wine selection** Very small. **Dress** Casual chic. **Disabled access** Yes. **Customers** Locals, ethnic, sushi lovers. **Hours** Sunday–Wednesday, 5:30 p.m.–midnight; Thursday–Saturday, 5:30 p.m.–1 a.m.

SETTING AND ATMOSPHERE Clean and crisp presentation of both food and the décor. No ceremony needed as Sachiko's gives off an air of quiet confidence.

The simple wooden decorations attest to the saying that 'less is more.' A lovely back garden and patio for dining in decent weather. Diners can either sit at the small-ish sushi bar, or choose from several tables in two adjacent spaces.

HOUSE SPECIALTIES Crab cream croquet; kushiage; gomadofu; soba with duck soup; sake cocktails.

OTHER RECOMMENDATIONS Anything from the sushi bar; sasazushi (bamboo leaf–wrapped sushi); soba salad.

SUMMARY AND COMMENTS The sushi is wonderfully fresh, but there's plenty on the menu for those not interested in raw sea life. The kushiage, a variety of meat or vegetables dipped in panko (light breadcrumbs), fried, and often placed on skewers, is special and can't be found in many New York kitchens. Service is very attentive and, if you're lucky, you might meet Sachiko herself who talks proudly to diners about the cuisine.

Sahara East ★★½

MIDDLE EASTERN	MODERATE	QUALITY ★★★★	VALUE ★★★★

184 First Avenue, The East Village; ☎ 212-353-9000

Reservations Accepted. When to go Warm weather. Entrée range $10.95–$16.95. Payment Cash only. Service rating ★½ Friendliness rating ★★★★ Bar Beer and wine. Wine selection Small. Dress Casual. Disabled access Poor (big step at front door). Customers Locals, ethnic. Hours Daily, 9 a.m.–midnight.

SETTING AND ATMOSPHERE A narrow little cafe, but pass through to the large garden in back decorated with lights and hanging knickknacks.

HOUSE SPECIALTIES Falafel, grape leaves, fattoush (salad with pita croutons), lamb or chicken shish kebab, lamb or chicken couscous.

OTHER RECOMMENDATIONS Shisha (aromatic tobacco, optionally flavored with apple), smoked from ornate water pipes fueled by glowing coals; bargain lunch specials.

ENTERTAINMENT AND AMENITIES Live music on Friday and Saturday, 9–11:30 p.m.

SUMMARY AND COMMENTS Sahara can turn out some high-quality food, but the tiny kitchen gets overwhelmed when things are busy. The dilemma is that the place is most fun when crowded, so one must weigh food against ambience when choosing a time to eat here (busy nights are Thursday through Sunday). On nice clear evenings, the garden fills up, and the perfumed shisha smoke wafts as snakily as the music. Older Middle Eastern guys and East Village hipsters blend effortlessly into the scene, and it feels wonderful to be a part of it all. On these busy kitchen nights, stick with the dishes we've listed and you'll do fine. If, however, food is more important to you than setting, go on off nights and ask the friendly chef about the day's specials. In any case, service is very friendly but maddeningly slack. Put yourself on the same slow track, puff an apple shisha (try it—it's much mellower than cigarettes; this is the place that made shisha chic), and relax into the Egyptian groove.

kids Saigon Grill ★★★

VIETNAMESE	INEXPENSIVE	QUALITY ★★★★½	VALUE ★★★★★

620 Amsterdam Avenue (at 90th Street), Upper West Side;
☎ **212-875-9072; www.saigongrill.com**
1700 Second Avenue (at 88th Street), Upper East Side; ☎ **212-996-4600**

Reservations Only for five or more (not accepted on weekends). **When to go** Avoid peak hours, especially on weekends. **Entrée range** $8.50–$14.95 (much less at lunch). **Payment** All major credit cards. **Service rating** ★½ **Friendliness rating** ★★ **Bar** Beer only. **Wine selection** None. **Dress** Casual. **Disabled access** No. **Customers** Local. **Hours** Daily, 11:30 a.m.–midnight (until 11:30 p.m. on Second Avenue).

SETTING AND ATMOSPHERE Clean, bright, no-frills bustling venue. The relaxed atmosphere and ample space make it a good choice for dining with kids.

HOUSE SPECIALTIES Barbecue spare ribs, barbecue pork chops, barbecue chicken, crispy whole sea bass, grilled boneless chicken, summer rolls, coconut sticky rice, pickled vegetable salad.

SUMMARY AND COMMENTS "Grill" is right: This place turns out some of the best grilled dishes around. Most Vietnamese restaurants in New York are run by Vietnamese of Chinese ethnicity, but here the two traditions run together. The wonderful barbecue spare ribs with peanut–plum sauce, for example, taste pretty Chinese. Hybrid or no, this is a real find, especially in an area where good Asian food is rare. Great as the grilled meats are, perhaps the best dish of all is the crispy whole sea bass (sweetly subtle sauce, ultra-flaky, and very fresh). Kids and adults will both like the wonderful coconut sticky rice (strewn with ground peanuts). Many of the other rice dishes are also very popular for young palettes.

Sea ★★★

THAI	INEXPENSIVE/MODERATE	QUALITY ★★★	VALUE ★★★½

114 N. Sixth Street, Williamsburg, Brooklyn; ☎ **718-384-8850;**
www.spicenyc.net

Reservations For parties over six. **When to go** Mid- to late afternoon. **Entrée range** $7–$15. **Payment** MC, V. **Service rating** ★★★½ **Friendliness rating** ★★★ **Bar** Full service with creative cocktails. **Wine selection** Limited. **Dress** Casual chic. **Disabled access** Yes. **Customers** Locals, hipsters, party-people. **Hours** Sunday–Thursday, 11:30 a.m.–1 a.m.; Friday and Saturday, 11:30 a.m.–2 a.m.

SETTING AND ATMOSPHERE A cool and fun vibe awaits as soon as you give your name to the host and are handed a number. Your number appears on a digitized screen when the table is ready, so in the meantime you should aim to score one of the two swings where you can wait. One swing is like a hanging pod and the other is less fun since it's simply a two-person suspended plank. You could also have a lychee martini at the round bar at the front. Sea is cavernous, but is full of energy and music with good beats.

HOUSE SPECIALTIES Seafood dumplings; shrimp fritters; 'volcanic' chicken; drunk man's noodle.

OTHER RECOMMENDATIONS Pad Thai; shrimp in a clay pot; summer rolls; Siamese fried rice.

SUMMARY AND COMMENTS This is not the type of place you go to have serious conversation or prime Thai food, but it is a fantastic place for decent Thai food and a rollicking good time. If you like spicy, then be sure to ask, otherwise the food won't be as flavorful as you might like. The strongest part of the menu are the appetizers, although a spicy pad thai and a red curry are pretty good. The service is efficient and be sure to go to the toilets so you can spy on your friends from inside the cubicle (each cabin has a monitor with live camera feeds to places in and outside the restaurant). The sink is communal for men and women. There's a much smaller Sea in the East Village at 75 Second Avenue; ☎ 212-228-5505.

kids Second Avenue Deli ★★½

JEWISH DELI	MODERATE	QUALITY ★★★★	VALUE ★★★

156 Second Avenue, The East Village; ☎ 212-677-0606; www.2ndavedeli.com

Reservations Not accepted. When to go Anytime. Entrée range $10–$26. Payment All major credit cards. Service rating ★★★ Friendliness rating ★★★ Bar Wine and beer. Wine selection Limited kosher. Dress Casual. Disabled access Good. Customers Locals, tourists. Hours Sunday–Thursday, 7 a.m.–midnight; Friday and Saturday, 7 a.m.–3 a.m.

SETTING AND ATMOSPHERE Classic deli, with wisecracking, kvetching meat slicers working up front and booths and pickle-filled tables. Ample space allows for stroller-maneuvering, and kids will like the simple, tasty soups and sandwiches.

HOUSE SPECIALTIES Freebie pungent health salad; great smooth chopped liver; authentic matzo ball soup; knishes; derma (rich stuffing—here with globs of paprika—in sausage casing); cholent (an ultra-slow-cooked meat and potato stew); sweet, orangy stuffed cabbage; homemade applesauce. There's much debate over the corned beef; theirs is very lightly "corned," but this allows more beefy flavors to emerge.

OTHER RECOMMENDATIONS Skip dessert; the deli may be open Friday nights and Saturdays, but they're kosher nonetheless, and desserts made with dairy substitutes aren't worth the calories.

ENTERTAINMENT AND AMENITIES They'll ship food anywhere via mail order.

SUMMARY AND COMMENTS When people think of New York City restaurants, they think of delis. Ha. It's actually easier to find good corned beef in Montreal or Los Angeles than here. While Second Avenue Deli's offerings are spotty, it still makes a few dishes very well. Don't stray from our suggestions and you'll have the authentic New York deli experience, if not a fantastic taste experience. You'll find better consistency at Mr.

Broadway Kosher Deli (see profile), but they have none of the history and little of the soul of this very traditional place.

Shun Lee West, Shun Lee Café ★★★½

CHINESE   MODERATE/EXPENSIVE   QUALITY ★★★★   VALUE ★★★★

43 West 65th Street, Upper West Side; ☎ 212-595-8895 or 212-769-3888 (Café)

Reservations Recommended. **When to go** Anytime. **Entrée range** $16–$32.50; in the cafe, most entrées are $16–$25. **Payment** All major credit cards. **Service rating** ★★ **Friendliness rating** ★★ **Bar** Full service. **Wine selection** Good. **Dress** Dressy, business; casual in the cafe. **Disabled access** Yes. **Customers** Locals, business, Lincoln Center. **Hours** Daily, noon–midnight.

SETTING AND ATMOSPHERE Dark and dramatic: Large silver-white dragons with little red eyes chase each other across black walls above luxurious black banquettes and black floors, and soft halogen lighting flatters the complexion. Silver-white monkeys swing over the small bar in the entrance, where you are greeted by tuxedoed maître d's. This is a snazzy take on the Chinese scene, and the clientele seems to revel in it.

HOUSE SPECIALTIES Szechuan wonton; steamed dumplings; beggar's chicken (order 24 hours in advance); Grand Marnier prawns; Cantonese sausage with Szechuan sausage; dim sum (cafe only).

OTHER RECOMMENDATIONS Sliced duckling with young ginger root; lobster in black bean sauce; rack of lamb, Szechuan-style.

SUMMARY AND COMMENTS High-style chinoiserie, with high-style Chinese cooking to match, make this an upscale Lincoln Center favorite. Both food and mood are elegant, and both are reflected in the prices. Some of the same excellent food is available in the more casual cafe, which has its own entrance, for a lot less. The cafe, black-and-white checked from floor to ceiling, also offers very good dim sum from wandering carts and abrupt but rapid service.

66 ★★★

CHINESE   EXPENSIVE   QUALITY ★★★★   VALUE ★★½

241 Church Street (between Leonard and Worth streets), Tribeca; ☎ 212-925-0202

Reservations Necessary, but first come, first served at the long communal table by bar. **When to go** Dinner for the glitz; lunch for a cheaper, less crowded experience. **Entrée range** $18–$32; prix-fixe lunch available. **Payment** All major credit cards. **Service rating** ★★★ **Friendliness rating** ★★★ **Bar** Full service; interesting cocktails. **Wine selection** Good. **Dress** Business casual day, chic night. **Disabled access** Yes. **Customers** Fashionistas, curious foodies, celebs, hipsters with thick wallets. **Hours** Monday–Saturday, noon–3 p.m. and 5:30 p.m.–midnight; Sunday, noon–3 p.m. and 5:30–10 p.m.

SETTING AND ATMOSPHERE Sleek, geometric, and minimalist are the first adjectives that come to mind when describing 66. Once you pass the long and high-topped communal dining table, you enter the main dining space that has three partitions and high ceilings. Small aquariums with colorful tropical fish are in view from any table across one panel, as is the well-lit and immaculate kitchen, viewed through glass above several tanks. The tables are made of a semitranslucent material that blends well with the white, silvery gray, and black décor. The similarities between 66 and a neighborhood Chinese restaurant begin and end with the lazy susans found on some of the large, round tables. Lunch is calmer and less crowded; dinner can be frenzied and a real scene.

HOUSE SPECIALTIES Peking duck; scallion pancakes; 66 sesame noodles; sweet and sour two-flavored shrimp (with condensed milk, mayonnaise, ginger); steamed cod with caramelized onions, ginger, and soy sauce; lobster.

OTHER RECOMMENDATIONS Marinated eggplant; Asian greens; lobster noodles; chili prawns; molten chocolate cake with spiced coconut ice cream; Vietnamese coffee-flavored sorbet.

SUMMARY AND COMMENTS 66 is a recent addition to the famed chef Jean-Georges Vongerichten's empire. The story is that he decided to open a Chinese restaurant that would celebrate flavors in the food without overwhelming a dish with too much indescribable sauce. Many of the dishes are well executed with interesting combinations of flavors, but there is an ongoing debate as to whether 66 can justify the prices charged; some of the food has been likened to glorified cheap Chinese fare at top-dollar prices. We'd disagree with the "glorified cheap Chinese fare" bit, but the prices are steep. In contrast, critics have lauded 66 as a pioneering space that takes Chinese food to a new and exciting level. The dishes are carefully presented, and for those that require a bit of scene whilst munching on a steamed shrimp dumpling, then 66 is the place for you. The à la carte lunch menu is cheaper than the dinner menu, but the portions are smaller; if you wish to enjoy varied tastes and also fill your belly, several dishes must be ordered. The lunch prix fixe is an inexpensive though light feed. Sake is served with a hefty price tag and a frugal pour.

Soba-ya ★★★½

JAPANESE   INEXPENSIVE/MODERATE   QUALITY ★★★½   VALUE ★★★★

229 East Ninth Street, The East Village; ☎ 212 533-6966

Reservations None. **When to go** Anytime. **Entrée range** $8–$16. **Payment** All major credit cards. **Service rating** ★★★½ **Friendliness rating** ★★★ **Bar** Beer and sake. **Wine selection** None. **Dress** Casual/trendy. **Disabled access** No. **Customers** Locals, ethnic, those in search of good soba and broth. **Hours** Daily, noon–3:50 p.m. and 5:30–10:30 p.m.

SETTING AND ATMOSPHERE Down a few steps, you enter a square-sized room filled with wooden tables and chairs in neat rows. Across from the till is an extensive display of traditional Netsuke figurines. The décor is minimal, but fresh with hints of bamboo and lots of wood and a few hangings with Japanese characters. A sit-down counter bar is located in the far corner.

HOUSE SPECIALTIES Anything with soba (buckwheat) or udon noodles accompanied with fresh scallions in either a vegetable, meat, or fish broth (the extra ingredients vary depending on which broth you choose).

OTHER RECOMMENDATIONS Goma ae (spinach with sesame sauce); tempura; extensive sake selection.

SUMMARY AND COMMENTS Although it is possible to order sashimi, one tends not to come here for sushi, but for other types of Japanese fare, especially the noodle soups. A whole bowl is easily a meal, so relax and enjoy the whole slurping experience. During peak dinner times, you may have to wait for a table, but patience is worth having as the food is delicious. Service is fast and staff are helpful in talking through any menu confusion.

Soul Fixins' ★★★

SOUTHERN/SOUL FOOD   INEXPENSIVE   QUALITY ★★★★   VALUE ★★★★

371 West 34th Street, Chelsea; ☎ 212-736-1345

Reservations Not accepted. When to go Anytime. Entrée range Lunch, $6–$7; dinner, $6.95–$9.95. Payment AE, MC, V. Service rating ★★ Friendliness rating ★★½ Bar None. Wine selection None. Dress Casual. Disabled access Good. Customers Locals. Hours Monday–Saturday, 11 a.m.–10 p.m.; closed Sunday.

SETTING AND ATMOSPHERE Minimal—this is mostly a take-out joint, but there are a bunch of self-service tables and chairs both inside and out on the sidewalk.

HOUSE SPECIALTIES Chicken in all forms—particularly barbecued; candied yams; collard greens; macaroni and cheese; cornbread; lemonade.

SUMMARY AND COMMENTS It almost defies the imagination to realize that plates of truly soulful victuals can be had within a couple blocks of the Empire State Building (a neighborhood considered bereft of good eats) for five bucks. Soul Fixins' makes soul food as good or better than nearly any served Uptown for a loyal and largely African American clientele of Midtown workers. Everything's cooked with deft aplomb: chicken and pork chops are reliably tender and flavorful, collard greens have lots of smoke and are not at all mushy. Candied yams are individual halves of spuds neither overspiced nor oversweet, done to the perfect texture (no mean feat when you're cooking ahead for steam-table service). Homemade lemonade and iced tea are just right: smooth, not too sweet, and refreshing. Even the cornbread (often a throwaway in soul food take-outs) is very good. The kitchen takes a relatively healthy approach, using minimal pork and fat.

Stan's Place ★★★

CREOLE   INEXPENSIVE/MODERATE   QUALITY ★★★   VALUE ★★★

411 Atlantic Avenue, Brooklyn; ☎ 718-596-3110

Reservations Not necessary. When to go Anytime. Entrée range $8–$18 or $25 prix-fixe dinner. Payment Cash only. Service rating ★★★½ Friendliness rating ★★★★ Bar BYOB. Wine selection BYOB. Dress Casual. Disabled access Yes.

Customers Locals, ethnic, regulars. **Hours** Tuesday–Friday, 7:30 a.m.–10 p.m.; Saturday, 8 a.m.–10 p.m.; Sunday, 9 a.m.–5 p.m.

SETTING AND ATMOSPHERE Labeled a New Orleans–style cafe, Stan's Place has an open, airy warmth without being precious. A high-ceilinged space with a small balcony in the back and a long coffee-dessert bar in the front. Dark wooden tables line the sides of the space along with a few tables in the middle.

HOUSE SPECIALTIES Creole cafe; chicory au lait; cheese grits; saffron bouliiabasse; catfish po' boys; Cajun scrambled eggs.

OTHER RECOMMENDATIONS Fried chicken; chicken and andouille jambalaya; boudin blanc; crab cakes.

SUMMARY AND COMMENTS Although much of the brunch menu has food preceded by the word 'cajun,' some would call the dinner dishes more 'creole'; others would say there's hardly a distinction. We'll suffice to say that however one calls it, the fare is tasty and should be eaten. Tabasco is eagerly served with breakfast eggs, and the cheese grits are wonderfully smooth and savory. Weekend brunch is a great time to bring the kids. The New Orleans ties are strong here, as shown in the recent aftermath of Hurricane Katrina when Stan's wasn't able to contact any Creole cafe to place orders; their supply came straight from the city. The chicory coffee is good, but the Creole coffee is mixed with chicory and real coffee beans for a special taste. The beignets available are fresh, but so far a bit too stodgy compared to their Southern counterparts. Stan's sometimes has live music on Thursday nights.

Sushi-Ann ★★★½

JAPANESE	EXPENSIVE	QUALITY ★★★★	VALUE ★★★★

38 East 51st Street (between Madison and Park avenues), Midtown East; ☎ 212-755-1780

Reservations Recommended. **When to go** Anytime. **Entrée range** $16–$33; sushi available à la carte. **Payment** All major credit cards. **Service rating** ★★ **Friendliness rating** ★★★ **Wine selection** Minimal. **Dress** Casual, business. **Disabled access** No. **Customers** Ethnic, business, locals. **Hours** Monday–Friday, noon–2:15 p.m. and 5:30–10 p.m.; Saturday, 5:30–9:30 p.m.

SETTING AND ATMOSPHERE Startlingly simple, sharp-angled, and bright with off-white and light wood walls, and light wood tables. Understated Japanese floral arrangements add spots of vibrant color here and there, and a large, 20-seat sushi bar, manned by six sushi chefs and jammed with Japanese businessmen at lunch, forms the centerpiece.

HOUSE SPECIALTIES Special deluxe bento (appetizers, sushi, and sashimi served in an elegant lacquer box); special makimoto (three kinds of rolled sushi); sea urchin hand roll, spicy codfish sushi, Japanese mackerel sushi, and anything else that appeals on the à la carte sushi list.

OTHER RECOMMENDATIONS Cooked sushi assortment (good for sushi beginners); chirashi (assorted fish fillets on vinegar-seasoned rice); sushi deluxe (an assortment of fresh and cooked items).

SUMMARY AND COMMENTS Celestial sushi and sashimi draws praise and crowds. Formerly called Sushisay, an excellent Midtown choice for the freshest of fresh fish. Order the preselected assortments, or make individual selections from the extensive à la carte list of sushi and hand rolls. The ambience and service are friendly; the high prices reflect the location.

kids Symposium ★★★

GREEK	INEXPENSIVE/MODERATE	QUALITY ★★★½	VALUE ★★★★

544 West 113th Street (between Broadway and Amsterdam avenues), Morningside Heights; ☎ 212-865-1011

Reservations Recommended. When to go Anytime you have a yen for a stuffed grape leaf. Entrée range $8–$20. Payment MC, V. Service rating ★★★★ Friendliness rating ★★★★½ Bar Limited. Wine selection Small but includes Greek selections (besides ouzo) and sangria. Dress Casual. Disabled access No. Customers Regulars, Columbia University staff and students, ethnic. Hours Monday–Thursday, noon–11 p.m.; Friday and Saturday, 11 a.m.–12:30 a.m.; lunch specials served noon–3 p.m.

SETTING AND ATMOSPHERE The main dining room has a tavern feel with closely arranged dark wooden tables, a few booths, wood floor, paintings on the walls, and low ceiling. What it lacks in sleek modernity, it gains in sheer coziness and warmth. A feeling of dining community pervades: Everyone is there to have a good time and eat good Greek food. The enclosed garden practically doubles the amount of tables. It's cheerful and bright and hosts several hanging plants, white and green vinyl tablecloths, and wooden chairs, and two large trees have grown to a considerable height and girth there (the tree's canopies are way above the enclosure's roof).

HOUSE SPECIALTIES Mixed appetizer plate (especially the stuffed grape leaves, taramosalata, and eggplant dip); shish kebab (lamb and vegetables on a skewer); mousaka.

OTHER RECOMMENDATIONS Pastitsio (baked pasta and ground meat); vegetarian mousaka; spanakopita (spinach and feta pie).

SUMMARY AND COMMENTS It's clear that the owners (it's family-run) have a lot of confidence when the only route to the enclosed garden is through the kitchen. Symposium has been around for over 20 years and proclaims to serve genuine Greek cuisine, which we can't dispute. The best bet is to order the Symposium salad for the table so you can sample a mixture of dips with a few olives and delectable stuffed grape leaves; warm pita bread accompanies the dish. The spinach pie is the right combination of spinach and feta, but sometimes the phyllo dough is not as crunchy as it could be. It's best to stick with the tried-and-true Greek specialties; rice and vegetables are served with the main dishes. The vegetarian mousaka is pretty decent as well. Service is very friendly. Plenty of space, a casual atmosphere, and a friendly and welcoming staff make Symposium kid-friendly.

Tabla ★★★★

INDIAN FUSION	EXPENSIVE	QUALITY ★★★★½	VALUE ★★★★

11 Madison Avenue (at 25th Street), Madison Square; ☎ 212-889-0667

Reservations Recommended for main dining room. **When to go** Anytime. **Entrée range** three-course prix-fixe dinner, $57; five- and seven-course tasting menus, $75 and $88. **Payment** All major credit cards. **Service rating** ★★★ **Friendliness rating** ★★★ **Bar** Full service. **Wine selection** Well chosen for food; fairly priced. **Dress** Casual or better. **Disabled access** Bread bar, yes; dining room, no. **Customers** Locals, business, ethnic. **Hours** Monday–Thursday, noon–11 p.m.; Friday and Saturday, noon–11:30 p.m.

SETTING AND ATMOSPHERE A dizzyingly beautiful crimson wood staircase separates two levels of space, each with its own distinct personality. The upstairs dining room is formal but hip, buzzing with excitement and alive with voluptuous colors—a perfect setting for the meal that follows. The room overlooks the street-level Bread Bar, which is more casual and doesn't require reservations.

HOUSE SPECIALTIES Goan spiced crab cake; tuna and seared baby squid, chickpea hummus, jicama, pickled ramps and peppers; rice-flaked crisped halibut; eggplant-stuffed braised Vidalia onion; vanilla bean kulfi.

OTHER RECOMMENDATIONS Nova Scotia lobster; foie gras torchon; lentil-crusted wild striped bass; rawa-coated soft-shell crabs; warm chocolate date cake.

SUMMARY AND COMMENTS Danny Meyer, king of New York's New American establishments Gramercy Tavern, Union Square Café, and Eleven Madison Park, now brings you Indian fusion, and this may well be the best of the bunch. Perhaps realizing that New American just isn't that new anymore, Meyer hired Floyd Cardoz, a native of India, to literally add some spice to what is becoming an increasingly tired cuisine. Cardoz took him at his word, using ingredients like kokum, cumin, tamarind, and tapioca to breathe new life into dishes like crab cake, foie gras, and fettucine. Even the tandoori breads come in bizarre flavors like buckwheat honey and horseradish. Though fusion is more often than not a failed experiment, Tabla manages to pull it off with style. You've never tasted anything quite like the food here, and that's why you're sure to come back. But be warned, Tabla is not for everybody; some people love it, while others hate it, though everyone agrees the vanilla bean kulfi is one of the best desserts in Manhattan. Lunch upstairs can be a bit of a disappointment due to meager portions, so go for the awesome Bread Bar downstairs instead.

Tamarind ★★★½

INDIAN	EXPENSIVE	QUALITY ★★★★	VALUE ★★★

41 East 22nd Street (between Park Avenue and Broadway), Madison Square; ☎ 212-674-7400; www.tamarinde22.com

Reservations Recommended. **When to go** Anytime. **Entrée range** $14–$30. **Payment** All major credit cards. **Service rating** ★★★½ **Friendliness rating**

★★★★½ **Bar** Full service. **Wine selection** Good with varied prices. **Dress** Smart casual, chic, or business. **Disabled access** Yes. **Customers** Business, regulars, foodies on expense accounts. **Hours** Sunday–Thursday, 11:30 a.m.–11:30 p.m.; Friday and Saturday, 11:30 a.m.–midnight.

SETTING AND ATMOSPHERE   This restaurant has a lot of style and warmth with a fresh, clean atmosphere. The style can be attributed to several elements, including the large glass windows at the front, skylight in the back, the fully stocked and well-appointed bar, the glass-enclosed kitchen, modern chairs, white-linen tablecloths, and freshly cut orchids on each table. The warmth is due to cream colors and soft lighting for the evening. You can eat at a table across from the bar in the narrow section of the restaurant, or you can sit at a table that opens out into a larger space towards the back. Private round tables are available around the periphery of the open room.

HOUSE SPECIALTIES   Raji's tandoori scallops; lobster masala; raan e chengesi (lamb in garlic, ginger, and spices); murgh kola puri (spicy chicken with peppercorns); crab soup; tandoori items.

OTHER RECOMMENDATIONS   Rosemary naan; lemon rice; luckhnow ki bhajia (incredibly crisp and light fritters with spinach, banana, and cheese); bhagarey baigan (eggplant with coconut, sesame, and peanut sauce); shrimp moiley (coconut-based sauce with mustard seeds, ginger, and curry leaves).

SUMMARY AND COMMENTS   Opened in 2001, Tamarind earned its culinary stripes almost immediately. The combination of spices is a treat to the senses. Luckily, there's a lot more than a linen tablecloth that sets this Indian restaurant apart from the other tasty and less expensive Indian counterparts. The difference lies in the delicate consideration of the ingredients used, the utmost freshest ingredients, and the daring to include lobster! The meats are as tender as the homemade cheese cubes that melt in the mouth. Presentation excels with the appetizers more than with the entrées; the succulent tandoori scallops are presented in a fried potato lattice cup that has become a signature dish. For a variety of chutneys and spices, try the vegetarian thali. Desserts range from chocolate soufflé to gulab jamun (pastry with dried milk and honey). The owner and manager are proud of their venture and are often seen shmoozing amongst the diners and ensuring customer happiness. The tearoom next door offers a wider selection of teas, desserts, and sandwiches in a more casual, cozy setting.

Tartine ★★★

FRENCH BISTRO	INEXPENSIVE	QUALITY ★★★★	VALUE ★★★½

253 West 11th Street (corner of West Fourth Street), Greenwich Village;
☎ **212-229-2611**

Reservations Not accepted. **When to go** Anytime. **Entrée range** $7.75–$16.95.
Payment Cash only. **Service rating** ★★ **Friendliness rating** ★★ **Wine selection**
Bring your own wine or beer. **Dress** Casual. **Disabled access** For outside tables.

Customers Locals. **Hours** Monday–Friday, 9 a.m.–4 p.m. and 5:30–10:30 p.m.; Saturday and Sunday, 10:30 a.m.–4 p.m. (brunch) and 5:30–10:30 p.m.

SETTING AND ATMOSPHERE This cute corner bistro on a pretty West Village street attracts lots of locals. There's usually a line waiting for the ten Formica-topped tables squeezed into the small exposed brick interior or for space in the outside cafe (weather permitting).

HOUSE SPECIALTIES Desserts—dacquoise, tarte tatin à la mode, custard-filled fruit tarts—are all made on the premises and are top-notch; salade basquaise; grilled salmon with citrus vinaigrette; croque monsieur made with brioche; beef mignonette aux poivres with frites.

OTHER RECOMMENDATIONS Onion tart, beet and endive salad; check daily specials.

SUMMARY AND COMMENTS Basic bistro fare at very fair prices, the added savings of BYOB, and the cozy setting make Tartine a very popular place. Appetizers are hit-and-miss. Go with one of the salads or check out the daily specials, and skip the escargots. Of the entrées, beef mignonette aux poivres is very good, tender, and spicy, and accompanying frites are crisp and tasty, though a bit oversalted. Save room for desserts, though, especially the tarte tatin à la mode, served warm with caramelized apples. Service can be both charming and indifferent, depending on a variety of factors. Saturday and Sunday brunch at $10.95 is a great deal and very tasty; the prix-fixe lunch is $12.95.

Tea & Sympathy ★★★

BRITISH	INEXPENSIVE/MODERATE	QUALITY ★★★½	VALUE ★★★

108–110 Greenwich Avenue (between Jane and Horatio streets), Greenwich Village; ☎ **212-989-9735; www.teaandsympathynewyork.com**

Reservations No. **When to go** Anytime. **Entrée range** $6.50–$14.50. **Payment** AE, MC, V. **Service rating** ★★★½ **Friendliness rating** ★★★★ **Bar** No, but lots of tea. **Wine selection** BYOB. **Dress** Casual or avant-garde. **Disabled access** Yes, but not for bathroom. **Customers** Regulars, locals, homesick Brits, occasional celebs. **Hours** Daily, 11:30 a.m.–10 p.m; Sunday dinner, $18.95 or $25 with dessert and drink, served after 1:30 p.m. until they sell out.

SETTING AND ATMOSPHERE As you might imagine, with a name like Tea & Sympathy and a purpose to serve tea and comfort food, the décor is anything but minimalist. The restaurant is a cozy, square room with ten small tables and a 22-seat capacity. A chalkboard lists the daily desserts, teas, and entrée specials. On the walls hang items of British kitsch, including caricatures of famous British icons, old-fashioned posters advertising British products, and shelves of mismatched china. The small kitchen is visible over the dessert case.

HOUSE SPECIALTIES Full afternoon tea (served anytime and includes watercress and egg salad, cream cheese and cucumber, chicken and tuna salad finger sandwiches, scones with clotted cream and jam, assorted cakes and cookies); shepherd's pie; bangers and mash (sausages and mashed potatoes);

rhubarb crumble with custard; Sunday dinner (choice of roast beef, lamb or chicken, Yorkshire pudding, potatoes, and vegetables).

OTHER RECOMMENDATIONS Victoria sponge cake; baked beans on toast; Welsh rarebit (cheddar with mustard on toast); Stilton and walnut salad with beets; cheese and onion quiche; chicken and leek pie; tuna melt. The macaroni falls a little short.

SUMMARY AND COMMENTS Due to the small size and addictive and delicious comfort food, it's not uncommon to have to wait outside for a table. The wait is well worth it, and since Tea and Sympathy is located in such a groovy part of town, you'll see interesting things to keep you occupied. This is not the place for a person on a strict diet; the tempting baked goods on display will entice you before you even look at the menu. Nicky, the owner, is often seen wandering between the restaurant and the shop next door, making sure customers are satisfied (and that they're behaving). She refuses to allow people to take a table unless everyone in the group is present; a few more of "Nicky's Rules" are displayed prominently on the front door window. The British selections excel, especially the shepherd's pie and vegetarian renditions. There aren't many places in NYC where you can find hot ribena and a Scotch egg on the menu. The afternoon tea is super and costs $19.95 for one person or $38 for two; if there are certain sweet things you don't like, let the server know beforehand so the selection can reflect your preferences. If you'd prefer fish and chips, the **A Salt and Battery** chip shop (also owned by Nicky) is adjacent to the tea shop.

Tomoe Sushi ★★★½

JAPANESE/SUSHI	MODERATE	QUALITY ★★★★	VALUE ★★★★

172 Thompson Street (between Houston and Bleecker streets), Greenwich Village; ☎ 212-777-9346

Reservations Not accepted. When to go Anytime. Entrée range $15–$25. Payment All major credit cards. Service rating ★★ Friendliness rating ★★★ Bar Beer and sake. Wine selection Stick to sake and beer. Dress Very casual. Disabled access No. Customers Ethnic, locals. Hours Monday–Tuesday, 5–11 p.m.; Wednesday–Saturday, 1–3 p.m. and 5–11 p.m.; closed Sunday.

SETTING AND ATMOSPHERE The quintessential Village hole-in-the-wall with a few Japanese touches—lantern lights, prints on the wall, and a small sushi bar that seats a lucky five people at a time. Tomoe is about as big as the upper right-hand section of a bento box, but that's part of its charm.

HOUSE SPECIALTIES Without a doubt, anything from the sushi bar; toro (fatty tuna), hamachi (yellowtail) belly; fresh salmon; amaebi (sweet shrimp); fresh king crab legs.

OTHER RECOMMENDATIONS Skip everything else. The shumai (boiled shrimp dumplings) are standard and the zaru soba (cold buckwheat noodles with dipping sauce) is subpar and much better elsewhere (try **Yodo** on 47th and Madison). Going to Tomoe for anything but raw fish is like going to a concert only for the opening act.

SUMMARY AND COMMENTS Tomoe gives the phrase "fresh off the boat" new meaning. The sushi and sashimi here are wonderfully fresh, clean, and delicious. Pieces are big but not Yama-esque, just big enough to get the whole thing in your mouth comfortably. From there, just close your eyes and let the fish dissolve away. Buttery toro will melt in your mouth, and the huge king crab legs are so sweet and juicy you'll start to hear waves crashing around your eardrums. Tomoe boasts a great selection and reasonable prices, but get there early. Be prepared for small talk with those waiting in line; you might stand up to an hour, and it's worth every minute.

Tre Pomodori ★★½

PASTA	MODERATE	QUALITY ★★★★	VALUE ★★★★★

210 East 34th Street, Midtown East; ☎ 212-545-7266

Reservations Recommended for large parties or at peak hours. **When to go** Anytime. **Entrée range** $8.95–$16.95; $5.95–$6.95 prix-fixe lunch. **Payment** Major credit cards. **Service rating** ★★½ **Friendliness rating** ★★★½ **Bar** Beer and wine. **Wine selection** Small; South America's best. **Dress** Casual. **Disabled access** Fair. **Hours** Sunday–Thursday, noon–4 p.m. and 5–10:30 p.m.; Friday and Saturday, noon–4 p.m. and 5–11:30 p.m.

SETTING AND ATMOSPHERE A very narrow, cozy parlor with tiled floor, framed pictures dotting the walls, and candles flickering on tables.

HOUSE SPECIALTIES All pastas, especially linguine vongole (baby clams, oil, garlic), agnolotti al porcini (ultra-mushroomy pasta pockets), and linguine fra diavolo (black linguine with calamari and spicy tomato sauce); risotto; apple tart.

SUMMARY AND COMMENTS This is not a great restaurant, but it is a useful one. If you're looking for a low-key place to get surprisingly tasty plates of pasta at bargain prices without getting gussied up (but you don't feel like a no-frills hole-in-the-wall either), this is a top choice, particularly when you're in East Midtown—where restaurants fitting that bill are hard to come by. The waiters will serve quickly for those rushing back to work (or out to shows), but lingering is never discouraged. Avoid the spotty appetizers and pricier entrées and cut straight to what they cook best: pasta. The linguine with baby clams is a splendid, classic version, very satisfying, and there's a broad range of other choices—18 in all. Risotto, sometimes a special, is also very good, as are the gratis crunchy toasts with tomato and basil. Desserts are only fair (best: apple tart). Service can be slightly confused but is always good-natured.

kids The Tree House Restaurant ★★

MEDITERRANEAN	INEXPENSIVE/MODERATE	QUALITY ★★★½	VALUE ★★★½

273 City Island Avenue, City Island; ☎ 718-885-0806; www.treehousecityisland.com

Reservations Not necessary. **When to go** Anytime. **Entrée range** $7–$23. **Payment** All major credit cards. **Service rating** ★★½ **Friendliness rating** ★★★★½ **Bar** Full service. **Wine selection** Very small. **Dress** Casual. **Disabled access** Yes, except bathrooms. **Customers** Locals. **Hours** Sunday–Thursday, 11:30 a.m.– 10 p.m.; Friday and Saturday, 11:30 a.m.–11 p.m.

SETTING AND ATMOSPHERE An average-sized space opens up once you pass the bar on your right. The décor is pleasant, but nothing particularly worth mentioning apart from the lovely sea-view mural on one of the back walls. Tables are suitably spaced apart from each other, and the setting is clean. Little white lights in the front windows make the storefront look particularly homey.

HOUSE SPECIALTIES Chevapas (a favorite for expats of former Yugoslavia, also known as skinless char-grilled beef sausage); shunka wrapper (cheese rolled with bacon); warmed stuffed grape leaves; brick-oven pizza.

OTHER RECOMMENDATIONS Romanian steak marinated in Balsamic vinegar, olive oil, and spices; Mediterranean chicken (chicken marinated in garlic and lemon and seasoned with peppercorns).

SUMMARY AND COMMENTS What the Tree House lacks in presentation it gains in truly tasty dishes ranging from shunkas, grape leaves (absolutely fabulous—especially when served warm), chevapas, and Romanian steak. The Tree House also has the "best brick-oven pizza on City Island," featuring topping combos like the Ortolana (tomato sauce, mozzarella, smoked meat, eggplant, summer squash, onions, and fresh tomatoes). The chef hails from Montenegro, and he takes pride in preparing dishes from all over the Mediterranean region. Fish dishes are hit-and-miss, as is the pasta. Sticking with either the above dishes or a daily special is the best way to make the most of your meal. Don't bother with dessert. Part of the appeal of this place is simply going to City Island and checking out some of the little colonial houses, seeing the marina, and wandering along the main street, City Island Avenue. It's a welcome change of pace, which may also explain why the service is so friendly. If you stay late enough, you may even be offered a swig of something strong from the home country.

Union Square Café ★★★★

NEW AMERICAN   EXPENSIVE   QUALITY ★★★★½   VALUE ★★★★

21 East 16th Street (between Union Square and Fifth Avenue);
☎ **212-243-4020**

Reservations Recommended. **When to go** Anytime. **Entrée range** $16.50–$29. **Payment** All major credit cards. **Service rating** ★★★★ **Friendliness rating** ★★★★ **Bar** Full service. **Wine selection** Excellent, both by the bottle and by the glass. **Dress** Casual, business. **Disabled access** Fair. **Customers** Locals, business. **Hours** Sunday–Thursday, noon–2:15 p.m. and 5:30–9:45 p.m.; Friday and Saturday, noon–2 p.m. and 5:30–10:45 p.m.

SETTING AND ATMOSPHERE Airy dining spaces—a few steps down, a small flight up—with creamy beige walls, dark green chair rails, vibrant modern paintings, a mural of many merry maidens ("The Women of USC"), and bright bunches of fresh flowers. The cherrywood floors and a long, dark wood bar add to the warm, welcoming ambience. All is stylish without trying too hard.

HOUSE SPECIALTIES Be sure to check the daily specials; hot garlic potato chips; black bean soup; Union Square Café's calamari; crispy risotto cake; grilled, marinated filet mignon of tuna; crabmeat and artichoke tortelli; warm banana tart with honey-vanilla ice cream.

OTHER RECOMMENDATIONS Roasted lemon-pepper duck; peach pot pie. For lunch: yellowfin tuna burger with creamy cabbage slaw and the U.S.C. hamburger.

SUMMARY AND COMMENTS For years, Union Square Café has been one of New York's most desired dining destinations. But one caveat, when Union Square Café is billed as New York's best restaurant, it's not for the food but the overall experience. Owner Danny Meyer and chef Michael Romano have set the standard for flawless, informed, amiable service in a laid-back setting, as well as dependable, usually delicious New American food. U.S.C. has all the elements of a classic, and it's one that's sure to keep running for years to come.

Veritas ★★★★

NEW AMERICAN	EXPENSIVE	QUALITY ★★★★½	VALUE ★★★★

43 East 20th Street (between Park Avenue South and Broadway), Gramercy Park; ☎ 212-353-3700; www.veritas-nyc.com

Reservations Necessary. **When to go** Anytime. **Entrée range** Prix-fixe three-course dinner, $68. **Payment** All major credit cards. **Service rating** ★★★★ **Friendliness rating** ★★★★ **Bar** Full service. **Wine selection** Unbelievable and incredibly reasonable. **Dress** Dressy casual, business. **Disabled access** Yes. **Customers** Locals, business, oenophiles. **Hours** Monday–Saturday, 5:30–10:30 p.m.; Sunday, 5–9:30 p.m.

SETTING AND ATMOSPHERE This small one-room space has an elegant, modern look but a thoroughly comfortable feel. The room is decorated simply, with colorful hand-blown glass objets d'art set smartly into random spaces in the wall. The clean modesty of Veritas quickly translates itself into a relaxing and pleasant atmosphere; people seem genuinely happy to be here. Hint: Check out the bathrooms and the very cool sinks.

HOUSE SPECIALTIES Hamachi tartare with mint, green onions, soy, and osetra caviar; roasted sweetbreads; crisp skate, saffron-chive sauce, pistou, and orzo; braised veal; seared salmon with sautéed Asian greens and curry nage; caramelized peach tarte tatin; praline parfait.

OTHER RECOMMENDATIONS Seared foie gras, rhubarb compote, pistachio oil, and 20-year-old balsamic vinegar; sweet corn chowder with steamed clams; farm-roasted chicken; grilled black angus New York strip steak; crème fraîche panna cotta; warm raspberry almond tart.

SUMMARY AND COMMENTS Veritas has a small problem, though it's a problem most restaurants wished they had. When people think of Veritas, they think of wine, and with good reason. But because of that reputation, people might not go there to eat, and that would be a shame, because Veritas turns out some of the best food in the city. Chef Scott Bryan (also of Siena and West Village sleeper Indigo) is a master at using fresh, clean ingredients to mask the underlying complexity of his dishes. Sweet corn chowder sounds like it should be warm and comforting, but Bryan wakes it up with a sharp, lively hot broth and crunchy, juicy whole kernels of corn, then softens it with creamy clams—the perfect summer soup. Seared foie gras and hamachi tartare share a similar sensuality. And there's no dropoff with desserts either, as Cameron Irvin makes, among other things, a superb caramelized peach tarte tatin. The food at Veritas more than stands on its own, even if you don't order wine. But how can you do that? The size of a small bible, the wine list runs the gamut and has something for everyone, including a surprising number of quality bottles in the $18 to $20 range. But perhaps the most pleasant surprise of Veritas is its lack of pretension. Despite the Ivy League-evoking name and the dedication to oenophilia, a subject traditionally associated with snobbery, Veritas goes out of its way to keep things down to earth. Eighteen-dollar bottles still bring out their top-of-the-line stemware; wine director Ben Breen and each of his four sommeliers are more than happy to pick out just the right bottle for you, and the entire staff is almost friendly to a fault. So go to Veritas, but don't just go for the wine. The wine list is great, but the food's even better.

Woo Chon ★★★

KOREAN	MODERATE	QUALITY ★★★★	VALUE ★★★★

8 West 36th Street (near Fifth Avenue), Midtown East; ☎ 212-695-0676

Reservations Accepted. **When to go** Anytime. **Entrée range** $10–$20. **Payment** AE, MC, V. **Service rating** ★★★ **Friendliness rating** ★½ **Bar** Beer and wine only. **Wine selection** Very limited. **Dress** Nice casual or better. **Disabled access** Good. **Customers** Korean businessmen, aficionados. **Hours** Daily, 10:30 a.m.–6 a.m.

SETTING AND ATMOSPHERE Two levels: a rather intense downstairs space (spotlit and dramatically appointed with lacquered calligraphy, dark wood, and Asian ink prints) and a slightly more laid-back upstairs room.

HOUSE SPECIALTIES Attention centers on the great bulgogi, sweetish garlic-marinated rib-eye prepared on the grill set into each table (wrap the beefy chunks in lettuce leaves with a little rice and dab on sweet soybean paste). Unfortunately, the tableside grills are outfitted for gas flame rather than glowing coals, but Woo Chon's awesome marinade—so delicious they bottle the stuff for sale—and top-quality meat easily compensate. Kalbi (beef short ribs) are equally recommended. Panchan, the traditional gratis assortment of little vegetable and fish starter plates, are unparalleled in their freshness, all flavors clearly focused and balanced (feel free to ask for extra helpings of your favorites).

Yookgaejang (a restorative spicy beef soup) and dduk guk (a hearty dumpling soup) are both good choices, as are rice and noodle dishes that come with toppings for mixing in (look for "bibim" as a prefix), but be aware that the cold buckwheat noodle items serve more as palate-cleansers than main courses. Woo Chon elevates lowly pajun (crunchy/spongy pancakes with optional extras like seafood or kim-chee) to an almost highbrow level, evoking subtle flavors from this snacky favorite. Also try gooksoo, a lot like shabu-shabu.

OTHER RECOMMENDATIONS Special $50 and $60 feasts may be ordered 48 hours in advance (bring a group and reserve a private room for the full effect).

SUMMARY AND COMMENTS Though Woo Chon is a venerable name in New York Korean food, it's important to be aware of where its strengths lie. As in many Korean restaurants, the menu stretches well beyond those strengths in an effort to please a broad audience, so stick with the recommended dishes and avoid stews (jigae), intricate seafood or vegetable preparations, and homier items—this is no grandma kitchen; for down-home Korean try Han Bat or Cho Dang Gol. Management's haughty manner has unfortunately been adopted by many of the waiters. Woo Chon has a branch in Flushing at 41–19 Kissena Boulevard (☎ 718-463-0803).

Xunta ★★★

SPANISH/TAPAS	MODERATE	QUALITY ★★★★	VALUE ★★★★

174 First Avenue, The East Village; ☎ 212-614-0620; www.xuntatapas.com

Reservations Only for four or more. When to go Before 7 p.m. to avoid crowds (Tuesdays are also light). Entrée range $8–$23. Payment All major credit cards. Service rating ★★½ Friendliness rating ★★½ Bar Full service. Wine selection Good, Spanish. Dress Nice casual. Disabled access Very poor (three steps down). Customers Young locals. Hours Sunday–Thursday, 4 p.m.–midnight; Friday and Saturday, 4 p.m.–2 a.m.

SETTING AND ATMOSPHERE Funky basement with Iberian touches and a young clientele. This seems more like a hangout than a restaurant; you'd certainly never expect to find good food here. This small space gets crowded on weekends.

HOUSE SPECIALTIES Pulpo a feira (octopus with paprika), tortilla española con cebolla (Spanish potato omelet with onion), lulas rechaeas (stuffed calamari), gazpacho, sardines, sangria, gambas ala plancha (grilled shrimp), cheeses, and hard-to-find Galician white wines (Albariños).

ENTERTAINMENT AND AMENITIES Live flamenco show on Thursdays at 8:30 p.m.; Flamenco Guitars on Tuesday, 9 to 10 p.m., and Afro-Cuban entertainment on Wednesday, 10 p.m. to midnight.

SUMMARY AND COMMENTS The tapas craze hit New York in a big way, but this Galician bar is the only place that makes the Real Stuff. Holy grail tapas like octopus and potato omelet are closer to true Spanish style than at any other tapas bar in town. And the Albariños (young, tart white wines) are sipped the authentic way, out of white ceramic bowls. Items can be ordered either as small dishes (tapas) or larger raciones. Bear in mind that genuine tapas are unpretentious lusty accompaniments to drink, not haute cuisine, so the rollicking bar scene and crude seating are part and parcel of the experience.

Zen Palate ★★½

VEGETARIAN/ASIAN	INEXPENSIVE	QUALITY ★★★½	VALUE ★★★★

34 Union Square East (16th Street); ☎ 212-614-9345
663 Ninth Avenue (Corner of 46th Street), Midtown West;
☎ 212-582-1669
2170 Broadway (between 76th and 77th streets), Upper West Side;
☎ 212-501-7867; www.zenpalate.com

Reservations Not accepted. **When to go** Anytime. **Entrée range** $8–$10; $2.50–$9 for pastas and soups. **Payment** All major credit cards. **Service rating** ★★★ **Friendliness rating** ★★ **Wine selection** No liquor license; BYOB. **Dress** Casual. **Disabled access** Upper West Side, yes; Midtown, yes; Downtown, no. **Customers** Ethnic, locals. **Hours** *Upper West Side:* Monday–Saturday, 11 a.m.–10:30 p.m.; Sunday, noon–10 p.m.; *Midtown:* daily, 11:30 a.m.–11 p.m.; *Downtown:* Monday–Saturday, 11:30 a.m.–3 p.m. and 5:30–11 p.m.; Sunday, 11:30 a.m.–3 p.m. and 5–10:30 p.m.

SETTING AND ATMOSPHERE This laid-back trio offers pockets of peace, with soft ocher walls, clouds on the ceiling in Midtown, patterned lattice-work Uptown, and dramatic architecture in the Union Square branch.

HOUSE SPECIALTIES Vegetable dumplings; spinach linguine salad with sesame-peanut dressing; Zen lasagna; eggplant in garlic sauce; tofu honey pie.

OTHER RECOMMENDATIONS Basil moo-shu rolls; stir-fried fettuccine; Zen ravioli with special sauce; fresh-squeezed vegetable juice.

SUMMARY AND COMMENTS An inexpensive oasis for noncarnivores, but you don't have to be a vegetarian to get the good karma and good vibes that come with the more than soul-satisfying cuisine here. The veggie variations are flavorfully inventive, and some are surprising in their intensity.

PART NINE

SHOPPING

KEEPING *your* EYES *on the* PRIZE *(and the Price)*

IT MAY SEEM ALMOST REDUNDANT TO TALK ABOUT a shopping guide to Manhattan. In fact, it's almost impossible *not* to shop in a city whose souvenirs—miniature Statues of Liberty, Empire State Buildings, (little) Big Apples—are so instantly familiar. There are Fifth Avenues in a million cities, but no dedicated follower of fashion will mistake that address for any other. Nearly every toney hotel lobby now comes complete with a fancy gift shop, if not a couple of name-brand boutiques. And then there are the street vendors, the shopping marts, the jewelry malls, the flea markets . . . . There's even a fashion delivery business—carryout clothing, so to speak—called **Caravan,** which drives the latest outfits to you.

In fact, if you're not careful—even if it's exactly what you have in mind—you could find yourself spending your whole visit, and more than your budget, haphazardly acquiring things. That seems like a waste in more ways than one. When every city you visit seems to have the same designer shopping malls filled with the same stores and labels, New York is a treasure trove of specialty items, one-of-a-kind gifts, and real connoisseur's delights. We can't list them all (have you hefted a *Manhattan Yellow Pages* lately?), but we have picked out some we particularly like.

And as usual, we have tried to pick out ways that you can combine your shopping expeditions with explorations of neighborhoods, which have much nicer views than all those prepackaged malls and dispense with some of the hype in favor of the rich variety of New York. Sure, this is prime window-shopping territory, and you can see, and buy, a little of almost everything just by wandering around; but intriguingly, communities of merchants seem to have evolved that coincide with great walking opportunities, so if you know what sort of purchases you want to make, you can look them over for hours and see history at the same time.

For example, are you longing to personalize your suburban townhome with unusual furniture and home accessories? Head to Soho. Love gazing at art galleries? You could spend a whole visit in Soho and its sibling rival, Chelsea. Designer couture? Fifth Avenue, of course, but also upper Madison Avenue. You can get discounts on clothes at a factory-shop mall, but why not wander the Lower East Side, the neighborhood that made discount shopping famous? New York is well-known for gourmet foods, and supermarkets such as Dean & Deluca and Zabar's are classics, but what about noshing on real pickles or fresh-from-the-oven matzo? And if you're looking for a real ethnic experience, skip the markets in Little Italy in favor of Arthur Avenue in the Bronx and see the neighborhood groceries out there.

For those collectors who are more single-minded, we have included a selection of stores and purveyors of specific goods. Rare books, black ties, vintage rock and roll—you want it, we got it.

ALL TOGETHER NOW:
Department Stores, "Malls," and Flea Markets

THE BIG NAMES

unofficial **TIP**
If you want to get that souvenir stuff out of the way in a hurry, you might just want to hustle through the company-logo superstores that are the gift shop equivalents of amusement parks.

WE'RE NOT BY ANY MEANS SUGGESTING that you settle for department-store shopping in New York, but sometimes traveling is a matter of so many gifts, so little time. In that case, you need a lot of options at one address. Besides which, there are some stores in New York so famous in and of themselves that they almost qualify as tourist attractions. (And there are a couple, perhaps not so well-known, that might change your vision of department stores.) Or you may like the spontaneity and treasure-hunt aspect of flea markets.

Probably the best-known names in more traditional department-store shopping in Manhattan are Barney's, Bergdorf Goodman, Bloomingdale's, Lord and Taylor, Macy's, and Saks.

Barney's original Chelsea store has become the transcendent Rubin Museum of Himalayan Art, but the uptown Barney's, a

$100-million Midtown megastore on Madison Avenue at East 61st (☎ 212-826-8900), is more than compensation.

The B&G logo of **Bergdorf Goodman** (☎ 212-753-7300) has been at the cornerstones of Fifth and 57th, both literally and metaphorically, for generations; and maybe that's exactly the reason it recently embarked on a very modern retooling. The seventh-floor housewares department, already a magnet for forward-thinking brides and newly promoted partners, is now 3,000 square feet larger and arranges its own exhibitions. Famed chef Daniel Boulud helped set up the new tea salon, and while so many stores are cutting back on either prices or service, Bergdorf is booming: It now has a whole men's store, called simply **Bergdorf Goodman Men,** dedicated to the best in ready-to-wear couture, on the opposite side of the street. Bergdorf is so dependable that should you suddenly discover that the dinner you're invited to is black-tie, you can call the gender-appropriate store to dispatch a personal shopper to your hotel with an armful of outfits for you to try on.

Bloomingdale's is the designer version of a department store, and it looks it. Everything is name-brand—you could hang your clothes out in the living room and never worry about feeling label-challenged—from Polo to Petrossian (yup, a caviar stand). It even has an American Express office (on Third Avenue at East 59th Street; ☎ 212-705-2000) and 504 Broadway at Spring Street in Soho (☎ 212-729-5900).

Lord & Taylor is the oldest specialty shop in the country, and still a standard (Fifth Avenue between 38th and 39th; ☎ 212-391-3344).

Macy's may be a giant—it covers more than a million square feet—but it's the most moderately priced of the bunch. Perhaps its merchandise isn't as cutting-edge as some; but it covers nearly all the bases, from kitchen goods (and carryout) in the basement to antiques on the ninth floor, and from haircuts to pedicures. And its rather stubborn nostalgia is fairly represented by that famous Thanksgiving Day Parade (Broadway between West 34th and 35th; ☎ 212-695-4400).

Saks Fifth Avenue (☎ 212-753-4000) is just where you'd expect it to be, on Fifth between 49th and 50th streets next to St. Patrick's Cathedral. This is an old-money outlet with an old-money outlook on fashion, jewelry, fine foods, and even lunch; the Café SFA on the eighth floor has views of the cathedral and Rockefeller Center across the street.

Henri Bendel remains a temple for the haute and the ultra-hip (712 Fifth Avenue, between 55th and 56th streets; ☎ 212-247-1100).

Our personal favorite is much less famous, far more limited in stock, and on the expensive side, but it is so beautifully appointed— even the store hardware is gorgeous—that it's worth a look. **Takashimaya** (Fifth Avenue between East 54th and 55th; ☎ 212-350-0115), in a fine six-story townhouse, begins with a tea shop in the basement and rises through a flower shop, spa, and art galleries to men's, women's, and home furnishings. One visit, and you'll have a whole new respect for interior design.

MALLS AND ALL

EVEN LESS DO WE SUGGEST YOU LOOK FOR A shopping mall in Manhattan (especially as the streets are already full of Gaps, etc.). If you must run off a quick list, however, there are a couple of shopping towers ("malls" in the city are more likely to be vertical than horizontal) that won't be far off your path.

Manhattan's version of a super-mall is **The Shops at Columbus Circle** (☎ 212-823-6300), a seven-story honeycomb of boutiques—and several of the city's most expensive restaurants as well—including **A/X Armani Exchange, Hugo Boss, Eileen Fisher, Thomas Pink, Joseph Abbond, Coach, Tourneau,** and a huge **Whole Foods** store, not to mention the **Mandarin-Oriental Hotel** and **CNN.** It's even the new home of the Jazz at Lincoln Center nightclub stage. It's located at 10 Columbus Circle in the Time-Warner Building (☎ 212-823-6300).

The **Manhattan Mall** at Sixth Avenue and 33rd Street has about 120 shops on nine levels, a typical food court, and a useful brochure-heavy visitors center on the seventh floor (☎ 212-465-0500). Even handier, it's right next to Macy's. The fourth and fifth floors of **Trump Tower** (☎ 212-832-2000) on Fifth Avenue between 56th and 57th streets are full of shops: The really big names—**Bruno Magli, Ferragamo, Chanel,** etc.—are right at street level; and the pink marble atrium with its astonishing waterfall/waterwall is something of a tourist attraction in itself. **Rockefeller Center** (☎ 212-332-6868) also has a minimall that you can tour while admiring the Plaza display of the moment, the skating rink, the Deco buildings, and so on (just off Fifth between 49th and 50th). And the renovated **South Street Seaport** (☎ 212-732-8257), part of the built-up Lower Manhattan area near the Fulton Fishmarket at Water Street, is now an attractive, if somewhat predictable, mall of shops, restaurants, and marine-history souvenir stores.

The most attractive one-stop shopping destination for now is the renovated **Grand Central Station** (☎ 212-340-2210), which has more than 120 boutiques, service stores, coffee shops, and carryouts. And of course, it also has several serious restaurants to choose from, including Michael Jordan's Steakhouse, with its view of the Grand Concourse; a mezzanine bar; the famed Grand Central Oyster Bar; the third-floor cocktail lounge in the long-neglected Campbell Apartment, built in the 1920s as a private office and modeled on a 13th-century Florentine palazzo; and a trendy faster-food and trattoria concourse on the lower level complete with fish and meat markets.

FLEA MARKETS

WE DO RECOMMEND THIS VERY CHARACTERISTIC diversion. What would shopping in Manhattan be without a visit to the flea markets? Of course, we mean semi-pro shopping—not the sort of amateur souveniring you can do anywhere, but spot, dash, and bargain stuff. Frequently there are serious antiques dealers as well (see more on antiques centers later in this section), but with flea markets, you need to be a little more careful about derivations and aging.

Some flea markets are regularly scheduled, some are more impromptu (especially in good weather), and a few are more like block parties with vendors involved, especially downtown. These are the most dependable spots to shop, but the Weekend section of the *New York Times* may mention some special fairs; also check the classified ads.

The most famous, the original, is the **Annex Antiques Fair and Flea Market** (☎212-243-5343)—popularly known as the "26th Street flea market"—which brings more than 500 vendors together every weekend in a trio of parking lots that stretch along Sixth Avenue from West 24th toward West 27th (☎ 212-243-5343). The antiques area, around 26th, is open both Saturdays and Sundays from sunrise to sunset, but the general market at the southern end is open only on Sundays—and that's the one to see if you're hoping to celebrity-hunt while you're trying to distinguish the Tiffany from the trash. From there it's a short walk to the **Chelsea Antiques Annex,** a.k.a. "the Garage" (☎ 212-647-0707), along West 25th Street between Sixth and Seventh, which is run by the same people and is open Saturday and Sunday, 7 a.m. to 5 p.m.

But unless you are a flea-market veteran, you may find it easier to grasp the opportunities at the somewhat smaller **Soho Antiques Fair and Flea Market** (☎ 212-682-2000), which sets up Saturdays and Sundays from 9 a.m. to 5 p.m. at the corner of Broadway and Grand Street. Another good smaller flea market is the **Greenwich Village Flea Market** at P.S. 41 on Greenwich Avenue near Seventh; it is open Saturdays only from noon to 7 p.m.

If you have the stamina, you can do the East Side/West Side two-step over the weekend by swinging through the upscale flea markets at **P.S. 183** on East 66th Street between First and York avenues (☎ 212-721-0900; Saturday only, 6 a.m.–6 p.m.) and the **"Greenflea"** indoor/outdoor market on Columbus Avenue at West 77th (☎ 212-721-0900; Sunday only, 10 a.m.–6 p.m.; ☎ 212-721-0900). Or look into the newer, in-crowd **Hell's Kitchen** gathering of 175 or so vendors along 39th Street between Ninth and Tenth avenues (Saturdays and Sundays, 9 a.m.–5 p.m.; ☎ 212-242-1217).

unofficial **TIP**
A few general rules apply to all flea markets: Don't expect dealers to accept credit cards, although a few whose merchandise is particularly expensive (antique furniture and so on) might. In most cases, expect to pay cash and carry your prize off with you. If you want to skim off the cream of the crop, go early; if you're hoping to score a real bargain, wait until the afternoon, when some dealers may be willing to shave the price so they don't have to pack everything up. Some markets may charge a nominal entrance fee of a dollar or two.

unofficial **TIP**
The Annex Antiques Fair and Flea Market is a good place to learn more about flea-market merchandise, as many of the dealers are extremely professional.

ONE-STOP SHOPPING:
Museum Shops and Theme Stores

ART-IFACTS: THE MUSEUM SHOPS

IF YOU'RE SICK OF THE COOKIE-CUTTER GIFT LIST, treat yourself to a mall of the mind, so to speak. Along two straight lines, one in Midtown and the other on the East Side, are clusters of the smartest—meaning chic and brainy—shops, all a little different and all, so to speak, of museum quality.

The first line, of course, is along Museum Mile, that stretch of Fifth Avenue between 82nd and 104th streets along which nine major collections are assembled. All have some sort of gift shop, but it's fair to say that the **Metropolitan Museum of Art** at 82nd Street (☎ 212-535-7710) has one of the most stunning collections anywhere, filled with not only merchandise relating to current and hit exhibits—replica jewelry, Egyptiana, art-design scarves, notepaper, and the like—but also classic reproduction posters, decorative glass, books, T-shirts, desk accessories, card cases, calendars, vases, reproduction statuary, Impressionist umbrellas, Munch and Dalí wristwatches, and even rugs. It has its own bridal registry, too. Check out some of the art being sold on consignment upstairs. And if you don't make it up to Museum Mile, the **Metropolitan Museum** has a two-story branch in Rockefeller Center at 15 West 49th Street (☎ 212-332-1360), where you can find a full selection of its merchandise, rugs and all; there's also an outpost in Macy's (☎ 212-268-7266).

The **Jewish Museum** on Fifth at 92nd (☎ 212-423-3200) has a small but striking collection of jewelry, menorahs, and scarves, many with designs adapted from religious or historical works.

The **Cooper-Hewitt National Museum of Design** at 91st (☎ 212-849-8300) is design central for those whose taste in silver, platters, and small personal and office items such as pens, bath luxuries, salt-and-peppers, and coasters tends to an earlier, more sensual age than the sleek modernity of MoMA's collection (this is, after all, the former Carnegie mansion). But if you do like that smart postmodern look, step into the shop at the **Guggenheim** at 89th Street (☎ 212-423-3615) and peruse their fine selections of posters, notepapers, jewelry, and textiles.

A short stroll away, though not literally in "the Mile," are the **Frick Collection** (Fifth and 70th), which has lovely notepaper, calendars, postcards, and notebooks; the **Whitney Museum's** (Madison and 75th) store with its sometimes elegantly spare (Shaker-influenced), sometimes witty assortment of ties, toys, and other home and closet whimsy; and the **Asia Society** bookstore has been newly renovated and expanded (Park Avenue between 70th and 71st; phone ☎ 212-517-2742; **asiasociety.org**), and stocks not only adult and children's books on Asian culture, cooking, language, and design but also toys, jewelry, teapots, chopsticks, Indonesian carvings, and unusual paper goods.

Along a somewhat more imaginary aisle in Midtown Manhattan, on a line that cuts from West 53rd to West 49th streets between Fifth and Sixth avenues (though closer to Fifth), you'll find half a dozen more museum shops within easy reach.

The **Museum of Art and Design** on West 53rd is both exhibit spaces and among the finest art-gift shops in town (45 West 53rd; ☎ 212-956-3535). Though the selection is not large, the jewelry is particularly attractive, sometimes spectacular, and there are often some glassworks as well as paperweights, books, and other decorative items.

The **MoMA Design Store** (44 West 53rd Street; ☎ 212-767-1050) has for good reason inspired one of the great mail catalogs of our box-stuffing era. Every one of these products—glassware, writing pens, kids' flatware, vases, photo frames, even watches and ties— have passed such muster with the museum's design mavens that they have become part of the permanent collection. And smart as they are, they are frequently great bargains: Among our personal favorite acquisitions have been spiral-twist stretch bracelets, something like Slinkies for the wrist, for $8 to $12. And **MoMA's bookstore** (across the street in the lobby at 11 West 53rd; ☎ 212-708-9700), which stocks more than 6,000 coffee-table books, catalogs, and quality paperbacks, is also packed with educational videos, software, art posters, calendars, and so on. For downtowners, there is another MoMA shop in Soho at 81 Spring Street (☎ 646-613-1367).

Just around the corner (straight through the block, if you could do it) on 52nd Street is the **Museum of Television and Radio** (☎ 212-621-6800), which has a small store ideally suited to those whose kids (or spouses) still have crushes on Mary Tyler Moore or Captain Kirk. It stocks videos, T-shirts, posters, vintage radio shows, and stocking stuffers with character, so to speak.

The **International Center for Photography** at Sixth Avenue and 43rd Street (☎ 212-857-0000) is the only museum anywhere that collects and exhibits only photographs; its calendars, prints, and coffee-table books are first-rate. The **Museum of the City of New York** has such urban memorabilia as stickball sets and vintage posters (Fifth Avenue at 103rd Street; ☎ 212-534-1672).

Among other attractive stops are the trio of stores at the **Metropolitan Opera House** in Lincoln Center: the Met shop on the main floor (☎ 212-580-4090); the broader Performing Arts shop on the lower level (☎ 917-441-1195); and the Poster Gallery (☎ 212-580-4673), which stocks not only great records and biographies but also diva (and danseur) T-shirts, mugs, and the sort of unabashed art lover's accessories that fill PBS catalogs. The shop at the **National Museum of the American Indian** (☎ 212-514-3700) in the old Custom House at 1 Bowling Green downtown near Battery Park has Native

American music and meditation tapes, beadwork kits, and turquoise jewelry of the sort that is once again popular with young people, plus T-shirts, arrowheads, and reproductions of famous paintings of the West. And if you're headed down that way, you might want to check out the maps, model ships, and other old-salt stuff at the **South Street Seaport Museum Shops** (☎ 212-732-8257).

The new **Rubin Museum of Himilayan Art** has beautiful jewelry, purses, cabinets, and rugs (150 West 17th Street at Seventh Avenue; ☎ 212-620-5000). Vaguely exotic jewelry, shawls, inlaid boxes, and leather-bound goods are among the attractions at the **Dahesu Museum** shop on Madison Avenue at 57th Street (☎ 212-759-0606).

BRAND LOYALTY: THEME STORES

THE 1990S GAVE BIRTH TO A WHOLE NEW BOOM in merchandising: stores specializing in movie and television tie-ins, corporate brand names, celebrity properties, and so on. They are virtually theme parks disguised as stores, and if your kids are determined to have these sorts of souvenirs, there are several along almost any major tour route.

kids Along Fifth Avenue near the foot of Central Park are the **Coca-Cola Store,** the **Warner Bros. Studio Store,** and the **World of Disney** store. (Both Disney and Warner Bros. have stores in Times Square as well.) The multistory **Niketown** is on 57th just around the corner toward Madison Avenue, as is the **Original Levi's Store.** There are **NBA/WNBA** stores in Times Square and on Fifth at 52nd. The **WWF New York** at Broadway and 43rd has floor-to-ceiling TV screens for video replays and a stage for live "performances," frequent in-house and celeb drop-bys as well as paraphernalia and food (☎ 212-398-2563).

The **NBC Studio Store,** in Rockefeller Center, is stocked with T-shirts, coffee mugs, and caps from *Seinfeld, Frasier, Friends, The Tonight Show, Saturday Night Live,* and so on.

And since more and more restaurants have their own in-house merchandise stores, check out the **Jekyll & Hyde Club** (Sixth and 57th; ☎ 212-541-9505), **Planet Hollywood** (☎ 212-333-7827) at Broadway and 45th, and the **Hard Rock Cafe** (1501 Broadway; ☎ 212-343-3355). These are all close enough to serve as an instant playground pub tour.

Of course, if your particular brand loyalty lies with a famous designer, you're headed uptown, so see the following sections on Fifth Avenue and Madison Avenue.

GREAT NEIGHBORHOODS
for SHOPPING

WINDOWS ON THE WORLD: FIFTH AVENUE

THERE ARE A FEW STREETS WHOSE STORES and window displays

are so famous that they don't even need city names attached. Rodeo Drive. Champs-Elysées. Via Veneto. And Fifth Avenue.

Fifth Avenue was nicknamed "Millionaire's Row" at the turn of the century, when the Vanderbilts, Astors, and Goulds all built palaces for themselves along the road, and it's never quite given up that expensive spirit. A few of the 19th-century mansions are still standing, and the churches of the area give you an idea of the luxury such tycoons expected even in their houses of worship. (Remember that Fifth Avenue is the east-west dividing line, and don't let addresses on the numbered streets confuse you. Cartier at East 52nd Street faces B. Dalton at West 52nd.)

To get a serious sense of both the retail and historical beauties of Midtown, start at the corner of 49th Street and head north toward Central Park. On your left sits **Rockefeller Center,** which fills the blocks between Fifth and Sixth avenues and West 48th and 51st streets and incorporates Radio City Music Hall and the NBC Studios (look around the corner onto West 49th and you'll see that famous window into the *Today* show). There are also many shops in the lower levels of the complex, and the famous ice rink/outdoor café (a Jekyll-and-Hyde trick that follows the seasons) and gardens, as well as many seasonal displays on the plaza. There is actually a minimuseum of the complex on the concourse level at 30 Rockefeller Plaza, with photos and video, and a walking tour guide is available free at the information desk in the lobby. Notice the gilded gods of industry on the front, the bas relief, and the Art Deco detailing.

Across the street are **Saks Fifth Avenue,** one of the city's finest department stores, and St. Patrick's Cathedral, which was built by James Renwick Jr. in the 1880s. Just above that is the elaborate facade of the famous jeweler **Cartier** at the corner of East 52nd, which is one of the few turn-of-the-19th-century mansions still intact. Legend has it that the original owner traded the house to Pierre Cartier for a string of pearls.

The French Gothic St. Thomas Church at the corner of Fifth and 53rd was built in 1914; the University Club at 54th was built in 1899 by Charles McKim (a partner of Stanford White) in imitation of the Italian palazzos. McKim also designed what is now the Banco di Napoli across the street. The Fifth Avenue Presbyterian Church, built in 1875, was where the Roosevelts, Auchinclosses, and Walcotts worshiped, helping give it the reputation of being the city's most influential congregation.

Now the credit-card boutiques begin to thicken: **Christian Dior** and **Pucci,** both at the corner of Fifth Avenue and East 55th; **Takashimaya** (discussed earlier) and **Elizabeth Arden** between East 54th and 55th; **Gucci** at East 54th; and **Henri Bendel** between West 55th and 56th.

De Beers, the first name in diamonds (it invented the phrase "Diamonds are forever") has opened an American flagship store at Fifth and 55th (☎ 212-906-0001). **Harry Winston,** diamond designer to the rich and famous, is on Fifth at West 56th, and the other three famous "Four Carat" neighbors, **Tiffany, Van Cleef & Arpels,** and **Bulgari,** are all at the intersection of 57th. (The building that houses Bulgari at 730 Fifth was the first home of the Museum of Modern Art.) Between 56th and 57th look for **Ferragamo** and O.J. favorite **Bruno Magli; Steuben,** the art-glass company; **Burberry's; Chanel;** and **Fendi. Norma Kamali** is just around the corner on 56th.

Bergdorf Goodman and **Bergdorf Goodman Men** (discussed earlier) fill the blocks from West 57th to 58th. And as you get to the bottom of the park, where Fifth meets 58th Street, you'll see **FAO Schwarz,** one of the most famous (though now insolvent) toy stores in the world.

CLOTHING ON THE HIGH SIDE: THE EAST SIDE

IF YOU LOVE THAT ITALIAN-LABEL LOOK BUT DON'T have time to fly to Rome, relax. These days, the signs along Madison Avenue in the 60s and 70s read like satellite transmissions from the Via Veneto, with just enough American and international designer boutiques to keep you grounded.

Some of the big-name stores have set up along the numbered streets between Madison and Fifth avenues, so that the old couture row, the new Madison, and the museum district are beginning to merge. As an example, start east along 57th Street from Fifth Avenue and you will see the signs for **Christian Dior, Chanel, Charivari, Yves Saint Laurent, Hugo Boss, Jil Sander, Montblanc, Burberry's, Coach, Prada, Holland & Holland** hunting clothiers, and **Louis Vuitton;** turn the corner onto Madison for **Tourneau,** the watch temple. **Emporio Armani** is on Madison at 58th; **DKNY** and the **Calvin Klein** flagship are on the corner at East 60th near the custom shirtmaker **Borrelli. Hermès** is on Madison at 62nd, along with **Luca Luca; Shanghai Tang** at 63rd; **David Yurman** at 64th; and **Emilio Pucci** is just around the corner on 64th Street between Madison and Fifth.

But the real name-label parade begins at the northwest corner of West 65th and Madison with the **Giorgio Armani** boutique, a stunning white four-story showplace that resembles the National Gallery's East Building (not to mention Armani couture itself). It gazes serenely across at the **Krizia** and **Valentino** boutiques and shelters the **BCBG/Max Azria** shop on its left.

Paul & Shark, the nautical-minded Italian sportswear, is at 66th and Madison (☎ 212-452-9868). Across 66th are the new **Bulgari** showroom, **Cerutti** children's clothing, **David Berk Cashmere, Jean-Paul Gaultier,** and **Nicole Miller,** who is to ties as the *New Yorker* is to cartoons. **Emmanuel Ungaro** holds down the corner of Madison and 67th. Cross 67th to **Kenzo, Moschino, Davide Cenci,** and **Frette** Italian linens, and peek around the corner to 21 East 67th for the classic English country tweeds, cufflinks, and other gentry goods at the boutique of the 150-year-old **House of Dormeuil.**

Above 68th Street are the complete ready-to-wear collections of **Gianni Versace** (in a negative-image Roman temple with black capitals and silver-gilded capitals); **MaxMara; Malo,** the European cashmere king; **Jaeger** sportswear; **Donna Karan; Bogner** ski couture; and **TSE Cashmere.** The **Dolce & Gabbana** store at the corner of Madison and 69th is 7,000 square feet of retro-rococo chic; **Prada** preens nearby at Fifth (☎ 212-664-0010) and Madison (☎ 212-327-4200).

Cross 69th to **Missoni, Chloë, Maraolo** Italian shoes, **Romeo Gigli, Miu Miu, Fila,** and **Andrea Carrano.** If you're crazy for natural fibers or custom-woven linens, it's dueling designer labels: the Italian **Pratesi** versus the French **D. Porthault.**

Yves Saint Laurent's couture store and his **Rive Gauche** boutique are side by side on Madison between 70th and 71st streets, along with **Gianfranco Ferre, Sonia Rykiel, Frederic Fekkai,** the hairdresser-cum-designer, and **Santoni's** handmade Italian footwear.

Ralph Lauren has four floors of Polo clothing, accessories, and home luxuries on the west side of Madison between 71st and 72nd streets and a whole second building full of Polo Sport casualwear and his trademark weathered look on the east side. At **Stubbs & Wooten** around the corner at 22 East 72nd (☎ 212-249-5200), you can have your handmade slippers monogrammed, needlepointed with dogs, stars, or cocktail glasses. **Givenchy's** haute couture store is on Madison at East 75th near **Carolina Herrerra,** and **Issey Miyake**'s is at 76th along with **Michael Kors.**

Not surprisingly, perhaps, the Upper East Side has also spawned a cluster of "pre-owned" fashion boutiques, some of them charitable to boot. **Out of the Closet** (220 East 81st Street) supports AIDS groups; the **Sloan-Kettering Memorial Thrift Shop** at Third Avenue and 81st Street benefits the hospital; but **Encore** (1132 Madison Avenue at 84th) and **Elle W** (Lexington at 64th) are just in it for the goods.

CLOTHING ON THE HIP SIDE: SOHO

FASHION- AND/OR BARGAIN-CONSCIOUS visitors have a great reason to wander the Soho area—aside from the fun of the street theater, that is. Retro, nouveau, haute, and so-so, Soho and surroundings are big boutique territory, so unless you want to have an Armani T-shirt just like everybody else's, you can get more in-circle designerwear at places such as **Scoop** (532 Broadway; ☎ 212-925-2886); **Morgane Le Fay,** Liliana Ordas's splendidly mysterious cave of dresses and capes (67 Wooster Street; ☎ 212-219-7672); and Laura Whittcomb's **Label** (265 Lafayette Street; ☎ 212-966-7736).

Other specialty shops include **Kate Spade** (59 Thompson Street; ☎ 212-274-1991) and her husband **Jack Spade's**

unofficial **TIP**
Soho shops and names play musical addresses so often that you may have to wander around to find again that great find you found before. And remember that weekends are prime wandering time, so quite a few Soho shopkeepers close on Monday.

men's shop around the corner (56 Greene; ☎ 212-625-1820); **Alexander McQueen** (417 West 14th Street; ☎ 212-645-1797); **Anna Sui** (13 Greene; ☎ 212-941-8406); the lower-case upper-class **agnes b.** (13 East 16th; ☎ 212-741-2585) and **agnes b. homme** (79 Green; ☎ 212-431-4339); Rei Kawakubo at **Commes des Garçons** (520 West 22nd; ☎ 212-604-9200); the pricey but irresistibly distinctive **Yohji Yamamoto** (103 Grand; ☎ 212-966-9066); rock-star child **Stella McCartney** (429 West 14th Street; ☎ 212-255-1556); neo-Mod **Cynthia Rowley** (112 Wooster; ☎ 212-334-1144); **Balenciaga** (54 West 23rd Street: ☎ 212-206-0872); **Vivienne Tam** (99 Greene; ☎ 212-966-2398); **Diane von Furstenberg** (385 West 12th; ☎ 212-486-4800); and Miuccia Prada at **Miu Miu** (100 Prince Street; ☎ 212-334-5156). An amalgam of Miu Miu, Jil Sander, Prada, Fendi, etc. is all in one at **Jeffrey New York** (449 West 14th Street; ☎ 212-206-1272); while former Vivienne Westwood designer Sonya Rubin and ex-Armani Kip Chappelle have merged into **Rubin Chappelle** (410 West 14th; ☎ 212-647-8636). One of **Betsey Johnson's** several New York locations is 138 Wooster (☎ 212-995-5048); **Nicole Miller Soho** is at 77 Greene Street (☎ 212-219-1825). Also check out **Kirna Zabête** (96 Greene Street; ☎ 212-941-9656); **Palma** (521 Broome Street; ☎ 212-966-1722); **Alpana Bawa** (41 Grand Street; ☎ 212-965-0559); and **John Varvatos** menswear (149 Mercer Street; 212-965-0700). Custom dressmaker **Shannon McLean** works out of her atelier at 7 East 81st (☎ 212-988-4210).

Perhaps a symbol of the next consumer boom is the huge **Prada** flagship at Broadway and Prince (☎ 212-334-8888), a $40-million, 23,000-square-foot art loft with computers in the racks, stadium seating in the shoe department, and handbags in the elevators. The other over-the-top trendy spot might be the 4,600-square-foot **Burton** boutique, which specializes in high-tech name ski equipment, accessories, clothing, and knickknacks—and even has a "cold room" where you can test out the chill factor (Spring and Mercer; ☎ 212-966-8068).

The first name in vintage chic, of course, is **Harriet Love,** author of the best-selling guide to the stuff and maven of the store that outfitted onetime-employee-turned-pop-singer Cyndi Lauper (126 Prince Street; ☎ 212-966-2280). **Cherry** might be the second name; you might even find Cyndi's seconds there (19 Eighth Avenue; ☎ 212-924-1410). And punky, edgy **Resurrection** is the third (217 Mott Street; ☎ 212-675-1374). **What Comes Around Goes Around** stocks more than 60,000 vintage pieces, designer to denim (351 West Broadway; ☎ 212-343-9303). **Mary Efron** (68 Thompson Street; ☎ 212-219-3090) goes the classic route: Dior, Bergdorf Goodman, etc. Also check out **Screaming Mimi** (382 Lafayette; ☎ 212-677-6464) and **Stellas Dallas** (218 Thompson; ☎ 212-674-0447). **De Leon Collection** specializes in vintage accessories, especially couture handbags, scarves, clutches, and more (40 West 25th Street in the Antiques Showplace; ☎ 212-675-1574). For the traditional Japanese look, as opposed to Tokyo modern couture, try **Kimono House** (131 Thompson Street; ☎ 212-505-0232).

There are also hot spots for last year's, or even last season's, designer consignments and sell-offs: check **INA** (21 Prince; ☎ 212-334-9048) and **INA Men** (262 Mott; ☎ 212-334-2210), for high style—Prada, Helmut Lang, Joseph—at cut-rate prices. Also look into **New and Almost New** (65 Mercer; ☎ 212-226-6677), **Cherry** (185 Orchard; ☎ 212-358-7131), and **Yu** (151 Ludlow; ☎ 212-979-9370) to score Yohji Yamamoto and Commedes Garçons on the rebound.

As with home furnishings, art, and hipness in general, the neighborhood is filling out through Little Italy, making Mott and Elizabeth streets a trendy transition to the bargain-minded Lower East Side. Imelda Marcos wannabes must make a beeline for **Sigerson Morrison** (28 Prince Street; ☎ 212-219-3893), unless you already have kid leather pumps the color of a swashbuckler's wine and velvet loafers for your dinner jacket.

Milliner **Kelly Christy** (235 Elizabeth Street; ☎ 212-965-0686) makes hats to order from a set of designs with names Ben & Jerry would love (though not at ice cream prices), such as the Jackie Kennedy–style pillbox called O and the fruit-topped Cherry Swirl. Softer chapeaux of fleece and fake fur and felt come in both adult and baby sizes at **Lisa Shaub**'s hat store (232 Mulberry; ☎ 212-965-9176). **Milena** does the Imelda Marco thing (252 Mott; ☎ 212-226-4711). As does **Shoe** (197 Mulberry; ☎ 212-941-0205). **Mayle** delivers the casual chic assembled by former model Jane Mayle (252 Elizabeth Street; ☎ 212-625-0406), while traditional ethnic prints and sari scarves are put together in untraditional ways at **Ca-**

> *unofficial* **TIP**
> If you have a certain craving for name-brand architecture as well as couture, skip down to 119 Hudson Street in Tribeca and see the Frank Gehry–designed **Issey Miyake** boutique, with its titanium "ribbons" that run from cellar to ceiling (☎ 212-226-1334).

lypso (280 Mott; ☎ 212-965-0990). **Zero** showcases Modernist designer Maria Cornejo (225 Mott Street; ☎ 212-925-3849), and **P.A.K.** hangs out Corey Pak (229 Mott; ☎ 212-226-5167). The oddest may be **Plate NYC,** however; it's a boutique by day, fusion nibblery and lounge by night (264 Elizabeth Street; ☎ 212-219-9212).

CLOTHING ON THE BARGAIN SIDE: THE LOWER EAST SIDE

THE LOWER EAST SIDE HAS BEEN FAMOUS FOR years as the place bargains are best; serious shoppers flew in to gawk along Orchard Street, where last season's department store and even designerwear could be had for, well, if not a song, then a chorus or two. These days, with sales so much more common and outlet malls thriving, the trek is a little lower on some visitors' itineraries, but the merchants of the neighborhood, now being more aggressively promoted as the Historic Orchard Street Bargain District, have banded together to raise their profile again. So if you do have that bargain bug—and, after all, how many of your office mates can tell last year's classics from this year's?—head east from Soho into this evocative old section.

*un*official **TIP**
While shopping on the Lower East Side, you should remember that many of the sidewalk vendors are hawking bootleg or counterfeit goods. And maybe you shouldn't flash your cash too carelessly.

More than 300 businesses in this neighborhood are still family-owned, and with just a little imagination (and maybe a stop in the Lower East Side Tenement Museum or other historic landmark), you'll be able to see it as it was when the pushcart and peddler era was melding into the wholesale world—especially if you go on a Sunday, when a lot of the area streets are blocked off for pedestrian traffic and turned into open-air vendor markets. And you'll definitely still hear the rhythms of the Yiddish millions of East European Jews stamped on the bargaining patter of the vendors, even though the community's ethnicity now ranges from South American to Southeast Asian. You may find 19th-century echoes in some stores' cash-only, or at least no credit card, policies and the haggling over prices you may get into every once in a while. If you like the hurly-burly of contact-sport shopping, this is the place, and you might get a real bargain if you work at it.

To keep from getting disoriented in all this retail abundance, stop by the offices of the **Historic Orchard Street Shopping District** at 261 Broome Street (☎ 212-226-9010) and pick up a brochure/map of the neighborhood; or if you drop by **Katz's Deli** at the corner of Ludlow Street and East Houston (☎ 212-254-2246) any Sunday at 11 a.m. from April through December, you can hook up with a free hour-long shopping tour. (If Katz's looks particularly familiar to you, it's probably because the most famous scene in *When Harry Met Sally*—the, uh, loud one—was shot here.) Meanwhile, following are few spots to get you started.

Check into the likes of **Giselle Sportswear** (143 Orchard; ☎ 212-673-1900); vintage couture at **Frock** (148 Orchard; ☎ 212-594-5380); and the really big-name double-breasteds at **Jodamo International** menswear (321 Grand Street; ☎ 212-219-1039). Lingerie lovers linger at **A. W. Kaufman** (73 Orchard; ☎ 212-226-1629) and **Louis Chock** across the street (74 Orchard; ☎ 212-473-1929). Try on the leather coats at **Carl & Sons** (172 Orchard; ☎ 212-674-8470). Actually, you can't escape leather shops on Orchard Street, any more than you will run out of any other kind of clothing; walk around a little before you buy, or at least try to bargain a little.

Do a hat trick at **Stetson's** (101 Delancey; ☎ 212-473-1343). For designer handbags, look to **Fine & Klein** (119 Orchard; ☎ 212-674-6720). If you really just want another Samsonite or American Tourister rollalong, there's plenty of that stuff to be found as well. On the other hand, there's just one place for umbrellas, **Salwen's** (45 Orchard; ☎ 212-226-1693), because if you don't hear Irving Salwen play Yiddish folks songs on the guitar, you haven't really gotten the Lower East Side experience.

That Soho chic-boutique thang is headed east, so keep your eyes peeled for iconoclastic designers setting up shop. A good example of creeping sticker shock is the fine collection of Elie Tahari at **Zao** (175 Orchard Street; ☎ 212-505-0500). The fabric stores are clustered along Hester and Orchard streets, and the tailoring shops are clustered north of Delancey toward East Houston along Rivington Street, Allen Street, and Stanton; get something custom-made. If you sew yourself, or even if you don't, take a gander at the incredible variety of zippers at **A. Feibusch,** from doll-sized to double-length (27 Allen Street; ☎ 212-226-3964).

Thanks to chic creep, so to speak, the strip of Orchard Street between Houston and Delancey is on the verge of becoming another youth-oriented bar-and-boutique area—O-Ho, perhaps. Many of these are retro-hip spots, with overtones of funk and psychedelia as well as hip-hop and sometimes a little ethnic or one-world flavor. If the shopping expedition covers two generations, this could be the answer.

ART GALLERIES: CHELSEA AND SOHO

WHILE "STARVING" IS NOT A REQUIRED ATTRIBUTE for an artist, it does help explain why it's the run-down neighborhoods that harbor artists until the rents go up with the hip quotient. It's also the reason that these two old villages, which are still battling for the art scene crowd, are being threatened by Brooklyn's DUMBO buzz. Still, there's more than enough to see here.

Soho is estimated to house 250 art galleries; its art scene has grown so rapidly that its annual September arts festival boomed from 60 events in 1965 to 200 in 1996 and spread out to 11 days of visual arts exhibits, performances, and dance in 1997.

Almost any Soho block has an art, photography, or print shop mixed in with the boutiques, if you just want to trust to chance. The two buildings at 415 and 420 West Broadway by themselves house well over a dozen galleries. **Louis K. Meisel** is at 141 Prince, **Martin Lawrence** at 457 West Broadway, and a branch of **Pace Gallery** at 142 Greene.

But a stroll down Broadway between Prince and Houston offers more than a full day's worth of art-gazing and architectural interest. The six-story loft at 575 Broadway, formerly used as the Guggenheim Museum Soho, was originally designed for owner John Jacob Astor II as a garment manufacturing and retailing complex. The **New Museum of Contemporary Art** is planning to move to a larger building on the Bowery at the terminus of Prince Street. Meanwhile, it's bunking with the **Chelsea Art Museum.**) The **Alternative Museum** is only one of several galleries inside 594 Broadway, but it sometimes mixes poetry readings and music with the visuals.

unofficial **TIP**
Soho arts festival director Simon Watson puts out a monthly newsletter called "Simon Says" (available at neighborhood galleries) listing 40 recommendations for art-gazing, and he also organizes Saturday afternoon museum and gallery walks led by area dealers.

Although the cast-iron facade of the **Museum for African Art** at 593 Broadway, which moved from its smaller Upper East Side space in 1993, is original, the interior spaces were designed by Maya Lin, architect of the Vietnam Veterans Memorial (the "black wall") in Washington, D.C. It is the only museum other than the Smithsonian's Museum of African Art that focuses on sub-Saharan cultural artifacts: life-sized carvings, masks, weavings, jewelry, and so on. (A new site is being prepared at Fifth Avenue at East 110th Street.)

Chelsea now has more than 200 galleries of its own, and the easiest way to take in some of the major ones is to stroll back and forth along the streets from West 20th to West 26th streets between Tenth and Eleventh avenues. The four-story **Dia Center for the Arts,** which arguably sparked the neighborhood movement when it expanded here from Soho, is at 535 West 22nd.

In the 500 stretch of West 21st Street, for example, **Bonakdar Jancou Gallery** has joined **Paolo Baldacci** at 521 West 21st Street near **Paula Cooper** (521 and 534 West 21st Street). Former Cooper Gallery directors **Christopher D'Amelio** and **Lucien Terras** now have their own eponymous gallery around the corner at 525 West 22nd Street, which is also the address of Lisa Spellman's **303 Gallery** and **Jason McCoy. Matthew Marks Gallery** has spaces at 521 West 21st, 522 West 22nd, and 523 West 24th; **Max Protetch** is at 511 West 22nd (leasing part of the space to the Wild Lily Tearoom); **Sikkema Jenkins** is at 530 West 22nd. **Fredericks Freiser** is at 504 West 22nd.

unofficial **TIP**
Note that most Soho galleries are open on Saturday and closed on Sunday and Monday; Chelsea galleries used to be open on Sunday, but many are now shifting to Saturday hours instead. Be sure to check ahead if you have weekend wandering in mind.

The stunning Art Deco building across 11th Avenue stretching from 26th to 27th is the Starrett-Lehigh Building, originally constructed over the Lehigh Valley Railroad yards and with elevators that hauled whole freight cars, fully loaded, into the warehouse. It is now a multigallery complex that includes not only visual arts spaces but also **Jan van der Donk** rare books and the even more fantastic **Bound and Unbound** conceptual art bookstore.

If you prefer to stick to Midtown, you can spend a lot of time amid the old, fine, and famous cluster of galleries in the area bounded by 56th and 57th streets and Park and Sixth avenues, particularly the **Fuller Building** at the corner of Madison; though most of these are also closed on Sundays, a fair number are open on Mondays. Among the most prominent galleries are **Pace Wildenstein** (which also has a branch at 534 West 25th Street) at 34 East 57th; **Marian Goodman,** who specializes in prominent foreign artists, at 24 West 57th; **Edwynn Hook,** which specializes in big-name photography, at 745 Fifth Avenue; modern art specialists at **Joseph Helman** at 20 West 57th; **David Findlay Jr.,** where you may spot a John Singer Sargent, at 41 East 57th; and a branch of the international **Marlborough** galleries at 40 West 57th.

HOME FURNISHINGS AND INTERIORS: SOHO

THE LOWER END OF SOHO AROUND Greene and Broome streets sweeps the market in cool furniture and home design, a number of them partial boutiques from the artisans who own them, including **Moss** (146 Greene Street; ☎ 212-204-7100), **Aero Studios** (419 Broome; ☎ 212-966-4700), **Design by Mary Jaeger** (51 Spring Street; ☎ 212-941-5877), **Armani Casa** (97 Greene; ☎ 212-334-1271), and **Todd Hase** (261 Wooster Street; ☎ 212-334-3568; **toddhase.com**). A little more commercial but still intriguing are the multi-culti **Coconut Co.** (250 Hudson; ☎ 212-539-1940); **Anthropologie** (375 West Broadway; ☎ 212-343-7070), which mixes clothing for the urban frontierfolk with artistically weathered furniture; **Portico Home** (72 Spring; ☎ 212-941-7800); and **Dialogica** (484 Broome; ☎ 212-966-1934). The new **Interiology** collection at 476 Broome stocks high-end European contemporary furniture.

Astonishing varieties and textures of tile, including platters and planters, are on display at the 3,500-square-foot branch of Milan's prestigious **Bisazza** (43 Greene Street; ☎ 212-463-0624), **Artistic Tile** (79 5th; ☎ 212-727-9331), and around the corner at **Country Floors** (15 East 16th; ☎ 212-627-8300). **Jeffrey Ruesch's** Art Deco and Nouveau furniture is upstairs from **Fred Silberman's** Art Deco furniture and lighting (39 Bond Street; ☎ 212-226-4777); the **Wooster Gallery** also caters to Deco-dent redecorators (86 Wooster; ☎ 212-219-2190).

Urban-country outfitters (particularly in the southwestern and neo-Italian styles) include **Distant Origin** (153 Mercer; ☎ 212-941-0025) and **Modern Stone Age** (54 Greene; ☎ 212-219-0383). Italy is the spiritual home, and often the actual one as well, of the ceramic designs and linens at **Ceramica** (59 Thompson Street; ☎ 212-941-1307); while the décor deluxe at **Jamson Whyte** (139 Charles Street; ☎ 212-255-7737) hails from Singapore and Southeast Asia. Deco-devoted celebrities head to **Depression Modern** (150 Sullivan Street; ☎ 212-982-5699).

But the home furnishings neighborhood is expanding—don't they always?—and in the single block of Lafayette Street between East Houston and Prince (which was once considered Little Italy, but is rather rapidly shifting toward the city's hip pocket), you can find astonishing antique etched-glass doors, Deco lighting fixtures, huge marble tubs, wrought-iron gates, ritzy toilet paper holders, and even the occasional elevator box at **Urban Archaeology** (143 Franklin; ☎ 212-431-4646); custom retro at **Salon Modern** (281 Lafayette; ☎ 212-219-3439); late–19th- and 20th-century antiques at **Secondhand Rose** (138 Dwayne; ☎ 212-393-9002); and one-of-a-kind Howdy-Doody-meets-the-Mad-Hatter-in-Manhattan accessories and furniture at **Lost City Arts** (18 Cooper Square; ☎ 212-375-0500). **BAC** has some of the most important names in mid-20th-century French design on its books (16 Crosby Street; ☎ 212-431-6151); and **Saigoniste** deals in, as the name suggests, Vietnamese trays, bowls, pillows, and chopsticks (239 Mulberry; ☎ 212-925-4610).

If you wander beyond Lafayette toward the Lower East Side, look for **Just Shades** (21 Spring Street; ☎ 212-966-2757), which stocks exactly what it says; here you can dress your windows with rice paper, silk, burlap, parchment, and a host of custom designs. And at the **Apartment,** the medium truly is the message . . . it's hard to tell whether it's a shop or someone's co-op (101 Crosby Street; ☎ 212-219-3066).

If there is any possibility that you have not found what you want in the Soho neighborhood—or at **ABC Carpet and Home** on Broadway at East 19th (☎ 212-473-3000)—there is also a large number of home furnishing shops in the East Village, especially along East 9th Street and on Duane and Franklin streets in Tribeca. Among the Franklin Street high spots are another branch of **Mod** (71 Franklin; ☎ 212-925-5506); **Antik** (104 Franklin; ☎ 212-343-0471); **R 20th Century** (82 Franklin; ☎ 212-343-7979); **Dune** (88 Franklin; ☎ 212-925-6171); and **Intérieurs** (151 Franklin; ☎ 212-343-0800).

SPECIALTY SHOPPING

IF YOU'RE ALREADY A COLLECTOR OR ARE shopping for someone who is, you can almost certainly find whatever it is in New York. In fact, you can probably find too many or get waylaid by all the other goodies in town. There are whole volumes devoted to shopping in Manhattan, and we ain't just talking the phone book; but unless shopping is your life, or you plan to move to town permanently, this list should help you get started.

ANTIQUES It would be impossible to pick the finest antiques dealers in a city like this, so we've only mentioned a few and their specialties. (Also look through this section for specific items.) Don't overlook the auction houses, especially **Christie's,** which has a 24-hour hotline for auction information (20 Rockefeller Plaza; ☎ 212-636-2000); its somewhat lower-scale—relatively speaking—branch, **Christie's East** at 219 East 67th (☎ 212-606-0400); **Sotheby Parke Bernet** (York Avenue at East 72nd Street; ☎ 212-606-7000) and its junior gallery, **Sotheby's Arcade** (☎ 212-606-7409); and **Swann Galleries** (104 East 25th Street; ☎ 212-254-4710). All of these and several other reputable firms advertise previews and auctions in the *New York Times.* Also be sure to refer to the "Flea Markets" section, since one person's flea is often another person's find.

If you like just to walk in and out of shops to see what catches your eye, the area around East 60th Street between Second and Third avenues is treasure alley. If you like to ground yourself in a single building and see as many dealers as possible, head for the **Chelsea Antiques Building** at 40 West 25th Street (☎ 212-929-0909), which has 150 dealers spread over three floors; or the **Manhattan Art and Antiques Center,** with 100 galleries of Asian, African, American, and European works (1050 Second Avenue between 55th and 56th; ☎ 212-355-4600). **Antiques at the Showplace** houses 100 dealers on two huge floors (40 West 25th Street; ☎ 212-633-6063), but like its neighboring flea markets, it's open only on weekends.

Among the Upper East Side galleries are the John Rosselli group: **JR Antiques** (255 East 72nd Street; ☎ 212-737-2252), **John Rosselli International** (423 East 73rd; ☎ 212-772-2137), and his lighting and accessory store, **John Rosselli & Associates** (979 Third Avenue, Suite 700; ☎ 212-593-2060).

Down in Soho, one of the big names in designer circles is **Niall Smith,** who specializes in late–18th- and early–19th-century European neoclassical furniture (96 Grand Street; ☎ 212-941-7354). **Eileen Lane** refurbishes Deco for redecoration (150 Thompson; ☎ 212-475-2988). For something your neighbors will never be able to get from Pier 1, look into **Rabun & Claiborne Gallery**, which specializes in late–19th-century American pieces and iron furniture by Omer Claiborne, whose daughter Leslie Cozart co-owns the gallery (115 Crosby Street; ☎ 212-226-5053). And **Les Pierre Antiques** in Greenwich Village continues the legacy of the (late) Pierres Deux—as has been said, the Julia Child of French provincial décor (369 Bleeker Street; ☎ 212-243-7740).

ARCHITECTURAL REMNANTS In addition to Soho's **Urban Archaeology,** mentioned earlier, Brooklyn's **Architectural Salvage Warehouse** in the Williamsburg area (☎ 718-388-4527) was established by the New York Landmarks Preservation Commission to supply historically minded New Yorkers (you don't have to show ID) with doors, mantels, wrought iron, chandeliers, and so on. The trick here is that you'll have to arrange your own shipping. Also check out **Demolition Depot** (216 East 125th Street; ☎ 212-860-1138).

ASIAN ART AND ANTIQUES For Japanese woodblocks, contact **Ronin Gallery** (605 Madison Avenue, fourth floor; ☎ 212-688-0188); **Things Japanese** (127 East 60th Street, upstairs; ☎ 212-371-4661); or the very fine **Joan B. Mirviss, Ltd.** (by appointment; ☎ 212-799-4021). New Orleans's prominent Asian art and textiles specialist **Diane Genre** shows in New York several times a year; call ☎ 504-595-8945 for an appointment. **Art of the Past** (1242 Madison Avenue; ☎ 212-860-7070) specializes in Asian art and antiques.

For chinoiserie, try **Ralph M. Chait Galleries** (724 Fifth Avenue, tenth floor; ☎ 212-758-0937). The **Chinese Porcelain Gallery** also handles Vietnamese and Cambodian pieces (475 Park Avenue; ☎ 212-838-7744).

AUTOGRAPHS Forget those mall stores with their preframed sports photos and replicated signatures. Head to the East Side to **James Lowe** (by appointment, 30 East 60th; ☎ 212-759-0775) or **Kenneth Rendell** (989 Madison Avenue; ☎ 212-717-1776) for authentic signed letters, manuscripts, photographs, and other documents. Inquire about their searching for specific persons' autographs or professional evaluations if you have such items to insure or sell.

BABY AND CHILDREN'S CLOTHING If you coo over pictures of babies in medieval lace, head for **La Layette et Plus** (170 East 61st Street; ☎ 212-688-7072) or **Jacardi** (787 Madison; ☎ 212-535-3200). **Calypso Enfant & Bebe** goes the fairy-princess route with tutus and French bassinets (426 Broome Street; ☎ 212-966-3234).

BEADS Agate, cinnabar, ivory, porcelain, faux and real amber, jade, amethyst, seed, brass, silver—all sizes, types, and prices of beads are at **Leekan Designs** in Soho (Mercer and Spring; ☎ 212-226-7226) along with sake and tea sets and wonderful bargain trinkets from Asia.

kids **BONES** Since the auctioning of Sue the *T. rex* at Sotheby's, bones have become big business. Actually, they already were starting to be, but for most tourists, the skeletons, teeth, fossils, and anatomical charts at **Maxilla & Mandible** will be a revelation (451–55 Columbus Avenue; ☎ 212-724-6173). It's just around the corner from the American Museum of Natural History, where dinosaurs are truly king, Rex or no; so this is a natural for kid's day. M&M owner Harry Galiano used to work at the American Museum of Natural History, in fact, and his museum-quality merchandise is impeccably treated.

If you're down in Soho, look into **Evolution,** which also has a fascinating assortment of bugs, skulls, horns, feathers, shells, and fossils—plus T-shirts to match (120 Spring Street; ☎ 212-343-1114).

BOOKS If you have the title, they have the book, or at least they can get it for you (and maybe at wholesale cost). Manhattan is crammed with general-interest bookstores, of course, including the original **Barnes & Noble, B. Dalton,** and **Doubleday** stores; and most neighborhoods have at least one hangout that caters to night owls. **Rizzoli** (31 West 57th; ☎ 212-759-2424) must be one of the prettiest stores in town, especially now that the big megastores have pretty much dispensed with décor.

But not surprisingly, the capital of American publishing is also a haven for fine antique, rare, used, and specialty books, several of them on the Upper East Side. Contact **Bauman Rare Books** (535 Madison Avenue, ☎ 212-751-0011, and 301 Park Avenue, Waldorf-Astoria Hotel, ☎ 212-759-8300); **Imperial Fine Books** (790 Madison Avenue, second floor; ☎ 212-861-6620); **Ursus Books** (981 Madison, ☎ 212-772-8787); **Martayan Lan** (70 East 57th Street; ☎ 212-308-0018); or **James Cummins** (699 Madison Avenue, seventh floor; ☎ 212-688-6441). The most famous secondhand bookstore in New York is the **Strand** (828 Broadway; ☎ 212-473-1452), which has an estimated 18 miles of shelves with books at rock-bottom prices, plus some first editions, autographed copies, and serious rare books (on the third floor) for those on lavish budgets. The prestigious, old-line **Gotham Book Market** has moved into larger digs—into the home of the old

H.P. Kraus antiquarian bookshop, in fact—at 16 East 46th Street (☎ 212-719-4448). **Argosy Books** (59th Street between Park and Lexington; ☎ 212-753-4455) has six floors of maps, posters, antiquarian books, political cartoons, and autographs: It was here that one collector purchased the boundary papers for Washington, D.C., signed by then–Secretary of State Thomas Jefferson, but most items are more affordable than that.

Manhattan's three leading gay bookstores are all downtown: the **Oscar Wilde Bookshop** in Greenwich Village (15 Christopher Street; ☎ 212-255-8097), **Creative Visions** in the West Village (548 Hudson Street; ☎ 212-645-7573), and **Bluestockings Women's Bookstore** on the Lower East Side (172 Allen Street; ☎ 212-777-6028).

Strand Books has a huge inventory of books on fine and decorative arts, architecture, techniques, and you-name-it (45 West 57th Street, fifth floor; ☎ 212-688-7600). **Biography Bookshop** in Greenwich Village is just what it sounds like, incorporating not only straight biographies but also diaries, children's versions, and biographical fiction (400 Bleecker Street; ☎ 212-807-8655). Just off Time's Square, **Drama Book Shop** (723 Seventh Avenue, second floor; ☎ 212-944-0595) is the place to go for titles on the performing arts.

Books of Wonder in Chelsea is the sort of children's bookstore you never grow out of, one where authors and illustrators pop in for pleasure as well as for autographings (16 West 18th Street; ☎ 212-989-3270). **Printed Matter Bookstore** (535 West 22nd Street; ☎ 212-925-0325) is a nonprofit outlet for books designed and produced by artists, often by hand; but most of the thousands of volumes are quite inexpensive.

With homestyle fare back on the trend menus (and container gardening, a Martha Stewart–style craze), you may be furrowing your brow for just that particular zucchini casserole recipe. **Joanne Hendricks Cookbooks** is heaven for culinary wannabes, including those who remember their moms working out of treasures that have long been out of print (488 Greenwich Street; ☎ 212-226-5731). An even larger selection, more than 7,000 titles both in and out of print, is available at **Kitchen Arts and Letters,** the love child of former Harper & Row editor Nachum Waxman (1435 Lexington Avenue; ☎ 212-876-5550).

Kinokuniya is a shop in Rockefeller Plaza that sells books on Japanese food, culture, art, martial arts, and fine literature in both English and Japanese; it's a branch of the Japanese Barnes & Noble, so to speak (10 West 49th Street; ☎ 212-765-7766). And in the Rockefeller Center Promenade is the **Librarie de France/Libreria Hispanica,** a.k.a. the Dictionary Store, which has thousands of French- and Spanish-language records, books, magazines, and newspapers, and more (610 Fifth Avenue; ☎ 212-581-8810).

Murder Ink (2486 Broadway, between 92nd and 93rd; ☎ 212-362-8905) is so full of mystery choices it's a crime to miss it—unless you're a Sherlockian, in which case you should head to the **Mysterious Bookshop** of Baker Street irregular Otto Penzler (129 West 56th Street; ☎ 212-765-0900); or find your Watson at **Partners & Crime** (44 Greenwich Avenue; ☎ 212-243-0440). Science fiction fans head to the **Forbidden Planet** (840 Broadway; ☎ 212-473-1576). For comic books (admittedly a paperback of a different color) head down to **Village Comics** (214 Sullivan Street; ☎ 212-777-2770) or **St. Mark's Comics,** which carries underground, limited-edition, and other hard-to-find copies (11 St. Mark's Place; ☎ 212-598-9439).

BRIDAL GOWNS Here the first (and second) name in wedding designs is **Vera Wang** (by appointment only, 991 Madison Avenue; ☎ 212-628-3400). For more downtown tastes, try **Jane Wilson-Marquis** in Soho (by appointment only, 155 Prince Street; ☎ 212-477-4408), **Mika Inatome** (11 Worth Street; ☎ 212-966-7777), or **Mary Adams** (159 Ludlow; ☎ 212-473-0237). For the bridesmaids, try the **Bridal Garden** (by appointment only; 54 West 21st Street, ninth floor; ☎ 212-252-0661). And if you don't mind playing Secondhand Rose, go see **Michael's** (see Consignment Clothing below).

CAVIAR Petrossian is the most famous name in mail-order caviar, and for good reason, but their headquarters are proof that good taste goes both ways. Whether you're buying beluga by the tin or just dropping by for a snack, this beautiful marble room, something like an ice cream parlor for sophisticates, is a great stop-off. The building itself is like a Moorish palace. There's a classic dinner menu as well, and it's a fine one, ideal for a pretheater meal before going to Carnegie Hall next door (West 58th Street at Seventh Avenue; ☎ 212-245-2214). Over on the East Side, try **Caviarteria** (10 Lexington Avenue; ☎ 212-759-7410); or **Caviar Russe** (Madison between West 54th and 55th; ☎ 212-980-5928).

CHEESE For those who consider cheddar the vanilla of cheeses, New York is *fromage* heaven. Check out the tasting menus at **Artisinal** (East 32nd Street and Park Avenue; ☎ 212-725-8585), **Ideal Cheese** (942 First Avenue; ☎ 212-688-7579), or **Murray's Cheese** (757 Bleecker Street; ☎ 888-692-4339). Don't worry about smelling up your suitcase; they ship.

CHOCOLATE AND CONFECTIONS Designer desserts? But of course! One look at the petits-fours at **Ceci-Cela** (55 Spring Street, ☎ 212-274-9179; and 166 Chambers, ☎ 212-566-8933), or the 200 chocolates in 25 flavors Kee Ling Tong sets out at her **Chocolate Garden** (80 Thompson Street; ☎ 212-334-3284), and you'll never waste your money on grocery-store candy again. Can't wait? Indulge in *and* carry out at the **Chocolate Bar** (48 Eighth Avenue; ☎ 212-366-1541); **Jacques Torres,** Soho's own see-it-made Willie Wonka (Hudson Street at King; ☎ 212-414-2462); or **Dylan's Candy Bar** (Third Avenue at 60th Street; ☎ 646-735-0078) from the scions of Ralph Lauren and F.A.O. Schwarz.

CLASSIC RECORDS One of the city's oldest and most early-rock-vinyl purist stores is **Subterranean Records** on Cornelia Street. For another fine selection in vintage vinyl, particularly rock and roll, try **Strider Records** (22 Jones Street; ☎ 212-675-3040) in Greenwich Village; or head to **St. Marks Sounds** (16 St. Marks Place; ☎ 212-677-3444). For early jazz, try **Jazz Record Center** (236 West 26th; ☎ 212-675-4480). **Academy Records** emphasizes classical, jazz, and rock (12 West 18th Street; ☎ 212-243-3000). But for sheet music, the real mecca is **Joseph Patelson Music House,** just behind Carnegie Hall on West 56th Street (☎ 212-582-5840).

CONSIGNMENT CLOTHING This is one town where resale is still high-fashion, so you can really come back from a New York trip wearing designer clothing at department-store prices. A lot of them, not surprisingly, are uptown. Big-name evening dresses are the hottest items at **Designer Resale** (324 East 81st Street between First and Second; phone ☎ 212-734-3639) and **Encore** (1132 Madison Avenue between 84th and 85th; ☎ 212-879-2850). In the same general neighborhood are **Michael's** (1041 Madison, second floor, between 79th and 80th; ☎ 212-737-7273), **Tatiana** (767 Lexington; ☎ 212-755-7744), and the just-as-chic men's designer boutique called **Gentlemen's Resale** (322 East 81st, between First and Second; ☎ 212-734-2739). Farther downtown you can slide into **Riflessi's** for Armani, Ermenegildo Zegna and Cerutti, and in sizes up to 60XL (260 Madison; ☎ 212-679-4875). (Look also at the section on shopping in Soho, above.) For kids' consignments try **Second Act Childrenswear** (1046 Madison Avenue; ☎ 212-988-2440).

COOKWARE AND KITCHEN GOODS The hottest styles in stoves, namely the porcelain-coated, restaurant-quality Garland stoves that the chefs, chef's critics, and celebrities with private chefs now buy for home use, are sold with a smile at **Mazer Store Equipment** in the Lower East Side (207 Bowery; ☎ 212-674-3450). **Broadway Panhandler** (477 Broome; ☎ 212-966-3434) gives "baker's dozen" a whole new meaning: It stocks not just dozens but hundreds of kinds of cake pans. For serious cookware in the French style, try **Bridge** (711 Third Avenue; ☎ 212-688-4220). **Fish's Eddy** has overstocked, de-accessioned, and leftover lots of plates, glassware, and platters from restaurants and hotels, and sometimes even ships; they have fun designs and logos and in many cases are institutionally sturdy (Broadway and 19th, ☎ 212-420-9020; and Broadway at 77th, ☎ 212-873-8819; **www.fishseddy.com**).

COSMETICS AND SKIN CARE Nobody cares more about facial products and cosmetics than Big Apple women (and men); none are more into earth-friendly brands than those in and around Soho. Try **Aveda** (233 Spring Street; ☎ 212-807-1492) or **M.A.C. Soho** (113 Spring Street; ☎ 212-334-4641) for new looks and counseling (ask for a discount if you're in the modeling or theatrical biz) or **Face Stockholm,** with its palette of 140 eye shadows (110 Prince Street; ☎ 212-966-9110). If you don't mind a few puns, the **Cowshed** spa in Soho House New York (☎ 212-627-9800) can re-moove the stress. For all-natural herbal cosmetics and body products, try **Erbe** (Prince and Spring streets; ☎ 212-966-1445) or the Estée Lauder–owned but still honorable **Origins** (402 West Broadway; ☎ 212-219-9764). A little farther north on Union Square is **Sephora,** where you can try on almost anything (45 East 19th Street; ☎ 212-995-8833).

Farther uptown, **Bergdorf Goodman** carries several cult lines of cosmetics from other countries, such as Japan's Kanebo and Paris's Yon-Ka, as well as the Spa to Go goods from top resorts (Fifth Avenue at 57th; ☎ 212-753-7300). It's also home to the **Susan Ciminelli Day Spa** on the ninth floor (☎ 212-872-2650).

For deeper treatments—facials, peels, aromatherapies, and the like—book some time at **Bliss** (568 West Broadway, second floor; ☎ 212-219-8970), **Bliss47** (Lexington at 47th Street; ☎ 212-219-8970), or **Bliss57** (9 East 57th Street; ☎ 212-219-8970), the **Oasis Day Spa** (108 East 16th; ☎ 212-254-7722), **Anuslaka Spa and Cellulite Clinic** (51 Madison Avenue; ☎ 212-355-6406), **Greenhouse Spa** (127 East 57th Street; ☎ 212-644-4449), **Qiora** (926 Madison Avenue; ☎ 212-744-5050), the Korean-style **Juvenex** (25 West 32nd Street, fifth floor; ☎ 212-733-1330), **Ula Day Spa** in Tribeca (8 Harrison Street; ☎ 212-343-2376), or the **Aveda Esthetique** (456 West Broadway; ☎ 212-473-0280). (Many high-end hotels have their own in-house spas, of course, some quite elaborate.)

While most high-end spas serve both sexes, men get their (spa) day alone at **Nickel** (77 Eighth Avenue at 14th Street; ☎ 212-242-3203), the first U.S. branch of a Parisian pair of spas. Ultra-premium shaving products are available—along with the shave itself—at **The Art of Shaving** at 373 Madison Avenue; two other stores in The Shops at Columbus Circle and on East 62nd have the goods but not the barber (☎ 800-696-4999).

And if you're tired of trying to find that perfect lipstick, check out **Giella Custom Blends** (at Henri Bendel, 712 Fifth Avenue, or one-on-one by appointment; ☎ 212-247-1100). They can custom-blend lipsticks or glosses to your specification (two for $50), matching something you always loved but can't find anymore, or a make-up artist will spend about one hour working with you for your own color ($25); or you can choose from their ready-to-wears ($16 apiece). If you left that old favorite at home, just go to Bendel and ask for one of the mail-back packages.

Kiehl's Since 1851 (109 Third Avenue; ☎ 212-677-3171) has, as the name implies, been a Manhattan watchword for nearly a century and a half, still owned and operated by the same family and still making its body treatments, shampoos, and skin care items by hand from all-natural ingredients.

DECORATIVE ARTS With all the revived interest in imperial Russia, Fabergé, and so on, it's fascinating to step into **A La Vielle Russie** (781 Fifth Avenue; ☎ 212-752-1727), which has been selling Russian enamels, icons, porcelain, fine jewelry, and, yes, Fabergé, since the Romanovs were in power.

If it's early-20th-century style you seek, you can indulge your craving for Art Deco at **DeLorenzo** (956 Madison Avenue, 55 East 65th; ☎ 212-249-7575) or **Barry Friedman** (32 East 67th; ☎ 212-794-8950). Tiffany classics are the house specialty at **Macklowe Gallery & Modernism** (667 Madison Avenue; ☎ 212-644-6400). And the artists at **Zuber et Cie** still hand-paint panoramic wallpapers from the company's mid-19th-century designs (979 Third Avenue; ☎ 212-486-9226).

FURS The center of the retail fur trade in Manhattan is on Seventh Avenue between 28th and 29th streets in Chelsea, a neighborhood often called (a little grandly) the Fur District. Among the most reliable names here are **G. Michael Hennessy** (☎ 212-249-7575) and **Gus Goodman** (☎ 212-244-7422), both in the 345 Seventh Avenue building, though on different floors—Hennessy on the 5th and Goodman on the 16th. But the greatest bargain, especially for the nonrich and unknown, is the **Ritz Thrift Shop** at 345 Seventh Avenue between 29th and 30th (☎ 212-265-4559), which buys, refits, and reconditions estate-sale furs, turns antique coats into linings or novelty coats, and sometimes just offers nice but not premium new coats at half-price or even lower. They'll buy their own coats back, too, although at a very much lower price and so long as they're still in very good condition; so you can keep trading up. Bargain hunters should also look into **Frederick Gelb** at 345 Seventh Avenue between 29th and 30th, 19th floor (☎ 212-239-8787).

GOURMET FOODS In search of the perfect pickle or real old-fashioned sauerkraut? Where else but the Lower East Side, where **Guss Pickle Products,** the city's oldest (and one of the major "characters" of the film *Crossing Delancey*), is still dishing 'em out (35 Essex Street; ☎ 212-254-4477). With that get the matzo to go at **Streit's Matzo Company** (150 Rivington Street; ☎ 212-475-7000). From dried fruit to nuts, go nuts at **A. L. Bazzini's** in Tribeca, which smells like honey-roasted heaven and sells a real PB&J sandwich that would have given Proust fits (339 Greenwich Street; ☎ 212-334-1280).

Greenwich Village is dangerous territory for foodies. Olives, all colors, sizes, and brines of them, are the hot items at the **Gourmet Garage Catering in Soho** (453 Broome Street; ☎ 212-941-5850). Imported coffees are easy enough to come by these days, but **McNulty's Tea and Coffee Co.** in Greenwich Village also stocks a few hundred types of tea leaves (109 Christopher Street; ☎ 212-242-5351); **Aphrodisia** has a few hundred leaves to choose from, too—in this case herbs, spices, and herbal remedies (264 Bleecker Street; ☎ 212-989-6440).

Of course, if you like all your temptations under one roof, there are New York's three most famous names in food: **Zabar's, Balducci's,** and **Dean & DeLuca.** Zabar's, on the West Side, just goes to show you what a serious Jewish deli can be (2245 Broadway; ☎ 212-787-2000). Balducci's may not be the Village veggie stand any more, but it's still run by the same folks (West 14th and Eighth Avenue; ☎ 212-673-2600). D&D, the Bloomingdale's of food, is located at 560 Broadway (☎ 212-226-6800). And now there's France's first name in fine prepared foods as well: **Fauchon,** the venerable Paris institution, has opened its first U.S. branch at 442 Park Avenue (☎ 212-308-5919). For foie gras, head to that other French standard, **d'Artagnan** (152 East 46th Street; ☎ 212-687-0300); carry out from below or indulge in the dining room upstairs.

JEWELRY If you want diamonds, you have to cruise the **Diamond District,** a continuous wall of glittering store windows and mini-malls along 47th Street between Fifth and Sixth avenues, traditionally operated by Orthodox Jewish and (increasingly) Middle Eastern dealers, where somehow if you cannot find just the setting you want, it can be made in about 24 hours. The most eye-bulging pieces already set with precious and semiprecious stones are in an even more glittery row along Fifth Avenue between 55th and 57th, including **Tiffany & Co.** (☎ 212-755-8000), **Harry Winston** (☎ 212-245-2000), **Bulgari** (☎ 212-315-9000), **De Beers'** new flagship at 703 Fifth (☎ 212-906-0001); and **Van Cleef & Arpels** (in the Bergdorf Goodman building; ☎ 212-644-9500). **Cartier** is a few blocks away at 52nd (☎ 212-753-0111) and on Madison Avenue at 69th (☎ 212-472-6400).

But if you want the one-of-a-kind look without the Indian-curse pedigree or the shah of Iran price tag, visit **Reinstein/Ross,** Susan Reinstein's boutiques in Soho (122 Prince Street; ☎ 212-226-4513) or the upper East Side (by appointment; 29 East 73rd; ☎ 212-772-1901); **Doyle & Doyle Estate and Fine Jewelry** on the Lower East Side (189 Orchard Street; ☎ 212-677-9991); **Me and Ro,** the Robin Renz/Michele Quan shop in NoLiTa (29 Elizabeth; ☎ 212-237-9215); **Ted Muehling's** studio at 27 Howard Street in Soho (☎ 212-431-3825); or **Pedro Boregaard** in Midtown (18 East 53rd Street, 15th floor; ☎ 212-826-3660). For custom-made pieces, go to **Belenky Brothers,** still in family hands after more than a century and now showcasing contemporary art as well as fine jewelry in its Soho building (151 Wooster Street; ☎ 212-674-4242); or, check out **Stuart Moore,** near Reinstein's (128 Prince; ☎ 212-941-1023).

And for fine and unique cuff links, head to **Seaman Schepps,** 100 years old and thriving (485 Park Avenue; ☎ 212-753-9520).

Mikimoto's pearls are the most famous, of course (730 Fifth Avenue; ☎ 212-457-4600), but **Sanko Cultured Pearls** (45 West 47th Street; ☎ 212-819-0585) also has a fine reputation, though you have to make an appointment.

JUKEBOXES Refurbished Wurlitzers, slot machines, and soft drink dispensers are among the nostalgia for sale at **Back Pages Antiques** (Coney Island, Brooklyn; ☎ 718-375-1980).

MUSICAL INSTRUMENTS More than a dozen specialty instrument, sheet music, and repair shops line Times Square's "Music Row." Its worth a stroll even if you're not in the market. The **Steinway & Sons** store on West 57th is as much museum as shop, and it's not alone: Even the rankest amateur would recognize the names on the violins and cellos at **Morel & Gradoux-Matt** (250 West 54th; ☎ 212-582-8896). And anyone whose taste runs to blues and rock and roll will know the more modern names (Muddy Waters, Peter Frampton) on the guitars at **Sam Ash** (155 West 48th; ☎ 212-719-2625). For less common international string and percussion instruments, try **Music Inn World Instruments** (169 West 46th; ☎ 212-243-5715).

NEON If you've discovered the artsy side of neon (and argon, and all the other colors of the electrified rainbow), head for **Let There Be Neon** in Tribeca (38 White Street; ☎ 212-226-4883), home of artist Rudi Stern.

PERFUMES Depending on your allegiance, try **Floris of London** (703 Madison Avenue; ☎ 212-935-9100), the all-American **Caswell-Massey** (518 Lexington Avenue; ☎ 212-755-2254), London-based **Jo Malone** in the Flatiron Building on 23rd (☎ 212-673-2220), or the **Anglo-French Creed** (9 Bond Street; ☎ 212-228-1732)—perfumeries to Hollywood and European royalty.

PHOTOGRAPHY Cindy Sherman is just one of the big names whose work can be found at **Metro Pictures** in Soho (519 West 24th; ☎ 212-206-7100), and hours of browsing won't begin to exhaust the fine options at **Laurence Miller Gallery** (20 West 57th; ☎ 212-397-3930). Although it's really a little farther south in Tribeca, the **Soho Photo Gallery** is the oldest, most comprehensive co-op in the country (15 White Street; ☎ 212-226-8571). Uptown, your best bets include **Pace Wilderstein MacGill** (32 East 57th Street; ☎ 212-421-3292), **Goodman** (24 West 57th; ☎ 212-977-7160), and **ICP** (Sixth Avenue at 43rd; ☎ 212-857-0000).

kids **SPORTS SOUVENIRS** Athletic logo clothing is in every shopping mall these days, but "official" T-shirts, warm-up jackets, and even home-game tickets can be scooped up at one of five **Yankees Clubhouse** stores (including 110 East 59th Street between Lexington and Park; ☎ 212-768-9555 and 245 West 42nd between Seventh and Eighth; ☎ 212-768-9555) or the **Mets Clubhouse** (143 East 54th; ☎ 212-888-7508). Or, of course, you could go to a real game . . .

TEA Try **Fauchon,** the famous Parisian tratteur with more than 100 kinds of tea, as well as caviar, candies, and pastries (442 Park Avenue at 56th; ☎ 212-308-5919).

TIES Longtime mens' clothier **Paul Stewart** now offers ties custom-woven to your choice of color, pattern, length, width, and lining (Madison Avenue at 45th Street; ☎ 212-682-0320).

kids **TOYS** Everyone knows FAO Schwarz, of course, and its year-long renovation has once again made it a landmark (Fifth Avenue and 58th Street; ☎ 212-644-9400); but more people should know **The Enchanted Forest** in Soho (85 Mercer Street; ☎ 212-925-6677), which describes itself as "a gallery of beasts, books, and handmade toys celebrating the spirit of the animals, the old stories, and the child within." And it is. The equally imaginative **Dinosaur Hill** in the East Village (306 East Ninth Street; ☎ 212-473-5850) is intentionally hard to find, like a fairy tale treasure; look for the name set in marbles in the sidewalk. But the buzz these days is all about the four-story **Toys R Us** store in Times Square (☎ 800-869-7787), with its 60-foot-high Ferris wheel, toy-themed cars, and Lego versions of the Empire State and Chrysler buildings.

More sedate young ladies who have become "mothers" to one of the various American Girl dolls may have tea (or pizza or a burger) with their child by making a visit to the **American Girl Place** at Fifth Avenue and 69th in the third-floor cafe: The $20 three-course lunch isn't much for a $100 doll. In a similar interactive mode, the newly renovated **World of Disney** store at Fifth and 55th (☎ 212-702-0702) is not only crammed with character merchandise and novelties featuring Disney, Muppet, and Pooh characters but is also the home of Cinderella's Princess Court, a sort of American Girls' tea with a tiara.

VINTAGE POSTERS AND CARTOONS The best collection of Toulouse-Lautrec and the like—in fact, the only complete collection of his "advertising" posters—belongs to *Wine Spectator/Cigar Aficionado* tycoon Marvin Shenken. Unfortunately, unless you're invited to his offices, you probably won't be able to see them, but you can pick up a few items almost as rare at **La Belle Epoque** on the Upper West Side (Columbus Avenue at 73rd Street; ☎ 212-362-1770) and **Carrandi Gallery** (138 West 18th Street; ☎ 212-242-0710). Movie buffs can try **Triton Gallery** (323 West 45th Street; ☎ 212-765-2472); or for foreign titles, try **Chisholm Larsson Gallery** (145 Eighth Avenue; ☎ 212-741-1703).

Fans of the *New Yorker* can make an appointment to view some of the famous cartoon collection for sale at the Times Square offices (☎ 212-286-5795). If it's animation cels you want, head for **Animazing Gallery** in Soho (461 Broome; ☎ 212-226-7374), an authorized Disney and Warner Bros. art gallery.

WATCHES Counterfeit Rolexes, Piagets, and Movados are all over town, and for $25 or $30 bucks they can be a fun souvenir, although whether they'll run for 24 hours or 24 months is a matter of pure chance. So is whether the hands work, incidentally. For guaranteed models of those luxury names—the ones that shout platinum!

titanium! white gold! and so on—visit **Tourneau,** whose double-page ads in the *New York Times* and luxury magazines are whole catalogs in themselves. In fact, it's practically an avenue in itself, with stores along Madison Avenue at 52nd, 57th, and 59th, as well as West 34th and Seventh Avenue and the new Shops at Columbus Circle; you can reach any of them through the main switchboard (☎ 212-758-3671). For more unusual vintage timepieces and clocks, try **Fanelli Antique Timepieces** (790 Madison Avenue; ☎ 212-517-2300), **Central Watch Band Stand** (Grand Central's Roosevelt Passage; ☎ 212-685-1689), or **Aaron Faber** (666 Fifth Avenue; ☎ 212-586-8411).

WINES **Sherry Lehmann's** inventory is famous, and not by accident; it's probably the largest in the world. The catalogs, which come out every couple of months, make great souvenirs and gifts as well (Madison Avenue at East 61st Street; ☎ 212-838-7500). But for atmosphere, and for a wine bar right next door, try **Morell & Co.** at 1 Rockefeller Plaza (☎ 212-688-9370), one of Manhattan's best-respected shops (and host of free tastings on Saturdays between 2 and 5).

Vintage New York in Soho stocks only wines produced in the state, as many as 150 labels (482 Broome Street, ☎ 212-226-9463; and 2492 Broadway between 92nd and 93rd, ☎ 212-721-9999). **Crush** boasts one wall holding more than 3,000 bottles by itself and has such up-to-date amenities as computerized advice about food and wine pairings (153 East 57th between Lexington and Third; ☎ 212-980-9463).

Manhattan is also home to a new kind of wine store, **Best Cellars,** where the less label-conscious can find help and hope. Here, wines are arranged not simply by varietals (since having drunk a lot of California Chardonnay will not necessarily give you a fair concept of French or Australian Chardonnay) but by "taste"—that is, "fresh" (light-bodied), "luscious" (round, richly flavored), and so on. So you just go after the sort of wine you like. And most of them are bargain-priced, to boot (Lexington at 87th; ☎ 212-426-4200).

WROUGHT IRON Not the old, but the old-style new-custom stuff: beds, lamps, étagères, and fencing from brother Carfaro, whose grandfather smithed in Turin, at **Desiron** (139 West 22nd Street; ☎ 212-414-4070).

PART TEN

EXERCISE *and* RECREATION

DOUBLE *your* PLEASURE, DOUBLE *your* FUN

A FEW YEARS AGO, IT WOULD HAVE SEEMED SILLY to put a chapter on exercise in a vacation guide—particularly a guide to a city as famous for self-indulgence as New York. But most of us at the *Unofficial Guides* are into some form of aerobic exercise, if only as a matter of self-preservation. It reduces stress, helps offset those expense account and diet-holiday meals (no, it's not true that food eaten on vacation has no calories), and even ameliorates some of the effects of jet lag. Even more remarkably, we have discovered that jogging, biking, and just plain walking are among the nicest ways to experience a city on its own turf, so to speak; and we're happy to see that more and more travelers feel as we do.

Even more intriguingly, New York is a paradise for workout buffs, since the gyms and exercise clubs in this town are often on the front lines of alternative routines. If you've read about Pilates or capoeira or some other new style but you haven't seen a lesson offered in your hometown yet, this is the place.

One good thing about indoor workout gear is that is takes up relatively little room and, at least until that step class, may double as walking-about wear. And if you're caught short, there are certainly T-shirts and shorts to be had on the street, if not at the gym.

If you are an outdoor type, however, consider the seasonal weather that time of year when you're packing. In the summer months, when it

unofficial **TIP**
If you are staying in one of the ritzier hotels, such as the New York Palace, the fitness center may have T-shirts and even shoes you can borrow for your workout, thus lightening your load.

can be not only hot but extremely humid, it's really a good idea to schedule exercise early in the day or in the first cool of the evening;

unofficial **TIP**
If you plan to exercise on summer or early fall evenings, pack some bug spray—better yet, double up and get some of that sunscreen with repellent built in.

those late-afternoon showers can make a nice difference. Holiday decorations can make for wonderful jogging in cold weather, if the sidewalks aren't slick; but again, it may be damp, so be sure to pack a weather-resistant layer. And remember that first-aid kit: We go nowhere without sports-style adhesive strips (get the flexible ones), ibuprofen or some other analgesic, petroleum jelly, and a small tube of antiseptic. And consider doubling your socks.

CHELSEA PIERS *and* CENTRAL PARK

THE REDEVELOPMENT OF THE OLD HUDSON RIVER pier area between 17th and 23rd streets into the **Chelsea Piers Sports and Entertainment Complex** may have cost millions, but it's sure bringing it back in now. Among its attractions are one of those Japanese multi-level golf driving ranges with 52 stalls and a 200-foot fairway—

unofficial **TIP**
There's an Origins spa next door to the *Sports Center at Chelsea Piers* for post-workout massages, manicures, and so on (☎ 212-336-6780), a sundeck and a brewpub for rewards (☎ 212-336-6440).

which, considering how crowded the courses are in the neighboring boroughs, is likely to be your best shot (☎ 212-336-6400); two outdoor roller rinks (☎ 212-336-6200) and two indoor ice rinks (☎ 212-336-6100); a huge field house with basketball, yoga, spinning, volleyball, batting cages, gymnastics bars, and the like (☎ 212-336-6500); and a mega–workout club, the **Sports Center at Chelsea Piers** (☎ 212-336-6000), with running track, boxing ring, bowling alley, pool, 10,000-square-foot rock-climbing wall, and weight-training areas—even indoor horseback riding and blading fitness classes. Sports club passes are $50 a day; skating costs $7 to $14 for adults, $6 to $10 for kids, and $15 to $25 for skate rental. Spend the whole day.

Central Park is where all outdoor sports meet—and meet up with Ultimate Frisbee, softball, pick-up flag football, and the like. Within Central Park, just for starters, there are rowboats at **Loeb Boathouse** (☎ 212-517-2233), which is also where rental bikes are found; rock-climbing classes around 97th Street; a half-dozen baseball diamonds and four soccer fields; tennis courts; regulation croquet (the competitive game, not the backyard version) near West 67th and lawn bowling near West 69th; the **Wollman ice-skating/roller-skating rink** (☎ 212-439-6900); and a front nine of miniature golf, thanks to Donald Trump, near the Wollman Rink in summertime.

If you're fond of **folk-dancing,** you'll find plenty of partners for a Sunday evening near the East 81st Street entrance toward Turtle Pond. There is even a **bird-watching** hotline that keeps up with unusual sightings and nestings (☎ 212-979-3070), and with more than 100 species hanging around, that can be a lot. We once thought we had caught a young man yelling obscure obscenities at a playground full of kids in the park; eventually we realized he was practicing bird calls. For information on other areas to play, call the **Manhattan Department of Parks and Recreation** (☎ 212-360-8133). Also read the description of Central Park in Part Six, New York's Neighborhoods.

WORKING OUT

WORKOUT CLUBS AND GYMS

AS WE'VE SAID, NEW YORK HAS SUCH A body-conscious culture that you can try out almost anything—and since that world overlaps with the competitive business world, there are even 24-hour clubs where the most obsessive of networkers can go in the wee hours.

Among the hottest workout clubs—the ones always written up in fitness magazines—are **The Sports Center at Chelsea Piers** (see above); the 24-hour **Crunch Fitness** clubs (404 Lafayette, ☎ 212-614-0120; 1109 59th Street, ☎ 212-758-3434; 162 West 83rd Street, ☎ 212-875-1902; and 54 East 13th Street, ☎ 212-475-2018); **Equinox Fitness** clubs (344 Amsterdam Avenue, ☎ 212-721-4200; 897 Broadway, ☎ 212-780-9300; and its new flagship at the Shops at Columbus Circle); the **IP PowerStrike Studios** (115 West 74th Street; ☎ 212-496-1254), founded by aerobics pro Patricia Merno and black belt Ilaria Montagnani; and the **Reebok Sports Club** (160 Columbus Avenue; ☎ 212-362-6800). If you go with a member, you can get a one-day pass for either Equinox Fitness or Reebok Sports Clubs.

Yoga is incredibly hot in New York (and we don't just mean the steamy bikram classes, either); check out the studio list at **www.yogaalliance.com** for the closest studio.

Even hotter is Pilates, and the most cutting-edge studio, where traditional Pilates meets modern medical research, is **IM=X Pilates** at Madison and 39th Street (☎ 212-997-5550). The introductory session is free, so you can learn the mechanics and then use it as your gym next trip around.

Buffing is a particularly strong draw for gay New Yorkers, and the most gay-friendly gyms are toward the Village and Chelsea, among them the **YMCA** branch at 224 East 47th Street (☎ 212-756-9600; one-day pass for $25) and **19th Street Gym** (22 West 19th Street; ☎ 212-929-6789; one-day pass for $25).

For more traditional swimming, racquetball, track, etc., the big **West Side YMCA** is the largest of the 19 branches, with two pools, basketball and volleyball, racquetball and squash, massage rooms, free weights, and more included in a $20 daily pass (5 West 63rd Street; ☎ 212-875-4100). Other popular branches are the **Midtown YWCA** (610 Lexington; ☎ 212-755-4500; $20 daily pass) and the **Vanderbilt YMCA** (224 East 47th; ☎ 212-756-9600; $25 daily pass). Also check out the **92nd Street YMHA** (1395 Lexington; ☎ 212-996-1100; $25 daily pass).

So far less famous, and so not crowded, is the gym and track facility at **Staten Island's Pier 6.**

WALKING

CONSIDERING HOW STRONGLY WE'VE URGED you to do your touring on foot, you may have already guessed that we find not agony but ecstasy in de feet. It's almost impossible not to enjoy the sidewalks of New York, and it's unfortunate that many of its most beautiful sections, particularly downtown, have been so reduced to the tour-stop circuit that most tourists never experience it. If you go out a little early, say 7:30 or 8 p.m., before the sidewalks get so crowded, you can walk Fifth Avenue or Madison Avenue at a fairly brisk pace, too; but you'll have to deal with the traffic signals.

The most obvious walking area, of course, is **Central Park,** where you can either stick to the seven-mile Outer Loop, the four-mile Middle Loop (from 72nd Street south), or the one-half-mile reservoir track; but it's even more fun to just take whatever asphalt trails attract you. You can't really get lost—some part of the outer world's skyline is almost always visible, and you'll come back across the main road several times—but there is always something new to discover that way: statues (have you found the Mad Tea Party yet?), lakes, ornate old bridges, gingerbread-trimmed buildings, the carousel, flower beds, dancing dogs, tiny transmitter-driven sailboats reminiscent of *Stuart Little,* chess players, stages, and so forth.

The Esplanade, which runs for about a mile from Battery Park along the Hudson River to Battery Park City, is one of the prettiest greenways in the area, and it has the added benefit of having parts of the way divided so that walkers don't have to contend with bladers or bikers.

Another popular park for walkers is **Riverside Park** on the Upper West Side between West 72nd and 145th streets, so if you're really interested in seeing the natural sights, you can turn out of Central Park along the main crossroads at West 86th, 97th, or even at the top of the park—110th Street/Cathedral Parkway—and go four blocks to the Hudson and Riverside Park, which is another four miles long.

RUNNING AND JOGGING

IF YOU HADN'T ALREADY GUESSED THAT CENTRAL PARK was also runners' central, a quick glance will convince you. Central Park Drive, which has a dedicated biking/running lane, is about seven miles long, or you can come in halfway at 72nd Street and do the southern part of the loop for about four miles; the famous track around the Reservoir (now with a beautifully restored fence) is just over a mile-and-a-half-long. The road is closed to traffic from 10 a.m. to 3 p.m. every weekday (except, please note, during the holidays, when the traffic crush is too heavy), and all weekend, starting at 7 p.m. Friday. There are runners there at most any (daylight) hour, especially on weekends; feel free to join the pack. For group therapy, call the **New York Road Runners Club** (☎ 212-860-4455; **www.nyrrc.org**), or hook up with their regular runs: about 6:30 and 7:15 p.m. weekdays and 10 a.m. Saturdays and Sundays. Meet at the club at East 89th Street or catch up at the starting point, just inside the park at Fifth and 90th.

unofficial **TIP**
Handicapped joggers can hook up with the *Achilles Track Club* at 42 West 38th Street for safe runs through Central Park (☎ 212-354-0300).

Another popular stretch for runners, as for walkers, is Riverside Park by the Hudson River, discussed in the preceding section. There is another two-mile stretch along the **Hudson Promenade** in the Village near the piers at the foot of Christopher Street; there's a track along the East River between the **Queensboro Bridge** and Gracie Mansion; Brooklyn's **Prospect Park** has a three-and-a-half-mile trail that begins near the boathouse entrance. If you'd like a short but sharp and visually stunning interval run, take the mile-long **Brooklyn Bridge** over and back, and consider the view of the Manhattan skyline a reward for chugging that high curve.

BIKING AND BLADING

NEW YORK HAS SOME OF THE MOST ELABORATE bike stores in the country, including **Metro Bicycles,** which will rent some of its models out for the day (360 West 47th and other locations; ☎ 212-581-4500), and **Pedal Pusher Bicycle Shop** (1306 Second Avenue, between 68th and 69th; ☎ 212-288-5592). If you're sticking with Central Park (a good idea, especially for newcomers), you can rent bikes right at the **Loeb Boathouse,** which is near East 74th Street (☎ 212-517-2233). A few of the bike-tour organizers—such as **Bite of the Apple Central Park Bike Tours** (☎ 212-541-8759), which lead two-hour rides through the lower part of Central Park—include bike rental in the fee ($30 adult, $20 child). Really experienced riders who prefer longer tours or races should contact the **New York Cycle Club** (☎ 212-828-5711).

Central Park is the place for recreational biking not only for its beauty but also because it has a designated biking/jogging lane that stretches for about seven miles. (See the preceding section, "Running and Jogging," for auto-free hours.) You must stick to the road, however; no impromptu mountain or trail riding allowed. If you'd like to see the park by moonlight, and you're in town on the last Friday of the month, wheel over to Columbus Circle at 10 p.m. Or you can combine the **Riverside Park** path from West 110th Street to West 72nd down the bike lane through **Hudson River Park** all the way to **Battery Park City.**

Both the **Five Borough Bicycle Club** (☎ 212-932-2300, x115) and the **New York Cycle Club** (☎ 212-828-5711) organize weekend group rides).

If you're more into blades, either ice or in-line, **Blades** has a half-dozen locations that teach, rent, and sell ice skates and rollers (they also equip you with protective gear). Among the most convenient locations are those at Columbus and Broadway at 72nd (☎ 212-787-3911); in the Village at Bleecker and Third (☎ 212-477-7350); at the Chelsea Piers development (☎ 212-336-6299); and at the Sky Rink itself at the Piers (☎ 212-336-6100). Blades also sponsors free clinics at the 72nd Street entrances, both East and West, weekend afternoons from April to October. The **Achilles Track Club,** mentioned above, also escorts in-line skaters through the park.

kids Central Park's **Wollman Rink** is open for in-lining in summer and, more famously, ice skating in winter (☎ 212-439-6900); you can hear the music almost any time. Adults skate there for $8.50 or $11 on weekends; kids skate for $4.50. You can rent skates for the rink or for the rest of the park. There is also a less famous and less expensive roller skating–ice rink at the northern end of the park, **Lasker Rink** at 107th Street; there adults skate for $4.50 and kids for $2. Even more famous, of course, is the **Rockefeller Plaza** ice rink, also seasonal. As the most famous, it's also the costliest; adults pay $11 weekdays, $13 weekends; kids under age 11 skate for $7 weekdays, $8 weekends, exclusive of skate rentals (☎ 212-332-7654). And yet another Midtown rink is being tried out in Bryant Park. **Riverbank Skating Rink** at 145th Street charges $4.50 for adults. For group skates and lessons, contact **Sky Rink** at Chelsea Piers, which offers lessons (☎ 212-336-6100) and a little pickup hockey as well.

If you are a serious blader, into the semiguerilla sorts of expeditions, contact the **Night Skates,** who meet at various sites around town, including Columbus Circle, Union Square, or skate shops (ask for information), and pick a route for the night. Also look over the biking and running routes mentioned in the preceding sections.

OTHER RECREATIONAL SPORTS

DESPITE THE SUCCESS OF NEIL SIMON'S "Brighton Beach" trilogy, many tourists are surprised to discover that New York has beaches. They are easily accessible by subway: the **Rockaways** by the A train; **Coney Island** by the B, D, F, or N; and nearby **Brighton Beach** itself by the D or Q.

Only a few hotels have swimming pools; so if lapping is your thing, check into Chelsea Piers or Asphalt Green, another of those we-do-it-bigger sports facilities. They have an Olympic-sized lap pool at York Avenue at 91st Street (☎ 212-369-8890; $20), but the pool is members-only between 3 and 8 p.m.

There are 30 Har-Tru **tennis courts** in Central Park that you can get for $5 an hour, though you need a permit and you have to sign up on a first-come, first-served basis. Sheets go up on the half-hour for the next hour's slot. Riverside Park's clay courts are maintained by volunteers (do your part) and also operates in a first-come, first-served manner. If you don't mind paying for your time, call **Crosstown Tennis** (14 West 31st Street; ☎ 212-947-5780) or **Sutton East Tennis Club,** favored by clay-courters (York Avenue at 60th Street; ☎ 212-751-3452), where rates go as high as $125 an hour. The **Midtown Tennis Club** has four courts inside and four outside (on the roof, which is a lot of fun) for $50 to $80 an hour (341 Eighth Avenue; ☎ 212-989-8572; **www.midtowntennis.com**). The Whitehall Street branch of the **New York Health and Raquet Club** has ten indoor courts (☎ 212-269-9800).

Horseback riding through the park is legendary, and so is the Clare-mont Riding Academy on West 89th, a couple of blocks from the park (☎ 212-724-5100). Rental for experienced riders is $45 an hour; $50 buys you a 30-minute private lesson or one-hour group lesson.

You'll see **rock climbing** in Central Park—they call it Rat Rock, and it's near Fifth Avenue around 62nd Street—but if you want something tougher, drop $15 at the **Manhattan Plaza Health Club** (482 West 43rd Street; ☎ 212-974-2250), **Extra Vertical Climbing Center** (61 West 62nd Street; ☎ 212-586-5718), or check the gyms mentioned above.

Romantics can go *en garde* at **Metropolitan Fencing** (45 West 21st Street, Chelsea; ☎ 212-463-8044) or master the art of the flying trapeze at the **Trapeze School of New York** on the Hudson River (☎ 917-797-1872).

Pickup softball, basketball, and **volleyball** are visible all over town, but the competition is really tough, especially when it comes to B-ball: Just watch a few minutes outside the cages at West Fourth and Sixth Avenue near Washington Square, famous as the original stomping grounds of Dr. J. There are more than a dozen golf courses in the city, but if you wish to waste most of a day in New York leaning over a little white ball, you're on your own. (There is a driving range at Chelsea Piers, if you just can't stand it.)

Kayakers should check out **Manhattan Kayak Company** at Pier 63 (☎ 212-924-1788), the **Riverside Park boathouse** at 72nd Street, or the **Downtown Boathouse** at Pier 26 (☎ 646-613-0375).

There is even a **bowling alley** in the Port Authority Bus Terminal (625 Eighth Avenue; ☎ 212-268-6909) and one near Union Square, the retro-funky **Bowlmor Lanes** (☎ 212-255-8188). For more opportunities to join in, pick up the weekly sports handout in gyms and sports stores around town.

SPECTATOR SPORTS

NEW YORK'S PRO SPORTS TEAMS ARE LEGENDARY and seemingly legion; it's no wonder that Madison Square Garden is a cable network as well as a venue. However, this is one time when "New York" means all five boroughs, and a little more. Both NFL teams, the **New York Giants** and the **New York Jets,** play "at home" at Giants Stadium in the Meadowlands of New Jersey—although the two teams have agreed to build a new, $800-million stadium that will be home to both and named for neither—and frankly, tickets are almost impossible to get, unless you're visiting friends with connections (or you're willing to pay a high price to a scalper). Besides, unless your friends are also driving, you'll have to catch a bus from the Port Authority to the stadium. However, if you feel like making a stab at it, you can call the Meadowlands box office at ☎ 201-935-3900. You can also see if there are any odd seats left with TicketMaster at ☎ 212-307-7171 or check the newspaper classified ads for tickets or ticket resale packagers.

The more frankly named **New York/New Jersey MetroStars** also play their soccer matches at the Meadowlands, but tickets may be easier to come by. Ditto another NBA team, the **New Jersey Nets** (which may relocate to Brooklyn as part of an ambitious proposal to revitalize the Fort Greene neighborhood), and one of three area NHL teams, the **New Jersey Devils;** call the box office (☎ 201-935-3900) or TicketMaster. Another NHL team, the **New York Islanders,** is actually in New York—Long Island's Nassau Coliseum—but farther out in Uniondale, and it takes both the Long Island Railroad (to Uniondale) and then a bus (N70, 71, or 72) to get there, so only fanatics need apply (☎ 516-501-6700). On the other hand, they did win four straight Stanley Cup titles in the 1980s.

But you don't have to leave town to score. If you aren't lucky enough to live in an area where you can see baseball live, you have never seen baseball. (And you'll never see baseball fans the way you'll see them in New York, for good or evil.) **Yankee Stadium**—the House that Ruth Built—is in the Bronx, hence the nickname "Bronx Bombers," though at the end of so easy a subway ride that going to a game there is on our list of recommended things to do. If you're staying on the West Side, catch the B or D line; if you're on the East Side, get the No. 4 train. All deliver you right to the 161st Street/Yankee Stadium station. (*Hint:* Transfer to the D line at Columbus Circle or 125th Street, as it's an express during peak times.) Do not take a taxi; it's not only about 20 times more expensive, it might also take you 5 times longer to get there. Besides, you'd miss an essential part of the experience: joining the fan crowd. Call the box office at ☎ 718-293-

unofficial **TIP**
There are occasional behind-the-scenes tours of Yankee Stadium; call and see if you might be able to catch one during your visit (☎ 718-579-4531).

6000 or TicketMaster at ☎ 212-307-7171. Get there early enough to wander around and check out the plaques beyond the outfield saluting Mickey Mantle, Babe Ruth, Lou Gehrig, Joe DiMaggio, and others. They used to be actually in play, flat in the turf, but cooler heads prevailed.

The **New York Mets'** Shea Stadium is in Queens—in Flushing Meadow, alongside the U.S. Tennis Association complex, where the U.S. Open is held—and is also easily reached by subway. To get to Shea, take the 7 line from the big 42nd Street station (Times Square) right to the Willett Street/Shea Stadium stop. You can quite possibly walk up and get tickets, but it might be better to call the stadium box office at ☎ 718-507-8499.

But minor-league baseball, which many aficionados swear is better, is all around the town. There are three stadiums, each holding around 6,500 seats, opening in the boroughs. The Mets have a brand-new $30 million stadium for their Class A minor-league baseball team, the **Cyclones,** on the Boardwalk at Brooklyn's Coney Island, which repaid the investment by winning the New York–Penn League pennant its first year out (☎ 718-449-8497). The Yankees, not to be outdone, spent $71 million to put a Class A team (also called the **Yankees**) on Staten Island, accessible via the tourist-friendly ferry (☎ 718-720-9265). And the **Newark Bears,** a team of baseball veterans (both Canseco brothers) owned by former Yankees catcher Rick Cerone, play in the Atlantic League (☎ 973-848-1000).

Both the NHL **New York Rangers** and the NBA **New York Knicks** call Madison Square Garden home. Unfortunately, they have a pretty regular following, so tickets are problematic. Call ☎ 212-465-6741 for Rangers info, ☎ 212-465-JUMP for the Knicks, or TicketMaster at ☎ 212-307-7171.

Even hotter these days is women's pro basketball, and the **WNBA New York Liberty** also tend the Garden (☎ 212-564-9622). So do the **Golden Gloves** boxing cards in January and February; the **National Invitational Tournament** college basketball championships in March; and the **Women's Tennis Association Tour championships** (what used to be known as the Virginia Slims Championship) every November. For any of these events, call the Garden box office (☎ 212-465-6741) and TicketMaster (☎ 212-307-7171).

The **U.S. Open** is held in the weeks leading up to Labor Day weekend at the U.S. Tennis Center in Flushing Meadow, and even with its new Arthur Ashe grandstand court, it's frequently a sellout. Unless you're already in the loop for finals tickets, they'll cost you a very close haircut, but earlier tickets may be around. Call the office at ☎ 718-760-6200 for more information or check in with our friends at TicketMaster. If you're curious about cricket, take the orange line subway (1 or 9) to **Van Cortlandt Park** at 242nd Street on a Saturday or Sunday afternoon.

Horse racing has a long and aristocratic tradition in New York, and though the crowds may be more democratic these days, the thoroughbred bloodlines are as blue as ever. You can take the subway (Far Rockaway A) to **Aqueduct Stadium** in Queens from mid-October to May (☎ 718-641-4700) or the Long Island Railroad's Belmont Special from Penn Station to **Belmont Park** (☎ 718-641-4700) from May to July and again from Labor Day to mid-October. (In between, the very old-style racing circuit moves upstate to hallowed Saratoga Springs.) The Belmont Stakes, the third jewel of the Triple Crown, is the first or second Saturday in June.

If you prefer harness racing, the standardbreds wheel around **Yonkers Raceway** Mondays, Tuesdays, Thursdays, Fridays, and Saturdays year-round; for race and schedule information call ☎ 914-968-4200. To get there you'll have to catch the Liberty Line's BXM4C bus from Madison Avenue at 39th Street. The **Meadowlands** has both thoroughbred racing in the fall and harness racing from mid-December through August (☎ 201-935-8500).

PART ELEVEN

ENTERTAINMENT *and* NIGHTLIFE

▌ LIGHTS, TICKETS, ACTION . . .

IT'S HARD TO BEAT THE SCOPE AND BREADTH of entertainment options in NYC, and if you haven't already figured it out, there are countless events, free or otherwise, occurring every single day and night. Modern, classical, jazz, international, and experimental forms of dance, music, opera, and theater (including comedy) are presented in all areas and many venues. Some performances are even found in the subway, on the sidewalk, and especially in the parks, particularly with good weather.

To try and combat the overwhelming feeling of not knowing where to start, you can break down the options before delving into the choices. Consider the following: area of town you'd like to be in, budget, genre of entertainment, how late you're prepared to stay out, and ticket availability. Once you've assessed these parameters, you can peruse the columns of listings with confidence; alternatively you could mark a random point on a page and act on a whim. For the latest information, check either the Web sites or the papers including *Time Out, Village Voice, 'L' Magazine,* the *New Yorker,* and *New York* magazine. The *New York Times* has an informative Arts & Leisure section, which expands over the weekend for some of the latest previews and reviews. Keep in mind that the latter part of this chapter profiles several club and bar options that can be enjoyed either before or after your chosen diversion, or even be the main entertainment of the night.

Embrace the spirit of the city's offerings, and be open to a bit of spontaneity. If you can't get tickets to one thing, there are other options, and you may end up going to something even better. Talk to people and see if you can pick up any suggestions. NYC is your palette to paint the town red, so get creative, use large brush strokes, and go forth!

TICKET TIPS

THERE'S A CERTAIN CACHET TO HAVING opening-night seats for a big performance. Often with big-time events, such seats are taken up by the press, luminaries, and those with connections and/or deep pockets. However, the performance takes precedence over the night you see it. Below you'll find some useful numbers and Web sites, and possible ways of how you can avoid going bankrupt in the process.

NYC/On Stage (☎ 212-768-1818) gives recorded listings and schedules for a variety of performing arts and will transfer you to the phone-charge company that handles the selected tickets. **Theatre Direct** (☎ 212-541-8457 or 800-BROADWAY; **www.theatredirect.com**) offers group ticket sales at reduced prices, as long as you have a group of at least ten people (sometimes more depending on the show).

The main ticket handling agencies for New York are **Telecharge** (☎ 212-239-5258 or 800-545-2559; **www.telecharge.com**), **TicketMaster** (☎ 212-307-4100 or 212-307-7171; **www.ticketmaster.com**) and **New York City Center CityTix** (☎ 212-581-1212; **www.nycitycenter.org**). Be warned that all of these agencies charge a handling fee, and sometimes there are additional "convenience fees" up to $9 per ticket.

Other ways of trying to snag otherwise sold-out seats is to go directly to the venue's box office about an hour and a half before show time (you can call the box office to confirm) and stand in (or start) the

unofficial **TIP**
It's a common occurrence for venues, arts and sports included, to release house seats.

"returns and cancellation" line. Such tickets, if available, are released soon before the curtain rises and are a real coup to acquire. Depending on the reason for the return, the tickets are either resold or given free (usually as a result of an extra press pass, or a kind soul approaches you on the line to offer an extra ticket). Broadway shows, Lincoln Center, and Carnegie Hall have nightly cancellation lines too, but remember: There's no guarantee of getting a seat by depending on the kindness of strangers.

You're also more likely to score a ticket if you are willing to sit alone, or if you can go at an off-peak time, such as Monday, Tuesday, or after (but not during) holidays.

There are plenty of ticket resellers who are sort of corporate scalpers; they manage to find tickets to sold-out shows (look under "Tickets" in the yellow pages, or do a Web search). And there are other "convenient" ticket centers at places like the Plaza Hotel, which bank on the idea that you don't have the patience or leisure to call the big, automated phone-charge networks yourself; however, one round with the surcharges may dissuade you from this convenience. Still, if money's no object or time is at a premium, they are easy and reliable sources. Among some reputable firms are **Prestige Entertainment** (☎ 800-243-8849); **Who Needs Tickets?** (766 Eighth Avenue at 47th Street; ☎ 212-278-8700); and **Manhattan Entertainment** (☎ 212-382-0633).

If you have an American Express gold card, call ☎ 800-448-8457 to see if there are any special promotional seats available (this usually applies only to hot, trendy shows). A final caveat: You are apt to find scalpers outside theaters and big sports events offering tickets, but this can be tricky; an increasing number of these tickets are counterfeit.

ECONOMIZING

IT "AIN'T CHEAP PUTTIN' ON A SHOW," and ticket prices, often, reflect the costs. Whether the venue is off-off Broadway or at the Metropolitan Opera House, salaries and/or rent needs to be paid; costumes, lights, and props need to be rented, borrowed, made, and/or insured; and publicity needs to be generated. Chances are that an off-off Broadway production won't cost more than $20 and will more likely be $5 to $12. However, the bigger the event, the more expensive, and tickets for some events can be, easily, upwards of $100 before a handling or scalping fee is even added. An average Broadway or Lincoln Center ticket costs about $60, though the full range is about $26 to $90. But deals do exist.

A good place to start is **TKTS** (☎ 212-221-0013). This is a place where same-day tickets to various theater and other cultural events are available for 25% to 50% off, plus a $3 surcharge; the only trick is that you have to go in person and take your chances on getting into a show you want to see. The best idea is to have three alternatives, in order of preference, already in your head; that way, if your first choice is sold out and there are only obstructed or nosebleed seats for your second choice, you'll still have something else to go for.

The main TKTS outlet is located at the north end of the Times Square area at 47th and Broadway, a striped tent on its own little island in the traffic, officially called Duffy Square. (The statue there, incidentally, is of George Cohan, who wrote "Give My Regards to Broadway," among other songs.) The day's options are listed on a board overhead; you can study it while in line. Windows open at 3 p.m. and stay open until 8 p.m. (which just gives you time to sprint for the theater door) Monday through Saturday; they open for matinee tickets (Wednesday and Saturday) from 10 a.m. to 2 p.m., also curtain time; and Sundays from 11 a.m. to 6 p.m. The other TKTS outlet is located by the South Street Seaport, at the corner of John and Front streets (☎ 212-768-1818); hours are Monday through Friday, 11 a.m. to 6 p.m.; Saturday, 11 a.m. to 7 p.m.; and Sunday, 11 a.m. to 4 p.m. Wednesday matinee tickets are sold on Tuesday evening, but only at this location. Saturday matinee tickets are sold on Friday only and

unofficial **TIP**
Beware that TKTS is not a secret to residents or tourists; the formidable queues at Times Square form some time before the actual opening.

Sunday matinee tickets are sold on Saturday only. Note that TKTS does not take credit cards, but traveler's checks are as good as cash.

Other ways to trim costs: Go directly to the box office of the show you want to see with cash or a credit card and avoid the handling charge; this also frequently allows you to look at a seating chart and pick the best ticket available. There might even be some really good tickets that have been turned in by patrons who could not use them: New Yorkers, being from such a long theatrical tradition, are good about that. If you are interested in one of the longer-running shows rather than a new hit, or don't care so much which show you see, look for discount coupons (some coupons are known as "twofers," that is, two for one) at the various Convention and Visitors' Bureau branches and stalls.

You might consider tickets to previews (full dress run-throughs of shows that have not officially opened yet and are still being polished), which are frequently less expensive, or matinees—although since older New Yorkers favor these earlier hours, they can be crowded. Or you might just go for a rehearsal, like those of the New York Philharmonic (see below).

Some of the cultural institutions have discounts for students or senior citizens, but be sure to carry ID when you go to seek tickets. And if you are a sturdy sort, inquire about standing-room tickets at the bigger venues; they aren't always free, but it's a show (and some people will probably leave at intermission . . .).

CAMERAS AND CLOSE-UPS

IF IT'S ONE OF THE TELEVISION TALK SHOWS you're interested in, you most likely need to try to get tickets ahead of time—say, six or eight weeks. In the case of **Saturday Night Live,** it's a matter of seasons rather than weeks. Tickets for the whole taping season are awarded by a lottery drawing every August, meaning that e-mail requests gathered in the 11 months previous are also in the pot, and even then winners only get two seats. For tickets call ☎ 212-664-3056 or email *SNL* at **SNLtickets@nbc.com.**

Most shows are a little easier, but almost all requests should be sent in at least two or three months in advance, and probably longer. Of course, if you regularly watch the shows, you probably already know this. What happens if your favorite personality gets canceled in the meantime? Hey, that's showbiz.

On the other hand, nobody likes empty chairs, even a couple, to show in the audience. So if you're still longing for that wild and crazy *SNL* moment, and you feel lucky, go over to Rockefeller Plaza no later than 7 a.m. on Saturday morning, stand around on the sidewalk on 49th Street between Fifth and Sixth, get your face on television in the background of the **Today Show,** and keep an eye on the 49th Street entrance to 30 Rockefeller Plaza. At about 9:15 a.m., not every week and with no guarantees, a few standby tickets to *Saturday Night Live* may be passed out. If you do get in, prepare to be seated at 8:30 p.m. for the dress rehearsal and 11:30 p.m. for the taping. You could also duck inside the main NBC lobby at 30 Rockefeller Plaza and hope for passes to *Late Night with Conan O'Brien,* which tapes Tuesday through Friday at 6:30 p.m. These tickets may be handed out at 9 a.m., but the line is already long by 7:30 a.m. *The Daily Show with Jon Stewart* tapes Monday through Thursday starting at 5:45 p.m. at 513 West 54th Street (between Tenth and Eleventh avenues). Call ☎ 212-586-2477 and leave a message to request tickets.

The Late Show with David Letterman tapes Mondays to Thursdays at 5:30 pm (twice on Thursday, 5:30 p.m. and 8 p.m. to cover the Friday show). For advance tickets, go to **www.cbs.com/latenight/lateshow** and submit an online form or visit the theater at 1697 Broadway between West 53rd and 54th streets Monday through Friday, 9:30 a.m. to 12:30 p.m. and Saturday and Sunday, 10 a.m. to 6 p.m. Don't line up prior to 9 a.m. or you will not be eligible for tickets. You can also show up for standby tickets for *The View* by going to ABC Studios at 320 West 66th Street at the audience entrance door between 8:30 a.m. and 10 a.m.; first come, first served.

Martha Stewart tapes at 10 a.m. on Tuesdays and 10 and 2 p.m. Wednesdays and Thursdays. You'll have to go to her Web site (**www.marthastewart.com**) well in advance to get confirmed seats, but you can go to Chelsea Television Studios at 221 West 26th Street, between Seventh and Eighth avenues, about two hours before showtime and hope for an opening.

Or just horn in on the al fresco audiences for the morning shows; see the section on Times Square in Part Six, New York's Neighborhoods.

For more information on how to get future tickets to *Montel Williams,* call ☎ 212-989-8101 or email your request on **www.montelshow.com/ misc/tickets**; for *Regis and Kelly,* call ☎ 212-456-2410 or try on the day for standby tickets at studio 7 Lincoln Square (Columbus and 67th Street)—arrive by 7 a.m. to get a standby number; for *Total Request Live* on MTV, call ☎ 212-398-8549 or arrive at the MTV studios (1515 Broadway) early and be prepared to answer trivia questions; you must be between the ages of 16 and 24; and for *Tony Danza,* write the show at Ansonia Station, P.O. Box 234095, New York, NY 10023.

PERFORMING ARTS

THE BIG TICKETS: LINCOLN CENTER
AND CARNEGIE HALL

Live from Lincoln Center IS ALMOST AN UNDERSTATEMENT. This venue draws an estimated 5 million patrons a year, and even if you only worked your way through all its programs and never set foot farther down Broadway, you could still fill up most of a week. Since the

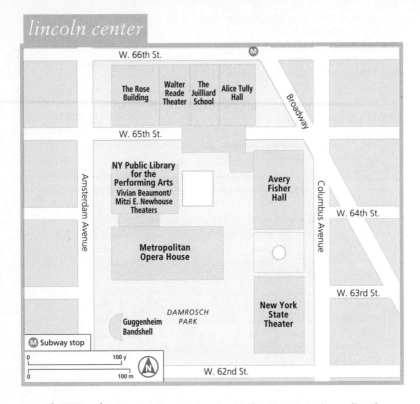

mid-1960s, the **Lincoln Center for the Performing Arts (www.lincoln center.org)** has been home to New York's most prestigious companies: the New York Philharmonic, the Metropolitan Opera and the New York City Opera, the New York City Ballet and American Ballet Theater, the Repertory Company of Lincoln Center, Wynton Marsalis's Lincoln Center Jazz Orchestra (now housed down the block in a three-stage complex at Time Warner Center), the Chamber Music Society, the Lincoln Center Film Society, and, for several years, though no longer, the New York Shakespeare Festival, plus the Juilliard School and the School of American Ballet.

The six-building complex, a cluster that looks out toward Broadway and Columbus Avenue between West 62nd and 65th, includes five theaters; the opera house, Bruno Walter Auditorium concert hall, and Alice Tully Recital Hall; two theaters and a recital hall within Juilliard; an outdoor bandshell; and branches of the New York Public Library and the Library and Museum for the Performing Arts. Huge renovations estimated at $1.5 billion are due to take place over the next few years to give some buildings a face-lift and improve acoustics.

Despite a near split, the Philharmonic, under the direction of Lorin Maazel, is still in residence at **Avery Fisher Hall** from September to June, with its popular and relaxed "Mostly Mozart" festival series during the summer. Open rehearsals during the season are held Thursdays at 9:45 a.m. For more information call ☎ 212-875-5030.

The **Metropolitan Opera House,** with its crystal chandeliers and Chagall murals, is worth a tour of its own (see Part Seven, Sightseeing, Tours, and Attractions). The Met Company, directed by James Levine, holds the stage from mid-September to April; the American Ballet Theater has been using it the rest of the year, and sometimes performs at City Center (see below). For more information, call ☎ 212-362-6000.

The **Vivian Beaumont Theater,** next to the opera house behind the reflecting pool with the Henry Moore sculpture, is shining after a $5 million renovation (☎ 212-239-6277). Under the Beaumont is the smaller (only 325 seats) and more cutting-edge **Mitzi Newhouse Theater** (☎ 212-239-6277).

The **New York State Theater** (☎ 212-870-5570), on the south side of the opera house, was designed by Philip Johnson and looks it, with its sequential entrances like layers of architectural curtains drawing back, its gilded ceiling, and its four banks of balconies. The New York City Ballet is in residence from around Thanksgiving through February (the *Nutcracker* pretty much fills up the schedule until January) and again from April through June. The New York City Opera, under the direction of Paul Kellog, performs July through November.

Alice Tully Hall is the home of the Lincoln Center Chamber Music Society and also often hosts concerts by Juilliard students; it turns cinematic in fall for the International Film Festival (☎ 212-875-5050), and the **Walter Reade Theater** upstairs hosts the New York Film Festival (☎ 212-875-5600). Special recitals are sometimes held in the three venues at Juilliard (☎ 212-799-5000). Check out the library exhibits, costumes, stage sets, prints, and scores.

kids The plaza outside is called **Damrosch Park** and is the site of various fine arts and crafts shows during the year and the Big Apple Circus in winter. It is also where the Guggenheim Bandshell is located and where free concerts, dance programs, and family shows organized by Lincoln Center Out-of-Doors pop up all through the summer; watch the papers.

Few concert halls have attracted as many legends as **Carnegie Hall** (**www.carnegiehall.org**) and no wonder: The premier concert was conducted by Tchaikovsky; the New York Philharmonic played here in the heyday of Mahler, Toscanini, Stokowski, and Bernstein; and a concert date here has for the past century been recognized as a mark of supreme artistry. Nowadays it hosts pop concerts as often as classical, but its astonishing acoustics—it was overhauled in the late 1980s—and its displays of memorabilia make it a genuine experience. Its newer $50-million, 700-seat underground venue, **Zankel Hall,** is a more intimate space that already has bookings for Yo-Yo Ma, Emmylou Harris, Emmanuel Ax, the Juilliard String Quartet, the

New World Symphony, and Mitsuko Uchida. Carnegie Hall is at 154 West 57th, near Seventh Avenue (☎ 212-247-7800).

Nearby is the **City Center of Music and Drama** at 131 West 55th (☎ 212-581-7907), which is once again drawing touring shows, dance performances, and concerts. (The Moorish-Spanish facade is a hint that it was originally a Shriners' Temple.)

Three other frequently star-studded venues may seem a little less accessible to first-timers but are often astonishing in their offerings (and not hard to get to): The **Brooklyn Academy of Music** (☎ 718-636-4100; **www.bam.org**), affectionately known as BAM, hosts film, theater, dance, opera, and music from local and international companies, as well as the Brooklyn Philharmonic. **Aaron Davis Hall,** on the campus of CCNY at West 135th Street and Convent Avenue, is a two-stage venue, the intimate 260-seat Black Box theatre and the 760-seat Marian Anderson hall: It brings in well-known jazz and pop performers (☎ 212-650-7000). The **New Jersey Performing Arts Center** in Newark (☎ 973-642-8989; **www.njpac.org**) stages many major international ballet, opera, and dance touring companies, not to mention world-class jazz and classical concerts.

BROADWAY

SO WHEN THE LIGHTS "GO OUT" ON BROADWAY, which happened most recently in March 2003, for a musicians' strike and later that same year in August, during the blackout, people around the world know. Besides having a large number of theaters opening up in the Times Square area, the arrival of the *New York Times* Building in 1904, changed the name of the former Long Acre Square to Times Square. More theaters, including the opening of the Empire Theater at 1430 Broadway at West 40th Street, increased traffic to and human interest in the area. With the increased illumination of Broadway and Times Square, along with the new *New York Times* Building, the area was dubbed "The Great White Way" in deference to all of the lights. Recently, the Broadway and Times Square area are often in the news because of the increasingly advanced technology of the billboards, news screens, and visible television studios.

The "official" Broadway theater district spans a 12-block stretch with a southern boundary at West 41st Street where the Nederlander stands, to the northern boundary of Broadway and West 53rd. Iron-ically, there are only four theaters situated on Broadway itself: The **Marquis** at 46th, the **Palace** at 47th, the **Winter Garden** at 50th, and the **Broadway** at 53rd Street. All other theaters are located to the east or west of this stretch.

unofficial **TIP**
For current shows, schedules, and phone numbers of all theaters, check the local newspapers or the listings at the beginning of this chapter.

For the record, Broadway is the only "true" north–south thoroughfare in Manhattan that crosses the city diagonally, thus shaping the

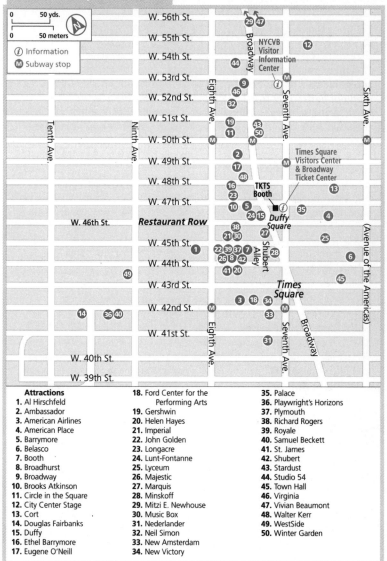

broadway theaters

0   50 yds.
0   50 meters

ⓘ Information
Ⓜ Subway stop

W. 56th St.
W. 55th St.
W. 54th St.
W. 53rd St.
W. 52nd St.
W. 51st St.
W. 50th St.
W. 49th St.
W. 48th St.
W. 47th St.
W. 46th St.
W. 45th St.
W. 44th St.
W. 43rd St.
W. 42nd St.
W. 41st St.
W. 40th St.
W. 39th St.

Tenth Ave.
Ninth Ave.
Eighth Ave.
Broadway
Seventh Ave.
Sixth Ave.
(Avenue of the Americas)

NYCVB
Visitor
Information
Center

Times Square
Visitors Center
& Broadway
Ticket Center

TKTS
Booth

Duffy
Square

Restaurant Row

Shubert
Alley

Times
Square

Attractions
1. Al Hirschfeld
2. Ambassador
3. American Airlines
4. American Place
5. Barrymore
6. Belasco
7. Booth
8. Broadhurst
9. Broadway
10. Brooks Atkinson
11. Circle in the Square
12. City Center Stage
13. Cort
14. Douglas Fairbanks
15. Duffy
16. Ethel Barrymore
17. Eugene O'Neill

18. Ford Center for the
    Performing Arts
19. Gershwin
20. Helen Hayes
21. Imperial
22. John Golden
23. Longacre
24. Lunt-Fontanne
25. Lyceum
26. Majestic
27. Marquis
28. Minskoff
29. Mitzi E. Newhouse
30. Music Box
31. Nederlander
32. Neil Simon
33. New Amsterdam
34. New Victory

35. Palace
36. Playwright's Horizons
37. Plymouth
38. Richard Rogers
39. Royale
40. Samuel Beckett
41. St. James
42. Shubert
43. Stardust
44. Studio 54
45. Town Hall
46. Virginia
47. Vivian Beaumont
48. Walter Kerr
49. WestSide
50. Winter Garden

irregular (though regularly named) Times Square, Union Square, Columbus Circle, Dante Park by Lincoln Center, and the oddly shaped area around West 72nd Street.

OFF- AND OFF-OFF-BROADWAY

THE SPIRITUAL LINE BETWEEN SOME ON-BROADWAY and off-Broadway venues is getting fuzzier. Many of the more "uptown" off-Broadway houses have pretty much been assimilated, whereas the downtown off-Broadway troupes, many of whom may once have been rather anti-establishment, are threatening to mellow into the high-culture circuit. And yet such theaters as the **Playwright's Horizons** (416 West 42nd; ☎ 212-564-1235) and **Roundabout** (231 West 39th; ☎ 212-719-9393), despite their central White Way addresses, have off-Broadway attitudes.

Among the best-known venues are the **Provincetown Playhouse,** famous as Eugene O'Neill's first dramatic home; the ambitious **Minetta Lane Theater** (18 Minetta Lane; ☎ 212-420-8000); **Cherry Lane,** founded by Edna St. Vincent Millay (38 Commerce Street; ☎ 212-989-2020); the **WPA Theater** (159 West 25th Street; ☎ 212-206-0523); **Classic Stage Company** (136 East 13th Street; ☎ 212-677-4210); **Jean Cocteau Repertory** (Bowery and Bond; ☎ 212-677-0060); **Joyce Theater** (175 Eighth Avenue at West 19th; ☎ 212-242-0800), featuring many dance genres; Joseph Papp's six-hall **Public Theater** in the onetime free library near Astor Place (425 Lafayette Street; ☎ 212-398-8383), and the lower-profile **Astor Place Theatre** across the street (434 Lafayette; ☎ 212-254-4370); **Players Theatre** near Washington Square (115 MacDougal Street; ☎ 212-475-1237); **Union Square Theater** (100 East 17th Street and Park Avenue; ☎ 212-505-0700); **Actors Playhouse** (100 Seventh Avenue South; ☎ 212-463-0060) and the **Sheridan Square Playhouse** across the street (99 Seventh Avenue South).

Again, off-off-Broadway refers less to an address (generally downtown, though it may be Village, East Village, Soho, etc.) than to a mind-set. It used to imply experimental or avant-garde productions, satires, debut productions, and sometimes just deeply serious art, and to a great extent it still does; but sometimes productions that are destined (or at least intended) to make their way to Broadway get their final editings here. Among the most interesting venues are the **Performing Garage,** home of the Wooster Group (33 Wooster Street; ☎ 212-966-3651); **Manhattan Theater Club** (261 West 47th Street, the Biltmore, and Stage I and II at City Center; ☎ 212-399-3000; **www.mtc-nyc.org**); the multimedia-minded **Kitchen Center** (512 West 19th Street; ☎ 212-255-5793); and **Ohio Theater** in Soho (66 Wooster Street; ☎ 212-966-4844); the four-stage **Theater for the New City** (155 First Avenue; ☎ 212-254-1109); and nearby **P.S. 122**—not Public School, here, but Performance Space—in the East Village (150 First Avenue at East Ninth; ☎ 212-477-5288); and **Theatre Workshop** (79 East Fourth Street; ☎ 212-460-5475).

SOMETHING FOR FREE?

IT MAY BE HARD TO BELIEVE, BUT NEW YORK does have free theater, and it is commonly known as **Shakespeare in the Park.** Central Park's Delacorte Theater is the summer home to the company that otherwise holds forth at the Papp Public Theater. It's a matter of principle, or at least of sentiment, for some of the biggest stars of stage and screen to do their stint in the open air: Patrick Stewart, Andre Braugher, Kevin Klein, and Michelle Pfeiffer have all bellowed the bard here.

Tickets are given out on a first-come, first-served basis at the Delacorte Theater beginning at 1 p.m. the day of show, but you'd better be there long before that. You might double your chances of getting in by sending a confederate down to the Public Theater box office (☎ 212-398-8383) between 1 and 3 p.m.; you can only get two tickets, but that's better than none. Furthermore, on selected dates, tickets will be distributed in each of the five boroughs; call ☎ 212-539-8750 or visit **www.publictheater.org** for details.

unofficial **TIP**
Even in winter, the Public Theater is a great, steeply intimate place to see innovative productions of Shakespeare with equally big-name stars.

The **New York International Fringe Festival** (☎ 212-279-4488) (**www.fringenyc.org**), although not free, offers premieres, improvisations, lectures, readings, storytellings, Shakespearean declamations, character studies, one-person shows, comic interpretations, and dance performances for relatively decent prices. You may even be surprised by the quality of the free subway entertainment. Although some performances aren't officially sanctioned by the MTA (Metropolitan Transit Authority), the MUNY (Music Under New York) program allows musicians to perform "legally" and grants them a special banner to prove that they have succeeded in getting through the application process that includes a competitive audition. Over 100 acts, individuals or ensembles, are sanctioned and perform over 150 times, somewhere in the subway system, during the week; locations change, although Times Square and Union Square are usually fixed spots. Impromptu, free entertainment can also be found during the summer months in many of the NYC parks.

OTHER MAJOR VENUES

AS MENTIONED EARLIER, THE NEW YORK CITY BALLET calls Lincoln Center home; but that is far from the only premier dance troupe that plays Manhattan. The **American Ballet Theater** (☎ 212-477-3030; **www.abt.org**) and **Alvin Ailey American Dance Theater** (☎ 212-767-0590; **www.alvinailey.org**) use **City Center** at 130 West 56th (☎ 212-581-1212); other companies book into the **Joyce Theater** (175 Eighth Avenue; ☎ 212-242-0800), which is home to the Eliot Feld Ballet, or the **Sylvia and Danny Kaye Playhouse** at Hunter College (695 Park Avenue; ☎ 212-772-4448). The **Florence Gould Hall** at the French Institute (55 East 59th Street; ☎ 212-355-6160), hosts some theatrical and literary performances; **Makor** (35 West 67th Street; ☎ 212-601-1000; **www.makor.org**) shows films and hosts lectures, music, and discussions. The **Aaron Davis Hall** at City College (West 135th Street and Convent Avenue; ☎ 212-650-6900) hosts ethnic dance troupes. Also watch for listings for such locally based companies as **Merce Cunningham** (☎ 212-255-8240), **Dance Theater of Harlem** (☎ 212-690-2800), and **Dance Theater Workshop** (☎ 212-924-0077). Also, be on the lookout for the **Baryshnikov Arts Center.** This arts complex with rehearsal and performance studios aims to be a creative home for dancers, musicians, composers, choreographers, designers, filmmakers, and others (450 West 37th Street; ☎ 646-731-3200).

Various chamber, orchestral, and recital performances take place at **Juilliard** in Lincoln Center (☎ 212-799-5000) and the nearby **Merkin Concert Hall** (129 West 67th; ☎ 212-501-3303); in the **Tisch Center** at the 92nd Street Y (at Lexington Avenue; ☎ 212-996-1100); in Miller Theater at **Columbia School of the Arts** (Broadway at 116th Street; ☎ 212-854-7799); and at the **Harlem School of the Arts** (645 St. Nicholas Avenue at West 141st; ☎ 212-926-4100). The **Amato Opera Theater,** a weekend-only venue, is very popular with serious music lovers (Bowery at Second Street; ☎ 212-228-8200). By far the most unusual venue is **BargeMusic**—just what it sounds like, a boat transformed into a concert hall—but the acoustics, and the names on the schedule, will make a believer out of you (across the East River at Fulton Ferry Landing just south of the Brooklyn Bridge; ☎ 718-624-2083).

> *unofficial* **TIP**
> Plans are in the works to construct a permanent home for *Cirque du Soleil* on 42nd Street west of Broadway.

Major rock, pop, reggae, soul, and country concerts are apt to be held, like most everything else, in **Madison Square Garden** (☎ 212-465-6741); but other common concert venues include MSG's smaller annex, the **Paramount;** the **Orpheum** (126 Second Avenue; ☎ 212-307-4100); the revived **Apollo** (West 125th and Frederick Douglass Boulevard; ☎ 212-531-5300); the **Beacon Theater** (2124 Broadway; ☎ 212-496-7070); the **Hammerstein Ballroom** at Manhattan Center (311 West 34th Street; ☎ 212-564-4882); **Symphony Space** (Broadway and 95th; ☎ 212-864-5400); **Roseland** (239 West 52nd Street; ☎ 212-247-0200); and the **Westbeth Center** in Chelsea(111 West 17th Street; ☎ 212-691-2272). For a taste of world music, check out the **World Music Institute** (**www.worldmusic.org**; ☎ 212-545-7536) for upcoming concerts. Occasionally more mainstream names show up in **Town Hall** (123 West 43rd Street; ☎ 212-840-2824), Avery Fisher Hall.

If lectures, poetry, and readings are your bag, call the **92nd Street Y** (1395 Lexington Avenue; ☎ 212-415-5440); **Poets House** (72 Spring Street; ☎ 212-431-7920), whose vast library is open to the public Tuesday through Friday, 11 a.m. to 7 p.m.; and Saturdays, 11 a.m. to 4 p.m.; the **Bowery Poetry Club** (308 Bowery; ☎ 212-614-0505); the home of the "poetry slam," the **Nuyorican Poet's Café** in the East Village (236 East Third Street; ☎ 212-505-8183); or the **New School/Academy of American Poets** series (66 West 12th; ☎ 212-229-5600). Or call the **Academy of American Poets** headquarters at ☎ 212-274-0343 to inquire about its poetry readings around town.

NEW YORK NIGHTLIFE

IF YOU'D LIKE TO BE AN ACTIVE PARTICIPANT in your evening's events, as opposed to an audience member, then you'll need to do a bit of bar/club hopping. This can be fun or tiresome depending on the distances between your chosen destinations, but you're bound to have some sort of an adventure, either on foot, in a taxi, or on the subway, between venues. There's a place and space for all types of people any night of the week.

unofficial **TIP**
There are several quality bars and clubs above 34th Street, but there is a tendency for more nightlife activity and variety to be concentrated downtown; keep this in mind if you feel like simply walking around and finding a place.

To wet your whistle, we suggest places that offer good beer, sake, sumptuous cocktails, jazz, rock, cabaret, country, alternative sounds, comedy, cigars, hookah pipes, and literary discussions. It's just a taste of the options, but a good place to start.

For those who still smoke and aren't quite sure how to drink and puff simultaneously in public since the smoking ban of March 2003, we offer a few options:

If you'd like something stronger than a hookah pipe at **Kush** (see profile), then you can opt for cigars at **Club Macanudo** (see profile) and **Velvet Cigar Lounge** (80 East Seventh Street; ☎ 212-533-5582). For cigarettes and a taste of Art Deco try **Circa Tabac** (32 Watts Street; ☎ 212-941-1781).

We hope that with this bit of insider advice and an added incentive to get out, you'll be motivated to do some regular New York City night-owl exploration. We hope to see you on the dark side. . . .

JAZZ

JAZZ MAY HAVE ORIGINATED IN NEW ORLEANS, but for decades New York has been the center of the jazz universe. If you have even the slightest interest in this style, you'll want to check out one or two of the following clubs; be prepared to stay up late, especially if you'd like to catch a jam session.

See profiles for **Village Vanguard, Smoke, Blue Note, Kavehaz, Knitting Factory, Tonic, Smalls,** and **Zinc Bar.**

CLEOPATRA'S NEEDLE (2485 Broadway at 92nd Street; ☎ 212-769-6969) has live music nightly and jam sessions Wednesday through Saturday, 12:30 a.m. until 3 a.m.; $10 minimum per person.

55 BAR (55 Christopher Street; ☎ 212-929-9883) is a no-nonsense Greenwich Village joint with music that is often surprisingly good. Two-drink minimum.

FAT CAT BILLIARDS (75 Christopher Street; ☎ 212-675-6056) offers jazz, pool, ping-pong, and chess. Jam sessions nightly at 1:30 a.m.

IRIDIUM (1650 Broadway at 51st Street; ☎ 212-582-2121), with its over-the-top ultramodern décor, is a trippy exception to the rule that jazz is often played in drab spaces.

LENOX LOUNGE (288 Lenox Avenue between 124th and 125th streets; ☎ 212-427-0253) is an historical jazz spot with an Art Deco feel and continues to serve good food and music regularly.

SWEET RHYTHM (88 Seventh Avenue South; ☎ 212-255-3626) was formerly the jazz-only Sweet Basil, but it now hosts world music with a bit of jazz thrown in.

ROCK AND ALTERNATIVE

ROCK CLUBS IN MANHATTAN MOSTLY FIT into three categories. There are the bar venues that host big-name acts for big cover charges—places like **Irving Plaza** (17 Irving Place; ☎ 212-777-6800), **Bowery Ballroom** (6 Delancey Street; ☎ 212-533-2111; **www.bowery ballroom.com**), and **Roseland** (239 West 52nd Street; ☎ 212-247-0200). Then there are the showcase places where newly signed bands preen for industry insiders—**Southpaw** (125 Fifth Avenue, Brooklyn; ☎ 718-230-0236; **www.spsounds.com**) and **Mercury Lounge** (see profile). At the bottom of the ladder are the vanity clubs where amateurish weekend warriors and ambitious startups play short sets at the **Baggot Inn, Pyramid,** and **Kenny's Castaways.** The multiband nights are hit-and-miss; one good band in a lineup of four is a welcome surprise.

The country's best bar bands have long played their hearts out in nearby New Jersey and Long Island (remember the origins of Southside Johnny, Bruce Springsteen, the Rascals, etc.), but Manhattan, right between those two areas, has few groups (or venues to present them) dedicated to entertaining a bar. The showcasing kids angle more for A&R attention than for a grooving good time for the house crowd, and an evening in one of the name venues means buying expensive tickets and standing amid rapturous crowds; you're basically at a concert, not hanging out in a bar.

*un*official **TIP**
If you just want to have a beer and listen to professional-quality local guys who play live for a living—a real *bar* band—you're in the wrong place.

If you don't mind your rock filtered through other influences, **Rodeo Bar** (see profile) presents good, professional hang-out bands (most are rockabilly/country/funky). **Hank's Saloon** (46 Third Avenue at Atlantic Avenue, Brooklyn; ☎ 718-625-8003) offers country music and a divey saloon vibe. Other venues include:

ARLENE'S GROCERY (95 Stanton Street; ☎ 212-995-1652) has cover charges on Friday, Saturday, and sometimes Sunday; price is dependent on the event. Considered a prestigious showcase for indie bands; medium to heavy rock; rock karaoke on Mondays.

BITTER END (147 Bleecker Street; ☎ 212-673-7030; **www.bitter end.com**) has been around for years, hosting some great and not-so-good music. Worth a visit just for the tradition it represents.

CB'S 313 GALLERY (313 Bowery; ☎ 212-677-0455; **www.cbgb.com**) sports a $5 to $15 cover. Mostly acoustic bookings in this "nice" twin (hung with paintings) to the legendary punk and music mecca CBGB's (☎ 212-982-4052) next door. It's important to note that at press time, the fate of both CBGBs and the 313 Gallery are in limbo, as the owner has been having lease issues with its landlord. The lease has expired, but they're still operating, and a huge save CBGB campaign is underway; **www.cbgb.com**.

LIVING ROOM (154 Ludlow Street; ☎ 212-533-7235) charges no cover; one-drink minimum. Medium rock to folk with focus on singer/songwriters.

NORTHSIX (66 North Sixth Street, Williamsburg, Brooklyn; ☎ 718-599-5103) adds to the mix with varied music sets and lots of energy.

SIDEWALK CAFÉ (94 Avenue A; ☎ 212-473-7373) no cover, two-drink minimum. Medium rock to folk. Avoid Monday's open-mic night.

unofficial **TIP**
Regardless of your age, always bring ID with you … some of these places wouldn't let in Rip Van Winkle without photo ID.

South of Houston Street, the music is often edgier and more experimental. **Tonic** (see profile) is a bastion of quality performances.

DANCING

APART FROM WEIRD CABARET LAWS PROHIBITING dancing in bars unless they're licensed, dancing is alive and well in NYC. Clubs, both underground and mainstream, abound and satisfy all music and style tastes. Herein lies the rub—some of the best beats are spun by DJs who travel and host club parties at various venues; some stationary clubs have nonstop style, but not always the best music, as hip takes precedence over harmonics. We won't list the DJ parties, as they often change, but *Time Out* has a good weekly clubs section listing. As for the trendy clubs, we'll give you an intro, but blink and they may already be passé.

Avalon (47 West 20th Street; ☎ 212-807-7780), moving in where Limelight once reigned, is harking back to the 1980s heyday of glitter and disco. **Glass** (287 Tenth Avenue; ☎ 212-904-1580) has an exclusive club feel, with house-lounge music (sometimes Latin). **Cielo** (18 Little West 12th Street; ☎ 212-645-5700) in the still hot Meatpacking District, takes dancing and DJs seriously, but this you can only appreciate once you get past the bouncers. Glass has neat unisex bathrooms so passersby on the street can see you preening in the two-way mirror. Other clubs include **Crobar** (530 West 28th Street; ☎ 212-629-9000) and **Quo** (511 West 58th Street; ☎ 212-268-5105) just across the street. Also try **Glo** (431 West 16th Street; ☎ 212-229-9119) and **Spirit** (530 West 27th Street; ☎ 212-268-9477). For pre-dance cocktails in swish surroundings, head for **Salon** (505 West Street; ☎ 212-929-4303). Finally, for no scene and lots of fun, try **B3** (33 Avenue B; ☎ 212-619-9755) for dancing in the basement.

For salsa dancing in a setting more down-home than glossy, choices include nightspots such as **S.O.B.'s** (see profile); or warm, artsy **Nuyorican Poets Café** (236 East Third Street; ☎ 212-505-8183). There's also **LQ** (511 Lexington Avenue in the Radisson Hotel; ☎ 212-593-7575) and the **Copacabana** (560 West 34th Street; ☎ 212-239-2672). Yet another option is **Swing 46** (see profile).

CABARET

SOME OF NEW YORK'S NOTABLE CABARET BARS include **Joe's Pub** (see profile), and, notably, **Feinstein's at the Regency Hotel** (540 Park Avenue; ☎ 212-339-4095) featuring namesake/owner Michael Feinstein and other legends. Old standbys (and we mean *old;* some of the following have been in operation for decades) include **The Duplex** (61 Christopher Street at Seventh Avenue; ☎ 212-255-5438), **Danny's Skylight Room** (346 West 46th Street; ☎ 212-265-8133; skip the Thai food), **the Oak Room** (see "Hotel Bars" below), **Don't Tell Mama's** (343 West 46th Street; ☎ 212-757-0788), and **Café Carlyle** (see profile).

unofficial **TIP**
For more info on NYC cabaret, check out www.svhamstra.com and www.cabaret.org.

IRISH

IRISH PUBS ARE A SAFE BET TO FIND GOOD BEER, pub grub, and fine "craic." You may even get some live music, complete with a fiddle or two. The following are of particular interest:

AN BEAL BOCHT CAFE (445 West 238th Street; Riverdale, Bronx; ☎ 718-884-7127) offers great music Wednesday through Saturday; it's a trek to get to, but they serve the best Guinness of all (warm fire too).

MONA'S (224 Avenue B; ☎ 212-353-3780), a real ultra-dive, serves cheap beer and hosts Monday-night jam sessions starting at 10:30 p.m.

PADDY REILLY'S (519 Second Avenue; ☎ 212-686-1210) has music nightly.

SWIFT HIBERNIAN LOUNGE (34 East Fourth Street; ☎ 212-260-3600) has music on Tuesdays, and great beer to boot.

THADY CON'S (915 Second Avenue; ☎ 212-688-9700) serves up authenticity and good Bass Ale.

FINE DRINKS

ONE OF THE BEST THINGS ABOUT NEW YORK is the substantial number of people who seek out the best food and drink with an obsessive zeal and passion. Mind you, the city has a plethora of corner bars where Bud Lite is drunk unrepentantly. But for those on a mission to enjoy only the finest drinks, there are zillions of places whose selection will astound. And for those who aren't professional bon vivants, the true believers populating these bars will gladly help clueless novices. New Yorkers may be rude and blasé, but once they start enthusing, it's hard to keep 'em down.

unofficial **TIP**
If you're online, the NYC Beer Guide provides exhaustive annotated listings of pubs, tastings, and local microbrews at **www.nycbeer.org**.

The best bars and restaurants for good beer:

BLIND TIGER ALE HOUSE (518 Hudson Street; ☎ 212-675-3848) has 26 quality taps, plus hand-pumps.

THE BROOKLYN BREWERY (79 North 11th Street; ☎ 718-486-7422; **www.brooklynbrewery.com**) in Williamsburg offers free brewery tours on Saturday at 1, 2, 3, and 4 p.m. Worth a visit.

BURP CASTLE (41 East Seventh Street; ☎ 212-982-4576) is all about beer, and the bartenders are dressed in monks' robes to ensure a reverential feeling toward the brew.

CAFÉ DE BRUXELLES (118 Greenwich Avenue; ☎ 212-206-1830) fries great pommes frites and offers a small but smart selection of Belgian bottles.

CHUMLEY'S (86 Bedford Street; ☎ 212-675-4449) is located in a hidden former speakeasy.

DBA See profile.

EAR INN (326 Spring Street; ☎ 212-226-9060) is a bohemian little cafe with especially good Guinness.

THE GINGER MAN See profile.

MCSORLEY'S (15 East Seventh Street; ☎ 212-473-9148) is a tourist fave, with old New York ambience and mediocre beer swilled alongside rambunctious frat boys.

OLD TOWN BAR (45 East 18th Street; ☎ 212-529-6732) has a halfway decent beer selection, plus great, traditional ambience.

PECULIER PUB (145 Bleecker Street; ☎ 212-353-1327) is expensive and incredibly mobbed on weekends, but the selection's amazing.

SILVER SWAN (41 East 20th Street; ☎ 212-254-3611) cooks terrific German food and stocks plenty of good German bottles.

SPUYTEN DUYVIL (359 Metropolitan Avenue; ☎ 718-963-4140) offers a superb array of brews both bottled and on tap, and the atmosphere is friendly and just a tad cool-kitsch.

WATERFRONT ALE HOUSE (540 Second Avenue; ☎ 212-696-4104 and 155 Atlantic Avenue; ☎ 718-522-3794) has an excellent tap selection, with some ultra-rare specials and good pub food.

HEARTLAND BREWERY (35 Union Square West; ☎ 212-645-3400) and **Chelsea Brewing Company** (Pier 59, Chelsea Piers; ☎ 212-336-6440) are half-decent microbreweries but very popular, and both have outdoor seating in the summer.

JAPANESE AND SAKE

THERE ARE TWO LOCI OF JAPANESE CULTURE in Manhattan: the East Village, where hip bohemian Japanese kids live and hang out, and Midtown, where a more suit-and-tie crowd have their bars and restaurants, many private. Each scene has its own custom-tailored sake bar. **Decibel** (240 East Ninth Street; ☎ 212-979-2733) is a knick-knack-filled haven in a very cool little basement space to talk and drink any of tons of sakes from your choice of unique cups. You can also try plum wine or a lychee martini. For other Japanese-flavored nightlife, see profiles for **Angel's Share** and **Chibitini.**

HOTEL BARS

SOME OF THE MOST ELEGANT BARS IN TOWN are located in hotels. These are places where beer takes a back seat to the gin, mojito, and martini hybrids.

THE ALGONQUIN (59 West 44th Street; ☎ 212-840-6800) was built in 1902 and was where the famed Literary Round Table was formed. Authors included Dorothy Parker and Robert Benchley. The bar is full of good drinking options: There's the famous Oak Room, as well as their elegant and relaxing lobby bar and the woody/clubby Blue Bar.

THE CARLYLE HOTEL (35 East 76th Street; ☎ 212-744-1600) contains not only the famous Café Carlyle (see profile) but also Bemelmans Bar, which features tinkling piano and a clubby atmosphere, with watercolors on the walls. Bemelman's also offers Madeline's tea Friday through Monday, from noon until 4 p.m. Bemelman created the *Madeline* children's books and drew large murals in the bar of Central Park.

GRAND BAR at the Soho Grand Hotel (310 West Broadway; ☎ 212-965-3000) has a very atmospheric lounge area, all inside the hotel lobby; very hip.

THE HUDSON BAR See profile.

MONKEY BAR at the Elysee Hotel (60 East 54th Street; ☎ 212-838-2600) is anything but restrained and stuffy; it attracts an exuberant crowd, and laughter—sometimes even singing, if you get there late enough—drowns out clinking glasses.

MORGANS BAR at the Morgan Hotel (237 Madison Avenue; ☎ 212-726-7755) serves up attitude, romantic atmosphere, and pricey but good mixed drinks below the hotel lobby. Alternatively, above on street level, Morgan Hotel's **Asia de Cuba** (☎ 212-726-7755) has a very popular but small bar as well as a lively, stylish restaurant. Try the martinis.

THE BAR AT 44 RESTAURANT IN THE ROYALTON See profile.

THE TOP OF THE TOWER AT BEEKMAN TOWER HOTEL (see profile) is a blessedly mellow spot for a late-night drink with a handsome East Side view, especially enjoyable at one of the outdoor tables.

TOWN BAR See profile.

THE VIEW AT THE MARRIOTT MARQUIS (1535 Broadway; ☎ 212-398-1900) is the only revolving bar in New York, so there's never a static vantage point. Don't eat the food.

SEX

THE BIG APPLE OFFERS MANY OPPORTUNITIES to either sow your wild oats or have a great time in places that don't flaunt the pickup vibe. For those who want to try out some smooth moves on strangers there are ample choices. Try **Bounce** (1403 Second Avenue; ☎ 212-535-2183); **Asia de Cuba** (see above); **Tao** (42 East 58th Street; ☎ 212-888-2288); **Meet** (71–73 Gansevoort Street; ☎ 212-242-0990); **Divine Bar** (244 East 51st Street; ☎ 212-319-9463); **The Bubble Lounge** (see profile); and the chic and grown-up **King Cole Bar** at the St. Regis Hotel (2 East 55th Street; ☎ 212-339-6721) for power pickups.

For those looking for something a little racier, fancy strip clubs like **Scores** (333 East 60th Street; ☎ 212-421-3600 and 536 West 28th Street; ☎ 212-868-4900); **Hustler Club** (641 West 51st Street; ☎ 212-247-2460); and **VIP Club** (20 West 20th Street; ☎ 212-633-1199) offer super examples of plastic surgery gone wild (and very steep bar tabs).

Beware of clip joints like **Legz Diamond** (622 West 47th Street; ☎ 212-977-3200), many of which pass out promotional flyers on Midtown streets; these are full-nudity places that bypass restrictions by serving no alcohol. Your cranberry juice will cost you dearly, and talkative women hired by the bar will attempt to pressure you into buying them even more outrageously priced drinks (and, eventually, fake champagne).

GAY NIGHTLIFE

THE LATEST SCENES CHANGE AT A DIZZYING PACE; widely available publications like *Time Out* (**www.timeout.com**) and *New York Blade* (**www.nyblade.com**)are good sources for information, as is the **Lesbian, Gay, Bisexual, and Transgender Community Center** (208 West 13th Street; ☎ 212-620-7310; **www.gaycenter.org**). The following are some spots with longevity.

The granddaddy of all piano bars is **Don't Tell Mama** (343 West 46th; ☎ 212-757-0788). **Stonewall Bar** still stands at 53 Christopher Street (it's since gone through several incarnations; ☎ 212-463-0950).

New York Nightclubs by Neighborhood

NAME	DESCRIPTION
SOHO AND TRIBECA	
The Bubble Lounge	Champagne bar
The Knitting Factory	(Very) alternative music club
S.O.B.'s	Latin and world music/dance nightclub
Zinc Bar	Bar and jazz club
CHINATOWN, LITTLE ITALY, AND THE LOWER EAST SIDE	
Chibitini	Hip sake bar
Kush	Funky Moroccan-themed bar
Tonic	Grungy but chic new music club
GREENWICH VILLAGE	
The Blue Note	Jazz club
Bowlmor Lanes	Hip bowling with attitude
Cornelia Street Café	Intimate performance space
Smalls	Jazz club for cool cats
Village Vanguard	Jazz club
THE EAST VILLAGE	
Angel's Share	Secret hideaway cocktail oasis
DBA	Mecca for ultra-high-quality drinks
Joe's Pub	Lush nightclub
Lava Gina	Offbeat music and drink bar
Mercury Lounge	Rock showcase
Mo Pitkin's	Bar with Judeo-Latino restaurant and cabaret
Remote Lounge	Voyeur theme bar
Webster Hall	Disco theme park
CHELSEA	
Bongo	Trendy hangout/oyster bar
Kavehaz	Gallery/jazz cafe

A walk down Christopher Street and environs will reveal a plethora of clubs and bars. **The Monster** (80 Grove Street; ☎ 212-924-3558) has an upstairs piano bar for an older crowd, plus a downstairs mirrored disco that's more of a pickup joint. The crowd's diverse, and while things can get silly, it's always fairly tasteful and safe. **The Cock** (188 Avenue A; ☎ 212-777-6254) may be dark and divey, but it's *very* serious about partying.

NAME	DESCRIPTION
GRAMERCY PARK AND MADISON SQUARE	
Flatiron Lounge	Chic cocktail lounge
The Ginger Man	Giant-sized beer bar
Rodeo Bar	Cowboy bar with high-quality eclectic live music
MIDTOWN WEST, TIMES SQUARE, AND THE THEATER DISTRICT	
Carolines	Comedy club
O'Flaherty's Ale House	Irish pub after-show hideaway
Swing 46	Swing dance club
Town	Chic cocktail bar
MIDTOWN EAST	
Campbell Apartment	Sophisticated bar/lounge
Pen-Top Bar at the Peninsula Hotel	Rooftop hotel bar
PJ Clarke's	Old-time New York bar
Sakagura	Hidden suave sake bar
Top of the Tower	Romantic bar/restaurant with superb views
UPPER WEST SIDE	
Hudson Bar	Chic hotel bar
Smoke	Jazz club
UPPER EAST SIDE	
Café Carlyle	Sophisticated New York nightspot
Club Macanudo	Upscale cigar and whisky bar
Lenox Room	Well-heeled lounge and restaurant
BROOKLYN	
Barbès	Welcoming, innovative bar/performance space
Excelsior Bar	Swish, neighborhood gay bar
Galapagos	Bar and performance space
Ginger's	Friendly gay bar with pool table

Boy's Room (9 Avenue A; ☎ 212-228-5340) is a tad sleazy, loads of fun, and not for the bashful. **Barrage** (401 West 47th Street; ☎ 212-586-9390) and **Splash Club, Bar and Lounge** (50 West 17th Street; ☎ 212-691-0073), have good pickup potential.

On the Upper East Side: **The Townhouse** (236 East 58th Street; ☎ 212-754-4649) is a place where Young Men Who Want to Meet Guys Who Wear Coats and Ties meet guys who wear coats and ties

At-a-glance Club Guide

SAKE BARS/JAPANESE

Angel's Share

Chibitini

Sakagura

WHISKEY/COCKTAILS/ CHAMPAGNE

Angel's Share

The Bubble Lounge

Campbell Apartment

Club Macanudo

DBA

Flatiron Lounge

Hudson Bar

Lenox Room

Town

ARTY

Barbès

Cornelia Street Café

Galapagos

Kavehaz

The Knitting Factory

Kush

Mercury Lounge

Tonic

MUSIC VENUES—VARIOUS GENRES

Barbès

Cornelia Street Cafe

Galapagos

Joe's Pub

The Knitting Factory

Lava Gina

Mercury Lounge

S.O.B.'s

Tonic

CHIC/TRENDY

Bongo

Campbell Apartment

Excelsior

Flatiron Lounge

Hudson Bar

JAZZ CLUBS

The Blue Note

Smalls

Smoke

Village Vanguard

Zinc Bar

who want to meet Young Men Who Want to Meet Guys Who Wear Coats and Ties.

The Roxy (515 West 18th Street; ☎ 212-645-5156) hosts gay roller disco on Wednesday nights, and a gay disco party on Saturday. **Henrietta Hudson** (438 Hudson Street; ☎ 212-924-3347) has live bands and DJs. **Starlight** (167 Avenue A; ☎ 212-475-2172) is hip and suits all crowds.

Girl's Room is filling in where Meow Mix left off, with go-go dancers, DJs, and a disco ball. **Cubby Hole** (281 West 12th Street; ☎ 212-243-9041) is more mellow and intimate.

Out of Manhattan, check out **Excelsior** (see profile) and **Ginger's** (see profile) both in Park Slope, Brooklyn.

DANCE/DISCO
Joe's Pub
Lava Gina
Rodeo Bar
S.O.B.'s
Swing 46
Webster Hall

HOTEL
The Bar at 44 Retaurant–Royalton Hotel
Café Carlyle–Carlyle Hotel
Hudson Bar–Hudson Hotel
Pen-Top Bar at The Peninsula
Top of the Tower at the Beekman Tower Hotel
Town–Chambers Hotel

GAY
Excelsior
Ginger's

COZY
Angel's Share
Barbès
The Bubble Lounge
Chibitini
O'Flaherty's Ale House
Pen-Top Bar at The Peninsula

BOWLING
Bowlmor Lanes

THEME
Café Carlyle
Carolines
Comedy/Cabaret
Mo Pitkin's
Remote Lounge

BEER/NEW YORK LANDMARKS
The Ginger Man
O'Flaherty's Ale House
PJ Clarke's

COMEDY

COMEDY CLUBS ARE OFTEN LOOKED DOWN UPON by Manhattanites as strictly for tourists (or, worse, for Bridge-and-Tunnelers—the derisive name for suburbanites drawn to the island for weekend entertainment). Indeed, the average New Yorker is at least as funny as some kid working the mike at Larry's Laughter Lounge. But if you must indulge in such shamefully uncosmopolitan pleasures, there are a few nationally known clubs, plus some intriguing cutting-edge comedy venues where you can both yuck it up and feel hip.

The best mainstream clubs are **Carolines** (see profile), **Gotham Comedy Club** (34 West 22nd Street; ☎ 212-367-9000), and **the Comic Strip Live** (1568 Second Avenue; ☎ 212-861-9386). Gotham feels serious and intimate—upscale but no baloney or showbiz touches; just a room with mic and audience. The Comic Strip, best on weekends, is even less slick. Celebs are fairly common at the Monday night showcase at the Comic Strip, but otherwise the show's very hit-or-miss. Those three get the best-known acts and have the most upscale ambience. Beware "new talent nights" at the big clubs: Audiences paying a hefty cover and two-drink minimum often see not the brightest young talent but those new-comers who've promised club owners they'll pack the club (and thus its coffers) with friends and family. **Laugh Lounge** (151 Essex Street; ☎ 212-614-2500) is a relative newcomer and boasts that it's the only comedy club on the Lower East Side. **The Comedy Cellar** (117 MacDou-gal Street; ☎ 212-254-3480) and **Stand-up NY** (236 West 78th Street; ☎ 212-595-0850) are also worth visiting.

unofficial **TIP**
For information on all fla-vors of comedy, *Time Out* (www.timeout.com) magazine features very complete listings.

Another place offering comedic sketches and improv stylings is the **Upright Citizens Brigade Theater** (307 West 26th Street; ☎ 212-366-9176; **www.ucbtheatre.com**); chances are you won't be disappointed, and performances are fairly inexpensive.

NIGHTCLUB PROFILES

Angel's Share

SECRET HIDEAWAY COCKTAIL OASIS

8 Stuyvesant Street (second floor), The East Village; ☎ 212-777-5415

Cover None. **Minimum** None. **Mixed drinks** $6–$8. **Wine** Bottles $25–$60. **Beer** $5–$18. **Dress** Elegant casual or anything black. Dress-up's fine, but not flashy. **Food available** Small menu of excellent Korean/Japanese snacks; great fried oys-ters. **Hours** Daily, 6 p.m.–2:30 a.m.

WHO GOES THERE   25–45; the beautiful, the hipsters, and the bohemian East Village Japanese.

WHAT GOES ON You go up steps with pink neon banisters, turn left through the sushi restaurant, and open an unmarked door to enter a mega-atmospheric little den of hip urbanity. Inside, there are suave young Asian bartenders crafting cocktails with single-minded intensity (they sample your drinks and tweak, often several times, before serving), soothing jazz played over a fine sound system, a few romantic tables with great views, and a bar filled with an interesting, intelligent, attrac-tive clientele. Martinis are awesome, as are gimlets and fresh fruit daiquiris (not too sweet), plus you'll find wonderful selections of spirits like whisky and bourbon—there's not a single dumb bottle in the room. Service is classy but utterly unpretentious. The bristling intensity of the bartenders electrifies the place; it's the ideal choice for an intelligent date. The "no-standing" rule can make it frustratingly difficult to get in (especially on crowded weekends), but provides uncommon tranquility when you do.

SETTING AND ATMOSPHERE A narrow sliver with a bar on one side and a dramatic view up Third Avenue through tall, draperied windows on the other. A huge mural of an Asian angel baby sets the tone of elegance with a sardonic twist. Tables are mostly for two—this isn't a destination for groups.

IF YOU GO Fridays and Saturdays you may find Japanese jazz duos strumming in a cramped corner, but the stereo is far more pleasing (yet another reason to avoid weekend prime time).

The Bar at 44 Restaurant (Royalton Hotel)

SWANKY BUT STRANGELY COZY HOTEL LOBBY BAR

44 West 44th Street, Midtown West; ☎ 212-944-8844

Cover None. Minimum None. Mixed drinks $10–$15. Wine $14–$17 by the glass; $35–$390 for bottles. Beer $10. Dress Mostly suits in evenings; looser later. Food available Light fare and desserts (from the kitchen of adjacent Restaurant 44). Hours Daily, noon–1:30 a.m.

WHO GOES THERE 30s–60s; tourists, businessmen, predinner drinkers.

WHAT GOES ON This is an ideal break-the-ice meeting place for a predinner drink, be your companions business associates, in-laws, or a hot date. It's just swanky enough to set an elegant tone, but comfy enough (lots of well-cushioned couches and chairs positioned for maximum intimacy) not to intimidate. Urbane conversation flows easily; as you look around the room, you notice that everyone seems very very engaged, very very glib. It's not just the clientele; it's the room. Good lighting combined with the atmospheric coziness also make this a choice spot for a late-night tête-à-tête.

SETTING AND ATMOSPHERE The cocktail area occupies a dramatic, long, sunken strip to your left as you walk through the narrow lobby. Toward the back, the lounge morphs into an airily open restaurant of similar design. Décor is what used to be called "futuristic": beige Jetsons couches, love seats, and chairs of odd shape in off-white fabrics. Jaded types might describe the look as Early Airport Club.

IF YOU GO Peer into the tiny vodka/champagne/grappa bar hidden to the right as you come in the front door. This claustrophobic sci-fi transporter room sports circular padded walls and flickery candles. Check out the bathrooms.

Barbès

WELCOMING, INNOVATIVE BAR/PERFORMANCE SPACE

376 Ninth Street (near Sixth Avenue), Park Slope, Brooklyn; ☎ 718-965-9177; www.barbesbrooklyn.com

Cover Only for the event space; suggested donation of $8. Minimum None. Mixed drinks $6–$8. Wine $4–$8. Beer $3–$6. Dress Casual or cool. Food available No, just peanuts. Hours Sunday–Thursday, 5 p.m.–2 a.m.; Friday and Saturday, 5 p.m.–4 a.m.

WHO GOES THERE   20s and up; locals, musicians, artists.

WHAT GOES ON   Socializing, hanging out, contemplation, and an interesting array of live events.

SETTING AND ATMOSPHERE   Entrance is right off the street in a residential neighborhood, so loud crowds and events are not encouraged. One enters the main area which features a long bar along one wall with tables and stools narrowly opposite as well as a nook with stools and table on the side between the end of the bar and front window. The performance space is past the bar into a smaller enclosure and this is where events such as poetry readings, art house films, acoustic guitars, and unplugged brass bands squeeze in.

IF YOU GO   Know that space gets tight when a popular event takes place, but if you persevere, you'll find a nook or standing position from where you can at least drink your beer.

The Blue Note

JAZZ CLUB

131 West Third Street, Greenwich Village; ☎ 212-475-8592; www.bluenotejazz.com

Cover $5–$55 at tables, $5–$45 at bar; brunch: $20/person. Minimum $5 at tables, one drink at the bar. Mixed drinks $6–$12. Wine Bottles, $30–$200. Beer $5. Dress Fancy shmancy. Specials Monday nights are bargains; Fridays and Saturdays after the last set, late-night show until 4 a.m. for $5 cover. No minimum till 4 a.m. Food available Full menu, for the gastronomically reckless. Hours Shows at 9 and 11:30 every night. Saturday and Sunday; jazz brunch, noon–6 p.m., with shows at 1 and 3:30 p.m.

WHO GOES THERE   22–90; tourists.

WHAT GOES ON   It's amazing how many tourists think that the Blue Note is a historic jazz institution, even though the place didn't open until the late date of 1981. But hordes of them continue to pay stratospheric prices to sit in uncomfortable chairs packed *way* too close together in a small, dark, boxy room. It's worth it, however, when they bring in acts who normally don't play clubs (Herbie Hancock, etc.), many of whom shine in the more intimate setting. But the entertainment here can be more "jazzish" than jazz; people like Roberta Flack, Tito Puente, and Steve Allen have played here. The Village Vanguard (see profile) and Iridium (see introduction to this chapter) are far more pure-minded in their bookings.

SETTING AND ATMOSPHERE   Claustrophobic and tacky, done in dark tones and mirrors. A cheesy neon Manhattan skyline is the only "classy" touch.

IF YOU GO   As at all jazz clubs in New York, avoid crowds by arriving for the last set or during bad weather (budget option: the revamped bar area now has good sight lines). Late jam sessions are cheap and sometimes quite good.

Bongo

299 Tenth Avenue, Chelsea; ☎ 212-947-3654

Cover None. **Minimum** None. **Mixed drinks** $6 and up (but they're huge). **Wine** $6–$8. **Beer** $4–$5. **Dress** Cool; suits may feel out of place after 8 p.m. **Specials** None. **Food available** Superb oysters on the half shell, perhaps the best in town. **Hours** Monday–Tuesday, 5 p.m.–12 a.m.; Wednesday, 5 p.m.–1 a.m.; Thursday–Saturday, 5 p.m.–3 a.m.

WHO GOES THERE Stylish small groups, couples, singles.

WHAT GOES ON While there are times when one wants to be in the center of things (and there's no better place than Manhattan for feeling "plugged in"), there are times when one prefers to retreat to the sidelines. Bongo is a tiny storefront hardly worth a second look from the outside. Yet despite the gritty area, you'll certainly not be roughing it inside, where cool ambience, great shellfish, and oversized cocktails are in the offing. It's no bargain, but there is a compelling coolness factor of knowing to take your date or business associate to this hip little place on the West Side. For those who like to nurse their drinks (pace is slooow here) and turn the intensity down a notch—and chat up companions away from bustling crowds and prying ears—this alluring scene is a five-minute cab ride from Midtown.

SETTING AND ATMOSPHERE A tiny but chic storefront with ironically retro couches and chairs, soft lighting, and sultry music. The comfortable bar faces a backlit stage of trendy vodka bottles and other intriguing drinks. Staff is aloof and cooler-than-thou (chalk it up to mystique).

IF YOU GO Don't miss the extraordinarily good (and well-priced) oysters, especially rich, sweet kumamotos. Mixed drinks are good (they spray your glass with atomized Vermouth for a *really* dry martini). The place can get crowded later, though there's usually space at the bar. Skip the expensive lobster rolls (lots of fresh lobster, but overwhelmed by olive oil and basil).

Bowlmor Lanes

110 University Place, Greenwich Village; ☎ 212-255-8188; www.bowlmor.com

Cover Monday through Thursday, $7.45 per person per game before 5 p.m., $8.45 after 5 p.m.; Friday night before 5 p.m., $8.45; Friday after 5 p.m., Saturday, and holidays, $8.95; Sunday, $8.45 ($5 for shoes). Ages 21 and over after 5 p.m. daily. **Minimum** None. **Mixed drinks** $6.50–$8.50. **Wine** $5.50 and up. **Beer** $4.75–$7. **Dress** Jeans and T-shirts (though some do dress up). **Specials** Monday night, unlimited bowling for $20 per person, ages 13 and up; kids' birthday parties available weekend afternoons. **Food available** Surprisingly good (eat at the bar or take delivery directly to your lane!), including some of Manhattan's better burgers;

beware the $25 credit card minimum. Hours Monday, 11 a.m.–3 a.m.; Tuesday and Wednesday, 11 a.m.–1 a.m.; Thursday, 11 a.m.–2 a.m.; Friday and Saturday, 11 a.m.–4 a.m; Sunday, 11 a.m.–midnight.

WHO GOES THERE Stylishly pierced and ironic 20–30-somethings.

WHAT GOES ON Very very hip, very very ironic bowling, with a crowd of chic 20–30-somethings sprinkled with some oblivious oldsters. As the place is fond of saying, "this is not your father's bowling alley."

SETTING AND ATMOSPHERE A real old-time bowling alley (built in 1938) partially morphed into a way-cool hangout. Just because the ball-return lanes are painted baby blue and balls and pins are fluorescent pink and yellow doesn't mean Uncle Ernie and Aunt Ethel (who've come here for 30 years) don't feel at home bowling a few frames among the packs of 22-year-olds. There's a handsome old semicircular bar and old-fashioned tile floors. The place hasn't been totally revised—this is not so much a complete MTV makeover of a 1950s bowling alley as a slightly trippy touch-up. Enough of the old remains that the effect is more eerie than contrived.

IF YOU GO Call ahead to check lane availability . . . this is not Paramus, New Jersey, so there's only space for a limited number of lanes. Try glow-in-the-dark bowling night (call for schedule).

The Bubble Lounge

CHAMPAGNE BAR

228 West Broadway, Soho; ☎ **212-431-3433;**
www.bubblelounge.com

Cover None. Minimum $25 at tables. Mixed drinks $7–$10. Wine Champagnes $7–$35/glass, less for half-glasses. Beer $6 and up. Dress Way chic, dark colors. Dress code is strictly inforced. No sneakers, gym or workout garments, sandals, baseball caps, military or combat fatigues, or swimwear. Specials Live jazz Tuesdays at 7:30 p.m. Food available Typical champagne accompaniments like oysters, caviar, salmon, foie gras, sorbets; all quite pricey. Hours Closed Sunday and Monday but available for private parties. Tuesday–Thursday, 5 p.m.–2 a.m.; Friday and Saturday, 5 p.m.

WHO GOES THERE 21–60; slinky well-heeled lounge chicsters and locals.

WHAT GOES ON A champagne and cigar bar (excellent ventilation tames the smoke) where chic poseurs peacefully coexist with more down-to-earth locals, all feeling very very grown-up. The bubbly itself is quaffed more as a style thing than as serious wine pursuit (sniff and swirl your glass like an oenophile here and you'll get some strange looks), but there's no denying that sipping Dom Perignon without shelling out big bucks for a whole bottle is a good thing. Twenty-three champagnes are available by the glass, 280 champagnes and sparkling wines by the bottle.

SETTING AND ATMOSPHERE An L-shaped space lush with red velvet draperies, exposed brick, couches, flickering candles, highly lacquered wood, and highly preened waitresses. Dracula would feel at home.

IF YOU GO Check out the downstairs Krug room, a champagne/wine cellar with waitress service. Reservations are strongly recommended for parties of six or more.

Café Carlyle at the Carlyle

SOPHISTICATED NEW YORK NIGHTSPOT

35 East 76th Street, Upper East Side; ☎ 212-744-1600; www.thecarlyle.com

Cover $50–$90/table, $10/bar. **Minimum** None. **Mixed drinks** $12 and up. **Wine** $10–$13.50 by the glass. **Beer** $10–$12. **Dress** Jackets required, of course, but you'd do well to pull out all the stops and wear your very best duds. **Specials** Save $20 on the cover charge by watching from the cafe (reservations aren't accepted, though, and you'll pay full price even if there's only standing room). **Food available** Old-fashioned New York food served by old-fashioned professional New York waiters—expensive and available 6 p.m.–midnight. **Hours** Monday–Saturday, 7 p.m.–1:30 a.m., shows at 8:45 p.m. and 10:45 p.m. (no second show Monday and Tuesday); Sunday, noon–3 p.m.

WHO GOES THERE 25–90; grown-ups.

WHAT GOES ON Performer Bobby Short was synonymous with Café Carlyle, and his death has left a void which aims to be filled by other talented musicians, including the Eddy Davis New Orleans jazz band.

SETTING AND ATMOSPHERE One of the most famous cabarets in the world, Café Carlyle sets a nearly unreachable standard of elegant and intimate supper-club ambience. A splendid assortment of Vertes murals adds greatly to the magic.

IF YOU GO Have a low-key drink before or after the show (or instead of the show entirely if you're on a budget) in the hotel's Bemelmans Bar, an urbane time capsule of an older New York with fine—if less famous— piano entertainment.

Campbell Apartment

SOPHISTICATED BAR/LOUNGE

15 Vanderbilt Avenue, entrance at Grand Central Station, Midtown East; ☎ 212-953-0409; www.hospitalityholdings.com

Cover None. **Minimum** None. **Mixed drinks** $10–$14. **Wine** Per glass, $7–$12 (champagne also available). **Beer** Bottled only, $6–$10. **Dress** Business, chic (smoking jacket and ivory-handled umbrellas not necessary). **Food available** No, just peanuts. **Hours** Monday–Saturday, 3 p.m.–1 a.m.; Sunday, 3–11 p.m.

WHO GOES THERE 20s–60s; commuters, after-work suits, the style-conscious.

WHAT GOES ON Drinking, socializing, and refined cruising.

SETTING AND ATMOSPHERE Apart from when the bar is buzzing with after-work socializing, the vibe is well suited for indulging in a vintage cocktail and admiring the scenery. Formerly an office/social area bought by a successful businessman in the terminal of Grand Central

Station (the station itself being an architectural marvel), the space features a beamed ceiling with intricate painted detail, a stone fireplace, and a huge multipaned lead-glass window behind the bar. It's worth visiting just to see the grand interior, even if you don't want a drink.

IF YOU GO   Unless you're commuting, try to arrive out with the rush hour, which would be either pre-5 p.m. or post-9 p.m. The timing will give you a better chance to find a seat and enjoy the décor as opposed to rubbing elbows or backs with dozens of standing patrons eager for a drink. Specialty cocktails include the Vanderbilt Punch and the Oxford Swizzle. The bar also encourages daydreams of putting on the ritz.

Carolines

COMEDY CLUB

1626 Broadway, Times Square; ☎ 212-757-4100; www.carolines.com

Cover $15–$40, depending on the act. Must be 18 or older to attend. Minimum Two drinks. Mixed drinks $5–$8. Wine $6–$8. Beer $4–$8. Dress Casual. Food available TGIFridays-type menu (with cutesy comedy-theme dish names) in the monstrously commercial upstairs Comedy Nation restaurant. Snack menu in the club. Hours Daily, 5:30 p.m.–until, shows at about 8 and 10:30 p.m. weekdays, 12:30 a.m. weekends. Show times vary by performance (call for info). Box office hours are Saturday through Wednesday, 10 a.m.–11 p.m.; Thursday and Friday, 9 a.m.–11 p.m.

WHO GOES THERE   21–60s; suburbanites on weekends, tourists and fans during the week.

WHAT GOES ON   With a location smack-dab in the middle of Times Square, Carolines 10:30 p.m. late set is a magnet for theatergoers insatiable for more entertainment. Like Broadway these days, the club relies on a steady diet of Big Names to pull in crowds, and this well-run operation—the most "upscale" of the big New York comedy clubs—gives them their money's worth.

SETTING AND ATMOSPHERE   Though the Comedy Nation restaurant at street level is an utterly soulless space (comedy insiders call it "Planet Ha-Ha-Hollywood"), the actual club area, downstairs, is a nice loungey hangout, a decent place for drinks even if you're not attending the show. The room doesn't have the mic-and-a-room pure minimalism of Gotham, but on entering it one feels that something exciting is about to occur—and with the top-flight talent booked here, it often does. Handicap accessible.

Chibitini

HIP SAKE BAR

63 Clinton Street (between Rivington and Stanton), Lower East Side; ☎ 212-674-7300; www.chibitini.com

Cover None. Minimum None. Mixed drinks $8–$10. Wine Not much selection but LOTS of sake, $7–$13 per glass. Bottles of sake range from $20–$105. Beer

Bottled only—seven to choose from, including Belgian, $4–$9. **Dress** Casual or cool. **Specials** None. **Food available** Light snacks, including sweet and savory dumplings, $9–$13. **Hours** Sunday and Tuesday–Thursday, 5 p.m.–midnight; Friday and Saturday, 5 p.m.–1 a.m. Closed on Mondays.

WHO GOES THERE 20s–50s; locals, hipsters, sake lovers (this brings the age up).
WHAT GOES ON Socializing and sake.
SETTING AND ATMOSPHERE Small and intimate place: six bar stools and padded benches along two walls with tables and chairs. Candles on each table, red-orange walls and a prominent photo of Chibi, the owner's French bulldog and the bar's namesake. Jazz or trippy electronica is usually playing in the background.
IF YOU GO This is the place to wise up on the sake scene by ordering a flight (a selection of three different sakes), either regular or deluxe at $15 or $20, respectively. It's a good way to try unfiltered sake, sake with an apple taste, and even a lightly sparkling sake. All sakes available here are served cold.

Club Macanudo

UPSCALE CIGAR AND WHISKY BAR

26 East 63rd Street, Upper East Side; ☎ 212-752-8200; www.clubmacanudonyc.com

Cover None. **Minimum** None. **Scotch** $9–$300. **Wine** Vintage/tawny ports $12–$40. **Beer** $9. **Dress** Jackets for men, no sneakers or jeans. **Food available** Overpriced; stick with appetizers/tapas. **Hours** Monday and Tuesday, 5 p.m.–12:30 a.m.; Wednesday–Saturday, 5 p.m.–1:30 a.m.; Sunday, closed.

WHO GOES THERE 30s–65; middle-aged suits, often stag but some towing either bored wives or trophy babes; some younger shmoozers.
WHAT GOES ON Some might expect that cigars and whisky are fun things to be enjoyed lightheartedly. These people will not dig Club Macanudo. This place takes itself seriously. If it all wasn't very very serious, people might not be inclined to fork over $800 a year to rent tiny personal humidors here (complete with a shiny brass nameplate), they might wince at the over-the-top chummy/clubby/woody interior, or they might even break a smile. But the scotch selection *is* pretty serious stuff—it's America's only bar serving rare bottlings from the Scotch Whisky Society—and the friendly bartenders (as devoted to scotch 'n' smoke as many regulars) are knowledgeable guides for neophytes. Go late enough that plenty of scotch has already been ingested, and you may strike up a stogie-based friendship with an exec who'd otherwise never take your calls. Varying genres of live music are featured.
SETTING AND ATMOSPHERE It's like being in an enormous cigar box (complete with wooden Indians) or spending time in an exclusive men's club.
IF YOU GO Don't worry too much about ordering the wrong thing; there are few dumb choices, drink- and cigar-wise. But do bone up on proper stogie cutting and lighting; do it wrong and you'll elicit gasps of horror.

Cornelia Street Café

INTIMATE PERFORMANCE CAFE

29 Cornelia Street (between Bleecker and West Fourth streets), Greenwich Village; ☎ 212-989-9319; www.corneliastreetcafe.com

Cover Only downstairs; varies from $5–$20. **Minimum** One drink per set. For food there is a $25 minimum for credit card use. **Mixed drinks** $6–$8. **Wine** $5–$9. **Beer** $4–$7. **Dress** Casual. **Food available** Yes, from snacks to full menu; $7–$18. **Hours** Daily; restaurant open from 10 a.m., but downstairs space usually open from 6 p.m. (unless there's an afternoon event); closes at 12:45 a.m.

WHO GOES THERE 20s–60s; regulars, the avant-garde.

WHAT GOES ON Listening, watching, and/or conversation.

SETTING AND ATMOSPHERE Although the cafe has several eating spaces, including sidewalk dining in fair weather, the profile focuses on the snug downstairs performance space, which feels a bit like a blue-tinged wine cellar. The narrow space allows for customers to sit at the long sides of the rectangular-shaped room. In spite of what seems like a miniscule stage, performers and five-plus person bands use it and entertain happy audiences.

IF YOU GO Have an objective to see or hear an interesting, potentially experimental, performance. The cafe has been in operation since 1977 and is very much a Greenwich Village institution, especially for artists and free thinkers. The restaurant offers breakfast through dinner and is especially popular for brunch. The downstairs space, which is often only open in the evenings, showcases events almost nightly. The cover is reasonable, and if the event isn't sold out and sounds appealing, give it a try.

DBA

MECCA FOR ULTRA-HIGH-QUALITY DRINKS

41 First Avenue, The East Village; ☎ 212-475-5097; www.drinkgoodstuff.com

Cover None. **Minimum** None. **Mixed drinks** $6.00 and up. **Wine** $7 by the glass. **Beer** $5–$25. **Dress** Casual but hip. **Specials** Happy hour every day, 1–7:30 p.m. ($1 off everything). **Food available** None. **Hours** Daily, 1 p.m.–4 a.m.

WHO GOES THERE 21–50; drink freaks, ranging from nerdy homebrewers to assured sybarites.

WHAT GOES ON No Schlitz here; rather, you'll find hand-pumped British (and British-style) ales, a whole bunch of taps (dated, so you can gauge freshness), and zillions of bottles. This is the only place in New York that serves properly poured ales and lagers at the proper temperature (never frigid, hand-pumps at cellar temperature) in the proper glasses, and there's a fine bourbon, scotch, and tequila collection as well. Servers have attitude, as do some of the customers.

SETTING AND ATMOSPHERE Low-lit, contemporary, and spare, this invariably crowded spot doesn't have much décor to distract the reverent drinking, but it's certainly far more refined than your average skanky beer hall. Nice garden out back, open only in warm weather.

IF YOU GO Not sure what to order? Ask advice from any of the beer geeks at the bar and you'll be guided by some of the city's most knowledgeable drinkers.

Excelsior Bar

SWISH, NEIGHBORHOOD GAY BAR

390 Fifth Avenue (between Sixth & Seventh streets), Brooklyn; ☎ 718-832-1599

Cover None. **Minimum** None. **Mixed drinks** $6–8. **Wine** $6–$7. **Beer** On tap and bottled. **Dress** Casual or cool. **Specials** Happy hour, Monday–Friday, 6–8 p.m.; Saturday and Sunday, 2–7 p.m. **Food available** None, but you may call for deliveries. **Hours** Monday–Friday, 6 p.m.–4 a.m; Saturday and Sunday, 2 p.m.–4 a.m.

WHO GOES THERE 20s–50s; locals, gay, straight, and hip.

WHAT GOES ON There's usually a good rapport at the bar—whether you're here for just a drink or to do some subtle cruising. From pretty boys to straight men and everything in between, all will enjoy themselves.

SETTING AND ATMOSPHERE Friendly, relaxed, and sophisticated cool atmosphere. Sleek décor that mixes pseudo-Mondrian-esque designs with 1970s tackiness. There's a lot of red and angular lines; overall the setting is crisp and clean. Old fans on the ceiling loom over clean wooden floors.

IF YOU GO Check out the jukebox, and after your selection has played, spend some time outside on the deck, or go downstairs into the garden and admire the two plastic pink flamingoes. You could also bar-hop to **Ginger's** across the street or get an order of tasty french fries at the **Chip Shop** (383 Fifth Avenue; ☎ 718-832-7701).

Flatiron Lounge

CHIC, SPECIALIST COCKTAILS

37 West 19th Street, Gramercy Park; ☎ 212-727-7741; www.flatironlounge.com

Cover None. **Minimum** None. **Mixed drinks** $8–$12. **Wine** $8–$12. **Beer** $8 but you don't come here for beer. **Dress** Chic or suited. **Specials** Downstairs room may be on offer for parties and special events. **Food available** Only free bar nibbles. **Hours** Sunday–Wednesday, 5 p.m.–2 a.m.; Thursday–Saturday, 5 p.m.–4 a.m.

WHO GOES THERE 20s–40s; cocktail connoisseurs, chic lounge-types mixed with business suits and professionals.

WHAT GOES ON Cocktail consumption, socializing, looking fantastic.

SETTING AND ATMOSPHERE Great setting that comes at a price for the drinks. The space is Art Deco inspired and designed, with an arched ceiling at the entrance, dark wood, and plush, private group banquettes along the wall, beside open tables and a 30-foot bar. The bar was renovated to its "original splendor" from its origin in the 1920s. There's a romantic quality to the place.

IF YOU GO Indulge in one or two of their special cocktails using some of their own infused spirits; alternatively, you could order a flight of cocktails ($18) that provides a selection and avoids excessive alcohol consumption. The mixologist prepares drinks such as a "Metropolis" that includes pearl vodka infused with green apples and finished with a touch of French apple brandy cider. A spiced pear drink is made with vodka infused with pear and cloves. Some drinks are prepared for certain seasons only.

Galapagos

BAR AND PERFORMANCE SPACE

70 North Sixth Street, Brooklyn; ☎ 718-782-5188; www.galapagosartspace.com

Cover Free, except back room performances, including music, theater, dance, and films (usually $5–$10). Minimum None. Mixed drinks $6–$9. Wine $6–$8. Beer $5–$8. Dress Grunge, casual, or simply cool. Specials Frequent special events; happy hour Monday–Saturday, 6–8 p.m. Food available None, but you may call for deliveries. Hours Sunday–Thursday, 6 p.m.–2 a.m.; Friday and Saturday, 6 p.m.–4 a.m.

WHO GOES THERE 20s–50s; locals, art set, hipsters.

WHAT GOES ON Galapagos is a solid reason to get out of Manhattan for an evening. It has won several awards of distinction for its performance space, its bar, and for being a top nightclub destination. These accolades are well-deserved. There's almost always something going on—whether it be a DJ, art installation, film, music, theater, or dance performance. You can go simply for a drink or to soak up a bit of culture, no pressure—it's all very laid-back and comfortable.

SETTING AND ATMOSPHERE Housed in an old mayonnaise factory, Galapagos suitably fills the lofty space. You'll either be taken aback or mesmerized by the expanse of water that meets you as you enter. An art piece usually hovers over the water. The water has been described as a "reflecting pool," but it's easy to get caught in the optical illusion tricking you to think that the water is bottomless. Lighting is dimmed and full of candles and colored lights. For those not wanting beer, the bartender makes a good vodka lemondrop. High tables and stools are close to a stage in the main space, and a few lower tables are arranged by the reflecting pool. The back room has several theater-style seats in the back and round tables near the stage. Although the music may be loud in back, the front room usually is quiet enough for conversation.

IF YOU GO Have a drink in the main space and then take a peek in the back room to see if the scheduled event strikes your fancy. The lovely and simple women's restrooms are candlelit, fragranced with fresh flowers, and have stalls hidden only by white muslin curtains. North Sixth Street has several bars, and Bedford Avenue is a nightlife hotbed; combine your visit to Galapagos with an exploration of Williamsburg.

The Ginger Man

GIANT-SIZED BEER BAR

**11 East 36th Street, Gramercy Park; ☎ 212-532-3740;
www.gingerman-ny.com**

Cover None. **Minimum** None. **Mixed drinks** $7 and up. **Wine** $5–$12. **Beer** $4.75–$10. **Dress** Casual. **Food available** Salads, soup, sandwiches, and Guinness Stout stew. **Hours** Monday–Wednesday, 11:30 a.m.–2 a.m.; Thursday–Friday, 11:30 a.m.–4 a.m.; Saturday, 12:30 p.m.–4 a.m.; Sunday, 3 p.m.–midnight.

WHO GOES THERE 21–60; throngs of businessmen and yuppies after work, varied at other times.

WHAT GOES ON On paper, this is New York's best beer hall. It boasts a mind-boggling 60 taps, nearly all well chosen; decent Guinness stew to eat; friendly bartenders; and a comfy living room in the back. Prices are fair, and this is a late hang in an early-closing nabe. But there are problems: The beer's too cold (fine for light lagers, but some of the fancier British and Belgian ales turn flavorless at ballpark temperature), and peak hours—5:30 to 10 p.m. and all night on weekends—can be a crowded hell of noise, so time your visit carefully. Off-peak times you can order your beer in peace.

SETTING AND ATMOSPHERE The huge, high-ceilinged space is classic New York, dominated by a mile-long bar and copper-plated Wall o' Taps. There are tables up front by the floor-to-ceiling windows and a relaxing parlor in back with sofas and armchairs.

IF YOU GO Mid-afternoons and late weeknights you'll have the place largely to yourself; bring 20 or 30 friends, no problem!

Ginger's

FRIENDLY GAY BAR

**363 Fifth Avenue (between Fifth and Sixth streets), Brooklyn;
☎ 718-788-0924**

Cover None. **Minimum** None. **Mixed drinks** $6–$9. **Wine** $6. **Beer** $4–$7. **Dress** Anything goes. **Specials** Monthly drink specials. **Food available** None. **Hours** Monday–Friday, 6 p.m.–4 a.m.; Friday and Saturday, 2 p.m.–4 a.m.

WHO GOES THERE 20s–70s; locals, gay, straight; truly diverse crowd.

WHAT GOES ON This is a great neighborhood bar, embracing all kinds. Lesbians are especially welcome. Amenities include a pool table, an outdoor garden, and the jukebox. Many have hailed the jukebox as being quite varied, but it sometimes plays a little too much Melissa Etheridge. Camaraderie is rampant, and you needn't sip your drink alone for long.

SETTING AND ATMOSPHERE The front part of the space is narrow with the bar spanning one side. This is a very lively area and tends to get noisy and crowded quickly. The regulars know each other and it's a good place to people-watch. The back room is more spacious and conducive to a quieter conversation—unless there's a dispute at the pool table. Ginger's is packed with knickknacks on the walls and loads of black-and-white photos. It's an incredibly cozy and homey space. The bar staff are very friendly and pour a good pint.

IF YOU GO Consider playing pool in the back room–but beware that some of the ladies take their game very seriously. When it's warm, you can enjoy the outdoor garden.

Hudson Bar

CHIC HOTEL BAR

356 West 58th Street; ☎ 212-554-6500; www.hudsonhotel.com

Cover None. Minimum None. Mixed drinks $10–$15. Wine Bottles $50 and up; $7–$15 by the glass; cognac $9–$35 by the glass. Beer $6–$7. Dress Casual dressy to ultra-chic or interestingly different; black always works. Specials None. Food available None, but hotel has restaurant and other food options. Hours Sunday–Thursday, 4 p.m.–2 a.m.; Friday and Saturday, 4 p.m.–3 a.m.

WHO GOES THERE 22–50; the beautiful, the trendy (and wannabes), and those interested in modern architecture.

WHAT GOES ON This is a great place to go on an expense account, expensive date, or out for some extravagant fun. The Hudson Bar oozes cool and style, and it still manages to offer a genuinely friendly staff. The DJ nights aren't particularly stunning–many prefer the CDs pumped through the speakers on other evenings.

SETTING AND ATMOSPHERE Expectations are high when you enter an Ian Schrager hotel, and you won't be disappointed with the Hudson. Subtlety is key from the sidewalk until you enter through the glass doors and proceed up the chartreuse-hued, illuminated escalators. Once off the escalators, turn around and walk up a few stairs to the Hudson Bar. Before the stairs there are a few tables in hidden corners with low light. Up the stairs you're met with a long bar and a vast floor comprised of large, illuminated square tiles. There's plenty of space–one wall has pillowed banquettes with clear tables and a mixture of faux-period and ultra-modern, clear-plastic high-backed chairs. The ceiling isn't too high, but you won't mind as you sip a strawbellini (strawberry puree and champagne) and gaze at the dozens of candles throughout the room; your eyes may even happen upon a famous face.

IF YOU GO Don't go if you're having a bad hair day. Also visit the Hudson Private Park Bar–a beautifully decorated outdoor bar which can be viewed through the lobby. This bar is open Monday–Friday, 7:30 a.m.– 1 a.m. and Saturday and Sunday, 8:30 a.m.–1 a.m.; the bar is closed during colder months. It has incredibly comfy chairs and love seats; you could easily become addicted to the atmosphere. Coffee and food available. During the winter you could also try the Hudson Library Bar, which is wood-paneled and cozy but not particularly chic.

Joe's Pub

NIGHTCLUB

**425 Lafayette Street, The East Village; ☎ 212-539-8770
(x778 for reservations, x454 for show schedule); www.joespub.com**

Cover $10–$35 (call to check). **Minimum** Usually two drinks or $12 food minimum (call to check). **Mixed drinks** $9–$12. **Wine** $10 and up. **Beer** $5–$9. **Dress** Elegant on cabaret nights, elegantly sexy on dance nights. **Specials** Pretheater prix-fixe dinner, 6–7:30 p.m. **Food available** Full menu until midnight. **Hours** Daily, 6 p.m.–4 a.m.; shows usually start around 8 and/or 11:30 p.m.

WHO GOES THERE A smart, chic set (younger later).

WHAT GOES ON Lots of cabaret (the more theatrical style, à la Ute Lemper—this is no piano bar). Also some rock-ish (Ricki Lee Jones has played here), jazz-ish, and well-chosen alternative bands (with music kept at a reasonable volume). Late Wednesday nights are a high point, with dancing to hot live salsa bands; likewise Tuesdays for reggae. Cabaret attracts a mixed audience, late and dance nights an especially attractive crowd. The name is a joke—"Joe" is Joseph Papp, the highly respected director of the Public Theater, and this certainly is no mere pub . . . though it makes a good pun.

SETTING AND ATMOSPHERE Carpeted with high ceilings, French windows, and softly glowing lamps. Highly atmospheric (where are the fog machines?) and very dramatic (not surprising, given their locale inside the Public Theater), Joe's Pub feels like a 1930s musical set—Marlene Dietrich would fit in well here. Yet it's not at all kitsch or contrived; it's just a great dark, sexy transportive place to dance, drink, or listen to music.

IF YOU GO Reserve tickets ahead of time. And don't forget to mix your low culture with some high culture by enjoying a film or theater performance in the Public Theater.

Kavehaz

GALLERY AND JAZZ CAFE

37 West 26th Street, Chelsea; ☎ 212-343-0612; www.kavehaz.com

Cover None. **Minimum** Two-drink minimum except at the bar. **Mixed drinks** $6–$10. **Wine** Bottles $20 and up, big selection; $6–$8 by the glass. **Beer** Five beers on tap as well as bottled; $5–$8. **Dress** Casual to chic. **Specials** Each night hosts at least one band. **Food available** Full menu, including salads, pastas, sandwiches, and tasty desserts; served until half-hour before closing. **Hours** Daily, noon–2 a.m.

WHO GOES THERE 22–90; locals, artsy folk, jazz- and blues-minded people.

WHAT GOES ON Each visit to the Kavehaz is a little different, since the artwork on the walls changes every month, and the featured bands change nightly. Daytime finds the Kavehaz mellow and somewhat sophisticated, and by night it becomes more sultry as a jazz cafe. Wednesday nights are especially busy due to performances by the Ray Vega Latin Jazz band; Vega used to play with Tito Puente. Monday nights feature a singer's showcase.

SETTING AND ATMOSPHERE   Formerly located in Soho, the new Kavehaz has pretty much the same vibe, but the space is a little smaller. The artwork often dictates the mood. Photographs tend to make the scene seem sophisticated, while the paintings give the space a very avant-garde feel. The ambience in the evening is subdued with candlelight. Above all, the service is friendly, and the atmosphere is more focused on a cafe-style relaxed vibe—it's never pretentious and is usually enjoyable.

IF YOU GO   Try one of the featured wines by the glass. If you decide to teetotal and simply absorb the atmosphere, have a cappuccino, served in a bowl.

The Knitting Factory

(VERY) ALTERNATIVE MUSIC CLUB

74 Leonard Street, Tribeca; ☎ 212-219-3055; www.knittingfactory.com

Cover Varies by show. **Minimum** None. **Mixed drinks** $5 and up. **Wine** $5 and up. **Beer** $4 and up. **Dress** Black T-shirts and black jeans always work. **Specials** Happy hour, 5–7 p.m., free live music in downstairs bar every night from 11 p.m. until late. **Food available** None. **Hours** Vary, call for info.

WHO GOES THERE   21–45; varies with the music, black-clad hipsters to shaved heads and multiple piercings; a broad age range for the less rock-ish groups.

WHAT GOES ON   A world-famous venue for alternative music and klezmer to thrash. Some of the jazzier and more intellectual performers have switched their allegiance to upstart **Tonic** (see profile) across town, but this is still a mecca for those open-minded enough to listen to "free" jazz, traditional Hanukkah melodies deconstructed by punk groups, or tuba quartets covering Jimi Hendrix. The staff has tons of attitude.

SETTING AND ATMOSPHERE   A nice mellow bar at street level, large two-level performance space within (very European), and a tiny Alterknit Room presenting groups of still narrower appeal. The old office's downstairs bar is dark, atmospheric, and quite the destination on late nights when hipper-than-hip bands set up there.

IF YOU GO   Check your e-mail or surf the web for free at the club's Internet connection in the main corridor. Try and see what's happening on every level of the space.

Kush

FUNKY, MOROCCAN-THEMED BAR WITH VARIED ENTERTAINMENT

191 Chrystie Street (between Stanton and Rivington streets), Lower East Side; ☎ 212-677-7328 www.kushlounge.com

Cover None. **Minimum** None. **Mixed drinks** $8–$14. **Wine** Not big selection, but has Lebanese wine, $8. **Beer** Bottles $5–$10. **Dress** Casual hip. **Food available** Middle Eastern snacks, including fresh mint tea. **Hours** Monday–Friday, 5 p.m.–4 a.m.; Saturday, 7 p.m.–4 a.m.; Sunday, 9 p.m.–4 a.m.

WHO GOES THERE   20s–40s; locals, hipsters, smokers, and those interested in world music, international DJs, and belly-dancing.

WHAT GOES ON Live, DJ, or "organic electronic" music played each night. Kush offers interesting entertainment, including belly-dancing, world-class DJs, percussion, and Bulgarian harmonics. This is one of the few places where smoking (albeit hookahs) is permitted.

SETTING AND ATMOSPHERE Since moving a few blocks away, Kush has maintained its essential funky vibe, but it has gone a bit upscale and has: (shock, horror) a velvet rope outside. Luckily, the rope isn't very hard to pass, so it may be in place to keep an eye on capacity. The same Moroccan feel pervades, with dark lighting and Moorish touches. The space is bigger than before with a front and back bar and a central space that gets roped off for special events. All sections are connected by narrow passages.

IF YOU GO Make sure you catch some of the entertainment, and if you are inclined to smoke, rent a hookah with a choice of specially flavored tobaccos for $18 (inhaling not required).

Lava Gina

OFFBEAT MUSIC AND DRINK BAR

116 Avenue C (between Seventh and Eighth streets), The East Village; ☎ 212-477-9319; www.lavagina.com

Cover Not usually. Minimum None. Mixed drinks $7–$10. Wine By the glass $6.50–$10; bottles from $24. Beer Bottled only $6–$10. Dress Casual, cool, or funky. Specials Happy Hour drink specials Monday–Thursday all night; Friday until 10 p.m. Food available Yes, tapas selection $6–$8. Hours Monday–Saturday, 6:30 p.m.–4 a.m.

WHO GOES THERE 20s–40s; locals, world music DJ junkies; varied.

WHAT GOES ON Sipping, socializing, and music appreciation.

SETTING AND ATMOSPHERE Unless one is averse to genitalia nuance, the distinct v-shaped bar and overwhelming red hues in the room create a welcoming and positive vibe. Wooden African sculptures adorn the walls, as do velvet curtains by the windows. Although there's no grit, there's no cookie-cutter look for the clientele either. DJs spin nightly in the far corner, beyond the V. A medium-sized space, which makes the V-bar a definitive centerpiece.

IF YOU GO Don't be put off by the name. The eclectic music choices (modern world sounds, including material from Asia, the Middle East, Eastern Europe, South America, and Africa) are deftly spun, and sometimes features live music. Bartenders aren't warm, but they are certainly efficient. Specialty cocktails include the spicy Lavapolitan and the Giant Gina, which is a nod toward a communal drink-fest for close company, as it's 48 ounces of martini and costs $65.

Lenox Room

WELL-HEELED LOUNGE AND RESTAURANT

1278 Third Avenue, Upper East Side; ☎ 212-772-0404; www.lenoxroom.com

Cover None. Minimum None. Mixed drinks $10–$13. Wine $7–$9 per glass; good bottle selection, $25 and up. Beer Bottled only $6–$8. Dress Relaxed business casual. **Food available** Wide selection, including raw bar, salads, and burgers, $8–$18; also three-plate tastes for $24–$27. **Hours** Monday and Tuesday, 5 p.m.–2:30 a.m.; Wednesday–Saturday, 5 p.m.–3 a.m.; Sunday, 5 p.m.–2 a.m. Note that these hours are for the lounge and not the restaurant. Food is available until 11 p.m. daily.

WHO GOES THERE 20s–60s; locals, lounge lizards.

WHAT GOES ON Refined lounging, cocktails, nibbles, and socializing.

SETTING AND ATMOSPHERE The space is fairly large, although most of it is dedicated to the restaurant. The lounge area offers simple dark wooden tables with plush, upholstered modernist-style chairs and padded banquettes. Reds and browns are the dominant colors, which add to the lounge feel. Sidewalk dining/drinking available in warm weather.

IF YOU GO Avoid looking scruffy. If you're confident in your outfit, then the vibe is fairly relaxed, and you can enjoy the well-mixed cocktails in style. Some of the lounge favorites are a sake julep, a velvet rosa (white rum, peach schnapps, cranberry juice), and a mandatory (Absolut mandarin, mandarin puree, tangerine juice, and vanilla). The food is well presented, high-quality, and flavorful.

Mercury Lounge

ROCK SHOWCASE

217 East Houston Street, The East Village; ☎ 212-260-4700; www.mercuryloungenyc.com

Cover $8–$22. **Minimum** None. **Mixed drinks** $5.50–$7. **Wine** $5. **Beer** $5. **Dress** Black and hip. **Food available** None. **Hours** Sunday–Wednesday, 7 p.m.–2 a.m.; Thursday– Saturday, 7 p.m.–4 a.m.

WHO GOES THERE 21–40; serious music fans, bohemian Lower East Side clubbers, some grunge.

WHAT GOES ON A showcase for newly signed (and hot about-to-be-signed) rock bands with an excellent sound system. The performance space is perfect for listening to an eclectic mix of groups, from surprisingly big names (playing here to maintain their hip credentials) to up-and-comers and cult favorites. If you've never heard of a band playing here, you probably will soon.

SETTING AND ATMOSPHERE You enter through a mysterious-looking black bar with black curtains, and the music's through a door in the back. It's basically a box of a room, but exposed brick and great sound (blessedly, never head-bangingly loud) and lighting create an ambience that feels right.

IF YOU GO Walk down nearby Ludlow Street after the show to explore some cafes, music clubs, and late-night shops.

Mo Pitkin's House of Satisfaction

BAR WITH JUDEO-LATINO RESTAURANT AND CABARET

34 Avenue A (between Second and Third streets), The East Village; ☎ 212-777-5660; www.mopitkins.com

Cover Only for cabaret space; tickets range from $5–$15. **Minimum** None. **Mixed**

drinks $7–$19. **Wine** Glass of sangria, $7. **Beer** Bottles and tap, $3–$6. **Dress** Casual and/or comfortable. **Specials** Early 2-for-1 drink specials for those who can prove local residency. **Food available** Yes, snacks to full menu, $8–$24. **Hours** Bar open daily, 5 p.m.–4 a.m.; cabaret open a half hour before shows.

WHO GOES THERE A truly mixed crowd; those in need of comfort food and cabaret.

WHAT GOES ON What doesn't go on in this two-level space offering a restaurant and bar. Check out Sadie's Hideaway either for private functions or a relaxed drink, and the cabaret area accommodates 65 seats. Mo's is a recent addition to the East Village, but it already features an impressive selection of talent ranging from comedy troupes, lectures, readings, singers, and bands.

SETTING AND ATMOSPHERE The cabaret space up the stairs (Upstairs at Mo's) is wonderfully old-school cabaret/comedy style with brick walls, an only slightly elevated small stage with obligatory upright piano, and straight rows of tables for the audience. The bar downstairs is casual, and the restaurant has chairs and banquettes perfect for wallowing in after a huge meal.

IF YOU GO Save some room to sample some food (fried macaroni and cheese, ceviche, or matzo ball soup) or try a novelty cocktail. It is unlikely you'll find another place in NYC that serves a cocktail with the infamous sweet kosher Passover wine known as Manischevitz—Mo's calls it a Manischevetini, and apart from a splash of its namesake, it contains vodka and fresh orange juice.

O'Flaherty's Ale House

IRISH PUB AFTER-SHOW HIDEAWAY

334 West 46th Street, Theater District; ☎ 212-581-9366; www.oflahertysnyc.com

Cover None. **Minimum** One drink. **Mixed drinks** $4.50–$5. **Wine** $4.50. **Beer** $4–$4.50. **Dress** Anything from suit and tie to jeans and T-shirt. **Food available** Surprisingly extensive Irish menu (shepherd's pie in several incarnations, stews, fried stuff). **Hours** Daily, noon–4 a.m. Happy hour daily, 4–7 p.m. with $3 pints, $3 champagne, and $3 warm cocktails.

WHO GOES THERE 25–55; locals and tourists until the 11 p.m. influx of the after-theater crowd (many actors and musicians).

WHAT GOES ON The beer's not super, but one of the selections is an interesting house-brewed honey lager. This is a great spot because among the windy passageways and copious alcoves there's an ambience to please almost anyone. The energy level picks up as theater people stop by for an after-work drink, and much of the crowd stays late. Part of the draw are the old-fashioned Irish bartenders, probably hired as much for their brogues as for their gregariousness. Live music daily from 10:30 p.m.–2:30 a.m.

SETTING AND ATMOSPHERE Choose your surroundings: a book-filled study in the back with comfortable chairs and a pool table; a front corner of couches (great for groups); a handsome wraparound bar with adjoining dart board; an outdoor garden with antique-style park benches. There's a nook or cranny for any occasion. It's all alcoves; there's no "main section" to speak of.

IF YOU GO If you're looking for a livelier time on this same block, see the profile for **Swing 46,** a jive-talking swing-dancing nightspot.

Pen-top Bar and Terrace at the Peninsula Hotel

ROOFTOP HOTEL BAR

700 Fifth Avenue (at 55th Street), Midtown East; ☎ 212-247-2200; www.peninsula.com

Cover None. Minimum None. Mixed drinks $10–$15. Wine $15 and up, by the glass. Beer $10 and up. Dress Sophisticated and expensive. Food available Small selection of upscale snacks like smoked salmon, cheese platter, and shrimp; good freebie bar snacks come with drinks. Hours Monday–Thursday, 5 p.m.–midnight; Friday and Saturday, 5 p.m.–1 a.m.; closed Sunday.

WHO GOES THERE 30–65; after-workers, trystin' smoochers, one-last-drinkers.

WHAT GOES ON There are higher bars with more breathtaking views, but the great thing about this 23rd-floor perch is that you see Manhattan not from the bottom or top but from the middle. You're surrounded by the top thirds of buildings (like the beautiful St. Regis Hotel across the street), an odd and striking geometric landscape cluttering the nighttime sky. It's a dramatic setting for an outdoor drink in good weather, and the indoor bar is hyper-romantic when it snows. Friendly, professional service.

SETTING AND ATMOSPHERE A romantic little bar surrounded by three outdoor spaces, each with its own great view: a large spillover area (full after work) with plastic tables and chairs; a standing-only balcony with a view up Fifth Avenue (good for cooing couples); and an elegant green carpeted rectangle with comfortable chairs and flickering lamps.

IF YOU GO Go on the late side; from 5 to 7 p.m. the office crowd takes over. The bar's essentially hidden: take the elevator to the top floor, then ascend the dramatic glassed-in circular staircase.

PJ Clarke's

OLD-TIME NEW YORK BAR

915 Third Avenue, Midtown East; ☎ 212-317-1616; www.pjclarkes.com

Cover None. Minimum None. Mixed drinks $7 and up. Wine $6–$8. Beer $4–$8. Dress Anything. Specials None. Food available Raw bar plus full menu, including burgers, fries, salads, chicken, steak, desserts. Hours Daily, 11:30 a.m.–4 a.m. (dining room closes at 3 a.m.).

WHO GOES THERE Businessmen after work, extremely varied later.

WHAT GOES ON A real New York legend, and one of the only old-time bars that hasn't turned cloyingly self-conscious. PJ's is a magnet for advertising people after work, but later the crowd turns amazingly diverse, from tourists to hard-boiled old guys to corporate moguls to Ratso

Rizzo, with lots of interaction. A great jukebox plays well-chosen show tunes, swing, and rock.

SETTING AND ATMOSPHERE   "Renovation" was a dirty word for the regulars, but after a year's closure, the place looks surprisingly similar, except with stronger floorboards and an upstairs bar/dining room. Luckily, this single skinny little brick building has stubbornly remained. The atmosphere inside is so authentically old New York it's practically gas-lit. There's an oversized wooden bar; big foggy mirrors plastered with photos of presidents, Irishmen, and deceased bartenders; and smoke-filled dining rooms where meals are served on tables with red-checkered tablecloths.

IF YOU GO   Check out the antique men's urinals—tourist attractions in their own right. On the subject, other notable restrooms are the unisex see-through (until you close the latch) stalls at **Bar 89** and the stalls at **SEA** (see dining profile).

Remote Lounge

VOYEUR THEME BAR

327 Bowery (between Second and Third streets), The East Village;
☎ **212-228-0228; www.remotelounge.com**

Cover Monday–Thursday, $5; Friday and Sunday, $10; Saturday, $10–20. **Minimum** None. **Mixed drinks** $10–$12. **Wine** Not advisable. **Beer** $5–$8. **Dress** Casual or cool. **Specials** Sometimes between 10 p.m.–midnight. **Food available** Yes. **Hours** Daily, 6 p.m.–4 a.m. (check ahead to ensure won't be closed for private parties).

WHO GOES THERE   20-somethings, singles, and the techie curious.

WHAT GOES ON   Voyeurism, scoping, drinking, self-promotion.

SETTING AND ATMOSPHERE   At first glance, you might think you're in a 1960s-style internet cafe, as the equipment and seating looks as though it all came straight off a *Star Trek* shoot. The bar is full of 'cocktail consoles' that allow patrons to scan remote-controlled cameras around the room, using joysticks, to find an object either of desire or derision. If you wish to make your opinions known, you can call another console with a handset. The bar has multiple screens overhead that display random camera feeds within the room.

IF YOU GO   Check your inhibitions at the door and use the technology. First-timers almost always appreciate the novelty of the consoles, but the only way to keep the customers returning is to feature theme nights, special DJs, and/or abstract art and colors on the plasma screens. If there's not a lot of extra stimuli, then the consoles can get tiring quickly. There are a few video games to play as well.

Rodeo Bar

COWBOY BAR WITH HIGH-QUALITY ECLECTIC LIVE MUSIC

375 Third Avenue, Gramercy Park; ☎ **212-683-6500; www.rodeobar.com**

Cover None. **Minimum** None. **Mixed drinks** $5–$11. **Wine** $4. **Beer** $4–$5. **Dress** Jeans and whatever. **Specials** Happy hour, 4–7 p.m. weekdays. **Food available**

Tex-Mex (full meals or bar munchies). **Hours** Monday–Saturday, 11:30 a.m.–4 a.m.; Sunday, 11:30 a.m.–2 a.m. Shows start at 10 p.m. nightly.

WHO GOES THERE Aging hippies, urban cowboys, music fans.

WHAT GOES ON Rodeo Bar isn't taken terribly seriously by New York music scene cognoscenti, but it offers something extremely rare: good bar bands in regular rotation. Styles range from electric to rockabilly to country rock, but the musical sensibility is always more New York hip than the saddles 'n' barrels décor would suggest; even the most country acts are *funky* country. The same bands play regularly, building audience and repertoire and honing skills. As a result, performances here are more polished than at nearly any other club in town, and there are loyal fans who come here first when they want to drink a beer and hear some dependably solid tunes without dropping dozens of dollars.

SETTING AND ATMOSPHERE So Wild West that you half expect Calamity Jane to come whooping past the bar; this place is tricked out with barrels, stirrups, rope-handle door knobs, peanut shells, the works. Someone was decorating for a square dance, but thank goodness the music's much hipper than Cowboy Bob. A huge bull stares inquisitively at the performers from the side of the stage. Yee-haw.

IF YOU GO If the cow-punching vibe is too much for you, cross over to the adjoining restaurant next door for a quick city fix.

Sakagura

HIDDEN SUAVE SAKE BAR

211 East 43rd Street, Midtown East; ☎ 212-953-SAKE; www.sakagura.com

Cover None. **Minimum** $10. **Mixed drinks** $7–$15. **Wine** $4–$25 for sake. 200 kinds of sake imported from Japan. **Beer** $5–$8 (Japanese only). **Dress** Most people in jackets, but nice casual will do. **Food available** Excellent simple Japanese dishes like udon (noodle soup) and kinpira (marinated burdock root). **Hours** Monday–Thursday, noon–1 a.m.; Friday, noon–2 a.m.; Saturday 6 p.m.–2 a.m.; Sunday, 6 p.m.–midnight.

WHO GOES THERE 30–55; Japanese businessmen, sake aficionados.

WHAT GOES ON A treasure trove of sakes, plain, pricey, and odd. The drier sakes are usually the most interesting, and those who find sake an overly subtle drink should try nama zake, which has a much wider flavor of considerable complexity. If you can afford them, the aged koshu sakes (a particularly good one is kamo izumi koshu, for $15 a glass) have the length and complexity of great wine. Don't make the faux pas of ordering your rice wine hot; the good stuff is drunk cold or at room temperature (very dry ones can be warmed a little). A couple of options: You can choose to sip from a masu (wooden box) rather than a cup, or a hire (nontoxic blowfish fin) can be added to impart a mellow, smoky flavor.

SETTING AND ATMOSPHERE Enter through a glarey office building lobby, walk back toward the elevators, and descend a dank staircase to get to this supremely inviting inner sanctum that's all sleek lines and open space. There are some secluded tables, but there's lots more action at the big handsome bar. It's sexy and peaceful, rarely crowded. Restrooms are hidden inside huge round wooden fermenting barrels.

IF YOU GO Try to talk your way into the odd private karaoke club; the door is just to your left as you enter the building's lobby.

Smalls

JAZZ CLUB FOR COOL CATS

183 West Tenth Street, Greenwich Village; ☎ 212-675-7369; www.fatcatjazz.com

Cover $10–$15. Minimum Two drinks. Mixed drinks $5–$9. Wine $5–$8. Beer $4–$6. Dress Casual. Specials One cover charge allows you to go to Smalls and sister club Fat Cat (75 Christopher Street). Food available Snacks. Hours Daily, 10 p.m.–5 a.m.; note that early shows on weekends start at 8 p.m.

WHO GOES THERE 21 and up; jazz aficionados, insomniacs, music students.

WHAT GOES ON Jamming, jazz, and listening. Each night highlights a different set of musicians.

SETTING AND ATMOSPHERE Smalls is back after having been closed for over a year, and the vibe is very much the same as it used to be although the renovations have made space for a full-bar service. Walk down a set of stairs and enter an intimate mecca of avant-garde and free jazz. In spite of the new bar, the focus is on the small stage, and stools and chairs are provided.

IF YOU GO Don't expect mainstream jazz. Old regulars are delighted at the resurrection, and newcomers are likely to get hooked on the caliber of musicians. For those who want to attend a jam session, you'll need to go to the affiliated **Fat Cat** jazz club (see above) at 1:30 a.m.

Smoke

JAZZ CLUB AND LOUNGE

2751 Broadway (between 105th and 106th streets), Upper West Side; ☎ 212-864-6662; www.smokejazz.com

Cover Varies, usually $10, but no cover Tuesday–Thursday, 5–8 p.m. Minimum Varies; sometimes a $10 "cover" is good for two drinks, sometimes it's separate. Mixed drinks $6–$7. Wine $6–$8. Beer Bottled and draft, $5–$6. Dress Casual; lounge and/or accessorize with instrument, sheet music, or drum sticks. Specials "Retro Happy Hour," Monday–Saturday 5–8 p.m.; $2 pints of cider and $4 apple martinis. Food available None, but you're welcome to order in. Hours Monday–Saturday, 5 p.m.–4 a.m.; Sunday 5 p.m.–2:30 a.m.

WHO GOES THERE All ages; jazz lovers, musicians, and any other affiliates.

WHAT GOES ON There's music every night of the week, most of it incredibly good. Smoke takes over from where the former Augie's Jazz Bar left off, so a great music tradition continues in this renovated space. You'll never know who'll be in the crowd listening or who'll come to the stage for a jam set, so no visit is ever the same.

PART ELEVEN ENTERTAINMENT AND NIGHTLIFE

SETTING AND ATMOSPHERE An intimate, warm, relaxed setting for some great music; space can get tight since there's only seating for 70, but the overflow crowds at the bar, and everyone gets a decent view. There's a real jazz-club ambience, with bar and lounge area complete with small octagonal tables, plush sofa and chairs, dark wood, red velvet curtains, candle sconces, and a few low-hanging, unobtrusive chandeliers; the only missing accoutrement is the club's namesake (eliminated by the smoking ban). Musicians and listeners alike praise the sound system; performances, including jam sessions, are given due respect and attention.

IF YOU GO Be prepared to listen, relax, and perhaps even be inspired.

S.O.B.'s

LATIN AND WORLD MUSIC/DANCE NIGHTCLUB

204 Varick Street, Soho; ☎ 212-243-4940; www.sobs.com

Cover Varies ($10–$25, more or less). Minimum $10 at tables. Mixed drinks $9–$10. Wine $7–$8 per glass; $19–$350 per bottle. Beer $5–$7. Dress Colorful and flashy. Specials Free entrance Fridays before 7 p.m., Tuesday before 9 p.m.; free salsa dance lessons Monday, 7–8:30 p.m. (stay free for the show). Food available Pretty good overpriced Pan-Latino and Brazilian dishes. Hours Monday–Saturday, 6:30 p.m.–4 a.m. (closed Sunday in fall and winter); music usually starts after 9 p.m.

WHO GOES THERE 21–40; music fans, salsa dancers, ethnic music trollers like David Byrne.

WHAT GOES ON This is a fun enough club just for hanging out and listening, but for those who like to dance, it's one of the best parties in town. Monday nights smoke with famous salsa groups (the dance class will get your hips up to speed); other nights feature music from Brazilian to reggae—anything funky and tropical. The bands are tops in their genres; this is a great place for world music neophytes to familiarize themselves with different styles. It's more nightclub than disco; bands are listened to as much as danced to, and even unaccompanied women feel "safe" on the dance floor.

SETTING AND ATMOSPHERE Large stage with sunken dance floor; the bar faces the stage, but visibility is bad in crowds. There are tables to the side of the stage. Bright and colorful, with lots of tropical touches.

IF YOU GO Bear in mind that things can get crowded; meet the $15 minimum by ordering a bottle from the surprisingly good wine list. FYI, S.O.B.'s stands for "Sounds of Brazil."

Swing 46

SWING DANCE CLUB

349 West 46th Street, Midtown West; ☎ 212-262-9554; www.swing46.com

Cover $5–$15. Minimum Two drinks at tables. Mixed drinks $6–$10. Wine $6–$8. Beer $5–$7. Dress Anything goes; dancers dress up. Specials Free dance lessons every night after first set. Food available Expensive dinners plus reasonably priced snacks (burgers, etc.). Hours Daily, 5 p.m.–2 a.m.

WHO GOES THERE 25–90; swing-dance aficionados old and young, cool barflies.

WHAT GOES ON Live music seven nights a week; big bands and combos playing swing. Lindy hoppers and jitterbugs are as hot as the music, and the place bristles with energy even on weeknights. The bar is as cool as the dance floor is hot, populated by older swing fans who prefer to sit and take it all in without getting personally involved. If you can overlook all the silly hepcat daddy-o spiel, it's all a pretty wild good time (neophyte dancers will not feel uncomfortable). Tap jam on Sunday.

SETTING AND ATMOSPHERE The bar's up front, cut off from the frenzied action further inside, but the bands can be clearly heard. The dance/nightclub room, framed with beige paneling, has a low ceiling and is close but not overly so. Tables have flickering candle lamps, and the dance floor is right up next to the band. An outdoor sunken terrace in front of the club is filled with tables in summer.

IF YOU GO Restaurant Row is actually a better block for bars than for restaurants. On this same street, check out **O'Flaherty's Ale House** (see profile).

Tonic

QUALITY ALTERNATIVE MUSIC CLUB

107 Norfolk Street, Lower East Side; ☎ 212-358-7501; www.tonicnyc.com

Cover $10 and up. Minimum One drink minimum with some shows. Mixed drinks $5–$8. Wine $5. Beer $5. Dress In black. Specials None. Food available Limited; sandwiches, desserts, soup at bar. Hours Show times vary; call. Box office opens at 7:30 p.m.

WHO GOES THERE Intellectual music fans and scenesters.

WHAT GOES ON The **Knitting Factory** (see profile) is still the best-known name in the city's avant-garde music scene, but it has lost a good deal of its creative edge. Tonic now plays host to many of the Knit's former performers and draws many of the new music scene's most cutting-edge bands. Programming runs the gamut, from semi-acoustic jazz to klezmer to "free" jazz to that hard-to-categorize point where many diverse styles meet.

SETTING AND ATMOSPHERE An arty narrow space with high ceilings, rough semipainted concrete, red velvet curtains, and red scrimlights. A small bookstore near the entrance sells 'zines and books on subjects you never knew existed. Sound is good; staff is friendly.

IF YOU GO Have a drink afterward at **DBA** (see profile), take a walk down nearby Ludlow Street (lots of bars, cafes, shops, and music), or catch some less-challenging East Village music (see the "Alternative Rock" section in this chapter's introduction). Visit the downstairs space, Subtonic, to see DJs spin in a trippy dimension—oftentimes way off the map.

Top of the Tower

3 Mitchell Place at 49th Street and First Avenue (Beekman Tower Hotel), Midtown East; ☎ 212-980-4796; www.topofthetowernyc.com

Cover None. **Minimum** None. **Mixed drinks** $7–$14. **Wine** By the glass, $7–$11. **Beer** Bottled only, $6–$9. **Dress** Upscale casual to business. **Food available** Yes, full menu $9–$27. **Hours** Sunday–Thursday, 4 p.m.–1 a.m.; Friday and Saturday, 4 p.m.–2 a.m.

WHO GOES THERE 30s–70s; tourists, lovers, vista seekers.

WHAT GOES ON Gazing, light canoodling, sipping, relaxing.

SETTING AND ATMOSPHERE The Top of the Tower is a perfect setting for either a date or a friendly tête-a-tête. Right off the elevator you're immediately in the middle of an open area complete with bar, baby grand piano (played from 9 p.m. onwards, except Mondays), small tables, and spacious high windows with Art Deco designs. There's no pretension in the air, but sneakers are not encouraged.

IF YOU GO Aim to get a table by a window during a sunset or later in the evening to see Midtown and the East River twinkle. The restaurant serves decent food, but the views are the main draw whilst you sip a drink or glass of champagne. You're sufficiently high enough up to be away from the fray.

Town Bar

15 West 56th Street (between Fifth and Sixth avenues), in Chambers Hotel, Midtown East; ☎ 212-582-4445; www.townnyc.com

Cover None. **Minimum** None. **Mixed drinks** $10–$22. **Wine** Good selection, $8–$20. **Beer** Bottled only, and what's the point when the drink and wine selection is so extensive? **Dress** Smart casual, cool, elegant, or chic. **Specials** None. **Food available** Delicious light meals, prepared in the Town restaurant kitchen, $12–$24. **Hours** Sunday–Friday, noon–midnight; Saturday, 5 p.m.–1 a.m.

WHO GOES THERE 20s–60s; professionals, deep-pocketed chicsters, hip hotel guests, cocktail aficionados.

WHAT GOES ON Town is bustling with a well-heeled, after-work crowd between 6 and 8 p.m.; afterwards, the scene is less frenetic and decidedly sophisticated. This is not the place to indulge recession blues, with quality champagne flowing in many a cocktail and gold leaf floating in drinks that sell for $22 a pop. Cocktails are taken seriously, and the mixers, from fruit puree to infusions, are all fresh.

SETTING AND ATMOSPHERE Ultra-chic environment, with a choice of four areas to drink: the lobby, main bar, mezzanine, or balcony. The main bar is small and narrow; warm, subtle lighting helps everyone look their absolute best. The staff are friendly and knowledgeable.

IF YOU GO Understand and accept that even though you may part with more cash than is normally sane for a round of drinks, you will enjoy the experience (unless you order beer). Ask the bartender (a.k.a. bar chef) about any recently concocted potions and request an explanation of the myriad infusions, spices, and ingredients displayed on the bar. A look at the vanilla-infused rum used for the mojitos is enough to make a sworn vodka tippler try a change of pace.

Village Vanguard

JAZZ CLUB

178 Seventh Avenue South, Greenwich Village; ☎ 212-255-4037; www.villagevanguard.com

Cover $30–$35 (includes $10 drink minimum). **Minimum** $25 for tables, $10 plus two drinks at bar. **Mixed drinks** $5–$10. **Wine** $5–$7. **Beer** $4.50–$5. **Dress** Dressy or nice casual. **Food available** None. **Hours** Open 8 p.m. every night, closing time varies. Sets start at 9 and 11 p.m.; call to see if a third set is scheduled.

WHO GOES THERE 25–90; jazz pilgrims and Japanese tourists.

WHAT GOES ON This is it—the most famous jazz club in the world. Over the last 60 years almost every major jazz musician has gigged in this room (many recorded landmark live albums here as well), and the ghosts are palpable. The service is crabby and the seating's cramped, but you become a tiny part of jazz history simply by walking in the door. The music is *finally* straying from strictly straight-ahead jazz and bebop: fusion, Latin, and even fresh blood are being heard here.

SETTING AND ATMOSPHERE Dank basement with a small bar in back . . . but the acoustics are wonderful, and it feels like jazz. Table service.

IF YOU GO Check out the Monday Night Vanguard Jazz Orchestra (Thad Jones/Mel Lewis's band, sans leaders). On any night, reservations are a good idea; this small club fills up fast. No talking is allowed during performances, no photography, no video taping, no audio recording, and no cell phones.

Webster Hall

DISCO THEME PARK

125 East 11th Street, The East Village; ☎ 212-353-1600; www.websterhall.com

Cover None–$30. **Minimum** None. **Mixed drinks** $6.50–$8. **Wine** $6.50. **Beer** $6–$7. **Dress** No sneakers, baseball hats, ripped jeans, or boots; dress to impress. **Specials** $15 admission discounts are available through their Web site. **Food available** Probably somewhere; look around. **Hours** Thursday–Saturday, 10 p.m.– 5 a.m.; Sunday–Wednesday, closed.

WHO GOES THERE 21–35; equal parts NYU freshmen, beautiful party people, and paunchy 30-somethings clutching beers and looking wistful.

WHAT GOES ON An enormous disco theme park with dance floors, lounges, a (temporary) tattoo parlor, and a coffee bar. There are spending opportunities everywhere you look; even the bathroom attendants reign over little concession stands, selling candy, mouthwash, and hair products. Fridays and Saturdays are monstrously crowded mainstream disco free-for-alls, and Thursdays have a psychedelic 1960s theme. The staff seems to be instructed to act as peevish as possible. Lots of DJs; ladies get in free all Thursday night, while men get in for $10 before 11:30 p.m.

SETTING AND ATMOSPHERE Ground level is mostly a classic disco, complete with a go-go girl behind the bar. Upstairs you enter a cavernous ball-room, like a junior high school auditorium taken over by aliens with superior technology: amazing lighting tricks and a SenSurround-style bass response that makes your chest feel like it's going to explode. More go-go girls, and androgynous characters on stilts. Still further upstairs is a balcony with tarot readings, temporary tattoos, body paint-ing, and a tranquil lounge (wicker chairs, ferns) that hosts live bands Thursday and Friday nights (also check the bar here for drink specials). In the basement, yet another dance floor, this one with burning incense.

IF YOU GO Conceal no weapons (or beer bottles)—no happening disco would be complete without a security pat-down at the front door, and this is no exception.

Zinc Bar

BAR AND JAZZ CLUB

90 West Houston Street, Soho; ☎ 212-477-8337; www.zincbar.com

Cover $5. **Minimum** One drink. **Mixed drinks** $7–$12. **Wine** Bottles $25 and up; $6–$8 by the glass. **Beer** $7–$8. **Dress** Casual to chic. **Specials** None. **Food available** None. **Hours** Sunday–Thursday, 6 p.m.–3:30 a.m.; Friday and Saturday, 6 p.m.–4 a.m.

WHO GOES THERE 22–55; locals, night-owls, and jazz aficionados.

WHAT GOES ON This is a great place to watch some purely amazing musicians in an intimate setting. Occasional impromptu audience participation occurs during performances. It's also cozy for a tête-à-tête with drinks. You can sit in the back room if you don't want to watch the set—but you will hear it. Poetry readings take place on Sundays at 6:30 p.m.

SETTING AND ATMOSPHERE Once you go down a few steps, pass the curtain and move into a low-light, narrow bar, you will already be in a mood to hear music. The Zinc Bar has two rooms—the first room hosts the main bar with stools on one side, and small round tables with a padded bench, along the wall, on the other side. This is where the musicians perform. The dominant color is red. The second room is a little more sizable and exposes red brick and wooden floors. One side has banquettes—perfect for groups—and the other side, once again, has a padded bench along the wall with a few cocktail tables.

IF YOU GO Make sure you manage to catch at least one set; the last one can start as late as 2 a.m.

ACCOMMODATION INDEX

NIGHTCLUB INDEX

RESTAURANT INDEX

SUBJECT INDEX